BT
7.92

THE SPEECHES

OF

Charles Dickens

THE SPEECHES

OF

Charles Dickens

EDITED BY

K. J. FIELDING

OXFORD
AT THE CLARENDON PRESS
1960

Oxford University Press, Amen House, London E.C.4

GLASGOW NEW YORK TORONTO MELBOURNE WELLINGTON
BOMBAY CALCUTTA MADRAS KARACHI KUALA LUMPUR
CAPE TOWN IBADAN NAIROBI ACCRA

PRINTED IN GREAT BRITAIN

PREFACE

THE purpose of this edition of Dickens's public speeches is simply to present them in the most readable and reliable form, and in a far more complete collection than any which has been made before. The first collected edition, put together by R. H. Shepherd and John Camden Hotten in 1870, and which has since been frequently reprinted, included fifty-six speeches; the last, edited by Walter Dexter, and printed in the *Collected Papers* of the Nonesuch edition of the complete works, in 1938, had an additional nine. The present edition, without claiming to be finally complete, has one hundred and fifteen. Of the additional fifty, eighteen have been republished at some time in various periodicals, chiefly the *Dickensian*; while the remainder are given for the first time since their initial appearance. None of them has been reprinted without reference to the original authorities, all have been corrected, and many greatly expanded and even almost entirely altered. Textually a completely fresh start has been made.

In annotating, the aim has been to put the reader, as far as possible, on equal terms with a fairly well-informed contemporary, without distracting his attention from the speaker by too many notes.

I am particularly indebted to the late Mr. Humphry House for his advice and encouragement in carrying out the present work; and also to Professor Ada B. Nisbet of the University of California, Mr. L. C. Staples, the editor of the *Dickensian*, and Mr. W. J. Carlton. As, formerly, one of the editors of the forthcoming *Pilgrim Edition* of Dickens's letters I was able to consult a number of original manuscripts and copies, which I might not have been able to see otherwise, and for this I am indebted to my fellow members of the Editorial Committee.

Special thanks are due to Mr. H. C. Dickens, O.B.E., for his generous permission to quote from all Dickens letters and manuscripts still subject to copyright. I also received great kindness from the late Comte de Suzannet, who allowed me to consult a number of rare pamphlets in his collection, which I gladly acknowledge; and I am no less grateful to many owners of letters and papers whose names are given in the actual note or reference to each passage quoted. In investigating Dickens's association with various societies I have been assisted by the kind co-operation and interest of their representatives. I am also greatly indebted to the trustees and officials of the Henry E. Huntington Library, San Marino, California, and of the Pierpont Morgan Library, New York, for permission to quote from many of their letters and manuscripts, to which further reference is also made in the notes.   K. J. F.

CONTENTS

ABBREVIATIONS, ETC.   xiii

TEXTUAL INTRODUCTION   xv

DICKENS AS A SPEAKER   xix

1837
3 *May*. Literary Fund: Anniversary Festival   1

1838
12 *May*. Artists' Benevolent Fund   2

1839
20 *July*. Banquet in Honour of W. C. Macready   2

1840
2 *December*. Southwark Literary and Scientific Institution   4

1841
12 *May*. Literary Fund: Anniversary Festival   6
25 *June*. Banquet in His Honour: Edinburgh   8

1842
29 *January*. Presentation to Captain Hewett: Boston   15
1 *February*. Banquet in His Honour: Boston   17
7 *February*. Banquet in His Honour: Hartford   22
18 *February*. Banquet in His Honour: New York   26
14 *March*. Private Dinner in His Honour: Washington   32
18 *March*. 'Social Supper' in His Honour: Richmond   34

1843
4 *April*. Printers' Pension Society   36
6 *May*. Hospital for Consumption and Diseases of the Chest   40
23 *May*. Charitable Society for the Deaf and Dumb   41
29 *June*. The Sanatorium   42
5 *October*. First Annual *Soirée* of the Athenaeum: Man-   44
chester

1844

26 *February*. *Soirée* of the Mechanics' Institution: Liverpool   52

28 *February*. Conversazione of the Polytechnic Institution: 58
Birmingham

20 *April*. Governesses' Benevolent Institution   65

11 *May*. Artists' Benevolent Society   67

4 *June*. The Sanatorium   68

1846

6 *April*. General Theatrical Fund   73

1847

29 *March*. General Theatrical Fund   77

1 *December*. *Soirée* of the Mechanics' Institution: Leeds   80

28 *December*. First Annual *Soirée* of the Athenaeum: Glas-   85
gow

1848

17 *April*. General Theatrical Fund   92

1849

21 *May*. General Theatrical Fund   94

19 *June*. United Law Clerks' Society   97

7 *July*. Banquet at the Mansion House   98

21 *November*. Newsvendors' Benevolent Institution   100

1850

6 *February*. Metropolitan Sanitary Association   104

25 *March*. General Theatrical Fund   110

1851

1 *March*. Banquet in Honour of W. C. Macready   113

14 *April*. General Theatrical Fund   118

10 *May*. Metropolitan Sanitary Association   127

9 *June*. Gardeners' Benevolent Institution   133

1852

27 *January*. Newsvendors' Benevolent Institution   135

5 *April*. General Theatrical Fund   138

4 *May*. Meeting for the Removal of Trade Restrictions on the Commerce of Literature   142

14 *June*. Gardeners' Benevolent Institution   143

31 *August*. Banquet to the Guild of Literature and Art: Manchester   148

2 *September*. Opening of the Free Library: Manchester   151

1853

6 *January*. Presentation to Dickens and Banquet to Literature and Art: Birmingham   154

22 *March*. Royal General Theatrical Fund   162

30 *April*. Royal Academy Banquet   163

2 *May*. Banquet at the Mansion House   164

30 *December*. At a Reading of the *Carol*: Birmingham   166

1854

28 *December*. At a Reading of the *Carol*: Bradford   168

30 *December*. Commercial Travellers' Schools   169

1855

14 *March*. Royal Literary Fund: Annual General Meeting   176

2 *April*. Royal General Theatrical Fund   184

21 *May*. Newsvendors' Benevolent Institution   188

16 *June*. Royal Literary Fund: Special General Meeting   192

27 *June*. Administrative Reform Association   197

22 *December*. After a Reading of the *Carol*: Sheffield   208

1856

12 *March*. Royal Literary Fund: Annual General Meeting   209

13 *March*. Meeting of the Dramatic Profession on Dulwich College   215

17 *March*. Royal General Theatrical Fund   220

5 *June*. Royal Hospital for Incurables   222

1857

11 *March*. Royal Literary Fund: Annual General Meeting 225

6 *April*. Royal General Theatrical Fund 228

21 *May*. Royal Hospital for Incurables 232

25 *May*. Royal Geographical Society 236

31 *July*. After Reading the *Carol* for the Jerrold Fund: Manchester 237

24 *August*. After a Performance of *The Frozen Deep*: Manchester 238

5 *November*. Warehousemen and Clerks' Schools 238

1858

19 *January*. At a Reading for the Athenaeum: Bristol 245

9 *February*. Hospital for Sick Children 246

10 *March*. Royal Literary Fund: Annual General Meeting 253

26 *March*. At a Reading of the *Carol* for the Philosophical Institution: Edinburgh 258

29 *March*. Royal General Theatrical Fund 260

29 *April*. At the First Reading for His Own Profit 263

1 *May*. Royal Academy Banquet 264

8 *May*. Artists' Benevolent Fund 265

1 *June*. Playground and General Recreation Society 269

21 *July*. Meeting for the Foundation of the Dramatic College 275

27 *and* 28 *September*. At Two Readings in Edinburgh 277

3 *December*. Prize-Giving of the Institutional Association of Lancashire and Cheshire: Manchester 278

4 *December*. Presentation and Banquet in His Honour: Coventry 285

1859

22 *December*. Commercial Travellers' Schools 288

1860

8 *March*. Royal Society of Musicians 294

17 *April*. Lecture by A. H. Layard for the Mechanics' Institute: Chatham 298

18 *December*. Reading for the Mechanics' Institute: Chatham 298

1861

1 *April.* Banquet at the Mansion House   299

1862

16 *January.* Reading for the Mechanics' Institute: Chatham   301

29 *March,* Artists' General Benevolent Fund   301

20 *May.* Newsvendors' Benevolent Institution   305

1863

4 *April.* Royal General Theatrical Fund   310

6 *May.* Royal Free Hospital   319

1864

6 *April.* Printers' Pension Society   323

12 *April.* University College Hospital   326

11 *May.* Meeting for the Establishment of the Shakespeare   333
Foundation Schools

1865

9 *May.* Newsvendors' Benevolent Institution   337

20 *May.* Newspaper Press Fund   342

29 *July.* After the Opening of the Guild Houses: Knebworth   349

1866

16 *January.* Banquet at the Mansion House   352

14 *February.* Dramatic Equestrian and Musical Sick Fund   353
Association

28 *March.* Royal General Theatrical Fund   358

7 *May.* Metropolitan Rowing Clubs   359

1867

5 *June.* Railway Benevolent Institution   361

17 *September.* Printers' Readers' Association   366

2 *November.* Farewell Banquet Before Visit to the United   368
States

xii   *Contents*

1868

3 and 7 February. First and Farewell Readings: Washington   375

20 February. Before a Reading: Providence, R.I.   376

8 April. Farewell Reading: Boston   377

18 April. Banquet in His Honour: New York   378

20 April. Farewell Reading: New York   383

1869

10 April. Banquet in His Honour at St. George's Hall: 384
Liverpool

30 August. Banquet to the Oxford and Harvard Crews   394

27 September. Birmingham and Midland Institute: Annual   397
Inaugural Meeting: Birmingham

1870

6 January. Birmingham and Midland Institute Prize-Giving: 409
Birmingham

15 March. Farewell Reading   412

5 April. Newsvendors' Benevolent Institution   414

30 April. Royal Academy Banquet   419

NOTES ON TEXT AND SOURCES   423

INDEX   445

ABBREVIATIONS, ETC.

BM	From manuscript in the British Museum.
DH	From manuscript in the Dickens House, 48 Doughty Street, London, W.C.1.
F	John Forster, *The Life of Charles Dickens*, 2 vols., 1876; reference by book and chapter; earlier editions were differently divided.
FC	From manuscript in the Forster collection, Victoria and Albert Museum.
H	From microfilm of manuscript in the Henry E. Huntington Library, San Marino, California.
M	From microfilm of manuscript in the Pierpont Morgan Library, New York.
MS	From manuscript, followed by name of owner.
RLF	From manuscript in the records of the Royal Literary Fund.
S	From manuscript in possession of the late Comte de Suzannet.
Shepherd	*The Speeches of Charles Dickens* [*1841–1870*], ed. R. H. Shepherd, 1884.
[ ]	Square brackets enclosing any form of reference show that though the text is taken from a better source, the letter referred to has been published by W. Dexter, *Letters of Charles Dickens*, 1938.

When the reference is given without these brackets, it indicates that (as far as is known) the letter or manuscript has not been published before.

Quotations from Dickens's letters, unless otherwise stated, are from Dexter's edition.

The place of publication is usually mentioned only when other than London.

TEXTUAL INTRODUCTION

PREVIOUS PUBLICATION

THE present edition has been undertaken to replace the one put together for John Camden Hotten in 1870.[1] For, with all its imperfections, it has been this edition that has been reprinted, in various guises, without a single alteration or correction ever since. In a few cases additional speeches have been inserted, but no changes in the old text have ever been made. The reports in the old edition, and all subsequent reprints, were inadequate, incomplete, badly transcribed, and often no more than a travesty of what Dickens actually said. But both the general reader, and Dickens's biographers, have accepted them quite uncritically and no one has ever questioned the way in which they were edited, with the result that many of the mistakes caused by Hotten's haste to profit by Dickens's death have been perpetuated.

The old edition, which was at first anonymous, has always been ascribed to Richard Herne Shepherd. Hotten died in 1873, and Shepherd attributed it to himself in his *Bibliography of Dickens* (1880), and published a new edition over his own name in 1884.[2] Although it was alleged to be 'revised and enlarged', it was no more than a rearrangement of the old one. This original and reprinted version, by Hotten and Shepherd, has so long been accepted without comment, that a brief explanation of its origin may help to account for its peculiar character.

It can hardly be said to have been edited at all. It was a successful piece of journalism, but quite disreputable in its origin and results. Hotten was a literary pirate at heart, but usually afraid of the risks. At the time his edition was published it was uncertain how far public speeches were protected by copyright. Already, in 1865, by rushing out a reprint of Carlyle's inaugural address as Lord Rector of Edinburgh University, Hotten had spoilt the sale of the official edition, and had escaped without trouble. Then, in 1868, he had begun planning a whole series of collected speeches. He had selected Dickens as a suitable victim; and, according to his own account, 'at once despatched an order to America to search there for every public speech made by him both upon the occasion of his 1st and 2nd visit to that country'.[3]

[1] *Speeches Literary and Social by Charles Dickens*, Now First Collected, London: John Camden Hotten, Piccadilly.
[2] *The Speeches of Charles Dickens*, London: Chatto & Windus.
[3] Letter from Hotten to Chapman & Hall, 7 July 1870. (MS., Sir Leslie Farrer, K.C.V.O.)

By February 1870 he was canvassing for advertisements, and it was thus that Dickens first heard of what was going on. His only response was to have a threatening letter sent to Hotten by his solicitor.

Hotten was full of innocent indignation. 'The letter,' he wrote, 'astounded me! At that time the Speeches were half printed—the Preface is dated Decr. last.'[1] He wrote a short pamphlet, entitled *Letters on Copyright*, to test the ground; but, before it could appear, Dickens was dead. Routledge was then allowed to publish G. A. Sala's obituary pamphlet, *Charles Dickens*, which included a few of the speeches, and Hotten wrote to Chapman and Hall to tell them that he had decided to risk it. There was really very little danger— he was legally in a strong position; and although Dickens had referred the affair to Chapman and Hall while he was alive, by this time they were interested only in the copyright of his major published works, and the executors had more important things to worry about. Hotten's edition of Dickens's *Speeches Literary and Social*, therefore, was rushed out with some last minute, scissors-and-paste additions, and there the matter was left.

There were fifty-six speeches in the original edition; two more were added to the National edition, of 1908; and a further seven to the *Collected Papers*, edited by Walter Dexter, for the Nonesuch Press, in 1938. Others have been reprinted in various periodicals, and in a valuable series of 'Uncollected Speeches', in the *Dickensian*, 1939–51. Their republication has been recorded separately in the *Notes on Text and Sources*.[2] As far as can be seen, none of these previous reprints has ever been taken from more than a single source. They are no longer of any value.

EDITORIAL METHOD

Editing the speeches has not been simply a matter of collecting those that may have reappeared in periodicals, and tracing others which were previously unknown. As far as possible all the better reports of any speech that could be found have been consulted, and an attempt has been made to combine them in a text which may take something from several different versions. The general principles of editing speeches, under such conditions, are obvious, and can briefly be summarized.

Dickens never wrote out his speeches before they were given, and only rarely did so afterwards. When they were important they were carefully considered beforehand; but although he occasionally consulted notes for figures and quotations, his speeches were never

---

[1] Letter from Hotten to Chapman & Hall, 7 July 1870. (MS., Sir Leslie Farrer, K.C.V.O.)

read. In the case of the speech at the banquet of the Metropolitan Sanitary Association of 10 May 1851, which was written out afterwards for Henry Austin, and the final speech at the Royal Academy banquet, there is no doubt that the text should be based exclusively on Dickens's manuscripts. His verbal memory was remarkable, and his report of the 1851 speech is incomparably better than any other. The manuscript of his last speech was one Dickens wrote out for *The Times*; and since *The Times* was the only newspaper at that time allowed to have shorthand reporters present—and its report was passed on to the others—the question whether any further authorities should be used can be put aside.

There are other cases, recorded separately in the notes, when Dickens is known (or can reasonably be supposed) to have corrected the proofs of reports that were sent to him. Here again, although other reports have always been consulted, it has been found in practice that the version Dickens corrected can be relied upon.

There remain reports in the press which were not corrected by Dickens. Their value ranges widely: some are worthless, and others almost completely accurate. In many cases it is quite clear that the reporters were incompetent; in others they were possibly working under difficulties; and at some of the banquets they probably joined in the toasts rather too whole heartedly. The speeches were often taken down in summary by the reporters themselves, and what was left was liable to be cut up again by the sub-editor. The convention of giving them in the third person made it easy to abbreviate and alter; and now often makes it impossible to enjoy the speeches as they were given, even when we have a full report.

Even the best reporter is never completely accurate: words may be lost in laughter or applause, a neighbour may cough, or in the haste of transcribing a few words may be illegible, and mis-read by the compositor. But even the worst report, as long as it was independent, may help to correct or confirm a better one.

Without having the chance to compare half a dozen accounts of the same speech, it is difficult for anyone to realize how widely they may vary. Any one of them by itself might be accepted as reasonably accurate, if the others were not completely different. In some cases the variations are unimportant; in others the final text is still so far from what Dickens can have said, that any additional notes on what he could not possibly have said would be useless. When sense is available, under these conditions, there is no point in recording nonsense. In theory it would have been possible to compile a textual variorium: in practice it would have been so complicated that it would have been almost impossible to do, and quite impossible to read.

The problem is confused by ignorance of how the reporting was undertaken. Very occasionally the work may have been sent in by penny-a-liners, who sold the same report twice over. At times some of the newspapers may have co-operated, or their reporters may have unofficially joined forces to make the work easier. There are numerous instances where one newspaper or periodical has copied from another without acknowledgement, which are usually easy to detect. In many ways it is easier to edit a text when all the reports are different, since they are then known to be independent. The difficulty arises when they are suspiciously the same, and it is impossible to be sure whether one really confirms another.

For these reasons, spelling, capitalization, punctuation, and paragraphing have been considered as fairly subject to standardization and editorial revision. But in the case of the two texts based on Dickens's manuscripts, such alterations have not been made; and when they are based on publications which he is known to have revised, they have been made very sparingly. In most cases when a speech has been published in any collected edition before, in order to make comparison with earlier texts as easy as possible, paragraphing has not been altered.

For ease of reading, the notes on the reports on which the text of each speech is based have been separated from the text. But although the *Speeches* have a certain unity, it must also be stressed that they are still no more than a series of separate reports. Most of them were never corrected by Dickens, and many are still very faulty. He might have disapproved of their being reprinted: 'These things', he once wrote to Forster, 'are so ill done.'[1]

In presenting them with some account of the occasions on which they were given, and a general explanation of their context, an attempt has been made to keep the fact that they were speeches constantly before the reader. For this reason, the interjections, applause, and laughter of the audience have been given, and also because they were part of the vocal punctuation of the speeches, which were always addressed to the people who were present and never merely to reporters for republication.

No such edition can ever hope to be complete. A few more speeches might be found, but it is unlikely that more than a few ever will be. Negative results have not been recorded, but it can be assumed that the chief national daily newspapers have always been consulted when the speech was given in London. Many other newspapers and periodicals have also been examined, as shown in the *Notes on Text and Sources*, pp. 423–43.

[1] F, VII. ii.

DICKENS AS A SPEAKER

DICKENS never had a Boswell; all his biographers have based their work chiefly on his letters. Yet he was not only a public spokesman in the sense of being a champion of all kinds of movements for charities, self-help, and reform. As no other author before him, or since, he succeeded in combining a reputation as both a writer and speaker. The first time he was given a public reception, it was reported that 'his speeches . . . were the best'.[1] Of his last public speech, at the Royal Academy dinner in 1870, Gladstone wrote, 'it was one of the most finished performances of its kind that I ever knew'.[2] 'He spoke so well', recorded Trollope, 'that a public dinner became a blessing instead of a curse, if he was in the chair.'[3]

The record of what Dickens said will be left largely to speak for itself. His speeches show his opinions about political affairs, education, and public health; about his fellow authors, the duties and status of a pro-fessional writer, the need for self-help in an age of uncertainty, and his relations with his public both in England and the United States. They display his sense of the need for charity in public affairs, as well as his scorn for obstructionists; and they reveal something of what he aspired to treat in *Household Words*, 'the enterprises, triumphs, joys and sorrows' of his times.[4] They allow us, moreover, to see the importance of Dickens's career as a great public figure, and to judge him in relation to outside issues and to other men. His speeches, in fact, give us what he was prepared to stand up and say in public, which was not always the same as what he expressed as his opinions to his correspondents, or what he published in the guise of fiction.

As an orator there is no doubt he was outstanding. Edmund Yates wrote, 'Dickens was by far the best after-dinner speaker I have ever heard.' Yates was echoed by Serjeant Ballantine, William Blanchard[5] Jerrold, and Justin McCarthy;[6] while Robert Mackenzie, writing for Americans, more cautiously claimed that he was merely 'the best after-dinner speaker in England'.[7] Lord Granville, the Liberal leader of the House of Lords, used to tell the story that he once asked Dickens who he thought was 'the best after-dinner speaker of the day'. Dickens replied, 'Well, there are many great orators . . . but if you want a really bright, witty, genial speech for a banquet, commend me to Bishop Wilberforce.' A few days later, Lord Granville asked the bishop the same question.

[1] *Scotsman*, 30 June 1841.
[2] F. G. Kitton, *Charles Dickens by Pen and Pencil*, 1890, p. 165.
[3] 'Charles Dickens', *St. Paul's Magazine*, July 1870, vi. 375.
[4] *Household Words*, 30 Mar. 1850, i. 1.
[5] *Recollections and Experiences*, 1884, ii. 111.
[6] W. Ballantine, *Some Experiences of a Barrister's Life*, new ed. 1898, p. 95; W. B. Jerrold, *London, A Pilgrimage*, 1872, pp. 183–4; Justin McCarthy, *Reminiscences*, 1899, i. 32–33.
[7] *Life of Charles Dickens*, Philadelphia, 1870, p. 132.

'Oh,' he answered, 'Gladstone, the Duke of Argyll, Disraeli and John Bright . . . are great speakers, but for a charming after-dinner speech give me Charles Dickens.'[1]

Charm was certainly one of his qualities as a speaker. Justin McCarthy writes of his hearers being 'carried away by the extraordinary charm' of one of his speeches.[2] Sir Arthur Helps, who had edited the speeches of the Prince Consort, wrote that Dickens had a presence 'conveying the idea of courage and honesty, which gives much effect to public speaking'.[3] Trollope, again, said that he despaired of giving 'any idea' of 'the general charm of his manner'.[4] His voice was rich and full, capable of either humour or pathos, and there was never any question of its being audible. 'His deep eyes seemed to flash upon every listener among the audience whom he addressed';[5] and, without undue gesticulation, he was able to give 'additional force and meaning to what he said' by the slightest movement of his wonderfully expressive hands. 'Indeed,' says Helps, 'when he read, or when he spoke, the whole man read or spoke.'

Yet nothing ever surprised new hearers more than his restraint. Although Dickens had trained himself as an actor, there was rarely anything histrionic about his speaking. The Duke of Argyll, who heard him give a speech in 1853, and who then went to one of his Readings, draws a clear distinction between them. 'In acting', he wrote, Dickens 'was really wonderful.' But, 'as a speaker, he was quite peculiar. It was the very perfection of neatness and precision in language—the speaking of a man who knew exactly what he was going to say, and how best to say it. But it was without fire or tones of enthusiasm, or flights of fancy; there was nothing that makes the orator.'[6] The contrast was all the more marked for the duke, perhaps, because Dickens intentionally eschewed the conventional style of parliamentary eloquence—the manner of the 'very circuitous and prolix peer', and of 'my honourable friend the Member for Drowsyshire'.[7]

His style was always direct. After his first speech at Edinburgh, in 1841, everyone had remarked on his impressive calmness, and how he spoke as if he were 'dictating to an amanuensis';[8] while Dickens wrote of himself on the same occasion, 'I was quite self-possessed', and 'as cool as a cucumber'.[9] Several years later, he maintained to Miss Burdett Coutts that he was never carried away when he spoke, and that 'as to my being tempted into any hot public assertion, I believe if you had ever seen me under any speechifying circumstances, you would have perfect confidence in my composure'.[10]

[1] Lord Redesdale, *Memories*, 1915, ii. 535.

[2] *Reminiscences*, 1899, i. 32–33.

[3] 'Charles Dickens: In Memoriam', *Macmillan's Magazine*, July 1870, xxii. 239.   [4] Op. cit.

[5] Justin McCarthy, *Reminiscences*, i. 32–33.

[6] *Autobiography and Memoirs*, ed. Dowager Duchess of Argyll, 1906, i. 416–17.

[7] 'A Few Conventionalities', *Household Words*, 28 June 1851, iii. 313–15.

[8] R. S. Mackenzie, *Life of Dickens*, 1870, p. 131.

[9] F. II. x.   [10] 15 May 1855.

All his speeches were carefully prepared, though he seemed almost equally at ease when they were extempore. Yet he never referred to any notes except for facts and figures or when he was giving a quotation. Before presiding at the annual meeting of the Birmingham and Midland Institute in 1869, he wrote to the editor of the *Daily News* to say that he would willingly help his reporter to revise his notes when the meeting was over, but that he had already assured two correspondents representing Birmingham papers that he would have no manuscript address in his possession, and 'that such notes as I make on such occasions would be illegible to everyone but myself'.[1] In fact, it was noticed when he gave the speech, 'that no note of any kind was referred to by Mr. Dickens—except the quotation from Sydney Smith'.[2]

Even so he had no doubt carefully thought out what he was going to say, and his verbal memory was remarkable. He wrote a report of his speech at the dinner of the Metropolitan Sanitary Association for his brother-in-law, Henry Austin, so he told him, 'I believe word for word, *exactly as it was given.*'[3] Although he could have aided his memory by referring to newspaper reports, it is very unlikely that he did. After the dinner given by the New York Press Club in April 1868 he went back to the hotel and repeated to Mrs. James T. Fields, 'every word of his speech without dropping one'.[4] He told Mrs. Fields and her husband that he would give no thought to what he was to say until shortly before one of his speeches was to be given. Then, says James T. Fields, he would 'take a walk into the country, and the thing was done. When he returned he was all ready for the task.'[5]

The fullest account of 'the art of speech making', as expounded by Dickens, was given to his Reading manager, George Dolby. According to this, Dickens confirmed that before he had to give a speech,

'his habit was to take a long walk . . . during which he would decide on the various heads to be dealt with. These being arranged in their proper order, he would in his 'mind's eye', liken the whole subject to the tire of a cart wheel—he being the hub. From the hub to the tire he would run as many spokes as there were subjects to be treated; and during the progress of the speech he would deal with each spoke separately, elaborating them as he went round the wheel; and when all the spokes had dropped out one by one . . . he would know that he had accomplished his task, and that his speech was at an end.

Dolby adds that he often heard Dickens speaking in public after this, and that he had been 'amused to see him' dismiss each spoke from his mind 'by a quick action of the finger as if he were knocking it away'.[6]

The custom of giving vast banquets in aid of a good cause was peculiarly Victorian; and it was typically Victorian that almost everyone

[1] *Fifty Years of Fleet Street, Being the Life . . . of Sir John R. Robinson*, ed. F. M. Thomas, 1904, pp. 249–50.
[2] *Shepherd*, p. 297, quoting 'one who was present'.
[3] 18 May 1851, M.
[4] *Memories of a Hostess*, ed. M. A. de Wolfe Howe, 1922, p. 184.
[5] *Yesterdays with Authors*, London, 1872, p. 240.
[6] George Dolby, *Charles Dickens as I Knew Him*, 1885, pp. 272–4.

realized its absurdity, and yet agreed to keep it going for want of a practical alternative. Dickens had been familiar with it from his days as a reporter, when he wrote about 'Public Dinners' in *Sketches by Boz*. He was hardly at ease in such surroundings. At the great banquet in aid of sanitary reform, for example, which was held in 1851, he had to listen to the 'Loud Cheers' that greeted Lord Carlisle's remark that preventable disease especially threatened 'those that fill the more humble walks of life'. It is not difficult to imagine, as Humphry House suggested, that he had a conscious delight in pointing out, in his speech that followed, that not all diseases knew such class distinctions.[1] As far as possible, Dickens kept away from mere charities and confined his help to provident societies and hospitals; but it was of a hospital dinner that he once expressed his opinions most frankly, in a letter to Douglas Jerrold:

> O Heaven, if you could have been with me . . . There were men there—your City aristocracy—who made such speeches . . . as any moderately intelligent dustman would have blushed through his cindery bloom to have thought of. Sleek, slobbering, bow-paunched, over-fed, apoplectic, snorting cattle and the auditory leaping up in their delight! I have never seen such an illustration of the Power of the Purse, or felt so degraded and debased by the contemplation, since I had eyes and ears. The absurdity of the thing was too horrible to laugh at.[2]

Thackeray was more typical of his age. He was an inveterate diner-out, somewhat ashamed of the practice, but prepared to speak up in defence of 'the honest good old English use of eating and drinking, which brings us together for all sorts of good purposes—do not suppose that I laugh at it any more than I would at good old honest John Bull, who has under his huge boisterous exterior, a great deal of kindness at the heart of him'.[3]

Dickens was too sensitive and too self-conscious ever to expose himself in quite this way.

At the same time he was by no means consistent. Although he disliked being lionized in private society, he was obviously attracted by appearing before the public he had created. Though he detested official display and ridiculed ostentation in others, he was showy at a time when everyone else was drab and, to strangers, he always appeared to have a faintly theatrical air. Yet once he had passed his first period of success when he was often the exuberant 'inimitable Boz', he was always somewhat self-consciously, Charles Dickens.

Self-consciousness, in fact, almost entirely absorbed Dickens except when he was engaged in his imaginative work; and it is largely because

---

[1] House, *The Dickens World*, 1941, p. 196.

[2] 3 May 1843 [S]. It was a dinner in aid of the Charterhouse Square Infirmary, patronized particularly by aldermen, merchants, and directors. In the absence of the Lord Mayor the chairman was Lieut.-Gen. Sir James Law Lushington. Dickens may have spoken, but there are only brief reports in *The Times* and *Morning Post*, 2 May.

[3] *Thackeray, The Humourist and Man of Letters*, ed. Theodore Taylor [pseud.], 1864, p. 216.

of this that it might easily be misleading to try to point out all the supposed cross-references one can see between his speeches and his novels.
Of course they abound. But it is more essential to realize that, although
he was deeply concerned about contemporary affairs in both his public
life and his fiction, they never quite correspond. It may have been this
which made Dickens sometimes deny a relation between them even when
it was clearly there. He flatly and incorrectly told his friend, Peter
Cunningham, for instance, that his visit to Preston had nothing to do
with *Hard Times*, and declared that part of the mischief that lay in
leading the public to suppose that it did was that, firstly, it encouraged
them 'to believe in the impossibility that books are produced in that
very sudden and cavalier manner (as poor Newton used to feign that he
produced the elaborate drawings he made in his madness, by winking at
his table)', and secondly that 'it localizes . . . a story which has a direct
purpose in reference to the working people all over England'.[1]

It is true that both his novels and his speeches deal with the contemporary scene, but there is no necessary significance in the fact that
they sometimes overlap. Betty Higden's grandson Johnny dies in the
Children's Hospital for which Dickens had spoken so earnestly a few
years earlier. Henry Gowan is evidently related to some of the members
of the committee of the Royal Literary Fund. The speech on Administrative Reform and the chapter on 'How Not To Do It', in *Little Dorrit*
are obviously closely linked. On the other hand, much of Dickens's
public life and private philanthropy does not seem to be directly related
to his imaginative writing. None of his experience in directing Miss
Burdett Coutts's 'Home for Fallen Women', for example, was used in
his novels.[2] His investigation of slum property in Westminster and other
parts of London seems to have had no direct connexion even with Mr.
Pancks and Bleeding Heart Yard.

Dickens himself once wrote of the art of the novelist, 'It does not
seem to me to be enough to say of any description that it is the exact
truth. The exact truth must be there; but the merit or art in the narrator,
is the manner of stating the truth. As to which things in literature, it
always seems to me there is a world to be done.'[3] Similarly, in inter-
preting his life or his novels, it is not enough to say that there is this, or
that, correspondence. The merit and art in the novelist lay in the way
he used his experience; and the merit and art needed to show how he did
so, would need another writer and another book.

Indeed, as well as the fact that there was some such relation it must
be borne in mind that his public life was a refuge and relief from what he
regarded as the desperate necessity to hold his place as the first writer of

---

[1] 11 Mar. 1854.

[2] Alice Marwood in *Dombey*, Little Emily and Martha Endell in *David
Copperfield*, and the street-walker in *Little Dorrit* (ch. xiv), who all came after
the Home was started, are no less melodramatic than Nancy in *Oliver Twist* or
Lilian in *The Chimes*. Even the sketches of situations involving prostitutes,
that Dickens noted for possible use in his memorandum book, are distinctly
stagey. (F, ix. vii.)   [3] F, ix. i.

his time. He saw himself as 'the modern embodiment of the old En-
chanters, whose Familiars tore them to pieces. I weary of rest, and have
no satisfaction but in fatigue. Realities and idealities are always comparing themselves before me, and I don't like the Realities except when
they are unattainable.'[1] Some of the realities he could never attain were
to be found in his work for social reform and in the illusions of the
theatre; and by immersing himself in all the practical details concerned
with both he found a kind of rest in fatigue as well.

Dickens's interests were always active and never reflective. He was
never merely content with homage and applause. In journalism,
amateur dramatics, practical philanthropy, and in public speaking, he
was ever intent on expressing himself and on avoiding what he called his
'restlessness' which overtook him when he stopped.

Not his genius only [said John Forster], but his whole nature, was too exclusively made up of sympathy for, and with, the real, in its most intense form,
to be sufficiently provided against failure in the realities around him. There
was for him no 'city of the mind' against outward ills. . . . It was in and from the
actual he still stretched forward to find the freedoms and satisfactions of an
ideal, and by his very attempts to escape the world he was driven back into the
thick of it.[2]

It is with this opinion of Forster in mind that these speeches have been
edited, chiefly as a contribution to Dickens's biography and in the belief
that a man's public speeches may sometimes be as revealing as his
private papers.

[1] To Hon. Mrs. R. Watson, 7 Dec. 1857, H. Compare to Mrs. M. Winter,
3 Apr. 1855.   [2] F, VIII. ii.

THE SPEECHES OF
CHARLES DICKENS

THE LITERARY FUND: ANNIVERSARY
FESTIVAL
3 *May* 1837

THE dinner was held at the Freemasons' Tavern, with the Duke of Somerset[1] in the Chair. According to *The Times* 'a host of persons associated with the literature of the country were present' including—among those known to Dickens—W. H. Ainsworth, Father Prout, John Macrone, Richard Bentley, William Lover, William Jerdan, and R. H. Horne. 'In the galleries were numbers of elegant females, and the whole scene was most lively and festive.'[2] Dickens acted as a steward, and spoke in reply to a toast from the Chair to 'The health of Mr. Dickens and the rising Authors of the Age', which was received with long-continued cheering.

HE spoke unaffectedly, he said, when he declared that his feelings were overpowered by receiving such an honour from such a company. [*Hear.*] He felt peculiarly embarrassed in acknowledging the toast, from the language in which it was couched. Wherever he looked around him he saw many more distinguished for ability than he could ever hope to be, to whom that honour might with far more justice have been awarded. He was proud to receive so friendly a shake of the hand from the old stagers, who sought to raise him up to their own level. The great discrepancy in the toast that had been drunk would have been in coupling them with 'the rising authors of the day'. Now, the difference was that they had risen, while he at the most was only rising. [*Hear, hear.*]

He hoped that the rising authors would all feel it an honour to be connected with that institution [*hear, hear*], and that should he ever leave any literary work that should carry his name to posterity (a circumstance the least likely to happen) that it would also be known that the flattering encouragement he had that night received from his literary brethren had nerved him to future exertions, smoothed his path to the station he had gained, and animated

---

[1] Edward Adolphus Seymour, 11th Duke of Somerset (1775–1855), President of the Literary Fund, 1801–38.   [2] *The Times*, 4 May.

his endeavour not to do other than justice to their kind praise. [*Cheers.*]

Dickens's first subscription to the society was in 1837; and his diaries show that he was also attending dinners of the Literary Fund Club at about this time. He was elected a member of the General Committee on 13 March 1839, retained his seat the following year, and then allowed his official membership to lapse. He was re-elected to the committee from 1845 to 1850, allowing his membership to lapse again in 1851 when he was elected a member of the council. He resigned from this merely honorary office on 5 June 1854. About the same time he began a campaign to reform the society in alliance with John Forster and C. W. Dilke, and opened his attack at the Annual General Meeting in 1855. From 1855 to 1860 they kept up a bitter struggle with the more conservative members, in an attempt to capture control of the society or discredit its administration, which ultimately resulted in their own failure and the complete vindication of the General Committee.

ARTISTS' BENEVOLENT FUND

12 *May* 1838

THE anniversary festival was held at the Freemasons' Tavern, with the Duke of Cambridge[1] in the Chair. During the course of the evening, after the usual proceedings, one of the toasts proposed was 'The health of the Royal Academicians', which was acknowledged by their president, Sir Martin Archer Shee. 'A Similar compliment to the Stewards', says the *Examiner*, 'was acknowledged by Mr. Dickens, whose presence we may add, gave no slight additional *éclat* to the affair, and whose name was received as a donor to the fund with such a burst of enthusiasm, again and again renewed, as we have never heard equalled in a meeting of this sort.'

BANQUET IN HONOUR OF W. C. MACREADY

20 *July* 1839

MACREADY'S[2] three-year management of Convent Garden came to an end with the farewell performance of *Henry V* on 16 July 1839. A few

---

[1] Frederick Adolphus, Duke of Cambridge (1774–1850), seventh son of George III; Viceroy of Hanover, 1816–37; active and efficient administrative philanthropist.

[2] William Charles Macready (1793–1873), one of Dickens's closest friends. *Nicholas Nickleby* was dedicated to him, Oct. 1839. After thirteen years at Drury Lane from 1823 to 1836, he had opened at Covent Garden under his own management in Sept. 1837; but although entirely successful he was unwilling to undertake a third season. See also Dickens's speeches of 29 Mar. 1847, pp. 77–79, and 1 Mar. 1851 at the farewell banquet, pp. 113–18. On leaving the stage he retired to Sherborne, but steadily maintained his friendship with Dickens.

days later a public dinner in his honour was given at the Freemasons' Tavern 'in testimony of the eminent service he had rendered to the legitimate drama'.

Dickens and Forster had been among Macready's closest friends and warmest supporters during his management. They had attended rehearsals, assisted him with reviews, and had been granted the freedom of the theatre. Dickens was among those who crowded into Macready's dressing-room after the last performance, and was filled with regret at his 'abdication'. He had written to Laman Blanchard on the 11th:

> I know no more than that there *is* to be a dinner to Macready on Saturday week, and that I am a steward. . . . Macready has, as Talfourd remarked in one of his speeches, 'cast a new grace round joy and gladness, and rendered mirth more holy!' Therefore we are preparing crowns and wreaths here, to shower upon the stage when that sad curtain falls and kivers up Shakespeare for years to come. I try to make a joke of it, but upon my word, when the night comes I verily believe I shall cry.

Macready listed Dickens, in his *Diaries*,[1] among those present at his table; and in expressing his thanks to all his friends, at the close of his speech, referred to him by name with Bulwer, Stanfield, Talfourd, and T. J. Serle.

The dinner was entirely successful, but was very unevenly reported. Most of the speeches can be found in full, but, as frequently happened, those who spoke last were reported least. Dickens rose almost last of all. The *Examiner* records that he 'was received with reiterated bursts of applause', and that in proposing 'The Members of the late Company of Covent Garden Theatre' his speech 'gracefully blended seriousness with pleasantry'.[2] According to another report, he declared that 'the public owed them a debt of gratitude for the intellectual and rational enjoyment which they had afforded during the last two seasons'.[3]

But while the newspaper reporters of the day failed in their task, Mary Cowden Clarke could still remember, nearly forty years later, how Dickens looked and spoke the first time she saw him. Watching from the gallery she noted particularly his 'perpetually discursive glances' and observant eye:

> No spoonful of soup seemed to reach his lips unaccompanied by a gathered oddity or whimsicality, no morsel to be raised upon his fork unseasoned by a droll gesture or trick he had remarked in some one near. But when it was his turn to speak, his after-dinner speech was one of the best in matter and style of delivery then given—though there were present on that occasion some practised speakers. His speech was like himself, genial, full of good spirit and good spirits, of kindly feeling and cheerful vivacity.[4]

There is somehow an element of mystery about the lost speech, for Forster mentions it only to say that he 'spoke with that wonderful instinct of knowing what to abstain from saying as well as what to say, which made his after-dinner speeches unique'.[5]

[1] *The Diaries of William Charles Macready*, ed. W. Toynbee, 1912, ii. 15–19.
[2] *Examiner*, 27 July, p. 475.   [3] *Morning Advertiser*, 22 July.
[4] Charles and Mary Cowden Clarke, *Recollections of Writers*, 1878, pp. 295–6.
[5] F, ii. v.

SOUTHWARK LITERARY AND SCIENTIFIC INSTITUTION

2 *December* 1840

To celebrate the foundation-laying of the new building of the institution, a banquet was given at the Bridge House Hotel, Southwark, with Henry Kemble,[1] M.P., in the Chair. After a number of other speakers, Dickens rose amid loud cheering to propose the toast of the evening.

HE was, he said, so confused by the warmth of the reception which he had met with, that he should have felt considerable difficulty in addressing a few words to them, if he were not relieved by the nature and subject of the toast which had been entrusted to him. The subject of the toast had been, indeed, exhausted by the chairman. The toast was 'success to the Southwark Literary and Scientific Institution', and although there were many gentlemen in that room who could more ably advocate the interests of that society, there was no one, however, no individual in Southwark—no one in London—no one in all England, more devoted to the success of Literary and Scientific Institutions, or who more desired to promote the welfare of the association to sustain which they were that day assembled. [*Cheers.*]

For he felt assured that such societies tended not only to enlarge the mind and awaken the best energies of our natures, but to improve and ameliorate the hearts of mankind. [*Applause.*] The chairman had alluded to the laying of the foundation stone of their building; but he would say, if they had never laid that stone—if they had met in a shed—nay, in the open fields—not only if they had not laid a foundation stone, but if they had not laid a single brick, nor an atom of straw, as the commencement of their edifice, still they had laid a moral foundation calculated to promote the best uses amongst what was styled the 'many-headed', but which by the aid of such institutions would soon be designated the 'many-thoughted, monster'. [*Applause.*]

The Reverend Professor near him had adverted to the opinions of Lord Bacon. He also remembered a doctrine of that illustrious man, which was by no means inapplicable to the present subject, on the present occasion. He stated that the qualities of the loadstone were discovered by the test of the needles formed from the rod of iron—not of the bar itself.[2] So in that and the like institutions, the few bright and brilliant individuals who originated them, drawn

---

[1] Henry Kemble (1787–1857), M.P. for East Surrey, 1837–47.

[2] The idea is Baconian, but the exact reference—if Dickens quoted it correctly—elusive: cf. *Advancement of Learning*, ii. ¶ 190, *De Augmentis Scientiarum*, VII. i; also, *Adv. of Learning*, ii. ¶ 86, *De Aug.* v. ii.

from the multitude, were those who ultimately consolidated their paramount utility as regarded the multitude itself. [*Great applause.*]

Had institutions similar to this existed long since, that one disgraceful leaf of dedication which formed the blot upon the literature of past ages, would have been torn from its pages. [*Cries of 'Hear, hear.'*] That huckstering, peddling, pandering to patronage for the sale of a book, the offspring of intellect and genius, would not now remain a stain upon their most brilliant productions. [*Hear, hear.*] Oh! it was sickening to see a man whom God had made a poet, crouching to those whose only title to eminence was derived from the achievements of the great great grandfather of those little, little sons. [*Great applause.*] The poet—for it was his natural avocation—was entitled to worship the stars; but when they contemplated him paying his adoration to stars and garters too, that was indeed a very different thing. [*A laugh and cheers.*]

If such institutions had existed in times gone by, Milton might have been appreciated in the age which he adorned, Otway might have lived and dined a few years longer [*a laugh*], and he knew not but that even Wordsworth might have been drawn from the dust of those shelves where until lately he had lain unnoticed and unmarked. [*Hear, hear.*] Nay, many of the illustrious dead, whose works were destined to illuminate posterity, might not have died the wretched inmates of the madhouse, or the asylum for the destitute. [*Loud cheers.*] For these, and for many other reasons, he hailed with sincere gratification the brilliant prospects of their institution—for brilliant they were, despite the paltry, pitiful incumbrance of £1,000. [*Hear, hear.*]

Those prospects were still more encouraging, when looking around him he perceived gentlemen who entertained the most opposite views upon political questions joining together to sustain and support a society constituted for such objects. [*Hear, hear.*] It was gratifying to find that this was a neutral ground upon which all shades of political opinions might mingle without a political compromise, proving satisfactorily—and a gratifying circumstance it was—the desire of those gentlemen rather to be elected by an enlightened constituency than to be representatives of ignorance and grovelling stupidity. [*Applause.*]

It was also gratifying to see amongst them so many ladies, they who on all occasions bestowed a grace and charm upon society, but who, upon the present occasion, lent to it an additional lustre. They came there to advocate claims of the highest and purest order—they came there not only to promote the demands of society for increased means for the dissipation of knowledge and the advancement of literature, but also by such means to cement more closely the dearest bonds by which society was united—in bestowing an additional charm upon the hearth and fireside of all, and giving to their household gods an additional claim to their worship and adoration. [*Cheers.*]

Thus a new spirit would be infused into the heart of society—a new soul would be breathed into the huge brick and mortar body of the metropolis; and if they wanted a spur to their exertions—if their energies required excitement—let them but recollect that in the churchyard not far distant from that place our Chaucer was entombed,[1] and that not a stone's throw from that room Shakespeare's own theatre once stood. [*Cheers.*] He would not say another word, but would conclude by proposing 'Success to the Southwark Literary and Scientific Institution.' [*Applause.*]

The celebrations concluded with a toast to the Ladies, which was given by the chairman, and to which Dickens replied. He wrote to Forster next day, mentioning the banquet: '*I believe you*—as to my own brilliancy. . . . Speeches excellent. I wish you had been there, for you can form no conception of what these bodies are. I never saw such a good meeting, or a thing so well and handsomely done.'[2]

THE LITERARY FUND: ANNIVERSARY FESTIVAL

12 *May* 1841

DICKENS was once again invited to be one of the stewards at the anniversary dinner. He took the Chair at a meeting of the stewards and the sub-committee on 11 May. Among the toasts then arranged was 'Mr. Charles Dickens and The Novelists', followed by 'Dr. Forbes and Medical Literature', and 'Mr. Macready and the Drama'. He attended the dinner next day with Macready, who noted in his diary, 'The speeches were mostly good, excepting Croly's—oh! and mine—oh!'[3] Unfortunately there is apparently no record of what Dickens said; for it was only the following year, when Prince Albert presided, that the society began to engage a reporter for the evening, and publish its own complete account of the annual proceedings. The *Morning Post* simply records: 'Mr. Charles Dickens made his acknowledgements, with a warm appeal in favour of the charity, and an eloquent indication of the benevolence of the institution.'[4]

Dickens attended the anniversary dinner only once more, in 1843

---

[1] Chaucer is buried in Westminster Abbey, which is over a mile and a half away; his friend John Gower, was buried in the church of St. Saviour's, Southwark; neither was entombed in a churchyard. It seems to have been a straightforward mistake by Dickens; but if it was due to a misreading of the reporter's shorthand—which it might well have been—one would have expected a reference to Chaucer's pilgrims and the Tabard, which would be more appropriate in association with the Globe Theatre, and more inspiring than a cemetery.

[2] F.C.   [3] *Diaries*, ed. Toynbee, ii. 136.   [4] 13 May.

when he was not called upon to speak.[1] He recalled the occasion later, at the Annual General Meeting of 1856, when he said:

I myself, at a dinner some twelve years ago, felt like a sort of Rip Van Winkle reversed, who had gone to sleep backwards for a hundred years; and waking, found that Literature instead of being emancipated, had to endure all manner of aristocratic patrons, and was lying at the feet of people who did nothing for it, instead of standing alone and appealing to the public for support.[2]

Yet this does not appear to have been his opinion at the time. Although he never attended another of the society's dinners, this at first seems to have been due to accident rather than principle. In 1842 he replied to an invitation forwarded by the secretary:[3]

I have delayed acknowledging the courtesy of the Committee, not because I was the least degree insensible to it, but because I deemed it probable that I might be leaving town . . . and in case I should not do so I wished to accept the Invitation with which I have been honoured. But although I am not going away just now . . . I regret that I *am* prevented by . . . an intolerable cold . . . which would render the sharpening of a saw, an infinitely more agreeable sound to the Literary Fund Diners than any observations from me.
Pray assure the Committee of my obligation to them.[4]

In 1845 he was in Italy. In 1846 he wrote to say 'it will be quite out of my power to attend the Literary Fund Dinner, otherwise I should have had great pleasure in returning thanks for the Novelists'.[5] It was only in 1847 that his replies began to grow curter, until in 1854 he simply wrote, 'As I do not attend the Dinner, I return the tickets.'[6]

Shortly after this, he opened his campaign to reform the society, and resigned from the council. From 1855 reporters were admitted to the annual General Meetings, and the reformers made the best of their opportunities for publicity. They nearly succeeded in capturing control of the Fund, and at one point the Rev. Whitwell Elwin, the editor of the *Quarterly*, urged Dickens not to offend the society's officers and members of the committee by abstaining from the dinner. Dickens replied that he could 'hardly be there without speaking', and that if he did he would probably offend them much more.[7]

Although there is no report of his remarks at the annual dinner of 1841, therefore, it deserves record with his later speeches against the society as the last time that he spoke at a festival on its behalf.

---

[1] 10 May, when Charles Lever replied for the Novelists.
[2] See p. 213.
[3] The Secretary was Octavian Blewitt (1810–84), author, and secretary of the Fund, 1839–84. His permanent engagement and salary were later attacked as an extravagance by Dickens and other 'reformers' of the society, but its increased efficiency and the preservation of its records were entirely the result of his services.   [4] 6 May, RLF.
[5] 10 May, RLF.   [6] 5 Apr., RLF.   [7] 1 May 1855.

BANQUET IN HIS HONOUR: EDINBURGH

25 *June* 1841

AFTER *Master Humphrey's Clock* had been running successfully for a year Dickens began to think of a holiday, deciding eventually in favour of a visit to the north and a tour in the Highlands. An Edinburgh correspondent had already written to tell him of a general desire to welcome him there, and that Lord Jeffrey was driving about declaring that there had been 'nothing so good as Nell since Cordelia'. And when Jeffrey arrived in London a week or two later they at once became fast friends, arranging definitely for the visit to be made in June.

It was decided to give a public banquet. Jeffrey, who was in ill health and hated dining-out, found affairs taken out of his hands, and Professor John Wilson,[1] 'Christopher North' of *Blackwood's*, was made chairman in his place. On 17 June Jeffrey wrote inviting Dickens to stay with him at Craigcrook, and explained:

> But the immediate business is this.—They will have you at a Public Dinner, you see, on Friday the 25th. Now I am not strong enough to go to such things—and I think that they are generally tantalising—and I suspect indeed that you would have been better pleased to have been let alone—at least until you knew a little who was who, and what was what in these latitudes.[2]

Dickens, in fact, was delighted by public recognition, and as soon as he and Mrs. Dickens had arrived kept Forster enthusiastically informed of all that went forward. They reached Edinburgh on Tuesday the 22nd. The banquet was to be on Friday. 'I have been this morning to the Parliament-house', he wrote, 'and am now introduced (I hope) to everybody in Edinburgh. The hotel is perfectly besieged and I have been forced to take refuge in a sequestered apartment . . . wherein I write this letter. They talk of 300 at the dinner.'[3]

It was held in the Waterloo Rooms. Professor Wilson entered the hall with Dickens on his arm, 'a little, slender, pale-faced, boyish-looking individual, and perhaps the very last man in the room whom a stranger to his portrait could have picked on as being the author of Pickwick'.[4] As soon as the dinner was over Mrs. Dickens, accompanied by 150 other ladies, was introduced into the gallery, where they were welcomed with loud cheers, and the speech-making then began.

After the usual toasts, which were enthusiastically received, the chairman rose amid long-continued cheering, to propose the health of their guest. In an eloquent and earnest speech he praised Dickens for his originality. He spoke of his just popularity, attained 'during an age more prolific of great men in poetry, and in all the various walks of

---

[1] John Wilson (1785–1854), Professor of Moral Philosophy, Edinburgh University; Tory controversialist, and principal contributor to *Blackwood's* from its first number in 1817.   [2] H.   [3] F, II. x.

[4] R. Shelton Mackenzie, *Life of Charles Dickens*, Philadelphia, 1870, pp. 130–1, quoting from 'a private letter written at the time'.

fiction than any other which illustrated the annals of this country'; and said that like Defoe, Richardson, Fielding, Smollett, he 'dealt with the common feelings and passions of ordinary man, in the common and ordinary paths of life'. The toast was received with loud and prolonged cheering; and, on rising, Dickens was greeted with enthusiastic applause. Then, it is said:

There *was* silence, deep as in the tomb—not a breath stirred, or a muscle moved in that crowded room—every eye was riveted on that wonderful man—every ear painfully on the alert to catch the first tones of the voice of that mighty magician; and soft were those tones, and calm that voice, as though he were dictating to an amanuensis the next number of Humphrey's Clock.[1]

He said:

IF I felt your warm and generous welcome less, I should be better able to thank you. If I could have listened, as you have listened, to the glowing language of your distinguished chairman, and if I could have heard, as you have heard, the 'thoughts that breathe and words that burn',[2] which he has uttered, it would have gone hard but I should have caught some portion of his enthusiasm, and kindled at his example. But every word which fell from his lips, and every demonstration of sympathy and approbation with which you received his eloquent expressions, render me unable to respond to his kindness, and leave me at last all heart and no lips. [*Great cheering.*] Yearning to respond as I would do to your cordial greeting—possessing, Heaven knows, the will, and desiring only to find the way.

The way to your good opinion, favour, and support, has been to me very pleasant—a path strewn with flowers and cheered with sunshine. I feel as if I stood amongst old friends, whom I have intimately known and highly valued. I feel as if the deaths of the fictitious creatures, in which you have been kind enough to express an interest, had endeared us to each other as real afflictions deepen friendships in actual life; I feel as if they had been real persons, whose fortunes we had pursued together in inseparable connexion, and that I had never known them apart from you.

It is a difficult thing for a man to speak of himself or of his works. But perhaps on this occasion I may, without impropriety, venture to say a word on the spirit in which mine were conceived. I felt an earnest and humble desire, and shall do till I die, to increase the stock of harmless cheerfulness. I felt that the world was not utterly to be despised; that it was worthy of living in for many reasons. I was anxious to find, as the Professor has said, if I could, in evil things, that soul of goodness which the Creator has put in them. I was anxious to show that virtue may be found on the by-ways of the

---

[1] R. S. Mackenzie, *Life*, p. 131. [2] Gray, 'Progress of Poesy'.

world, that it was not incompatible with poverty and even with rags, and to keep steadily through life the motto, expressed in the burning words of your Northern poet

> The rank is but the guinea's stamp
> The Man's the gowd for a' that.

[*Loud cheers.*] And in following this track, where could I have better assurance that I was right, or where could I have stronger assurance to cheer me on than in your kindness on this, to me, memorable night? [*Loud cheers.*]

I am anxious and glad to have an opportunity of saying a word in reference to one incident in which I am happy to know you were interested and still more happy to know, though it may sound paradoxical, that you were disappointed: I mean the death of the little heroine. When I first conceived the idea of conducting that simple story to its termination, I determined rigidly to adhere to it, and never to forsake the end I had in view. Not untried in the school of affliction, in the death of those we love, I thought what a good thing it would be if in my little work of pleasant amusement I could substitute a garland of fresh flowers for the sculptured horrors which disgrace the tomb. If I have put into my book anything which can fill the young mind with better thoughts of death, or soften the grief of older hearts; if I have written one word which can afford pleasure or consolation to old or young in time of trial, I shall consider it as something achieved—something which I shall be glad to look back upon in after life. Therefore I kept to my purpose, notwithstanding that towards the conclusion of the story, I daily received letters of remonstrance, especially from the ladies. God bless them for their tender mercies! The Professor was quite right when he said that I had not reached to an adequate delineation of their virtues; and I fear that I must go on blotting their characters in endeavouring to reach the ideal in my mind. [*Cheers.*] These letters were, however, combined with others from the sterner sex, and some of them were not altogether free from personal invective. But notwithstanding, I kept to my purpose, and I am happy to know that many of those who at first condemned me are now foremost in their approbation.

If I have made a mistake in detaining you with this little incident, I do not regret having done so; for your kindness has given me such a confidence in you, that the fault is yours and not mine. I come once more to thank you; and, here, I am in difficulty again. The distinction which you have conferred upon me is one which I never hoped for, and of which I never dared to dream. That it is one which I shall never forget, and that while I live I shall be proud

of its remembrance, you must well know. I believe I shall never
hear the name of this capital of Scotland without a thrill of gratitude and pleasure. I shall love while I have life her people, her hills,
and her houses, and even the very stones of her streets. And if, in
the future works which may lie before me, you should discern—God
grant you may—a brighter spirit and a clearer wit, I pray you to
refer it back to this night, and point to that as a Scottish passage
for evermore. [*Loud cheers.*] I thank you again and again, with the
energy of a thousand thanks in one, and I drink to you with a
heart as full as my glass, and far less easily emptied, I do assure
you. [*Great laughter and cheering.*]

Other speeches followed, including one by Patrick Robertson[1] to the
memory of Scott. His speech was typical of others, on which James
Hedderwick remarked, that they would have 'been more appropriate at
a Burns Club or a St. Andrew's Society dinner', as, 'the spirit of the
worthy Caledonian who maintained that Shakespeare . . . must have had
Scotch blood in his veins, was manifest throughout'.[2]

The memory of Burns, which was proposed by J. T. Gordon,[3] was not
forgotten. Dickens then rose to propose the health of the chairman, and
said:

I have the honour to be entrusted with a toast, the very mention
of which will recommend itself to you I know, as one possessing no
ordinary claims to your sympathy and approbation, and the proposing of which is as congenial to my wishes and feelings as its
acceptance must be to yours. It is the health of our Chairman [*loud
cheering*], and coupled with his name I have to propose the 'Literature of Scotland': a literature which he has done much to render
famous through the world, and of which he has been for many
years—as I hope and believe he will be for many more [*loud cheers*]
—a most brilliant and distinguished ornament. Who can revert to
the literature of the land of Scott and Burns without having directly
in his mind, as inseparable from the subject and foremost in the
picture, that old man of might, with his lion heart and sceptred
crutch, Christopher North? [*Loud cheers.*] I am glad to remember
the time when I believed him to be a real, actual, veritable old

---

[1] Patrick Robertson (1794–1855), advocate; Lord of Session, 1842; versifier
and wit; described to Forster, by Dickens, as 'a large, portly, full-faced man
with a merry eye, and a queer way of looking under his spectacles which is
characteristic and pleasant'.

[2] *Backward Glances*, 1891, p. 88. Hedderwick was assistant-editor of the
Scotsman.

[3] John Thomson Gordon (1813–65), advocate, son-in-law of Professor
Wilson, and Jeffrey's nephew; Sheriff of Midlothian, 1848; later a personal
friend of Dickens, who described him on this occasion, to Forster, as 'a very
masterly speaker indeed, who ought to become a distinguished man'.

gentleman, that might be seen any day hobbling along the High Street, with the most brilliant eye—but that is no fiction—and the greyest hair in all the world, who wrote not because he cared to write, not because he cared for the wonder and admiration of his fellow men, but who wrote because he could not help it [*loud cheers*], because there was always springing up in his mind a clear and sparkling stream of poetry which must have vent, and like the glittering fountain in the fairy tale, draw what you might, was ever at the full, and never languished even by a single drop or bubble. [*Loud cheers.*] I had so figured him in my mind, and when I saw the Professor two days ago, striding along the Parliament House, I was disposed to take it as a personal offence—I was vexed to see him look so hearty, I drooped to see him twenty Christophers in one. I began to think that Scottish life was all 'light' and no 'shadows' [*loud cheers*],[1] and I began to doubt of that beautiful book to which I have turned again and again, always to find new beauties and fresh sources of interest. [*Cheers.*]

It has been the happy lot of Scotland that her great writers have loved to exhibit her in various forms, whether in scenes of solitary grandeur or her simple village ways. The mighty genius[2] who lately departed from you was equally at home in the wild grandeur of Highland scenery or the burning sands of Syria, and in the low haunts of London life; while there is not a shepherd or a peasant who has not his type immortalized in the verse of him whose hand was on the plough while his heart was with the muse. There is not a glen of a lonely haunt in the Highlands which has not been visited by Christopher North in his shooting jacket, with a heart as free and as wild as the winds that swept over him. His voice has been heard from the lonely heaths and the snow drifts of the mountains, in the highways of Edinburgh, and in the caves of the Covenanters. By his genius every foot of ground in Scotland has been pictured to dwellers afar off as a fairy land. [*Cheers.*] It is difficult to follow the Professor through all the scenes which he has depicted with such exquisite beauty, from the varied stores of his rich and teeming fancy; so that the epitaph of Goldsmith may be applied to him, that there was no subject but he touched, and nothing which he touched that he did not adorn. [*Cheers.*]

But the literature of Scotland comprises other names which are

---

[1] Referring here, and in the next paragraph, to Professor Wilson's *Lights and Shadows of Scottish Life*, 1822.

[2] As an admirer of Scott, Dickens had already joined in a dispute about his reputation between Lockhart and the Ballantynes, in the *Examiner*. In *Barnaby Rudge* he was then paying him the compliment of imitation and attempting a challenge.

familiar to you: poets, historians, critics, all of the foremost rank.
The learned Lord whom I am proud to call my friend [*cheers*], to
whom, by his fine taste and just appreciation of the beauties of an
author, literature owes so much, and to the generosity of whose
nature those who are opposed to him have borne high testimony;[1]
the author of *Matthew Wald* and *Adam Blair*, who has lately depicted with vivid colouring the last days of the mighty genius who
departed on the banks of the river he loved so well;[2] the gentleman
who is present amongst us, and who under the signature of 'Delta'
[*loud cheers*] has given the world assurance of a poet, and who has
raised in us all admiration which we would fain be at liberty to
increase still further by meeting him oftener;[3] these, and other
great names, are all included in the toast, which we drink to do
honour, not to them, but to ourselves. [*Loud cheers.*]

Professor Wilson replied; and proposed a toast to the Fine Arts.
Peter Robertson read a mock report of the meeting, and some verses
referring to various characters in Dickens's works which 'excited great
laughter and cheering'. A toast was proposed to Lord Jeffrey; and
Dickens then rose for the last time, and said:

I am less fortunate than the two gentlemen who have preceded
me in their toasts, for I have to mention a name known to all
present, but which I cannot utter at this time without deep sorrow
—a name in which Scotland had a high and endearing pride, which
England delighted to honour, and which was cherished in the breast
of every reflecting man throughout the whole civilized world. From
among the gifted spirits of our times a gentle, honest, generous and
true one has passed away, as it were but yesterday. The life of one
devoted to all that was true and beautiful, and elevating, in art and
nature, hath come to an end. I will give you the memory of Wilkie.[4]
It is not as one whom many of us knew and loved; it is not as one
whose simple nature his high fame and fortune never spoiled or
changed; it is not as one who acted up to what he taught, and who
made the domestic virtues and duties his daily practice, that I
think of him tonight. I think of him as one—and you should do so
too—who has left behind him unwonted fire, who has left an undying and imperishable name, who made the cottage hearth his

[1] Lord Jeffrey.
[2] John Gibson Lockhart (1794–1854), editor of the *Quarterly*, author of the
Life of Sir Walter Scott, 1836–8. He and Dickens were on friendly terms.
[3] David Macbeth Moir (1798–1851), physician and author, member of the
Blackwood's coterie.
[4] Sir David Wilkie (1785–1841), Scottish painter; god-father of Wilkie
Collins; had died suddenly, on returning from Alexandria, on 1 June, shortly
after leaving Gibraltar, and had been buried at sea; personal friend of Dickens.

grave theme, and who surrounded the lives, and cares, and daily toils, and occupations of the poor, with dignity and beauty: who indeed found 'books in the running brooks, sermons in stones, and good in everything', and who has left behind in all his works the same breathing of health, as of the air wafted from the heather of his native land. [*Cheers.*]

However desirous one may be on an occasion like the present to separate his memory from these mournful associations which gather around it, it is impossible, they are peculiarly inseparable from him: the painter's study with the empty easel, the brush and palette which he was wont to use, now lie idly by, his unfinished pictures turn their faces to the wall, and that bereaved and affectionate mourner whom he loved in his days to honour, will look upon him no more. He is gone, and has left behind him, particularly to his countrymen and all who knew him, a name and fame as pure and unsullied as the bright sky which shines over the painter's grave. He has filled our minds and memories with what is mournful, yet as soothing as the roll of the blue waters over his honoured head. Mindful of his only sister, I cannot help expressing the hope that the time will shortly come when she, like us, will feel a solemn pleasure in speaking of his goodness and greatness, and when she will have the grateful recollection that he died in the fulness of his powers, before age or sickness had dimmed his sight, or had bowed his head.

Dickens was said to be 'much affected in the delivery of this speech',[1] particularly when he referred directly to Sir David Wilkie's death. The toast was drunk in silence. Among other speakers, Angus Fletcher briefly proposed the health of Mrs. Dickens, to which Dickens replied saying that his wife was a Scotswoman, and born in the city of Edinburgh. The meeting broke up about twelve o'clock.

It was Dickens's first triumph in public speaking. Everyone was delighted. His hearers were surprised at his ability as a speaker, and described his eloquence enthusiastically. One wrote: 'He is as happy in public speaking as in writing—nothing studied, nothing artistical; his were no written speeches, conned, and got by heart, but every sentence seemed to be suggested on the impulse of the moment.'[2] The *Scotsman* thought his speeches the best of the evening, and his address 'earnest, unaffected, and even touching'; and the *Evening Courant* agreed that his words seemed entirely spontaneous, and that there was nothing elaborate in his style: 'It is simple and inartificial, and seems to be suggested by circumstances as they arise, having entirely a conversational tone.'

Dickens was as pleased as anyone, and dashed off several short

[1] *Edinburgh Evening Courant.*
[2] R. S. Mackenzie, *Life of Dickens*, p. 131.

accounts to his friends. 'It was a most magnificent show', he wrote to George Cattermole, 'and the shouting perfectly awful.' Edward Chapman was told, 'The whole place rings today with the noise of the affair', and Jerdan, 'the dinner was a very brilliant affair indeed—they say the best on record'. Forster received a fuller report: 'The great event is over; and being gone, I am a man again. It was the most brilliant affair you can conceive. . . . I think (ahem!) that I spoke rather well. It was an excellent room, and both the subjects (Wilson and Scottish Literature, and the Memory of Wilkie) were good to go upon.'[1]

After being elected 'a burgess and guild brother of the city', and a brilliant round of private engagements, they left Edinburgh on Sunday, 4 July, for a ten days' tour in the Highlands, under the guidance of their Scots friend, Angus Fletcher.

PRESENTATION TO CAPTAIN HEWETT: BOSTON
29 *January* 1842

THE *S.S. Britannia*, in which Dickens had embarked at Liverpool on 4 January, arrived at Boston on the 22nd. 'We had a dreadful passage', Dickens wrote to his friend Thomas Mitton, 'the worst, the officers all concur in saying, that they had ever known. We were eighteen days coming; experienced a dreadful storm which swept away our paddle-boxes and stove our lifeboats; and we ran aground besides, near Halifax, among rocks and breakers where we lay at anchor all night.'[2]

The day before their arrival the passengers held a meeting to get up a subscription to buy a piece of silver plate to present to the captain, 'As a slight acknowledgement of His great ability and skill . . . and as a feeble token of Their everlasting gratitude'.[3] Lord Mulgrave[4] took the Chair at the meeting, while Dickens acted as secretary and treasurer.

A week after landing a meeting was held in the saloon of the Tremont Theatre to witness the presentation of the plate—a silver goblet, pitcher, and salver. Captain Hewett, Dickens, and one of the other members of the committee came forward, and were greeted with great applause. As soon as it had subsided, Dickens addressed the meeting, and said:

LADIES and gentlemen, I am assured by your presence here this morning that you have become acquainted with the nature of the welcome duty which I have to discharge, and which is most

---

[1] F, II. x.   [2] 31 Jan. 1842.

[3] Inscription for the salver, agreed on at the meeting, and recorded by Dickens in the Minutes. (*Dickensian*, 1929, xxv. 288–9, in facsimile.)

[4] George Augustus Constantine Phipps (1819–90), styled Viscount Normanby 1831–8, the Earl of Mulgrave, 1836–63, 2nd Marquis of Normanby, 1863; officer in Scots Fusilier Guards. Later, Liberal whip, and Lord-in-waiting; Governor, successively, of Queensland, New Zealand, and Victoria, 1871–84. Had first met Dickens on board ship, and joined him again a few months later in Montreal. They kept up their friendship thereafter. Dickens also came to know Lord Mulgrave's father, the 1st Marquis of Normanby (1797–1863).

pleasantly commended to me in a double sense: firstly because it cannot fail to be gratifying to a worthy man who has established a strong claim upon my interest and esteem; and, secondly, because it affords me an opportunity of meeting you, whom I have a thousand reasons for longing to see, here, or anywhere.

It may be known to you, perhaps, that passengers on board the *Britannia* Steamship which bore me and some four score others to these happy shores, held a meeting together the day before our arrival, the object of which to do honour to Captain Hewett, the able commander under whose guidance we had crossed the wide Atlantic. I, and two other gentlemen, (one of whom stands near me, and the other of whom is prevented by business from attending here today) had the honour to be deputed by that meeting to carry its intention into effect. In the execution of the trust reposed in us by our fellow passengers, we are most desirous to impress you with the fact that this is very far from being an ordinary or matter of course proceeding: that it is not a matter of form, but of good sound substance; that in presenting Captain Hewett with these slight and frail memorials, we are not following out a hollow custom, but are imperfectly expressing the warmest and most earnest feelings, being well assured that with God's blessing we owe our safety and preservation under circumstances of unusual peril, to his ability, courage, and skill.

You will please to understand that these tokens on the table are an acknowledgement, not in themselves, but in the feeling which dictates their presentation, of many long and weary nights of watching and fatigue, of great exertion of body, and much anxiety of mind, and of the prompt and efficient discharge of arduous duties such as do not often present themselves. In a word, this is anything but an extraordinary return for really extraordinary services; and we wish you to regard it in that light that our present may have the value which it was intended to bear, and which is far enough removed, Heaven knows, from its intrinsic worth or beauty.

Captain Hewett [*turning to him*], I am very proud and happy to have been selected as the instrument of conveying to you the heartfelt thanks of my fellow passengers on board the ship entrusted to your charge, and of entreating your acceptance of this trifling present. The ingenious artists who work in silver do not always, I find, keep their promises even in Boston. I regret that instead of two goblets, which there should be here, there is at present only one. This deficiency, however, will soon be supplied; and when it is, our little testimonial will be, so far, complete.

You are a sailor, Captain Hewett, in the truest sense of the word; and the devoted admiration of the ladies, God bless them, is a sailor's first boast. I need not enlarge upon the honour they have done you, I am sure, by their presence here. Judging of you by myself, I am certain that the recollection of their beautiful faces will cheer your lonely vigils upon the ocean for a long time to come.

In all time to come, and in all your voyages upon the sea, I hope you will have a thought for those who wish to live in your memory by the help of these trifles. As they will often connect you with the pleasures of those homes and firesides from which they once wandered, and which, but for you, they might never have regained, so they trust that you will sometimes associate them with your hours of festive enjoyment; and that when you drink from these cups, you will feel that the draught is commended to your lips by friends whose best wishes you have, and who earnestly and truly hope for your success, happiness, and prosperity in all the undertakings of your life.

Captain Hewett briefly replied. Dickens had a sincere respect for him, and recalled him affectionately, in the first chapter of *American Notes*, as 'a well-made, tight-built, dapper little fellow, with a ruddy face . . . and with a clear, blue honest eye, that it does one good to see one's sparkling image in'.

BANQUET IN HIS HONOUR: BOSTON

1 *February* 1842

DICKENS'S first impressions of the United States were favourable. He received a welcome which left 'no time . . . for exercise', and little for correspondence, but that was his only complaint as he sat down to write to Macready:

It is impossible to tell you what a reception I have had here. They cheer me in the Theatres; in the streets; within doors; and without. I have a public dinner here tomorrow—another at Hartford on Wednesday—another at New-haven on Thursday—a great Ball in New York on Monday the Fourteenth, a great public dinner at the same place in the same week—another dinner in the same place with a club—and entertainments of all kinds in perspective all through the States. Deputations and Committees wait upon me every day—some have come 2000 miles.[1]

He had been invited to a public dinner by a committee of the Young Men of Boston before he left England, and directly he arrived he accepted its invitation. The banquet was given in the drawing-rooms of Papanti's Hall. Immediately on Dickens's arrival he was received by the committee, and the proceedings commenced: a full band in the gallery struck up 'Washington's March', followed by 'God Save the Queen', and the

---

[1] 31 Jan. 1842, M.

company took their places. Josiah Quincy, Jr.,[1] took the Chair as president of the occasion, assisted by various vice-presidents, including Oliver Wendell Holmes.

As soon as the cloth was removed, Quincy rose and gave the first toast. Among the guests was James T. Fields[2]—then a young man of twenty-five, later one of Dickens's closest friends—who vividly recalled the whole occasion many years later as 'a glorious episode'.

Did ever mortal preside with such felicitous success as did Mr. Quincy? . . . And how admirably he closed his speech of welcome, calling upon the young author amid a perfect volley of applause 'Health! Happiness! and a Hearty welcome to Charles Dickens!' . . . And when Dickens stood up at last to answer for himself, so fresh and handsome with his beautiful eyes moist with feeling, and his whole frame aglow with excitement, how we did hurrah, we young fellows![3]

Dickens replied:

GENTLEMEN, If you had given this splendid entertainment to anyone else in the whole wide world—if I were tonight to exult in the triumph of my dearest friend—if I stood here upon my defence to repel any unjust attack—to appeal as a stranger to your generosity and kindness as the freest people on the earth—I could, putting some restraint upon myself, stand among you as self possessed and unmoved as I should be alone in my own room in England. But when I have the echoes of your cordial greeting ringing in my ears; when I see your kind faces beaming a welcome so warm and earnest as never man had, I feel—it is my nature—so vanquished and subdued, that I have hardly fortitude enough to thank you. If your President, instead of pouring forth that delightful mixture of humour and pathos which you have just heard with so much delight had been but a caustic, ill-natured man—if he had only been a dull one—if I could only have doubted or distrusted him or you, I should have had my wits at my fingers' ends, and, using them, could have held you at arm's length. But you have given me no such opportunity; you take advantage of me in the tenderest point; you give me no chance of playing at company, or holding you at a distance, but flock about me like a host of brothers, and make this place like home. Indeed, gentlemen, indeed, if it be

---

[1] Josiah Quincy (1802–82), lawyer; President of the State Senate, 1842; mayor, 1846–8.

[2] James Thomas Fields (1817–81), author and publisher, junior partner in Ticknor, Reed & Fields, of which, after 1854 when it became Ticknor & Fields, he was the head. He first met Dickens in England in 1859; they took a great liking to each other; and on Dickens's second visit to America, Fields and his wife showed him the greatest kindness and consideration. They were also associated in publishing transactions, and in the arrangements for Dickens's readings.

[3] James T. Fields, *Yesterdays with Authors*, London, 1872, pp. 129–30.

natural and allowable for each of us, on his own hearth, to express his thoughts in the most homely fashion, and to appear in his plainest garb, I have a fair claim upon you to let me do so tonight, for you have made my house an Aladdin's Palace. You fold so tenderly within your breasts that common household lamp in which my feeble fire is all enshrined, and at which my flickering torch is lighted up, that straight my household gods take wing, and are transported here. And whereas it is written of that fairy structure that it never moved without two shocks—one when it rose, and one when it settled down—I can say of mine that, however sharp a tug it took to pluck it from its native ground, it struck at once an easy, and a deep and lasting root into this soil, and loved it as its own. I can say more of it, and say with truth, that long before it moved, or had a chance of moving, its master—perhaps from some secret sympathy between its timbers, and a certain stately tree that has its being hereabout, and spreads its broad branches far and wide—dreamed by day and night, for years, of setting foot upon this shore, and breathing this pure air. And trust me, gentlemen, that if I had wandered here unknowing and unknown, I would—if I know my own heart—have come with all my sympathies clustering richly about this land and people—with all my sense of justice as keenly alive to their high claims on every man who loves God's image—with all my energies as fully bent on judging for myself, and speaking out, and telling in my sphere the truth, as I do now when you rain down your welcomes on my head.

Your President has alluded to those writings which have been my occupation for some years past; and you have received his allusions in a manner which assures me—if I needed any such assurance—that we are old friends in the spirit, and have been in close communion for a long time.

It is not easy for a man to speak of his own books. I dare say that few persons have been more interested in mine than I; and if it be a general principle in nature that a lover's love is blind, and that a mother's love is blind, I believe it may be said of an author's attachment to the creatures of his own imagination, that it is a perfect model of constancy and devotion, and is the blindest of all. But the objects and purposes I have in view are very plain and simple, and may easily be told. I have always had, and always shall have, an earnest and true desire to contribute, as far as in me lies, to the common stock of healthful cheerfulness and enjoyment. I have always had, and always shall have, an invincible repugnance to that mole-eyed philosophy which loves the darkness, and winks and scowls in the light. I believe that Virtue shows quite as well in rags and patches as she does in purple and fine linen. I believe that she and every beautiful object in external nature, claim some sympathy in the breast of the poorest man who breaks his scanty loaf of daily bread. I believe that she goes barefoot as well as shod. I believe that she dwells rather oftener in alleys and by-ways than she does in courts and palaces, and that it is good, and pleasant, and profitable to track her out, and follow her. I believe that to lay one's hand upon some one of those rejected ones whom the world has too long forgotten, and too often misused, and to say to the proudest and most thoughtless,—these creatures have the same elements and capacities of goodness as yourselves, they are moulded in the same form, and made of the same clay; and though ten times worse than you, may, in having retained anything of their original nature amidst the trials and distresses of their condition, be really ten times better.—I believe that to do this is to pursue a worthy and not useless avocation. Gentlemen, that you think so too, your fervent greeting assures me. That this feeling is alive in the Old World as well as in the New, no man should know better than I—I, who have found such wide and ready sympathy in my own dear land. That in expressing it we are but treading in the steps of those great master-spirits who have gone before, we know by reference to all the bright examples in our literature, from Shakespeare downward.

There is one other point connected with the labours (if I may call them so) that you hold in such generous esteem, to which I cannot help adverting. I cannot help expressing the delight, the more than happiness it was to me to find so strong an interest awakened on this side of the water, in favour of that little heroine of mine, to whom your President has made allusion, who died in her youth. I had letters about that child, in England, from the dwellers in log-houses among the morasses, and swamps, and densest forests, and deepest solitudes of the Far West. Many a sturdy hand, hard with the axe and spade, and browned by the summer's sun, has taken up the pen, and written to me a little history of domestic joy or sorrow, always coupled, I am proud to say, with something of interest in that little tale, or some comfort or happiness derived from it; and my correspondent has always addressed me, not as a writer of books for sale, resident some four or five thousand miles away, but as a friend to whom he might freely impart the joys and sorrows of his own fireside. Many a mother—I could reckon them now by dozens, not by units—has done the like, and has told me that she lost such a child at such a time, and where she is buried, and how good she was, and how, in this or that respect, she resembled Nell.

I do assure you that no circumstance of my life has given me one-hundredth part of the gratification I have derived from this source. I was wavering at the time whether or not to wind up my Clock, and come and see this country, and this decided me. I felt as if it were a positive duty, as if I were bound to pack up my clothes, and come and see my friends; and even now I have such an odd sensation in connexion with these things, that you have no chance of spoiling me. I feel as though we were agreeing—as indeed we are, if we substitute for fictitious characters the classes from which they are drawn—about third parties, in whom we have a common interest. At every act of kindness on your part, I say to myself 'That's for Oliver; I should not wonder if that were meant for Smike; I have no doubt that is intended for Nell'; and so I become a much happier, certainly, but a more sober and retiring man than ever I was before.

Gentlemen, talking of my friends in America, brings me back, naturally and of course, to you. Coming back to you, and being thereby reminded of the pleasure we have in store in hearing the gentlemen who sit about me, I arrive by the easiest, though not by the shortest course in the world, at the end of what I have to say. But before I sit down, there is one topic on which I am desirous to lay particular stress. It has, or should have, a strong interest for us all, since to its literature every country must look for one great means of refining and improving its people, and one great source of national pride and honour. You have in America great writers— great writers—who will live in all time, and are as familiar to our lips as household words. Deriving (as they all do in a greater or less degree, in their several walks) their inspiration from the stupendous country which gave them birth, they diffuse a better knowledge of it, and a higher love for it, all over the civilized world. I take leave to say, in the presence of some of those gentlemen, that I hope the time is not far distant when they, in America, will receive of right some substantial profit and return in England from their labours; and when we, in England, shall receive some substantial profit and return for ours. Pray do not misunderstand me. Securing for myself from day to day the means of an honourable subsistence, I would rather have the affectionate regard of my fellow men, than I would have heaps and mines of gold. But the two things do not seem to me incompatible. They cannot be, for nothing good is incompatible with justice. There must be an international arrangement in this respect: England has done her part, and I am confident that the time is not far distant when America will do hers. It becomes the character of a great country; *firstly*, because it is justice; *secondly*, because without it you never can have, and keep, a literature of your own.

Gentlemen, I thank you with feelings of gratitude such as are not often awakened, and can never be expressed. As I understand it to be the pleasant custom here to finish with a toast, I would beg to give you 'America and England—and may there never be anything but the Atlantic between them.'

When the applause had subsided the president proposed 'The Health of the Lady of our Distinguished Guest.—If she were the model of the pure and elevated females of his works, it might well be said that she was the better half, *even* of Charles Dickens'. The toast was drunk with nine cheers, the company all standing.

A steady succession of further speakers then followed, including Josiah Quincy, President of Harvard University, Thomas Colley Grattan, British Consul in Massachusetts, Richard H. Dana, father and son, Washington Allston, the painter, George Bancroft, historian and Collector of the Port of Boston, and Jonathan Chapman, the mayor. There were many other speakers. Oliver Wendell Holmes sang some verses of his own, and James M. Fields, of the Tremont Theatre, gave 'The Werry last Obserwations of Weller, Senior'.

The president finally gave the toast of 'A speedy return to Charles Dickens', and they then withdrew together.

'It was a most superb affair,' Dickens wrote to Forster, 'and the speaking *admirable*.'[1] He left Boston on 5 February, with happier memories of his visit there than of anywhere else in America when four months later he returned to England.

BANQUET IN HIS HONOUR: HARTFORD

7 *February* 1842

THE dinner was given at the City Hotel, with William J. Hammersley[2] in the Chair. It was variously reported by the local press to be 'a very neat affair',[3] 'a grand affair',[4] and 'a splendid affair . . . which gave the highest satisfaction both to the illustrious guest, and to those who assembled on the occasion to pay him a tribute of respect'.[5]

Following the dinner, the proceedings began with a list of 'Regular Toasts', which were duly honoured by the company. Some of the more 'irregular' ones, that came later, give a curious idea of what Dickens's hosts expected from their guest. He was a 'Nobleman of Nature', one of 'Those whose greatness is created by the hand of God'; 'The Great Republican of the Literary World'. His 'Genius and Talent', were to advocate the cause of 'The Poor and the Oppressed'; Literature was a

---

[1] F, III. iii.

[2] William James Hammersley (1808–77), publisher, bookseller, and local politician; mayor, 1853–4, and 1862–4; representative to the Connecticut General Assembly, 1850, 1867, and 1870.

[3] The *Daily Times*, Hartford, 9 Feb. 1842.

[4] *Hartford Daily Courant*, 10 Feb. 1842.

[5] *New England Weekly Review*.

'neutral ground on which men of every clime might meet'—without copyright fee—and he was welcomed as a visitor unlike 'those illiberal mercenaries who have travelled through these States only to discover and . . . magnify our foibles'. It was all too much to expect of anyone.

The president of the occasion at length rose to give a toast to 'The Health of Charles Dickens.—Elected by the world's suffrage to an elevated station in the great republic of letters. His fame is written on the heart, and the head approves the record.' It was received with loud and long continuous applause; and, when the cheering had at last subsided, Dickens rose and said:

GENTLEMEN, to say that I thank you for the earnest manner in which you have drunk the toast just now so eloquently proposed to you; to say that I give you back your kind wishes and good feelings with more than compound interest, and that I feel how dumb and powerless the best acknowledgements would be beside such genial hospitality as yours—is nothing. To say that in this winter season, flowers have sprung up in every footstep's length of the path which has brought me here, that no country ever smiled more pleasantly than yours has smiled on me, and that I have rarely looked upon a brighter summer prospect than that which now lies before me now—is nothing. [*Applause.*]

But it is something to be no stranger in a strange place; to feel, sitting at a board for the first time, the ease and affection of an old guest, and to be at once on such intimate terms with the family as to have a homely, genuine interest in its every member; it is, I say, something to be in this novel and happy frame of mind. And as it is of your creation, and owes its being to you, I have no reluctance in urging it as a reason why, in addressing you, I should not so much consult the form and fashion of my speech, as I should employ that universal language of the heart which you, and such as you, best teach and best can understand. Gentlemen, in that universal language—common to you in America, and to us in England, as that younger mother tongue which, by means of, and through the happy union of our two great countries, shall be spoken ages hence, by land and sea, over the wide surface of the globe—I thank you.

I had occasion, gentlemen, to say the other night in Boston, as I have more than once had occasion to remark before, that it is not easy for an author to speak of his own books. If the task be a difficult one at any time, its difficulty certainly is not diminished when a frequent occurrence to the same theme has left one nothing new to say. Still I feel that, in a company like this, and especially after what has been said by the President, that I ought not to pass over those labours of love which, if they have no other merit, have been the happy means of bringing us together.

It has been often observed that you cannot judge of an author's personal character from his writings. It may be that you cannot— I think it very likely, for many reasons, that you cannot—but, at least, a reader will rise from the perusal of a book with some defined and tangible idea of the writer's moral creed and broad purposes, if he has any at all; and it is probable enough that he may like to have this idea confirmed from the author's lips, or dissipated by his explanation. Gentlemen, my moral creed—which is a very wide and comprehensive one, and includes all sects and parties—is very easily summed up. I have faith, and I wish to diffuse faith in the existence—yes, of beautiful things, even in those conditions of society which are so degenerate, degraded, and forlorn that, at first sight, it would seem as though they could not be described but by a strange and terrible reversal of the words of Scripture—God said, Let there be light, and there was none. I take it that we are born and that we hold our sympathies, hopes, and energies in trust for the many, and not for the few. That we cannot hold in too strong a light of disgust and contempt, before the view of others, all meanness, falsehood, cruelty, and oppression, of every grade and kind. Above all, that nothing is high, because it is in a high place; and that nothing is low, because it is in a low one. [*Loud applause.*] This is a lesson taught us in the great book of nature. This is the lesson which may be read, alike in the bright track of the stars, and in the dusty course of the poorest thing that drags its tiny length upon the ground. This is the lesson ever uppermost in the thoughts of that inspired man, who tells us that there are

> Tongues in trees, books in the running brooks,
> Sermons in stones, and good in everything. [*Cheers.*]

Gentlemen, keeping these objects steadily before me, I am at no loss to refer your favour and your generous hospitality back to the right source. While I know, on the one hand, that if, instead of being what it is, this were a land of tyranny and wrong, I should care very little for your smiles or frowns, so I am sure upon the other, that if, instead of being what I am, I were the greatest genius that ever trod the earth, and had exerted myself for the oppression and degradation of mankind, you would despise and reject me. I hope you will, whenever, through such means, I give you the opportunity. Trust me that whenever you give me the like occasion, I will return the compliment with interest.

Gentlemen, as I have no secrets from you, in the spirit of confidence you have engendered between us, and as I have made a kind of compact with myself that I never will, while I remain in America, omit an opportunity of referring to a topic in which I and all others of my class on both sides of the water are equally interested—equally interested, there is no difference between us—I would beg leave to whisper in your ear two words, International Copyright. I use them in no sordid sense, believe me, and those that know me best, best know that. For myself, I would rather that my children coming after me, trudged in the mud, and knew by the general feeling of society that their father was beloved, and had been of some use, than I would have them ride in their carriages, and know by their banker's books that he was rich. But I do not see, I confess, why one should be obliged to make the choice, or why fame, besides playing that delightful *reveille* for which she is so justly celebrated, should not blow out of her trumpet a few notes of a different kind from those with which she has hitherto contented herself.

It was well observed the other night by a beautiful speaker, whose words went to the heart of every man who heard him, that if there had existed any law in this respect, Scott might not have sunk beneath the mighty pressure on his brain, but might have lived to add new creatures of his fancy to the crowd which swarm about you in your summer walks and gather round your winter evening hearths.

As I listened to his words there came back fresh upon me, that touching scene in the great man's life, when he lay upon his couch surrounded by his family, and listened, for the last time, to the rippling of the river he had so well loved, over its stony bed. I pictured him to myself, faint, wan, dying, crushed both in mind and body by his honourable struggle, and hovering round him the ghosts of his own imagination—Waverley, Ravenswood, Jeannie Deans, Rob Roy, Caleb Balderstone, Dominie Sampson—all the familiar throng—with cavaliers, and Puritans, and Highland chiefs innumerable overflowing the chamber, and fading away in the dim distance beyond. I pictured them, fresh from traversing the world, and hanging down their heads in shame and sorrow that, from all those lands into which they had carried gladness, instruction, and delight for millions, they had brought him not one friendly hand to help to raise him from that sad, sad bed. No, nor brought him from that land in which his own language was spoken, and in every house and hut of which his own books were read in his own tongue, one grateful dollar-piece to buy a garland for his grave. Oh! if every man who goes from here, as many do, to look upon that tomb in Dryburgh Abbey, would but remember this, and bring the recollection home!

Gentlemen, I thank you again, and once again, and many times to that. You have given me a new reason for remembering this day, which is already one of mark in my calendar, it being my birthday;

and you have given those who are nearest and dearest to me a new reason for recollecting it with pride and interest. Heaven knows that, although I should grow ever so grey, I shall need nothing to remind me of this epoch in my life. But I am glad to think that from this time you are inseparably connected with every recurrence of this day; and, that on its periodical return, I shall always, in imagination, have the unfading pleasure of entertaining you as my guests in return for the gratification you have afforded me tonight. [*Loud applause.*]

Dickens's speech was enthusiastically received, being 'cheered loudly during the delivery, and at the conclusion of every sentence'.—Songs were sung; complimentary letters were read; and some verses, written for the occasion by Mrs. Lydia Sigourney, were recited in Dickens's honour. A long succession of 'volunteer toasts' then followed the official speeches.

All went well except the allusions to international copyright. Dickens was determined to drag the question forward whenever he could, although, as he said, his American friends 'were paralysed with wonder at such audacious daring'.—'I wish you could have seen,' he wrote to Forster, 'the faces that I saw, down both sides of the table at Hartford, when I began to talk about Scott. I wish you could have heard how I gave it out. My blood so boiled . . . that I felt as if I were twelve feet high when I thrust it down their throats.'[1] His campaign was beginning to have an effect. The Hartford *Daily Times* commented rather ominously: 'Mr. Dickens alluded in his remarks to an international copyright law. . . . It happens that we want no advice upon this subject, and it will be better for Mr. Dickens, if he refrains from introducing the matter hereafter. But it is not pleasant to pursue the question further at this time.'

BANQUET IN HIS HONOUR: NEW YORK

18 *February* 1842

DICKENS arrived in New York by steamboat from New Haven, on the 13th. On the 14th he was at the 'Boz Ball', at the Park Theatre; and a few days later he attended the public banquet in his honour, at the City Hotel. He had received an invitation to it, signed by Washington Irving and over forty other New York notabilities, while he was still at Boston. The dinner committee were alarmed at the outcry following Dickens's demand for international copyright—although they all said they agreed with him—and begged him to give it up. But, he replied—so he told Forster—'that nothing should deter me . . . that the shame was theirs, not mine; and that as I would not spare them when I got home, I would not be silenced here'.[2]

[1] F, III. iii.   [2] F, III. iii.

The occasion was, nevertheless, a great success. Washington Irving[1] took the Chair. The scene in the hall was said to be brilliant, and the decorations 'in the most neat and chaste style imaginable', including 'two beautifully painted transparencies'—left over from the Boz Ball— 'in richly carved antique frames', showing Pickwick addressing the club, and Ralph Nickleby introducing Kate to his friends. Nearly 250 guests sat down to dine; many more were present; and when once the speaking had begun, Mrs. Dickens and a number of ladies were quietly admitted on the platform behind the upper table.

As soon as the cloth was removed, Irving rose to give the toast of the evening. He had prepared a lengthy speech in the full conviction that he would break down without being able to deliver it. He was almost inaudible, and his conviction soon became a certainty. But the toast, to 'Charles Dickens—Literary Guest of the Nation', was received with deafening applause. Dickens rose, and replied:

MR. PRESIDENT and Gentlemen, I don't know how to thank you—I really don't know how. You might, perhaps, suppose that by the dint of custom and from the experience your kindness has heaped upon me since my arrival in this country, that the difficulty would have been somewhat diminished or dwindled into nothing but I do assure you the fact is exactly the reverse. Unlike that rolling stone which gathers no moss, I have, in my progress to your city, collected around me such a heap of obligation and weight of acknowledgement, that in my power of expressing it I have grown more and more unwieldy every hour! [*Loud applause.*] I picked up such a quantity of fresh moss—so to speak—at a certain brilliant scene on Monday night, that I thought I never could, by any possibility, grow any bigger. [*Great laughter.*] But crowded upon that, there comes again tonight a new accumulation of such extent and magnitude, that I am fairly at a standstill and can roll no more! [*Laughter and enthusiastic applause.*]

Gentlemen, we know from all the authorities, that whenever a fairy stone, or ball, or reel of thread, stopped of its own accord— which I do not—some catastrophe was sure to be at hand. Its precedent, however, holds good in my case. For, remembering the short time I have before me in this land of mighty interest, and the

---

[1] Washington Irving (1783–1859), author of *A History of New York*, by 'Diedrich Knickerbocker', 1809; *The Sketch Book of Geoffrey Crayon, Gent.*, 1819–20; *Bracebridge Hall*, 1822; *Tales of a Traveller*, 1824; *Life of Columbus*, 1828; *Conquest of Granada*, 1829; *The Alhambra*, 1832, and other works, variously referred to by Dickens in his speech. Irving had visited Europe in 1815, and returned to America in 1832; he had been nominated to the Senate as Minister to Spain on 10 Feb., and had accepted the appointment on the 18th. After reading the *Old Curiosity Shop* he had written enthusiastically to Dickens. He was to regret the warmth of his admiration after the publication of *American Notes* and *Martin Chuzzlewit*.

poor opportunities I can have at best of acquiring a knowledge of,
and making myself acquainted with it, I have felt it almost a duty
to decline the honours which my generous friends elsewhere would
heap upon me, and henceforth to pass through the country more
quietly. Argus himself, though he had but one mouth for his hundred eyes, would have found the reception of a public entertainment once a week somewhat relaxing to his vigilance and activity.
[*Great laughter and applause.*] And as I would lose no scrap or jot
from the rich mines of gratification and instruction which await
me, I know, on every hand—and of which I have already derived
no small instalment from your hospitals and common jails—I have
resolved to take up my staff, and go upon my way rejoicing, and
for the future to shake hands with Americans not at parties, but
at home. [*Long continued cheering.*] And therefore, gentlemen, I say
tonight, with a full heart and an honest purpose and grateful feelings, that I bear with me, and shall ever bear with me, a deeper
sense of your kind, affectionate and noble greeting, than it is possible to convey in words; that no European sky without, and no
cheerful home or well-warmed room within shall ever shut out this
land from my vision; that I shall often hear your words of welcome
in my quiet room, oftenest when it is most quiet, and shall see your
faces in the winter evening fire; that if I should live to grow old,
the light of this hall and others like it will shine as brightly to my
dull eyes fifty years hence as it does tonight; and that when my
course is run the sympathy you have shown to me shall be well
remembered and paid back, so please God, in my undying love and
honest endeavours for the good of my race. [*Loud and enthusiastic
applause.*]

Gentlemen, one other word with reference to this tiresome first
person, and I close that theme. I came here in an open, honest, and
confiding spirit, if ever man did, and because I heartily inclined
toward you; had I felt otherwise I should have kept away. As I
came here, and *am* here, without the least admixture of the hundredth portion of a grain of base alloy, without the faintest unworthy reference to self in any word I have ever addressed to you,
or in any sentiment I have ever interchanged with you, I assert
my right tonight, in regard to the past for the last time, my right
in reason, truth, and justice, to appeal to you, as I have done on
two former occasions, on a question of universal literary interest
in both countries. And, gentlemen, I claim this justice: that I have
made the appeal as one who has a most righteous claim to speak
and to be heard; and that I have done so in a frank, and courteous,
and good-humoured spirit of deference to those who frankly, court-
eously, and good humouredly differed from me in any or every

respect. [*Cheers.*] For myself, gentlemen, I have only to add that I will ever be as true to you as you have been to me. [*Loud cheers.*] I recognize in your enthusiastic approval of the creations of my fancy, as in a glass, your enlightened care for the happiness of the many, your tender and gentle regard for the afflicted and helpless, your sympathy for the downcast, your plans for the correction and improvement of the bad, and the encouragement and solace of the good—the education and advancement of every member of society. [*Great cheering.*] My constant and increasing devotion to the end of my life to these ends, and to every other object, to the extent of my humble capacity, having the common good in view, shall prove to you that in this you do not mistake me, and that the light you have shed around my path was not unworthily bestowed. [*Cheers.*]

And now that I have said this much in reference to myself, let me have the gratification I have long expected of saying a few words in reference to somebody else. [*Laughter.*] There is in this city a gentlemen who, at the conclusion of one of my books—I well remember it was the *Old Curiosity Shop*—wrote to me in England a letter so generous, so affectionate, and so manly, that if I had written the book under every circumstance of disadvantage, discouragement, and difficulty, instead of with everything to cheer and urge me on, I should have found in the receipt of that letter my best and happiest reward. [*Cheers.*] I answered him, and he answered me [*laughter*], and so we kept shaking hands autographically [*laughter*], as if no ocean rolled between us [*laughter*], until I came here on Saturday night, longing and eager to see him. And [*laying his hand on Irving's shoulder*[1]], here he sits! [*Cheers.*] And I need not tell you that it is the crowning circumstance to me of the night, that he is here in this capacity. [*Great cheering.*]

Why, gentlemen, I don't go upstairs to bed two nights out of seven, as I have a credible witness very near at hand to testify [*laughter*[2]],—I say, gentlemen, I do not go to bed two nights out of seven without taking Washington Irving under my arm upstairs to bed with me [*uproarious laughter*]; and when I don't take him I take his next of kin—his own brother—Oliver Goldsmith. [*Cheers.*]

---

[1] One report adds—'said Dickens, with all the velocity and volubility of a young "going, going, gone", and slapping Washington Irving on the back with most extraordinary Sam Wellerish gusto, amidst most terrific laughing and cheering.' (*New York Herald*, 20 Feb.)

[2] 'Here Boz gave a funny Sam Weller *sort* of side look out of one eye half round at his wife, who sat behind Bryant, and laughed; she blushed, hid her face in her handkerchiefs, and laughed; Miss Sedgwick who sat next her, laughed most immoderately—the Mayor laughed intolerably—altogether too much for a Mayor— . . . the parson laughed, and all laughed, like true Pickwickians.' (Ibid.)

Washington Irving! Why, who but he was in my thoughts the other day as I approached your city in the steamboat from New Haven, when I was looking out for the Hog's Back, the Frying Pan, and Hell Gate and all those horrible places of renown that were a terror to the Dutch navigators? [*Laughter and cheers.*] Washington Irving! Why, when I visited Shakespeare's birthplace not long ago, and went beneath the roof where he first saw light, whose name but *his* was the first that was pointed out with pride upon the wall? —Washington Irving!—Diedrich Knickerbocker, Geoffrey Crayon! Why, where can we go that they have not been before us? In the English farmhouse, in the crowded city, along the beautiful lanes, across the pleasant fields of England, and amidst her blessed, happy homes, his name above every name rises up with hallowed recollections of his virtues and talents, and like his memory will continue to be hallowed in those bright and innocent sanctuaries, until the last tick of the clock of Time! [*Tremendous cheering.*]

If we go into the country are there no Bracebridge Halls in existence? If we visit the crowded city, has Little Britain never had a chronicler? Is there no Boar's Head in Eastcheap?[1] Why, gentlemen, when Mr. Crayon left England he left sitting in the small back parlour of a certain public house near that same Boar's Head, a man of infinite wisdom, with a red nose and an oilskin hat, who was sitting there when I came away. Yes, gentlemen, it was the same man—not a man that was very *like* him, but the self-same man—his nose in an immortal redness, and his hat in an undying glaze.[2] [*Laughter.*] Why, Mr. Crayon was also on terms of intimacy, in a certain village near that same Bracebridge Hall, with a certain radical fellow, who used to go about very much out at elbow, with his hat full of old newspapers. Gentlemen, I knew the man.[2] [*Laughter.*] He's there to this very hour, with the newspapers in his hat, very much to the dissatisfaction of Mr. Tibbets the elder.[3] [*Great laughter.*] And he has not changed a hair; and when I came away he charged me to give his best respects to Washington Irving!

Gentlemen, leaving the town and 'Rural Life in England,' and forgetting for a moment, if anybody can, 'The Pride of the Village,' and 'The Broken Heart',[4] let us cross the water again and ask who has associated himself most closely with the Italian Post-House,[5] and the Bandits of the Pyrenees? When the traveller beyond the Alps is lighted to his little chamber, along dark, echoing, and

[1] 'The Boar's Head Tavern, Eastcheap', is one of the papers in the *Sketch Book*.   [2] 'A Village Politician', *Bracebridge Hall.*
[3] See 'Ready-Money Jack', though he was the *son* of old Tibbets—Dickens's mistake.   [4] Various papers in the *Sketch Book.*
[5] The post-house was 'The Inn at Terracina', in 'The Italian Banditti', *Tales of a Traveller*, Part III.

spacious corridors, damp, gloomy, and cold; when he has sat down
by the fire to watch the gradual change of his room from misery
to comfort; when he has drawn his curtains, such as they are,
moth-eaten and mouldy, and hears the tempest beating with fury
against his window; and when all the ghost stories that ever were
told crowd around and in upon him—amid all his thick-coming
fancies—who is it he thinks of at such a time? Why, Washington
Irving! [*Cheers.*]

Go further away still, to the Moorish fountain, sparkling full in
the moonlight, with a few water carriers and village gossips lingering about it still, as in days of old, for its refreshing coolness,
and the voices of others going to the village dying away in the
distance, like bees. Who, at such an hour, takes his silent stand
beside the traveller, and points with his magic wand to the walls
of the Alhambra? Who awakens in every cave the echoing music,
the tread of many twinkling feet, the sound of cymbals, the rattling
clang of armour, the tramp of mailed men, and bids legions which
for centuries have slept a dreamless sleep within the earth, or
watched unwinkingly for buried treasure—who bids them start up
and pass in grim array before your eyes? [*Loud Cheers.*]

Or, leaving this, who embarked with Columbus in his gallant ship,
traversed with him the dark and mighty ocean, leaped into the
main, upon the land, and planted there the flag of Spain? [*Loud
cheers.*] Who but this same man now sitting by my side. And who,
to come to your own coast, is a more fit companion for the bucca-
neers, and money-diggers[1] [*laughter*], or who more fit to accompany
Rip Van Winkle in his fearful journey to the mountains, where the
uncouth crew did play at ninepins on that thundery afternoon?
[*Roars of laughter.*] What pen but his could call such spirits from
the vasty deep—make them come, too, at his call—peopling those
Catskill mountains until they seem as much a part of them as any
crag that ever frowned, or torrent that ever darted headlong from
their heights. [*Cheers.*]

But, gentlemen, this is a most dangerous theme for me, for I
have been enchanted with these people from my boyhood, and my
glass slipper is on me still. Lest I should be tempted now to talk
too long about them I will, in conclusion, give you a sentiment,
most appropriate in the presence of Bryant,[2] Halleck,[3] and—but

---

[1] 'The Money-Diggers', *Tales of a Traveller*, Part IV.

[2] William Cullen Bryant (1794–1878), poet, and editor of the *New York
Evening Post*; his verse was greatly admired by Dickens.

[3] Fitzgreene Halleck (1790–1867), poet and confidential clerk employed by
John Jacob Astor. 'Halleck is a merry little man', Dickens wrote to Forster,
'Bryant a sad one'. Halleck wrote of Dickens to a friend about the same time,
in a letter quoted by Forster: 'I am quite delighted with him. . . . I wish you

I suppose I must not mention the ladies here[1]—I will give you 'The Literature of America,—She well knows how to honour her own literature, and to do honour to that of other lands, when she chooses Washington Irving for her representative in the country of Cervantes!' [*Enthusiastic applause.*]

Among the remaining speeches, the most remarkable was by Cornelius Mathews, one of the editors of *Arcturus*. It was given in reply to a toast by Washington Irving, to 'International Copyright'. American writers and American literature, he declared, were also sufferers from the absence of an agreement between the two countries: 'There is at this moment waging in our midst a great war between a Foreign and a Native Literature. The one claims pay, food, lodging and raiment: the other battles free of all charges . . . has neither a mouth to cry for sustenance . . . or a head to be sheltered.' He concluded with the sentiment, 'International Copyright—The only honest turnpike between the readers of two great nations'.

This was the last time Dickens spoke on the subject. 'When the night came', he told Forster, 'I asserted my right, with all the means I could command to give it dignity, in face, manner, or words; and I believe that if you could have seen and heard me, you would have loved me better than you ever did in your life.'[2] He stayed in New York two weeks longer, left for Philadelphia, and then went on to Washington.

PRIVATE DINNER IN HIS HONOUR: WASHINGTON

14 *March* 1842

DICKENS arrived in Washington on the evening of the 9th, and next day at once began to make the most of a single week's stay in the capital. He was not greatly impressed by it. Part of his business there was to continue his private campaign for international copyright; and he handed over a petition in its favour, signed by American authors, to be presented to the House of Representatives, and left another with Henry Clay to be brought before the Senate.

No public reception was arranged, but he was invited to a private dinner at Boulanger's on Monday the 16th. John Quincy Adams was also a guest, and George M. Keim[3] took the Chair. Apparently no record of the occasion was given by the press, but a fairly full account was entered in his diary by Benjamin Brown French, which was reprinted by Robert Shelton Mackenzie in his *Life of Charles Dickens*.[4]

had listened to his eloquence at the dinner here. It was the only real specimen of eloquence I ever witnessed. Its charm was not in its words, but in the manner of saying them.'

[1] Probably referring to, at least, Catherine Maria Sedgwick (1789–1867), novelist of domestic life, who was seated next to Mrs. Dickens.

[2] F, III. iii.

[3] George May Keim, Major-General of the Pennsylvanian militia, U.S. Marshall for East Pennsylvania, 1841–9; noted for his wit.

[4] Philadelphia, 1870.

According to the diarist, on proposing Dickens's health the chairman gave the toast of 'Philanthropy and Genius, and a representative of both now our guest in Washington, whom Washington himself would have rejoiced to welcome'. Dickens replied:

IF this were a public dinner, he said, he supposed he would be expected to make a speech; as it was but a social party, surely no such effort would be expected of him; and when he looked about the table, and saw gentlemen whose positions in public life rendered it unavoidable that they should either speak themselves or listen to the speeches of others every day, his refraining upon this occasion must be far more acceptable, and surely possess more novelty than any remarks he might make—and he must be allowed to assume that here, in the enjoyment of a social hour, they would be happy to give their ears some rest, and he should therefore consider himself relieved from making a speech. He would, however, say that like the Prince in the Arabian tales he had been doomed, since he arrived in this hospitable country, to make new friendships every night, and cut their heads off the following morning. But the recollection of this night—wherever he might go—should accompany him, and like the bright smiles of his better angel, be treasured in his mind as long as memory remained.

Other toasts included, 'The health of John Quincy Adams', 'The City of Boston', and 'The Old Curiosity Shop'. Then, according to French, after the toast to 'The Queen of Great Britain' had been drunk standing, Dickens said, 'Allow me to assume the character of Mr. Pickwick, and in that character to give you "The President of the United States".'[1] This was also drunk standing. There were further toasts, among them one to Mr. Pickwick by his creator, when a messenger arrived from the hotel to say that the long-delayed mail from England had arrived at last. It had originally been embarked in the *Columbia*, but she had met such heavy storms that she had been forced to put back, and being so long overdue had almost been given up for lost. About eleven o'clock Dickens rose, and, 'in the most feelingly beautiful manner possible', said:

I rise to propose to you one more sentiment; it must be my last; it consists of two words—'Good Night!' Since I have been seated at this table I have received the welcome intelligence that the news from the dear ones has come at last—that the long-expected letters have arrived. Among them are certain scrawls from little beings across the ocean, of great interest to me, and I thought of them

---

[1] Presumably, since the company was already standing, he imitated Mr. Pickwick by mounting his chair to give the next toast, 'with one hand gracefully concealed behind his coat tails, and the other waving in the air to assist his glowing declamation', as shown in Seymour's first sketch 'Mr. Pickwick Addresses the Club'.

for many days past, in connexion with drowned men and a noble
ship, broken up and lying in fragments upon the bottom of the
ocean. But they are here, and you will appreciate the anxiety I feel
to read them.

Permit me, in allusion to some remarks made by a gentleman
near me, to say that every effort of my pen has been intended to
elevate the masses of society; to give them the station they deserve
among mankind. With that intention I commenced writing, and I
assure you that as long as I write at all, that shall be the principal
motive of my efforts. Gentlemen, since I arrived on your hospitable
shore, and in my flight over your land, you have given me everything I can ask but *time*—that you cannot give me, and you are
aware that I must devote some of it to myself. Therefore, with the
assurance that this has been the most pleasant evening I have passed
in the United States, I must bid you farewell, and once more repeat
the words, Good Night!

He left for the hotel where he found Mrs. Dickens had kept the letters
for him unopened; and they sat up together reading them until two
o'clock in the morning.

'SOCIAL SUPPER' IN HIS HONOUR: RICHMOND
18 *March* 1842

DICKENS had already refused an invitation to a public dinner sent him
by the local citizens before his arrival in Richmond on 17 March. As well
as wishing to keep his public vow to avoid official functions, he had
privately resolved to accept no hospitality while in the slave states.
But a deputation waited on him to renew their request, and he accepted
an invitation to a social supper 'to meet a few of his friends'—to the
number of nearly a hundred. 'I was obliged to accept a public dinner in
this Richmond,' he wrote to Forster, 'and I saw plainly enough, there,
that the hatred which these Southern States bear to us as a nation has
been fanned up and revived again by this Creole business, and can
scarcely be exaggerated.'[1]

The supper was held at the Exchange Hotel, where Dickens was staying. Thomas Ritchie,[2] the editor of the *Richmond Enquirer*, took the

---

[1] F, III. iv. In November 1841, slaves on the *Creole*, sailing from Hampton
Roads Va., to New Orleans, had overpowered the crew, and put into the British
port of Nassau. They had all been given their freedom, except for a minority
who were charged with the murder of an owner. The U.S. demanded their sur-
render. Gt. Britain refused, but paid an indemnity in 1853. There were several
other outstanding causes of dispute at this time.

[2] Thomas Ritchie (1778–1854), journalist and politician; prominent as
secretary at public meetings, chairman at dinners, and welcomer of distinguished guests.

Chair. As soon as the 'viands and substantials had been pretty well cleared off', Ritchie rose to give the toast of the evening in an eloquent address of praise and welcome, tempered only by his final prayer that Dickens would never allow his success to 'turn his head or paralyse his pen'. He proposed 'Charles Dickens, the Literary Guest of the Nation.— We welcome him to the hearths and hearts of the Old Dominion.'

Dickens rose, amid great applause, and said:

MR. PRESIDENT and Gentlemen, I am most truly grateful and obliged to you for the kind welcome which you have given me. I receive and acknowledge with gratitude this testimonial of your kindly feelings towards me. If it were possible to convey to you my sense and appreciation of your favours, I would indeed acknowledge, as I receive, your good wishes an hundred fold. But, as I said at a social party a few nights since at Washington—a party somewhat similar to this—it is my misfortune to be passing through this country with almost as rapid a flight as that of any bird of the air— the American Eagle excepted. [*Cheers.*] I find, in my career amongst you, no little resemblance to that far-famed Sultan of the thousand-and-one nights, who was in the habit of acquiring a new friend every night and cutting his head off in the morning. I find another resemblance to what we read in the history of that Sultan. He was diverted from his bad habit by listening to the tales of one who proved a favourite above all the rest; so I am stopped in my original intention by the hospitalities of the Americans. [*Cheers.*]

I say that the best flag of truce between two nations having the same common origin, and speaking the same language, is a fair sheet of white paper inscribed with the literature of each. [*Cheers.*] If, hereafter, I think of this night, if I remember the welcome which you have assured me, believe me, my small corner, my humble portion of that fair sheet shall be inscribed with the hospitalities I have received from the friends I have seen and made here. [*Cheers.*] It has been said, gentlemen, that an after-dinner speech may be too long. [*Laughter.*] If so, it may be said with more truth, that an after-supper speech cannot be too short [*laughter*], and especially to those with whom to listen to a speech is no novelty [*laughter*], and among whom a man of few words is a rare and almost literal 'phenomenon'. [*Great laughter and cheering.*] I therefore deem it only necessary to say to you that I am most deeply and sincerely obliged to you for your kindness. [*Cries of 'Go on'.*]

In reference to the admonition tendered to me by my worthy friend, your President, I will say that it has long been a thing near my heart. But I hope I shall never need the monitor of which he reminds us. My situation forbids all paralysis of my pen—as I hope you will discover from November next, when I shall resume my literary labours. The hospitalities of America can never be forgotten among them: your kindness, certainly never. Imagine me thinking of you tomorrow; imagine me on the road to Fredericksburg—on that Virginia road from Fredericksburg to the Potomac.[1] [*Here the laughter and cheering was overpowering. The President exclaimed,* '*No more of that Hal, an you love me*'.] In fact throughout all my travels in these parts I shall think of the pleasure I have enjoyed in the bosom of your society. [*Great cheering.*]

Several other speakers followed, proposing the usual toasts and sentiments: either on the kinship of England and America, and the aristocracy of genius, or jocosely Dickensian. Ritchie, who had Dickens sitting next him, was no doubt the author of the concluding remarks in the report given in the *Richmond Enquirer.* From these they seem to have indulged in unrestrained facetiousness. 'The sallies' between Dickens and Ritchie, we are assured, 'were constant and amusing. In one instance, when the latter complimented a character in the "Curiosity Shop", Mr. D. retorted by denominating him a living "curiosity". . . . It was an Attic Supper—which no one present will be able to forget.' The final toast was to 'Charles Dickens, the "artful dodger"—He has dodged Philadelphia and Baltimore; but he could not dodge the "Old Dominion"'.

It was the last time he was to speak in public in the United States for twenty-five years. From Richmond he and Mrs. Dickens continued their tour, on to Baltimore, and then to Pittsburg. He was now completely disillusioned, and, 'On Board the Steamboat from Pittsburg to Cincinnati', wrote once more to Macready, to say 'I have not changed—I cannot change . . . my secret opinion of this country. I have said to Forster that I believe the heaviest blow ever dealt at Liberty's Head, will be dealt by this nation in the ultimate failure of its example to the Earth.'[2]

From Cincinnati they went on to Louisville, St. Louis, Columbus, Cleveland, Buffalo, Niagara, and thence to Canada. They left Montreal for New York on 30 May, visited Lebanon and West Point, embarked on the *George Washington* on 7 June, and were home again in London by the 29th.

PRINTERS' PENSION SOCIETY
4 *April* 1843

THE anniversary festival was held at the London Tavern, with Dickens in the Chair. There were the usual loyal toasts, which were received with great applause, to 'The Queen'—'His Royal Highness Prince Albert'—

---

[1] The journey from Washington to Potomac Creek was by steamer, and from Fredericksburg to Richmond by rail; but the two were linked up by an appalling stage-coach ride, over a plank road and through muddy swamps, vividly described in *American Notes,* ch. ix. Dickens had meant to take a different route on his return, but was now well aware that he would have to go back the same way.   [2] 1 Apr. 1842, M.

'Her Majesty the Queen Dowager, and the rest of the Royal Family', and to 'The Dukes of Sussex and Cambridge, and the Duke of Northumberland,—the Patrons of the Printers' Pension Society'. The chairman then rose to give the toast of the evening.

IT had, he observed, a more immediate reference to the object for which they were that day assembled. The Printers' Pension Society had existed, as most of them no doubt knew, about sixteen years, and was founded for the purpose of maintaining the widows of deceased printers, or decayed printers themselves. The amounts awarded in the estimation of some might be said to be small,—the good that was done was great. [*Applause.*] It afforded to many, and the most deserving persons, relief in the hour of distress,—that distress which sooner or later comes to most of us. [*Hear, hear.*] But the printers were peculiarly liable to premature decay, to injury to their faculties when many others were still able to earn their daily bread (which was a fact known to most of them) from the character of their occupation—the late and arduous hours during which they were obliged to tax powers that were often of the most delicate nature.

That peculiar liability to decay gave printers powerful claims to their sympathy and support. [*Hear, hear, hear.*] But that claim was largely enhanced when they recollected that by the printers' means they were enabled to scatter throughout the world the loftiest efforts of intellect—the 'thoughts that breathe, the words that burn'—to send to every part of the universe the great imaginings of the most accomplished minds, to instruct and regenerate mankind. [*Loud applause.*] When they reflected thus—and who could avoid it ?—the claims of the printers became irresistible. [*Applause.*] He felt quite assured from what took place at the last election for pensioners, and from what he saw now in that room, that everyone would promptly put his hand into whatever pocket he had, and thereby enable their Treasurer to make a most favourable report. [*Cheers.*] He was sure it was unnecessary to add more to arouse their sympathies; but he could assure them that the knockings at the door of the institution were very numerous.

Be it borne in mind that this institution gave no encouragement to thoughtlessness and extravagance; for every claimant must have contributed to the funds for some years before he was qualified should necessity arise to appeal for aid. [*Hear.*] Many had belonged to it from its foundation. He knew many who were so circumstanced. The institution was further valuable as generating good feeling among the workmen themselves. [*Hear, hear.*] On every account they deserved the respect and consideration of every honest man, to the truth of which he could bear ample testimony from considerable intercourse with that valuable body of men. There was an asylum for warriors who had fought the battles of their country, and most justly and properly; but, in God's name, let them sustain an asylum for those who suffered in struggles, in the bloodless contests, of promoting knowledge, of civilizing or of improving mankind, and of advancing the peaceful superiority of human beings. [*Cheers.*] He gave them 'The Printers' Pension Society, and prosperity to it'. [*Loud applause.*]

Robert Bell[1] then proposed 'The Health of the Chairman'—a gentleman to whom society and literature were so much indebted. The toast was received with loud applause, and Dickens replied:

He felt deeply obliged, he said, for the kindness thus shown, and the enthusiastic manner in which it had been evinced. There were few proceedings which went so home to his heart, as such testimonies of kind regards. [*Cheers.*]

He then continued:

He had, he said, to propose another toast, and he would introduce it with a remark or two, not because they were requisite, but because such a toast on such an occasion ought not to be named without some observation. [*Hear, hear.*]

I now give 'The Press', that wonderful lever Archimedes wished for, and which *has* moved the world! which has impelled it onward in the path of knowledge, of mercy, and of human improvement so far that nothing in the world can ever roll it back! [*Loud applause.*] The mass of the people, said Dr. Johnson very truly, in any country where printing is unknown, must be barbarous; and Sir Thomas More, the best, and wisest, and the greatest of men, who, before the press was established, died what was almost the natural death of the good, and the wise and the great—Sir Thomas More so clearly saw into futurity, and descried from afar off the stupendous influence of the press, that he went out of his way to set up a printing-press in Utopia, knowing that without it even the people of that fancied land would not bear competition in the course of years with the real nations of the earth. [*Cheers.*] If they looked back only for two hundred years, to that time when the Dutch citizen carved letters on the bark of the beechen tree, and took off impressions of them on paper as toys to please his grand-children—he little knew the wonderful agent which, in scarcely a century, was about to burst on mankind; what a strong engine in the course of time it

---

[1] Robert Bell (1800–67), journalist and miscellaneous writer; popular speaker at similar functions; friend of Thackeray; as representative of the General Committee was Dickens's chief opponent in his controversy with the Royal Literary Fund, 1855–60.

must become, even in the land where the ruthless vices and crimes of the annointed ruffian who spread More's bloody pillow were to acquire him an immortality of infamy. [*Cheers.*]

I thank God that it has been so; from that hour no good has been devised, no wonderful invention has been broached, no barbarism has been struck down, but that same press has had its iron grip upon it, and has never once let go till it was done. If we look at our social and daily life, we shall see how constantly present the press is, and how essential an element it has become of civilized existence. In great houses, and even in lowly huts, in crowds, and in solitudes, in town and country, in the nursery of the children and by the old man's elbow chair—still, in some shape or other, there it is! Now it is an alphabet, with its fat black capital letters; now in the form of whole words; now in the story of *Puss in Boots*; now as *Robinson Crusoe*; now as the tale of the Caliph Haroun al-Raschid; now as a Lindley Murray; now as a *Tutor's Assistant*; then as a Virgil, a Homer, or a Milton; now in the form of the labours of the editor of a popular newspaper: in some shape or other the press is constantly present and associated with our lives, from the baptismal service to the burial of the dead. [*Cheers.*]

I know that to some its power is obnoxious. There are some gentlemen of a patriotism so unselfish that they would put the newspaper press of their native country on the equality of efficiency with that of another nation which, as long ago as Benjamin Franklin wrote, was a unique, a distinct and a singular thing. But as we have means of judging for ourselves every morning and evening of the newspaper literature, it is satisfactory to know that there never was a righteous cause but the same men have hated it; and there never was a disappointed man or a discontented patriot, anxious to pass upon a people determined not to recognize him as such, but he has bemoaned the privileges of the press in the same crocodile's tears.[1]

With regard to the influence of the press on public men, I only leave you to judge from what public men often are even with this engine in full operation, what sort of characters they would be

---

[1] Referring to a recent dispute. The reviewer of *American Notes* (James Spedding) in the *Edinburgh Review*, had favourably compared the American Press with the English, saying: 'We cannot but regard the condition of our own Daily Press, as a morning and evening witness against the moral character of the people.' *The Times* and other newspapers, were indignant. Dickens expressed his own view publicly in his letter to *The Times* of 15 Jan., and privately to Lord Brougham (25 Jan.), saying: 'The English Press is bad enough—a great part of it very bad—but it can no more be compared with Amèrican Journalism than a silver fork can be likened to a bowie knife, or a gold bracelet to an iron handcuff.' (MS. Brotherton Collection, Brotherton Library, University of Leeds.)

without it. I give you then,—'The fountain of Knowledge and the bulwark of Freedom, the founder of free states and their preserver —the Press!' [*Loud cheers.*]

Dickens then continued:

He had next to propose, he said, 'The Stationers' Company'. He believed that notwithstanding what had been declared by a Noble and learned Lord, 'a friend of ours elsewhere', the Stationers' Company were alive and doing well, and that Stationers' Hall still stood where it did. [*Laughter and applause.*] He gave, with great pleasure, 'The Stationers' Company, the steady supporters of the Printers' Pension Society'. [*Applause.*]

Various other toasts followed.

Thomas Hood replied on behalf of himself, Douglas Jerrold and the other authors present; Clarkson Stanfield responded for 'The Arts'; and John Forster proposed 'The Extension of General Education'.

HOSPITAL FOR CONSUMPTION AND DISEASES OF THE CHEST

6 *May* 1843

THE second annual dinner of the hospital, which had been opened only in September 1842, took place at the London Tavern with the Earl of Arundel and Surrey in the Chair.[1] There was the usual series of speeches. Dickens proposed the toast of the evening.

THE institution, he said, although at this time but a very young plant almost in the bud, had struck a deep root and taken a strong hold in the bosoms of tens of thousands of our fellow creatures. Little more than six months, according to the report just read, had passed since the hospital was open for the reception of patients, and within that short time no fewer than sixty or seventy patients had occupied its beds, while the number of out-patients—many of whom they had been delighted to learn had, by the skill and timely aid they had received, been enabled to resume their accustomed occupations—amounted to no fewer than 750. [*Cheers.*]

If this charity had not existed, the doors of no sick house within London's wide bounds would have been open to these poor persons. [*Hear, hear.*] Before the hospital was founded they would have suffered, lingered, pined, and died in their poor homes, without a hand stretched out to help them in their slow decay. Remembering

[1] Henry Granville Fitzalan Howard (1815–60), styled Lord Fitzalan until 1842; then known as the Earl of Arundel and Surrey; 14th Duke of Norfolk, 1856.

that the classes of suffering which the charity purposed to alleviate were of all others peculiarly the growth and produce of the country; that they were often the inheritance of the youngest, fairest, best amongst us, that they deprived fair England of those whom it could least afford to lose, struck down the objects of our dearest hopes when in their youthful prime, and when it was hardest to lose them—remembering these things who could doubt that such a charity must be munificently endowed? [*Cheers.*] He now called upon them to drink 'Prosperity' to the institution, not as an unmeaning toast, but as a pledge that nothing on their parts should be wanting to aid and urge it onward in its prosperous course. [*Cheers.*]

The toast was drunk with three times three and one cheer more, and was briefly acknowledged by Dr. W. A. Guy.[1]

CHARITABLE SOCIETY FOR THE DEAF AND DUMB

23 *May* 1843

THE seventh anniversary festival of the Charitable and Provident Society for the Aged and Infirm Deaf and Dumb was held at the London Tavern under the presidency of Lord Dudley Coutts Stuart.[2] Dickens was one of the chief speakers, and wrote to Serjeant Talfourd a few days before:

. . . I am a steward at the Dinner of the Deaf and Dumb charity, which comes off that evening. *That* I wouldn't mind; but most unhappily one Dr. Howe[3] from America, who invented the means of communicating with Laura Bridgeman, the deaf, dumb, and blind girl at Boston, has come to London, just when I don't want him, for the express purpose of being carried to that dinner (in pursuance of a wild engagement made four thousand miles off) by me. But for this he would have remained another week at Liverpool—as I devoutly wish he had. . . .

I swear I will shun them like a Pestilence, and that I will make this, my Third Public Dinner this year, my final appearance on the London Tavern Stage.[4]

Dickens proposed the health of the chairman:

IT was, he said, with particular gratification that he had attended that celebration and witnessed its proceedings. It was a matter for

---

[1] William Augustus Guy (1810–85), Professor of Forensic Medicine, King's College, London.

[2] Lord Dudley Coutts Stuart (1803–54), Liberal M.P. 1831–7, and 1847–54; energetic advocate of Polish independence, and philanthropist; cousin of Dickens's friend Miss Burdett Coutts.

[3] Dr. Samuel Gridley Howe (1801–86), founder of Perkins Institution for the Blind, at Boston, 1832. The education of Laura Bridgeman is described in *American Notes*, ch. iii.

[4] 20 May 1843, *Maggs Bros., Catalogue 312*, 1913, item 2262.

just rejoicing to contemplate the healthy and promising appearance of that institution. Its objects were of the most useful and praiseworthy character; and the nobleman who presided, distinguished as he was for his amiability and usefulness, had never been engaged in a more valuable manner than on this occasion.

A number of those present were themselves deaf and dumb, and in the course of the evening one or two of them also addressed the Chair, in silence, using their manual signs. Dickens is said to have alluded in a very pathetic manner, in his speech, to these addresses, which were warmly applauded by the rest of the company.

THE SANATORIUM

29 *June* 1843

THE Sanatorium, or 'Home in Sickness', had been founded in 1840 by Dr. Southwood Smith.[1] Dickens's aid was enlisted the following year, and in 1842 it was opened at Devonshire House, York Gate, very close to the Dickens's residence at 1 Devonshire Terrace. The aims of the society were more fully described in his speech at the anniversary dinner of 1844.[2]

After it had been running for only a year it found itself in difficulties, and the committee decided to organize a dinner to obtain subscriptions and to gain publicity. Dickens made strenuous efforts to enlist what help he could. 'It has been a matter of Life or Death with the Sanatorium', he wrote to Macready, 'which has done a world of Good, and if it can weather the storm, will do worlds more'.[3] Maclise had agreed to attend; and Macready consented to have his name put down as a steward, with various other notabilities, including Robert Browning, Dickens, G. R. Porter, John Forster, Lord Robert Grosvenor, Matthew Davenport Hill, the Marquis of Lansdowne, Lord Sandon, Lord Dudley Coutts Stuart,

---

[1] Thomas Southwood Smith (1788–1861), sanitary reformer; Benthamite, one of the projectors of the *Westminster Review*, and member of original committee of the Society for the Diffusion of Useful Knowledge; on the central board for inquiry into the condition of factory children, 1832; wrote reports for the Poor Law Commissioners on the causes of sickness and mortality among the poor; one of the principal founders of both the Health of Towns Association, 1839, and the Metropolitan Association for the Improvement of the Dwellings of the Industrial Classes, 1842; served on the children's employment commission, 1840; and appointed medical member of the General Board of Health, 1848–54. He was well acquainted with Dickens, not only through their association as officers of the Sanatorium, but from other common interests, especially in the conditions of the employment of children, and in housing and sanitary reform. In the fifties, he helped Dickens in deciding on a site and drawing up the plans of the Columbia Estate—Miss Burdett Coutts's flats for working men in Bethnal Green.   [2] See pp. 148–58.   [3] 2 June 1843, M.

and Dr. Southwood Smith. The dinner was held at the London Tavern, with Lord Ashley in the Chair.[1]

On the removal of the cloth the usual loyal toasts were given, including the health of Prince Albert as president of the society. The chairman then gave the toast of the evening in a speech which was warmly applauded, and Dickens rose to reply.

H E had been asked to perform this duty, he said, and he did it most cheerfully. Of the merits and advantages of the institution he was fully convinced; and in his desire to promote the success of such establishments he could assure them he was second to no man. He hoped they would not deem it presumptuous in him to say that he knew something of the classes for which this institution was intended. It was to provide for those classes refuge in sickness, and to restore them to peace of mind, health of body, and reinstatement in their positions in society. Its objects were so noble and so interesting, that to be successful it only required to be known in the highest and most active classes. [*Cheers.*]

He then proposed the health of their chairman, for who so fit to be their president as he who had sacrificed party spirit and politics that he might advance the cause and interests of the neglected and forlorn,—who had boldly stood forward among seven hundred legislators, and maintained that women should not be compelled to do the work of harnessed brutes? To Lord Ashley the most oppressed and neglected classes would have to return thanks for ages to come.—'Lord Ashley, the chairman of the day.' [*Loud and long continued applause.*]

Lord Ashley replied, saying that it 'was most gratifying to him to aid in the advance of any effort to ameliorate the condition of society; and it was peculiarly gratifying to have it thus acknowledged by one who had done so much, and so successfully, to arouse the sympathies of all for the situation and wants of the different classes of life'.

[1] Antony Ashley Cooper, Lord Ashley (1801–85), 7th Earl of Shaftesbury, 1851. Dickens had already been in correspondence with him on factory legislation, and, in his support, had savagely reviewed Lord Londonderry's *Letter to Lord Ashley on the Mines and Collieries Bill*, in the *Morning Chronicle* of 20 Oct. 1842. They met rarely, though working independently for many of the same causes, especially the Ragged School movement and Public Health. Shaftesbury wrote of Dickens to Forster, 'God had given him, as it were, a "general retainer" for all suffering and oppression' (17 December 1871, MS., Mr. W. J. Carlton). For Dickens's opinion of Shaftesbury see p. 132.

FIRST ANNUAL *SOIRÉE* OF THE ATHENAEUM: MANCHESTER

5 *October* 1843

THE Athenaeum had been founded in 1835, and after a brilliant beginning its membership dropped and its debts mounted until it was in danger of being dissolved; but a new committee energetically set to work to raise funds, organized a great bazaar, and arranged the *soirée* at which Dickens agreed to preside. A detailed account of the part Dickens played, has been left by one of the organizers, Edward Watkin.[1]

According to Watkin, it was Dickens's sister, Mrs. Burnett,[2] who had persuaded him to come; and it was at her home in Manchester that he first met Dickens in order to discuss the arrangements. Dickens, 'went into the history of the Athenaeum—spoke of the class to be benefited by it—of their sufferings and wants'. He appeared to take a great interest in it all, and modestly disclaimed any merit for taking part. 'Such institutions', he said, 'are most necessary and most useful, and there is too general a desire to get the utmost possible work out of men instead of a generous wish to give them the utmost possible opportunity of improvement. . . . *I must put it into them strong.*' Speaking of future plans, he said that if they could once ensure success for the Athenaeum, it 'will of itself establish others elsewhere'.

Next morning he was shown the Free Trade Hall where the meeting was to be held that night. He was pleased with it, and, 'immediately on entering it said he *felt* he could make himself exceedingly well heard in it'. That evening, in the carriage that took Dickens to the Hall, Watkins had time to look at Dickens more closely. He thought that his face was not 'strictly speaking, *handsome*', but that his eyes were 'dark and full of fire, and, when turned upon you give a light . . . such as I have seldom seen before'. He shrewdly noticed that he had a good deal 'of the eyebrow elevating, shoulder-shrugging, and head-nodding peculiar to people who have travelled a great deal'.

The scene in the Free Trade Hall was impressive. When the whole company had assembled, 'its appearance', said a local reporter, 'was extremely imposing, the elegant and chaste appearance of the new decorations in white and gold harmonising agreeably with the brilliant assemblage of beauty and fashion'.[3] Dickens entered the hall accompanied by several of the stewards, and, after shaking hands with Cobden,[4]

---

[1] Edward William Watkin (1819–1901), later a successful railway promoter; knighted 1868. His account was given in his reminiscences, *Alderman Cobden of Manchester*, 1891, pp. 123–30.

[2] Fanny Elizabeth Dickens (1810–48), his elder sister; concert singer and pianist; married Henry Burnett (1811–93) also a singer, in 1837; they retired from the stage on religious principles. After severe illness, she died of consumption. [3] *Manchester Guardian*.

[4] Richard Cobden (1804–65), statesman; from 1836 leading spirit of the Anti-Corn Law League; from 1841 M.P.; in Manchester, he was one of the founders of the Athenaeum, and alderman 1838–44. His presence, in the Free

promptly rose to open the business of the evening. He was greeted with the most enthusiastic cheering; and, on the applause subsiding, said:

LADIES and Gentlemen, I am sure that I need scarcely tell you that I am very proud and happy, and that I take it as a great distinction, to be asked to come amongst you on an occasion such as this, when even with the brilliant and beautiful spectacle I see before me, I can hail it as the most brilliant and beautiful circumstance of all that we assemble together here, even *here*, upon neutral ground [*Hear, hear,—from Cobden and others*], where we have no more knowledge of party differences [*hear, hear*], or public animosities between side and side, or between man and man, than if we were a public meeting in the commonwealth of Utopia. [*Hear, hear, and loud applause.*]

Ladies and gentlemen, upon this, and upon a hundred other grounds, this assembly is not less interesting to me, believe me— although personally almost a stranger here—than it is interesting to you; and I take it, that it is not of greater importance to all of us, than it is to every man who has learned to know that he has an interest in the moral and social elevation, the harmless relaxation, the peace, happiness, and improvement, of the community at large. [*Applause.*] Not even those who saw the first foundation of your Athenaeum laid, and watched its progress, as I know they did, almost as tenderly as if it were the progress of a living creature, until it reared its beautiful front, an honour to the town—not even they, nor even you who within its walls have tasted its usefulness, and put it to the proof, have greater reason, I am persuaded, to exult in its establishment, or to hope that it may thrive and prosper, than scores of thousands at a distance, who—whether consciously or unconsciously matters not—have, in the principle of its success and bright example, a deep and personal concern. [*Applause.*]

It well becomes, particularly well becomes, this enterprising town, this little world of labour, that she should stand out foremost in the foremost rank in such a cause. [*Hear, hear.*] It well becomes her that among her numerous and noble public institutions, she should have a splendid temple sacred to the education and improvement of a large class of those, who, in their various and useful stations, assist in the production of our wealth, and in rendering her name famous through the world. [*Hear, hear.*] I think it is grand to know that while her factories re-echo with the clanking of

Trade Hall, with his supporters, on the same platform as Disraeli and many prominent local Tories, accounts for Dickens's opening remarks. He was later contemptuous of Dickens's political reliability, on his refusal to support the campaign against Taxes on Knowledge, and dismissed him—with Sir John Bowring, Lamartine, and Thackeray—as belonging to 'the *genus sentimentalist*'.

stupendous engines and the whirl and rattle of machinery, the immortal mechanism of God's own hand, the mind, is not forgotten in the din and uproar, but is lodged and tended in a palace of its own. [*Loud applause.*] Ladies and gentlemen, that it is a structure deeply fixed and rooted in the public spirit of this place, and built to last, I have no more doubt, judging from the spectacle I see before me, and from what I know of its brief history, than I have of the reality of these walls that hem us in, and the pillars that spring up about us. [*Hear, hear.*]

You are perfectly well aware, I have no doubt, that the Athenaeum was projected at a time when commerce was in a vigorous and flourishing condition, and when those classes of society to which it particularly addresses itself were fully employed, and in the receipt of regular incomes. A season of depression almost without parallel ensued, and large numbers of young men employed in warehouses and offices suddenly found their occupation gone, and themselves reduced to very straightened and penurious circumstances. This altered state of things led, as I am told, to the compulsory withdrawal of many of the members, to a proportionate decrease in the expected funds, and to the incurrence of a debt of £3,000. By the very great zeal and energy of all concerned, and by the liberality of those to whom they applied for help, that debt is now in rapid course of being discharged. [*Great applause.*] A little more of the same indefatigable exertion on the one hand, and a little more of the same community of feeling upon the other, and there will be no such thing; the figures will be blotted out for good and all; and, from that time, the Athenaeum may be said to belong to you and to your heirs for ever. [*Loud applause.*]

But, ladies and gentlemen, at all time, now in its most thriving, and in its least flourishing condition—here, with its cheerful rooms, its pleasant and instructive lectures, its improving library of six thousand volumes; its opportunities of discussion and debate, of healthful bodily exercise, and, though last not least (for by this I set great store, as a very novel and excellent provision) its opportunities of blameless rational enjoyment [*hear, hear*]—here it is, open to every youth and man in this great town, accessible to every being in this vast hive, who, for all these benefits, and the inestimable ends to which they lead, can set aside one sixpence weekly. [*Hear, hear, and applause.*] I do look upon the reduction of the subscription to that amount, and upon the fact that the number of members has considerably more than doubled within the last twelve months, as strides in the path of the very best civilization, and chapters of rich promise in the history of mankind. [*Applause.*]

I do not know, ladies and gentlemen, whether, at this time of day and with such a prospect before us, we need trouble ourselves very much to rake up the ashes of the dead-and-gone objections,—the palsied, halting, blind, deaf, everything but dumb objections, that were wont to be urged by men of all parties against institutions such as this whose interests we are met to promote; but their philosophy was always to be summed up in the unmeaning application of one short sentence. How often have we heard, from that large class of men, wise in their generation, who would really seem to be born and bred for no other purpose than to pass into currency counterfeit and mischievous scraps of wisdom, as it is the sole pursuit of some other criminals to utter base coin,—how often have we heard from them as an all-convincing and self-evident argument, that 'A little learning is a dangerous thing'? [*Hear, hear.*] Why, a little hanging was considered a very dangerous thing, according to the same authorities [*laughter*], with this difference, that because a little hanging was dangerous, we had a great deal of it; and because a little learning was dangerous, we were to have none at all. [*Applause and laughter.*] Why, when I hear such cruel absurdities gravely reiterated, I do sometimes begin to doubt whether the parrots of society are not more pernicious to its interests than its birds of prey. I should be glad to hear such people's estimate of the comparative danger of 'a little learning' and a vast amount of ignorance [*hear, hear*]; I should be glad to know which they consider the most prolific parent of misery and crime. [*Hear, hear, and applause.*] Descending a little lower in the social scale, I should be glad to assist them in their calculations, by carrying them into certain jails and nightly refuges I know of, where my own heart dies within me when I see thousands of immortal creatures condemned, without alternative or choice, to tread, not what our great poet calls 'the primrose path to the everlasting bonfire', but one of jagged flints and stones, laid down by brutal ignorance, and held together like the solid rocks by years of this most wicked axiom. [*Great applause.*]

Would we know from any honourable body of merchants, upright in deed and thought, whether they would rather have ignorant or enlightened persons in their employment, we have their answer in this building; we have their answer in this company; we have it emphatically given in the munificent generosity of your own merchants of Manchester, of all sects and kinds, when this establishment was first proposed. [*Applause.*] But, ladies and gentlemen, are the advantages derivable by the people from institutions such as this, only of a negative character? If a little learning be an innocent thing, has it no distinct, wholesome, and immediate influence upon the mind? [*Hear, hear.*] The old doggerel rhyme, so often written in the beginning of books, says that

> When house and lands are gone and spent,
> Then learning is most excellent.

But I should be strongly disposed to reform that adage, and say that

> Though house and lands be never got,
> Learning can give what they can *not*.

[*Hear, hear, and applause.*] And this I know, that the first un-purchaseable blessing earned by every man who makes an effort to improve himself in such a place as the Athenaeum is self-respect [*hear*]—an inward dignity of character which once acquired and righteously maintained, nothing, no, not the hardest drudgery, nor the direst poverty, can vanquish. [*Applause.*] Though he should find it hard for a season even to keep the wolf of hunger from his door, let him but once have chased the dragon of ignorance from his hearth, and self-respect and hope are left him. [*Applause.*] You could no more deprive him of those sustaining qualities by loss or destruction of his worldly goods, than you could, by plucking out his eyes, take from him an internal consciousness of the bright glory of the sun. [*Loud applause.*]

The man who lives from day to day by the daily exercise in his sphere of hand or head, and seeks to improve himself in such a place as the Athenaeum, acquires for himself that property of soul which has in all times upheld struggling men in every degree, but self-made men especially and always. [*Applause.*] He secures to himself that faithful companion which, while it has ever lent the light of its countenance to men of rank and eminence who have deserved it, has ever shed its brightest consolations on men of low estate and almost hopeless means. [*Applause.*] It took its patient seat beside Sir Walter Raleigh in his dungeon-study in the Tower; and it laid its head upon the block with More. But it did not disdain to watch the stars with Ferguson, the shepherd's boy; it walked the streets in mean attire with Crabbe; it was a poor barber here in Lancashire with Arkwright; it was a tallow-chandler's son with Franklin; it worked at shoemaking with Bloomfield in his garret; it followed the plough with Burns; and, high above the noise of loom and hammer, it whispers courage, even at this day, in ears that I could name in Sheffield and Manchester.[1] [*Loud applause.*]

---

[1] Of the less easily remembered of these, James Ferguson (1710–76), the astronomer, Sir Richard Arkwright (1732–92), the inventor of textile machinery, and Robert Bloomfield (1766–1823), author of the poem *The Farmer's Boy*, like the others, were self-taught men.

The more a man who improves his leisure in such a place learns, the better, gentler, kinder man he must become. [*Hear, hear.*] When he knows how much great minds have suffered for the truth in every age and time, and to what dismal persecutions opinion has been exposed, he will become more tolerant of other men's belief in all matters, and will incline more leniently to their sentiments when they chance to differ from his own. [*Hear, hear.*] Understanding that the relations between himself and his employers involve a mutual duty and responsibility, he will discharge his part of the implied contract cheerfully, faithfully, and honourably; for the history of every useful life warns him to shape his course in that direction.

The benefits he acquires in such a place are not of a selfish kind, but extend themselves to his home, and to those whom it contains. Something of what he hears or reads within such walls can scarcely fail to become at times a topic of discourse by his own fireside, nor can it ever fail to lead to larger sympathies with men, and to a higher veneration for the great Creator of all the wonders of this universe. [*Applause.*] It appeals to his home and his homely feeling in other ways; for at certain times he carries there his wife and daughter, or his sister, or, possibly, some bright-eyed acquaintance of a more tender description. [*Hear, hear.*] Judging from what I see before me, I think it is very likely [*applause*]; I am sure I would if I could. [*Laughter and applause.*] He takes her there to enjoy a pleasant evening, to be gay and happy. Or, sometimes, it is possible he may happen to date his tenderness from the Athenaeum. [*Laughter.*] I think that it is a very excellent thing, too, and not the least among the advantages of the institution. [*Hear, hear.*] In any case I am quite sure that the number of bright eyes and beaming faces which grace this meeting tonight by their presence, will never be among the least of its excellences in my recollection. [*Applause.*]

Ladies and gentlemen, I shall not easily forget this scene, the pleasing task your favour has devolved upon me, or the strong and inspiring confirmation I have tonight, of all the hopes and reliances I have ever placed upon institutions of this nature. In the literary point of view—in their bearings upon literature—I regard them as of great importance, deeming that the more intelligent and reflective society in the mass becomes, and the more readers there are, the more distinctly writers of all kinds will be able to throw themselves upon the truthful feeling of the people, and the more honoured and the more useful literature must be. [*Applause.*] At the same time, I must confess that, if there had been an Athenaeum, and the people had been readers years ago, some leaves of dedication in your library, of praise of patrons which was very cheaply bought, very dearly sold, and very marketably haggled for by the groat,[1] would be blank leaves, and posterity might probably have lacked the information that certain monsters of virtue ever had existence. [*Hear.*] But it is upon a much better and wider scale; it is, let me say it once again, in the effect of such institutions as these upon the great social system, and the peace and happiness of mankind, that I delight to contemplate them [*applause*]; and, in my heart, I am quite certain that long after this institution, and others of the same nature, have crumbled into dust, the noble harvest of the seed sown in them will shine out brightly in the wisdom, the mercy, and the forbearance of another race. [*Loud applause.*]

Ladies and gentlemen, I will not detain you any longer; but, in virtue of my office, which entitles me to subvert, I suppose, for the time being, all rational and proper modes of proceeding, I will beg to introduce you to Mr. Cobden. [*Laughter and great applause.*]

Speeches followed from Cobden, Thomas Milner Gibson,[2] Dr. Lyon Playfair and Disraeli. The last speaker before the interval was John Roby[3] of Rochdale, who gave an amusing account of how he had over-heard a lady, after a former *soirée* in Manchester, saying that she liked all the speeches but his. He wound up by facetiously proposing to give a lecture for the Athenaeum, 'upon some subject—whenever it may be thought advisable'. Dickens then announced that the meeting was about to carry out another object of the Athenaeum, and that was to have a short interval for refreshment. [*Applause.*]

Dessert was placed on the table, and 'the band played some lively airs', meanwhile, Dickens 'was literally besieged by bevies of fair applicants for his autograph'. Someone offered him a sovereign for the bazaar fund, in exchange for his signature and 'the chairman at once complied . . . modestly adding below his name the words "Very Dear". The gentleman, however, handed his sovereign to Mr. Watkin . . . exclaiming very emphatically, "I don't think so".' Henry Burnett also described the scene, saying that Dickens began his work 'with a smile of good nature and acquiescence . . . and continued until the table began to look golden'.[4]

Dickens resumed the proceedings by calling on the Rev. John Eustace Giles. He was the younger brother of the Rev. William Giles, Dickens's first schoolmaster, and had been his fellow pupil twenty years before, in Chatham. He recalled the time 'when they were no strangers to each

---

[1] *groat*: alternatively, 'great'.

[2] Thomas Milner Gibson (1806–84), politician; M.P. for Manchester since 1841; ally of Cobden and orator of the Anti-Corn Law League. Later he and his wife were friends of Dickens, in spite of her keen interest in spiritualism of which he strongly disapproved.

[3] John Roby (1793–1850), banker, author of *Traditions of Lancashire*, 1829.

[4] F. G. Kitton, *Charles Dickens by Pen and Pencil*, 1890, p. 143.

other, when they rambled together through the same Kentish fields, and mingled in the same sports'. Dickens's place in the Chair was then taken by James Crossley,[1] and a vote of thanks to Dickens was proposed, seconded, and carried by acclamation. He came forward, and said:

Ladies and Gentlemen, I am most deeply, and cordially, and earnestly obliged to you for this kind and hearty welcome. And let me say that only one thing has made me at all uncomfortable for a moment this evening, and it is this—that gentlemen who have spoken should have preserved the fiction that any merit exists on my part in being here tonight; for, trust me, that of all the rewards and honours which you could give, or I could possibly receive, a request to preside at such an assembly as this would be the highest. [*Applause.*] And pray remember that in any future time a similar request to be useful in like manner, I should take to be the very highest mark of your favour and distinguished regard. [*Loud applause.*]

Ladies and gentlemen, when Mr. Roby delivers that lecture he has promised, at the Athenaeum, I engage to attend [*loud laughter*]; and, at its close, I will deliver another [*renewed applause*], and I shall be most happy, in conjunction with Mr. Disraeli, to write the best description of Mr. Roby, as he appeared when delivering the lecture [*applause and roars of laughter*] that our joint abilities can possibly produce. Ladies, I am happy to say that the time for discussing Mr. Roby's speech in corners and by-places has now arrived, and that I can dismiss you to those more whispered and low invocations, after the very brilliant and eloquent one which was delivered to you as the Lancashire Witches[2] by Mr. Disraeli. [*Laughter and applause.*] Gentlemen, I am instructed to inform you that there is still at the bazaar, 'a most excellent stock of goods', which are to be procured at 'the most reasonable prices', and 'on the lowest possible terms',—consistent with the interests of the establishment. [*The quiet humour with which Mr. Dickens, after a significant pause, added the saving clause, was at once and generally appreciated by the assembly, as was evinced by a general burst of laughter.*] And, ladies and gentlemen, once again I beg to return you most heartfelt thanks. [*Loud applause.*]

Dickens then retired, and dancing commenced. It was kept up until an early hour.

Although he was elected an honorary life member of the Athenaeum, Dickens was never able to fulfil his promise to appear on its behalf again.

---

[1] James Crossley (1800–83), author and bibliophile; prominent local Tory; President of the Athenaeum, 1847–50; introduced to Dickens by W. H. Ainsworth.   [2] A conventional compliment to the ladies.

He accepted an invitation to attend the fifth annual *soirée* in 1847, and at the last minute it was announced that he could not come. He was invited the following year, when Emerson took the Chair, but he was again unable to attend.

The financial difficulties of the Manchester Athenaeum, and the need to resort to bazaars and *soirées* to raise funds and gain publicity, were typical of the dilemma in which all such institutions found themselves. It was impossible for them to be attractive and useful enough to attract large numbers of working-men, and to be self-supporting at the same time. As well as this, the committees of management invariably came under the control of the more respectable middle-class, and the lectures were mainly attended by shopkeepers' sons, apprentices, and clerks. As a result, workers or mechanics gave up attending almost altogether. In Manchester this social change was particularly marked, and some 'Lyceums' had been started, in 1838, to cater for the poorest classes; but they failed for the usual reason that their members preferred entertainment to instruction.

An awareness of these tendencies is implicit even in Dickens's earlier speeches; and, later, he was outspoken in demanding that working-men should not be 'patronized', but that they should have some say in the management of institutions conducted in their name.

SOIRÉE OF THE MECHANICS' INSTITUTION: LIVERPOOL

26 *February* 1844

F o r Dickens's convenience, as he was to speak at Birmingham a few days later, the annual Christmas *soirée* of the Liverpool Mechanics' Institution had been postponed until February. A few days beforehand Dickens wrote to Forster: 'I think I shall have grounds for a very good speech at Brummagem; but I am not so sure of Liverpool: having misgivings of over-gentility.'[1] On arriving there on the 25th he joined an old friend, T. J. Thompson,[2] who made up a small party with Dickens, his sister Fanny, and her husband Henry Burnett.

The next morning he went to look over the institution where he was to preside that evening. He wrote to his wife that it was 'an enormous place', but that he thought it would be easy to speak in. It was being fitted with gas, 'after the manner of the ring at Astley's', and he was somewhat appalled to think that it would have 'eight hundred ladies tonight, in full dress. I am rather shakey just now, but I shall pull up, I have no doubt.'[3]

[1] F, iv. iii.

[2] Thomas James Thompson (18?–1881); Dickens had probably met him through Charles Smithson, who had married Thompson's sister. Smithson was a partner of Thomas Mitton—formerly Dickens's fellow clerk—who was about this time acting as Dickens's solicitor.

[3] *Mr. & Mrs. Charles Dickens*, ed. W. Dexter, 1935, p. 94.

In the evening, as he appeared on the platform, the organ played 'See the Conquering Hero Comes', and the whole company rose to welcome him with the most enthusiastic cheering.

As soon as the applause had subsided, Dickens rose and said:

LADIES and Gentlemen, It was rather hard of you to take away my breath before I spoke a word; but I would not thank you, even if I could, for the favour which has set me in this place or for the generous kindness which has greeted me so warmly; because my first strong impulse still would be—although I had that power—to lose sight of all personal considerations in the high intent and meaning of this numerous assemblage in the contemplation of the noble objects to which this building is devoted, of its brilliant and inspiring history, of that rough upward track, so bravely trodden, which it leaves behind, and that bright path of steadily increasing usefulness which lies stretched out before it. [*Cheers.*] My first strong impulse still would be to exchange congratulations with you, as members of one united family, on the thriving vigour of this strongest child of a strong race. My first strong impulse still would be, though everybody here had twice as many hundreds of hands as there are hundreds of persons present, to shake them in the spirit every one [*cheers*],—always, allow me to say, excepting those hands (and there are a few such here) which, with the constitutional infirmity of human nature, I would rather salute in some more tender fashion. [*Laughter and applause.*]

When I first had the honour of communicating with your Committee with reference to this celebration, I had some selfish hopes that the visit proposed to me might turn out to be one of condolence, or, at least, of solicitous inquiry; for they who receive a visitor in any season of distress are easily touched and moved by what he says, and I entertained some confident expectation of making a mighty strong impression upon you. But, when I came to look over the printed documents which were forwarded to me at the same time, and with which you are all tolerably familiar, these anticipations very speedily vanished, and left me bereft of all consolation but the triumphant feeling to which I have referred. For what do I find on looking over those brief chronicles of this swift conquest over ignorance and prejudice, in which no blood has been poured out, and no treaty signed but that one sacred compact which recognizes the just right of every man, whatever his belief, or however humble his degree, to aspire, and to have some means of aspiring, to be a better and a wiser man? [*Loud cheers.*] I find that in 1825 certain misguided and turbulent persons proposed to erect in Liverpool an unpopular, dangerous, irreligious, and revolutionary establishment, called a Mechanics' Institution [*cheers*]; that, in

1835, Liverpool having somehow or other got on pretty comfortably in the meantime in spite of it, the first stone of a new and
spacious edifice was laid; that in 1837 it was opened; that it was
afterwards, at different periods, considerably enlarged; that, in
1844, conspicuous among the public beauties of a beautiful town,
here it stands triumphant—its enemies lived down; its former
students attesting in their various useful callings and pursuits the
sound, practical information it afforded them; its members
numbering considerably more than 3,000, and setting in for 6,000
at least; its library comprehending 11,000 volumes, and daily
sending forth its hundreds of books into private homes; its staff of
masters and officers amounting to half a hundred in themselves;
its schools, conveying every sort of instruction, high and low,
adapted to the labour, means, exigencies, and conveniences of
nearly every class and grade of persons. I was here this morning,
and in its spacious halls I found stores of wonders worked by nature
in the air, in the forest, in the cavern, and in the sea; stores of the
surpassing engines devised by science for the better knowledge of
other worlds and the greater happiness of this; stores of those
gentler works of art which, though achieved in perishable stone, by yet
more perishable hands of dust, are in their influence immortal. With
such means at their command, so well directed, so cheaply shared,
and so extensively diffused, well may your Committee say, as they
have done in one of their Reports, that the success of this establishment has far exceeded their most sanguine expectations. [*Cheers.*]

But, ladies and gentlemen, as that same philosopher whose
words they quote—as Bacon[1] tells us—instancing the wonderful
effects of little things and small beginnings, that the influence of the
loadstone was first discovered in particles of iron and not in iron
bars, so they may lay it to their hearts that when they combined
together to form the institution which has risen to this majestic
height, they issued on a field of enterprise the glorious end of which
they cannot even now discern. Every man who has felt the advantages of, or has received improvement in, this place, carries its benefits into the society in which he moves, and puts them out at compound interest; and what the blessed sum may be at last, no man
can tell. [*Cheers.*] Ladies and gentlemen, with that Christian prelate
whose name appears on your list of honorary members;[2] that good
and liberal man who once addressed you within these walls, in a
spirit worthy of his calling and of his High Master, I look forward
from this place, as from a tower, to the time when high and low,

---

[1] See p. 4.

[2] Edward Stanley (1779–1849), Bishop of Norwich, 1837–49; vigorous
Liberal reformer; especially active in extending education.

and rich and poor, shall mutually assist, improve, and educate each other. [*Applause.*]

I feel, ladies and gentlemen, that this is not a place, with its 3,200 members, and at least 3,200 arguments in every one, to enter on any advocacy of the principle of Mechanics' Institutions, or to discuss the subject with those who do or ever did object to them. I should as soon think of arguing the point with those untutored savages whose mode of life you last year had the opportunity of witnessing; indeed, I am strongly inclined to believe them by far the more rational of the two. Moreover, if the institution itself be not a sufficient answer to all such objections, then there is no such thing in fact or reason, human or divine. [*Hear.*] Neither will I venture to enter into those details of the management of this place which struck me most on the perusal of its papers; but I cannot help saying how much impressed and gratified I was, as everybody must be who comes to their perusal for the first time, by the extraordinary munificence with which this institution has been endowed by certain gentlemen. [*Cheers.*]

Amongst the peculiar features of management which made the greatest impression on me, I may observe that that regulation which empowers fathers, being annual subscribers of one guinea, to introduce their sons who are minors; and masters, on payment of the astoundingly small sum of five shillings annually, in like manner their apprentices, is not the least valuable of its privileges, and certainly not the least valuable to society. And, ladies and gentlemen, I cannot say to you what pleasure I derived from the perusal of an apparently excellent report in your local papers of a meeting held here some short time since, in aid of the formation of a girls' school in connexion with this institution. [*Cheers.*] This is a new and striking chapter in the history of these institutions; it does equal credit to the gallantry and policy of this, and disposes one to say of it with a slight parody of the words of Burns, that

> Its 'prentice han' it tried on man,
> And then it *taught* the lasses, O.

That those who are our best teachers, and whose lessons are oftenest heeded in after life, should be well taught themselves, is a proposition few reasonable men will gainsay; and, certainly, to breed up good husbands on the one hand, and good wives on the other, does appear as reasonable and straightforward a plan as could well be devised for the improvement of the next generation. [*Loud cheers.*]

This, and what I see before me, naturally brings me to our fairer members, in respect of whom I have no doubt you will agree with me that they ought to be admitted to the widest possible extent,

and on the lowest possible terms; and, ladies, let me venture to say
to you that you never did a wiser thing in all your lives than when
you turned your favourable regard on such an establishment as
this [*cheers*], for wherever the light of knowledge is diffused, wherever there is the clearest perception of what is beautiful, and good,
and most redeeming amid all the faults and vices of mankind, there
your character, your virtues, your graces, your better nature will be
the best appreciated, and there the truest homage will be proudly
paid to you. [*Loud applause.*] You show best, trust me, in the clearest
light; and every ray that falls upon you at your own firesides, from
any book or thought communicated within these walls, will raise you
nearer to the angels in the eyes you care for most. [*Much cheering.*]

I will not longer interpose myself, ladies and gentlemen, between
you and the pleasure we all anticipate in hearing other gentlemen,
and in enjoying those social pleasures with which it is a main part
of the wisdom of this society to adorn and relieve its graver pursuits. We all feel, I am sure, being here, that we are truly interested
in the cause of human improvement and rational education, and
that we pledge ourselves—everyone as far as in him lies—to extend
the knowledge of the benefits afforded in this place, and to bear
honest witness in its favour. To those who yet remain without its
walls, but have the means of purchasing its advantages, we make
appeal, and in a friendly and forbearing spirit say, 'Come in, and be
convinced: "Who enters here, leaves *doubt* behind."' If you,
happily, have been well taught yourself, and are superior to its
advantages, so much the more should you make one in sympathy
with those who are below you. Beneath this roof we breed the men
who, in time to come, must be found working for good or evil in
every quarter of society. If mutual forbearance among various
classes be not found here, where so many men are trained up in so
many grades to enter on so many roads of life, dating their entry
from one common starting-point, as they are all approaching, by
various paths, one common end, where else can that great lesson be
imbibed? Differences of wealth, of rank, of intellect, we know there
must be, and we respect them; but we would give to all the means
of taking out one patent of nobility, and we define it in the words
of a great living poet, who is one of us, and who uses his great gifts,
as he holds them in trust, for the general welfare:

> Howe'er it be, it seems to me,
> 'Tis only noble to be good.
> Kind hearts are more than coronets,
> And simple faith than Norman blood.[1]

[1] Tennyson, 'Lady Clara Vere de Vere'.

Dickens sat down amid loud and continued applause. As soon as it had subsided he rose again, and introduced a member of the Institution who sang *The Ivy Green*.

The chairman then said: 'I am requested to introduce you to a lady whom I have some difficulty and tenderness in announcing—Miss Weller [*laughter and applause*], who will play a fantasia on the piano-forte.' [*Applause.*] Miss Weller is said to have played 'with all her accustomed delicacy, power, and beauty', while Dickens, 'during the time she was delighting the audience with her exquisite playing, . . . kept his eyes firmly fixed on her every movement'. Before leaving the platform they were introduced, and Dickens shook hands with her and her father, 'at the same time making some observation which created much laughter among those immediately around'.[1] Later in the evening he introduced Miss Weller once more, saying that 'The god-child, of whom I am so proud, will oblige again'.

After further speeches, songs, and an interval for refreshment and a promenade, Dickens resigned his seat to the President of the Institution. The secretary proposed a vote of thanks, it was seconded and passed by acclamation, and was then succeeded 'by such a scene of enthusiasm as had never been seen within the walls of that institution before'.[2] The cheering was prolonged for several minutes. When it had at last subsided and Dickens stepped forward to reply, it broke out again. At last he was able to say:

The height of gratification to which you have raised me, places me in that situation of disadvantage to which I jocularly referred at the beginning of my address. Believe me,—believe me, the obligation, the delight, and pride in this case are all on my side— that it is a delight and happiness to me to connect myself with such an institution as yours. It is—as those who know me best, best know—a reward to which I attach the best and proudest value. I should be ashamed of myself, and care very little for those belonging to me, if I did not make all my children, as they grow up, feel and estimate the value of such institutions as Mechanics' Institutions, and become members of them. Which I will. [*Applause.*]

In reference to one point referred to by the eloquent gentleman who has just addressed you, which is, the objection that used to be urged against such institutions that they might possibly confound the distinctions of society, and render people dissatisfied with the grades into which they have fallen, allow me to say that after mature consideration I am convinced there is no fear of that in England. The distinction of the different grades of society are so accurately marked, and so very difficult to pass, that I have not the slightest fear of any such result. [*Applause.*]

In the path I have trodden, which has met with your approval,

---

[1] *Liverpool Mercury.*   [2] Ibid.

I will continue to tread so long as God grants me health and life; but I fear there is one quality for which my books have been praised, in which they will be terribly deficient in time to come,—and that is *Heart*. I felt a loss of heart when I first entered this room; more still when I went upstairs; and the last remnant of my heart went into that piano. [*—Pointing to the instrument on which Miss Weller had been playing.—Laughter and cheers.*] Ladies and Gentlemen,— Good night. In certain words contained in a little book referred to so often and so kindly, allow me for once to quote myself and add, 'And so, as Tiny Tim observed, God bless Us Every One!' [*Enthusiastic applause.*]

As soon as he had returned to the hotel Dickens finished his letter to his wife, telling her of his 'vigorous, brilliant, humorous, pathetic, eloquent, fervid, and impassioned speech'. The following day he was invited to lunch by Mr. Weller to his house at the Breck, where he met the other members of his family, and when—according to the editor of the *Liverpool Mercury*—'further and further evidences of their extraordinary abilities and acquirements in various charming ways were witnessed by the delighted party, and made an impression on Mr. Dickens which will not soon be obliterated'. In the evening he attended a fancy-dress ball, which ended with a Sir Roger of forty couples at three o'clock in the morning.

The same day Dickens left for Birmingham, where he was to speak that night, while his friend Thompson remained behind. That evening, Dickens wrote to him, quite seriously:

I cannot joke about Miss Weller; for she is too good; and interest in her (spiritual young creature that she is, and destined to an early death, I fear) has become a sentiment with me. Good God, what a madman I should seem, if the incredible feeling I have conceived for that girl should be made plain to anyone!

Thompson, however, was no less susceptible, and had the advantage of being a widower. He stayed on in Liverpool, won her affection, and married her some time next year. Dickens became related to the family only through the marriage of his brother Frederick with her sister Anna, which was not a success. Mrs. Thompson long outlived Dickens, and was the mother of two daughters who became Elizabeth Lady Butler, and Alice Meynell.

CONVERSAZIONE OF THE POLYTECHNIC INSTITUTION: BIRMINGHAM

28 *February* 1844

THE Polytechnic Institution had been started in Birmingham in 1843, after the failure of a Mechanics' Institute and an Athenaeum. In order to raise funds, and to excite interest in the new society, it was decided to hold a conversazione in the Town Hall, at which Dickens consented to preside. The scene at the meeting was described by a local reporter:

Never have we seen our noble Hall to greater advantage. . . . The rich festoons of flowers . . . gave it . . . the appearance of some enchanted scene of romance . . . and the 'Welcome Boz!' which was formed in flowers in front of the great gallery, gave something like an anticipatory notice of . . . the loud, long, hearty and enthusiastic cheers, with which the Chairman was greeted.[1]

Dickens himself was delighted with his reception, and wrote to his sister, Mrs. Burnett, that the moment he appeared, 'the whole assembly stood up, with a noise like the rustling of leaves in a wood; and then began to cheer in the most terrific manner I ever heard: beginning again and again and again'.[2] When the applause had subsided, he said:

Y o u will think it very unwise, or very self-denying in me, in such an assembly, in such a splendid scene, and after such a welcome, to congratulate myself on having nothing new to say to you; but I do so notwithstanding. To say nothing of places nearer home, I have had the honour of attending at Manchester shortly before Christmas, and at Liverpool only the night before last (whence I have brought with me a slight hoarseness), for purposes similar to that which bring you together now; and, looking down a short perspective of similar engagements, I feel immense satisfaction in the thought that I shall very soon have nothing at all to say; in which case I shall be content to stake my reputation, like the Spectator of Addison, and that other great periodical Spectator, the Speaker of the House of Commons, on my powers of listening.

That feeling, and your earnest reception of me, are not my only reasons for feeling a genuine, cordial, and sincere pleasure in the proceedings tonight. The Polytechnic Institution of Birmingham is now in its infancy, struggling into life under all those adverse and disadvantageous circumstances which, to a greater or less extent, naturally beset all infancy [*laughter*]; but I would much rather connect myself with its records now, however humble, in its days of difficulty and danger, than look back upon its origin when it may have become strong, and rich, and powerful. I should prefer an intimate association with it now, in its early days and apparent struggles, to becoming its advocate and acquaintance, its fair-weather friend, in its high and palmy days. I would rather be able to say to it, 'I knew you in your swaddling clothes. [*Laughter.*] Your two elder brothers had drooped and died, their chests were weak. [*Renewed laughter.*] About your cradle nurses shook their heads, and gossips groaned; but up you shot apace, up, up, indomitable in your constitution, strong in your tone and muscle, well-knit in your figure, steady in your pulse, wise and temperate in your

---

[1] *Birmingham Advertiser.*   [2] 1 Mar. 1844 [DH].

speech, of good repute in all your doings, until you have grown a
very giant.' [*Loud applause.*] Birmingham is, in my mind, and in
the minds of most men, associated with many giants; and I can no
more believe that this young institution will turn out sickly,
dwarfish, or of stunted growth, than I can that when my glass
slipper of chairmanship falls off, and the clock strikes twelve tonight, that this hall will be turned into a pumpkin! [*Applause.*]
I found that strong belief upon the splendid array of grace and
beauty by which I am surrounded, and which, if it only had one
hundredth part of the effect upon others it has upon me, could do
anything it pleased, with anything and anybody. [*Cheers.*] I found
my strong conviction, in the second place, upon the public spirit of
the town of Birmingham—upon the name and fame of its capitalists
and working men; upon the greatness and importance of its merchants and manufacturers; upon its inventions, which are constantly in progress; upon the skill and intelligence of its artisans,
which are daily developing; and the increased knowledge of all
portions of the community. All these reasons lead me to the conclusion that your institution will advance, that it will and must
progress, that the town will stride in advance of time and will not
content itself with lingering leagues behind.

I have another peculiar ground of satisfaction in connexion with
the object of this assembly, and it is this: that the resolutions about
to be proposed do not contain in themselves anything of a sectarian
or class nature; that they do not confine themselves to any one
single institution, but assert the great and omnipotent principles
of comprehensive education everywhere, and under each and every
circumstance. I beg leave to say that I concur heart and hand
in those principles, and will do all in my power for their advancement; for such imperfect knowledge as I possess of the mass of my
fellow creatures, and their condition in this country, weds me to
this principle heart and hand, beyond all power of divorcement but
one. I hold that for any fabric of society to go on day after day, and
year after year, from father to son, and from grandfather to grandson, unceasingly punishing men for not engaging in the pursuit of
virtue and for the practice of crime, without showing them the way
to virtue, has no foundation in justice, has no foundation in religion, has no foundation in truth, and has only one parallel in
fiction that I know of,—which is the case of an obdurate old Genie,
in the *Arabian Nights,* who was bent on taking the life of a certain
merchant, because he had struck out the eye of his invisible son.
Again, if I may refer to another tale in the same book of charming
fancies—not inappropriate to the present occasion—there is the
case of a powerful spirit who had been imprisoned at the bottom of

the sea, shut up in a casket with a leaden cover, sealed with the seal
of Solomon upon it. There he lay neglected for many centuries,
and during that period made many different vows: at first, that he
would reward magnificently those who should release him, and, at
last, that he would destroy them. Now, there is a spirit of great
power, the Spirit of Ignorance, long shut up in a vessel of Obstinate
Neglect, with a great deal of lead in its composition, and sealed
with the seal of many, many Solomons, and which is exactly in the
same position. Release it in time, and it will bless, restore, and re-
animate society; but let it lie under the rolling waves of years, and
its blind revenge at last will be destruction.[1] [*Loud applause.*]

That there are classes which, rightly treated, are our strength,
and wrongly treated are our weakness, I hold it impossible to deny;
and that for these industrious, intelligent, and honourably independent classes, in whom Birmingham is especially interested,
there are no means of mutual instruction and improvement so
peculiarly adapted to their circumstances as a Mechanics' Institute,
is a proposition which I take to be, by this time, quite beyond dis-
proof. Far be it from me, and here I wish to be most particularly
understood, to attempt to depreciate the excellent Church instruction Societies, or the worthy, sincere and temperate zeal of those
reverend gentlemen by whom they are usually conducted. [*Hear.*]
On the contrary I believe that they have done, and are doing,
much good, and are deserving of high praise; but I hope it may be
said, without offence, that in a community such as Birmingham,
there are other objects not unworthy in the light of heaven—and
objects of recognized utility—which are worthy of support, but
which lie beyond their influence: principles which are practised in
word and deed in Polytechnic Institutions, principles for the diffusion of which honest men of all degrees and of every creed may
associate together on an independent footing and on neutral
ground, and at small expense, for the better understanding and the
greater consideration of each other, and for the better cultivation
of the happiness of all. For it surely cannot be allowed that those
who labour day by day, surrounded by machinery, shall be permitted to degenerate into machines themselves; but, on the
contrary, they should be able to assert their common origin in that
Creator from whose wondrous hands they came, and unto whom,
responsible and thinking men, they will return. [*Applause.*]

---

[1] The idea of releasing the Spirit of Ignorance was hardly a happy one. It had
been better expressed in the *Christmas Carol*, where the Ghost of Christmas
Present shows Scrooge Ignorance and Want personified as two ragged children,
a boy and a girl. Behind both the book and the speech was the sincere conviction
that education must be extended before it was too late.

There is, indeed, no difference in the main with respect to the dangers of ignorance, and the advantages of knowledge, between those who hold different opinions; for, it is to be observed, that those who are most distrustful of the advantages of education, are always the first to exclaim against the results of ignorance. This fact was pleasantly illustrated on the railway, as I came here. In the same carriage with me there sat an ancient gentleman (I feel no delicacy in alluding to him, for I know that he is not in the room, having got out far short of Birmingham), who expressed himself most mournfully as to the ruinous effects and rapid spread of railways, and was most pathetic upon the virtues of the slow-going old stage coaches. Now I, entertaining some little lingering kindness for the road, made shift to express my concurrence with the old gentleman's opinion, without any great compromise of my own. Well, we got on tolerably comfortably together; and when the engine, with a frightful screech dived into the darkness, like some strange aquatic monster, the old gentleman said this would never do [*laughter*], and I agreed with him. When it parted from each successive station with a shock and a shriek, as if it had had a double tooth drawn, the old gentleman shook his head, and I shook mine. [*Renewed laughter.*] When he burst forth against such new fangled notions, and said that no good could come from them, I did not contest the point. But I invariably found that when the speed of the engine was abated, or there was the slightest prolongation of our stay at any station, the old gentleman was up in arms, and his watch was instantly out of his pocket, denouncing the slowness of our progress.[1] [*Laughter.*] Now I could not help comparing this old gentleman to that ingenious class of persons who are in the constant habit of declaiming against the vices and crimes of society and at the same time are the first and foremost to assert that vice and crime have not their common origin in ignorance and discontent. [*Laughter and cheers.*]

The good work, however, in which whatever may be your parties and opinions you are all deeply interested, has been well begun. We are all interested in it, it is advancing and cannot be stopped by any opposition although it may be retarded, in this place or that, by the indifference of the middle classes, with whom its successful progress chiefly rests. Of this success I cannot entertain a doubt;

[1] The Grand Junction Railway from Liverpool to Birmingham had been open since July 1837; the last stage of the journey is also described in 'Fire and Snow,' *Household Words*, 21 Jan. 1854. A great deal has been written about Dickens's supposed distaste for railways and regret for the stage-coach which is rather misleading. 'A Child's Dream of a Star' (1850) was conceived 'coming down the railroad', Dickens wrote to Forster, 'always a wonderfully suggestive place to me when I am alone.' *Dombey and Son* (1846-8) was to deal with the Railway Age.

for whenever the working classes enjoy an opportunity of effectu-
ally rebutting accusations which falsehood or thoughtlessness have
brought against them, they always avail themselves of it, and show
themselves in their true characters; and it is this which made the
damage done to a single picture in the National Gallery in London,
by some poor lunatic cripple, a mere matter of newspaper notoriety
and wonder for some few days. This has established a fact evident
to the meanest comprehension, that any number of thousands of
persons of the humblest condition of life in this country, can pass
through that same National Gallery, or the British Museum, in
seasons of holiday making, without damaging in the slightest degree, the smallest rarity, in either wonderful collection. [*Applause.*]
I do not myself believe that the working classes were ever the
wanton or mischievous persons they have been so often and so long
represented to be [*applause*]; but I rather incline to the opinion
that some wise men took it into their heads to lay it down as a
matter of fact, without being particular about the premises; and
that the idle and prejudiced, not wishing to have the trouble of
forming opinions for themselves, took it for granted—until the
people had an opportunity for disproving the stigma and vindicating themselves before the world. [*Applause.*]

Now this assertion is well illustrated by what has occurred respecting an equestrian statue in the metropolis, with respect to which a
legend existed that the sculptor hanged himself, because he had neglected to put a girth to the saddle. This story was currently believed
for many years, until it was inspected for a different purpose, and it
was found to have had a girth all the time. [*Cheers and laughter.*]

But surely if, as it is stated, the people are ill disposed and
mischievous, surely that is the best reason that can be offered for
teaching them better; and if they are not, surely that is a reason
for giving them every opportunity of vindicating their injured
reputation; and they cannot possibly, I think, have a better one
than the opportunity of associating together voluntarily for such
high purposes as it is proposed to carry out by the establishment of
the Birmingham Polytechnic Institution. [*Cheers.*] In any case,
and in every case, if you would reward honesty, if you would give
encouragement to good, if you would stimulate the idle, eradicate
evil, or correct what is bad, education—comprehensive liberal
education—is the one thing needful, and the one effective end.
[*Applause.*] And if I may apply to my purpose, and render into
plain prose, some words of Hamlet, not with reference to any
government or party (for party being, for the most part, an
irrational sort of thing, has no connexion with the object we have
in view), and if I might apply those words to education as Hamlet

applied them to the skull of Yorick, the King's Jester, I would say, 'Now hie thee to the council chamber, and tell them, though they lay it on in sounding language and fine words an inch thick, to this complexion they must come at last'.

Dickens resumed his seat amid enthusiastic and repeated cheering. He was followed by the president of the institution, and several other speakers, who proposed and supported various resolutions in favour of education. On Dickens leaving the Chair, his place was taken by the president; and it was moved, seconded, and carried with acclamation:

That this meeting, while conveying its cordial thanks to Charles Dickens Esq., for his presence this evening, cannot separate without tendering that warmest expression of its gratitude and admiration to one whose writings have so eloquently inculcated the lessons of benevolence and virtue, and so richly contributed to the stores of public pleasure and instruction.

Dickens then rose, and replied:

Ladies and Gentlemen, We are now even, for if I have ever been so fortunate as to touch your feelings, you have amply returned the compliment. But I am as little disposed to say to you, 'Go, and sin no more', in this wise, as I am to promise for myself that 'I will never do so again'. As long as I can make you laugh or cry, I will; and you will easily believe me when I say that you cannot do too much on your parts to show me that we are still cordial and loving friends. To you, ladies of the institution, I am—as who is not?— especially and deeply indebted. I have sometimes [*pointing to the word 'Boz' in front of the great gallery*] thought that much of whatever little magic lies in that short name yonder *must* be attributable to its having as many letters in it as there were three Graces, and to the Graces having been of your fair sisterhood.

A story is told of an eastern potentate of modern times, who, for an eastern potentate, was a tolerably good man—sometimes bowstringing his friends rather indiscriminately in his moments of anger, but burying them with great splendour in his moments of penitence—that whenever intelligence was brought him of any new plot or turbulent conspiracy, his first inquiry always was, 'Who is she?'—meaning that there must be a woman at the bottom of it. In my small way, I differ from that potentate. Whenever any good is to be done, and any great end is to be attained, any ministering angel's hand is needed, my first inquiry always is, 'Where is she?' And the certain answer is, 'She is here'. Ladies and gentlemen, you have made me very proud and happy, and with all my heart I thank you for your heartfelt generosity,

A thousand times, good night:
A thousand times the worse to want your light![1]

[1] *Romeo and Juliet*, II. ii.

As soon as he returned to his hotel, Dickens wrote to Thompson, whom he had left behind in Liverpool, to say how he wished he had come, and that the passage 'about the Genie and the casket' had been introduced 'with marvellous effect, and was applauded to the echo. . . . A better or quicker audience never listened to man.' Next day he was on his way home again, as he told his sister, 'perfectly exhausted, dead, worn-out, and spiritless'.[1]

GOVERNESSES' BENEVOLENT INSTITUTION

20 *April* 1844

THE Governesses' Benevolent Institution had recently been founded by the Rev. David Laing.[2] Dickens readily accepted an invitation to speak at its first anniversary festival, replying to Mrs. Laing:

I have found it necessary . . . to decline attending many projected dinners in behalf of charitable Institutions. But I will most certainly make an exception in favor of the Governesses. Their cause has my warmest sympathy; and I should perform Lord Castlereagh's feat of turning my back upon myself, if I hesitated for an Instant.[3]

The dinner was held at the London Tavern with the Duke of Cambridge in the Chair. After the usual series of speeches, Lord Sandon[4] proposed the health of the chairman, the Rev. David Laing read the first list of subscriptions, and he was followed by Dickens.

THE toast he was about to propose, he said, had reference to the means by which the end they had in view was to be attained, and to the delicacy with which the helping hand of the society was extended to objects of its sympathy: it was, 'the health of the Committees of ladies and gentlemen who manage its affairs'. He took the great end and object of this institution to be the recognition, at last, of the claims and merit of a class whose office is in reason and in right high, but which has been made in folly and injustice low. [*Loud cheers.*] It had been stated by Dr. Goldsmith,[5] who had painful experience of the neglect which this class of instructor endures, that he knew no member of society more useful nor more honourable than the imparter of knowledge; at the same time he knew none who was so generally despised, and whose talents were so ill

---

[1] 1 Mar. 1844 [DH].

[2] Rev. David Laing (1800–60), chaplain to the Middlesex Hospital; see also p. 270.   [3] 1 Feb. 1844 [DH].

[4] Dudley Ryder, Viscount Sandon (1798–1882), 2nd Earl of Harrowby 1847; Tory M.P. of Liberal opinions; probably known to Dickens through Miss Burdett Coutts, whose cousin, Lady Frances Stuart, Lord Sandon had married in 1823.   [5] *The Bee*, 'On Education'.

rewarded. Now, if this were true in general, with what particular force did it apply to those unkind, ungenerous slights which 'patient merit of the unworthy takes' in the persons of governesses ? [*Cheers.*]

It was very well to say that 'knowledge is power', but how often did they forget that it was a source of weakness too ? [*Applause.*] Knowledge had not its right place in society, and he believed that it did not obtain a just recognition and reward for its services any-where. To take the case of those ladies in comparison with menial servants: they were worse paid than the cook; their salaries would bear poor comparison with the wages of the butler; they would appear but shabbily with the remuneration of the lady's-maid; and they were even lower than those paid to liveried footmen. [*Cheers.*] The power of governesses was acknowledged by the middle-aged lady in a turban—she felt the power of the governess's knowledge in the education of her daughters; gentlemen also felt the power of the governess's knowledge; but nobody thought of the poor fagged knowledge herself, her eyes red with poring over advertisements in search of a new situation; and, after having faithfully accomplished her task in one family, being thrown upon the world, and going forth again among strangers to educate others.

When he first received the prospectus of this institution, and perceived that to a committee of ladies was entrusted the care of considering the cases of distressed governesses and of relieving them with a delicacy suitable to their refined feelings, he began to hope for the improvement of the condition of governesses who were not distressed, and to hope that their position in society would be elevated as it ought to be. He considered that those ladies and gentlemen who engaged in this good work virtually pledged them-selves, by their influence and example, to elevate the moral con-dition of governesses; and from that moment he conceived in that institution a heartfelt interest, and a hope of future benefit, that he felt for very few. He took that to be the great end of the institution, for it would otherwise do but little at the best. They might relieve the physical sufferings of governesses in distress—they might cheer them on the bed of sickness, and soften the asperities of their condi-tion in declining age; but, unless the society exerted its energies to render governesses more respected, it would fall far short of the great end which he conceived it had in view. From first to last he had a confidence that the society would do its duty; and he hoped by its means to see blotted out a national reproach, and that the profession of education would be placed on that honourable footing which in any civilized and Christian land, it ought to hold. [*Con-tinued cheering.*]

'The health of the Committees' was then drunk with loud cheers.

Benjamin Bond Cabell,[1] the treasurer, replied; other toasts followed; and it was announced with the second list of subscriptions that a total had been reached of more than £1,000.

Dickens would have been a fairly obvious choice as a speaker in any case, but just after the publication of chapter xxxvi of *Martin Chuzzlewit*, with the scene between Tom Pinch and his sister's employer, 'the brass-and-copper founder', his participation was particularly appropriate. Dickens's argument in fact, and Tom's in fiction, are closely allied; and it seems likely that fact and fiction were linked even more closely. Writing to her friend and former pupil, Lucy Sanford, in May 1844, Mary Carpenter gaily remarked that:

As Dickens's sister was your governess, there can be no doubt that she is Ruth, and thus it is evident that you are the young lady; the similarity between your Papa and the cannon-founder is of course striking. Mamma was quite shocked, and begged me not to tell you; but I thought you would not forgive me if I withheld from you such a compliment.[2]

The identification of Miss Sanford as 'the young lady', and her 'Papa' as 'the brass-and-copper founder', is obviously a joke; but apart from this, her remarks must have been made seriously, or Mrs. Carpenter would not have been so shocked. Dickens's younger sister, Letitia Mary, may well have been a governess for a short time.

He seems to have had no further connexion with the governesses after this, except to send a strong protest a few years later at the way the candidates were forced to apply for assistance. Each applicant had to be recommended by one of the subscribers. It was a practice adopted by many charitable societies, who found it a way of keeping up their supporters' interest. Dickens thought it humiliating, and complained that 'when anything of this kind attains a preposterous height, it is sure to stagger and fall; and I am convinced that a very few returns of the Governesses Institution contest must startle a great many supporters'.[3] However, the system was kept unchanged until 1938, and the society is still active and efficiently run.

ARTISTS' BENEVOLENT SOCIETY

11 *May* 1844

THE annual dinner of the society was held at the Freemasons' Tavern, with Lord Palmerston, then in opposition, in the Chair. The final toast of the evening, proposed by the chairman, was 'The Authors of England and Charles Dickens Esq.', which is said to have been given 'in a very

[1] Benjamin Bond Cabell (1781–1874), patron of art; M.P., 1846–57; F.R.S.; active institutional philanthropist and officer of various charitable societies including the Artists' Benevolent Society and the Royal Literary Fund.

[2] J. Estlin Carpenter, *Life and Work of Mary Carpenter*, 1879, p. 84. Miss Carpenter (1807–77) was a philanthropist and educationalist, resident of Birmingham, already interested in ragged schools, and later well known for her work on juvenile delinquency.

[3] 1 September 1847, MS., in the society's records.

complimentary manner'. Dickens returned thanks 'in an eloquent speech'.

There are no newspaper reports of what he said, but the Rev. W. H. Brookfield sent an amusing account of the dinner of the 'Artists' Malevolent' in a letter to his wife, in which he said that 'Dickens spoke shortly and well enough, but it had a very cut and dried air, and rather pompous and shapely in its construction and delivered in rather a sonorous deep voice. Not a jot of humour in it.'[1]

THE SANATORIUM

4 *June* 1844

THE anniversary festival was held at the London Tavern, with Dickens in the Chair. 'The Health of Her Majesty', and the other usual loyal toasts, were proposed in succession, and were received with all the honours. The chairman then rose to give the toast of the evening, and said:

LADIES and Gentlemen, I have now to propose to you a toast which may not only be assumed to have a real interest for us who are met here to advance the prospects of a young and struggling institution, but which I know concerns and deeply moves the welfare, comfort, mental ease, health, and life of a vast multitude of persons of both sexes, born and bred among the middle classes of society, who are dependent, under Providence, upon their own honourable exertions for subsistence in this great wilderness—London. The toast, ladies and gentlemen, is 'Prosperity to the Sanatorium'. [*Cheers.*]

I scarcely know whether it is necessary for me in this company to enter into any explanation of the objects and designs of this establishment, but its leading principle may be very easily and briefly stated. It is a home in sickness, founded and maintained upon the footing of a club, the expenses of which, by the voluntary contributions of many persons for a common welfare and advantage, are rendered so light that a weekly payment never exceeding two guineas, and in many instances not exceeding one guinea, secures to every inmate, gentleman or lady, a comfortable, genteel, and cheerful house; a quiet, well-ventilated, and wholesome chamber; the first medical advice that the skill and science of this city can supply; the diligent and careful nursing of persons trained and educated for the purpose; every possible comfort in illness, and every possible means towards recovery. This small weekly payment

---

[1] Charles and Frances Brookfield, *Mrs. Brookfield and Her Circle*, 1905, i. 137.

begins and ceases with the residence of the sick persons in the house, the qualification for a member being the annual subscription of only one guinea. If the patient have any relative or devoted friends anxious to minister to his or her afflictions, that friend can reside in the house on the same cheap and easy terms; and if the patient have a preference for any medical adviser not immediately connected with the institution, that gentleman can rely, as many have, and certify to it afterwards, on his instructions being honestly and faithfully carried out, and his treatment never being interfered with in the least degree; nay, the patient never even having heard of such a place as the Sanatorium, may have been induced to enter it—for this has happened also—by the advice of a medical professor most eminent and most honoured for his humanity and great attainments, who has said: 'You have to submit to a most terrible bodily trial, go into this place, in Heaven's name; for on nowhere else can I repose such perfect confidence in the treatment and attention you will receive and which will, therefore, lead to your ultimate recovery.'

Bear in mind, ladies and gentlemen, that all those benefits are extended to the recipients, not in charity, but as a just right which honest pride may claim without a blush. [*Cheers.*] Bear in mind that but for this Sick Home hundreds of persons, as sensitively and delicately nurtured as ourselves, would have had no choice between a public hospital and the uncertain supplies of strangers. Is it too much to claim, therefore, for an institution such as this the sympathy of every generous mind and feeling heart?

Let us suppose for a moment that there was no such place as the Sanatorium, as there was not two years ago, and that a lady who lives by imparting to others the accomplishments that she acquired in happier and more prosperous days, who is a governess in a family, is stricken down by illness. It is part of the lady's position that she should have no home to repair to in such a case, for her profession leads her, of necessity, to establish herself in the homes of others. It is, therefore, almost a part of that lady's position, very often to have no right to be ill; but, as that implied contract is an artificial one in which nature has no very great share, ill she is—and seriously. The lady in the family, Mrs. Wilkins we will say, takes an early opportunity of informing Mr. Wilkins of the circumstance, and Mr. Wilkins at first, does not very well know what to make of it, as it was not in the agreement; but he, after a little reflection, says that this sort of thing is very inconvenient to the family, as no doubt it is, and that he hopes it is not catching. [*Laughter.*] The family apothecary advises him, and says 'No, it is not catching; but it is a surgical disorder of long standing, not uncommon—not at all uncommon; but of a very serious nature, which will require time, the best medical advice, and a severe operation.'

Mr. Wilkins lives in a very good style; but his house is not larger than will comfortably accommodate his family, and he has to provide another governess for the instruction of his children. He is a tender-hearted man enough; but he cannot create out of a tender heart the room and attention which such a case requires. The poor lady is perfectly aware of that, resigns her situation, and takes a lodging. She is visited there by a surgeon, a most humane and liberal man, to whom this melancholy case is by no means strange, who entertains a great interest and compassion for her, and who more than confirms the statement of the apothecary. He feels for her desolate situation, and makes a few inquiries. Her family, of course, was broken up when she went out as a governess, or she never would have gone out. But has she no relative ? Yes, a brother, but he is a clerk in the City. She has a sister, but she went to Australia four years ago, with a husband and six children. The case must be proceeded with. Nobody dare venture to breathe in her anxious and excited ear of a hospital, and there is nothing for her but a lodging, which, for any provision that it has in its convenience for illness, might be a lodging for an immortal spirit wholly unencumbered by a body—where the good woman of the house is almost perpetually employed in the back parlour dotting down her accounts with pen and ink, adding them up and bringing them forward, and carrying them over. She is greatly assisted in the product of these items by an odious anomaly called a sick nurse, who has been hired to attend upon the poor lady, and who is a creature of that sort who never could continue to exist but for our deplorable propensity to take whatever does exist for granted, and to rest comfortably satisfied that, because it is very bad, it cannot be better.[1]

And so this poor lady struggles on, surrounded by every adverse circumstance at a time when everything should be propitious, and instead of kind feelings and fostering hope going hand in hand to speed her recovery, her home is gloomy, hopeless, and disconsolate. And even if her desolate situation should awaken, and Heaven forbid such circumstances should not awaken, the sympathies of those about her, leading them to be regardless of their own immediate profit in her great misery, even that is torture to an honourable mind; for in this miserable sacrifice of the poor, and the uncertainty

[1] Dickens's hearers would have appreciated that in his still current novel, *Martin Chuzzlewit*, Dickens had introduced Mrs. Gamp in a chapter which gave 'Valuable Hints in relationship to the Management of a Sick Chamber'. Mrs. Gamp's 'original' was a sick-nurse who had attended a companion of Miss Burdett Coutts in 1843.

of ever being able to repay the kindnesses, new causes of despondency and grief inevitably spring up. This is no idle picture, but one of every day's occurrence, and you may know of its existence. It is even stated here, in this little record which has been laid before you today, where a poor governess frightfully afflicted is cured, where the blind clerk recovers the inestimable blessing of sight, where the senseless is restored to health, where the gentleman and scholar, whose labours are connected with popular instruction through the press, does not disdain to seek refuge, where the dying man expatiates to his brother, day by day, upon the happiness and peace of such a place as this institution, begging him with his last breath to make it better known when he is in his grave. There is not one among us, I am confident, who can withstand this little simple history. There is not one among us, I know by myself, who can pass it wholly by—there is not one among us, having a brother or child, or any dear friend, who can dismiss the harrowing echoes of that faint voice from his mind.

This, ladies and gentlemen, is the Sanatorium we call upon you to assist. I am confident that the voice of which I have spoken will speak to you far more forcibly than I can ever hope to do of the high claims it has upon you. Its principle is self-support,—still, it appeals to you and the public for help; for to be self-supporting it must be thoroughly and well established, and there is no greater inconsistency in thus putting forth its pretentions and appealing to you for help, than there is in any young married couple who are to live upon their annual income wanting some assistance upon their first entering into the world. The directors of this Sanatorium, ladies and gentlemen, cannot offer you the luxury sometimes too freely offered, of the bestowing of charity in the common acceptance of the word, but they can offer you the gratification—and you will judge for yourselves whether there can be a higher or better one—of helping those who help themselves. [*Cheers.*] They offer you the gratification of enabling men and women of strong hearts to preserve an independent spirit and an upright mien, when that calamity, which is our common inheritance, stops the labour of their hands and heads. There can be no one here who does not owe a debt of sympathy for acts of kindness and affection in the hour of need, and I am persuaded that there is no one present to whom the prosperity of this institution, if it be rightly understood, can by possibility be a matter of indifference or slight regard. I beg, therefore, to propose to you to drink, 'Prosperity to the Sanatorium'.

The chairman resumed his seat amid loud applause. After giving 'The health of the Vice-Presidents of the Institution', he next proposed 'The Ladies', a toast of particular interest on this occasion, since, as the reporter remarked, it 'differed materially from the ordinary anniversary festivals, inasmuch as ladies graced the board, and added by their beauty to the harmony of the entertainment'.

When he had given that toast, he said, he should feel that the glory of his office was gone. He had often looked towards the gallery of that room and wondered why the ladies were consigned to that dismal, gloomy, and uncomfortable region, and considered whether there could be any good reason for sending them skyward. He had speculated again and again whether the custom was Chinese, Kamschatkan, Mahometan, or Ojibbeway, because he felt it was certainly not an English one, or, if it was, that it ought no longer to be so. He was lately conversing with a friend upon the subject, and he suggested as a reason for the custom a desire, on the part of the men, to etherealize the ladies, as they could not possibly suppose that they desired to eat and drink. It certainly was not that distance might increase the enchantment, as they were enchanting to us under any circumstances. He had consulted several ladies who sat around him on the subject, and they had told him we were mistaken in their views, and indeed it was high time the men set themselves right, or there was no knowing what tremendous consequences might ensue from the ladies' determined vows of celibacy.

They had, however, this evening set themselves right, and they might congratulate themselves upon the grace and lustre that were shed upon the meeting by the presence of 'our better angels', of our dearest companions and our constant and unchanging friends— those friends who were ever at our sides in the period of our success, the closest to us in triumph and defeat, and to whom, let us roam through the world as fiercely as we will, we must come back for comfort and help; and excellent as this establishment was with all its appliances and means to boot, it was nothing in comparison with the soothing kindness and affection of their gentle care.

The toast was enthusiastically acknowledged. Other speakers followed, including Clarkson Stanfield representing Art, W. H. Ainsworth Literature, and J. P. Harley the Theatre.

The following year Dickens was in Italy when plans were made for the next annual dinner, but he offered to attend if it could be delayed until early in July after his return. It was not held then, and the society gave up its house since the lease had expired. Attempts were made to rent another, or to raise the money to buy or build somewhere more suitable. Dickens organized a production of *Every Man in His Humour* by his amateur company at the St. James's Theatre on 15 November in its support; but in spite of the success of the play the sanatorium appears never to have been reopened.

GENERAL THEATRICAL FUND

6 *April* 1846

THE first anniversary festival of the General Theatrical Fund was held at the London Tavern, with Dickens in the Chair. As he explained, it had been founded seven years before, in imitation of the theatrical funds of Covent Garden and Drury Lane, which had been started in 1776. At that time, and for some while after, the Funds of the two great patent monopoly theatres had served for the whole dramatic profession. But while membership of their funds was still limited to actors who belonged to their regular companies, they no longer had a monopoly, the two theatres had been turned into opera-houses, they had no regular companies to belong to, and no one could possibly qualify to receive their help. The General Theatrical Fund, on the other hand, was open to all. Dickens had many theatrical friends, and soon after it was started he had been elected a Trustee, with Serjeant Talfourd[1] and Benjamin Bond Cabell.

On entering the room he was greeted with great applause, 'especially by a large number of ladies, who were congregated at both ends of the room'. There were the usual loyal and patriotic preliminaries: Captain Chappell replying on behalf of the Army and Navy,—a toast which the chairman introduced 'with a spirit-stirring reference to the recent victories on the banks of the Sutlej'—in the First Sikh War. In proposing the toast of the evening, he went on to say:

GENTLEMEN, in offering to you a toast which has not yet been publicly drunk in any company, it becomes incumbent on me to offer a few words in explanation,—in the first place premising that the toast will be, 'The General Theatrical Fund'. [*Cheers.*]

The association whose anniversary we celebrate tonight, was founded seven years ago, for the purpose of granting permanent pensions to such members of the *corps dramatique* as had retired from the stage, either from a decline in their years or a decay in their powers. [*Cheers.*] Collected within the scope of its benevolence are all actors and actresses, singers or dancers, of five years' standing in the profession. To relieve their necessities and to protect them from want is the great aim of the society; and it is good to know that for seven years the members of it have steadily, patiently, quietly, and perseveringly pursued this end, advancing by regular contribution moneys which many of them could ill afford, and cheered by no external help or assistance whatsoever. It has thus

---

[1] Thomas Noon Talfourd (1795–1854), made serjeant 1833; knighted and Justice of Common Pleas 1849; author of *Ion*, a tragedy, 1835, the *Letters* 1837, and *Memorials* 1848, of Charles Lamb; M.P. for Reading 1835–41 and 1847–9; had introduced the Copyright Bill of 1842. He was a close friend of Dickens, who dedicated *Pickwick* to him Sept. 1837.

served a regular apprenticeship; but I trust that we shall establish
tonight that its time is out, and that henceforth the Fund will enter
upon a flourishing and brilliant career.

I have no doubt that you are all aware that there are, and were
when this institution was founded, two other institutions existing,
of a similar nature—Covent Garden and Drury Lane—both of long
standing, both richly endowed. It cannot, however, be too distinctly
understood that the present institution is not in any way adverse
to those. How can it be, when it is only a wide and broad extension
of all that is most excellent in the principles on which they are
founded? That such an extension was absolutely necessary was
sufficiently proved by the fact that the great body of the dramatic
corps were excluded from the benefits conferred by a membership
of either of these institutions; for it was essential in order to
become a member of the Drury Lane society that the applicant,
either he or she, should have been engaged for three consecutive
seasons as a performer. This was afterwards reduced, in the case
of Covent Garden, to a period of two years; but it really is as exclusive one way as another, for I need not tell you that Covent
Garden is now but a vision of the past. [*Laughter.*] You might
play the bottle-conjuror with its dramatic company, and put them
all into a pint bottle.[1] [*Laughter.*] The human voice is rarely heard
within its walls save in connexion with Corn,[2] or the ambidextrous
prestidigitation of the Wizard of the North.[3] The only run there, is
the run of rats and mice. In like manner Drury Lane is so devoted
to foreign ballets and foreign operas that it is more deserving of the
name of the *Opéra Comique*, than of a national theatre; while the
statue of Shakespeare is well placed over its portal, since it serves
as emphatically to point out his grave as does his bust at Stratford-
upon-Avon. How can the profession generally hope to qualify for
the Drury Lane or Covent Garden institutions, when the oldest and
most distinguished members have been driven from the boards on
which they earned their reputations, to delight the town in theatres
to which the General Theatrical Fund alone extends?

I will again repeat that I attach no reproach to those other Funds,
with which I have had the honour of being connected at different
periods of my life.[4] At the time those associations were established,

---

[1] 'The Bottle Conjuror' had been billed to perform absurd impossibilities at
the Haymarket in 1749: a famous hoax by the Duke of Montagu which
resulted in a riot.

[2] Regular meetings of the Anti-Corn Law League were held at the theatre,
and in 1845, for the benefit of the League, even a Bazaar.

[3] John Henry Anderson (1815–74), conjuror and actor; also remembered as
the sub-lessee of Covent Garden when it was burnt down in 1856.

[4] Dickens had attended the anniversary festival of the Drury Lane Fund in

an engagement at one of those theatres was almost a matter of course, and a successful engagement would last a whole life; but an engagement of two months' duration at Covent Garden would be a perfect Old Parr of an engagement just now. It should never be forgotten that when those two funds were established the two great theatres were protected by patent, and that at that time the minor theatres were condemned by law to the representation of the most preposterous nonsense, and some gentlemen whom I see around me could have no more belonged to the minor theatres of that day than they could now belong to St. Bartholomew's Fair.

As I honour the two old Funds for the great good which they have done, so I honour this for the much greater good it is resolved to do. It is not because I love them less, but because I love this more—because it includes more in its operation.

Let us ever remember that there is no class of actors who stand so much in need of a retiring fund as those who do not win the great prizes, but who are nevertheless an essential part of the theatrical system, and by consequence bear a part in contributing to our pleasure. [*Cheers.*] We owe them a debt which we ought to pay. The beds of such men are not of roses, but of very artificial flowers indeed. Their lives are full of care and privation, and hard struggles with very stern realities. [*Hear, hear.*] It is from among the poor actors who drink wine from goblets, in colour marvellously like toast and water, and who preside at Barmecide feasts with wonderful appetites for steaks,—it is from their ranks that the most triumphant favourites have sprung. [*Cheers.*] And surely, besides this, the greater the instruction and delight we derive from the rich English drama, the more we are bound to succour and protect the humblest of those votaries of the art, who add to our instruction and amusement. [*Cheers.*]

Hazlitt has well said that 'There is no class of society whom so many people regard with affection as actors. We greet them on the stage, we like to meet them in the streets; they almost always recall to us pleasant associations.'[1] When they have strutted and fretted their hour upon the stage, let them not be heard no more,—but let them be heard sometimes to say that they are happy in their old age. When they have passed for the last time behind that glittering row of lights with which we are all familiar, let them not pass away into the gloom and darkness; but let them pass into cheerfulness and light, into a contented and happy home.

Feb. 1839. His friend John Pritt Harley, the comedian, was secretary. No doubt Dickens also attended, and possibly spoke, at other anniversary festivals of both the C.G. and D.L. funds, about 1837–9.

[1] 'On Actors and Acting', *The Round Table*, 1817, ii. 242.

This is the object for which we have met; and I am too familiar
with the English character not to know that it will be effected.
When we come suddenly in a crowded street upon the careworn
features of a familiar face, crossing us like the ghost of pleasant
hours forgotten, let us not recall those features in pain, in sad
remembrance of what they once were; but let us in joy recognize,
and go back a pace or two to meet it once again, as that of a friend
who has beguiled us of a moment of care, who has taught us to
sympathize with virtuous grief cheating us to tears for sorrows not
our own—and we all know how pleasant are such tears. Let such a
face be ever remembered as that of our benefactor and our friend.

I tried to recollect, in coming here, whether I had ever been in
any theatre in my life from which I had not brought away some
pleasant association, however poor the theatre; and I protest, out
of my varied experience, I could not remember even one from
which I had not brought some favourable impression—and that,
commencing with the period when I believed that the Clown was a
being born into the world with infinite pockets, and ending with
that in which I saw the other night, outside one of the 'Royal
Saloons', a playbill which showed me ships completely rigged,
carrying men and careering over boundless and tempestuous oceans.
And now, bespeaking your kindest remembrance of our theatres
and actors, I beg to propose that you drink as heartily and freely
as ever a toast was drunk in this toast-drinking city, 'Prosperity to
the General Theatrical Fund'.

Dickens sat down amidst loud applause. In reply to a toast to his
health, he said that, like Dogberry, if he were as tedious as a king he
could find in his heart to bestow it all upon their lordships; and briefly
thanked the company for the kind manner in which they had received
the toast.

The secretary having read the report, Dickens said that when the
Comic Muse found herself in reduced circumstances, she had taken
lodgings in the Haymarket, and placed herself under the protection of a
gentleman with whom she had previously resided without exciting a
breath of scandal. He concluded a humorous speech by proposing 'The
Health of Mr. Benjamin Webster'.[1] In Webster's absence, Douglas
Jerrold returned thanks, complimenting him on the great enterprise and
energy that he had displayed as a manager.

Dickens then proposed the health of J. B. Buckstone,[2] the treasurer of
the fund, the solvency of which had, he was happy to say, not been at all

[1] Benjamin Nottingham Webster (1797–1882), actor and dramatist;
manager of Adelphi and New Adelphi 1844–72, and of the Haymarket 1837–
53. Energetic supporter of dramatic charities; President of Dramatic College
1862–77; personal friend of Dickens.

[2] John Baldwin Buckstone (1802–79), comic actor and dramatist; manager
of Haymarket, 1853–76, where his ghost is said to walk.

impaired by the treasurer having been seen of late, in a place of great public resort, soliciting the loan of five shillings. This allusion to Buckstone's part in *Lend Me Five Shillings* raised 'bursts of laughter'. Buckstone replied, and a number of other toasts followed, before the proceedings finally came to an end 'at a convivial hour'.

GENERAL THEATRICAL FUND

29 *March* 1847

THE anniversary was held at the London Tavern, with W. C. Macready in the Chair. For several days past it had been feared that ill health would prevent him from presiding; but, as the *Morning Post* reported, 'despite considerable weakness, and we think much danger, he screwed his courage to the sticking place, and made the path of danger the road to honour'. He was greeted with great enthusiasm.

There was the usual programme of toasts. When it came to the main speech of the evening, Macready noted in his diary, it 'was heard with the deepest attention and interest, and with much applause'.[1] He vigorously stated the case for the General Theatrical Fund, as opposed to the exclusive benevolent funds of Drury Lane and Covent Garden. The last time a member had been enrolled in the latter had been in 1843, 'and from the present appropriation of the theatre and the laws of the Fund', no other could join it until 1855. 'In touching on the various disasters of the two great national theatres', it was reported, he was 'evidently moved by the hopeless state of our drama. His voice faltered and his frame shook.'[2]

Buckstone, the treasurer, followed, as 'the farce', so he said, 'after the tragedy'. Then Dickens rose to propose the health of the chairman, and said:

GENTLEMEN, it is well for me, and better for you, that the admirable exposition we have heard from my friend on my left of the claims and merits of the General Theatrical Fund, and its immense superiority in its freedom from exclusive restrictions to any other institution having any similar but narrower object, leaves nothing to be added on that head: though the case is so clear and so strong, and has always in its common sense and justice interested me so earnestly, that I could hold forth on this theme 'until my eyelids could no longer wag', and am happy to be relieved of the danger of producing any influence on *your* eyelids by dealing with it at all. As it has been written of Vice, that she is

A monster of such hideous mien,
As to be hated needs but to be seen.[3]

---

[1] *Diaries*, ed. Toynbee, ii. 361. [2] *Morning Post*, 30 Mar
[3] Pope, *Essay on Man*, ii.

so, I am sure, it might be written of the General Theatrical Fund, that its objects are:

> so worthy and so much its own
> As to be favoured, need but to be known.

And better known they never can be, than from the lips which have proclaimed them to the room this night.

There is, however, gentlemen, one point that seems to me to arise naturally out of the observations of our distinguished President, and at which I cannot help just glancing as I go along. Hope lingered at the bottom of a box in ancient days, as we are told: I cannot help fancying that I descry her lingering yet, at the bottom of those two strong-boxes of the Covent Garden and Drury Lane Theatrical Funds, to offer solid consolation to the General Theatrical Fund in time to come. For as the natural recipients of that treasure pass away in natural course, and no one among them bears in his hand 'a glass that shows me many more'—or any more—I cannot help fancying that some portion of the garnered wealth must come our way at last, and float into our roomy coffers. Gentlemen, I hardly think it possible that two such large golden camels can entirely pass through the eyes of two such little needles; and when an institution has arisen, so broad and free as this is, which extends its advantages, not to the pale shades of two dead and buried companies of actors, but to the whole theatrical profession through-out England, I hold it would be a faint-hearted blinking of the question not to avow what most of us here must surely feel—a confident belief that to such resources it may justly, and of right, look for valuable endowment in the days to come. It is ill 'waiting for dead men's shoes', I know; but it is quite another matter waiting for shoes that have been made for people who can never be born to try them on.

I come now, gentlemen, to propose to you a toast which is uppermost, I dare say, in the thoughts of everybody present, which is 'the very head and front' of the occasion, and the cause which brings us together; which is, and ever must be, inseparably asso-ciated with the honour, dignity, and glory of the English stage; with its revival in splendour and magnificence from ruin and rubbish, with its claims to be respected as an art and as a noble means of general instruction and improvement. To whom could such a toast apply, if not to our chairman, Mr. Macready ? Of whom, gentlemen— so graceful and appropriate is the position he now occupies among us—I would say, if I may paraphrase what he knows well, that nothing in the Chair became him like the taking of it. It is as generous and true in him—at the head of his profession, and at the zenith of a proud and prosperous career, to take part with this Fund, and to be heard in this place urging its claims with a manly earnestness, because it is not restrictive, and because it does not favour a few, and because it addresses itself to the great body of actors, and most of all to those who most need it,—as it must be of enduring service to the institution to receive such high and valuable testimony.

Gentlemen, it would be difficult for me to find terms in which to discharge the duty of proposing our chairman's health, in the difficulty I always feel as to the separation of his name from sentiments of strong personal affection and attachment, if I were not happily relieved by the knowledge that, in your breasts as well as mine, the mere mention of Mr. Macready's name awakens a host of eloquent associations,—Hamlet, Macbeth, Othello, grey-haired Lear, Virginius, Werner, and a host of others, speak for him within us, like spirits. We once again forget the encircling walls of his Covent Garden Theatre, or of Drury Lane—theatres then with nothing infamous to mock the lesson that the poet taught or shame the woman-student of it—and look upon old Rome, its senate and its army, or the Forest of Arden with its gnarled and melancholy boughs, or Swinstead Abbey Gardens with the cruel king upon his death-bed, or Prospero's enchanted island, or any of those scenes of airy nothings that he made plain and palpable. Oh! if one touch of nature makes the whole world kin, think, gentlemen, for how much of the kindred feeling that is amongst us tonight, or at any time, we are indebted to such an art, and such a man! May we be more and more indebted to him, year by year, for very many years to come! May we yet behold the English drama—this a hope to which I always cling—in some theatre of his own, rising proudly from its ashes, into new and vigorous existence. And may we, in the reception we now give his name, express all this, and twenty times as much; including the past, the present, and the future; and give him reason years hence to remember this occasion, with something of the pleasure and delight that we have through him derived from it ourselves! I beg to propose to you to drink the health of our chairman, Mr. Macready.

The toast was drunk with great enthusiasm, and all due honours. Among the remaining toasts were one to the trustees proposed by John Forster, and the 'Stewards', and the 'Ladies', proposed by the chairman. Macready left immediately after the last: 'Delighted to escape, and attended with the grateful homage of the committee and much applauded by the guests as I passed through them.'[1] Buckstone was requested to take his place in the Chair; and 'the evening was finished to the satisfaction of all parties'.[2]

[1] *Diaries*, ed. Toynbee, ii. 361.   [2] Official *Proceedings*.

SOIRÉE OF THE MECHANICS' INSTITUTION: LEEDS

1 *December* 1847

THE *soirée* was held in the Music Hall, Albion Street. It had been gaily decorated with festoons, wreaths and garlands of evergreens, and natural and artificial flowers; while above the platform was stretched a banner, upon which was inscribed in silver letters, 'The Sovereignty of Man lies Hid in Knowledge'.

Among the guests were George Stephenson,[1] Edward Baines father[2] and son,[3] James Crossley the President of the Manchester Athenaeum, and many local celebrities. Several of these were loudly cheered as they ascended the platform, but when Dickens himself appeared the whole audience rose, and the applause became almost deafening; and when, after a lapse of several minutes, partial silence had been obtained, another loud and hearty burst followed upon the call of a gentleman in the saloon, for 'one cheer more for the author of Little Nell'.[4]

As soon as Dickens had been introduced to the mayor and other gentlemen upon the platform, the president of the institution stepped forward and said, 'Ladies and Gentlemen, Mr. Dickens will now do us the honour of taking the Chair this evening'. When the tumultuous applause that greeted him had ceased, Dickens rose and said:

LADIES and Gentlemen, Believe me, speaking to you with a most disastrous cold, which makes my own voice sound very strangely in my ears, that if I were not gratified and honoured beyond expression by your cordial welcome, I should have considered the invitation to occupy my present position in this brilliant assemblage in itself a distinction not easy to be surpassed. The cause in which we are assembled and the objects we are met to promote, I take, and always have taken to be, *the* cause and *the* objects involving almost all others that are essential to the welfare and happiness of mankind. [*Applause.*] And in a celebration like the present, com-

---

[1] George Stephenson (1781–1848), inventor, and founder of railways; designer of the 'Rocket'.

[2] Edward Baines (1774–1848), journalist; proprietor of *Leeds Mercury*; M.P. for Leeds 1834–41.

[3] Edward Baines (1800–90), journalist and economist; editor of *Leeds Mercury*; M.P. for Leeds 1859–70; knighted 1880; active nonconformist Liberal, strong supporter of purely voluntaryist movement in education; principal founder of the institution, and President of the West Riding Union of Mechanics' Institutes.

[4] The incident was mentioned by Dickens in a letter to D. M. Moir of 17 June 1848, saying that he heard afterwards that the gentleman had lately lost a daughter of his own. He added—probably incorrectly—that it occurred *after* his speech.

memorating the birth and progress of a great educational establishment, I recognize a something, not limited to the spectacle of the
moment, beautiful and radiant though it be—not limited even to
the success of the particular establishment in which we are more
immediately interested—but extending from this place and through
swarms of toiling men elsewhere, cheering and stimulating them in
the onward, upward path that lies before us all. [*Hear, hear, and
loud applause.*] Wherever hammers beat, or wherever factory chim-
neys smoke; wherever hands are busy, or the clanking of machinery resounds; wherever, in a word, there are masses of industrious
beings whom their wise Creator did not see fit to constitute all
body, but into each and every one of whom He breathed a mind,
—there, I would fain believe, some touch of sympathy and encouragement is felt from our collective pulse now beating in this
Hall. [*Loud cheers.*]

Ladies and gentlemen, glancing with such feelings at the report of
your institution for the present year, sent to me by your respected
President—whom I cannot help feeling it, by-the-by, a kind of
crime to depose, even thus peacefully, and for so short a time
[*laughter*]—I say, glancing over this report, I found one statement
of fact in the very opening which gave me uncommon satisfaction.
It is, that a great number of the members and subscribers are
among that class of persons for whose advantage Mechanics' Institutions were originated, namely, persons receiving weekly wages.
[*Hear, hear.*] This circumstance gives me the greatest delight. I
am sure that no better testimony could be borne to the merits
and usefulness of this institution, and that no better guarantee
could be given for its continued prosperity and advancement. [*Loud
applause.*]

To such associations as this, in their darker hours, there may yet
reappear now and then the spectral shadow of a certain dead and
buried opposition; but before the light of a steady trust in them on
the part of the general people, bearing testimony to the virtuous
influences of such institutions by their own intelligence and conduct, the ghost will melt away like early vapour from the ground.
[*Loud applause.*] Fear of institutions such as these! We have heard
people sometimes speak with jealousy of them. With distrust of
them! Imagine here, on either hand, two great towns like Leeds,
full of busy men, all of them feeling necessarily, and some of them
heavily, the burdens and inequalities inseparable from civilized
society. In this town there is ignorance, dense and dark. In that
town, education—the best of education: that which the grown man
from day to day and year to year furnishes for himself and main-
tains for himself, and in right of which his education goes on all his

life, instead of leaving off, complacently, just when he begins to live in the social system.

Now, which of these two towns has a good man, or a good cause, reason to distrust and dread?—'The educated one', does some timid politician with a marvellously weak sight say—as I have heard such politicians say—'because knowledge is power, and because it won't do to have too much power abroad'. Why, ladies and gentlemen, reflect whether ignorance be not power, and a very dreadful power. [*Hear, hear, hear.*] Look where we will, do we not find it powerful for every kind of wrong and evil? Powerful to take its enemies to its heart, and strike its best friends down; powerful to fill the prisons, the hospitals, and the graves; powerful for blind violence, prejudice, and error, in all their gloomy and destructive shapes. [*Cheers.*] Whereas the power of knowledge, if I understand it, is to bear and forbear; to learn the path of duty and to tread it; to engender that self-respect which does not stop at self, but cherishes the best respect for the best objects; to turn an always enlarging acquaintance with the joys and sorrows, capabilities and imperfections of our race to daily account in mildness of life and gentleness of construction,[1] and humble efforts for the improvement, stone by stone, of the whole social fabric. [*Loud cheers.*]

I have never heard but one tangible position taken against educational establishments for the people, and that was, that in this or that instance, or in these or those instances, education for the people has failed. And I have never traced even this to its source but I have found that the term education, so employed, meant anything but education—implied the mere imperfect application of old, ignorant, preposterous spelling-book lessons to the meanest purposes: as if you should teach a child that there is no higher end in electricity, for example, than expressly to strike a mutton-pie out of the hand of a greedy boy [*laughter*]—and on which it is as unreasonable to found an objection to education in a comprehensive sense, as it would be to object altogether to the combing of youthful hair, because in a certain charity school they had a practice of combing it into the pupil's eyes. [*Loud cheers and laughter.*]

Now, ladies and gentlemen, I turn to the report of this institution, on whose behalf we are met; and I start with the education given there, and I find that it really is an education that is deserving of the name. [*Hear, hear, and applause.*] I find that there are papers read and lectures delivered, on a variety of subjects of interest and importance. I find that there are evening classes

1 *construction*: 'conversation'?

formed for the acquisition of sound, useful English information,
and for the study of those two important languages, daily becoming
more important in the business of life, the French and German. I
find that there is a class for drawing, a chemical class, subdivided
into the elementary branch and the manufacturing branch—most
important here. I find that there is a day school, at twelve shillings
a quarter, which small cost, besides including instruction in all that
is useful to the merchant and the man of business, admits to all the
advantages of the parent institution. I find that there is a school
of design established, in connexion with the Government School;
and that there was in January this year, a Library of between six
and seven thousand volumes of books. [*Applause.*] Ladies and
gentlemen, if any man would tell me that anything but good could
come of such knowledge as this, all I can say is, that I should
consider him a new and most lamentable proof of the necessity of
such institutions [*laughter*], and should regard him in his own person
as a melancholy instance of what a man may come to by never
having belonged to one or sympathized with one. [*Loud and long-
continued applause.*]

There is one other paragraph in this report which struck my eye
in looking over it, and on which I cannot help offering a word of
joyful notice. It is the steady increase which appears to have taken
place in the number of lady members [*applause*], among whom I
hope I may presume are included some of the bright fair faces that
are clustered around me. [*Applause.*] Gentlemen, I hold it is not
good for man to be alone [*applause and laughter*], even in Mechanics'
Institutions [*renewed applause*], and I rank it as very far from
amongst the last or least of the merits of such places, that he need
not be alone there, and that he is not. [*Applause.*] I believe that the
sympathy and society of those who are our best and dearest friends
in infancy, in childhood, in manhood, and in old age, the most
devoted and least selfish natures that we know on earth, who turn
to us always constant and unchanged, when others turn away,
should greet us here, if anywhere, and go on with us side by side.
[*Loud applause.*]

I know, gentlemen, by the evidence of my own proper senses at
this moment, that there are charms and graces in such greetings,
such as no other greetings can possess. I know that in every beautiful work of the Almighty hand, which is illustrated in your lectures,
and in every real or ideal portraiture of fortitude and goodness that
you find in your books, there is something that must bring you
home again to them for its brightest and best example. And therefore, gentlemen, I hope you will never be without them, or without an increasing number of them in your studies and your

commemorations; and that an immense number of new marriages [*laughter*], and other domestic festivals naturally consequent upon those marriages [*renewed laughter and applause*] may be traced back from time to time to the Leeds Mechanics' Institution. [*Loud applause and laughter.*]

Ladies and gentlemen, there are many gentlemen around me, distinguished by their public position and services, or endeared to you by frequent intercourse, or by their zealous efforts on behalf of the cause which brings us together; and to them I shall beg leave to refer you for further observations on this happy and interesting occasion; begging to congratulate you finally upon the occasion itself; upon the prosperity and thriving prospects of your institution; and upon our common and general good fortune in living in these times, when the means of mental culture and improvement are presented cheaply, socially, and cheerfully, and not in dismal cells or lonely garrets. [*Hear, hear.*] And lastly, I congratulate myself, I assure you, most heartily upon the part with which I am honoured on an occasion so congenial to my warmest feelings and sympathies, and I beg to thank you for such evidences of your good-will, as I never can coldly remember and never forget. [*Reiterated cheering.*]

Many other speakers followed, proposing and supporting various sentiments in favour of popular education. Finally the mayor replied to a proposal of thanks addressed to the guests, remarking good-humouredly that he was the least of them, as shown by the placard announcing the meeting; for the names of Charles Dickens and George Stephenson had been placed in giant characters at the head of it, while going down the bill, with the letters growing smaller and smaller, his name appeared in minute characters at the very end, as 'Francis Carbutt, Mayor of Leeds'. On Dickens vacating the Chair, the mayor took his place; and a vote of thanks to the late chairman was proposed, seconded, and carried with acclamation. Dickens replied:

Ladies and Gentlemen, it is a great satisfaction to me that this question has been put by the Mayor, inasmuch as I hope I may receive it as a token that he has forgiven me those extremely large letters [*laughter*], which I must say, from the glimpse I caught of them when I arrived in town, looked very like a leaf from the first primer of a very promising young giant. [*Loud laughter and applause.*]

I will only observe, in reference to the proceedings of this evening, that after what I have seen, and the many excellent speeches I have heard from gentlemen of so many different callings and persuasions, meeting here as on neutral ground, I do more strongly and sincerely believe than I ever have in my life—and that is saying a great deal—that institutions such as this will be the means of refining and improving that social edifice which has been so often mentioned tonight, until—unlike that Babel tower which would have taken heaven by storm—it shall end in sweet accord and harmony amongst all classes of its builders. [*Loud applause.*]

Ladies and gentlemen, most respectfully and heartily I bid you good night and good-bye, and I trust the next time we meet it will be in even greater numbers, and in a larger room, and that we shall often meet again, to recall this evening, then of the past, and remember it as one of a series of increasing triumphs of your excellent institution. [*Loud and prolonged applause.*]

Dickens was delighted, and wrote to Forster, 'A most brilliant demonstration last night, and I think I never did better'.[1]

FIRST ANNUAL *SOIRÉE* OF THE ATHENAEUM: GLASGOW

28 *December* 1847

GLASGOW was not far behind Manchester, Birmingham, and Leeds. Its Athenaeum had been founded earlier in 1847, taking the place of an Educational Association which had succumbed to the disadvantage of holding its classes at six o'clock in the morning. The inaugural *soirée*, at which Dickens had consented to preside, was held in the new City Hall; a temporary cross-gallery was especially erected for the occasion; and in less than half an hour after the doors had been opened it was completely filled with a company of 4,000, all seated at tea-tables.

The hall had been decorated with banners, drapery, and evergreens. The platform for the chairman and distinguished visitors was surmounted by a crimson canopy, while behind them was displayed an enormous allegorical tableau. The galleries were fringed with drapery of crimson and white, 'presenting gorgeous slips on which were inscribed . . . "The Glasgow Athenaeum"—"The Sovereignty of Man lies hid in Knowledge"—"Literature, Science, and Art". . . . Altogether the hall was adorned with a style of grace and lightsome beauty which was the admiration of all.'[2]

As Dickens entered the hall, he was received with the most enthusiastic applause, 'handkerchiefs were waved by hundreds of fair hands, the bagpipes playing "Welcome Royal Charlie"'. The cheering lasted several minutes. The proceedings were opened by the secretary. He was

---

[1] F, VI. i, n., incorrectly dated 4 Dec.
[2] *Glasgow Chronicle*.

succeeded by the chairman, who waited for the applause to subside and then said:

LADIES and Gentlemen, Let me begin by endeavouring to convey to you the assurance that not even the warmth of your reception can exceed in simple earnestness and cordiality the feelings with which I come among you. [*Applause.*] This beautiful scene and your generous greeting would naturally awaken within me no common feelings, but when I connect them with the high purpose of this brilliant assembly; when I regard it as an educational example and encouragement to all Scotland; when I regard it no less as a recognition on the part of everybody here to the right indisputable and inalienable of all those who are actively engaged in the work and business of life to elevate and improve themselves so far as in them lies by all good means, I feel as if I stood here to swear brotherhood to all the young men in Glasgow, and to all the young women too [*laughter and immense applause*],—being unfortunately in no position to take upon myself any tenderer vows in that respect. [*Renewed laughter and applause.*] I feel, I say, as though we were pledged from this time forth to make common cause together in one of the most worthy and laudable of all human objects. [*Cheers.*]

Ladies and gentlemen, common cause must be made in such a design as brings us together tonight: without it nothing can be done, but with it everything. It is a common cause of right, God knows, for it is idle to suppose that the advantages of such an institution as the Glasgow Athenaeum stop within its walls or are confined to its own members. Through all the society of this great and important city, upwards to the highest and downwards to the lowest, its influence I know must be felt for good [*loud cheers*]: downwards in a clearer perception of, and sympathy with, those social miseries that can be alleviated, and those wide open doors of vice and crime that can be shut and barred; and upward in the greater intelligence, increased efficiency, and higher character of all who partake of its benefits themselves, or who communicate, as all must do, in a greater or less degree, some portion of them to the circle of relatives and friends in which they move.

Nor, ladies and gentlemen, would I say of any man, however high his social position, or however great his attainments, that he might not find something to be learnt even by immediate contact with such an institution. [*Cheers.*] If he only saw the goddess Knowledge coming out of her secluded palaces and high places to mingle with the throng, and to give them shining glimpses of the splendour of the treasures she once kept closely hoarded up, he might learn something. If he only saw the energy and courage with which those who earn their daily bread by the labour of their hands or heads, come night after night, as to a recreation, to that which was perhaps the sole absorbing business of his youth, there might still be something very wholesome for him to learn. But, when he could see in such places, as anybody who chooses can see, their genial and reviving influences, their substitution of the contemplation of the beauties of nature and art and the wisdom of great men, for mere sensual enjoyment, then he might know and learn this—that it is at once the duty and interest of all good members of society to encourage and protect these institutions. [*Applause.*]

Ladies and gentlemen, I take occasion to say now, as I did at an Athenaeum meeting in Yorkshire a few weeks since—and I think it a point always to be borne in mind on occasions such as these— that when such associations are objected to or decried on the ground that, in the views of the objectors, education among the people has not succeeded, the term *education* is used with not the least reference to its real meaning, and is wholly misunderstood. Mere reading and writing are not education. [*Cheers.*] It would be quite as reasonable to call bricks and mortar, architecture; oils and colours, art; reeds and cat-gut, music; or a child's spelling-book the works of Shakespeare, Milton or Bacon, as to call the lowest rudiments of education, 'education', and to visit upon that much abused and slandered word their failure in any instance. To my thinking it is precisely because they are not education: because, generally speaking, the word has been misunderstood in that sense a great deal too long; because education for the business of life, and for the due cultivation of the domestic virtues, is at least as important from day to day to the grown person as to the child; because real education amidst the strife and contention for a livelihood, and the consequent necessity incumbent on a great number of young persons to go into the world when they are very young and having had no adequate opportunity for mental culture, is extremely difficult,— it is because of these things that I look upon Mechanics' Institutions and Athenaeums as vitally important to the well-being of society; and it is because the rudiments of education may there be turned to good account in the acquisition of sound principles, and in the practice of the great virtues of Faith, Hope, and Charity, to which all our knowledge tends: it is because of that, I take it, that we are met here in Education's name tonight. [*Cheers.*]

It is a very great satisfaction to me to occupy the place with which I am honoured in this meeting on behalf of an infant Institution,—a remarkably fine child no doubt [*laughter*], of thriving aspect, of vigorous constitution, but an infant still. [*A laugh.*] I esteem myself singularly fortunate in knowing it before its prime, in the hope that I may have the pleasure of remembering in its prime, and when it has attained to its lusty maturity, that I was a friend of its youth. [*Applause.*] It has already passed through some of the disorders to which childhood is liable. Succeeding to its elder brother, of a very meritorious character but of rather a weak constitution, who expired when only about twelve months old [*laughter*] from, it is said, the exhausting effects of getting up too early in the morning, it has fought manfully through a sea of troubles. Its friends have often been much concerned for it; its pulse has been so exceedingly low that it was only beating 1250, when it should have been 10,000. Several relations and friends have even gone so far as to walk off once or twice in the melancholy belief that it was dead. But notwithstanding all this, assisted by the indomitable energy of one or two kind nurses, to whom it can never be sufficiently grateful, it has come through triumphantly; and now, of all the youthful members of its family I ever saw, it has the strongest attitude, the healthiest look, the brightest and most cheerful air. [*Cheers.*]

I find it with lectures in prospect and in progress, in a great variety of sound, useful, and well-selected subjects; I find that already evening classes are in operation for the modern languages, French, German, Spanish, and Italian, as well as for Logic, Grammar, Music and Mathematics, and that these are now attended by upwards of five hundred persons. But best and foremost of all in the history of the institution, and far more satisfactory to me than anything else, I find that all this has been mainly achieved by the young men of Glasgow themselves, with very little assistance. [*Loud applause.*] And, ladies and gentlemen, as the axiom that Heaven helps those who help themselves is truer in no case than in this, I look to the young men of Glasgow, from such a past and such a present, to a noble future. [*Cheers.*] Everything that has been done in any other Athenaeum hitherto, I confidently expect to see done here; and when that shall be the case, and when there are great cheap schools connected with it, and when it has bound together for ever all its friends, and won over to itself all those who look distrustfully upon it now—then, but not till then, may the young men of Glasgow rest from their labours, and think their duty done. [*Renewed cheering.*]

If the young men of Glasgow look for any stimulus or encouragement in this wise, they have one already beside them in the presence of their fair townswomen: an incentive which is irresistible. [*Immense applause.*] It is a most delightful circumstance to me, and one fraught with inestimable benefits to institutions of this kind, that at a meeting of this nature those who in all things are our strongest aid, our best examples, our encouragers and friends, are not excluded. In ancient times abstract ideas of excellence were associated with those arts which refined and elevated mankind, and it was even conceived that the Graces themselves came down to encourage their cultivation by their example, and adorn them by their presence. But, now, we have the Graces with us themselves [*laughter*] for, I am happy to say, that in Glasgow there is a peculiar bond of union between its Athenaeum and the fairest part of creation. The present Library being a small one, and the necessary additions being difficult and expensive to make, I understand that the ladies generally have resolved to hold a fancy bazaar for the sale of the work of their own hands, and to devote the proceeds to the admirable purpose of its extension. And I learn, with no less pleasure, that Her Majesty the Queen, approving of this most excellent design, with a graceful and womanly feeling, has consented that the bazaar shall be held under her royal patronage. [*Great applause.*] After this I can only say, gentlemen, that if you do not find something very agreeable in your books, you are much duller scholars than I take you to be. [*Laughter.*] And you, ladies—the single ladies at least—however disinterested I know you are by sex and nature, will I hope reap advantages from your exertions to promote its interests, by never marrying any but members of the Athenaeum. [*Laughter.*] It seems to me that it ought to be the pleasantest library in the world. [*Cheering and laughter.*]

Hazlitt, in speaking of some of the graceful fancies of the writers of fiction, says:

> How long since I first became acquainted with these characters; what old fashioned friends they seem; and yet I am not tired of them, like so many other friends, nor they of me.

In this case the books will not only possess all the attractions of their own friendships and charms, but also the manifold—I had almost said the womanfold—associations connected with their donors. I can imagine now, in fact, from these fanciful associations, some fair Glasgow widow may be taken for the remoter one whom Sir Roger de Coverley could not forget [*laughter*]; I can imagine how Sophia's muff may be seen and loved, but not by Tom Jones, going down the High Street on any winter day; or I can imagine the student finding in every fair form the exact counterpart in the Glasgow Athenaeum; and I can imagine the *History of Europe* exciting the utmost interest without either the knowledge or consent of my friend Sheriff Alison.[1] [*Much laughter in which the learned Sheriff joined.*] I can imagine, in short, how through all the facts and fictions of this library, the ladies will always be active, and and that

> Age will not wither them, nor custom stale
> Their infinite variety.　　　　　　　　[*Applause.*]

I am surrounded by gentlemen to whom I shall soon give place, being at least as curious to hear them as you yourselves undoubtedly are; but before I sit down allow me to observe that it seems to me a most delightful and happy chance that this meeting should be held at this genial season of the year, when a new time is, as it were, opening up before us, and when we celebrate the birth of that divine and blessed Teacher, who took himself the highest knowledge into the humblest places, and whose great system comprehended all mankind. I hail it as a most auspicious omen, at this time of the year, when many scattered friends and families are reassembled, that we should be called upon to meet here to promote a great purpose, a general good will, and a general improvement; as I consider that such designs are worthy of the faith we hold, and I do believe they are a practical remembrance of the sacred words, 'On earth peace, good will towards men'.

I hope that every year which dawns on your institution, will find it richer in its means of usefulness, and greyer headed in the honour and respect it has gained. It can hardly speak for itself more appropriately than in the words of an English writer, when contemplating the English emblem of this period of the year, the Holly Tree:

> And should my youth, as youth is apt, I know,
> 　Some harshness show,
> All vain asperities I, day by day,
> 　Would wear away,
> Till the smooth temper of my age should be
> Like the high leaves upon the Holly Tree.
>
> And as when all the summer trees are seen
> 　So bright and green,
> The Holly leaves their fadeless hues display
> 　Less bright than they,
> But when the bare and wintry woods we see,
> What then so cheerful as the Holly Tree?

---

[1] Archibald Alison (1792–1867), historian and lawyer; Sheriff of Lanarkshire; author of the *History of Europe*, 1833–42.

So serious should my youth appear among
   The thoughtless throng,
So would I seem among the young and gay
   More grave than they,
That in my age as cheerful I might be
As the green winter of the Holly Tree.[1]

Dickens resumed his seat amid loud and continued applause.

He was succeeded by several other speakers: Lord Provosts and ex-Lord Provosts of Glasgow and Edinburgh, professors of their universities and various other local dignitaries, as well as Dr. Moir or 'Delta', author and contributor to *Blackwood's*, with whom Dickens had already made friends, at Edinburgh, in 1841. Finally Sheriff Alison proposed a vote of thanks to the chairman for the honour he had done the Athenaeum by presiding at its first annual celebration.

On rising, Dickens was received once more with deafening cheers, and said:

Ladies and Gentlemen, I am no stranger to Scotland, and—I say it with the deepest gratitude—I am no stranger to the warmth of Scottish hearts; but the warmth of your present welcome almost deprives me of any hope of acknowledging it. I will not detain you any longer at this late hour; let it suffice to assure you, that for taking the part with which I have been honoured in this festival, I have been repaid a thousandfold by your abundant kindness, and by the unspeakable gratification it has afforded me. I hope that, before many years are past, we may have another meeting in public [*great applause*] when we shall rejoice at the immense progress your institution will have made in the meantime, and look back upon this night with pleasure and satisfaction. I shall now, in conclusion, repeat most heartily and fervently the motto referred to by Dr. Ewing, 'Let Glasgow flourish' [*cheers*], which Bailie Nicol Jarvie, himself 'a Glasgow body', observed was 'elegantly putten round the town's arms'.[2]

Alison thought that Dickens's speech was 'extremely well received', considering that it 'contained nothing new and little striking'. Fortunately, he was self-satisfied with his own performance: 'I proposed a vote of thanks . . . and endeavoured, in a few sentences, to characterise and select the brilliant points of his writings, which gave general satisfaction, and was the more surprising as I was very little acquainted with them. I never had any taste for those novels the chief object of which is to paint

---

[1] Robert Southey, 'The Holly Tree'. Forster mentions that when Dickens was looking for a title for his projected weekly periodical, he considered *The Holly Tree*, with lines from the poem as a motto, before he decided on *Household Words*.

[2] Scott, *Rob Roy*, ch. xxvii.

the manners and foibles of middle and low life.' He admitted in his speech that, with the inevitable exception of Scott, there were no other great novelists whom he could sincerely praise.

As Dickens's host, on the other hand, he was delighted 'with the suavity of his manners and the variety and brilliance of his conversation. Indeed the flow of his ideas was so rapid . . . that it appeared to me that his writings'—which he had not read—'gave no adequate idea of his talents'. As an historian, Alison regretted that Dickens should have taken to a form of composition unworthy 'of his powers, and for which I could not anticipate durable fame'.[1]

Dickens was delighted with his success, which was spoilt only by the illness of his wife. The next day was divided between visits to the prison and lunatic asylum, lunch with the Town Council, and a dinner-party in the evening: 'Unbounded hospitality and enthoozymoozy the order of the day, and I have never been more heartily received anywhere, or enjoyed myself more completely.'[2]

GENERAL THEATRICAL FUND

17 *April* 1848

THE anniversary festival was held in the London Tavern, with Sir Edward Bulwer Lytton[3] in the Chair. Earlier in the year, Dickens had written to Lytton to ask him to preside.

The usual loyal toasts were given and received; and, in replying for the Navy, Captain Chappell caused some amusement by regretting that Dickens had not brought 'his friend Captain Cuttle'. Other speakers followed, including the chairman, who proposed 'Prosperity to the Trade and Commerce of the City of London', and Sheriff Hill, who replied. The sheriff made rather a strange speech, in which he said that 'in his official capacity he had made it his duty to enquire how many actors were employed in Newgate; and he had found there was not one, out of its 3,000 occupants'.

When Dickens rose to propose the health of the chairman, he began by replying to both the Captain and the sheriff:

[1] Sir Archibald Alison, *My Life and Writings*, 1883, i. 567–8.
[2] F, vi. i.
[3] Edward George Earle Lytton Bulwer (1803–73), assumed additional name of Lytton 1843, 1st Baron Lytton 1866; novelist, dramatist, statesman, poet. He was greatly admired by Dickens, who came to know him through Forster, who acted as a sort of agent between Lytton and Macready. Already Lytton had written several successful plays for Macready, including the *Duchesse de la Vallière* 1836, the *Lady of Lyons* and *Richelieu* 1838, and *Money*, a comedy, 1840. His friendship with Dickens developed slowly, until Dickens visited him at Knebworth with his amateur players in 1850. After that they were closely associated in the management of the Guild of Literature and Art, of which Lytton was president and Dickens vice-president.

HE had, he said, never been in *limbo*, and therefore his knowledge of the Old Bailey was limited; and as the sheriff had been pleased to remark that but few, if any actors, had been in 'durance vile', he thought he might return the compliment by saying that but few sheriffs had been resident in Newgate. [*Laughter.*] With respect to the speech of the gallant officer, who returned thanks for the Navy, he could assure him that though his friend Captain Cuttle was not present, he would most indubitably 'take a note of it'. [*Hear, hear, and laughter.*]

'Good wine', as Rosalind says, 'needs no bush'; so a good play needs no epilogue; a good book no preface; and a good toast but few words. It was conventionally supposed that actors were an improvident race; but he would maintain that it was more creditable to those who yielded up out of so many shillings so many pence to a fund for their decayed brethren, than those who hoarded up hundreds. [*Cheers.*] And he would assert that, in the profession, there were a number of highly honourable, talented and striving men and women, of whose daily lives many of the company then assembled might take an example. [*Hear, hear.*]

Dickens then pronounced a high eulogium on the talents of the chairman, who, he said, had written the best comedy since Goldsmith's time; and as to his works of fiction, they were known and appreciated by all the world. He concluded by calling on the company to drink his health.

The toast was responded to with all the honours. Later, Dickens also proposed the final toast of the evening:

He had, he said, but half a dozen words to say. The Muses were ladies; the Graces were ladies; some of the best writers were ladies; some of the best characters in tragedy and comedy were ladies; the brightest portion of our existence were ladies. He would, therefore, give 'The Ladies'.

The next day Dickens wrote an account of the proceedings for Forster:

The naval captain . . . made the best speech of the kind I ever heard in my life. The dinner went off capitally. Hirsute very good, but with that strange unfortunate manner in full force, and a dodge in the way of action which I will describe to you vivâ voce. Dickens was very good . . . both in reply to the Capting, and the Sheriff—who said a very odd thing—also to be described.[1]

'Hirsute' was presumably Lytton, whose unfortunate manner as a speaker was notorious. Fifteen years later Dickens still remembered Sheriff Hill's remarks, and his own rejoinder, and repeated them at the festival of the fund in 1863.

---

[1] 18 Apr. 1848 [FC].

GENERAL THEATRICAL FUND

21 *May* 1849

THE anniversary festival was held in the London Tavern, with Charles Kean[1] in the Chair. After a toast to the society itself, the chairman gave the health of the trustees and Dickens. 'To him', he said, 'is due much of the present prosperous condition and flattering prospects by which this institution is encouraged.' The toast was drunk by the company standing. In rising to reply, Dickens was received with a burst of applause, and said:

GENTLEMEN, in hope that you will not object to a Trustee with a cold, however naturally you might object to a cold Trustee [*laughter*], I beg, in behalf of my absent colleagues, to return you their thanks for the honour you have rendered them, and on my own part to acknowledge the honour you have rendered me. And I am well assured, gentlemen, that I express their feelings no less than my own, when I congratulate the General Theatrical Fund on the brilliant assembly by which I am surrounded; and on its being presided over by a gentleman who has a triple claim on its consideration and respect. [*Cheers.*] I do not mean to say, gentlemen, with Mrs. Malaprop's own happy confusion of ideas, that the chairman is 'like Cerberus, three gentlemen at once'[2] [*cheers and laughter*]; but I think I give utterance to the sentiment—to the general sentiment—of all this company, when I hail him as gracefully seated in his right place tonight, not only in consideration of his own talents and public position, but in memory of the genius of his immortal father [*tremendous cheering*], and in consideration of the many tender and sweet remembrances all England must associate with his accomplished wife. [*Enthusiastic applause, lasting for several minutes, the whole company rising, with waving of handkerchiefs and similar demonstrations.*][3]

Gentlemen, if, like some Trustees on an infinitely larger scale— some of those legislative Trustees who occasionally refresh them-

---

[1] Charles Kean (1811–68), actor, second son of Edmund Kean; as Macready's rival, he was mercilessly reviewed by Forster, and he was not among Dickens's theatrical friends; in 1842 he had married Ellen Tree (1805–80).

[2] Sheridan, *Rivals*, IV. ii.

[3] The *Era* notes: 'When he mentioned his *father*—when he referred to EDMUND KEAN, deafening were the shouts that drowned his voice. We hope the son saw his own importance—his own influence—his own attraction!' While when Dickens 'paid a merited and graceful compliment to Mrs. Kean . . . then, if possible, the uproar was greater than ever'. ('A Glance at the Theatrical Fund Dinner', *Era*, 27 May, p. 9.)

selves with odd vagaries elsewhere—I might espy 'strangers present'[1] [*cheers and laughter: Dickens casting his eyes to the Ladies' gallery*]; though Heaven forbid that the sudden sharpness of my eyesight should be attended with the disastrous House of Commons consequences, and lead to the withdrawal of those fair ornaments of our society; but I say, if, with the proverbial clearness of vision of an Irish member [*loud laughter*], I might espy 'strangers present,' I would appeal to them confidently as the best judges whether their sex has ever had a gentler, better, truer exponent than the lady of whom I speak. [*Immense applause.*] Perchance, gentlemen, I would appeal to them to say whether her sitting among us at this time is not the crowning grace of our festivity. [*Renewed cheering.*]

In common, gentlemen, both with the chairman and Secretary, I regret very much to miss at this board today the pleasant and familiar face of our Treasurer [*J. B. Buckstone*]; I regret it selfishly for our sakes, for I can guess to how many faces his is imparting something of its own delightful cheerfulness and mirth at this moment. [*Cheers.*] But as a less important officer of this institution, it is a great pleasure to me to confirm all that you have heard stated of its continued prosperity, and to bear my admiring testimony to the patience and perseverance with which its members contribute, many of them from very scanty and uncertain resources, those periodical sums which are to be a provision for their old age; to exult, as I annually do, in the refutation thus afforded to the sweeping charge of improvidence, which is somewhat thoughtlessly made, and as I conceive ungenerously, against the members of the theatrical profession, and other not dissimilar pursuits. Gentlemen, I always consider when I hear that charge made, that it is not sufficiently recollected that if you are born to the possession of a silver spoon, it may not be very difficult to apply yourself to the task of keeping it well polished on the side-board [*laughter*], but that if you are born to the possession of a wooden ladle instead [*laughter*], the process of transmuting it into that article of plate is often a very difficult and discouraging process. [*Cheers and laughter.*] And most of all we should remember that it is so at a time of general trouble and distress. 'Uneasy lies the head that wears a crown' indeed, in days when crowns of so many sorts, of gold, brass, and iron, are tumbling from the heads of the wearers; but the head that wears a mimic crown, and the hand that grasps a mimic sceptre, fare at such a season, worst of all; for then the peaceful, graceful arts of life go down, and the slighter ornaments

[1] John O'Connell, the Irish politician, M.P. for Limerick, had recently 'spied strangers' as a protest against unfair reporting by *The Times* in the House of Commons on 15 May.

of social existence are the first things crushed. [*Cheers.*] Therefore, gentlemen, if the King of Sardinia cannot get into trouble without involving the King of Mr. Daggerwood's Company;[1] and if the leader of the Austrian armies cannot make a movement without affecting the leader of the business at the Theatre Royal, Little Pedlington[2] [*laughter*], so much the more have we reason to rejoice in the continued prosperity of this institution—so much the more have we reason to rejoice in its floating on this sea of trouble; like the veritable sea-serpent,[3] according to Captain McQuhae [*laughter*], with which it tallies in all its essential features, for it is apparently bent on a vigorous and determined object [*laughter*], with its head considerably above water [*laughter*], and drawing easily behind it a long train of useful circumstances. [*Renewed cheers and laughter.*]

One other word, gentlemen, on the hopes of the Drama, and consequently on the hopes of the extended operations of this establishment, and I have done. When the chairman made his first admirable speech, I confess I had some doubts whether I quite agreed with him, but I was quite sure that if we did not agree, we should agree to differ;[4] but when he made that admirable other speech in reference to the Fund, I was happy to find that we were cordially agreed. Gentlemen, I allude to the regeneration of the Drama. I think it next to impossible but that it must come to pass, because the Drama is founded on an eternal principle in human nature. I say it respectfully, I do not think it within the power of any potentate on earth, however virtuous, however munificent, however strong in the love and honour of a people, to raise the Drama up, or to pull the Drama down. [*Loud cheers.*] In this room, in Windsor Castle, in an African hut, in a North American wigwam, there is the same inborn delight and interest in a living representation of the actions, passions, joys, and sorrows of mankind. [*Tremendous cheering.*] In England, of all countries on the earth,

[1] *Daggerwood's*: alternatively, 'Vincent Crummles''. (*Era.*)

[2] John Poole, *Little Pedlington and the Pedlingtonians*, 1839; its author (1793–1872), a successful dramatist and miscellaneous writer, was helped for the rest of his life, after a complete collapse, by Dickens, Talfourd, and Forster.

[3] Capt. McQuhae of H.M.S. *Daedalus* had reported a sea-serpent to the Admiralty, which he and several members of the ship's company had seen on a passage home from the East Indies. After much discussion in the press, and further reports, the matter was referred to Professor Owen, who decided that the serpent was a large seal.

[4] In proposing 'The Queen', Charles Kean had said that he recalled 'with pride and satisfaction' the numbers and the names of the actors who had taken part in the Civil War on the royalist side, and who had held commissions in the army. This was sure to be unwelcome to Dickens, as were also his allusions to the recent command performances at Windsor Castle, in which he had taken part, being 'a star of light' rising on 'the darkened horizon of the future'.

this interest is purified and exalted by the loftiest masterpieces of human fancy, and the proudest monuments of human wit. [*Renewed cheers.*] Such an art, gentlemen, I hold to be imperishable; reverses it may suffer, from many causes, but 'malice domestic, foreign levy, nothing', to my thinking, can root it out. [*Immense cheering.*]

As a friend of Forster and partisan of Macready, Dickens had been expected to say either too little or too much. In fact, both Kean and Dickens were careful not to give obvious offence; but the tory *Morning Post* was unwilling to let slip an opportunity to embitter their relations. It suggested that Kean's remarks about Dickens were 'clothed in such terms of rhapsody that great doubts were entertained by those present whether a covert satire was not intended. . . . Mr. Charles Dickens, in his reply, was strikingly ungrateful.'[1] The *Era*, on the other hand, was more generous to Dickens:

His words came fresh and flowing, as it were, from a living source, and they went home, telling of the genius of their author; for when such a man speaks, what he says is unlike all else you hear. It was something to hear 'Boz' . . . speak his mind, and in his mind honest truth predominates, though he may exaggerate occasionally 'for the fun of the thing'.[2]

UNITED LAW CLERKS' SOCIETY
19 *June* 1849

Several of Dickens's legal friends were benefactors of the society, and Dickens had been invited to speak in 1844, when he had been unable to attend. This year the dinner was held in the Freemasons' Tavern, with the Lord Chief Baron, Sir Jonathan Frederick Pollock,[3] in the Chair. In proposing Dickens's health, he said that 'they would be doing homage to genius. . . . It would be a waste of words on his part to enlarge upon the merits of that gentleman. It was sufficient to pronounce his name, for his genius was felt in all their breasts—his glowing words were in their memory, and found their way to every man's heart.' The toast was received with loud applause, and Dickens replied.

He was, he said, deeply sensible of the warmth and earnestness of the welcome he had received this evening, and of the distinguished compliment which had been paid to him by the Lord Chief Baron. He had been requested to propose a toast upon this occasion, and he did not know for what reason, unless it were that he was a law student without ever having studied the law, or that he once had the honour of being connected with a case, which was an action

---

[1] 22 May, p. 6.   [2] 27 May, p. 9.
[3] Sir Jonathan Frederick Pollock (1783–1870), Lord Chief Baron of the Exchequer 1844–66; knighted 1834; created baronet 1866.

for breach of promise of marriage—and which was only reported
in one book—a case in which he confessed that the pleading, the
evidence, the summing up, and the verdict were all equally wrong.[1]

He was extremely glad to be present, because it afforded him an
opportunity of entering into personal explanations. Some time ago
a gentleman had written to him stating that he thought he had been
'rather hard' upon the profession, and it would be an agreeable
sacrifice to offended justice if he would come here and confess that
he did not mean what he said. He was now ready to plead to that
accusation.

He then went on to make some amusing observations on the
subject of pleading, and facetiously alluded to the character of Dick
Swiveller as connected with the law. He concluded by proposing
'The Bar and the Profession'.

William Ballantine[2] returned thanks.

BANQUET AT THE MANSION HOUSE
7 *July* 1849

THE banquet to Literature, Science, and Art was given at the Mansion
House by the lord mayor, Sir James Duke.[3] For some reason, although it
followed the usual traditions, it was not entirely successful. There were
the customary toasts to various institutions of the arts and sciences and
their representatives, followed by others to the Church, the peerage, the
judges, and the House of Commons. The lord mayor then said he was
happy to see around him various gentlemen who had made themselves
widely and honourably known by their writings. He begged to propose
as a toast 'Honour and Prosperity to those engaged in the Pursuits of
Literature', and he would couple with that toast the name of Mr. Charles
Dickens.

IN reply Dickens said that he begged, on behalf of the distinguished
men included in the toast, to return thanks for this honour; an
honour which was not lessened by the fact of its being unusual
in that hall. [*Cheers.*] It would ill become him at that late period
of the evening to detain them by any lengthened observations, but
he could not help observing on behalf of his brethren engaged in

---

[1] 'Bardell and Pickwick.'

[2] William Ballantine (1812–77), barrister; serjeant-at-law 1856; author of
Some Experiences of a Barrister's Life, 1882; acquainted with Dickens.

[3] Sir James Duke (1792–1873), merchant; M.P. for Boston 1837–49, and for
the City of London 1849–65; had been Dickens's tenant in Devonshire Terrace
while he was abroad, 1846–7.

the pursuits of Literature, that they highly appreciated this graceful compliment, and that one of the best tributes which could be paid to them was to receive a recognition of their art at the hands of the Chief Magistrate of the City of London, and to partake of his sumptuous hospitality. [*Cheers.*]

The lord mayor's well-intentioned banquet nearly led to a display of literary pique, characteristic of Dickens and most of his fellow authors. They were all alike in complaining of lack of recognition when it was withheld, and rejecting it as patronage whenever it was offered. Forster tells the story, in the *Life*, from his own point of view—that of an author who had not been even invited:

In the summer of 1849 he [Dickens] came up from Broadstairs to attend a Mansion-house dinner, which the lord mayor of that day had been moved by a laudable ambition to give to 'literature and art', which he supposed would be adequately represented by the Royal Academy, the contributors to *Punch*, Dickens, and one or two newspaper men. On the whole the result was not cheering; the worthy chief magistrate, no doubt quite undesignedly, expressing too much surprise at the unaccustomed faces around him to be altogether complimentary. In general (this was the tone) we are in the habit of having princes, dukes, ministers, and what not for our guests, but what a delight, all the greater for being unusual, to see gentlemen like you! In other words, what possibly could be pleasanter than for people satiated with greatness to get for a while by way of a change into the butler's pantry? This in substance was Dickens's account to me next day, and his reason for having been very careful in his acknowledgement of the toast of 'the Novelists'.[1]

This is unfair to Sir James Duke. It is not true that the authors at the banquet were confined to contributors to *Punch*, although Thackeray, Lemon, Mayhew, Doyle, and Leech were all there. Also present were Sir Henry Ellis, Sir Frederick Madden, Panizzi, Samuel Rogers, J. G. Lockhart, G. R. Porter, Tom Taylor, and many lesser literary men. It was a constant difficulty, moreover, for anyone organizing such a banquet, to avoid having the same guests as everyone else. Some authors invariably rejected all invitations to dine out in public, and others were never known to refuse. On this occasion, certainly, Macaulay, Guizot, Monckton Milnes, Hallam, and Talfourd had all replied regretting their inability to attend; but the *Punch* contingent was always ready to dine.

But the *Daily News* found the idea of Literature being honoured in the City too extraordinary to pass without comment, and accompanied its normal report of the proceedings at the banquet with a stinging, heavy-handed editorial. It began:

'Le vrai Amphitryon est L'Amphitryon ou l'on dîne.' The great moral truth first announced by Molière was never more happily illustrated than at the Mansion House on Saturday last. Mr. Charles Dickens, in the bland moment of repletion, designated turtle and ice punch, 'a *graceful* recognition of the claims of literature', and vowed that 'no more gratifying compliment' could be paid to men of letters than 'such a tribute from the chief magistrate of the City of London'.

[1] F, VI. vi.

It went on to give a mock-report of a speech omitted by 'our own' reporter, made by 'the real *bonâ fide* Mr. Punch'.

Dickens, according to Forster, was 'nettled not a little' by this allusion in the *Daily News*, and sent him a letter from Broadstairs to be forwarded to the editor. Forster discreetly suppressed it at the time, but included it in the *Life*. Dickens wrote:

> I have no other interest in, or concern with, a most facetious article on last Saturday's dinner at the Mansion-house . . . than that it misrepresents me in what I said on the occasion. If you should not think it at all damaging to the wit of that satire to state what I did say, I shall be much obliged to you. It was this. . . . That I considered the compliment of a recognition of Literature by the citizens of London the more acceptable to us because it was unusual in that hall, and likely to be an advantage and benefit to them in proportion as it became in future less unusual. That on behalf of the novelists, I accepted the tribute as an appropriate one; inasmuch as we had sometimes reason to hope that our imaginary worlds afforded an occasional refuge to men busily engaged in the toils of life, from which they came forth none the worse to a renewal of its strivings; and certainly that the chief magistrate of the greatest city of the world might be fitly regarded as the representative of that class of our readers.[1]

The whole affair turned on the sensitivity of the authors of the period to class patronage, which they tried to counter by claims for 'the Rights of Literature'. Dickens was all the more exasperated by the *Daily News* satirist because, as he showed later in his dispute with the Literary Fund, no one was more sensitive or bitter on the same point than he.

NEWSVENDORS' BENEVOLENT INSTITUTION

21 *November* 1849

THE Newsvendors' Benevolent Institution had been founded in 1839. Its first anniversary dinner was held ten years later, at the Albion Tavern, with Dickens in the Chair.

After proposing the health of Her Majesty the Queen, Dickens gave 'Prince Albert and the rest of the Royal Family', reminding the company that as this was the anniversary of the birthday of the Princess Royal[2] they could not do less than wish her Royal Highness many years of health and happiness. The toast was received with enthusiastic applause.

HE then said it had now become his duty to give them what was usually called 'the toast of the evening'.—That 'duty', as Shakespeare said, 'cannot be silent'. But he would promise that what he might say should be said earnestly and to the purpose, and at once as much and as little as possible. [*Hear, hear.*] As he learned

---

[1] F. VI. vi.

[2] Victoria Adelaide Mary Louisa (1840–1901), eldest daughter of Queen Victoria; married Frederick William, 1858, who became Crown Prince of Prussia 1861, and Emperor Frederick II, 1888; their eldest son was the Emperor William III, 'the Kaiser'.

from the pamphlet which had been placed before him, it was ten years since the newsvendors, being a large and industrious body in London, established a Benevolent and Provident Institution 'for the granting of temporary relief and permanent assistance to masters and servants engaged as vendors of newspapers, who from age, infirmity, or distress, may require the aid of the benevolent'. And he observed that the institution so originated had this excellent feature—that only those were eligible as permanent pensioners who were members of the society, and had subscribed to its funds —which, as he thought, was a very salutary and wise regulation; not only as encouraging provident habits and the feeling of brotherhood, but also as sparing the reduced recipients of bounty any humiliation in availing themselves of those funds [*hear, hear*],—as inspiring (which he considered a most excellent thing) the thought: 'I can take the money without a blush; I did a just thing when I subscribed to this institution, and I did it for others no less than for myself. I did not then know that the hour of sickness and distress, which comes to so many of us, would come to me; but, being come, I can thank God I was mindful of it, and that I can take this pittance with an independent spirit, and an upright head.' [*Cheers.*]

This institution, although it had a portion of £1,000 hard money out at interest, which was a very tolerable fortune for so very young a creature, was still exceedingly young. Its whole life had been passed in the nursery. It was so young, indeed, that it had never until today come down to show itself after dinner. [*Hear, hear, and laughter.*] But as there was in the infancy of almost all young creatures a certain period when the frame was employed in gathering form and strength, so he believed that this young creature had been employed these ten years in taking the necessary amount of sleep and very mild sustenance; and that tonight a young giant was exhibited to them for the first time, which, like the giant in the *Arabian Nights*, would contemptuously kick over the casket which had contained it; yet, unlike that giant, would never be able to get into it again. [*Cheers and laughter.*]

The rapidity with which healthy children grew out of their clothes was, he believed, a frequent subject of complaint in many families—he knew it was in his own. [*A laugh.*] If this child did not grow out of its first suit of £1,000 while the nap was still new upon it, so as to compel them to measure him in quick succession for a suit of £2,000, or £5,000, or £10,000, all he meant to say was that the fault would be theirs alone, and they would deserve to be stigmatized as most unnatural parents. [*Cheers.*] For himself, as a friend of the family, he should never be satisfied unless he had an opportunity of saying to the grown-up bantling: 'I knew you when you were a baby with a very weak chest. [*Laughter.*] I sat at the head of the table on the first occasion when your pinafore was taken off; and now I see you a strong man, who (if I may adopt the phraseology of the sporting part of the press, with which you are all, no doubt, familiar) may be heard of once a year at the bar of the Albion, whose money is ready for all comers, and who would be very glad to meet with any customer who will do him the honour to call.' [*Laughter.*]

The claims of the Newsvendors, as a body, upon one another, and upon the public, to erect a provident institution of their own: and not only that, but to elevate themselves and those whom they employed, in the social scale, in intelligence and good conduct: seemed to him to be most undeniable. It was not that they toiled in all weathers—it was not that they were up early and late—that they were watching while others slept—that they were at our doors daily throughout the year ministering to our requirements—although this was much, and in virtue of which we owed them a debt of gratitude—it was not for this that they inherited this claim; but it was because they were connected with that great power which had become the axis on which the moral world turned round. [*Great cheering.*]—Humbly connected no doubt, but most usefully and inseparably. They were, to that fountain of knowledge to all men which was popularly called 'the Press', as conduits to a well of water; or what the pipes which undermined the streets of this city were to the great gas works from which the lights proceeded which turned our night into day. [*Cheers.*] It was that they went on for ever between us and those mighty engines which, working night by night, and all night long, were felt in their faintest throb throughout the civilized world. [*Cheers.*] It was that those men should be in a high degree worthy of their trade, and should not be behind the members of any other industrious calling, but should be up with the foremost. [*Cheers.*]

It was no more than two hundred and fifty years since the first idea of a newspaper was conceived in this island, to stimulate the people to resist the Spanish Armada.[1] It was not more than two hundred years since the first notion of a regular newspaper, in anything like its present form, was reduced to practice. One hundred and fifty years ago there did not appear to have been a single daily paper in England, and ten years later only one. When he compared such a state of things with that now existing, he felt as if the humble men connected with the vending of news ought to be in advance of those times in the same proportionate degree as

[1] *English Mercurie*, 1588: it had been shown to be an eighteenth-century forgery, in 1839.

the newspapers they dealt in, and that they ought to take their stand upon the footing of their useful trade, and be as much recognized and respected in that trade as the paper-maker or the printer. [*Cheers.*] Were they not indebted to the newsvendors almost for everything? If expresses came from different parts of the country, or steam-packets from foreign lands, did they not do so to deposit their treasures with the newsvendors, by whom their most important communications were laid thereafter before the public? [*Cheers.*] It was only last summer a member of their trade delivered at his door the astounding intelligence that the City of London was the best watered, the best drained, and the most wholesome city in the world; and, shortly after, the same gentleman, brought him the astounding intelligence that certain sages who said such was the case, were not locked up in the incurable cellars of Bethlehem Hospital. [*A laugh.*] Shortly after this the same newsvendor brought him the news that the city was a charnel-house;[1] and on yesterday morning an afflicted wife and family heard from the same source, that a husband and father was roaming about the world with an unsatiated thirst for human blood.[2] [*Laughter.*]

The object which brought them together at that meeting might at first sight seem small enough; but it was so great in its importance, and so comprehensive in principle, that it really deserved their best consideration. He thought that every follower, however humble, of that great plough, which was for ever turning up the world, and knew no season of pause in its work, was deserving of their best consideration; and therefore he asked them to drink most heartily and cordially, 'Prosperity to the Newsvendors' Provident and Benevolent Association.'

The toast was drunk 'with three times three, and one cheer more'. One of the Newsvendors then proposed the health of the chairman, and Dickens replied.

[1] General concern for public health, aroused by the cholera epidemic of 1848-9, was then at its height. Dickens had written to his brother-in-law Henry Austin on 19 Oct. 1849: '—Come and dine with me towards the end of next month, in the City, when I preside for the "News Wenders". I think it'll be a good occasion for making 'em a sanitary speech, and banging at the wooden headed, porpoise souled old Idols of aldermen, whom—I was going to say may God confound—but He has done it.' M.

[2] Evidently a reference to the recent controversy about capital punishment, which had flared up with the execution of the notorious murderers, Mr. and Mrs. Manning, on 12 Nov. Dickens had written a letter to *The Times* on the 13th, in which he described 'the atrocious bearing, looks and language, of the assembled spectators', at the execution. In another letter, written on the 17th, he had made it clear that he was simply against public executions; and because the all-out opponents of capital punishment thought that this did not go far enough, he suddenly found himself attacked as a presumably bloodthirsty 'supporter of secret hangings'.

He thanked the company most heartily, he said, for this very cordial mark of their good will, which he could not separate from something of the earnestness of a private greeting, rather than a mere public welcome. [*Hear.*] Having been himself a speaker so often already, he ought now to confine himself to calling forth divers unwilling gentlemen he saw around him, and contemplating their sufferings and their triumphs. [*Hear, hear, and laughter.*] In thanking them for the honour they had conferred upon him, he could not forget that his first entry into life, his first success in life, his first view of the bearings of life around him, were in connexion with a London daily newspaper, and that connexion had always lived in his remembrance as a source of pleasure, and he acknowledged it as a source of at once pride and pleasure.

After a pause during which a comic song was sung, the chairman again rose, and said he had an extremely comprehensive toast to propose, namely, 'The Press', which he supposed included everybody connected with it. On one side of him he saw several of the most successful gentlemen connected with it, and he would therefore give 'The Press in all its Ramifications, and Mr. Jerdan in connexion with Periodical Literature'. William Jerdan,[1] the editor of the *Literary Gazette*, replied.

METROPOLITAN SANITARY ASSOCIATION

6 *February* 1850

ON bringing forward his Health of Towns Bill in 1847, Lord Morpeth had been faced with such determined opposition to so-called 'centralization' that he had been forced to agree that it should not apply to London. It was only after many concessions and much conciliation that it was passed as the Public Health Act the following year. Lord Morpeth, Lord Ashley, and Edwin Chadwick had then been appointed members of the newly constituted Board of Health, which was at once faced by the cholera epidemic of 1848–9. Yet, in spite of the appointment of a Metropolitan Sanitary Commission when London was dropped from the Bill, little was done in the capital itself, where most action was needed.

A new public movement was started, therefore, under the title of the Metropolitan Sanitary Association, to arouse official bodies to action. It was not a new idea to Dickens. 'In all my writings', he had written, 'I hope I have taken every possible opportunity of showing the want of sanitary improvements in the neglected dwellings of the poor.'[2] At the

---

[1] William Jerdan (1782–1864), journalist; minor writer but leading figure in literary affairs; one of the founders of the Royal Society of Literature; active official of the Royal Literary Fund; former contributor to *Bentley's Miscellany*, when edited by Dickens.

[2] *Martin Chuzzlewit*, Preface to the cheap edition, Nov. 1849.

same time there is no doubt that his interest in the movement was stimulated by his brother-in-law, Henry Austin.[1]

Austin had been secretary of an association for the Improvement of the Dwellings of the Labouring Classes, and joint-secretary of the Metropolitan Commission of Sewers. He was now secretary to the General Board of Health. In this position he was able to keep Dickens in touch with official developments, send him the latest reports, and advise him about the numerous articles on the sanitary question written for *Household Words*. Austin had no official position on the Metropolitan Sanitary Association. The whole idea of the new society was that, being independent, it could attack other official bodies and public prejudice far more openly than dared the Board of Health itself. Yet there is no doubt that the two bodies were closely in league, and Austin probably often did business for both.

Its first public meeting was held at the Freemasons' Tavern, with the Bishop of London, Dr. Blomfield, in the Chair. He opened the meeting with a strong, well-reasoned speech. It was the purpose of the new association, he explained, 'to encourage and animate . . . the Legislature'. They had been 'taught an awful lesson by the visitation of cholera in the course of the last year'. He quoted from various reports showing the urgent need for sanitary reform, and referred to one especially which stated that: 'A survey had been made of a block of houses (including what is called Jacob's Island) which was most severely ravaged by cholera.' He went on to say that the report showed that 'the most important sanitary improvements might be obtained for these houses for an average rate of 1¾d. a week'. On the grounds of expense, therefore, reform was entirely practicable.

A number of resolutions were then proposed and passed demanding 'prompt, energetic, and carefully devised means of relief'. The Rev. Dr. John Cumming moved a resolution which deplored the number of deaths from preventable disease in London, and declared that 'this great sacrifice of human life is accompanied by an amount of physical degradation and mental depravity, which act as effective barriers to the inculcation either of social obligations or of Christian virtues'. On rising to second this resolution Dickens was received with loud and continued applause.

HAVING been requested to second the resolution, he said, he was happy to say that he would have but a very few words to address them in doing so, chiefly because all that was to be said upon the subject had been anticipated by the previous speakers. But they would excuse him if he so far followed in the footsteps of those who had preceded him, as to endeavour to impress upon the

---

[1] Henry Austin (1812–61), civil engineer; pupil of George Stephenson; close friend of Dickens; married Dickens's sister Letitia Mary in 1837. Later Chief Inspector to the General Board of Health, member of the Sewerage Commission, and attached to the Local Government Act Office. ('Memorial for Civil List pension for Mrs. Austin', drawn up by Dickens, Public Record Office, T. i. 64863.)

meeting that their great object was to bring the metropolis within the provisions of the Public Health Act, from the operation of which it had been most absurdly and monstrously excluded [*hear, hear*]— because it was their duty to diminish an amount of suffering and a waste of life which would be a disgrace to a heathen land, to atone for long years of neglect, of which they had all to a greater or less extent been guilty, and to redress a most grievous and cruel injustice. [*Hear, hear.*]

It was a common figure of speech when anything very important was left out of any great scheme, to say that it was the tragedy of *Hamlet* with Hamlet left out; but the existence of a Public Health Act with the metropolis excluded from its operation suggested something to him even more sad, and that was the representation of *Hamlet* with nothing in it but the gravedigger. [*Cheers and laughter.*] They had agreed that this was a state of things which must not be allowed to continue. They found every year 13,000 unfortunate persons dying unnaturally and prematurely around them.[1] They found infancy was made stunted, ugly, and full of pain; maturity made old, and old age imbecile; and pauperism made hopeless every day. They claimed for the metropolis of a Christian country that this should be remedied, and that the capital should set an example of humanity and justice to the whole empire. [*Cheers.*]

Of the sanitary condition of London at the present moment, he solemnly believed it would be almost impossible to speak too ill. He knew of many places in it unsurpassed in the accumulated horrors of their neglect by the dirtiest old spots in the dirtiest old towns, under the worst old governments in Europe. [*Hear, hear, and laughter.*] Great contrasts of rank, great contrasts of wealth, and great contrasts of comfort must, as every man of sense was aware exist among all civilized communities; but he sincerely believed that no such contrasts as were afforded by our handsome streets, our railroads and our electric telegraphs, in the year of our Lord 1850, as compared with the great mass of the dwellings of the poor in many parts of this metropolis, had ever before been presented on this earth. [*Hear, hear.*]

The principal objectors to the improvement of the sanitary condition of London—not to mention those noble and honourable friends of theirs who were that day at Westminster and elsewhere,

---

[1] 'Taking the last four years, more than 15,000 persons have, on an average, died prematurely in the metropolis, i.e. the mortality has exceeded 2 per cent. of the population (corrected for increase) by that amount.' (Note in the official report of the proceedings published by the Association, *Public Health a Public Question*.)

'letting I dare not wait upon I would'—the principal objectors to the sanitary improvement of the metropolis, might be divided into two classes. The first of these classes consisted of the small owners of small tenements, who pushed themselves forward on boards of guardians and parish vestries, and were clamorous about the ratings of their property. The other class was composed of gentlemen more independent and less selfish, who had a weak leaning to the words 'self-government'. [*Hear, hear.*] Now, the first of these classes proceeded generally on the supposition that the compulsory improvement of their dwellings, when exceedingly defective, would prove very expensive. But that was a great mistake, for nothing was cheaper than good sanitary improvement, as they knew in the case of 'Jacob's Island', which he had described in a work of fiction some ten or eleven years ago, and where the improvements had been made at a cost of less than the price of a pint of porter or two glasses of gin a week to each inhabitant. [*Hear, hear.*] With regard to the objectors on the principle of self-government, and that what was done in the next parish was no business of theirs, he should begin to think there was something in it when he found any court or street keeping its disease within its own bounds, or any parish keeping to itself its own fever or its own smallpox, just as it maintained its own beadles and its own fire-engine. [*Cheers and laughter.*] But until that time should have arrived, and so long as he breathed the same air as the inhabitants of that court, or street, or parish,—so long as he lived on the same soil, was lighted by the same sun and moon, and fanned by the same winds, he should consider their health and sickness as most decidedly his business, and would endeavour to force them to be pure and clean, and would place them under the control of a General Board for the general good. [*Hear, hear.*[

The Right Rev. prelate in the chair had referred in the most impressive manner to that charge frequently made, among other ill-considered charges, against the poor, that they liked to be dirty and to lead degraded lives. Now if that charge were true it would only present to him another proof of our living in a very alarming and a most unnatural state of society. But it was no more true of them than that when they first had public baths they would not bathe, and that when they first had washhouses their wives would not wash. [*Hear.*] We could not expect to gather 'grapes from thorns nor figs from thistles'; and we could not be surprised if the poor were not sensible of the decencies of life when they had no opportunity of being made acquainted with them. The main wonder in connexion with the poor was that they did so soon esteem what was really for their good when they had any fair experience of it.

No one who had any experience of the poor could fail to be deeply affected by their patience, by their sympathy with one another, and by the beautiful alacrity with which they helped each other in toil, in the day of suffering, and at the hour of death. [*Cheers.*] It hardly ever happened that any case of extreme protracted destitution found its way into the public prints without our reading at the same time of some ragged Samaritan sharing his last loaf or spending his last penny to relieve the poor miserable in the little room upstairs, or in the cellar underground. [*Renewed cheers.*] It was with a view to mitigate the sufferings of that class; to develop in these people the virtue which nothing could eradicate; to raise them in the social scale as they should be raised; to lift them from a condition into which they did not allow their beasts to sink, and to cleanse the foul air for the passage of Christianity and education throughout the land, that the meeting was assembled. He could not lay it to his heart, nor could he flatter any of those present with the idea that they had met there to plume themselves on their charity or their philanthropy. They could claim little merit for each other in such a cause, for the object of their assembling, as he regarded it, was simply to help to set that right which was very wrong before God and before man. [*Loud and prolonged cheers.*]

Further resolutions were passed, and, after a vote of thanks to the chairman, the meeting closed.

The Bishop of London's reference to Jacob's Island, and Dickens's remarks about its appearance in *Oliver Twist* as the place where Bill Sikes was brought to bay, had an amusing sequel. It was a river-side district of Bermondsey which, from being 'wholly unknown, even by name, to the great mass' of the population of London when Dickens first described it,[1] had since become notorious. The earliest fatal cases of cholera had occurred there both in 1832 and 1849.[2] Yet, a few days after the meeting of the Metropolitan Sanitary Association, the Marylebone vestry—which was equally notorious in its way—showed that it was still unknown to many even by name.

In the course of discussing what was to be done with parish children, it may have been difficult for some of the vestry's members to avoid an uneasy recollection of 'the board' of 'a certain town', presided over by a Mr. Limbkins. They were extremely doubtful whether they would be justified in 'spending the poor ratepayers' money' on providing the children with any education, and one of Dickens's old antagonists, Sir Peter Laurie,[3] rose to oppose such a measure with all his authority as an

[1] *Oliver Twist*, ch. 1.

[2] *Report of the General Board of Health on the Epidemic Cholera of 1848 and 1849*, Mar. 1850, Appendix B, pp. 92–94.

[3] Sir Peter Laurie (1778–1861), Chairman of the Union Bank; Master of Saddlers' Company; Lord Mayor 1832. As a magistrate he had given Dickens special access to London prisons as early as 1835. He had made himself notorious

ex-lord mayor. To illustrate how misguided and misinformed reformers of all kinds could be, he begged their permission to read out a passage from the recent speech by the Bishop of London about Jacob's Island: 'The Bishop of London, poor soul', said Sir Peter, 'in his simplicity, thought there really was such a place . . . whereas it turned out that it only existed in a work of fiction, written by Mr. Charles Dickens ten years ago [*roars of laughter*]. The fact was admitted by Mr. Charles Dickens himself at the meeting. . . . Mr. Dickens said ". . . nothing was cheaper than good sanitary improvements, as they knew in this case of 'Jacob's Island' [*laughter*], which he had described in a work of fiction some 10 or 11 years ago." [1]

The vestry was delighted. Another member agreed that 'It was all very well to listen to the rubbish of Mr. Charles Dickens who sold his work at a very high price, and got a good living out of it. . . . All that was cant and humbug.' It was only the following week that Sir Peter was challenged by a more widely read member, and indignantly defended his original remarks.

Dickens was no less delighted, and in writing the preface to the cheap edition of *Oliver Twist* next month, retaliated by telling the whole story, and quoting from Sir Peter's speech:

Reflecting upon this logic, and its universal application; remembering that when FIELDING described Newgate, the prison immediately ceased to exist; that when Smollett took Roderick Random to Bath, that city instantly sank into the earth . . . I was inclined to make this preface the vehicle of my humble tribute to SIR PETER LAURIE. But I am restrained . . . by no less a consideration than the impossibility of his existence. For SIR PETER LAURIE having been himself described in a book (as I understand he was, one Christmas time, for his conduct on the seat of justice), it is but too clear that there CAN be no such man.

Alderman Cute of *The Chimes*, who 'Put Down' everything,—'a sly fellow too! A knowing fellow. Up to everything. Not to be imposed upon.'[2]—was put down himself once more. Shortly after, Dickens mentioned him again, when writing to Henry Austin, as 'That incarnation of a Vulgar Soul and a thoroughly mean and sordid spirit'.[3]

The subsequent history of the association is not clear; but it was fully active throughout 1851, when Dickens spoke at a banquet on its behalf.[4] He had been elected a member of the General Committee; but this was a body of over 150. It had his full support, in principle, but he had no time to serve as an active member. On 12 May 1850 he wrote to Austin excusing himself from a meeting, called at short notice, to support the Metropolitan Interments Bill, simply because it interested him too much:

If I get fierce and antagonistic about burials, I can't go back to Copperfield for hours and hours. This is really the sort of condition on which I hold my inventive powers; and I can't get rid of it.

in 1844, just before Dickens began *The Chimes*, by saying that he would put down suicide by sending offenders to prison, and was consequently pilloried in the book as 'Alderman Cute.'

[1] *Observer*, 11 Feb., p. 3.   [2] *The Chimes*, 'First Quarter'.
[3] 21 Mar. 1850, M.   [4] See p. 127.

I am sincerely anxious to serve the cause, and am doing it now all the good I can, by side-blows in Household Words. . . . You will see next week, that I turned a paper called 'The Begging Letter Writer', to sanitary purposes.[1]

He would certainly have been fierce enough if he had gone to the meeting, since a mob of undertakers led a rush against the platform, the barriers were smashed, and it had been broken up in disorder. Three years later, however, 'the cause' owed even more to *Bleak House*.[2]

GENERAL THEATRICAL FUND

25 *March* 1850

THE anniversary festival was held at the London Tavern with Benjamin Webster[3] in the Chair. There were the usual loyal and patriotic toasts. In reviewing the society's progress, Buckstone paid a special tribute to 'the constant championship and attendance of our steadfast Trustee, Mr. Charles Dickens'. After other speeches Dickens rose to propose the health of the chairman. He was loudly cheered for some minutes, and said:

MR. CHAIRMAN and Gentlemen, Before I proceed to discharge the very simple office entrusted to me, you will perhaps allow me to congratulate you upon the very agreeable mode of spending Quarter Day—a day not always connected with agreeable associations, or devoted to such hilarity. [*Laughter and cheers.*] Perhaps you will also allow me, gentlemen, to renew my annual congratulations upon the prosperity of the General Theatrical Fund, and upon the courage and perseverance with which its members, many of them under very unpropitious circumstances indeed, continue to fulfil their task. [*Hear, hear.*] I never go into any of our smaller London theatres, or even into country theatres—such a one for instance as I was at the other night, where no particular piece belonged to the immense night in the bill, where generally people walked in and out, where a sailor fought a combat with anyone he chanced to meet and who happened to be in possession of a sword, —I never go into any of the neglected temples of the drama, where it is so hard to get a living, but I come out again with a considerably strengthened and increased admiration of those who are the members of this Fund [*cheers*], and who, with constancy and

---

[1] M. 'The Begging-Letter Writer' appeared in *Household Words*, 18 May 1850, and was collected in *Reprinted Pieces*, 1858.

[2] Dickens took a 'side-blow' at the incident in another paper in *Household Words*, 8 June 1850, i. 214–22, called 'The Raven in the Happy Family': 'It wasn't the undertakers who made a brutal charge at the platform, and overturned the ladies like a troop of horses. Of course not.'

[3] See p. 76.

perseverance, bear up under the greatest difficulties. [*Renewed cheering.*] It is, I say, an extraordinary and a remarkable fact. and an excellent example to the members of other and more lauded professions.

Gentlemen, I now come to the toast which I have to propose to you. I shall not express, as I ought to express according to all precedent, my sorrow that it has not fallen into better hands; for although it might easily have done that, to tell the truth, I am exceedingly glad to hold it in mine, as it gives me the opportunity of publicly rendering my humble tribute of respect to the character and exertions of a gentleman to whom this fund is much indebted, who is connected in no slight degree with the public enjoyment, and in no slight degree with the successes and hopes of the English Drama, its literature and art. I mean our chairman, Mr. Webster. [*Long continued cheering.*] I knew very well you would give a cordial reception to his name. [*Cheers.*] I was well assured of it because I esteem, as every friend of this institution must esteem, the very great importance of his encouragement, because I feel it is honourable to him and to it, that setting aside all considerations of this Fund or that Fund, of this theatre or that theatre, he puts himself at the head of a society which comprehends all theatres, and which includes all the members of a profession of which he is an old and great supporter. [*Cheers.*]

I felt assured, gentlemen, of the sympathy of all this company who are not connected with the profession, because our chairman has been now, for a long time, the manager of two admirably conducted theatres; because he has never been behind the public requirements in any respect, but has even outstripped them; and because he has a very strong demand upon our respect and admiration. [*Cheers.*] My friend, Mr. Buckstone, admirably expressed in one sentence a capital summary of his merits, that 'he not only employed a great number of actors, but paid them too' [*laughter*]; and really, gentlemen, in drinking such a toast as the present, we must not forget what a very difficult and arduous career such a manager has to encounter [*hear, hear*]; what untoward circumstances and great difficulties he has to struggle against, and how likely he is to be injured by any depression in the public mind, from whatever cause. Yet, notwithstanding all this, he has evinced a steadiness of purpose not to close his theatre, night after night, whatever may be the great temptations he has had to do so, being too mindful of the poor hangers-on dependent upon him for their daily bread, and who hope for the public support. Such a manager as this, gentlemen, Mr. Webster has always been; and when we add to this, that for many years he has fought a manly, stand-up English battle against very powerful rivals of various countries, English, Swedish, French, Italian, and has encountered all kinds of strange animals, lions, tigers, Ethiopians and Nightingales;[1] and when we add to this that it is sometimes softly whispered, though I do not believe it myself, that certain members of the theatrical profession, on rare and particular occasions, at great distances apart, are a little capricious and difficult to deal with: when we take all these circumstances into our consideration, I think we shall agree that he has come very nobly through his difficulties, and looks exceedingly well tonight after all that he has gone through. [*Laughter and cheers.*]

I cannot, gentlemen, in conclusion, express my sense of Mr. Webster's position in reference to the Drama, and in reference to this society, more to my own satisfaction, at all events, than by relating a little story (a very short one) that was told to me last night of an exceedingly intelligent and strictly veracious friend of mine, an American Sea Captain. [*A laugh.*] Gentlemen, once upon a time, he had as a passenger upon board his ship a young lady of great personal attractions, I use that phrase as one entirely new to you [*laughter*], and five young gentlemen, also passengers, and who in the course of a short voyage all fell desperately in love with the young lady. The young lady, liking all the five young gentlemen, and liking them all equally well, felt herself placed in a position of some difficulty, and in this emergency applied for advice to my friend the Captain. My friend the Captain, himself a man of an original turn of mind, proposed to the young lady that she should jump overboard, he having a well-manned boat alongside to prevent the possibility of accidents, and that she should marry the man that jumped in after her. She was very much struck by it, and it being summer time and fine weather, and naturally fond of bathing, decided to accept the proposition. Accordingly, on a certain morning, when her five admirers were all on deck, she went over the side head foremost. Four of the five immediately plunged in after her [*laughter*]; and, said the young lady to the Captain when they were all on deck again, 'What am I to do now? See how wet they are.' Said the Captain to the young lady, 'Take the dry one!' Which she did.[2]

Now the way in which I adapt this story to the present purpose

[1] The 'Ethiopian Serenaders', Jenny Lind, and various wild-beast shows, were all classed together as 'top-line' rivals of the legitimate drama.

[2] The captain was E. E. Morgan, the original of Captain Silas Jorgan of 'A Message from the Sea', by Dickens and Collins. See W. J. Carlton, 'Captain Morgan—*alias* Jorgan', *Dickensian*, 1957, liii. 75–82, who gives Morgan's version. Dickens wrote to tell Morgan that he had appropriated the story, 'and acquired an immense reputation from it' (*Scribner's Monthly*, xiv. 772). He told it again, in one of his speeches, in 1867, see pp. 364–5.

is simply by reversing it: that the British drama having gone overboard, and a great many admirers having looked on coolly, and one
having gone in and kept his head above water for a long time, my
advice to this society would have been, 'Take the wet one.' And
you have got him. I am thoroughly glad you have, and I beg to
propose to you, in all sincerity, to drink his health with acclamation.

Dickens resumed his seat amid loud cheering. Webster returned
thanks, and proposed the 'Health of the Trustees of the General
Theatrical Fund'. Dickens then rose to reply, and said:

On behalf of the Hon. Mr. Justice Talfourd, and my brother
Trustee,[1] I beg to return you my best thanks, and particularly to
my friend Mr. Webster, for his kind mention of my name. [*Cheers.*]
The only embarrassment that I feel on these occasions is that I
really don't know what we have to do. I might illustrate our position by a theatrical case. Perhaps you may have observed that
when a young lady performs a piece of horsemanship, there are
generally two or three ambiguous looking gentlemen who follow
Mr. Widdicombe[2] about, and who are indispensable to the performance, though the lady never knows why or in what particular, but
she is perfectly satisfied that they must be there, and that without
them the thing could not possibly be done. [*Laughter.*] I might
suppose my friend Mr. Buckstone, in reference to this institution,
to be the party representing Mr. Widdicombe, and Mr. Cullenford
performing the pleasing act of Secretaryship upon the highly
trained charger; while we, the Trustees, represent those attendants
looking on so very hard after them.

A number of other toasts, and unreported speakers, followed.

BANQUET IN HONOUR OF W. C. MACREADY

1 *March* 1851

MACREADY's farewell performance, as Macbeth, was given at Drury
Lane on 26 February. Dickens was present, and wrote next day to tell
him how as 'a mere boy' he had been one of his 'faithful and devoted
adherents in the pit', and how 'no light portion of my life arose before
me when the great vision to which I am beholden ... faded so nobly from
my bodily eyes last night'.

A banquet in his honour had been arranged for the following Saturday.
As a member of the organizing committee, Dickens had been active in
preparing for it for some weeks. Against Macready's advice, he and
Forster had decided to give it at the London Tavern, instead of somewhere larger, 'because', Macready noted, 'they get a better dinner and

---

[1] Talfourd, see p. 73 n., and Benjamin Bond Cabell, p. 67 n., were the other
two trustees.   [2] A ringmaster.

plenty of champagne'.[1] But it was not nearly big enough for the hundreds of admirers who wanted to hear Macready on his final public
appearance. About a week beforehand, therefore, it was decided to hold
it in the Hall of Commerce.

The Hall was not free for the organizers until the day of the banquet,
and no attempt was made at decoration except for two brilliant stars in
gas, with the ciphers 'V' and 'A' in the centre of the hall. Large as it
was, the tables were closely wedged together. Over 600 sat down to
dinner, and those on the outskirts who had some difficulty in hearing,
punctuated the proceedings of the evening with cries of 'order' and
'speak up'. The *Morning Post* complained that the stewards had been
less anxious about their duties than 'their own comforts and the convenience of their respective friends'.[2] And the *Illustrated London News*
made similar objections, that 'on a cold day, to take part in a cold
dinner, in an immense cold room . . . so lofty that the speakers were but
partly and tantalizingly heard, is a trial of no mean consideration. . . .
Yet the assembly came out like Mr. Dickens's *Mark Tapley* all the
stronger under their disadvantages.'[3]

When Macready appeared, accompanied by Sir Edward Bulwer
Lytton, the chairman, they were received with enthusiastic cheering.

A lively description of the proceedings was given, many years later, by
John Coleman, then a young actor.[4] On being told that all seats were
sold out, he had appealed to Dickens, who had sent him 'a characteristically courteous autograph letter enclosing a ticket'. He was fortunate
enough to be placed between Thackeray and the Prussian ambassador.

After the usual loyal toasts, the chairman proposed Macready's health
in a speech which, Coleman remarks, 'read famously in the papers next
day, but which sounded very badly that night'. Coleman went on:

> The speech of the night, however, was Macready's. When he arose a thunder
> of acclamation broke forth that shook tables and chairs, glasses, walls and
> windows, till verily, the latter seemed as if they were going to tumble about
> our ears. . . . His resonant sonorous voice rang round the place like the shrill
> blast of a clarion, and died away like the soft breathing of a lute ; but whether
> diminuendo or crescendo, every word was clearly articulated and made its
> mark. . . . As far as I could see through my own tears, there was not a single
> dry eye in the vicinity.

The next speaker was Dickens, who had to propose the health of the
chairman. He, too, said Coleman, 'was at his best . . . indeed his speech
was as florid as his costume. . . . He wore a blue dress-coat, faced with
silk and aflame with gorgeous brass buttons, a vest of black satin, with
a white satin collar, and a wonderfully embroidered shirt. When he got
up to speak, his long curly hair, his bright eyes, and his general aspect
of geniality and *bonhomie* presented a delightful picture. I made some
ingenuous remark upon the subject to Thackeray, who blandly rejoined,

---

[1] *Diaries*, ed. Toynbee, ii. 493.
[2] *Morning Post*, 3 May, p. 6. Other newspapers agreed.
[3] 8 Mar. 1851, p. 186.
[4] John Coleman, *Fifty Years of an Actor's Life*, 1904.

"Yes, the beggar is as beautiful as a butterfly, especially about the shirt-front".'

He was received with enthusiastic applause, and said:

GENTLEMEN, After all you have already heard, and have so rapturously received, I assure you that not even the warmth of your kind welcome would embolden me to hope to interest you if I had not full confidence in the subject I have to offer to your notice. [*Hear.*] But my reliance on the strength of this appeal to you is so strong that I am rather encouraged than daunted by the brightness of the track on which I have to throw my little shadow. [*Hear, and laughter.*]

Gentlemen, as it seems to me, there are three great requisites essential to the perfect realization of a scene so unusual and so splendid as that in which we are now assembled. The first, and I may say most difficult requisite, is a man possessing that strong hold on the general remembrance, that indisputable claim on the general regard and esteem, which is possessed by my dear and much valued friend, our guest. [*Cheers.*] The second requisite is the presence of a body of entertainers, a great multitude of hosts as cheerful and good humoured—under, I am sorry to say, some personal inconvenience [*cries of 'No, no!' and a laugh*]—as warm-hearted and as nobly in earnest, as those whom I have the privilege of addressing. The third, and certainly not the least of these requisites, is a president who, less by his social position which he may claim by inheritance, or by his fortune which may have been adventitiously won, and may again be accidentally lost [*a laugh*], than by his comprehensive genius, shall fitly represent the best part of him to whom honour is done, and the best part of those who unite in the doing of it. [*Hear, hear.*] Such a president I think we have found in our chairman of tonight [*loud cheers*], and I need scarcely add that our chairman's health is the toast I have to propose to you. [*Renewed cheering.*]

Many of those who now hear me were present, I dare say, at that memorable scene of Wednesday night last [*loud cheers*], when the great vision which had been a delight and a lesson, and, I dare say, very often to many of us—I know I can speak for myself—a support and a comfort, and which for many years has improved and charmed us, and to which we look back in elevated relief from the labours of our lives, faded from our sight for ever. [*Cheers.*] I will not stop to inquire whether our guest may or may not have looked forward through rather too long a period for us, to some remote and distant time when he might possibly bear some far-off likeness to a certain Spanish archbishop whom our old friend Gil Blas once served. [*A laugh.*] Nor will I stop to inquire whether it was a reasonable disposition in the audience of Wednesday night to seize upon the words:

> And I have bought
> Golden opinions from all sorts of people
> Which would be worn now in their newest gloss,
> Not cast aside so soon—[1]

but I will venture to intimate what has, in my own mind, mainly connected that occasion with the present. When I looked round on the vast assemblage, and observed the huge pit hushed into stillness on the rising of the curtain, and that mighty surging gallery, where men in their shirt sleeves had been striking out their arms like strong swimmers [*laughter*],—when I saw that boisterous human flood become still water in a moment, and remain so from the opening to the end of the play, it suggested to me something besides the trustworthiness of the English crowd, and the delusion under which those labour who are apt to disparage and malign it: it suggested to me, that in meeting here tonight, we undertook to represent something of the all-pervading feeling of that crowd through all its intermediate degrees, from the full-dressed lady, with her diamonds sparkling upon her breast in the proscenium-box, to the half-undressed gentleman [*great laughter*], who bides his time to take some refreshment in the back row of the gallery. [*Laughter.*] And I consider, gentlemen, that no one who could possibly be placed in this Chair could so well head that comprehensive representation, and could so well give the crowning grace to our festivities as one whose comprehensive genius has in his various works embraced them all [*hear, hear*], and who has in his dramatic genius, enchanted and enthralled them all at once. [*Cheers.*]

Gentlemen, it is not for me here to recall, after what you have heard this night, what I have seen and known in bygone times of Mr. Macready's management, and of the strong friendship of Sir Bulwer Lytton for him, of the association of his pen with his earliest successes, or of Mr. Macready's zealous and untiring services; but it may be permitted to me to say what, in any public mention of him I can never repress, that in the path we both tread I have uniformly found him from the first the most generous of men; quick to encourage, slow to disparage [*cheers*], ever anxious to assert the order of which he is so great an ornament; never condescending to shuffle it off, and leave it outside state rooms, as a Mussulman might leave his slippers outside a mosque. [*Cheers and laughter.*]

There is a popular prejudice, a kind of superstition, to the effect that authors are not a particularly united body, that they are not

---

[1] *Macbeth*, I. vii.

invariably and inseparably attached to each other. [*Laughter.*] I
am afraid I must concede half a grain or so of truth to that superstition; but this I know, that there can hardly be, that there hardly
can have been, among the followers of literature, a man of more
high standing further above those little grudging jealousies, which
do sometimes disparage its brightness, than Sir Edward Bulwer
Lytton. [*Cheers.*]

And I have the strongest reason just at present to bear my
testimony to his great consideration for those evils which are
sometimes unfortunately attendant upon it, though not on him.
For, in conjunction with some other gentlemen now present, I
have just embarked in a design with Sir Bulwer Lytton, to smooth
the rugged way of young labourers, both in literature and the fine
arts, and to soften, but by no eleemosynary means, the declining
years of meritorious age. [*Cheers.*] And if that project prosper, as
I hope it will, and as I know it ought, it will one day be an honour
in England where it is now a reproach [*hear*]; originating in his
sympathies, being brought into operation by his activity, and
endowed from the very cradle by his generosity.[1] [*Cheers.*] There
are many among you who will have each his own favourite reason
for drinking our chairman's health, resting his claim probably upon
some of his diversified successes. According to the nature of your
reading, some of you will connect him with prose, others will
connect him with poetry. One will connect him with comedy, and
another with the romantic passions of the stage, and his assertion
of worthy ambition and earnest struggles against

> those twin gaolers of the human heart
> Low birth and iron fortune.[2] [*Cheers.*]

Again, another's taste will lead him to the contemplation of Rienzi,
and the streets of Rome; another's to the rebuilt and repeopled
streets of Pompeii; another's to the touching history of the fireside
where the Caxton family learned how to discipline their natures
and tame their wild hopes down. [*Loud cheers.*] But however various

---

[1] The idea of a provident society for writers and artists was not a new one; it
had been in Lytton's mind for the past twenty years. When Dickens and his
amateur players visited Lytton at Knebworth in Nov. 1850, the old scheme
was brought to life under the name of the Guild of Literature and Art. Lytton
then set to work and wrote a comedy, called *Not So Bad As We Seem*, by acting
which the amateur players hoped to raise three or four thousand pounds before
the year was out. Their dramatic performances, this year and next, were an
entire success; but because of legal formalities there was a delay of seven years
before the Guild could begin to function; it never aroused any popular support;
and it was at last dissolved in 1897.

[2] Lytton, *Lady of Lyons*, III. ii, '. . . of the daring heart'.

their feelings and reasons may be, I am sure that with one accord each will help the other, and all will swell the greeting, with which I shall now propose to you 'The Health of our Chairman, Sir Edward Bulwer Lytton'. [*Loud and long continued cheering.*]

Lytton replied briefly. Other speakers included John Forster, who 'ladled out', said Coleman, 'or, I should say, roared forth', a sonnet written for the occasion by Tennyson. Among the last was Thackeray. He seemed likely to break down any minute from sheer nervousness. Nevertheless, he made a characteristically graceful elegiac speech, in which he said:

All triumphs must have an end—this triumph must end. These festivities cannot go on till morning—all must die out in time—we must go home. [*Cheers and laughter.*] Our entertainment is nearly over; I wish, however, it would come often again. The dinner was partly cold—it is now quite cold—it has gone the way of all dinners. . . . The bottles have been removed by Messrs. Bathe, the last toast has been said, and the last song sung; the lights will soon be put out, and when the lights are out, the man who has put them out will go out himself afterwards. [*Great laughter.*]

The point I wish to come to, is this. I wish to think of our friend Macready, who like Claude Melmotte is sighing for his Constance, and I shall not detain you longer, but propose to you the health of Mrs. Macready and family.

Macready replied briefly, Lord Dufferin proposed 'The Ladies', and the festivities came to an end. 'When all was over', wrote Coleman, Macready moved away 'through an avenue of overwrought men, excited and hysterical as women. . . . Many, who could not get near him, cried "God bless you, sir!" or "God bless you, Mac!" . . . That night, at the maturity of his powers and in the zenith of his fame, he passed for ever from the fierce light of public life.'

GENERAL THEATRICAL FUND

14 *April* 1851

MRS. DICKENS had been unwell earlier in the year, and about this time she visited the Spa at Malvern. Dickens spent much of his time with her there, but he was already deeply committed in the rehearsals of his amateur company for the first performance of *Not So Bad As We Seem*, to be played before the Queen. He was also in the middle of writing *David Copperfield*, and helping Miss Burdett Coutts with the administration of her Home for Fallen Women. Then, on 31 March, his father died. Great efforts were made to release him from his promise to take the Chair at the sixth annual dinner of the General Theatrical Fund. But the need was urgent; and, as no one else could be found at such short notice to take his place, Dickens consented to preside. Coming up by train from Malvern, he just had time to call at his home before leaving for the London Tavern. On his entry he was greeted with acclamation.

After dinner the chairman rose amid prolonged cheering, and said:

GENTLEMEN, in offering to you the loyal and always acceptable toast, 'The Queen', I have the pleasure of informing you that the Secretary has, this morning, received Her Majesty's usual annual donation of one hundred pounds to the funds of the Institution. [*Cheers.*] 'The Queen.'

Drunk with three times three, followed by 'God save the Queen'.

The chairman: Gentlemen, I am sure it will not be necessary for me in presenting to you the next toast, to remind any gentleman present—it being sufficiently known to all parties—of the great interest taken by the illustrious individual whose health I am about to propose, in all the arts and sciences, or the zealous co-operation which His Royal Highness Prince Albert has always shown to any measure devised for their encouragement. [*Cheers.*] At the present time, that is more particularly brought under the attention of the public through the exertions now being made on the suggestion of His Royal Highness, to open within a few days, an Exhibition of the world's progress in the arts and sciences in the magnificent and surprising Palace of Glass, which is, of itself, one of the most remarkable works of art of the age.[1] [*Cheers.*] 'His Royal Highness Prince Albert, Albert Prince of Wales, and the rest of the Royal Family.' [*Loud cheers.*]

Cheers were given, three times three, and a glee—All hail to the Prince.'

The chairman: Gentlemen, the next toast which I have to propose is one, in reference to which the gallant deeds of the members of the professions that are the subjects of it, speak sufficiently in themselves, and need no words of mine,—'The Army and Navy.' [*Cheers.*]

Representatives of the two services replied, and then the chairman rose to propose the toast of the evening, and said:

Gentlemen, I have so often had the gratification of bearing my testimony in this place to the usefulness of the excellent institution in whose behalf we are assembled, that I should be sensible of the disadvantage of having nothing new to say to you in proposing the toast you all anticipate, if I were not relieved by the conviction that nothing new needs to be said, inasmuch as its old grounds of appeal to you can neither be weakened or strengthened by any advocacy of mine.

Although the General Theatrical Fund, unlike some similar public institutions, is represented by no fabric of stone, or brick, or glass—

---

[1] Paxton's Crystal Palace was opened by the Queen on 1 May. The whole project had originated with Prince Albert, who was President of the Commissioners for the Exhibition.

like that wonderful achievement of my ingenious friend **Mr. Paxton**, of which the great demerit, as we learn from the best authorities, is, that it ought to have fallen down before it was quite built, and would by no means consent to do it. [*Cheers and laughter.*] Although, I say, the General Theatrical Fund is represented by no great architectural edifice, it is nevertheless as plain a fact, rests upon as solid a foundation, and carries as erect a front as any building in the world. [*Cheers.*] And the best that its exponent, standing in this place, can do, is to point it out to all beholders, saying simply, 'There it is! Judge of it for yourselves.' [*Cheers.*]

But, gentlemen, though there may be no necessity for me to state what the General Theatrical Fund *is*, it may be desirable (with reference to that portion of the present company who have hitherto had but a limited acquaintance with it), that I should state what it is *not*.[1] It is not a theatrical association whose benefits are confined to a small body of actors, while its claims to public support are uniformly preferred in the name of the whole histrionic art. [*Cheers.*] It is not a theatrical association adapted to a state of things entirely past and gone, and no more a feature of the present time than groves of highwaymen hanging in chains on Hounslow Heath, or strings of packhorses between London and Birmingham. [*Cheers and laughter.*] It is not a rich old gentleman, with the gout in his vitals, brushed up once a year to look as vigorous as possible, and taken out for a public airing by the few survivors of a large family of nephews and nieces, who keep him laid up in lavender all the rest of the year as a mighty delicate old gentleman: then ask his poor relations, whom they lock out with a double turn of the street door key, why they don't come in and enjoy his money? [*Cheers and laughter.*] It is not a theatrical association, which says to the poor actor, 'You have only to strut and fret your hour, for so many consecutive nights and for so many seasons, on this stage—whereon it is impossible you ever can set foot; you have only to declaim for so many consecutive nights, in English—here, upon these boards where the English tongue is never heard; you have only to force yourself between these bars (of music), and to make your way—you, an unwieldy Swan of Avon, into this aviary of singing birds—you have only to do this, and you shall come into your share of the advantages of the fund which was raised from the public, in the name, and for the love, of your all-embracing art.' [*Cheers.*]

No, gentlemen, if there be any such funds, this Fund is not of that kind. [*Cheers.*] This Fund is a theatrical association, addressed to the means, and adapted to the wants—and sore and dire those

[1] Referring, in what follows, to the Covent Garden and Drury Lane Funds; see p. 73.

often are—of the whole theatrical profession throughout England. It is a society in which the word 'exclusiveness' is unknown. [*Cheers.*] It is a society which says to the actor, 'You may be the Brigand, or the Hamlet, or the Ghost, or the Court Physician, or the King's whole army [*cheers and laughter*]; you may do the light business, or the heavy business, or the comic business, or the serious business, or the eccentric business; you may be the captain who courts the young lady, whose guardian unaccountably persists in dressing himself a hundred years behind the time [*laughter*]; or you may be the lady's young brother, in white kid gloves and trousers, whose position in the family would appear to be to listen to all the female members of it when they sing, and to shake hands with them between all the verses [*laughter*]; or you may be the Baron who gives the *fête*, and who sits on the sofa under the canopy, with the Baroness, to behold the *fête*; or you may be the peasant who swells the drinking chorus at the *fête*, and who may usually be observed to turn his glass upside-down immediately before drinking the Baron's health [*laughter*]; or you may be the Clown who takes away the door-step of the house where there's a dinner party; or you may be the first stout gentleman who issues forth out of that house, on the false alarm of fire, and precipitates himself into the area [*great laughter*]; or you may be a Fairy, residing for ever in a revolving Star, in the Regions of Pleasure, or the Palace of Delight [*cheers and laughter*]; or you may even be a Witch in *Macbeth*, bearing a marvellous resemblance to the Malcolm or Donaldbain of the previous scenes with his wig hind-side before. [*Great laughter.*] But, be you what you may; be your path in the profession never so high or never so humble, this institution addresses *you*, and offers you the means of doing good to yourself, and doing good to other people.' [*Loud cheers.*]

Nor let it be forgotten, gentlemen, that the General Theatrical Fund is essentially a Provident Institution. [*Cheers.*] Its members are of a class whose earnings are, at the best, precarious; and they are required to lay by, out of their weekly salary, when they get it, a certain small weekly sum. This they do through every difficulty, with a constancy that cannot be too much admired; and the first effect of the institution on them, is, to engender a habit of forethought and self-denial. [*Cheers.*] By becoming a member of this society the actor is placing himself in a position to secure his own right at no man's wrong; and when in old age or times of distress he makes his claim to it, he will be entitled to say, 'I do not compromise my independence herein; I do not disgrace my children; I am neither a beggar nor a suppliant; I come to reap the harvest from the seed which I sowed long ago.' [*Cheers.*] Therefore it is, gentlemen, that in asking you to support this Institution, I never will hold out to you the inducement, that you are performing an act of charity in the common acceptation of the word. Of all the abuses of that much abused term, none have so raised my indignation as some that I have heard in this room. [*Hear, hear.*] If you help this Fund you will not be performing an act of charity, but you will be helping those who help themselves, and you will be coming to the aid of men who put their own shoulders to the wheel of their sunken carriage, and did not stand idly by while it sank deeper in the mire. [*Cheers.*] If you help this Fund you will not be performing an act of charity, but you will do an act of Christian kindness, benevolence, encouragement. You will do an act of justice—you will do an act of gratitude. But I will not so wrong a body of men struggling so manfully for independence, as to solicit you to perform, in their behalf, an act of charity. [*Cheers.*]

Gentlemen, I have used the term 'gratitude'. Let any of us look back upon his past life, and say whether he owes no gratitude to the actor's art! Not because it is often exercised in the midst of sickness, poverty, and misfortune,—other arts, God knows, are liable to the like distresses! Not because the actor sometimes comes from scenes of affliction and misfortune—even from death itself—to play his part before us; all men must do that violence to their feelings, in passing on to the fulfilment of their duties in the great strife and fight of life. But because in the relief afforded to us by the actor's art, we always find some reflection, humorous or pathetic, sombre or grotesque, of all the best things that we feel and know. If any man were to tell me that he owed no great acknowledgement to the stage, I would only ask him the one question, whether he remembered his first play?[1] [*Cheers.*]

Oh, Gentlemen, if you can but carry back your thoughts to that night, and think a little of the bright and harmless world it opened to your view, full well assured am I that we shall hear of it expressively from Mr. Cullenford, when he comes to read out the donations by and by!

Gentlemen, this is the sixth year the members of this society have met together in this room. This is the sixth time your child

---

[1] Dickens's own earliest recollections went back to the theatre at Chatham, or 'Dullborough Town' of the *Uncommercial Traveller*, where 'Richard the Third ... had first appeared to me ... and had made my heart leap with terror by backing up against the stage-box in which I was posted, while struggling for life against the virtuous Richmond. ... Many wondrous secrets of Nature had I come to the knowledge of in that sanctuary; of which not the least terrific were, that the witches in Macbeth bore an awful resemblance to the Thanes and other proper inhabitants of Scotland; and that the good king Duncan couldn't rest in his grave, but was constantly coming out of it and calling himself somebody else.'

has been brought down and introduced to the company after dinner. [*Cheers and laughter.*] His nurse, a very worthy person of the name of Buckstone [*laughter*], with excellent characters from several places [*laughter*], is here, and will presently speak to you regarding the health of the child; and will, I have no doubt, be able to tell you that its chest is perfectly sound [*laughter*], and its general health in the best condition. [*Cheers.*] Long may it continue so—long may it thrive and grow! Long may we meet here to congratulate each other on its increased and increasing prosperity [*cheers*], and longer than the line of Banquo may the line of figures be, in which its patriotic share in the National Debt shall be stated a hundred years hence, in the account books of the Governor and Company of the Bank of England! [*Loud cheers.*] I beg to give you, 'Prosperity to the General Theatrical Fund!' [*Great cheering.*]

In reply Buckstone praised and thanked Dickens for his services to the fund; and, in a general report on the society, announced that it was intended to apply for a royal charter.

He was followed by John Forster,[1] who had to propose the health of the chairman. Already, half an hour before Dickens had risen to speak, he had had a far heavier responsibility thrust upon him, on being called out of the room to receive the news of the death of Dickens's youngest child. He described, in the *Life*, how 'it was the servant from Devonshire-terrace to tell me that his child Dora was suddenly dead.... My decision had to be formed at once, and I satisfied myself that it would be best to permit his part of the proceedings to close before the truth was told to him. But as he went on, after the sentences I have quoted, to speak of actors having to come from scenes of sickness ... aye, even of death itself, to play their parts before us, my part was very difficult. "Yet how often is it with all of us", he proceeded to say, and I remember to this hour with what anguish I listened to the words ... "how often is it with all of us, that in our several spheres we have to do violence to our feelings, and to hide our hearts in carrying on this fight of life, if we would bravely discharge in it our duties and responsibilities."[2]

Forster paid an eloquent and sincere tribute to Dickens as a writer and moralist, mentioning that he knew he was present 'at great personal sacrifice, which few men would have ventured to make'. In speaking of

---

[1] John Forster (1812–76), literary and dramatic editor of the *Examiner*, critic and historian; he was Dickens's closest friend, constant literary adviser, and most regular correspondent; the author of the *Life of Charles Dickens*, 1872–4, which in spite of certain limitations is still indispensable. He was a man of great ability, strong good sense, and tremendous energy; and though he is now most often thought of in connexion with Dickens, he performed similar services to other writers, and had great influence over them. Sometimes abrupt and pompous in manner, he could be no less kind and patient with his friends. He bequeathed his library and collection of manuscripts, including most of those of Dickens's novels, to the Department of Science and Art, now in the Victoria and Albert Museum. [2] F, VI. vi.

his works he declared that 'In whatever direction Mr. Dickens pursued his literary path, his practical philanthropy was ever palpable.' Considerable confusion was caused when someone at the end of the hall cried out 'Humbug!'[1] Forster, however, continued unperturbed, and finished his speech in his usual grandiloquent manner.

In reply the chairman begged to be allowed to offer them his deepest thanks for the manner in which the last toast had been responded to. He deeply felt the honour conferred upon him, having attended the meeting as a matter of duty, though placed from peculiar circumstances in a highly painful and difficult position. If his services were of any value to the institution, he said, he could assure its members that those services were always freely and heartily at their disposal. [*Cheers.*] He would say no more upon that subject, but proceed to a toast which he doubted not would be warmly received and responded to.

He had always taken the highest interest in the prosperity of the Drama, because he believed that a noble Drama tended to purify the human heart, and was a most important agent in the work of education and civilization. [*Cheers.*] He would not dismiss the hope that the British Drama would ultimately 'look up', after a pretty long contemplation of its feet; because he could not believe that any art which so appealed to the various passions and affections of human nature could become extinct. [*Cheers.*] A love of the Drama in some shape was implanted in the breasts of all people. When the officers of Captain Cook's ships, who had left their children enacting mimic plays in this country, arrived in the South Sea Islands, they found the untutored natives doing the same beneath the shadow of their broad-leaved trees. It constituted one of the distinctions which separated man from the brute creation, and he should continue in that belief until he heard of the monkeys producing a play, or the elephants coming out in a good jog-trot, see-saw comedy. [*Laughter.*]

It had often been his misfortune to hear the Drama decried by people of the best intentions because of its abuses. [*Hear, hear.*] No doubt the Drama had its abuses like other institutions, but so far from that being a reason why they should decry it, it was a reason why they should endeavour to improve and elevate it. [*Cheers.*] In some shape you would always have it; and, depend upon it, if you would not have it at its best, with your own help and consent, you would have it at its worst in your own despite. Perhaps the one reason why the Drama did not hold so good a position in this country as it ought to do, was to be found in the fact that, up to a comparatively recent period, English legislation had drearily

[1] *Daily News*, 15 Apr., p. 6.

discouraged it, and its professors had not been looked upon with the respect to which they were justly entitled. [*Cheers.*] But notwithstanding all discouragement, he hoped that it could, and believed that it would, be restored to its proper position among the Arts; and in no way could they better assist the endeavour to raise it, than by extending their support and assistance to those who had always shown their anxiety to maintain the respectability and honour of the Dramatic Profession. [*Cheers.*]

In giving them the toast of 'The Drama', he was sure they would be gratified by his connecting it with the name of a gentleman who had long been honourably distinguished for the manner in which he conducted himself with regard to it, and who had in his own person set a worthy example of probity, generosity and honour. Under all difficulties with which he had been surrounded, Mr. Webster had never deserted his post. [*Cheers.*] He had always maintained the confidence of all who had placed their trust in him, and had never made any engagement which he had not faithfully performed. As Mr. Webster had hitherto shared the fortunes of the Drama, when the sun did not altogether shine upon it, so he trusted he might yet partake of its prosperity in fairer and brighter weather; and he was sure that they would all feel with him, that they were only rendering to that gentleman a fitting tribute in drinking 'The Drama and Mr. Webster'. [*Loud cheers.*]

Webster replied briefly.

The chairman then said that it was now his duty to remind them of the importance to their institution of a body of gentlemen whose healths he was to have the pleasure of proposing; and, in discharging that duty, he might perhaps be allowed to relate a little theatrical anecdote, which was a favourite story of a very dear friend of his, newly lost to the stage.[1]

At a certain country theatre one night, when the play was *The Castle Spectre*, the gentleman who was to enact the part of Reginald was taken ill. Upon which the manager requested a certain other gentleman in the company—who had the peculiar power sometimes to be found, as he (the chairman) believed, in a country theatre, of going on for any part without knowing anything about it, and when anyone addressed him in the play, of replying in any terms that happened to occur to him [*laughter*],—requested this gentleman to fill the gap. He immediately dressed for the purpose, but on coming on the stage behind the act drop, thought it judicious to say, 'Stop a bit, what's it about?' [*Laughter.*] 'Oh!' said the

---

[1] W. C. Macready; see Lady Pollock, *Macready as I Knew Him*, 1884, pp. 18–20. Dickens used the story again, see p. 266.

other actors, 'there's nothing in it. You have been shut up in a dungeon on bread and water for fifteen years, and all that time you have never seen your daughter.' 'All right,' said Reginald; 'Ring up!' But on the act-drop being 'rung up' accordingly, he not only paralysed the audience with the astounding information that he had been shut up in that dungeon for fifteen years, without tasting a morsel of food during the whole of that time, but further stated as a remarkable effect of this lowering treatment, 'that he had become so weak as to be quite unable to drag his hind legs after him'. [*Great laughter.*]

Now, without entering into any details about numbers of years, lest he should involve himself in a similar confusion, he (the chairman) rejoiced to hail, sitting at that table near him, a gentleman whom they all undoubtedly had for many years associated with the Romantic Drama in its most picturesque and captivating forms, and who had never grown older during the whole of that time—Mr. James Wallack.[1] [*Loud cheering.*] Notwithstanding the late severe illness of his friend, Mr. Wallack, he rejoiced to see him there, with his gallant figure, his winning manner, and his buoyant spirits, all alike unimpaired, and heartily congratulated the Fund on having him for one of their vice-presidents. He begged to give them 'The Vice-Presidents of the Institution and Mr. James Wallack'. [*Cheers.*]

Wallack replied briefly.

The Chairman then said that the next toast he had to give was the Professional Ladies and Gentlemen who had delighted them with their exertions that evening. After what they had heard and witnessed he felt sure that he need do no more to recommend that toast to them, than to remind them that the whole of those Ladies and Gentlemen gave their assistance, not only gratuitously, but cheerfully, to aid the cause which they had met to promote, and he was sure that they wished for no greater reward than the knowledge that they had been instrumental in promoting the prosperity of the General Theatrical Fund. [*Loud cheers; followed by a Madrigal.*]

The Chairman said that he had now come to the last toast of the evening. There was a story told of an Eastern potentate, that when any intelligence of mischief having occurred was brought to him, he always used to exclaim, 'Who is she?'—invariably anticipating that it must be caused by a woman. In this country they had a somewhat better application of the same idea, for whenever there

[1] James William Wallack (1791?–1864), actor and manager in England and America.

was a cause of benevolence to be served, they had only to say 'Where is she?' and the answer was sure to be 'She is here.'[1] [*Loud cheers.*] The Drama was full of beautiful specimens of woman's love and woman's wit, but without stopping to draw comparisons between the characters of Desdemona, Juliet, or other interesting creatures of the poet's brain, he would conclude by giving them, 'The Ladies'.

Helped by Mark Lemon, Forster broke the news of his child's death to their friend. Dickens wrote to his wife next morning, and Forster went down to Malvern to bring her back to London. 'He did not break down', wrote his daughter Mary, 'until an evening or two after her death, some beautiful flowers were sent', and he 'was about to take them upstairs and place them on the little dead baby, when he suddenly gave way completely'.[2] Dickens wrote to Miss Burdett Coutts on the 17th, 'Our poor little Dora!—I had just been playing with her and went to preside at a Public Dinner at which I was pledged. Before it was over—even before they sang the Grace—she was dead. I left her well and gay.'

METROPOLITAN SANITARY ASSOCIATION
10 *May* 1851

THE first anniversary banquet of the Metropolitan Sanitary Association was held at Gore House, Kensington; it had once been well known to Dickens as the home of Lady Blessington, but was now opened for the exhibition year by M. Soyer, the great chef, as a Universal Symposium. The banquet was laid out in the 'baronial hall', newly erected in the grounds, which is said to have been 'elegantly fitted up for the occasion':

> Behind the chairman was a trophy emblematical of the grand banquet supplied by M. Soyer, at York, to His Royal Highness Prince Albert .... Chinese lanterns, suspended from the ceiling, diffused a mellow and pleasant light over the brilliant pageant below, and the tables were decorated with a profusion of plate, rare exotics in vases, and silvered mirror globes which multiplied and reflected the brilliant scene. A military band was in attendance, but concealed from the view of the spectators, and the gallery at the end of the hall was filled with ladies.[3]

The Earl of Carlisle, recently appointed Chancellor of the Duchy of Lancaster, and formerly Chief Commissioner of Woods and Forests, presided as chairman.[4] On conclusion of the dinner, there were the usual

---

[1] Dickens had told this story before, see p. 64.
[2] 'Charles Dickens at Home, by His Eldest Daughter', *Cornhill*, Jan. 1885, N.S. iv. 38.   [3] *Morning Herald*, 12 May, p. 6.
[4] George William Frederick Howard (1802–64), 7th Earl of Carlisle 1848, previously known by courtesy title of Lord Morpeth; M.P. 1836–41 and 1846–8; introduced Public Health Act 1848; friend of Dickens; Lord Lieutenant of Ireland 1855–8 and 1859–64.

loyal toasts. Then, in proposing 'The Church', the chairman regretted the unavoidable absence of the Bishop of London, Charles James Blomfield: recalling that it was at his request, in the House of Lords, in 1839, that the Poor Law Commissioners were instructed to extend their inquiries to the whole kingdom, when the actual principle of the responsibility of the Government for public health was first acknowledged. His place was taken by the Bishop of Ripon.

In rising to propose the toast of the evening, the chairman was received with great enthusiasm. Although it was so commonplace as to pass without comment at nearly all such public dinners, the speakers were well aware of the contrast between their aims and the splendour of their surroundings. The Earl of Carlisle reminded his hearers that the nearby Crystal Palace was 'itself a shrine of labour. . . . But, while we gaze on the large area of its vast extent, on the wondrous results of its harmonious and completed combinations . . . let us not refrain from tracing them back to that crowded workshop, that damp cellar, and that stifling garret.'

Lord Robert Grosvenor[1] replied. He congratulated the association on all it had already achieved, but warned its members in the words of Lord Castlereagh, that 'we should not halloo until we are out of the wood'. Viscount Ebrington responded to the toast of 'The Sanitary Reformers in Parliament'; and then Dickens rose to propose 'The Board of Health', and said:

M Y Lord and Gentlemen, I am placed in that peculiarly advantageous position for speaking, that I must either turn from the chairman or from the company. But, as the company includes that best and brightest part of all company, whose presence (I presume) we are supposed not to recognise on these occasions as we never address them—and, as I have abundant experience of the innate courtesy and politeness of my noble friend—I shall take the course which I am sure will be most agreeable to him, and turn to this assembly in general. Indeed, gentlemen, I have but a few words to say, either on the needfulness of Sanitary Reform, or on the consequent usefulness of the Metropolitan Sanitary Association.

That no one can estimate the amount of mischief which is grown in dirt; that no one can say, here it stops, or there it stops, either in its physical or its moral results, when both begin in the cradle and are not at rest in the obscene grave [*hear, hear*], is now as certain as it is that the air from Gin Lane will be carried, when the wind is Easterly, into May Fair, and that if you once have a vigorous pestilence raging furiously in Saint Giles's, no mortal list of Lady Patronesses can keep it out of Almack's. [*Hear, hear.*]

Twelve or fifteen years ago, some of the first valuable reports

---

[1] Lord Robert Grosvenor (1801–63), later 1st Baron Ebury; M.P. for Middlesex, whig, associate of Lord Ashley.

of Mr. Chadwick[1] and of Dr. Southwood Smith[2] strengthening and much enlarging my previous imperfect knowledge of this truth, made me, in my sphere, earnest in the Sanitary Cause. And I can honestly declare tonight, that all the use I have since made of my eyes—or nose [*laughter*]—that all the information I have since been able to acquire through any of my senses, has strengthened me in the conviction that Searching Sanitary Reform must precede all other social remedies [*cheers*], and that even Education and Religion can do nothing where they are most needed, until the way is paved for their ministrations by Cleanliness and Decency. [*Hear.*] Am I singular in this opinion? You will remember the speech made this night by the Right Reverend Prelate, which no true Sanitary Reformer can have heard without emotion. [*Hear, hear.*] What avails it to send a Missionary to me, a miserable man or woman living in a fœtid Court where every sense bestowed upon me for my delight becomes a torment, and every minute of my life is new mire added to the heap under which I lie degraded? To what natural feeling within me is he to address himself? What ancient chord within me can he hope to touch? Is it my remembrance of my children? It is a remembrance of distortion and decay, scrofula and fever? Would he address himself to my hopes of immortality? I am so surrounded by material filth that my Soul can not rise to the contemplation of an immaterial existence! Or, if I be a miserable child, born and nurtured in the same wretched place, and tempted, in these better times, to the Ragged School, what can the few hours' teaching that I get there do for me, against the noxious, constant, ever-renewed lesson of my whole existence. [*Hear, hear.*] But, give me my first glimpse of Heaven through a little of its light and air —give me water—help me to be clean—lighten this heavy atmosphere in which my spirit droops and I become the indifferent and callous creature that you see me—gently and kindly take the body of my dead relation out of the small room where I grow to be so familiar with the awful change that even *its* sanctity is lost to me— and, Teacher, then I'll hear, you know how willingly, of Him whose thoughts were so much with the Poor, and who had compassion for all human sorrow! [*Applause.*]

I am now, gentlemen, to propose to you as a toast a public Body without whose efficient aid this preparation so much to be desired, for Christianity at home, cannot be effected; and, by whom, if we

---

[1] Edwin Chadwick (1800–90), one of the commissioners to the General Board of Health 1848–54; had been secretary to the Poor Law Commissioners 1834– 46; the first sanitary commission had been appointed at his instigation, 1839; strong advocate of centralization. Continued active career as a reformer after official retirement in 1854. Referred to, at his own request, in *American Notes*, ch. xviii. [2] See p. 42 n.

earnestly desire such preparation, we must stand, giving them all the support it is in our power to render. I mean, the Board of Health. We have a transparent instance very near at hand of the mysterious arrangement that no great thing can possibly be done without a certain amount of nonsense being talked about it in the way of objection. Much as our respected friend the Ex-unprotected Female[1] was confounded, at that family dinner party where we last heard of her, by some alarming conversation respecting the sparrows in Mr. Paxton's gutters [*cheers*], and the casks of gunpowder sent to the Great Exposition under the semblance of coffee, so, I dare say, it has been the fortune of most of us to hear the Board of Health discussed in various congenial circles. I have never been able to make out, distinctly, more than two objections to it; the first is expressed in a long word which I seem to have heard pronounced with a sort of violent relish on two or three previous occasions—*Centralization.*

Now, gentlemen, in the year before last, in the time of the cholera, you had an excellent opportunity of judging between this Centralization on the one hand, and what I may be permitted to call Vestrylization [*laughter*] on the other.[2] You may recollect the Reports of the Board of Health on the subject of cholera, and you may recollect the Reports of the discussions on the same subject at some Vestry Meetings. [*Laughter.*] I have the honor—of which I am very sensible—to be one of the constituent body of the amazing Vestry of Marylebone [*laughter*]; and if you chance to remember (as you very likely do) what the Board of Health *did*, in Glasgow and other places, and what my vestry *said*, you will probably agree with me that between this so-called Centralization, and this Vestrylization, the former is by far the best thing to stand by in an emergency. My vestry even took the high ground of denying the existence of cholera in any unusual degree. [*Laughter.*] And though that denial had no greater effect upon the disease than my vestry's denial of the existence of Jacob's Island had upon the Earth about Bermondsey, the circumstance may be suggestive to you in considering what Vestrylization is, when a few noisy little landlords interested in the maintenance of abuses, struggle to the foremost ranks; and what the so-called Centralization is when it is a combination of active business habits, sound medical knowledge, and a zealous sympathy with the sufferings of the people.

But gentlemen there is, as I have said, another objection to the Board of Health. It is conveyed in the shorter and less alarming

---

[1] *Punch*, 3 May 1851, xx. 177–8, 'Scenes from The Life of An (Ex) Unprotected Female'.

[2] Cf. pp. 108–10.

word—*delay*.[1] Now, I need not suggest to you that it would surely be unreasonable to object to a first-rate chronometer that it wouldn't go—when its owner wouldn't wind it up. Yet I cannot help thinking, I must plainly avow, that the Board of Health is in the parallel position of being excellently adapted for going, and being very willing and anxious to go, but not being able to go, because its lawful master has fallen into a gentle slumber, and forgotten to set it a-going.[1] As a component particle of this association which my Noble friend in the chair considers useful as a gentle stimulus to governments, I must take leave to say that I do not, and can not, consider the Board of Health responsible for delay in sanitary reforms. Lord Robert Grosvenor referred just now to Lord Castlereagh's favourite adage, that you must never hallo until you are out of the Wood. It occurred to me that with a very slight addition that would be an excellent adage for all Sanitary Reformers: to wit, that you must never hallo until you are out of the Woods—and Forests. [*Laughter.*]

If I may venture to make the remark under the presiding of my Noble friend whom we are all glad to see, and would all have been so happy to retain, in those leafy regions, I would say that since the remote period when 'the noble Savage' ran wild there, some other Nobles—not Savages by any means, but gentlemen of high accomplishments and worth—have gone a little wild in the same districts and wandered rather more languidly out of the direct path than is quite good for the public. You will of course understand that in saying this, I merely express my own individual misgivings. But I will tell you why I entertain them. Considering the Report of the Board of Health on Intra-mural Interments[2] to be one of the most remarkable social documents ever issued under any Government, and an honour to the country and the time, I cannot but believe that the Board of Health would have advanced a little quicker in the carrying-out of the measure founded upon it but for some stoppage in the way above them which we don't clearly see.

[1] Dickens's manuscript, from which the text is given (see 'Notes on Text and Sources', p. 430), was written for his brother-in-law, Henry Austin, to whom it was sent on the 18 May. This passage, [1] . . . [1] was added later on the back of the page, after Dickens wrote to Austin on 21 May, 'I remember that I have omitted a little point about a chronometer. It lies in two sentences. If you will send me back the speech at any time, I will put them in.' A second note followed, the same evening, to say: 'I send you the Speech with the little Insertion made.' M.

[2] *Report on a General Scheme for Extra-mural Sepulture*, 1850. Austin had sent it to him as soon as it appeared, Dickens replying immediately, 27 Feb. 1850: 'Many thanks for the Report, which is extraordinarily interesting. I began to read it last night, in bed—and dreamed of putrefaction generally.' M. It was responsible for much in *Bleak House*.

Remembering the vigor and perspicuity with which they have indicated to us the chief Sanitary evils it is essential to remove, I cannot hold them responsible for the prolonged existence of those evils. As with omission, so with commission. Remembering how clearly they showed us the advantages of a continuous supply of soft water, and how they pointed out to us an abundant source of supply, I cannot cast upon them the blame of a measure which gives us only hard water. Remembering how they dwelt upon the necessity of a combination of water-works, I cannot charge them with the injury of perpetuated separation. Remembering how they demonstrated to us that disease *must* lurk in houses founded over cesspools or built upon foundations saturated with cesspool matter, I cannot hold them responsible for a system of drainage which does not remove these ills. And therefore, gentlemen, both for the good they have done, and for the good they may be fairly assumed to have had the will to do, but not the power, I commend the Board of Health to you as especially deserving and requiring the sympathy, the encouragement, and the support of the Metropolitan Sanitary Association.

I shall beg, in conclusion, to couple with the toast the name of a Noble Lord, one of its members, whose Earnestness in all good works no man can doubt, and who always has the courage to face the worst and commonest of all cants; that is to say, the cant about the cant of philanthropy and benevolence. I propose to you Lord Ashley and the Board of Health.

Lord Ashley, who was one of its members, replied, saying that he was pleased by the mention of the Board of Health, because he thought that generally speaking too little attention was paid to its exertions. He went on to speak of the close association between the moral, political, and social condition of the people.

At the second anniversary banquet, next year, Dickens was unable to attend. In proposing 'The Literary Supporters of Sanitary Reform', Chadwick coupled the toast with the names of both Dickens and F. O. Ward, whom he praised for 'the power and independence with which they had attacked the vested interests opposed to sanitary progress',[1] to which Ward replied.

[1] *Daily News*, 5 June 1852, p. 3.

GARDENERS' BENEVOLENT INSTITUTION

9 *June* 1851

THE dinner was held at the London Coffee House, with Joseph Paxton[1] in the Chair. There was a larger assembly than the Gardeners had ever had before, including, of the Dickens circle, Mark Lemon, Douglas Jerrold and W. H. Wills. The dinner, said the *Gardeners' Chronicle*, was 'all that could be desired . . . and the dessert . . . was magnificent'.

Douglas Jerrold proposed the health of the president, the Duke of Devonshire, and Paxton gave the toast of the evening. Dickens then rose to propose the health of the chairman.

HE could assure them, he said, that when he entered that room he had no idea of addressing them, but a member of the committee had asked him to propose the toast in a manner which evinced that he thought he required no *forcing* [*laughter*], and that he only required to be planted in that soil to flower immediately. [*Laughter.*] Though he was no gardener himself, he knew well and appreciated the repose and delight to be found in gardening, and amongst its productions. Probably there was no feeling in the human mind stronger than the love of gardening. The prisoner in his dismal cell would endeavour to raise a flower from the chinks in the floor of his dungeon; the invalid or lodger in the garret took delight in the pot of flowers on the parapet, or endeavoured to cultivate his scarlet runners in communication with the garret of his neighbour over the way; the miniature garden was one of the greatest amusements of childhood; and, again, gardening was one of the last and best pleasures of the aged. [*Cheers.*]

It was a holy duty in foreign countries to decorate the graves of the dead with flowers, and here, too, the resting-places of those who had passed away from us would soon be gardens. [*Cheers.*] Indeed, from that old time when the Lord walked in the garden in the cool of the evening, down to the day when a Poet Laureate sang

> Trust me, Clara Vere de Vere,
>   From yon blue heavens above us bent
> The gardener Adam and his wife
>   Smile at the claims of long descent,[2]

at all times and in all ages, gardens were among the objects of the greatest interest to mankind. [*Loud cheers.*] There might be a few,

---

[1] Joseph Paxton (1801–65), gardener and architect; manager of Chatsworth estate for the Duke of Devonshire; architect of Crystal Palace; railway director and speculator; had been closely associated with Dickens in the foundation of the *Daily News*; knighted, 23 Oct. 1851.

[2] Tennyson, 'Lady Clara Vere de Vere'.

but he believed they were but a few, who took no interest in the products of gardening, except perhaps in London Pride, or a certain degenerate kind of 'Stock', which was apt to grow hereabouts, cultivated by a species of frozen-out gardeners whom no thaw can ever penetrate [*hear, and laughter*]; except these, the gardeners' art had contributed to the delight of all men in their time. That there ought to be a Benevolent Provident Institution for gardeners was in the fitness of things, and that such an institution ought to flourish, and did flourish, was still more so.

He had risen to propose to you the health of a gentleman who was a great gardener, and not only a great gardener, but a great man [*cheers*], the growth of a fine Saxon root cultivated up with a power of intellect that was at this time the talk of the civilized world—he alluded, of course, to his friend, the chairman of the day. [*Laughter, and much cheering.*] He had taken occasion to say at a public assembly hard by, a month or two ago, in speaking of the wonderful building Mr. Paxton had designed for the Great Exhibition in Hyde Park, that it ought to have fallen down, but that it refused to do so. We were told that the glass ought to have been all broken, the gutters all choked up, and the building flooded, and that the roof and sides ought to have been blown away; in short, that everything ought to have done what everything obstinately persisted in not doing. Earth, air, fire and water all appear to have conspired together in Mr. Paxton's favour—all had conspired to one result, which, when the present generation was in dust, would be an enduring temple to his honour, and to the energy, the talent, and the resources of Englishmen.[1] [*Applause.*]

'But', said a gentleman to him the other day, 'no doubt Mr. Paxton is a great man, but there is one objection to him that you can never get over, that is, he is a gardener'. Now, that was their case tonight, that he was a gardener [*cheers*], and they were extremely proud of it. This was a great age, with all its faults, when a man by the power of his own genius and good sense could scale such a daring height as Mr. Paxton had reached, and composedly place his form on the top. This was a great age, when a man impressed with a useful idea, could carry out his project without being imprisoned, or thumb-screwed or persecuted in any form. [*Applause.*]

I can well understand, Dickens continued, that you, to whom the genius, the intelligence, the industry, and the achievements of our friend are well known, should be anxious to do him honour by placing him in the position he occupies tonight; and I assure you, you have conferred great gratification on one of his friends, in

[1] Destroyed by fire, at Sydenham, 30 Nov. 1936.

permitting him to have the opportunity of proposing his health, which that friend now does most cordially, and with all the honours. [*Applause.*]

Among the remaining toasts was 'The Literature of the Country, and Mr. Charles Dickens', proposed by the chairman, to which Dickens briefly returned thanks.

NEWSVENDORS' BENEVOLENT INSTITUTION

27 *January* 1852

THE second anniversary dinner of the institution was held at the Albion Tavern once again, with John Forster[1] in the Chair. Several of the Dickens circle were present, including John Leech, Mark Lemon, Charles Knight, Peter Cunningham, Bradbury and Evans, and Charles Whiting. After Forster had proposed the toast of the evening, and one of the officers of the society had replied, Dickens rose to give the health of the chairman.

HE approached the next task, he said, with much the same feelings as an ex-Lord Mayor contemplated a Lord Mayor in full glory, as he could not but remember that he had once occupied the exceedingly dignified, but, if his memory served him, somewhat uncomfortable post of honour, the Chair. He might be allowed, however, to congratulate the newsvendors present on the happy accident of their pursuing their avocations in the capital of a country which gave its name to the house in which they were then assembled rather than in the capital of a neighbouring country which should be nameless.[2] He had been told, that in the very improbable event of any one of the tightly muzzled newspapers opening its lips by any extraordinary effort, it was the intention of the paternal Government there immediately to hamstring all the newsmen. [*Cheers and laughter.*] It was felt, as he had learnt on the best authority, that in having been every day the dispensers of free speech, they had rendered themselves obnoxious to the 'cause of order', and that 'perfect liberty and freedom' (by which was to be understood, of course, perfect liberty to destroy liberty) could not possibly exist as long as the newsvendors continued to run about.

Not being so embarrassed themselves, however, he might perhaps be permitted to congratulate them on three grounds. In the first place, on the reappearance of their society in public. He thought

[1] See p. 123 n.
[2] The freedom of the French press had been severely restricted after Louis Napoleon's *coup d'état* of the 2 Dec. 1851. Dickens had met him several times, but had no liking for him.

it a very important thing that lights of this nature should not be hidden under bushels; but that they should sometimes shine in a cheerful atmosphere, like the present, to remind their friends that they were burning steadily. It was really important that the friends and patrons of the society should have such opportunities of meeting together, not only to encourage and stimulate one another, but to remind the public also of its modest existence, and of its very moderate appeal in behalf of a most trustworthy, useful, punctual, and reliable class of servants.

In the second place he must say that, while sitting there, it had been particularly pleasant to him to observe that so small a company contained so many gentlemen who were distinguished at that fountain-head whose waters were, by the agency of the newsvendors, dispensed to all England. It was a good and right thing that the great popular artist of the time, whose humour was so delicate, so nice, and so discriminating, and whose pencil like his observation was so graceful and so informed with the sense of beauty that it was mere disparagement to call his works 'caricatures', should be there tonight in the person of Mr. Leech.[1] [*Hear, hear.*] Passing over some other friends, whom he saw both on his right hand and his left, and who very fitly and properly represented the graces of our periodical literature, it was good also that they have a separate representation of that weekly picture of the age, that weekly necessary of life with which Mr. Leech was inseparably connected—of course he meant *Punch*—in the person of its editor, Mr. Lemon.[2] [*Applause.*] It was equally gratifying and appropriate that they should have their antiquarian literature, curious research, and various knowledge, represented by Mr. Peter Cunningham[3] [*applause*]; publishing enterprise, liberality, and a great deal more by Mr. Charles Knight[4] [*applause*]; and printing enterprise and success on a great scale by Mr. Evans[5] and Mr. Whiting.[6] [*Applause.*]

[1] John Leech (1817–64), humorous artist; best known through his long association with *Punch*; one of the illustrators of Dickens's Christmas books.

[2] Mark Lemon (1809–70), editor of *Punch*, journalist, and playwright; enthusiastic member of the amateur players; close friend of Dickens until, at her request, he acted for Mrs. Dickens, on their separation, in 1858.

[3] Peter Cunningham (1816–69), author of the *Handbook of London*, 1849, and many other works, chief clerk in the Audit office.

[4] Charles Knight (1791–1873), author; publishing agent for the Society for the Diffusion of Useful Knowledge, 1829–46; editor and publisher of many popular instructive works.

[5] Frederick Mullett Evans (1803 ?–70), printer and publisher, in partnership with William Bradbury (1800–69): although chiefly printers, they were proprietors of *Punch*, published the *Daily News*, co-proprietors of *Household Words*, 1850–9, and were Dickens's publishers until the final quarrel in 1858.

[6] Charles Whiting, later printer of *All the Year Round*.

It was so fitting that those gentlemen should be there, and their presence seemed to be inclusive of so much, and to be such a good testimony to the worth and vigour of the institution, that he could scarcely have felt disposed to congratulate them more if they had had representatives among them from the whole public, beginning with the young gentleman at the head of the third column of *The Times*, who for some years past had been conjured to return to his disconsolate parents, but had never yet however had time to do so [*cheers and laughter*], and ending with the wonderful man who lived somewhere over at Kennington, who was still engaged in gauging the rain and measuring the wind [*renewed laughter*]: if they were represented, he could not congratulate them more.

Thirdly, and lastly, he congratulated them upon their chairman [*applause*], of whom he would say in reference to his usefulness there that night, that no man could possibly descend from his station to be useful. However exalted his station he must ascend from it to be useful to mankind; and this was one of the greatest principles and greatest truths of the greatest history with which mankind was acquainted. On this occasion he proposed the health of their chairman with peculiar pleasure. He did so not only because of his admirable discharge of the duties of his office and his forcible exposition of the claims of their order and institution, but because he recognized in his being asked to fill the position of chairman, a peculiar significance which was most creditable to the society. It was a proof to him that they were resolved that their chairman on these occasions should mean something—that they were not disposed to look out for the commonplace aid of a mere title or a mere signpost; but that, remembering their calling, they desired to place in their Chair a worthy representative of the journals of England. Therefore it was that they had elected for their chairman a gentleman who was the editor of one of the most able, original, useful, upright, and honourable journals in the world.[1] In doing this they had done wisely and well, and he would venture to predict that if they were always as true to themselves the public would certainly be true to them. Besides the paramount claim of the chairman on their respect, at which he had already glanced, he might add that in his earliest work Mr. Forster was the fearless historian of freedom, and the plain speaker of plain truths long industriously concealed in mere moonshine and mystification, while in his latest works he had been the gallant champion of the dignity of literature and its common cause with the people against sordid patrons, hard taskmasters, empty headed noodles, and every description of froth and

[1] Dickens himself had frequently contributed to the *Examiner*, from 1838 to 1849.

foppery that could possibly surround them. He begged to propose the health of the chairman.

John Forster's earliest work had been the *Lives of the Statesmen of the Commonwealth* (1836–9), and 'his latest' was the *Life and Adventures of Oliver Goldsmith* (1848).[1] The campaign for 'the dignity of literature', with which he had concerned himself, had been getting fiercer. Its main contention, that 'authors by profession' should be treated with the same respect as other professional men, went back to Isaac D'Israeli and the beginning of the century, and it aroused strong support. Forster, Lytton, and D'Israeli had all associated it with their studies of eighteenth-century writers: D'Israeli in his *Calamities of Authors*, Lytton in the play he had written for the Guild, *Not So Bad As We Seem*, and Forster in his biography of Goldsmith. Lytton and Forster had also once intended to collaborate in a history of the age of Queen Anne, which would probably have dealt partly with the same theme.

When Thackeray, therefore, not only made several opportunities to sneer at 'the dignity of literature', but pointedly selected the 'English Humourists' of the previous century, including Goldsmith, as the subject for his first public lectures, in 1851, it had been intended as a challenge; and when he had made a further attack on the Guild, on the first night of *Not So Bad As We Seem*, for putting on a play about a 'miserable old literary hack of the time of George the Second', it was not surprising that he drove himself into isolation from his fellow authors. Although, even at this time, there was still no actual quarrel with Dickens, in speaking out in support of Forster and 'the dignity of literature', Dickens made it clear that there was open disagreement.

GENERAL THEATRICAL FUND

5 *April* 1852

THE seventh anniversary festival was held at the London Tavern. Macready had been asked to take the Chair, but was unable to attend. In his place Dickens managed to obtain Sir Edward Bulwer Lytton, writing to him on 4 March: 'I am heartily obliged to you, and . . . with reference to the Guild it is a particularly graceful and well-timed thing to render them this help. For it will suggest, both to the profession and the public, that the Curmudgeon Managers who grumble about us are unconscionable and thankless fools.' Their grumbles had been about the Amateur Players.

There were the usual loyal and patriotic toasts. Lytton spoke appropriately, Buckstone amusingly, and Forster vigorously in giving the health of the chairman. Lytton replied, and went on to propose a toast to Dickens and 'his brother Trustees', saying that he felt a particular pleasure in giving it on that occasion, 'because he had first become thoroughly acquainted with the real character of Mr. Dickens, in his

---

[1] Later expanded into a *Life and Times* of Goldsmith, 1854.

position as actor and stage manager of those gentlemen . . . who had endeavoured to promote the interests of the Guild of Literature to which Mr. Forster had referred'. The toast was received with loud cheering, which broke out again as Dickens rose to reply.

H E could assure them, he said, that he really was not using a common form of words, but was honestly expressing the feeling of the moment when he avowed himself at some loss, both to thank the company for their hearty greeting, and to thank his generous friend in the Chair for the terms in which he had referred to him. Sir Anthony Absolute was of the opinion that in love affairs it was best to begin with a little aversion; and if he (Mr. Dickens) could only have started with a little coldness on the part of his friend in the Chair, or even a moderate warmth on the part of the audience, it was quite unknown into what an admirable speech he should have presently soared. But a tribute so noble, and a welcome so cordial, he found to be very bad preparations indeed for such an achievement.

Before referring to the Fund, which was the main object of interest with all of them that evening, he would take leave to say that he was exceedingly glad that his friend, the chairman, had happened to allude to him in that company, in his Stage-Managerial capacity; because he did particularly desire to express his conviction in such a company, of all others, that the dramatic profession were very ill served by some misjudging friends, when they supposed that it could possibly be injured by, or could possibly regard with anything like resentment or jealousy, Amateur Theatricals. [*Cheers.*] He had, for a brief space, assumed the functions of an amateur manager and actor, in furtherance of a cause in which his warmest sympathies and aspirations were (like those of his friend in the Chair) enlisted; and to represent that the stage could possibly be injured, or could fairly claim any right to consider itself injured by such performances was to exclude it from the liberal position assumed in such wise by every other liberal art. [*Cheers.*] In literature there were received, freely and without cavil, amateurs of all kinds: physicians, lawyers, officers of the army and navy, merchants' clerks who travelled and saw strange countries, lords and ladies of various degrees,—anybody who had anything to say, and possibly, now and then, somebody who had nothing to say. [*Cheers and laughter.*] During the whole of the last season, a gallery was opened in Pall Mall for the exhibition of pictures of amateur artists; yet he never heard that the members of the Royal Academy were much aggrieved by the circumstance, or very desperately alarmed by its public patronage and success. So, in music: he believed it was generally acknowledged that some excellent lessons had been given to the public and the profession by the knowledge and patience of amateurs in chorus singing, and that the production of some of the most admired works of the old masters were due to the exertions of amateurs, without the least injury to the regular professors of the art. The liberal and generous feeling which thus distinguished other kindred arts, surely was to be claimed for the stage, as *its* just characteristic too; and could not be better claimed for it than at the anniversary celebration of its most comprehensive and its least restricted institution. [*Cheers.*]

With reference to the General Theatrical Fund, he had been so often before them as one of the Trustees, that he found it very difficult to say anything relative to it which he had not said before, or which they did not all know as well as himself. Independently of the fact that their Fund had been established seven years, and that their position was steadily improving every time they met, the eloquence of their chairman in proposing the toast of the evening, and their Treasurer's admirable acknowledgement of it, had completely exhausted the subject, and he now stood before them a bankrupt Trustee without a leg to stand upon. [*Laughter.*] If he could only have found one good vice in the management, he would have been well set up in business for the evening, and might have remained in a perfectly self-satisfied condition until next year. If, for instance, he could only have complained that the institution was expensively managed, that there was nobody connected with the management who had any sympathy with the unfortunate members of the Dramatic profession; that none of them had had any experience of the habits or struggles of poor actors; if he could only have said that their Treasurer was a stern, austere man [*laughter*], altogether a hard-favoured person, severe of countenance and very difficult to approach [*laughter*]; or if he could have said that the institution was exclusive in its nature, one that required candidates for admission to its benefits to have compiled with some trifling condition—reasonable, but not easy, such as having held an engagement for two or three consecutive years in the moon, or having appeared in Sir Edward Lytton's *Money* two or three hundred nights before the Esquimaux—if he could have found any such trifling ground of complaint, he would have been at no loss for a topic.[1] But, whereas in the General Theatrical Fund, the low comedian was not expected to have fulfilled those consecutive engagements in the moon; the tragedian was not expected to have played Evelyn two or three hundred consecutive nights in the icy regions of the North; Fenella, the sister of Masaniello, was not

[1] The usual allusions to the Drury Lane, and Covent Garden Funds, see p. 73, with a glance at the Royal Literary Fund.

refused relief because she was only a dancer, nor Masaniello himself because he was only a singer.[1] [*Cheers.*]

He had nothing left to say in lieu of that great speech he might, and indisputably would, under these happier circumstances have made, but that he wanted a grievance. [*Cheers.*] Indeed, he was so utterly at a loss for a grievance that he had had serious thoughts of abandoning these festivals altogether, and taking to attending those banquets which he sometimes saw advertised to take place in the neighbourhood of Freemasons' Hall, where he was informed that he could find all these causes of complaint ready made to his hand. [*Cheers and laughter.*] Like his friend, Mr. Buckstone, however, he did not wish to indulge in any unkind expressions towards the other theatrical funds, as some old and esteemed friends of his were connected with them, and as he would wish to make them also the friends of this institution. [*Cheers.*] What he would suggest, afar off, was that these Funds should make some change in their constitutions adopted to the altered times, and he thought there was nothing so likely to reconcile all differences, and to do so much good to all parties, as a happy marriage. [*Cheers and laughter.*]

All he would say in his official position was that the General Theatrical Fund was progressing steadily, that they had not the slightest difficulty to state to that company, and that the institution was steadily and gallantly supported by the members of the profession. [*Cheers.*] All who had the least theatrical experience must know how necessary it was to any play, in order to ensure success, that it should possess some female interest. No institution could succeed that was not backed by that influence [*cheers*]; and, therefore, it was with great pleasure that he learned from their worthy Secretary that a large portion of their subscribers consisted of the gentler sex. [*Cheers.*] Nor were they wanting there, to shed on the assembly a grace which nothing else could give to it; for whether he looked before or behind him (and here he might be allowed to say that he almost regretted to occupy one of the posts of honour, and wished he were situated among some of his friends in a more private situation at the side of the room)— [*laughter*], he met with nothing but beaming faces, encouraging and gentle looks. [*Cheers.*] On the part of his brother Trustees, and on his own behalf, he begged to acknowledge the toast with many thanks; and he begged to assure those present that they need not be in the least afraid, that evening, of troubling the Treasurer or the Trustees by swelling their contributions in support of the Fund to an inconvenient amount; for they were perfectly ready to bear,

---

[1] Fenella and Masaniello are in Auber's opera *La Muta di Portici*; Fenella, in the title-part, was clearly no singer.

with the utmost cheerfulness, the heaviest total with which they might think fit to burden them. [*Cheers.*]

MEETING FOR THE REMOVAL OF TRADE RESTRICTIONS ON THE COMMERCE OF LITERATURE

4 *May* 1852

THE relations between publishers and the public were still as undefined and unregulated as those between publishers and authors; and Dickens was naturally interested in the dispute which arose between the London Booksellers' Association, and John Chapman,[1] early in 1852. Briefly, the association demanded that all retailers should sell books at the price fixed by publishers, on penalty of their supplies being withheld, while Chapman insisted that he should at least be allowed to sell imported books at whatever price he wanted, and indeed any books at all. He came into conflict with the association, and engaged its members in public controversy. The Booksellers laid their case before Lord Campbell, Dr. Milman, and George Grote, who agreed to act as arbitrators. After refusing to attend a meeting, at too short a notice, on 14 April, Chapman announced a meeting of his own, to be held at his house and shop, 142 Strand, to decide whether 'the advocates of free trade in books' should lay their case before Lord Campbell as he proposed, on 17 May, and 'to agree upon such an expression of opinion as may hasten the removal of the present trade restrictions on the commerce of literature'.

There was a crush of eminent authors present; and, on the motion of Professor Owen, seconded by Robert Bell, Dickens was called to the Chair. He was warmly received by the meeting.

ON being requested to take the Chair, he said, he had in the first instance declined, on the ground that they had met to discuss what was a bookseller's question, and not an author's question. But further consideration suggested that he might, as being necessarily impartial in a contention between different classes of booksellers and publishers. [*Hear, hear.*] He was, on principle, most strongly opposed to any system, in any commercial direction, of exclusion or restriction. He held that every man, whatever his calling, must be left to the fair and free exercise of his own honest thrift and enterprise. Holding that opinion he was there tonight to make a protest against a particular system of restriction, and he trusted that a satisfactory result would be obtained. [*Cheers.*]

---

[1] John Chapman (1821–94), publisher, author, and editor of the *Westminster Review*, 1851–94; later qualified as physician, though his practice was 'open to strong suspicion of quackery'; close friend of George Eliot, see G. S. Haight *George Eliot & John Chapman*, New Haven, 1940.

Letters from various prominent authors, including Leigh Hunt, John Mill, and Carlyle, were then read supporting the objects of the meeting. John Chapman explained why it had been called, and various resolutions were put forward and hotly debated. A number of booksellers had been admitted who were members of the association, and they were prepared to support it vigorously. Dickens is said 'to have exercised the most consummate tact throughout the proceedings constantly threatening to take an unruly turn'.

Next day, George Eliot described the affair, in a letter to some friends. 'Dickens in the chair', she wrote, 'a position he fills remarkably well, preserving a courteous neutrality of eyebrows, and speaking with clearness and decision'. His appearance, however, she found disappointing: he was undistinguished phrenologically, and 'neither fat nor thin, neither tall nor short'. Still, he managed the 'vulgar, ignorant booksellers' well.[1]

Towards the close of the proceedings, Dickens called their attention to a proposal that a deputation should be formed to call on Lord Campbell, to state the views of the meeting. It was finally decided that this would be unnecessary, and that John Chapman should wait on him personally. The meeting closed with a vote of thanks to the chairman, and the last visitor left to the strains of 'See the Conquering Hero Comes', played on the piano by George Eliot, in honour of Chapman.

Lord Campbell gave a decision against the Booksellers' Association, and it was accordingly dissolved.

GARDENERS' BENEVOLENT INSTITUTION

14 *June* 1852

THE ninth anniversary festival was held at the London Tavern, with Dickens in the Chair. As usual the dessert and flowers were a special feature of the occasion. The cloth having been removed, Dickens rose and said:

THE first toast which our duty and our inclination alike prompt us to give, is the health of Her Majesty the Queen. Her Majesty often breathes the morning air in gardens; and it is not hard to imagine that there may be occasions when the results of the plain wood and iron spade, without the palace, may afford her a more agreeable relief from the cares of state than the gold and silver within. That Her Majesty has an interest in gardens we may venture to assume; and that she has a special interest in gardeners we know, in the most acceptable manner, by her having presented this institution with the sum of fifty pounds. [*Applause.*]

The toast having been duly acknowledged, the chairman gave 'Prince Albert, the Prince of Wales, and the rest of the Royal Family', which was drunk with all the honours; and then said:

[1] G. S. Haight, *Letters of George Eliot*, 1954, ii. 23–24.

When my friend, the late Reverend Sydney Smith[1] was taking leave of a friend going to New Zealand, he whimsically wished that he might disagree with any cannibal who might chance to eat him;[2] and although myself of a pacific disposition, I should like to disagree with any foreign gentlemen who would take away my personal liberty; and I should be disposed to differ with any foreign prince, potentate, or peasant who might venture to take any liberty with my liberty. Hence, gentlemen, I always hold in great respect our Army and Navy, and not least when it is by no means inappropriate to remember that no agriculture, no commerce, no art, could long be pursued if England were unable to defend herself, to repel invasion, and to make her name, as it ought to be, a name of fear to the tyrants of the world. [*Loud applause.*] I beg to give you 'The Army and Navy', and to couple with that toast the name of Captain Wrench.

The Captain briefly returned thanks; and Dickens rose to propose the toast of the evening, and said:

Gentlemen, I have to offer you a toast which expresses our interest in the institution in whose behalf we are met together. I feel in reference to the institution something like a counsel for the plaintiff with nobody on the other side; but even if it had existed instead of three times three, ninety times nine years, I should still feel it my duty to trouble you with a few facts from the very short brief which has been entrusted to me, for that desperate gardener, Old Time, does so transplant and remove, as to warrant the supposition that there are always some to whom it may be desirable to state the merits of the case.

The institution was founded in the year 1838; and for the first few years of its existence seems not to have been particularly robust, and to have been placed in rather a shaded position, receiving somewhat more than its needful allowance of cold water. [*Laughter.*] In 1843 it was removed into a more genial situation, and grafted on to a better managerial stock where it began to blossom; and it has now borne fruit and become such a vigorous

---

[1] Sydney Smith (1771–1845), canon of St. Paul's, wit, whig, and Edinburgh Reviewer; member of the Holland House circle, to which Dickens was admitted much later than he. They came to have a great mutual respect; Dickens's fourth son, Sydney Smith Haldimand was named after him, 1847.

[2] Lady Holland, *A Memoir of The Reverend Sydney Smith*, 3rd ed., 1855, i. 436: 'The advice I sent to the Bishop of New Zealand, when he had to receive the cannibal chiefs there, was to say to them, "I deeply regret, Sirs, to have nothing on my table suited to your tastes, but you will find plenty of cold curate and roasted clergyman on the sideboard;" and if in spite of this prudent provision his visitors should end their repast by eating him likewise, why I could only add, "I sincerely hoped he would disagree with them".'

tree that, at present, thirty-five old people daily sit within the shelter of its friendly branches.

It is to be observed of this institution, unlike some older and more renowned, that what it is in name it is in effect. The class for whose benefit it purports to have been devised has its full and entire advantage. All the pensioners upon the list have been veritable gardeners, or the wives of gardeners. It is managed by gardeners, and besides having upon its books this excellent rule: 'That gardeners who have contributed to the funds of the charity for fifteen years, and who from old age or misfortune become destitute, have claims upon this institution in preference to those who have never subscribed to it', I observe that every subscriber may be placed upon the pension list, if he will, without election, without canvass, without solicitation and as his independent right. I lay great stress upon this, because I hold that the main principle of every society such as this should be, in the first place, to help those who have helped themselves and helped others; and, secondly, to merge all considerations of its own importance in the sacred duty of relieving such persons when they fall into affliction, with the utmost possible delicacy, and without the least chance of carrying a pang to their hearts, or bringing a blush to their cheeks. [*Loud applause.*]

That the society's pensioners do not become such as long as they are reasonably able to toil is evinced by the significant fact that the average age of the present pensioners is 77. That they are not wastefully relieved is shown by the fact that the whole sum expended for their relief does not exceed five hundred pounds a year; that no narrow confines of locality are favoured in the selection will be clear when I assure you that pensioners are to be found in every part of the country, east, west, north, and south. That the expenses of the society are not disproportionate to the society's income is proved by their being all defrayed out of the annual subscriptions, while the sum at present in hand is £2,700, and we mean to make it up to three thousand at least. [*Applause.*]

Such is the institution which appeals to you through me as a most unworthy advocate for sympathy and support. That it has not addressed itself in vain to the employers is evident from its having for its President a nobleman whose whole possessions are remarkable for taste and beauty, and whose gardener's laurels are famous throughout the world.[1] And I notice with great pleasure, on the list

---

[1] William George Spencer Cavendish, 6th Duke of Devonshire (1790–1858), well-known to Dickens through his patronage of the Guild of Literature and Art; 'his gardener' was Sir Joseph Paxton (see p. 133) manager of the Chatsworth estates where he built the famous conservatory. The Duke was also the President of the Horticultural Society.

of Vice-Presidents, the names of many noblemen and gentlemen of great influence and station. I am particularly struck in glancing through the pages of this little book, with the number of nurserymen and seedsmen who have contributed, and the handsome sums written against their names. It is a very worthy example. The gardeners also muster very strong, and I do hope the day will come when no one will be left out, but every decent gardener in England will feel that this society is a part of his calling, and though he may never want its aid, that it is his duty to belong to it for the sake of others who may.

The gardener particularly needs such help as this society affords. His gains are not great; he often knows gold and silver better as the colours of fruit and flowers, than by their presence in his pockets; and it is easy to see how his exposure to changes of weather may render him peculiarly liable to sickness and infirmity. A gardener, of all men, should particularly appreciate the worth of such a society as this, for his continual observance of the changing seasons and declining days may well suggest to him the decline of life, and that it is a dictate both of worldly prudence and Christian kindness to provide for it.

Finally, to all here who are gardeners, and to all here who are not gardeners, except as we all trace our descent in a direct line from the first 'gardener Adam and his wife',[1] this institution forcibly appeals. The universality of the gardener's calling is one of its greatest characteristics. If any improvement be made in Her Majesty's garden, or in that of his Grace or my Lord, it is very soon transferred even to the costermonger. In the culture of flowers there cannot, by their very nature, be anything solitary or exclusive. The wind that blows over the cottager's patch sweeps also over the grounds of the nobleman; and as the rain descends on the just and the unjust, so it communicates to all gardeners, both rich and poor, an interchange of pleasure and enjoyment; and the gardener of the rich man, in developing and enhancing a fruitful flower of a delightful scent is, in some part, the gardener of everybody else. [*Cheers.*]

Flowers are the best picture books I know; and whenever I see them lying open at the labourer's door, I can always read in them that he is a better and happier man. It is not too much to say that the gardener is essential to all of us. The love of gardening is associated with all countries and all periods of time. The scholar and the statesman, men of peace and men of war, have agreed in all ages to delight in gardens. The most ancient people of the earth had gardens where there are now nothing but solitary heaps of earth. The

---

[1] Tennyson, 'Lady Clara Vere de Vere'.

younger ancients had crowns of flowers. In China hundreds of acres were employed in gardens. When we travel by our railways we see the weaver striving for a scrap of garden, the poor man wrestling with smoke for a little bower of scarlet runners; and those who have no ground of their own will carry on their gardens in jugs and basins. In factories and workshops, people garden; and even the prisoner is found gardening, in his lonely cell, after years and years of solitary confinement. Of the exponents of a language so universal as this, surely it then is not too much to say that the gardener who produces shapes and objects so lovely and so comforting should have some hold upon the world's remembrance when he himself becomes in need of comfort?

And so then, coming at last to three times three cheers for three times three years, I will call upon you to drink 'Prosperity to the Gardeners' Benevolent Institution', and I beg to couple with that toast the name of its President, the Duke of Devonshire, whose worth is written in all his deeds, and who has communicated to his title and his riches a lustre which no title and riches could confer. [*Great applause.*]

Sir Joseph Paxton replied. One of the guests proposed the health of the chairman, and Dickens replied.

He begged most unaffectedly and heartily to thank the company for the honour they had done him; but looking to the other toasts upon the list, he would at once proceed to say that it was important to all such charities to have the aid of efficient honorary officers who, not merely under the excitement of an occasional festival, but at all times, were prepared to do them service. Among such officers none were more important than the Vice-Presidents, and he had much pleasure in proposing their health.

This was duly acknowledged. The secretary then announced the subscriptions, and Dickens continued.

His office, he said, had compelled him to burst into bloom so often that he could wish there were a closer parallel between himself and the American Aloe. It was particularly agreeable and appropriate to know that the parents of the institution were to be found in the seed and nursery trade. And the seed having yielded such good fruit, and the nursery having produced such a healthy child, I have the greatest pleasure in proposing the health of 'The Nursery and Seed business—the Parents of the Institution', and to couple with that toast the name of Mr. James Thompson. [*Cheers.*]

This was also acknowledged; and Dickens then rose to propose the health of the treasurers.

His observation of the signboards of this country, he said, had taught him that its conventional gardeners were always jolly, and always three in number. [*Laughter.*] Whether that conventionality had any reference to the three Graces, or to those very significant letters £., s., d., he did not know. Those mystic letters were, however, very important, and no society could have officers of more importance than its Treasurers, nor could it possibly give them too much to do. [*Cheers.*]

Various other toasts followed, concluding with 'The Ladies'—'in proposing which the chairman delighted the company by the point and eloquence of his remarks; regretting, in reference to the last, that he could not address the meeting as "Ladies and Gentlemen" from the stupid conventionality which made the ladies spectators only, and not partakers in their festivities.'

Mrs. Hannah Brown—Miss Burdett Coutts's companion—wrote to congratulate him a day or two later, and Dickens replied:

I have not read the speech—I hope it is well done—but I have strong apprehensions that it may be sadly mangled. I can't help saying that I wish you (*and the new Subscriber*) could have heard it; for it was a pretty subject—and that, and the sunburnt faces, worked me up to my best pitch. It made quite a remarkable impression on the audience.[1]

BANQUET TO THE GUILD OF LITERATURE AND ART: MANCHESTER

31 *August* 1852

THE dramatic performances in aid of the Guild of Literature and Art culminated in a provincial tour at the end of August and the beginning of September 1852. At Manchester a local committee arranged a banquet, at the Athenaeum, in honour of the Guild. Sir Edward Bulwer Lytton, the president of the association, was able to attend; and he responded to the toast of the evening proposing its prosperity.

He began by explaining its origin and aims. 'Bulwer spoke brilliantly,' Dickens wrote to Forster, 'and his earnestness and determination about the Guild was most impressive. It carried everything before it.'[2] In the course of his speech Lytton went on to pay tribute to the amateur players, his fellow members, adding that:

... foremost among all operations, unwearied amidst all difficulties, confident amidst all sneers and cavils, has beat the great heart of that man who has done so much to render literature popular, and the people literary. More on another occasion I should say; but I content myself with this passing homage to a name that must be rising on every lip—I mean the name of Charles Dickens. [*Loud cheers.*]

[1] 17 June 1852, M.   [2] F, VI. v.

Dickens himself spoke in reply to a toast given by the mayor, to 'The Amateur Company of the Guild'. It was drunk with great cheering; and on rising he was received with loud applause.

MR. MAYOR and Gentlemen, On behalf of the company of friends who act with me in more senses than one, and on my own part, who am their representative and mouthpiece here, I beg to tender you our best thanks for the splendid recognition with which you have honoured us tonight. I do so with a feeling of unusual earnestness, because I am, believe me, in common with one and all of those friends, deeply and truly sensible of the heartfelt cordiality with which we have ever been received in this noble town. [*Applause.*] Gentlemen, from our first assumption of the actor's craft here, on behalf of a worn-out man of letters—the author of many excellent pieces still constantly produced upon the stage, but with no kind of advantage to himself, and with no kind of remembrance of him that I ever heard of—down to this happy hour, our Manchester audience has been so true to us, so heartily with us, so affectionate towards us, that in playing to it we have always felt as if we were playing to one great-hearted friend. [*Applause.*] And, I do assure you, that when our little curtain shall fall tomorrow night, for the last time, probably, upon that beaming countenance and that encouraging voice that have now so often gladdened us, we shall feel a sorrow of no mimic kind, and a regret at parting that will outlive the fiction of the scene.

Gentlemen, after what you have heard so eloquently said by my friend, Sir Edward Bulwer Lytton, on the scheme to advance which this little body of friends have been associated together, I feel it would not be reasonable in me to trouble you with any observations respecting its general claims, or the immense service which has been rendered to it by Manchester. In taking the field to promote that object, we thoroughly and sincerely knew it to be a good one; we thoroughly and sincerely knew it to be a just reproach to letters and to art that it had been too long neglected; and were thoroughly and sincerely resolved to do all that in us lay to help the need which we knew to exist. Gentlemen, our little labours have indeed been labours of love. Careful business consideration of every detail of this project, and the most solicitous regard to the more pressing exigencies and weaknesses of our order, must now constitute the strength of this Guild, and must now be the foundation of its steady claim to general public support. What we have done is merely to set it going, and to give it, as we hope and believe, a steady onward impulse. If I wanted—speaking in my managerial capacity—if I wanted any assurance, which I never did, for I hope I have long known better, that men of imaginative pursuits could co-operate

as steadily and staunchly as any other order of men, I should find
it in the undeviating punctuality, regularity, order, forgetfulness
of self, and consideration for others which, behind the scenes, off the
stage, in the bare daylight when the lamps were out and there was
no gilding on the gingerbread, have linked our little association
together in most unusual ties. [*Applause.*] And, gentlemen, if I
wanted any assurance to you that we were not likely to be very
wrong-headed and mistaken in the objects we have at heart, I
should find it in the fact that every one of the three eminent writers
to whom we had the high gratification of rendering most timely
assistance by our theatrical performances before the Guild was
devised, has since been placed on the Pension List;[1] and that, I
know, with a delicate consideration for their feelings, most truly
affecting to themselves and most truly honourable to Her Majesty
and Lord John Russell. [*Applause.*]

I have now the great gratification, with the chairman's leave, of
proposing to you to drink, 'Prosperity to the Manchester Athenaeum'. [*Applause.*] I cannot disguise from you that I feel a kind of
radiant godfatherly satisfaction in proposing the toast, for I can
never forget that I had the honour of presiding over the first of its
great meetings.[2] [*Hear, and cheers.*] I can never forget that I am
one of its honorary life members, and that my parchment of enrolment in that capacity occupies a proud position upon my study
wall at home. [*Applause.*] In short, gentlemen, I belong to the
family, and I contemplate the family greatness tonight with a glow
of family pride. [*Cheers and laughter.*] Long, therefore, gentlemen,
I most sincerely pray, may the Manchester Athenaeum flourish,
a pattern to the rising enterprise and energy of England, and a
vigorous branch of that great social tree, which, under the name and
form of such institutions, has happily for all sorts and conditions
of men, struck its roots deep in this land. [*Applause.*] Long may all
political divisions and party dissensions be forgotten here [*hear,
hear*], and very long may my old friend Mr. Crossley,[3] in the character of an allegorical lion, lie down with the radical in the form of
an allegorical lamb, on this peaceful neutral ground. [*Laughter and
applause.*] Long, very long, gentlemen, may the Manchester Athenaeum increase and prosper, work and strive—a noble emblem of the
wonderful place in which it rears its head; and long may its young
men be generously united to advance generous objects, and render
such faithful public service as they have rendered to the Guild of

---

[1] Leigh Hunt, James Sheridan Knowles, and John Poole, who had been
granted Civil List pensions in 1847, 1848, and 1851 respectively.
[2] See pp. 44 ff.
[3] See p. 51 n.

Literature and Art. [*Applause.*] I beg to call upon you to drink 'Prosperity to the Manchester Athenaeum.' [*Great cheering.*]

Among other members of the amateur players who also spoke were Frank Stone, who was a native of Manchester, Charles Knight, Robert Bell, and Peter Cunningham.

The performance the following night was a great success; and Dickens was able to write to Forster, 'They are now getting up annual subscriptions, and will give us a revenue to begin with. I swear I believe that people to be the greatest in the world.'[1]

OPENING OF THE FREE LIBRARY: MANCHESTER
2 *September* 1852

THE Public Libraries Act had been passed in 1850, and almost immediately Sir John Potter,[2] the mayor, set about founding one for Manchester. He bought the Hall of Science, which had belonged to the supporters of Robert Owen, published plans for a free library, and opened a subscription list. It was typical of the time that the former Socialists' Hall should be converted into a library; and at a meeting, in January 1851, it was generally recognized to be 'a pleasing idea . . . that an edifice so disastrous pecuniarily to the industrious, and for a long time shunned by the respectable and moral . . . might be made a centre from which there should issue forth the most humanizing and refining of influences'.[3]

The opening of the new library, at Camp Field, the following year, coincided with the visit of the amateur players. The mayor invited Dickens to attend, and he readily accepted though at first he was unwilling to speak as well: 'My engagements are very numerous, but the occasion is too important, and the example too noble, to admit of hesitation.'[4] On the day itself, however, he did not hold back.

Dickens was preceded by a number of other speakers, among whom were the Earl of Shaftesbury and Sir Edward Bulwer Lytton. He was received with loud applause, and said:

SIR JOHN POTTER, my Lords, Ladies, and Gentlemen, I have been so much in the habit within the last fortnight of relying upon the words of other people, that I find it quite a novel sensation to be here dependent solely upon my own. [*Laughter.*] I assure you that I feel at this moment in imminent danger of sliding into the language of my friend who addressed you last; and, from the mere force of habit, I rather miss the prompter. [*A laugh.*] For this reason, and

---

[1] F, vi. v.

[2] Sir John Potter (1815–58), business man; Mayor, 1848–51; knighted 1851; M.P. for Manchester 1857 until death.

[3] *Manchester Courier*, 4 Sept. 1852.

[4] 17 July 1852, MS., Manchester Central Library.

many others, I shall trouble you with a very short speech indeed in proposing the resolution with which I have the honour to be entrusted. It so fully expresses my feelings and hopes, and my convictions in association with this auspicious day, that I cannot do better than to read it to you at once:

> That as in this institution special provision has been made for the working classes, by means of a free lending library, this meeting cherishes the earnest hope that the books thus made available, will prove a source of pleasure and improvement in the cottages, the garrets, and the cellars of the poorest of our people.

[*Cheers.*] Ladies and gentlemen, limiting what I wish to say on this subject to two very brief heads, I would beg to observe, firstly, that I have been made happy since I have been sitting here by the solution of a problem which has long perplexed me. I have seen so many references made in the newspapers, in parliamentary debates, and elsewhere, to the 'Manchester School', that I have long had a considerable anxiety to know what that phrase might mean, and what the 'Manchester School' might be. [*Laughter.*] My natural curiosity on this head has not been diminished by the very contradictory accounts I have received respecting that same school; some great authorities assuring me that it was a very good one, some that it was a very bad one; some that it was very broad and comprehensive, some that it was very narrow and limited; some that it was all cant, and some that it was all cotton. [*Loud laughter.*]

Now, ladies and gentlemen, I have solved this difficulty, by finding here today that the 'Manchester School' is a great free-school, bent on carrying instruction to the poorest hearths. [*Cheers.*] It is this great free-school, inviting the humblest workman to come in and to be a student; this great free-school, most munificently endowed by voluntary subscriptions in an incredibly short space of time—starting upon its glorious career with twenty thousand volumes of books—knowing no sect, no party, no distinction—nothing but the public want and the public good. [*Hear, hear, and applause.*] Henceforth, ladies and gentlemen, this building shall represent to me the 'Manchester School' [*cheers*]; and I pray to Heaven, moreover, that many great towns and cities, and many high authorities, may go to school a little in the Manchester seminary, and profit by the noble lesson that it teaches. [*Cheers.*]

In the second and last place, ladies and gentlemen, allow me to observe that like my friend, Sir Edward Lytton, I exceedingly regret my inability to attend that other interesting meeting of this evening. I should have rejoiced to have seen in this place, instead of myself, and to have heard in this place, instead of my own voice, the voice of a working man in Manchester, to tell the projectors of this spirited enterprise with what feelings he and his companions regard their just and generous recognition here. [*Cheers.*] I should have rejoiced to hear from such a man, in the solid and nervous language in which I have often heard such men give utterance to the feelings of their breasts, how he knows that the books stored here for his behoof will cheer him through many of the struggles and toils of his life, will raise him in his self respect, will teach him that capital and labour are not opposed, but are mutually dependent and mutually supporting [*hear, hear and applause*]—will enable him to tread down blinding prejudice, corrupt misrepresentation, and everything but the truth, into the dust. [*Applause.*]

Ladies and gentlemen, I have long been, in my sphere, a zealous advocate for the diffusion of knowledge among all classes and conditions of men [*applause*]; because I do believe, with all the strength and might with which I am capable of believing anything, that the more a man knows, the more humbly, and with a more faithful spirit he comes back to the fountain of all knowledge, and takes to his heart the great sacred precept, 'On earth peace, good will toward men.' [*Loud applause.*] And well assured I am, that that great precept, and those other things I have hinted at as pleasant to have heard here today from a working man, will rise higher and higher above the beating of hammers, the roar of wheels, the rattle of machinery, and the rush of waters, and be the more and more clearly felt through every pulsation of this great heart, the better known and used this institution is. [*Applause.*]

Ladies and gentlemen, I have great pleasure in moving the resolution which I have already read to you. [*Renewed applause.*]

The resolution was seconded by Thackeray, who had had every intention of making a good speech. He began well, but came to a stop after a minute or two and sat down leaving a sentence unfinished. Other speakers included Sir James Stephen, Monckton Milnes, the Earl of Wilton, John Bright, Charles Knight, Peter Cunningham, James Crossley, and the Bishop of Manchester.

Later the same day Dickens wrote an account of his activities to Miss Burdett Coutts:

I sent you a paper from Manchester this afternoon, with a report in it of a dinner to the Guild. With that gallant people at my back—as they always are—I have a more fervent hope than ever, of setting right at last what is very wrong in my calling. I have the object so deeply at heart, and so strongly feel the advantage I have in my present power in such matters (which involves a great duty) that I am in a desperate earnestness which I think must produce something. I am afraid you hardly think with me now—but you will.

I wish you could have seen the opening of the Free Library for the people, at Manchester today. Such a noble effort, so wisely and modestly made; so wonderfully calculated to keep one part of that awful machine, a great working town, in harmony with the other![1]

A similar meeting, of 'the working classes', to which Dickens referred in his speech, was held the same evening, but most of the speakers were the same as those of the earlier meeting, and little was heard of 'the voice of the working man'.

PRESENTATION TO DICKENS AND BANQUET TO LITERATURE AND ART: BIRMINGHAM

6 *January* 1853

THE citizens of Birmingham had recently formed an association to award prizes in the Fine Arts. They had held a successful exhibition in 1852, and then formed a committee to organize a banquet. Meanwhile, a different committee had started a shilling subscription for a presentation to Dickens; and it had been decided to combine the two functions, so that he could attend them both on one visit.

The presentation took place at the rooms of the Society of Artists, Temple Row. A local reporter described them as 'crowded by as gay and distinguished an assembly as had ever met in Birmingham'. All eyes turned to the door, when the 'galaxy' of 'Dickens, Sir Charles East-lake,[2] John Forster and Professor Cockerell,[3] made their appearance'.[4] The chairman of the committee then explained the nature and circumstances of the presentation, which consisted of a silver-gilt salver and a diamond ring, and the secretary read an address.

It stated that the presentation was a result of their pride in Dickens 'as a national writer', no less than their admiration for 'the high moral purpose of his books'. In asking him to accept it, they expressed the hope 'that the day is not far distant when there shall be a national value set upon such services', and 'when, before even the bright chivalry of birth, there shall be a public recognition of . . . the sovereignty of genius'.

Dickens then replied:

GENTLEMEN, I find it very difficult, I assure you, to tender my acknowledgments to you, and through you to those many friends of mine whom you represent, for this honour and distinction which you have thus conferred upon me. I can most honestly assure you, that it is in the power of no great representative of numbers of people to awaken such happiness in me as is inspired by this token of good will and remembrance, coming to me direct and fresh from

---

[1] [M].

[2] Sir Charles Lock Eastlake (1793–1865), President of the Royal Academy, 1850; artist, writer, and public servant; secretary of the Fine Arts Commission, 1841–61; Keeper of the National Gallery, 1843–7, Director, 1855–65.

[3] Charles Robert Cockerell (1788–1863), Professor of Architecture, Royal Academy, 1840–57.   [4] *Birmingham Journal.*

the numbers themselves. [*Hear, hear.*] I am truly sensible, gentlemen, that my friends who have united in this address are partial in their kindness, and regard what I have done with too great favour. But I may say, with reference to one class—some members of which, I presume, are included there—that I should in my own eyes be very unworthy both of the generous gift and the generous feeling which has been evinced, and this occasion, instead of pleasure, would give me nothing but pain, if I was unable to assure them, and those who are in front of this assembly, that what the working people have found me towards them in my books, I am throughout my life. [*Hear, hear.*] Gentlemen, whenever I have tried to hold up to admiration their fortitude, patience, gentleness, the reasonableness of their nature, so accessible to persuasion, and their extraordinary goodness one towards another, I have done so because I have first genuinely felt that admiration myself, and have been thoroughly imbued with the sentiment which I sought to communicate to others. [*Hear, hear.*]

Gentlemen, I accept this salver and this ring, so far above all price to me, and so very valuable in themselves, as beautiful specimens of the workmanship of this great town, with much emotion I assure you, and with the liveliest gratitude. You remember something, I dare say, of the old romantic stories of those charmed rings which would lose their brilliance when the wearer was in danger, or would press his finger reproachfully when he was going to do wrong. In the very improbable event of my being in the least danger of deserting the principles which have won me these tokens, I am sure that diamond [*pointing to the presentation ring*] would assume a clouded aspect to my faithless eye, and would, I know, squeeze a throb of pain out of my treacherous heart. But I have not the least misgiving on that point; and, in this confident expectation, I shall remove my old diamond ring from my left hand, and in future wear the Birmingham ring on my right, where its grasp will keep me in mind of the good friends I have here, and in vivid remembrance of this happy hour. [*Hear, hear.*]

Gentlemen, in conclusion, allow me to thank you and the society to whom these rooms belong, that the presentation has taken place in an atmosphere so congenial to me, and in an apartment decorated with so many beautiful works of art, among which I recognize before me the productions of friends of mine, whose labours and triumphs will never be subjects of indifference to me. I thank those gentlemen for giving me the opportunity of meeting them here on an occasion which has some connection with their own proceedings; and, though last not least, I tender my acknowledgments to that charming presence which is here, without which nothing beautiful can be complete, and which is endearingly associated with rings of a plainer description [*laughter*],—and which, I must confess, awakens in my mind at the present moment a feeling of regret that I am not in a condition to make an offer of those testimonials. [*Renewed laughter.*] I beg you, gentlemen, to commend me very earnestly and gratefully to our absent friends, and to assure them of my affectionate and heartfelt respect.

At the close of these proceedings the company adjourned to the Royal Hotel, where they enjoyed 'a most sumptuous dinner'. The ladies had to be content with tea and coffee, but as soon as the meal was over they were allowed into the gallery, where they were received with cheers.

After the usual loyal toasts, 'The Church' was proposed, and Archdeacon Sandford[1] replied. He paid a general tribute to Literature and Art, but gave especial praise to Dickens for having done 'more than any living man to elevate the lighter literature of our country. . . . He had enforced precepts which we might venerate as Christians.'

Other toasts then followed, before William Scholefield[2] rose to propose 'The Literature of England', coupling with it 'the name of a gentleman present who was entitled to a high place among those who had not only most deeply interested and beneficially instructed their own country, but the people of every country of Europe, and of other parts of the world, . . . Mr. Charles Dickens'.

Dickens rose amid enthusiastic and long-continued cheering, and replied:

Mr. Mayor and Gentlemen, I am happy on behalf of many labourers in that great field of literature to which you have pledged the toast, to thank you for the tribute you have paid to it. Such an honour, rendered by acclamation, in such a place as this, seems to me, if I may follow on the same side as the venerable Archdeacon who has lately addressed you and who has inspired me with a gratification I can never forget [*cheers*], such an honour, gentlemen, rendered here, seems to me a two-sided illustration of the position that Literature holds in these latter, and of course 'degenerate' days. [*Cheers and laughter.*] To the great compact phalanx of the people, by whose industry, perseverance, and intelligence, and their result in money-wealth such places as Birmingham, and many others like it, have arisen—to that great centre of support, that comprehensive experience, and that beating heart—Literature has turned happily from individual patrons, sometimes munificent, often sordid, always few, and has found there at once its highest purpose, its natural range of action, and its best reward. [*Loud cheers.*]

[1] John Sandford (1801–73), Archdeacon of Coventry; formerly Warden of Queen's College, Birmingham.

[2] William Scholefield (1809–67), radical M.P. for Birmingham, 1847–67; first Mayor, 1838.

Therefore it is right also, as it seems to me, not only that Literature should receive honour here, but that it should render honour too, remembering that if it has undoubtedly done good to Birmingham, Birmingham has undoubtedly done good to it. [*Cheers.*] From the shame of the purchased dedication, from the scurrilous and dirty work of Grub Street, from the dependent seat on sufferance at my Lord Duke's table today, and from the sponging-house and Marshalsea tomorrow, from that venality which, by a fine moral retribution, has degraded statesmen even to a greater extent than authors, because the statesman entertained a low belief in the universality of corruption, while the author yielded only to the dire necessity of his calling,—from all such evils the people have set Literature free. And my creed in the exercise of that profession is, that Literature cannot be too faithful to the people in return— cannot too ardently advocate the cause of their advancement, happiness, and prosperity. [*Loud applause.*] Gentlemen, I have heard it sometimes said—and what is worse, as expressing something more cold-blooded, I have sometimes seen it written—that Litera- ture has suffered by this change, that it has degenerated by being made cheaper. I have not found that to be the case. [*Cries of ' Hear, hear.'*] Nor do I believe that you have made that discovery either. But let a good book in these 'bad times' be made accessible,—even upon an abstruse and difficult subject—and my life upon it, it shall be extensively bought, read, and well considered. [*Cheers.*]

Why do I say this? Because I believe there are in Birmingham at this moment many working men infinitely better versed in Shake- speare and in Milton than the average of fine gentlemen in the days of bought-and-sold dedications and dear books. I ask anyone to consider for himself who, at this time, gives the greatest relative encouragement to the dissemination of such useful publications as Macaulay's *History*, Layard's Nineveh *Researches*, Tennyson's *Poems*, the Duke of Wellington's published *Dispatches*, or the minutest truths (if any truth can be called minute) discovered by the genius of a Herschel or a Faraday. [*Great applause.*] It is with all these things, as with the great music of Mendelssohn, or a lecture upon art—delivered tomorrow by my distinguished friend the President of the Royal Academy—and how happy we should be if such were the case! [*great cheering*]—however small the audience, however contracted the circle in the water in the first instance, the people are now the wider range outside; and the Sister Arts, while they instruct them, derive a wholesome advantage and improvement from their ready sympathy and cordial response. [*Applause.*] I may instance the case of my friend Mr. Ward's[1] magnificent picture

[1] Edward Matthew Ward (1816–79), historical painter; friend of Dickens;

[*cheers*]; and the reception of that picture here is an example that it is not now the province of art in painting to hold itself in monastic seclusion, that it cannot hope to rest on a single foundation for its great temple—or the mere classic pose of a figure, or the folds of a drapery—but that it must be imbued with human passions and action, informed with human right and wrong, and, being so informed, it may fearlessly put itself upon trial, like the criminal of old, to be judged by God and its country. [*Cheers.*]

Gentlemen, to return and conclude, as I shall have occasion to trouble you again [*loud cries of 'Go on!'*], for this time, I have only once again to repeat what I have already said. As I begun with Literature I shall end with it. I would simply say that I believe no true man, with anything to tell, need have the least misgiving, either for himself or for his message, before a large number of hearers—always supposing that he be not afflicted with the coxcombical idea of writing down to the popular intelligence, instead of writing the popular intelligence up to himself, if, perchance, he be above it; and provided always that he deliver himself plainly of what is in him, which seems to be no unreasonable stipulation, it being supposed that he has some dim design of making himself understood. [*Cheers and laughter.*] On behalf of that Literature to which you have done so much honour, I beg to thank you most cordially, and on my own behalf, for the most flattering reception you have given to one whose claim is, that he has the distinction of making it his profession. [*Cheers.*]

John Forster then proposed 'The Birmingham Society of Artists' and praised the 'merchant princes' of Birmingham, Manchester, and Liverpool as the Medici of a new era. Other speakers included Lord Lyttelton,[1] who gave 'The Guild of Literature and Art', and W. H. Wills,[2] its secretary, who responded. They were followed by Dickens again, who rose and said:

I am requested to propose—or, according to the hypothesis of my friend Mr. Owen,[3] I am, in the temporary character of a walking

painted his portrait; had assisted the Guild of Literature and Art; his picture 'Charlotte Corday going to Her Execution' had won the Fine Arts Association's sixty guinea prize.

[1] George William Lyttelton (1817–76), 4th Baron Lyttelton, 1837; Lord Lieutenant of Worcestershire; Principal of Queen's College, Birmingham; first President of the Birmingham and Midland Institute; Under-secretary of state for Colonies, 1846; chairman of Canterbury association, 1850; and Chief Commissioner of Endowed schools, 1869.

[2] William Henry Wills (1810–80), journalist, dramatist, and miscellaneous writer; contributed to *Bentley's Miscellany* when under Dickens's editorship; one of the original staff of the *Daily News*; sub-editor of *Household Words* and later of *All the Year Round*.

[3] Rev. J. B. Owen, one of the previous speakers.

advertisement, to advertise to you—the educational institutions of Birmingham [*a laugh*], an advertisement to which I have the greatest pleasure in calling your attention. Gentlemen, it is right that I should, in so many words, mention the more prominent of these institutions, not because your local memories require any prompting, but because the enumeration implies what has been done here, what you are doing, and what you will yet do. I believe the first is the King Edward's Grammar School, with its various branches; and prominent among them is that most admirable means of training the wives of working men to be good wives and working wives, the prime ornament of their homes, and the cause of happiness to others—I mean those excellent girls' schools in various parts of the town, which, under the excellent superintendence of the Principal, I should most sincerely desire to see in every town in England. [*Cheers.*] Next, I believe, is the Spring Hill College, a learned institution belonging to the body of Independents, foremost among whose professors Literature is proud to hail Mr. Henry Rogers,[1] one of the soundest and ablest contributors to the *Edinburgh Review*. The next is the Queen's College, which, I may say, is only a new-born child; but in the hands of such an admirable Doctor, we hope to see it arrive at a vigorous maturity. [*Cheers.*] The next is the School of Design, which as has been well observed by my friend Sir Charles Eastlake, is invaluable to such a place as this; and, lastly, there is the Polytechnic Institution, with regard to which I had long ago an occasion to express my profound conviction that it was of unspeakable importance to such a community as this, when I had the honour to be present under the auspices of your excellent representative, Mr. Scholefield.[2] [*Hear, hear.*] They are all admirable in their kind; but I am glad to find that more is yet doing. A few days ago I received a Birmingham newspaper containing a most interesting account of a preliminary meeting for the formation of a Reformatory School for juvenile delinquents. You are not exempt here from the honour of saving these poor, neglected, and wretched outcasts. I read of one infant, six years old, who has been twice as many times in the hands of the police as years have passed over his devoted head. These are the eggs from which jail birds are hatched; if you wish to check that dreadful brood, you must take the young and innocent and have them reared by Christian hands. [*Great applause.*]

Lastly, I am rejoiced to find that there is on foot a scheme for a

[1] Henry Rogers (1806–77), Professor of English Literature and Language, Mathematics and Mental philosophy, 1839–58; Christian apologist; two vols. of his *Essays* contributed to the *Edinburgh Review* had been published in 1850.

[2] See pp. 58 ff.

new Literary and Scientific Institution,[1] which would be worthy
even of this place, if there was nothing of the kind in it: an institution, as I understand it, where the words 'exclusion' and 'exclusiveness' shall be quite unknown [*great cheering*]; where all
classes may assemble in common trust, respect and confidence;
where there shall be a great gallery of painting and statuary open
to the inspection and admiration of all comers; where there shall
be a museum of models in which Industry may observe its various
sources of manufacture, and the mechanic may work out new
combinations and arrive at new results; where the very mines
under the earth and under the sea shall not be forgotten, but presented in little to the inquiring eye; an institution, in short, where
many and many of the obstacles which now inevitably stand in the
way of the poor inventor shall be smoothed away, and where, if he
have anything good in him, he will find encouragement and hope.
[*Much applause.*]

I observe with unusual interest and gratification, that a body of
gentlemen are going for a time to lay aside their individual pre-
possessions on other subjects, and as good citizens, are to be engaged
in a design as patriotic as may well can be. They have the intention of
meeting in a few days to advance this great object, and I call upon
you, in drinking this toast, to drink success to their endeavours, and
to make it the pledge by all good means to promote it. [*Much cheering.*]

If I strictly followed out the list of educational institutions in
Birmingham I should not have done here; but I intend to stop,
merely observing that I have seen within a short walk of this place
one of the most interesting and practical institutions for the Deaf
and Dumb that has ever come under my observation. [*Hear, hear.*]
I have seen in the factories and workshops of Birmingham such
beautiful order and regularity, and such great consideration for the
work people provided, that they might justly be entitled to be
considered educational too. I have seen in your splendid Town
Hall, when the cheap concerts are going on there, also an admirable
educational institution. I have seen the results in the demeanour of
your working people, excellently balanced by a nice instinct, as free
from servility on the one hand, as from self-conceit on the other.
[*Hear, hear.*] It is a perfect delight to have need to ask a question,
if only from the manner of the reply—a manner I never knew to
have passed unnoticed by an observant stranger. Gather up those
threads, and a great many more I have not touched upon, and
weaving all into one good fabric, remember how much is included
under the general head of the Educational Institutions of your town.
[*Vehement cheering.*]

[1] The Birmingham and Midland Institute.

There were many further toasts and speeches during the evening, among them being another from Forster, who replied on behalf of the Periodical Press.

Dickens had been greatly interested by the project, to which he referred, for a new Industrial and Literary Institute in Birmingham. It had been started at a meeting on 10 June 1852, when a committee had been appointed to consider the best means of founding it successfully. It had decided that it would be necessary to raise at least £20,000; and the committee issued its report a few days after Dickens's visit.

He had already heard all about it from his hosts, and on the way to the station immediately after the banquet the idea occurred to him of offering to help to raise the money by giving a series of readings. He wrote to Arthur Ryland[1] next day, to confirm his offer to 'read the Christmas Carol next Christmas (we being, please God, all alive and well) to the Town Hall folk, either on one or two nights'. He emphasized that he would particularly like 'to have large numbers of working people in the audience. I should like to do it in some way for the benefit . . . of the new institution, and yet I should like the working people to be admitted free'. It would take 'about two hours', he thought, and 'there would be some novelty in the thing, as I have never done it in public, though I have in private, and (if I may say so) with great effect on the hearers'.[2]

Dickens's offer was gladly accepted. Eventually the sum was successfully raised; the new buildings were begun in 1855, and they were finished in 1858. Dickens was elected president in 1869, spoke at the following annual meeting,[3] and presided at the prize-giving in January 1870.[4]

He enlarged on his speech in a letter to Macready:

I know you would have been full of sympathy and approval, if you had been present at Birmingham, and that you would have concurred in the tone I have tried to take about the eternal duties of the Arts to the People. I took the liberty of putting the Court and that kind of thing out of the question, and recognizing nothing *but* the Arts and the People. The more we see of Life and its brevity, and the World and its Varieties, the more we know that no exercise of our abilities in any Art, but the addressing of it to the great ocean of humanity in which we are drops, and not to bye-ponds (very stagnant) here and there, ever can or ever will lay the foundation of an endurable retrospect. Is it not so? You should have as much practical information on this subject now, my dear friend, as any man.[5]

He was no less pleased with the presentation, writing some time later of the address which had accompanied the ring and salver, 'It has hung by my side ever since I received it, and please God, shall remain there, as long as I live and work.'[6]

---

[1] Arthur Ryland (1807–77), solicitor; founder of the Birmingham and Midland Institute; its President, 1861; Mayor, 1860.

[2] From a newspaper cutting of unidentified name and date, in *Birmingham and Midland Institute Newspaper Cuttings, 1864–82*, Birmingham Reference Library.

[3] See pp. 397 ff.   [4] See p. 409.   [5] 14 January 1853 [M].

[6] To J. Eaton Walker, date unknown. (*Aris's Birmingham Gazette*, 23 Oct. 1869.)

ROYAL GENERAL THEATRICAL FUND
22 *March* 1853

THE anniversary festival took place at the London Tavern, with the Hon. F. H. F. Berkeley M.P.,[1] in the Chair. On proposing the toast of the evening, the chairman explained that once again their hopes that Macready would have stood in his place were unavoidably disappointed. He made an amusing speech, referring to attacks on actors from the pulpit, particularly mentioning a pamphlet he had read recently which called them 'the devil's bird-catchers'.

Buckstone replied on behalf of the society; and then Dickens rose, amid great applause, to propose the health of the chairman:

ON a recent occasion, he said, they were informed that a respectable and active police officer had insinuated himself into the midst of an incorruptible election.[2] This very intellectual person had reason to believe, from information he had received, that if he proceeded in a certain direction he would encounter a sage, between whom and himself a most mysterious and magnetic influence would arise if he laid his hand upon his nose. He obeyed these instructions, and in reply to the gesture alluded to, the sage observed, 'It is all right, but there is something more'; whereupon the police officer repeated the necessary cabalistic sign, which secured his admission into the mysterious region, and he took the chief magician into custody.

If he might adapt this incident, of a not very agreeable or creditable nature, to the present very agreeable and creditable occasion, he would suggest it was all right, but there was something more. Without having applied their hands to their noses, they might be said to have placed them in grateful homage on their hearts, and also to their ears in listening to those sweet sounds produced by the musicians, and which gave delight, not only in themselves, but from the generous spirit in which they were uttered. They had used their hands in making those sounds very agreeable to the management of the fund, and in acknowledging the very admirable exposition of its claims they had heard from the Chair. In reference to the Chair, he would simply say that he hoped the 'devil's bird-catchers' might always be able to lime so good a bird. He was too

[1] Francis Henry Fitzhardinge Berkeley (1794–1870), M.P. for Bristol; prominent advocate of the ballot, and opponent of 'temperance'.

[2] At Derby, July 1852. Since the Reform Bill, bribery had become more complicated and better organized, as it was essential to keep up the fiction that the candidate was unaware what his agents were doing. See also Dickens's remarks on the election in ch. lx of this month's number of *Bleak House*, Mar. 1853, in which there was not the least exaggeration. After the last general election, in 1852, there had been over 100 petitions alleging bribery and corruption.

old a bird to be caught by chaff, whether of a celestial or infernal description.

The chairman had laid the fund under a very great obligation, and the cabalistic sign which he was advised as the next in order was, that every gentleman present should empty a wine glass in his honour. [*Loud cheers.*] They were so fortunate in having for their president a gentleman who was the representative of a large mercantile community, and his presence afforded a graceful expression of that union of sympathy which should exist between the busy pursuits of life and its wholesome recreations. They also had in their chairman of the night one who was personally and pleasantly acquainted with the objects of their assembly. He, therefore, called upon them to drink his health, and when they had done that, he hoped they would recollect that there was still 'something more'.

The Chairman responded briefly; Robert Bell replied to the toast of 'English Dramatic Literature'; the chairman gave 'The Ladies', and the proceedings came to an end.

ROYAL ACADEMY BANQUET

30 *April* 1853

THE annual dinner of the Royal Academy was held in the association's rooms in Trafalgar Square, with the president, Sir Charles Eastlake, in the Chair. There was the usual programme of speeches, which led at last to a toast to 'The Interests of Literature', to which both the Dean of St. Paul's,[1] and Dickens, were called on to reply. Dean Milman returned thanks appropriately before leaving the acknowledgement to be completed by Dickens.

In the course of his speech he paid a special tribute—as Viscount Hardinge had before him—to Clarkson Stanfield's[2] striking picture of the *Victory* being towed into Gibraltar harbour after Trafalgar, which had been obscured for the evening by the president's chair, the back of which was hung with crimson velvet.

AFTER tendering his acknowledgement of the toast, and the honour done him in associating his name with it, Dickens said that those acknowledgements were not the less heartfelt because he was unable to recognize in this toast the President's usual disinterestedness;

---

[1] Henry Hart Milman (1791–1868), Professor of Poetry, Oxford, 1821–31; poet, dramatist, historian; had many literary friendships, and was well known to Dickens.

[2] Clarkson Stanfield (1793–1867), marine and landscape painter, scene-painter, and former sailor; close friend of Dickens; painted scenery for *The Frozen Deep*, performed at Tavistock House; Dickens wrote an obituary, 'The Late Mr. Stanfield', for *All the Year Round*, 1 June 1867.

since English literature could hardly be remembered in any place, and certainly not in a school of art, without a very distinct remembrance of his own tasteful writings, [*cheers*] to say nothing of that other and better part of himself which, unfortunately was not visible upon these occasions. [*Renewed cheers.*]

If, like the noble lord, the Commander-in-Chief, he might venture to illustrate his brief thanks with one word of reference to the noble picture painted by a very dear friend of his, which was a little eclipsed that evening by the radiant and rubicund chair which the President now so happily toned down [*laughter*], he would beg leave to say that, as literature could nowhere be more appropriately honoured than in that place, so he thought she could nowhere feel a higher gratification in the ties that bound her to the sister arts. [*Cheers.*] He ever felt in that place that literature found, through their instrumentality, always a new expression, and in a universal language. [*Cheers.*]

BANQUET AT THE MANSION HOUSE
2 *May* 1853

A BANQUET to the judges and various official dignitaries was given by the lord mayor at the Mansion House. It was the occasion of a meeting between Dickens and Mrs. Harriet Beecher Stowe. Seated opposite each other, Mrs. Stowe thought that Dickens and his wife were 'people that one could not know a little of without desiring to know more',[1] but Dickens felt little liking for the author of *Uncle Tom's Cabin*.[2]

'The ceremonies of the dinner', wrote Mrs. Stowe, 'were long and weary'. But, at length, after the usual toasts, and after the lord mayor had proposed the healths of the American Minister, and the judges, he gave 'Vice-Chancellor Wood[3] and the Courts of Equity'. In returning thanks the Vice-Chancellor regretted the absence of some of his brother judges of the Court of Chancery, and he went on to say that the court had been blamed much more than it deserved. The parsimony of the public had long limited the Chancery judges to two—the number that had existed in the reign of George III—but its business had continued to increase. However, there were now seven judges, and each case would be examined on its merits. Everything brought before the court, he thought, would be decided within a few months.[4]

[1] H. E. Beecher Stowe, *Sunny Memories of Foreign Lands*, London, Sampson Low, i. 266.

[2] See H. Stone, 'Charles Dickens and Harriet Beecher Stowe', *Nineteenth-Century Fiction*, 1957, xii. 188–202.

[3] Sir William Page Wood (1801–81), Vice-Chancellor, 1853; he had been appointed Solicitor-General, member of the Chancery Commission, and knighted, in 1851; Lord Chancellor and 1st Baron Hatherley, 1868.

[4] *Bleak House*, to which everyone assumed the vice-chancellor was referring,

After the lord mayor had proposed a toast to 'The Bar', Sir Thomas Noon Talfourd rose, and spoke of the literature of England and America, 'alluding to the two distinguished authors then present'. One, he said, was a lady who had shed a lustre on the literature of America, and whose works were deeply engraved on every English heart, while with the other he associated the toast he had to propose, 'Mr. Charles Dickens and the Literature of the Anglo-Saxons'. Dickens rose to reply.

REFERRING to Mrs. Beecher Stowe, he said that in returning thanks he could not forget he was in the presence of a stranger who was the author of a noble book with a noble purpose. But he had no right to call her a stranger, for she would find a welcome in every English home.

He begged to say that he was delighted to hear from Vice-Chancellor Wood that the Court of Chancery would not in the future be what it had been in the past. [*A laugh.*] He had reason to hope that a suit which had been going on for some years past, and in which he was interested, might, by the learned judge's intervention, be brought to a satisfactory termination. [*Laughter.*]

Several other toasts followed before the ladies retired to the drawing-room, where Mrs. Stowe met Mrs. Dickens. She thought her, 'a good specimen of a truly English woman; tall, large, and well developed'—an opinion that greatly amused Dickens when Mrs. Stowe published it in her account of her travels.

The opinions of the Bench about *Uncle Tom's Cabin* were a sore point. Lord Denman, a former admirer, had recently published a biting attack on Dickens for slighting Mrs. Stowe. What was worse, the veteran Chancery reformer had compared *Uncle Tom* with *Bleak House*, to the disadvantage of the latter. Dickens disliked her style, distrusted her arguments and thought that the book was likely to do harm. Fearing a war in Europe, moreover, he was anxious for American support, and felt that Carlyle might say 'we have thrown this great and powerful friend away for the sake of the Blacks'.[1]

In spite of all this, however, he kept quiet. He was able to follow up his remarks on Wood's speech in his preface to *Bleak House*, next August. Dr. Walter Farquhar Hook, the vice-chancellor's friend, thereon sent Wood an amusing parody of Macaulay's *History*, in which he described

had been written as a deliberate period-piece of the eighteen-twenties when delays in Chancery were notorious. Even so, a week after the banquet, in spite of there being five new judges, seven cases were reported in a week 'in which there were no less than 74 counsel employed, one of which it transpired . . . had been before Lord Chancellor Lyndhurst in 1827'. (*The Times*, 28 Mar. 1854.) Or, in other words, when Dickens had finished *Bleak House* and started his next novel, cases were still being heard which he might have reported himself, when a short-hand writer in the chancellor's court, twenty-seven years before.

[1] Letter to Mrs. Cropper, Lord Denman's daughter, 20 Dec. 1852, quoted H. Stone, 'Dickens and Harriet Beecher Stowe', op. cit.

how: 'The Reformed Courts found a solitary defender. . . . It was at a lord mayor's feast, when, amidst the fumes of wine, even a Vice-Chancellor may be permitted to see double. . . . Dickens was disgusted, and dealt such summary justice to the offending judge that he did not again venture to appear at a lord mayor's feast for two whole years.'[1]

AT A READING OF THE *CAROL*: BIRMINGHAM

30 *December* 1853

DICKENS'S promise to read on behalf of the Birmingham and Midland Institute was redeemed soon after Christmas. The readings were given in the Town Hall, on 27, 29, and 30 December. The first and last were of the *Christmas Carol*, and the other was of the *Cricket on the Hearth*.

On the first night, even a heavy snow storm could not prevent an audience of over 1,700 reaching the Town Hall, which was brightly decorated with holly; and although, as he wrote to Mrs. Watson, Dickens was a little doubtful 'whether it was quite practicable to conceal the requisite effort', he soon found himself at his ease, 'and that we were all going on together . . . as if we had been sitting round the fire'.[2] On the part of his hearers, wrote a local reporter: 'Everybody was charmed by the way in which the story was told. How Mr. Dickens twirled his moustache, or played with his paper knife, or laid down his book, and leant forward confidentially, or twinkled his eyes as if he enjoyed the whole affair immensely!'[3]

On the last night, there was an audience of 2,000; for, in accordance with Dickens's wishes, the tickets had been sold at a price low enough for ordinary working men. The *Birmingham Journal* declared that 'the great compact body were working people, although you would scarcely have supposed it to look at them'. When Dickens appeared, they all 'rose up and cheered most enthusiastically, and then became quiet again, and then went at it afresh. . . . He was stopped at the very first word he spoke with a perfect hurricane of applause, and had to go back to the beginning again. At last he got in a few sentences.'

MY Good Friends, When I first imparted to the Committee of the projected Institute my particular wish that on one of the evenings of my readings here the main body of my audience should be composed of working men and their families [*cheers*] I was animated by two desires; first, by the wish to have the great pleasure of meeting you face to face at this Christmas time [*renewed applause*], and accompany you myself through one of my little Christmas books; and secondly, by the wish to have an opportunity of stating publicly in your presence, and in the presence of the Committee, my earnest hope that the Institute will, from the beginning, recognize

---

[1] W. R. W. Stephens, *Life of Hook*, 1878, ii. 471.
[2] 13 Jan. 1854 [H.]   [3] *Birmingham Journal*.

one great principle—strong in reason and justice—which I believe to be essential to the very life of such an Institution. It is, that the working men shall, from the first unto the last, have a share in the management of the institution which is designed for his benefit, and which calls itself by his name. [*Cheers.*]

I have no fear of being misunderstood—of being supposed to mean too much in this. If there ever was a time when any one class could of itself do much for its own good, and for the welfare of society—which I greatly doubt—that time is unquestionably past. It is in the fusion of different classes, without confusion; in the bringing together of employers and employed; in the creating of a better common understanding among those whose interests are identical, who depend upon each other, and who can never be in unnatural antagonism without deplorable results, that one of the chief principles of a Mechanics' Institution should consist. In this world a great deal of the bitterness among us arises from an imperfect understanding of one another. [*Cheers.*] Erect in Birmingham a great Educational Institution, properly educational; educational of the feelings as well as of the reason; to which all orders of Birmingham men can contribute; in which all orders of Birmingham men can meet; wherein all orders of Birmingham men are faithfully represented; and you will erect a Temple of Concord here which will be a model edifice to the whole of England. [*Loud cheers.*]

Contemplating as I do the existence of an Artisans' Committee, which not long ago considered the establishment of the Institute so sensibly, and supported it so heartily, I earnestly entreat the gentlemen—earnest I know in the good work, and who are now among us—by all means to avoid the great shortcoming of similar institutions; and in asking the working man for his confidence, to set him the great example and give him theirs in return. [*Great cheering.*] You will judge for yourselves if I promise too much for the working man, when I say that he will stand by such an enterprise with the utmost of his patience, his perseverance, sense and support; that I am sure he will need no charitable aid or condescending patronage; but will readily and cheerfully pay for the advantages which it confers; that he will prepare himself in individual cases where he feels it necessary; in a word, that he will feel his responsibility like an honest man, and will most honestly and manfully discharge it. [*Great cheering.*] I now proceed to the pleasant task to which I assure you I have looked forward for a long time.

The reading was a brilliant success. Dickens was delighted with his audience: 'They lost nothing, misinterpreted nothing, followed everything closely, laughed and cried with the most delightful earnestness',[1]—

---

[1] To Hon. Mrs. R. Watson, 13 Jan. 1854.

and they, in turn, were no less pleased with him. When the story was finished, and the chairman proposed a vote of thanks, the audience gave 'a deafening "aye", that sounded like a thunder-clap',[1] followed by three cheers for Dickens, and three for his wife.

When the applause had subsided, Dickens stepped forward and said:

You have heard so much of my voice since we met tonight, that I will only say, in acknowledgement of this affecting mark of your regard, that I am as truly and sincerely interested in you; that any little service to you I have freely rendered from my heart [*applause*]; that I hope to become an honorary member of your great Institution [*great applause*], and will meet you often there when it becomes practically useful; and I thank you most affectionately for this new mark of your sympathy and approval; and that I wish you many happy returns of this great birthday time, and many prosperous years. [*Great cheering.*]

Next day the visit was wound up by a special breakfast, given by the committee, at which Mrs. Dickens was presented with 'an elegant flower-stand, as a tribute of respect to her husband'.

On his return Dickens replied to Arthur Ryland, 'I think I was never better pleased in my life than I was with my Birmingham friends';[2] and to his old friend, de Cerjat, he declared that the readings were 'the most remarkable thing that England could produce, I think, in the way of a vast intelligent assemblage; and the success was wonderful and prodigious'.[3]

AT A READING OF THE *CAROL*: BRADFORD

28 *December* 1854

FOLLOWING his success at Birmingham, in December 1853 Dickens was overwhelmed with applications from similar institutions asking for readings on their behalf. Most of them he was compelled to refuse, but at Christmas the following year he arranged a small reading tour. He began at Reading, on 19 December, at the Literary and Mechanics' Institute at Talfourd's request; he then went on to Sherborne, on behalf of the Literary Institution, for Macready; and, finally, after spending Christmas at home, he travelled up to Bradford to read for the Educational Temperance Institute.

The reading took place in St. George's Hall. After inspecting it earlier in the day, Dickens wrote to Forster: 'The hall is enormous, and they expect to seat 3,700 people to-night! Notwithstanding which, it seems to me a tolerably easy place.'[4] At night it was crowded. Dickens was

---

[1] *Birmingham Journal.* [2] 18 Jan. 1854.
[3] 16 Jan. 1854. [4] F, VII. ii.

loudly cheered on his appearance, and began by giving a brief introduction:

IN reading this little book, he said, he should pause for at the most ten minutes as nearly half-way through as the prescribed divisions of the story would permit.

Allow me, he went on, before I commence, to express two wishes. The first is that you will have the kindness, by a great stretch of the imagination, to imagine this a small social party assembled to hear a tale told round the Christmas fire [*applause and laughter*]; and secondly, that if you feel disposed as we go along to give expression to any emotion, whether grave or gay, you will do so with perfect freedom from restraint, and without the least apprehension of disturbing me. [*Loud applause.*] Nothing can be so delightful to me on such occasions as the assurance that my hearers accompany me with something of the pleasure and interest I shall have in conducting them [*hear*]; and, believe me, I cannot desire anything so much as the establishment amongst us, from the very beginning, of a perfectly unfettered, cordial, friendly sentiment. [*Loud cheering.*]

Dickens then proceeded with the reading, which was followed with the closest attention, and received at the end with loud and repeated applause. A vote of thanks was proposed and seconded, the mayor put the motion, and it was carried with loud cheers. Dickens briefly replied.

They had, he said, been such an admirable audience for so long that he would only detain them by thanking them heartily for their cordial response to the proposition of the two gentlemen, and conclude by assuring them that he could not possibly have given them more pleasure than they had given him.

He was increasingly pleased with the experience of reading to such great audiences, and wrote to W. F. de Cerjat, in his usual New Year letter: 'I am but newly come home from reading at Reading, and at Sherborne in Dorsetshire, and at Bradford, in Yorkshire. Wonderful audiences! and the number at the last place three thousand seven hundred. And yet but for the noise of their laughter and cheering, they went like one man.'[1]

COMMERCIAL TRAVELLERS' SCHOOLS

30 *December* 1854

THE anniversary dinner was held at the London Tavern, with Dickens in the Chair. Preparations had been made for only about eighty to a hundred guests, 'but such was the interest excited by the announcement that Mr. Charles Dickens had kindly consented to preside, that as dinner hour approached the ticket bureau of the tavern was literally besieged by

[1] 3 Jan. 1855.

applicants . . . and upwards of two hundred gentlemen considered themselves fortunate in being allowed to join in the festivities'.[1] Even at such
short notice everyone was satisfied with the final arrangements, although
there was some delay before Dickens took the Chair, supported by his
friend George Moore, the treasurer,[2] Horace Mayhew,[3] Albert Smith,[4]
and Peter Cunningham.[5]

On rising to propose the first toast he was received with loud and
protracted cheering, and said:

I shall beg to suggest a reform in these proceedings at the outset
by addressing this assembly as 'Ladies and gentlemen'. [*Loud cheers,
in which the ladies in the gallery conspicuously joined.*] I beg to propose to you the health of a constitutional Sovereign of a free people,
the embodiment of the private virtues and public principles of the
English nation—a Sovereign who in her public contact fully appre-
ciates the national resolution never to allow the light of civilization and freedom to be quenched in the darkness of any irrespon-
sible will on the face of the earth. Gentlemen, I give you the Queen,
with all the honours. [*Loud cheers.*]

The chairman rose again, and said:

It does not require any extraordinary sagacity in a commercial
assembly to appreciate the dire evils of war.[6] The great interests of
trade enfeebled by it, the enterprise of better times paralysed by it,
all the peaceful arts sent down before it too palpably indicate its

[1] *Daily News*, 1 Jan., p. 3.

[2] George Moore (1806–76), formerly a traveller himself in the lace-trade,
then partner in prosperous lace-house; devoted to practical philanthropy, but
indifferent to public honours; friend of Dickens. In their different ways they
both assisted the Royal Hospital for Incurables, the Warehousemen and Clerks'
Schools, and the Royal Free Hospital—Moore's activities were almost unlimited—and Dickens's association with any of these institutions may have
been partly due to their friendship.

[3] Horace Mayhew (1816–72), journalist, and miscellaneous writer; for some
time sub-editor of *Punch*; younger brother of Henry Mayhew.

[4] Albert Richard Smith (1816–60), author and entertainer; after an ascent
of Mont Blanc in Aug. 1841, he wrote and gave an illustrated lecture on 'Mont
Blanc', at the Egyptian Hall, which remained popular from 1852 to 1858. He also
gave similar lectures on 'The Overland Mail', and 'China', in 1850 and 1858–9.
His brother Arthur Smith (1825–61) was later Dickens's Reading Manager.

[5] See p. 136.

[6] War against Russia had been declared in March, British troops had landed
in the Crimea in September, and the battles of Alma and Balaclava had been
fought. Dickens summed up his feelings, in a letter to the Hon. Mrs. Watson,
as 'mixed . . . admiration of our valiant men, burning desires to cut the
Emperor of Russia's throat, and something like despair to see how the old
cannon-smoke and blood-mists obscure the wrongs and sufferings of the people
at home' (1 Nov. 1854). He made it perfectly clear, however, that he had no
sympathy with men such as John Bright who had just declared that he believed
the war to be 'a terrible crime'.

character and results, so that far less practical intelligence than that by which I am surrounded would be sufficient to appreciate the horrors of war. [*Hear, hear.*] But there are seasons when the evils of peace though not so acutely felt are immeasurably greater, and when a powerful nation by admitting the right of any autocrat to do wrong sows by such complicity the seeds of its own ruin, and overshadows itself in time to come with that fatal influence which great and ambitious powers are sure to exercise over their weaker neighbours. [*Loud cries of Hear, hear.*]

Therefore it is, ladies and gentlemen, that the tree has not its roots in English ground from which the yard wand will be made that will measure—the mine has not its place in English soil which will supply the material of a pair of scales to weigh—the influence, that may be at stake in the war in which we are now straining all our energies. That war is at any time, and in any shape, a most dreadful and deplorable calamity we need no proverb to tell us; but it is just because it is such a calamity, and because that calamity must not for ever be impending over us at the fancy of one man against all mankind, that we must not allow that man to darken from our view the figures of peace and justice between whom and us he now interposes. [*Hear, hear.*]

Ladies and gentlemen, if ever there were a time when the true spirits of two countries were really fighting in the cause of human advancement and freedom—no matter what diplomatic notes or other nameless botherations, from number one to one hundred thousand and one, may have preceded their taking the field—if ever there were a time when noble hearts were deserving well of mankind by exposing themselves to the obedient bayonets of a rash and barbarian tyrant, it is now, when the faithful children of England and France are fighting so bravely in the Crimea. [*Loud cheers.*] Those faithful children are the admiration and wonder of the world so gallantly are they discharging their duty; and therefore I propose to an assembly emphatically representing the interests and arts of peace, to drink the health of the Allied Armies of England and France, with all possible honours. [*Cheers.*]

The toast was received with the loudest demonstrations of enthusiasm. The chairman then went on to propose 'His Royal Highness Prince Albert and the Royal Family'.

He had, he said, omitted the toast from the proper place on the list, partly because he had been engaged with one of the officers of the institution in conversation, and partly because he connected the name of his Royal Highness Prince Albert with the charity in which his Royal Highness had always taken so deep an interest. [*Cheers.*]

After a short interval the chairman then rose to give the toast of the evening, and said:

I think it may be assumed that most of us here present know something about travelling. [*Hear, hear, and laughter.*] I do not mean in distant regions or foreign countries, although I dare say some of us have had experience in that way, but at home, and within the limits of the United Kingdom. I dare say most of us have had experience of the extinct 'fast coaches', the 'Wonders', 'Taglionis', and 'Tallyhos', of other days. I dare say most of us remember certain modest post-chaises, dragging us down interminable roads through slush and mud, to little country towns with no visible populations except half a dozen men in smock frocks smoking pipes under the lee of the Town Hall; half a dozen women with umbrellas and pattens, and a washed-out dog or so shivering under the gables to complete the desolate picture. [*Cheers and laughter.*] We can all discourse I dare say, if so minded, upon our recollections of the 'Talbot', the 'King's Head', or the 'Lion' of those days. We have all been to that room on the ground floor on one side of the old inn yard, not quite free from a certain fragrant smell of tobacco, where the cruets on the sideboard were usually absorbed by the skirts of the box coats that hung from the wall [*great laughter*], where driving-seats were laid out at every turn like so many human mantraps, where county members framed and glazed were eternally presenting that petition which somehow or other made their glory in the county, though nothing else had ever come of it. [*Great laughter.*] Where the *Book of Roads*, the first and last thing always required, was always missing, and generally wanted the first and last dozen leaves, and where one man was always arriving at some unusual hour in the middle of the night, and requiring his breakfast at a similarly singular period of the day. [*Continued laughter.*] I have no doubt we could all be very eloquent on the comforts of our favourite hotel, wherever it was,—its beds, its stables, its vast amount of posting, its excellent cheese, its head waiter, its capital dishes, its pigeon-pies, or its 1820 port. [*Loud cries of Hear, hear.*] Or possibly we could recall our chaste and innocent admiration of its landlady, or our fraternal regard for its handsome chambermaid. [*Cheers.*] A celebrated dramatic critic once writing of a famous actress, renowned for her virtue and beauty, gave her the character of being 'an eminently gatherable-to-one's-arms, sort of person'. Perhaps someone amongst us has borne a somewhat similar mental tribute to the charms of the ladies associated with the administration of our favourite hotel. [*Cheers and laughter.*]

With the travelling characteristics of later times we are all, no doubt, equally familiar. We know all about that station of which

we have a clear idea although we were never there; we know that
if we arrive after dark we are certain to find it half a mile from the
town, where the old road is sure to have been abolished, and the new
road is going to be made, where the old neighbourhood has been
tumbled down, and the new one is not half built up. We know all
about that porter on the platform who with the best intentions in
the world cannot do anything particularly efficacious with the
luggage by looking at it with that bell in his hand. We know all
about that particularly short omnibus, in which one is to be doubled
up to the imminent danger of the crown of one's hat; and about
that fly, whose leading peculiarity is never to be there when it is
wanted. We know, too, how instantaneously the lights of the station
disappear the moment the train slips away, and about that grope
to the new Railway Hotel, which will be an excellent house when
the customers come, but which at present has nothing to offer but a
liberal allowance of damp mortar and new lime. [*Continued laughter.*]

I record these little incidents of home travel mainly with the
object of increasing your interest in the purpose of this assemblage.
Every traveller has a home of his own, and he learns to appreciate it
the more from his wandering. [*Cheers.*] If he has no home, he learns
the same lesson unselfishly by turning to the homes of other men.
He may have his experiences of cheerful and exciting pleasures
abroad; but home is best, after all, and its pleasures are the most
heartily and enduringly prized. [*Loud cheers.*] Therefore, ladies and
gentlemen, everyone must be prepared to learn that commercial
travellers as a body know how to prize those domestic relations
from which their pursuits so frequently sever them; for no one
could possibly invent a more delightful or more convincing testimony to this fact than that they themselves afford in founding and
maintaining a school for the children of deceased or unfortunate
members of their own body,—those children who now appeal to
you in mute but eloquent terms from the gallery. [*Hear, hear.*]

It is to support that school, founded with such high and friendly
objects, so very honourable to your calling, and so useful in its
solid and practical results, that we are here tonight. It is to roof
that building which is to shelter the children of your deceased
friends with one crowning ornament, the best that any building can
have, namely a receipt stamp for the full amount of the cost. [*Cheers.*]
It is for that your active sympathy is appealed to, for the completion
of your own good work. You know how to put your hands to the
plough in earnest as well as any men in existence, for this little book
informs me that you raised last year no less a sum than eight
hundred pounds; and while fully half that sum consisted of new
donations to the Building Fund, I find that the regular revenue of

the charity has only suffered to the extent of thirty pounds. After this I most earnestly and sincerely say that were we all authors together I might boast, if in my profession were exhibited the same unity and steadfastness I find in yours. [*Hear, hear.*]

I will not urge upon you the casualties of a life of travel, or the vicissitudes of business, or the claims fostered by that bond of brotherhood which ought always to exist amongst men who are united in a common pursuit. You have already recognized those claims so nobly, that I will not presume to lay them before you in any further detail. Suffice it to say that I do not think it is in your nature to do things by halves. I do not think you could so if you tried, and I have a moral certainty that you never will try. [*Cheers.*] To those gentlemen present who are not members of the travellers' body, I will say in the words of the French proverb, 'Heaven helps those who help themselves'. The Commercial Travellers having helped themselves so gallantly, it is clear that the visitors who come as a sort of celestial representatives ought to bring that aid in their pockets which the precept teaches us to expect from them. [*Hear, hear, and laughter.*] With these few remarks, which not even your good nature will induce me to prolong, I beg to give you as a toast, 'Success to the Commercial Travellers' School'.

The chairman sat down amidst vociferous cheering, while the toast was received with every demonstration of welcome and applause. *The Orphan's Prayer* was then sung by the children, who afterwards walked through the rooms; the toast of the chairman was proposed, and enthusiastically received—the company standing and cheering for several minutes; and Dickens replied:

Ladies and Gentlemen, You have made me tonight the representative of so many travellers rich in all kinds of enthusiasm, in addition to my own seven poor ones,[1] and that necessity has involved the necessity of your hearing my voice so often, that I shall confine myself to simply thanking you most sincerely for the very kind manner in which you have received my health. [*Hear, hear.*]

He then continued:

If the President of this Institution[2] had been here, I should possibly have made one of the best speeches you ever heard, but as he is not here, I shall turn to the next toast on my list, the Health of your worthy Treasurer, Mr. George Moore,—a name which is a synonym for integrity, enterprise, public spirit, and benevolence. [*Loud cheers.*] He is one of the most zealous officers I ever saw in my

---

[1] *The Seven Poor Travellers* was the Christmas Number of *Household Words* for 1854.

[2] John Masterman (1781–1862), banker; M.P. for City of London, 1841–57.

life; he appears to me to have been doing nothing during the last week but rushing into and out of railway carriages, and making eloquent speeches at all sorts of public dinners in favour of this charity. [*Cheers and laughter.*] Last evening he was in Manchester, and this evening he comes here, sacrificing his time and convenience, and exhausting in the meantime the contents of two vast leaden ink-stands, and no end of pens, with the energy of fifty bankers' clerks rolled into one. [*Cheers and laughter.*] But I clearly foresee that the Treasurer will have so much to do tonight, such gratifying sums to acknowledge, and such large lines of figures to write in his books, that I feel the greatest consideration I can show him is to propose his health without further observation, leaving him to address you in his own behalf. I propose to you, therefore, the health of Mr. George Moore, the Treasurer of this charity, and I need hardly add that it is one which is to be drunk with all the honours. [*Loud cheers.*]

Moore replied giving a report on the result of his visit to Manchester, and the general state of the society's finances. The first list of subscriptions was then read, after which the chairman said:

So many travellers have been going up Mont Blanc lately, both in fact and in fiction, that I have heard recently of a proposal for the establishment of a company to employ Sir Joseph Paxton to take it down. [*Cheers and laughter.*] Only one of those travellers, however, has been enabled to bring Mont Blanc to Piccadilly, and by his own ability and good humour so to thaw its eternal ice and snow, as that the most timid lady may ascend it twice a day 'during the holidays', without the smallest danger or fatigue. [*Laughter.*] Mr. Albert Smith, who is present among us tonight, is undoubtedly 'a Traveller'. [*Hear, hear.*] I do not know whether he takes many orders, but this I can testify, on behalf of the children of his friends, that he gives them in the most liberal manner. [*Loud cheers, and a general transmission of slips of paper towards Albert Smith.*]

We have also among us my friend Mr. Peter Cunningham, who is also a traveller, not only in right of his able edition of Goldsmith's *Traveller*, but in right of his admirable *Handbook*, which proves him to be a traveller in the right spirit through all the labyrinths of London. We have also amongst us my friend Horace Mayhew, very well known also for his books, but especially for his genuine admiration of the company at the end of the room [*pointing, amid cheers and laughter, to the ladies' gallery*], and who, whenever the fair sex is mentioned, will be found to have the liveliest personal interest in the conversation. [*Continued laughter.*]

Ladies and gentlemen, I am about to propose to you the health of these three distinguished visitors. They are all admirable speakers [*loud laughter*], but Mr. Albert Smith has confessed to me, that on fairly balancing his own merits as a speaker and a singer, he rather thinks he excels in the latter art. [*Immense laughter.*] I have, therefore, yielded to his estimate of himself, and I have now the pleasure of informing you that he will lead off the speeches of the other two gentlemen with a song. Mr. Albert Smith has just said to me in an earnest tone of voice, 'What song would you recommend?' and I replied, 'Galignani's Messenger'. Ladies and gentlemen, I therefore beg to propose the health of Messrs. Albert Smith, Peter Cunningham, and Horace Mayhew, and call on the first-named gentleman for a song. [*Loud cheers.*]

Albert Smith's singing was received with great applause, and Cunningham and Mayhew briefly returned thanks.

ROYAL LITERARY FUND: ANNUAL GENERAL MEETING
14 *March* 1855

RELATIONS had steadily been growing more strained between Dickens and the General Committee of the Literary Fund, until about 1854 they came to a head.[1] Early in June he resigned from the Council, and began to consider what could be done to make it change its policy. He and Forster formed an alliance with C. W. Dilke,[2] they went into council on their own, and planned an organized attack to be carried out at the next Annual General Meeting.

Their exact objections to the management of the Literary Fund are not easy to define. The reasons they gave, which no doubt satisfied themselves, were genuine enough, but do not account for the determination of their opposition and the bitterness it aroused. Personal antagonism to certain members of the committee was probably behind some of their animosity, and certainly there was the class hatred of self-made men for committee-minded officials who were quite content to be patronized by the aristocracy. Above all, they had the positive ideal of reorganizing the society so that it should be run by authors, for authors, and should help to make authorship a respectable profession instead of a precarious branch of journalism. Time after time they insisted that they wanted to raise the status of the whole literary profession; for although they were rebels and reformers they not only wanted respect, but respectability.

The same determination was expressed in several of the speeches, it is evident in the novels, and was a consistent theme throughout Dickens's career. His dedication of *Pickwick* to Talfourd for his exertions on behalf

---

[1] See also pp. 1–2 and 6–7.

[2] Charles Wentworth Dilke (1789–1864), proprietor of the *Athenaeum*; had been a clerk in the Navy Pay Office with John Dickens; manager of the *Daily News*, 1846–9; author of an important series of articles on Pope, and other articles on the identity of Junius.

of copyright in the House of Commons, the American speeches, the foundation of the Guild of Literature and Art, and his quarrel with the Literary Fund are all associated in his struggle for what were called 'the Rights of Literature'. Dickens was not alone in his disputes with publishers: as long as there were no royalty agreements antagonism and distrust between publisher and author was the rule rather than the exception. Professional writers were united in their dislike of amateurs who could make light of these difficulties and were not forced to write for pay; and to Dickens the bohemian and the dilettante were typified by Skimpole and Henry Gowan.

In comparison with other professions, authors were not well paid and their incomes were always insecure. Their social status had changed since the beginning of the century, but it was still uncertain. Several attempts had already been made to found writers' associations, but they had all been entirely impracticable or incompetently run.[1] Dickens, Dilke, and Forster recognized that it was almost impossible to start a new society, but hoped that they might be able to capture control of one already in being, change its constitution, and then carry out a policy of their own.

The tactics of the reformers need some explanation, since they involve a knowledge of the history of the society, and its constitution. The Literary Fund had been started about 1790 by the Rev. David Williams. It existed solely for the benefit of authors of works 'of approved literary merit . . . being in want or distress';[2] its grants were always made outright, and they were always supposed to be kept secret.[3] After long delay it had been granted a royal charter, in 1818, which defined its aims and constitution.

The case of the reformers was that the charter was hopelessly defective. Although it carefully provided for two governing bodies, a general committee and a council, through a mistake in drafting only the committee was given any effective power. This had not been discovered until 1848, when the question was laid before the Attorney General; and, thereafter, although members of the council were duly elected, they never met and had nothing to do. The reformers maintained, moreover, that the charter was also faulty in limiting the functions of the society so strictly. They held that the founder had intended that the Literary Fund should have a 'hall or college', which was actually mentioned in the charter, that it should engage in wider activities as well, and generally speaking keep up with the times. And as the society had no power to alter its own constitution, they proposed that it should obtain a new charter.

The Annual General Meeting was held on 14 March. A few days beforehand the reformers circularized their supporters asking them to attend,

---

[1] Among others, a National Association had been started by William Jerdan, in 1831, and an attempt was made at founding an Authors' Society by Charles Mackay in 1843. From the way it was run, Dickens was strongly opposed to the latter, and refused to take part.

[2] *Charter of Incorporation*, St. Albans, 1926.

[3] The rule was strictly kept by the committee, but several of those who received assistance had no objection to making it known, since it served as a guarantee of respectability in applying for further help.

as changes were to be proposed 'of great importance to literary men and to the legitimate objects of a society intended for their benefit'.[1] As far as they could they were anxious to preserve the element of surprise, and Dickens left it to the last minute before writing to the secretary to give notice of his intentions.[2]

The meeting was held at the society's house in Great Russell Street, with Sir Robert Harry Inglis[3] in the Chair. Sir Robert began by mentioning that he had received a very courteous intimation that other business than that upon the notice paper would be introduced, and that it would be dealt with as soon as the ordinary business had been disposed of.

After further proceedings, a vote of thanks was proposed to the auditors, when C. W. Dilke arose to move an amendment. He said that he wished to protest at the high cost of the administration of the society, especially in comparison with the Artists' Benevolent Fund. He moved that, 'this meeting is of the opinion that the expenses of managing the Literary Fund are unreasonable and enormous, and that a great change must be made in the administration of its affairs'. He was supported by Dickens, who explained that there was not the slightest intention to throw any obstacle in the way of the vote of thanks, but that they wished to put the matter to the vote. The amendment was seconded by Sir Edward Bulwer Lytton.

The Rev. Dr. Russell then replied with the explanation that almost the entire cost of the administration was due to the amount spent on the rent of the society's house and the salary of the permanent secretary, both of which were essential. After discussion, the amendment was put to the vote and lost by 32 votes to 28.

The next business was the election of officers. Dilke rose to say that in place of the present president, the Marquis of Lansdowne, he wished to propose Henry Hallam,[4] on the grounds that literary or scientific attainment was a better qualification for office than rank. On being challenged, he admitted that he had not received Hallam's consent to use his name, but maintained that this was irrelevant since it was a question of principle, not of personalities. There followed a dispute about electoral procedure, in which Dickens declared that he was 'one of the gentlemen then present, who held beyond all dispute that the society should be entirely in the hands of literary and scientific men, and that no other human being had any business there whatever'. Eventually, voting papers were given out and collected, and while they were waiting for the scrutineers to return and announce the result, Dickens rose to speak.

In the interval, he said, perhaps the chairman would permit him to

---

[1] Letter to Dr. William Smith of 12 Mar. 1855. Similar letters are known to Harrison Ainsworth, John Blackwood, and Peter Cunningham, from Dickens; and there is one in almost the same words, in the records of the Literary Fund, from Dilke to M. Delepierre, secretary to the Belgian consul.

[2] 14 Mar. 1855, RLF.

[3] Sir Robert Harry Inglis (1786–1855), M.P. for Oxford, 1829–54; commissioner on public records, 1831; active member of various learned societies.

[4] Henry Hallam (1777–1859), Whig historian.

proceed with a motion which he had to submit to the meeting. The resolution went to recognize the necessity of the society being re-incorporated under a new Charter, and he would state the grounds on which he moved it with all possible plainness. The existing Charter was so excessively ridiculous, so absurdly inconsistent, and so manifestly preposterous, that it ought to be abandoned by all men of sound mind, memory, and understanding. [*A laugh.*] Whether the construction that had been put upon it by the Committee were legal or illegal he did not know; but this he did know, that it was sheer nonsense, and he was therefore of the opinion that steps ought to be taken to procure an amended Charter from the Government.

He need scarcely remind them how this question arose. About seven years ago the administrative body of the Corporation, which then consisted of the Council and Committee together, ascertained that for thirty years or so all their proceedings had been illegal. The respected outlaws [*laughter*], on whose minds this conclusion had forced itself, immediately rushed off to the Attorney General, and, in the most laudable manner, exerted themselves otherwise to effect a reconciliation with the outraged majesty of the Law. [*Renewed laughter.*] The result of their deliberations was, that one of the governing bodies of the society called the Council, which had hitherto been recognized as having a right to sit and vote with the General Committee, was thenceforward entirely set apart as having no business to do so, was understood to be for ever banished from the light of the General Committee's countenance, and had taken no part in the management of the society.

Now, before he followed the Council into their extraordinary position in space, let him inquire under what authority these two bodies, the Council and the General Committee, had come into existence. Necessarily, under the authority of the Charter, which declared that there should always be a Council, General Committee, President, Vice-Presidents, and so forth, who, in the words of the Charter should have 'the entire direction and management' of the affairs of the institution. In the very next paragraph, the Charter referred to 'Meetings of the Council', regularly and plainly express-ing, in the most roundabout and the most homely English, that the Council should meet, and that it should have as much share in the government of the institution as the General Committee or the other officers of the society had. This intention the Charter further most emphatically expressed by requiring that the Council should be a very notable body indeed, composed of the 'most potent, grave, and reverend signiors' that the society could discover. [*Laughter.*] It demanded as a qualification that they should have dissected for years every limb of the cases brought before the General Committee, and it regularly stipulated that the Council should be composed of the President and Vice-Presidents and not more than twenty other members of the Corporation, who should 'have served for three years at least upon the General Committee'. The Council being, in this express manner, thus constituted and limited, he hoped they would excuse him for suggesting that outside the Literary Fund itself, and outside those two large establishments of St. Luke's and Bedlam [*laughter*], there surely could not be in the metropolis a single human being who could for one moment doubt that the Council was intended to have a real existence, and ought to have something to do. [*Hear, hear.*] But had it a real existence? Had it anything to do? Why, he appealed to facts which were within the knowledge of every gentleman at that table, and to his own personal experience too; for he had had the honour of being elected a member of that august body, and also of retiring from it as soon as he found out how it was situated. [*Laughter and cheering.*]

Having forfeited his seat on the General Committee, he received a most obliging letter from the secretary, in which he could detect nothing like latent pleasantry or a practical joke, asking if he would like to be elected a member of the Council. He felt extremely diffident about aspiring to such an honour. He pictured to himself a body of sages, peaceably meeting, whose large consumption of midnight oil for the benefit of the society and in administration of the Literary Fund might possibly account for the great expenditure which had been incurred. [*Laughter.*] After much thought he came to the conclusion that by study, and fasting, he might perhaps become fit for such companionship [*laughter*], and replied to the secretary that he would accept the office.[1] So much was he impressed with the importance of the function, that for months afterwards he never left home without leaving word where he might be found, in the event of the Literary Fund wanting him to take counsel with them. [*Laughter.*] He found, however, that they got on without requiring his assistance, and he was then induced to inquire when this Council met, where it met, and what it had to do when it did meet. To his inexpressible amazement he discovered that, according to the construction of the Charter, it never had met as a Council, that it never could and never did meet at any place whatsoever, that it had nothing to do, and that in short it was the only thing in all creation that had no end, purpose, or object in being in existence. [*Hear, and laughter.*]

I ask the meeting—Dickens continued—to consider what the public would say to such a mode of doing business in any other institution with similar pretensions: to a board of directors never meant to direct, to a body of highly qualified judges never allowed

---

[1] He was elected, 12 Mar. 1851.

to judge [*hear*], to a jury convened by solemn writ and summons, never to deliberate and find a verdict. Imagine a physician appointed never to prescribe—a surgeon, never to set a bone. Conceive a corps of firemen who are especially enjoined under no circumstances whatever to go within fifty miles of a fire [*laughter*], or imagine the picked officers of the Royal Humane Society particularly, and strictly, tied up by law from approaching the water. [*Increased laughter.*]

But this is the case of your Council at this moment—that Council which the Charter expressly mentions as one of the governing bodies which shall have 'the entire direction and management' of the affairs of the institution. Now I beg to suggest that if no such pretence would be tolerated in any other institution under the sun, it is least likely to be endured once known and understood out of doors, in the case of a public institution having control over the very large sum of money which has been subscribed by the public, with one plain, distinct, and undeniable object. Firstly, because anything like a false pretence of any kind in such an institution, most properly and justly lays it open to particular suspicion [*hear*]; and, secondly, because the continued endurance of this ridiculous and absurd state of things will always suggest most infallibly and dangerously either that the Council is used as a shelf on which to place uncomfortable members of the General Committee, or as a means of propping up the faults of the concern with the mere names of eminent literary men, who have and can have really nothing to do with it. [*Hear, hear.*]

I submit that this Charter is utterly defective and rotten, inasmuch as it appoints among the governing bodies of the institution a Council; inasmuch as it regulates and sets forth the duties and functions of the other governing bodies, but omits to name those of the Council; the consequence of which is, not only nonsense, as I have already said, but a distinct perversion both of the letter and the spirit of the Charter; and inasmuch as the Council does not discharge, and to the end of time never can discharge, these functions which we solemnly confide to it by the Charter, I have not only the hope—the present hope—but the ultimate certainty of setting this very foolish matter right; and, therefore, I beg to move:

That whether the General Committee's construction of the existing Charter be legal or illegal (as to which there are differences of opinion), it is manifestly absurd, as constituting a body expressly to be elected from Members of the General Committee, with at least three years' experience, called a Council, to which it confides no powers, and no duties, and which never meets, because it cannot even be called together, by any authority, for any purpose; and that it is, therefore, desirable to apply for a new Charter, and that a committee be specially appointed with this object.

At this point the scrutineers returned to announce that the entire official list of officers had been elected. John Forster rose to say that he seconded Dickens.

One of the members of the committee then suggested that a special meeting should be called to discuss the question of obtaining a new charter. He protested that it would be expensive. Sir John Forbes, the physician, thought that there could be no objection to the suggestion that a committee should be appointed merely to consider the matter, and he added that, 'Mr. Dickens who swayed the whole world by his writings, was equally likely to sway them by his speeches when he chose to speak. At least he had that effect on him.' [*Cheers.*]

Dickens agreed to the suggestion that the committee should consider whether an Act of Parliament might do as well as a new charter, and went on to reply to one of the officers of the society who had proposed that the matter should simply be left to the discretion of the General Committee:

He could not accede to this suggestion, he said, since that Committee had already reported against any alteration. As to the present constitution of the Corporation not being inconvenient, all he had to say was that everything foolish was inconvenient—a foolish arrangement just as a foolish person. He thought that members of the Council were now placed in a ridiculous position in relation to the public; and would be placed also in an inconvenient position when the truth, with respect to their want of duties or of power, became known. He should press his resolution, but would be ready to confer with the General Committee as to the names to be placed upon the special committee of the society.

After further discussion it was agreed that the committee should 'report the result of their deliberations to a Special General Meeting to be convened for the purpose', and the resolution was then passed unanimously. A committee was appointed consisting of the president,[1] the Dean of St. Paul's, B. W. Procter,[2] Sir Edward Bulwer Lytton, John Forster,

---

[1] Henry Petty Fitzmaurice (1780–1863), 3rd Marquis of Lansdowne; prominent though moderate leader of the Whig party for the past fifty years; member of the present Cabinet under Palmerston, without office; had the reputation of being a patron of literature and art.

[2] Bryan Waller Procter (1787–1874), author under the pseudonym of 'Barry Cornwall'; after practising as solicitor and conveyancer, he was appointed Metropolitan Commissioner in Lunacy, 1832–61; had many literary friends, including Dickens and Forster. Dickens wrote a preface for *Legends and Lyrics*, 1858, by his eldest daughter Adelaide Ann Procter, who was a regular contributor to *Household Words*.

W. M. Thackeray,[1] Dickens, Robert Bell, Rev. G. R. Gleig,[2] C. W. Dilke,
W. Tooke,[3] Sir Henry Ellis,[4] Sir John Forbes, and J. Auldjo.[5] Dilke announced that he and his friends would offer no further opposition to the
election of officers nominated by the committee, and in the ballot for the
General Committee which followed, the old members were re-elected,
with the addition of Thackeray and Frederick Pollock.[6] After a vote of
thanks to the chairman, and the secretary, the meeting came to an end.

The reformers were jubilant at their victory. To John Blackwood
Dickens wrote: 'I did more than I expected yesterday, and have now a
confident hope of greatly increasing the usefulness of the Institution
without treading very heavily on any of its favorite corns.'[7] Their proposals appeared moderate, and were apparently well received. Certainly
the press was on their side. The *Athenaeum* of course continued to support its proprietor, but even the rival *Literary Gazette* gave its qualified
approval now that he was no longer in a party of one:

> The principal leader of the opposition to this state of things, and almost the
> only opponent up to the present time, is Mr. Dilke . . . but his calculations have
> been made with such rabid views of economy . . . that they have tended to
> invoke a conservative opposition. This year Mr. Dilke's efforts have been most
> gallantly supported by Mr. Dickens, Sir E. Bulwer Lytton, Mr. Forster and
> others, . . . and the work of reformation has commenced in a more . . . accept-
> able form.[8]

Even *The Times* came out in their support, linking the demand for
reform in the Literary Fund to its own attacks on administrative red-
tape, and 'our old enemy, routine, . . . flunkeyism and worship of rank'.[9]

[1] Thackeray played only a small part in the controversy within the Literary
Fund, but he had already been involved in a public dispute about 'The Dignity
of Literature', see p. 138. In Jan. 1850, the *Morning Chronicle*, supported by
Forster in the *Examiner*, had accused him of 'fostering a baneful prejudice'
against literary men. After hotly denying that the literary profession was
looked down on, he found himself black-balled when Milman proposed him for
the Athenaeum; and after saying that the fault lay principally with his fellow
authors for being over-sensitive, he resigned from the Literary Fund, in 1861,
because he was made to sit at a side-table at the anniversary dinner. He wanted
to be a social success and to maintain the 'dignity of literature' at the same
time; but he was so inconsistent that he failed in both.

[2] George Robert Gleig (1796–1888), Chaplain-General of the Forces, 1844–
75; Inspector-General of Military Schools, 1846–57; after active service as an
officer in the Peninsular and America, he had been ordained, 1820; became a
popular novelist and military historian; is best remembered for a biography of
the Duke of Wellington.

[3] William Tooke (1777–1866), solicitor, one of the treasurers of the Literary
Fund, and a minor historian.

[4] Sir Henry Ellis (1777–1869), Principal Librarian of the British Museum,
1827–56; scholarly, diligent, and amiable, but an inefficient administrator.

[5] John Auldjo, author of travel books.

[6] William Frederick Pollock (1815–88), Master of Court of Exchequer;
eldest son of the Lord Chief Baron, Sir Jonathan Frederick Pollock.

[7] MS. National Library of Scotland, Blackwoods' MSS.

[8] 17 Mar., p. 170.   [9] 16 Mar., p. 6.

The *Daily News* was equally outspoken. The reason why so few literary men were members of the society, it declared, was easily accounted for: 'When they open the society's reports, and observe the dazzling array of titles in the list of vice-presidents, and other officers . . . they shut the book and hesitate to obtrude themselves into such illustrious company.'[1]

It seemed as if the cause were won. It only needed the Special Committee to agree on its recommendations, one more General Meeting, and the old charter could be swept away and replaced by a new one. The more conservative members of the society would resign rather than admit that they were wrong, and Dickens and his friends would be left in command. Officially Dickens was still discreet; but privately he wrote to Wilkie Collins, 'I wish you could have seen your servant, last Wednesday, beleaguer the Literary Fund. They got so bothered and bewildered, that I expected to see them all fade away under the table: and the outsiders laughed so irreverently whenever I poked up the chairman that it was quite a facetious business. Virtually, I consider the thing done.'[2]

ROYAL GENERAL THEATRICAL FUND
2 *April* 1855

THE dinner was held at the London Tavern with J. B. Buckstone, the treasurer of the society, in the Chair. There were the usual loyal and patriotic speeches before Dickens rose to propose the toast of the evening, and said:

I DARE say, gentlemen, it is within the theatrical experience of most of us that upon some occasion when we have been at the play —when everything has progressed in the most satisfactory manner —when the principal actor has been a decided favourite—when every point has told with the people in front—when no one has had the misfortune to make one of those little mistakes which we call 'missing his tip' [*laughter*]—I dare say that, within the theatrical experience of most of you, on some occasion, the act drop being down, there has unexpectedly appeared before it, on one side, a gentleman in plain clothes, with his hat feelingly clasped in both his hands, and not without some appearances of the street upon his boots—a gentleman of pale aspect in sight of the audience which is partly referable to the agitation of his feelings, and partly to the strong action floating on features unprepared by the hare's foot—but before that gentleman has opened his lips in reference to the 'proverbial generosity of the British public', you immediately perceive with dismay that he has come forward to apologize. [*Hear, hear, and laughter.*]

[1] 15 Mar., p. 4.   [2] 19 Mar. 1855 [M].

Now, I am that gentleman on the present occasion. [*Renewed laughter.*] 'Ladies and gentlemen, therefore [*laughter*], I am commissioned by the management to inform you that Mr. Buckstone, owing to circumstances over which he has no control, has been put up for two parts in this piece, and finds himself unable to appear in both of them at the same time. [*Laughter.*] He is, at this present moment, making himself up for his favourite character—Treasurer to the General Theatrical Fund [*cheers, and laughter*], in which arduous impersonation he has, through several successive seasons at this establishment, been sustained by your applause. [*Hear.*] He therefore finds himself unable, for the moment, to appear in that other character of Chairman, for which he has been announced in the bill, and in which he would have delivered that well-known and spirit-stirring address, which would have so much affected you. [*Laughter.*] In this dilemma, relying on that consideration which was never appealed to in vain—I allude to the consideration of a British audience—perhaps you will permit me to walk through Mr. Buckstone's part.' [*Loud applause.*] Therefore, ladies and gentlemen, I have to say to you in this way, that perhaps you will allow me to state to you what Mr. Buckstone would have said. [*Laughter.*]

Ladies and gentlemen, on receiving from Mr. Toole the key note, 'Pray, silence—chair!' Mr. Buckstone would have risen to have proposed the toast of the evening, and in doing so he would have commenced by congratulating the members of the Theatrical Fund on the numerous and respectable assembly before him, testifying as it does to their sense of the merits of the institution itself, and to the fact that in the midst of wars and tumults the humanizing arts are not forgotten. [*Applause.*] Least of all, as is natural, that art,[1] that through the means of one little play, has made the battles of Poitiers and Agincourt more renowned than all the chroniclers and historians put together, and which—no disrespect to those 'thoughts that breathe and words that burn',[2] referred to by our chairman—has done more to stir the bold English blood in a just cause, than all the parliamentary speeches that were ever delivered, than all the debates which ever made the night hideous. [*Loud cheers.*] Surely you are not inappropriately asked to remember this object in a time of war, when it can present to you tangibly and in its glowing pictures the joys of military triumph, the sorrows of defeat, the constancy of noble minds, the misfortunes and unspeak-

---

[1] The report in the *Era*, reprinted in the *Proceedings* published by the society, reads: 'that art, the literature grub, through the means. . . .' Although clearly corrupt it is impossible to correct it by comparison with other reports. See Notes on Text and Sources, p. 432.

[2] Gray, 'The Progress of Poetry'.

able calamities of war [*hear, hear*], and the inappreciable blessings of peace. [*Cheers.*]

You are besought most worthily to remember this object of maintaining and encouraging a society which comprehends every grade of actors without limitation, which is fettered by no hard restrictions or impossible conditions, which embraces all theatrical professors, high and low, equally training them to be provident before they are independent, and which succours all who are responsive to its appeal. The resources of the society become their right, so that the proudest spirit need not blush to accept its aid. Lastly, gentlemen, and in a word you are asked to help those who under trouble and difficulty have helped themselves. You are asked to do this in tender remembrance of those efforts which have lightened our cares and have placed us for the time in a wider and less selfish world in lieu of that which is so much with us early and late. This is the sum and substance of Mr. Buckstone's case if he had been able to appear in that principal character for which he is put down in the bill. At the right moment you would have heard all that fervid eloquence which belongs to the part, and would have seen all the humour connected with it thoroughly performed. As I now have the pleasure of observing Mr. Buckstone at the wing, evidently well up in the part of Treasurer, with his property documents all ready, eager to come on, I will, with your permission, leave the stage to him, merely observing that I detect mischief in his treasury eye, and I would recommend to you the caution once regularly administered at the opening of the pit doors, 'Take care of your pockets!' I have now to propose to you 'Prosperity to the General Theatrical Fund!'

The toast was drunk with great enthusiasm, and Buckstone rose amid loud cheering to reply from the Chair. He was an excellent speaker, efficient in reviewing the state of the society, and amusing in recalling the hardship's of an actor's life. He described how he himself had once walked from Northampton to London, with no more than $4\frac{1}{2}d.$ in his pocket, wearing 'a pair of dancing pumps, tied up at the heel with pack-thread'. Dickens then rose to propose the health of the chairman.

He was sure, he said, that after the address they had just heard, he need say but little in proposing to them the health of their respected chairman, and prosperity to the Haymarket Theatre. If Mr. Buckstone were any ordinary chairman, he might pass the toast over without any further observations; but he was not so— he was a gentleman who had a special claim upon their regards. He could answer for it from his recollections as a boy, twenty-five years ago, how much the acting of that gentleman had enchanted him, as no doubt it then did many others, and how he went home to dream of his comicalities. When at the Adelphi, Mr. Buckstone was great in his most original boys, as he is excellent in everything. Who can forget at that time his leading home the inebriated Master Magog, the Beadle; or, in later days, his drunken man in *Presented at Court*; or his *Rough Diamond*,¹ with his huge shirt collar and most natural account of the doings at his village home? It was gratifying to notice the progress Mr. Buckstone had made in his profession since that time, but that was not the only claim the chairman had upon them—he had always shown himself most ready to urge the claims of their benevolent fund, and to support and aid a brother actor.

Mr. Buckstone had now become a manager, and it was to be hoped that by keeping everybody and everything in their proper places, he would command that success which he so much deserved. [*Cheers.*] If in the Crimea, or in the East at the theatre of war, they had met with some checks, and nothing was to be found that was required, it was gratifying to know that such was not the case at the Haymarket Theatre. If Mr. Buckstone had some slight comestibles and luxuries to present to his patrons, if he had to bring his ships upon the stage, they might depend upon it that everything good would not be found packed under 500 tons of iron, nor would he be unable to fire a shot because they had all been left somewhere where they were not wanted.² [*Cheers and laughter.*] It had given him great delight to witness the spirit with which Mr. Buckstone had conducted his house—to enjoy the acting of Miss Cushman,³ or the twinkling of the feet of the Spanish Dancers. [*Cheers.*] Again, wishing them every success, he begged to propose to them 'The health of Mr. Buckstone, and success to the Haymarket Theatre'.

Buckstone was able to continue his duet with Dickens by proposing his health as one of the trustees, 'our best friend and ally', in company with Macready and Benjamin Bond Cabell.⁴

The following day Dickens wrote a little sketch of the proceedings for Forster, rejoicing in the reception of his remarks on the Commissariat and the Crimea:

¹ *Presented at Court* was by J. S. Coyne, 1848, and the *Rough Diamond* by Buckstone, 1847.

² Such mistakes were being exposed by a committee of inquiry into the condition of the army, which had begun sitting at Chelsea, on 5 Mar. It had been set up in consequence of a motion by John Roebuck, carried on 29 Jan., when the Aberdeen administration was defeated. It is mentioned in the preface to *Little Dorrit*.

³ The American actress, Charlotte Cushman (1816–76), had appeared at the Haymarket as Romeo earlier in the season.

⁴ Macready had been elected a trustee after the death of Talfourd, Mar. 1854.

The Government hit took immensely, but I'm afraid to look at the report, these things are so ill done. It came into my head as I was walking about at Hampstead yesterday. . . . On coming away I told B. we must have a toastmaster in future less given to constant drinking while the speeches are going on. B. replied 'Yes sir, you are quite right sir, he has no head whatever sir, look at him now sir'—Toastmaster was weakly contemplating the coats and hats— 'do you not find it difficult to keep your hands off him sir, he ought to have his head knocked against the wall sir,—he should sir, I assure you sir, if he was not in too debased a condition to be aware of it sir.'[1]

In later editions of the *Life* Forster dropped the whole passage, except for the first sentence which was shuffled into the text. 'T.' was too obviously Toole, and 'B.'—from the marginal title 'Tavernkeeper and toastmaster'—the proprietor, Mr. Bathe.

NEWSVENDORS' BENEVOLENT INSTITUTION

21 *May* 1855

REMEMBERING the part he had played in their anniversary festivals of 1849 and 1852, the Newsvendors invited Dickens to become their president when the office fell vacant in April 1854. Dickens willingly agreed. They then asked him to preside at the next Annual General Meeting, in May. He managed to excuse himself, for the time being, but the following year he consented.[2]

The meeting was held at the Freemasons' Hall. On taking the Chair, Dickens was loudly cheered, and he immediately rose to say:

BEFORE proceeding with the business of the general meeting, it occurs to me that we should all refresh our memories as to what this institution is, what it wants, and why we have reason for hoping that its wants will, in the long run, be realized. In the first place your institution is a society—a benevolent and provident society—'for granting temporary relief and permanent assistance to masters and servants engaged as vendors of newspapers, who from age, infirmity, or distress may require assistance.' As I understand the society, although it grants temporary relief to those who are not members, it reasonably, as a matter of justice and right, only grants pensions to the persons and widows of those who are members. It appears one of the great merits of this institution that the qualification of membership is made so extremely small and easy, and within the access of everybody belonging to the trade, the subscription being five shillings annually, or a fraction more than a penny a week.

---

[1] F, VII. ii. n.
[2] *Minutes* of the society, 22 May 1854, and 9 Apr. and 8 May 1855.

Everybody knows, on the authority of 'the wisdom of our ancestors', that 'early to bed and early to rise, make a man healthy, wealthy, and wise'; and although the newsmen as a class are compelled to rise extremely early, which implies extremely early going to bed, still the financial operations of the newsmen do not materially affect the money market. [*Laughter.*] The society provides a qualification within the reach of all poor men, and therefore you commence with the very strong leverage of going upon a perfectly practicable plan. The management of the society is remarkably economical; its expenses are particularly small; it has three pensioners upon its list; and it has saved from its small beginnings £1,500.

Then we come to the question of what your infant struggling society wants? It wants, in the first place, as we all do, more money; it wants, as very few of us do with our current Parliamentary experience, more members. [*Cheers.*] This latter want I regard as by far the more important want of the two; for it is only by the support of the newsvendors themselves; it is only by your zealous exertions and devotion to your own cause; it is only, in short, by your uniting together for the benefit of your common calling, that this society can ever be raised into an extended sphere of usefulness; in fact it is only by your thoroughly helping yourselves that the public can ever be got to help you. [*Cheers.*] You may rely upon it that there is no principle more certain than this, that every man who becomes a member of your society communicates a moral support to it which is worth his five shillings a year fifty times told. [*Hear, hear.*] Every man owes a duty to the calling in which he is engaged no less than to himself, and it is only by this sense of double duty being diffused among the whole trade that your society can ever succeed. [*Cheers.*] Even if there be a man in your trade so sanguine as to believe that he himself will never want help in age, infirmity, or distress, you must inspire that man with the ambition to help his brothers all round, and to elevate the whole family by the brightness of that laudable example.

Well then, we come to the question, what grounds the society has for believing that it will ultimately come to the accomplishment of those wants which I have stated? Now, foremost in the future which is opening before you, I cannot but put the intelligence and enterprise of the principals engaged in the newsvending trade, and the business habits, the good sense, and the good feeling of their assistants. If certain gentlemen whom I see about me tonight—if Mr. Wild, for example, who is close to me, were a distributor of news for the two reasons that his great grandmother, the Dowager-dowager Mrs. Wild had been a distributor of news [*a laugh*], and that he himself had not the slightest knowledge of his own business, I should have slight hope of him.[1] Or if he had selected for his assistant a man who left me the *Morning Post* for last Christmas Day twelve months, instead of *The Times* of this morning [*laughter*], sent my copy of the *Examiner* to Bengal instead of to Tavistock Square, and insisted in serving me with publications I never wished to see, while keeping back those I am dying to read, I should have very small hope of him; and I should take the liberty of saying of such a master and man—as I have taken the liberty of saying pretty often lately of another master and man [*laughter*]: 'It is perfectly clear that no good whatever can come out of these people; they are a scarcely animated heap of confusion and imbecility, and they can no more become better than roses can bloom in the Great Desert, or than the Great Pyramid can stand on its head.' [*Cheers.*]

But newsmen cannot proceed in this manner. They must be steady, attentive, active, industrious, and efficient. The master, to succeed in his trade, must watch and be wary and attentive to every minute detail; and the assistant, to be an assistant worthy of his money—whether he be a man of middle age with a large family, or whether he be an undersized boy who gets a larger-sized boy to hold his oilskin portfolio while he refreshes himself by 'overing' all the posts on his beat [*laughter*]—must do his appointed task of work within his appointed time, or he must come out of the Cabinet altogether, and go to the father of all confusion and false principles. [*Laughter.*] And although the checktaker at a theatre never sees the play [*a laugh*], and similarly it is possible a newsman may never read the paper—though I have seen him at it often when he goes along the street—I cannot but believe that he derives some intelligence and instruction from the article in which he deals; and so

[1] Dickens's remarks have obvious political references. As further details were brought to light of the disaster in the Crimea, the sufferings of the troops, and the mismanagement that caused them, he had grown more angry and embittered. Although the Aberdeen administration had been defeated, and Palmerston had succeeded in forming a new Ministry to replace it—after the failure of Lord John Russell, and the Earl of Derby—it was little more than a rearrangement of the previous Cabinet. Dickens thereon wrote to Forster, on 3 Feb., 'I am hourly strengthened in my old belief that our political aristocracy and our tuft-hunting are the death of England. In all this business I don't see a gleam of hope.' More recently, in a debate on 14 May, the Government had been accused of packing the Cabinet with the members of a few great families, and Lord Ellenborough had asked for 'the selection of men for public employment without regard to anything but the public service'. Dickens relieved his exasperation by joining the Administrative Reform Association, and by a stream of articles in *Household Words*: 'Prince Bull' (17 Feb.), 'Gone to the Dogs' (10 Mar.), 'Fast and Loose' (24 Mar.), 'The Thousand and One Humbugs' (21 Apr., 28 Apr., and 5 May), 'The Toady Tree' (26 May) and 'Cheap Patriotism' (9 June).

long as he discharges his duties faithfully and efficiently, I cannot think it likely his trade will remain a peculiar or exceptional case in not having its own thriving provident institution, supported by the very best men. [*Cheers.*]

Then, lastly, if the members of the trade be only true to the trade itself and to themselves—which I again insist on, with your leave, to be the one thing needful in this business, and the solid ground on which alone your house can stand—we have to ask whether there is a reasonable hope that the public will be glad to help them? I am strongly of opinion that there is, since no one can doubt that the newsman is in his degree a public servant, and that the pack he carries up and down is of vital importance to the public interest. [*Cheers.*] There are near Westminster, at this very moment while I speak, some gentlemen—certain howling Dervishes [*a laugh*], who are observed to be particularly attentive at their devotions at the shrine of my friend Mr. Layard,[1] whose honesty of purpose stands unimpeached—who would hamstring every newsman in London, if they could do so with impunity. Why? Because the newsman, though he is humbly associated, still is usefully and necessarily associated with that great engine which puts a girdle round the earth in every twenty-four hours, [*cheers*], and because the newsman, going upon his daily way, lights up the whole country, as the bearer of a flaming cross used to call the Highland clans together.[2] [*Renewed cheers.*]

[1] Austen Henry Layard (1817–94), excavator of Nineveh, and politician. He had travelled in Persia, Turkey, and Albania, 1840–3; excavated various ancient Assyrian cities, 1845–51; was appointed attache to the Embassy at Constantinople, 1849; and published *Nineveh and Its Remains*, 1848–9, and *Nineveh and Babylon*, 1853, which had an immediate popular success. Was M.P. for Aylesbury, 1852–7; Under-secretary for Foreign Affairs, Feb.–May 1853; visited Constantinople later the same year, and the Crimea, where he observed the battle of Alma in 1854, on his return.

He was appointed a member of the Sebastopol Committee, under Roebuck's chairmanship, gave evidence before it, and led an attack on the conduct and mismanagement of the war, in the House of Commons. His evidence of administrative incompetency in both the civil service, and the army and navy, brought him great unpopularity within the House, particularly after his criticism of Captain Charteris, superintendent of Balaclava Harbour, who died before he could face a court of inquiry. He was received with great impatience, and a mistake in referring to the Captain's age was made an excuse for shouting him down.

Dickens got to know him, and at once offered his own support in *Household Words*, recruited Mark Lemon (of *Punch*), Shirley Brooks (*Illustrated London News*, and the *Weekly Chronicle*), Douglas Jerrold (*Lloyd's Weekly News*), and undertook to speak 'carefully' to Forster (of the *Examiner*). 'I most earnestly entreat you,' Dickens wrote to Layard, 'as your staunch friend and admirer, ... to count upon my being Damascus Steel to the core.' See also p. 198.

[2] Undoubtedly Dickens was thinking of the part the press, and particularly *The Times*, had recently played in exposing administrative incompetence.

We have had lately a strike among the gasworkers, and a strike among the cab-drivers; but consider what were those inconveniences compared with the light that would be dimmed, and the progress that would be stopped, by a strike of newsmen. [*Cheers.*] Humbly associated, I say again, but necessarily associated with that wonderful engine, that great result of civilization which is the terror of all humbugs, and the natural enemy of everyone and everything that cannot bear the light, the newsman is undoubtedly in his degree a good public servant, and the public never forgot a good public servant yet, if he took his right place.

And when I remember that this trade has grown to what it is from the days when some little, mean, poor broadside was issued occasionally, giving an account of certain wonderful appearances observed in the air by eighteen persons of credit down in North-amptonshire [*a laugh*]; when a dozen country gentlemen subscribed to a newsletter written by a person of learning, the news of which, seldom true to begin with, was six months old when they got it; when a copy of *The Times* would scarcely have made one night's curl papers for a young lady with a very moderate crop [*laughter*]; and when I look to the present day when the same newspaper is large enough for a carpet for a dining-room; and when I reflect that the daily press is the portal through which men of great ability, intelligence, and energy pass to win their way to distinction in every quarter of the world; I say—when I see all this—I cannot believe that an institution belonging to the trade, and plainly tending to its benefit, does not contain within it the capacity of being developed to a state of usefulness and credit worthy of the service in which newsmen were enlisted.

The business of the meeting then proceeded. On its conclusion a vote of thanks was given to the chairman, which was carried with loud applause, and briefly acknowledged.

Later in the year the secretary tried to persuade Dickens to give a public reading for the society's benefit, but he was unsuccessful. Dickens refused to preside at the anniversary festivals of 1856 and 1857, and did not appear on its behalf again until 1862.

ROYAL LITERARY FUND: SPECIAL GENERAL MEETING

16 *June* 1855

THE meetings of the Special Committee appointed at the Annual General Meeting went off without friction. Dickens acted as chairman, Forster and Dilke were induced to keep quiet, while Lytton made most of the proposals, which the rest of the members endorsed. They discussed the need for a new charter and agreed on various recommendations. In general, they decided to make the council a senior advisory-body, while leaving the committee with the ordinary work of running the society and administering its funds. They also proposed that the committee should have the power of granting annuities and loans as well as outright grants, in order to spare some of the applicants the sense of accepting charity.

Having set down these recommendations in a *Report of the Special Committee*,[1] which was drawn up by Dickens, a sub-committee was appointed 'to consider the feasibility of making the Literary Fund Society an Institution serviceable and creditable to the followers of Literature as a liberal profession, and not wholly restricted to the temporary relief of writers in distress'. The members of the sub-committee were Sir John Forbes, Dilke, Forster, Auldjo, and Dickens himself. At their meeting, on the 16 April, Dickens once again took the Chair, and they then drew up a further list of recommendations, embodied in a *Report of the Sub-Committee*. They suggested that if the society was to have a house of its own it should be used for literary meetings; that it might be made a literary centre, or club, with a writing-room and library; and that there should be a new class of honorary members, called 'Associates', which should include 'the most distinguished literary men of all countries'. Ultimately they might be able to raise a separate fund to build the 'Hall or College' envisaged by the founder, but for the time being they should use the society's house in Great Russell Street, until they could see whether the changes they proposed were likely to be successful.

The rest of the Special Committee accepted these recommendations; the report was sent to the General Committee, printed, and distributed to members; and an application was sent to the registrars for a Special General Meeting.

The reformers were still confident of their success; their proposals were intentionally modest, and they felt that they could afford to be magnanimous. Unfortunately they underestimated the strength of the opposition. The weakness of their case was that they put forward too many suggestions at once—each of which might have been accepted by itself—so that the report seemed more revolutionary than it was. The more conservative members decided that they disliked all change on principle. Many of the proposals, moreover, had already been rejected years ago when they had been submitted by Dilke, who had succeeded in making himself thoroughly disliked.

The chairman at the General Meeting was Benjamin Bond Cabell. After the usual preliminaries, he read a letter from the Marquis of Lansdowne to say that he would resign as president if the recommendations

[1] The *Report of the Special Committee* was printed by the society, and distributed to members before the Special General Meeting. MS, RLF. This full *Report* includes the *Report of the Sub-Committee*, of which there is also a separate manuscript. Both manuscripts are in Dickens's hand throughout. They were no doubt not merely drafted by him, as chairman, but largely his composition. The *Report* was reprinted in the *Athenaeum*, 9 June, pp. 675–6, and in other newspapers and periodicals.

of the report were accepted. Dickens then presented the report, and moved its adoption. He was seconded by Forster.

In reply, Monckton Milnes[1] moved an amendment, which gratefully acknowledged the work of the committee, but maintained that 'as the proposals . . . involve an entire alteration of the nature and interest of the society', and that as 'its means were inadequate' to effect the change, the proposal to apply for a new charter should be dropped. He made a temperate speech, which was seconded by Frederick Pollock, who said that though he had supported the motion for an inquiry at the last meeting, he could not accept the report: 'At that meeting certain subjects were alluded to by Mr. Dilke and Mr. Dickens, in a very amusing speech, which he should have no objection to hearing again', but he thought that the report went too far.

Dilke replied on behalf of the Special Committee in a speech concerned chiefly with the early history of the society, the intentions of its founders, and the great value of its endowments. He was followed by the Rev. Dr. Russell,[2] and Lord Stanley, who both spoke for the amendment, and then at last by Dickens.

As his speech, he said, was in the report which he had presented to the chairman, he would not be able to renew the gratification which the learned gentleman, the seconder of the amendment, said he felt at hearing his speeches. [*A laugh.*] He regarded, moreover, the complaint of the lamentable deficiency of their funds, after the astounding and unanswered statement made by Mr. Dilke of their financial resources, as about the most bitterly ironical thing which the human mind could conceive of that society.

The honourable gentleman who had moved the amendment had appeared, in common with other gentlemen who had addressed the meeting, to approach the proposal entirely in the character of a lender; but let him approach it in the character of a borrower [*hear, hear*], and put the question to them as a matter of feeling, whether they could not conceive the case of a high-spirited literary man, who would refuse to apply for a gift of money but who would be willing to come to the Fund for a loan to assist him in his difficulties. The noble lord had said, 'Oh! he can regard it as a loan, and can pay it back again in the form of a donation.' But, he would ask, was there a man in that room, who, having received a loan of, say,

---

[1] Richard Monckton Milnes (1809–85), created Baron Houghton, 1863; politician, poet, biographer of Keats; M.P. for Pontefract, 1837–63; had many literary friendships dating from his membership of the Cambridge 'Apostles', when he knew Tennyson, Hallam, and Thackeray, to the careful cultivation of a wider circle in his later years; was well known to Dickens, but though their relations were friendly, Dickens's views as a professional writer, and Milnes's as a professed dilettante, could never be reconciled.

[2] Dr. John Russell (1787–1863), Rector of St. Botolph's, Bishopgate, 1832–63; Headmaster of Charterhouse, 1811–32; Thackeray's headmaster.

a hundred pounds, would have the audacity to put down his name in the list of subscribers as a donor to the society of one hundred pounds, when he repaid it? [*Cheers.*] The suggestion was founded on a perfect misconception of the literary character and honour of the country which it was amazing to hear from such lips. [*Cheers.*]

A gentleman in the room interrupted to say that it was understood that Chateaubriand[1] had done so. DICKENS.—Then he did extremely wrong. JOHN MURRAY.—I would do so, too. DICKENS.—Then you would be extremely wrong, likewise. [*A laugh.*]

With respect to the proposal of the Committee to establish a place for the reunion of literary men, it had been objected by one honourable gentleman that the Athenaeum and other clubs already existed, to which literary men might resort. Why, there was also a fine building known as the London Tavern, which was equally open and accessible to literary men. [*A laugh.*] But did they think that Mr. Bathe, the respectable and enterprising owner of that establishment, would keep his house open for such a purpose? The accommodation proposed to be provided by the committee was of a character suited to the requirements of persons who were altogether unable to avail themselves of privileges such as those to which he had referred. [*Cheers.*] It had been said that the committee wished to take a very large proportion of the £30,000 belonging to the Fund, and appropriate it to other purposes. Nothing of the sort was intended; and the committee had expressly stated in their report that the funds required would be supplied by those persons who would avail themselves of the privilege of the proposed new institution. The object of the literary institution was to induce literary men at home and abroad to take a greater interest in the society, and in case of success the committee anticipated that the increased interest would ensure a corresponding increase in contributions to the Literary Fund; and they proposed that the experiment should first be made on a very small scale, and at almost nominal expense [*cheers*], and then, if unfortunately they should fail in exciting among the profession an increased interest in the objects of the institution, and so did not gain an accession of subscribers, no possible harm would have been done, and the project need not be carried any further. Mr. Milnes had asked the advocates of the scheme why they did not found such a society as

[1] François René de Chateaubriand (1768–1848), French author and statesman; created peer of France, 1815; had been an emigré in England, 1792–1802, when he had been assisted by the Literary Fund. He was said to have mentioned the fact—which was otherwise unknown—at the anniversary dinner of 1822 when he was present as ambassador of France. In fact there was never any question of his specifically repaying what he had received, as a subscription.

they wanted; but they might just as reasonably ask him, and the other conductors of that institution, why this was not done by them as they had their £30,000 of reserved fund, their £200 a year, with which to fulfil these original intentions of the founders that they now altogether blinked.

He would ask any gentleman present to consider whether the Literary Fund was capable of an extended interest among Literary men? Let him look around the room, and,—he said it without any disrespect—at the representatives of Literature on the platform, and ask himself whether he could not imagine a better representation of Literature, brought together under the name of the Literary Fund. [*Cheers.*] The alterations proposed in the report, in the mode of assisting literary men, were suggested by literary men animated with a feeling in favour of their art, who desired to do it good; and actuated also by an earnest desire to rouse up this slumbering society and make it do more for Literature than it had ever yet done, or was likely to do, if left to itself. [*Cheers.*] They knew well that being awakened was, at all time, and under any circumstances, an extremely disagreeable process.—They all knew this, for they objected to it every day of their lives. [*A laugh.*] But beyond all question the Literary Fund had overslept itself by a great number of years, and it was absolutely necessary to knock it up; and, please God, they would get it out of bed by some means or other. [*Cheers and laughter.*]

Dickens was followed by Sir John Forbes, who was for compromise; and then by Samuel Wilberforce, the Bishop of Oxford,[1] a staunch supporter of the regular committee, whose speech probably saved them the day. Sir Edward Bulwer Lytton spoke next. After trying to correct various misinterpretations of the reformers' intentions on the part of the previous speakers, he went on to say that:

Mr. Milnes had insinuated that the gentlemen connected with the Guild of Literature and Art wanted the society to lend its money for their objects. They wanted quite the reverse, because so much was it their object to have loans and pensions granted that if the General Committee had come heartily into their objects, it was the intention of the Guild to have handed over the

---

[1] Samuel Wilberforce (1805–73), Bishop of Oxford, 1845–69; Bishop of Winchester, 1869–73; had been Canon Chaplain to Prince Albert, 1841, and Sub-Almoner to Queen Victoria, 1843. Known as 'Soapy Sam', he had presided at the last anniversary dinner of the fund, on 22 May, when Dickens had given as one of his reasons for not attending: 'If I were there, I could hardly be there without speaking. The Bishop of Oxford is not wholly free from that kind of land-seamanship which is expert in wearing and tacking; and he *might* (I do not say he would) execute a manœuvre or so which I might feel it necessary to reduce to the level of an ordinary straightforward comprehension.' Letter to Rev. Whitwell Elwin, 1 May 1855 [S].

funds they had collected, and it would have been their pride to think that they could have given to the society immeasurably more than any sums the aristocracy had bestowed upon it. [*Cheers.*]

After the chairman had undertaken that whatever the result of the vote, the General Committee would give their best consideration to the question of granting annuities and loans, the amendment was then put to the vote and carried by a large majority.

There were no new arguments against the case for reform, but as soon as it was clear that Dickens and his friends had lost, the press went over to the other side. The attitude of the *Literary Gazette* is significant, since it had been strongly in favour of the demand for an inquiry at the Annual General Meeting, in March, and its proprietor and editor Lovell Reeve had written to congratulate Dickens on his success. It had even welcomed the changes suggested in the printed report, but now it swung round completely:

> The hope we had entertained of announcing some improvement . . . was early dispelled by the vapid proceedings of the Special Committee. Sir Edward Bulwer Lytton and Mr. Dickens . . . have had the misfortune to lend themselves to be the mouthpiece of a sort of conspiracy that has manifested itself against the authorities of the institution for some years past in a very offensive manner; and the arguments of the malcontents, though possessing some truth . . . have proved nevertheless injurious to the cause, from the captious spirit in which they have been brought forward.[1]

The General Committee made no attempt to consider the question of granting annuities and loans, as the chairman had promised, and the reformers were forced to retire and to consider what was to be done before the next Annual General Meeting in March 1856.

ADMINISTRATIVE REFORM ASSOCIATION

27 *June* 1855

THE miserable plight of the Army in the Crimea during the winter, the unremitting criticism of *The Times*, and the published evidence of the witnesses before the Sebastopol Committee, had left the country surprisingly unmoved. It showed little more than a sense of uneasiness; and Dickens was almost equally alarmed by defeat abroad and apathy at home:

> I believe the discontent [he wrote] to be so much the worse for smouldering instead of blazing openly, that it is extremely like the general mind of France before the breaking out of the first Revolution, and is in danger of being turned by any one of a thousand accidents—a bad harvest—the last strain too much of aristocratic insolence or incapacity—a defeat abroad—a mere chance at home—into such a Devil of a conflagration as never has been beheld since.[2]

---

[1] 23 June 1855, p. 395.
[2] To A. H. Layard, 10 Apr. 1855 [BM].

Slight ministerial re-adjustments were useless. The only permanent remedy was to reorganize the real administration of the country, in the Army, the Navy, and the Civil Service. A new society was started to advocate such reforms, and on 5 May the Administrative Reform Association held its first public meeting.

Its constitution, membership, and aspirations were indefinite. According to *The Times* it was chiefly composed of 'merchants and traders of the metropolis'. At first it aroused widespread support, but it failed to enlist any leader of eminence to serve it permanently, and was insufficiently political to be able to bring any force to bear on those in authority. The Government had already promised moderate reform; for the question of reorganizing the Civil Service was not new, Sir Stafford Northcote's and Sir Charles Trevelyan's Report had been issued in 1853 and it was no longer an issue to rouse the whole country. The association lacked power because it was supported by men of good will rather than men with a definite grievance.

Early in May Dickens promised the new association that he would speak on its behalf, and lent his help to A. H. Layard who was raising the same issue in Parliament. Layard's exchanges with Palmerston are referred to in Dickens's speech. He was determined to have the question argued in debate, but on asking the Prime Minister for a day on which to bring forward the motion, Palmerston had replied, 'Really, sir, I cannot undertake to find a day for the hon. gentleman, he must find one for himself.' It was eventually debated on 15 and 18 June, and rejected by 359 votes to 46.[1]

Meanwhile a second meeting of the Association had been held at Drury Lane Theatre, on 13 June. The chairman, Samuel Morley,[2] began by reading several letters from wellwishers who were unable to attend. They included one from Dickens, which was introduced with the announcement that he had promised to speak at their next meeting. Dickens had written:

I regret that I cannot attend the meeting at Drury-lane Theatre on Wednesday night, having a duty to discharge, to which I have been pledged for months. I have enrolled myself a member of the Administrative Reform Association,

[1] Palmerston's reply to Layard was made on 7 May. The motion was: 'That this House views with deep and increasing concern the state of the nation, and is of the opinion that the manner in which merit and efficiency have been sacrificed, in public appointments, to party and family influences, and to a blind adherence to routine, has given rise to great misfortunes and threatens to bring discredit on the national character, and to involve the country in grave disasters.' On 18 June Palmerston replied to Layard's accusation of flippancy, made at the second meeting of the A.R.A., 'Sir, I wonder that when the hon. gentleman made that statement, a blush of shame did not suffuse his face at making charges which his conscience ought to have told him . . . were the reverse of the truth. [*Cheers.*] I shall say no more about the Drury Lane private theatricals. [*Renewed cheers, and laughter.*]'

[2] Samuel Morley (1809–86), textile manufacturer, politician, and leading nonconformist; used his great wealth in philanthropy; became proprietor of *Daily News*, Liberal M.P., and staunch supporter of Gladstone, 1868–85.

because I believe it to be impossible for England long to hold her place in the world, or long to be at rest within herself, unless the present system of mis-managing the public affairs, and mis-spending the public money, be altogether changed; because I daily see stronger and stronger reason to entertain the con-viction that it never will be really amended in any essential respects, until a general determination that it must be, is so extended throughout the country, that it shall make itself plainly heard, even within the very thick party-walls of the House of Commons; because the steady union of great numbers of earnest men is essential to this result; and because I hope the association will effect such union by honestly instructing the people as to their real wrongs, and their peaceful means of righting them for the common good.

You know that literature is my profession—it is at once my business and my pleasure, and I shall never pass beyond it. The association can render me no service but as one of the community, and I join it in no other character, and with no other purpose.[1]

On 27 June the third meeting of the association was held, at which Dickens was able to redeem his promise. 'I am rather flustered about the thing just now,' he wrote to Wilkie Collins a few days before, 'not know-ing their ways or what kind of audience they are, or how they go on at all. But I'll try them, and the best can do no more.'[2]

The theatre was crowded. The Chair was again taken by Samuel Morley who opened the meeting. He was followed by Dickens, who was received with loud and protracted cheering, and said:

I CANNOT, I am sure, better express my sense of the kind recep-tion accorded to me by this great assembly, than by promising to compress what I shall address to it within the closest possible limits. It is more than eighteen hundred years ago, since there was a set of men who 'thought they should be heard for their much speaking'. As they have propagated exceedingly since that time, and as I observe that they flourish just now to a surprising extent about Westminster [*laughter*], I will do my best to avoid adding to the numbers of that prolific race. [*Hear, hear, and laughter.*] The noble lord at the head of the Government, when he wondered in Parliament about a week ago, that my friend, Mr. Layard, did not blush for having stated in this place what the whole country knows perfectly well to be true, and what no men in it can by possibility better know to be true than those disinterested supporters of that noble lord, who had the advantage of hearing him and cheering him night after night, when he first became Premier—I mean that he did officially and habitually joke at a time when this country was plunged in deep disgrace and distress [*hear, hear*]—I say, that noble lord, when he wondered so much that a man of this age, who has, by his earnest and adventurous spirit, done the most to dis-tinguish himself and it, did not blush for the tremendous audacity of having come so between the wind and his nobility, turned an airy period with reference to the private theatricals at Drury Lane Theatre. [*Cheers and laughter.*] I have some slight acquaintance with theatricals, private and public, and I will accept that figure of the noble lord. I will not say that if I wanted to form a company of Her Majesty's servants, I think I should know where to put my hand on 'the comic old gentleman' [*roars of laughter*]; nor, that if I wanted to get up a pantomime, I fancy I should know what establishment to go to for the tricks and changes [*renewed laughter*]; also, for a very extensive host of supernumeraries, to trip one another up in that scene of contention with which many of us are familiar, both on these and on other boards, in which the principal objects thrown about, are loaves and fishes. [*Hear, and laughter.*] But, I will try to give the noble lord the reason of these private theatricals, and the reason why, however ardently he may desire to ring the curtain down upon them, there is not the faintest present hope of their coming to a conclusion. It is this:—The public theatricals which the noble lord is so condescending as to manage, are so intolerably bad, the machinery is so cumbrous, the parts so ill distributed, the company so full of 'walking gentlemen' [*laughter*], the managers have such large families, and are so bent upon putting those families into what is theatrically called 'first business'—not because of their aptitude for it, but because they *are* their families, that we find ourselves obliged to organize an opposition. [*Cheers.*] We have seen the *Comedy of Errors* played so dismally like a tragedy that we cannot bear it. We are, therefore, making bold to get up the *School of Reform,*[1] and we hope, before the play is out, to improve that noble lord by our performance very considerably. [*Hear, hear, and laughter.*] If he object that we have no right to improve him without his license, we venture to claim that right in virtue of his orchestra, consisting of a very powerful piper, whom we always pay. [*Laughter.*]

Sir, as this is the first political meeting I have ever attended [*hear*], and as my trade and calling is not politics, perhaps it may be useful for me to show how I come to be here, since reasons similar to those which have influenced me, may still be fluttering, unbalanced, in the minds of others. [*Hear, hear.*] I want at all times, in plain sincerity, to do my duty by my countrymen. If I feel an attachment toward them, there is nothing disinterested or meritorious in that, for I can never too affectionately remember the confidence and friendship that they have long reposed in me. [*Cheers.*] Within my sphere of action—which I shall never change; I shall never overstep, further or for a longer period than I do tonight, the circle of my own pursuits, as one who lives by Litera-

[1] Thomas Morton, *The School of Reform, Or How to Rule a Husband,* 1805.

ture, who is content to do his public service through Literature, and who is conscious that he cannot serve two masters—within my sphere of action I have, for some years, tried to understand the heavier social grievances and to help to set them right. [*Cheers.*] When the *Times* newspaper proved its then almost incredible case, in reference to the ghastly absurdity of that vast labyrinth of misplaced men and misdirected things, which made England unable to find on the face of the earth, an enemy one-twentieth part so potent for the misery and ruin of her noble defenders as she has been herself, I believed that the gloomy silence into which the country fell, was by far the darkest aspect in which a great people had been exhibited for very many years. [*Cheers.*] With shame and indignation lowering among all classes of society, and this new element of discord piled on the heaving basis of ignorance, poverty and crime, which is always below us—with little adequate expression of the general mind, or apparent understanding of the general mind, in Parliament—with the machinery of the Government and legislation going round and round, and people fallen from it and standing aloof, as if they had left it to its last remaining function of destroying itself, when it had achieved the destruction of so much that was dear to them—I did believe, and I do believe, that the only wholesome turn affairs so menacing could take, was, the awakening of the people, the outspeaking of the people, the uniting of the people in all patriotism and loyalty to effect a great peaceful constitutional change in the administration of their own affairs. [*Cheers.*] At such a crisis this Association arose, and at such a crisis I joined it: considering its further case to be—if further case could possibly be needed—that what is everybody's business is nobody's business, that men must be gregarious in their good citizenship as in most other things, and that it is a law in nature that there must be a centre of attraction for particles to fly to, before any serviceable body with recognised functions can come into existence. Well! This Association has arisen, and we belong to it. What are the objections to it? I have heard in the main but three, which I will briefly glance at, in the order in which I have heard them. One.[1] It is proposed to exercise an influence, through the constituencies, on the House of Commons. I have not the least hesitation in saying that I have the smallest amount of faith in the House of Commons at present existing [*hear, hear*], and that I consider the exercise of such influence highly necessary to the welfare and honour of this country. Reading no later than yesterday, a favourite book of mine, I find Mr. Pepys, two hundred years ago, writing of the

[1] *One*: both pamphlets have 'Oh!' which cannot be correct, though apparently passed by Dickens in proof. Press reports have 'One'.

House of Commons in his time and its political contentions,
thus:

> My cousin Roger Pepys tells me that it is a matter of the
> greatest grief to him in the world that he should be put upon this
> trust for being a Parliament man; because he says nothing is
> done, that he can see, out of any truth or sincerity, but mere envy
> and design.[1]

Now, how comes it to pass that after two hundred years, and
especially many years after a Reform Bill, the House of Commons
is, in the gross, so little changed, I will not stop to inquire. I will
not ask how it happens that bills which cramp and worry the
people, and restrict their scant enjoyments, are so easily smuggled
through that place[2] [*cheers*], and how it happens that measures for
their real service are so very difficult to pass. [*Cheers.*] I will not
analyse the confined air of the lobby, or reduce to their primitive
gases, its deadening influences on the memory of that Honourable
Member who was once a candidate for the honour of your—and
my—independent vote and interest. I will not ask what Sectarian
figure that is, full of blandishments, standing on the threshold,
with its finger on its lips. I will not ask how it comes to pass that
personal altercations, involving all the removes and definitions of
Shakespeare's Touchstone—the retort courteous—the reply chur-
lish—the reproof valiant—the countercheck quarrelsome—the lie
circumstantial and the lie direct—[*laughter*]—are always of immeasurably greater interest in the House of Commons than the
health, the taxation, the education, of a whole people. [*Cheers.*]
I will not penetrate the mysteries of that secret chamber in which
the Bluebeard, Party, keeps his strangled public questions, straitly
charging his last bride, the new comer, on no account to open the
door. [*Laughter.*] I will merely put it to the humble practical
experience, recent and remote, of everybody here, whether the
House of Commons is not occasionally a little hard of hearing, not
a little dim of sight, not a little slow of understanding: whether,
in short, it is not in a sufficiently invalided state to require close
watching, and the occasional application of sharp stimulants; and
whether it is not capable of improvement? [*Cheers.*] I believe that,
in order to preserve it in a state of real usefulness and independence,
the people must be ever watchful and ever jealous of it; and it must
have its memory jogged; it must be kept awake; when it happens
to have taken too much Ministerial narcotic, it must be trotted

---

[1] *Diary*, 27 May 1664.
[2] Chiefly referring to the Sunday Trading Bill introduced by Lord Robert
Grosvenor, which had led to riots in Hyde Park, and was eventually withdrawn.

about, and must be hustled and pinched in a friendly way, as is the usage in such cases. [*Laughter*.] And I hold that no power can have so just a right to administer our functions as a body comprising electors from all parts of the country, who are associated together because their country is dearer to them than drowsy twaddle, unmeaning routine, or the absurdest worn out conventionalities. [*Cheers*.]

This brings me to objection number two. It is stated that this Association sets class against class.[1] Is this so? [*Cries of 'No.'*] No, it finds class set against class, and seeks to reconcile them. [*Hear, hear*.] I wish to avoid placing in opposition here, the two words Aristocracy and People. I am one of those who can believe in the virtues and uses of both, and, I would elevate or depress neither, at the cost of a single just right belonging to either. [*Cheers*.] I will use, instead of these words, the terms, the governors and the governed. These two bodies the Association finds with a gulf between them, in which lie, newly buried, thousands on thousands of the bravest and most devoted men that, even England ever bred. [*Cheers*.] It is to prevent the recurrence of innumerable smaller evils, of which, unchecked, that great calamity was the crowning height and the necessary consummation, and to bring together those two fronts looking now so strangely upon each other, that this Association seeks to help to bridge over that abyss, with a structure founded on common justice and supported by common sense. [*Cheers*.] Setting class against class! The old unmeaning parrot cry than which we remember nothing earlier in our lives! Try its justice in this case, by an illustration:—A respectable old gentleman with a large and costly establishment of servants, finds his household in complete disorder, and that he can get nothing done. When he asks his servants to give his children bread, they give them stones; when they are told to give those children fish, they give them serpents. What they are ordered to send to the East they send to the West; when they ought to be serving dinner in the North, they are consulting obsolete and exploded cookery books in the South; they break, lose, forget, waste, destroy; only tumble over one another when required to do anything; and make the respectable gentleman's house a scene of scandalous ruin. At last the respectable gentleman calls to him his house steward, and says, even then more

---

[1] Dickens had already tried out several of his arguments on Miss Burdett Coutts, who thought Layard's demands were ill timed and excessive. Dickens wrote to her, on 15 May: 'I differ from you altogether as to his setting class against class. He finds them already set in opposition. . . . You assume that the popular class takes the initiative. Now as *I* read the story, the aristocratic class did that, years and years ago, and it is *they* who put *their* class in opposition to the country—not the country which puts itself in opposition to *them*.' [M.]

in sorrow than in anger, 'This is a terrible business, no fortune can stand it—no mortal equanimity can bear it! I must change my system of appointing my servants; I must obtain servants who know and will do their duty.' The house steward throws up his eyes in pious horror, ejaculates 'Good God, here is my master setting class against class!' rushes off into the servants' hall, and delivers a long and melting oration on that wicked theme. [*Laughter.*]

And so we come to the third objection, which I have observed to obtain among that class of young gentlemen of good family, who are not particularly fit for anything but spending money which they have not got. [*Laughter.*] It is usually comprised in the observation, 'How very extraordinary it is that these Administrative Reform fellows can't mind their own business.' I think it will occur to most of us who are here, in final disposal of this alarming objection, that it is rather because we do mind our own business, and because we must have our business minded, and because those who undertake to mind it do not mind it properly, that we are an Association at all. [*Hear.*] I observe from the Parliamentary debates —which have of late, by-the-by, frequently suggested to me that there is this difference between the bull of Spain and the bull of Nineveh,[1] that, whereas, in the Spanish case, the bull rushes at the scarlet, in the Ninevite case, the scarlet rushes at the bull [*laughter and cheers*]—I have observed in the Parliamentary debates that, by a curious fatality, there has been a great deal of the reproof valiant and the counter check quarrelsome, in reference to every individual case, showing the necessity of Administrative Reform, by whomsoever produced, whensoever, and wheresoever. [*Cheers.*] I dare say I might have no difficulty in adding two or three cases to the list, which I know to be true, and which I have no doubt would be contradicted [*cheers*], but I consider it a work of supererogation; for, if the people at large be not already convinced that a sufficient general case has been made out for Administrative Reform, I think they never can be, and they never will be. [*Cheers.*] There is, however, one old indisputable, very well known story, which has so pointed a moral at the end of it that I will substitute it for a new case: by doing of which I may avoid, I hope, the sacred wrath of St. Stephen. [*Laughter.*] Ages ago a savage mode of keeping accounts on notched sticks was introduced into the Court of Exchequer; the accounts were kept, much as Robinson Crusoe kept his calendar on the desert island. [*Laughter.*] In course of

---

[1] The winged bull with a human head, was a common subject in Assyrian sculpture, and Layard had sent home two immense specimens for the British Museum. Layard as the Ninevite Bull was a gift for the political cartoonists, see *Punch*, 7 Apr., p. 135, 12 May, p. 186, and 19 May, p. 202.

considerable revolutions of time, the celebrated Mr. Cocker was born, and died. [*Laughter.*] Mr. Walkinghame, of *The Tutor's Assistant*, and a terrible hand at figures, was born, and died;[1] a multitude of accountants, book-keepers, actuaries, and mathematicians, were born, and died; and still official routine clung to these notched sticks, as if they were pillars of the constitution, and still the Exchequer accounts continued to be kept on certain splints of elm wood called 'tallies'. [*Hear, and laughter.*] Late in the reign of George III, some restless and revolutionary spirit originated the suggestion, whether, in a land where there were pens, ink, and paper, slates and pencils, and systems of accounts, this rigid adherence to a barbarous usage might not possibly border on the ridiculous? All the red tape in the public offices turned redder at the bare mention of this bold and original conception, and it took till 1826 to get these sticks abolished. [*Laughter.*] In 1843 it was found that there was a considerable accumulation of them; and the question then arose, what was to be done with such worn-out, worm-eaten rotten old bits of wood? I dare say there was a vast amount of minuting, memoranduming, and dispatch-boxing, on this mighty subject. The sticks were housed at Westminster, and it would naturally occur to any of us unofficial personages that nothing would have been easier than to allow them to be carried away for firewood, by some of the many miserable creatures in that neighbourhood. However, they never had been useful, and official routine could not endure that they ever should be useful, and so the order went forth that they were to privately and confidentially burnt. [*Laughter and cheers.*] It came to pass that they were burnt in a stove in the House of Lords. The stove, overgorged with these preposterous sticks, set fire to the panelling; the panelling set fire to the House of Lords; the House of Lords set fire to the House of Commons; the two houses were reduced to ashes; architects were called in to build two more; we are now in the second million of the cost thereof; the national pig is not nearly over the stile yet; and the little old woman Britannia, hasn't got home tonight.[2] [*Loud laughter and cheers.*]

[1] Edward Cocker (1631–75) and Francis Walkinghame (*fl.* 1751–85) were the reputed authors of *Cocker's Arithmetick* and *The Tutor's Assistant*, versions of which were still in use. 'According to Cocker' was one of the titles considered for *Hard Times*.

[2] The Houses of Parliament were burnt down on 16 Oct. 1834. The competition for a new design was won by Charles Barry in 1836, he was appointed architect, and work started in 1837. The House of Commons was not ready for use until 1852, when over £2,500,000 had been spent. The building was not completed until 1860.

Writing to Forster on 29 June (wrongly dated 29 Mar.) Dickens said: 'A

I think we may reasonably observe, in conclusion, that all-obstinate adherence to rubbish which time has long outlived, is certain to have in the soul of it more or less that is pernicious and destructive; more or less that will some day set fire to something or other; more or less, which, freely given to the winds would have been harmless, which persistently retained, is ruinous. [*Cheers.*] I repeat, with submission, that I think it is as unnecessary to set the Administrative Reform case up, as it is idle to hope to put it down, on this or that particular instance. The great, broad, true case that our public progress is far behind our private progress, and that we are not more remarkable for our private wisdom and success in matters of business than we are for our public folly and failure, I take to be as clearly established as the existence of the sun, moon, and stars. To set this right, and to clear the way in the country's cause for merit everywhere: accepting it equally whether it be aristocratic or democratic, and only asking whether it be honest or true: I take to be the object of this Association. [*Cheers.*] This object it seeks to promote by uniting together large numbers of the people, I hope, of all conditions, to the end that they may better comprehend, bear in mind, understand themselves, and impress upon others, the common public duty. Also, of which there is great need, that by keeping a vigilant eye on the skirmishers of Party, as they are thrown out from time to time by their Generals, they may see that feints and manœuvres do not oppress the small defaulters and release the great, and that they do not gull the public with a mere field-day Review of Administrative Reform, instead of an earnest hard-fought Battle. [*Loud cheers.*] I speak as an individual, wholly unconnected with the management of this Association, and having had no consultation with any one upon the subject, when I particularly wish that the directors might devise some means of enabling intelligent working men to join this body, on easier terms than subscribers who have larger resources. [*Cheers.*] I could wish to see great numbers of them belong to it, because I sincerely believe that it would be good for the common weal.

Said the noble lord at the head of the Government, when Mr. Layard asked him for a day for his motion, Let the hon. gentleman find a day for himself.[1] [*Shame, shame.*]

good illustration of a Government office. T—— very kindly wrote to me to suggest that Houses of Parliament illustration. After I had dined on Wednesday, and was going to jog slowly down to Drury Lane, it suddenly came into my head that perhaps his details were wrong. I had just time to turn to the Annual Register, and *not one of them was correct!*'—T. is unidentifiable; the initial is probably misleading.

[1] See p. 198.

Now, in the names of all the gods at once,
Upon what meat doth this our Cæsar feed,
That he is grown so great?[1]   [*Loud cheers.*]

If our Cæsar will excuse me, I would take the liberty of reversing
that cool and lofty sentiment, and I would say, 'First Lord, it is
your duty to see that no man is left to find a day for himself.
[*Cheers.*] See you, who take the responsibility of government, who
aspire to it, live for it, intrigue for it, scramble for it, who hold to it
tooth-and-nail when you can get it, see you that no man is left to
find a day for himself. [*Loud cheers.*] In this old country, with its
seething hard-worked millions, its heavy taxes, its crowds of
ignorant, its crowds of poor, its crowds of wicked, woe the day
which the dangerous man shall find for himself, because the head
of the Queen's Government failed in his duty of anticipating it by
a brighter and better one! [*Great cheering.*] Name you the day,
First Lord; make the day; work for a day beyond your little time,
Lord Palmerston, and History in return may then—not otherwise
—find a day for you; a day equally associated with the contentment
of the loyal, patient, willing-hearted English people, and with the
happiness of your Royal Mistress and her fair line of children.'
[*Loud and protracted cheering.*]

Dickens was followed by other speakers, including Layard, who said:

He could scarcely express the pleasure he felt at the presence of his friend
Charles Dickens. [*Loud cheers.*] His friend had taken that truly English view of
the question which so remarkably characterized him. He differed from his
friend when he said he had not been engaged on political questions. It was true
he had not made a trade of politics, but he had been engaged in true politics, in
teaching how the feelings of all classes ought to be respected.

A vivid description of Dickens's part at the meeting was given by
Alexander Southern, then a reporter on the London press:

. . . I early took up my station in the orchestra, where I could see and hear
everything to perfection. Mr. Austen Layard was supposed to be the 'trump
card' of the evening, but the appearance of Mr. Dickens was hailed with
rapturous delight and expectation.

Mr. Dickens, who was daintily dressed in a white waistcoat and evening dress,
came to the front, and in the course of his remarks alluded to the old woman who
wondered she couldn't get over the stile, comparing Britannia to the old lady of
our nursery rhyme; the point of the humour being its damaging criticism upon
the Government of the day, who were shifting the responsibility of what had
occurred from one to another, in the way of the Circumlocution Office. 'The
national pig is not nearly over the stile yet; and the little old woman, Britannia,
hasn't got home to-night,'—with a jump in the voice and an archness of expression which showed Dickens to be a consummate actor. . . . He was, however,
gravely in earnest, and his voice changed greatly to suit the occasion, when he

---

[1] *Julius Cæsar*, I. ii.

denounced Palmerston for his heartlessness and for his *insouciance* of behaviour, when he knew how disastrously the campaign had gone on in the Crimea, and that the whole nation was bowed down in grief at the calamitous crisis which had then just arrived.[1]

A month later Dickens began writing *Little Dorrit*. It is wrong to look for the origin of any of the themes in the novels simply in the author's activities in real life, since life and fiction were both closely twisted round the core of the writer's personality. In this case, Dickens would never have spoken for the association, if it had not expressed convictions he already held. Yet as well as 'the common experience of an Englishman', and the evidence given before the Sebastopol Committee—both of which he mentioned in the Preface to *Little Dorrit*—the origin of Circumlocution Office was no doubt closely associated with the campaign for Administrative Reform.

Dickens was too independent to co-operate with any established organization for long. But he had been particularly attracted by the new association, and he wrote to Macready:

> The subject is surrounded by difficulties. . . . But the great first strong necessity is to rouse the people up—to keep them stirring and vigilant—to carry the war dead into the Tent of such a creature as this Lord Palmerston, and ring into his soul . . . that the time for Dandy insolence is gone for ever. . . . For this, and to encourage the timid people to come in, I went to Drury Lane the other night—I wish you had been there, and had seen and heard the people![2]

The association published a number of pamphlets on the need for reform in various Government departments, but it gradually petered out. Morley resigned the chairmanship in June 1856, and was succeeded by John Roebuck. He announced that it was proposed to act through Parliament in future, rather than independently; and with that it certainly lost Dickens's interest, if not before.

AFTER A READING OF THE *CAROL*: SHEFFIELD

22 *December* 1855

THE reading was given for the benefit of the institute, in the Mechanics' Hall, where it was received with immense enthusiasm. 'Enormous success at Sheffield', wrote Dickens the next day, 'where they took the line "and to Tiny Tim who did NOT die"—with a most prodigious shout and roll of thunder.'[3] At the conclusion, it was reported, 'A universal feeling of joy seemed to pervade the whole assembly, who . . . greeted the renowned and popular author with a tremendous burst of cheering.' A vote of thanks was passed, amid further applause, and the mayor made a presentation of some articles of Sheffield manufacture 'as a manifestation of their gratitude to Mr. Dickens for his kindness in coming to Sheffield'.

[1] F. G. Kitton, *Charles Dickens by Pen and Pencil, Supplement*, 1890, p. 45.
[2] 30 June 1855 [M].   [3] To Hon. Mrs. R. Watson [H].

Dickens replied:

MR. MAYOR, I beg to assure you, and those gentlemen who are associated with you in this kind gift, that I accept with heartfelt delight and cordial gratitude such beautiful specimens of the work of your famous town. The kind expressions with which you have accompanied this presentation, and the response which they received from the assembly, will never be obliterated from my memory. You have heard my voice so much tonight that out of pure forbearance I will not say more than to assure you that these things shall be heirlooms in my family. They will be prized by those who love me as testifying not only to the work of Sheffield hands, but to the warmth and generosity of Sheffield hearts. [*Applause.*]

Believe me, ladies and gentlemen, that to the earnestness of my aim and desire to do right by my readers, and to leave our imaginative and popular literature more closely associated than I found it at once with the private homes and public rights of the English people, I shall ever be faithful,—to my death—in the principles which have won your approval. [*Loud applause.*] Allow me to take a reluctant leave, wishing you, one and all, many many merry Christmases, and many, many happy new years. [*Loud cheers.*]

He left immediately for Paris to be with the family for Christmas; writing, later:

Sheffield was a tremendous success and an admirable Audience. They made me a present of table-cutlery after the reading was over, and I came away by the Mail Train within threequarters of an hour—changing my dress and getting on my wrappers, partly in the Fly, partly at the Inn, partly on the Platform.[1]

ROYAL LITERARY FUND: ANNUAL GENERAL MEETING

12 *March* 1856

THE cause of the self-styled 'reformers' of the Literary Fund had already been lost, but none of them was willing to admit defeat. It was clear that they could never gain a majority within the society, but they seem to have had an idea that if they could only keep up their opposition long enough they might get public opinion on their side, and somehow force the committee to resign. They were determined to bring the matter forward at the next Annual General Meeting, and sent a letter announcing their intention well in advance.

They explained that it was their wish to call attention to the fact that, whereas from 1844 to 1854 the expenses of administering the Literary Fund had been over £5,600, during the same period it had cost

---

[1] To Mary Boyle, 8 Jan. 1856 [M].

the Artists' Benevolent Fund less than £1,000. They proposed, therefore, that the expenses of managing the society were 'unreasonable, and that a great change must be made in . . . its affairs'.[1] The notification was not only signed by the old guard of Dickens, Forster, Dilke, Dilke's son, Mark Lemon, B. W. Procter, and Peter Cunningham, but by new adherents, including Rev. Whitwell Elwin,[2] Hepworth Dixon,[3] Neil Arnott,[4] Professor Ansted,[5] and Sir Charles Pasley.[6]

Cabell again took the Chair. After the usual routine business, Dilke proposed the resolution of which they had given notification. He made a straightforward speech, which was seconded by Procter. Robert Bell then replied on behalf of the Committee, and showed that the expenses of the Literary Fund compared very favourably with those of many similar institutions, though they were not as low as those of the societies selected for comparison by the reformers. Dickens then rose to speak, in support of the resolution, and said:

Sir, I shall not attempt to follow my friend Mr. Bell—who, in the profession of literature, represents upon this Committee a separate and distinct branch of the profession, that like:

> The last rose of summer
> Stands blooming alone,
> His lovely companions
> All faded and gone,

—into the very ingenious maze of bramble-bushes with which he has contrived to beset this question. In the remarks I have to make I shall confine myself to four points. One, that it would appear from Mr. Bell's speech that the Committee find themselves in the painful condition of not spending enough money, and will presently apply themselves to the great reform of spending more. [*'No, no!'* *and a laugh.*] Two, that with regard to the house, it is a positive matter of history, that the house for which Mr. Williams was so anxious, was to be applied to uses to which it never has been applied, and which the administrators of the Fund decline to recognize. Three, that with respect to Mr. Bell's endeavours to

[1] Printed copy, RLF.

[2] Rev. Whitwell Elwin (1816–1900), editor of the *Quarterly Review*, and rector of Booton, Norfolk; close friend of Thackeray, and also of John Forster; acted as Forster's executor, and, in that capacity, was responsible for the destruction of many of Dickens's letters and other manuscripts.

[3] William Hepworth Dixon (1821–79), editor of the *Athenaeum*, historian and traveller.

[4] Neil Arnott (1788–1874), physician, inventor, and natural philosopher.

[5] David Thomas Ansted (1814–80), Professor of Geology, King's College, London.

[6] Sir Charles William Pasley (1780–1861), Lieutenant-General, writer on military subjects; Director of Royal Engineer establishment at Chatham, 1812–41; Inspector-General of Railways, 1841–6.

remove the Artists' Benevolent Fund from the ground of analogy which it unquestionably occupies in reference to the Literary Fund, by alleging that it continually relieves the same people, I beg to say that Mr. Bell, as well as every gentleman sitting at that table, knows perfectly well, that it is the business of this Fund to relieve the same people over and over again [*hear, hear*]; and, indeed, I hold in my hand a report for 1855, from which I find out that out of forty-eight cases relieved, thirty were those of persons relieved from the second to the tenth time.

Robert Bell interjected that the cases were entirely different, since a fresh inquiry was made every time the committee of the Literary Fund considered granting further relief. Dickens continued:

I can only oppose to that statement my own experience when I sat on that committee, and when I have known persons relieved, as a matter of course, on many consecutive applications, without further inquiry being made. As to the suggestion that we should select the particular items of expenditure that we complain of, I think it is according to all experience that we should first affirm the principle that the expenditure is too large. If that be done by the meeting, then I will immediately proceed to the selection of the separate items. [*Hear, hear.*]

Now, in rising to support this resolution, I may state at once that I have scarcely any expectation of its being carried, and I am happy to think it will not. Indeed, I consider it the strongest point of the resolution's case that it should not be carried, for it would be impossible to convey to the public a more convincing proof of mismanagement, and the determination of the managers to mismanage it to the death, than would be involved in the recital for the second time within twelve months, that the attention of the Committee had been called to the incontrovertible facts of its great expenditure, and that at the same time the Committee had asserted that it considered the expenses were not unreasonable. [*Hear, hear.*] I cannot conceive a stronger case for the responsibility of the reform urged for the second time and I rejoice that this statement of facts and the assertion that the expenses are not unreasonable will go forth together.

Now, to separate this question from details, let us remember what the Committee and their supporters asserted last year, and I hope will reassert this year: that it was rather a model kind of thing than otherwise now, that if you get £100 you are to spend £40 in management; and if you get £1000, of course you may spend £400 in giving the rest away. Now, in case there should be any ill-conditioned people here, who may ask what occasion there can be for all this expenditure, I will give you my experience. I went last year to a highly respectable place of resort, Willis's Rooms, in St. James's, to a Special General meeting of this Corporation, for the purpose of hearing and seeing all I could, and saying as little as I could prevail on myself not to say.[1] Allowing for the absence of the younger and fairer portion of the female sex, the general appearance of the place was very much like Almack's[2] in the morning. [*Laughter.*] A number of stately old dowagers were ranged in a row on one side, and old gentlemen sat on the other. The ball was opened with due solemnity by a real marquis, who walked a minuet with the Secretary, at which the audience were much affected. [*Laughter.*] Then another party advanced, who, I am sorry to say, was only a member of the House of Commons— but a gentleman highly connected—and he gracefully took the floor. To him, however, succeeded a distinguished lord, then a bishop, then the son of a distinguished lord; after which the minor church rose, with a member of the Stock Exchange and the Bar; and, at last, in an interval of the theatricals, a man more immediately connected with Literature, though not of course considered very respectable, was allowed to step in and sustain the part of Pangloss, in the adventures of *Candide*, and delight the audience by explaining that this was the best of all possible societies, conducted under the best of all possible managements, at the least of all possible expenditure from the best of all possible funds. [*Laughter.*]

It is in these things—it is in our fondness for being so stupendously genteel, by keeping up such a fashionable appearance, by giving way to the vulgar and common social vice of hanging on to great connexions at any price—that the money goes. [*Hear, hear.*] Why, sir, the very last distinguished writer of fiction[3] whom you caught for your public dinner, told you, in return for drinking his health, somewhere towards the small hours of the morning, that he felt like the servant in plush who is permitted to sweep the stage down, when there are no more great people to come on; and

---

[1] See pp. 192 ff.

[2] The exclusive assembly rooms in King Street, St. James's.

[3] Thackeray, at the anniversary dinner of 1852. His remarks were apparently made with entire good humour: 'We, from this end of the table, speak humbly and from afar off. We are the usefuls of the company, who over and over again perform our little part, deliver our little messages, and then sit down. . . . We resemble the individual in plush, whom gentlemen may have seen at the Opera, who comes forward and demurely waters the stage, to the applause of the audience—never mind who is the great Taglioni, or the Lind, or the Wagner, who is to receive all the glory! For my part I am happy to fulfil that humble office, and to make my little spurt, and to retire.' (*Thackeray, The Humourist and Man of Letters*, by Theodore Taylor [pseud.], 1864, pp. 215–16.)

I myself, at a dinner some twelve years ago,[1] felt like a sort of Rip Van Winkle reversed, who had gone to sleep backwards for a hundred years; and, waking, found that Literature instead of being emancipated, had to endure all manner of aristocratic patrons, and was lying at the feet of people who did nothing for it, instead of standing alone and appealing to the public for support. [*Hear, hear.*]

Why, this Bloomsbury house is another part of the same desire for show, and the officer who inhabits it. (I mean, of course, in his official capacity, for, as an individual, I much respect him.) When one enters the house it appears to be haunted by a series of mysterious looking ghosts, who glide about in some extraordinary occupation; and, after the approved fashion of ghosts, but seldom condescend to disclose their business. What are all these meeting and inquiries wanted for? As for the authors, I say, as a writer by profession, that the long inquiry said to be necessary to ascertain whether an applicant deserves relief, is a preposterous pretence, and that working literary men would have a far better knowledge of the cases coming before the board than can ever be attained by that Committee. [*Hear, hear.*] Further, I say openly and plainly, that this Fund is pompously and unnaturally administered at great expense, instead of being quietly administered at small expense; and that the secrecy to which it lays claim as its great attribute, is not kept; for through those 'two respectable householders', to whom reference must be made to enlighten the ignorance of the Committee, the names of the most deserving applicants leak out, and are, to numbers of people, perfectly well known.

The members have now got before them a plain statement of fact as to these charges; and it is for them to say whether they are unreasonable, or justifiable, becoming, and decent. I beg most earnestly and respectfully to put it to those gentlemen who belong to this institution, that they must now decide, and cannot help deciding, what the Literary Fund is, and what it is not—what it is for, and what it is not for. [*Hear.*] The question raised by the resolution is whether this is a public corporation for the relief of men of genius and learning, who may be reduced to distress by unavoidable calamities or deprived by enfeebled faculties or declining life of the power of literary exertion; or whether it is a snug, traditional, and conventional party, bent upon maintaining its own usages with a vast amount of unnecessary parade, upon its own annual puffery at costly dinner tables, and upon a course of expensive toadying once every twelve months, to one or two members of the aristocracy, with a view to recruiting its finances. This is the

[1] 12 May 1843, see p. 7.

question that you must decide today, and it is a question from which you cannot escape. [*Hear, hear.*]

Richard Blackmore[1] succeeded Dickens, supporting the committee. In the course of his speech, he said he was sure that: 'Mr. Dickens and those who supported him were friends to the society, but he must say it was time the fund cried, "Save me from my friends!"'—Dickens interrupted to say that he did not 'wish to be considered a friend of the fund [*cries of "Oh! oh!"*]—as it was conducted. [*Hear, hear, and a laugh.*]'

He was followed by John Forster and Monckton Milnes. Then, apart from a few less formal interchanges, the final speech was from John Murray, the publisher. He blamed Dickens and his supporters for the harm they were doing the society by their attacks, which had even been repeated in *Household Words*.[2] He begged to move an amendment, that while the meeting recognized 'the necessity and importance of a wise economy', it would be best attained by confiding it 'to the consideration of the Committee'. It was passed by 51 votes to 30, and so the original resolution was never put to the vote.

The trend of opinion against reform was again reflected by the *Literary Gazette*, once among its strongest supporters. According to its report the speeches made by all three of the reformers, 'certainly did the cause more harm than any adversary could have done':

> The majority we have occasion to know, was considerably augmented by the speeches of Mr. Dickens and Mr. Forster. Both forgot, to a degree painful to witness, the character of the audience they were addressing. The vapid jaunty facetiousness, which is quite in place in the pages of 'Household Words', is very much out of place in addressing an assemblage of educated gentlemen.[3]

Even the *Athenaeum*, as the official organ of the reformers, could do little to efface the evidence of the vote: Hepworth Dixon could merely declare that the amendment was carried only by the votes of the officers of the society, 'sixty-nine in number, a great many of whom were present'.[4] But, as the *Saturday Review*[5] pointed out, apart from the fact that there was no reason why the officers should not vote, only sixteen of them did so, while the majority in favour of the amendment was over twenty.

[1] Richard Doddridge Blackmore (1825–1900), later a novelist, and author of *Lorna Doone*, 1869; at this time, having given up the law, he was a schoolmaster and minor poet.
[2] 'The Royal Literary Fund', *Household Words*, 8 Mar. 1856, xiii. 169–72. Although attributed solely to Henry Morley in the 'Contributors' Book', Dickens revised it and added the last two paragraphs himself.
[3] 15 Mar. 1856, p. 63.
[4] 15 Mar. 1856, p. 328.
[5] 22 Mar. 1856, p. 411.

MEETING OF THE DRAMATIC PROFESSION ON DULWICH COLLEGE

13 *March* 1856

THE case of the endowment of Dulwich College and recently been brought before the public by the Charity Commissioners. They had issued a report early in January showing that when the college was founded by Edward Alleyn, in 1619, the annual value of the endowment was worth about £800. It had since increased until it was worth at least ten times as much, and might even be made £50,000 a year, by proper management. The statutes of the college, however, had remained unaltered, and it was notorious that the masters and the fellows of the college were overpaid and had little to do. The commissioners had suggested a new scheme of administration, therefore, under which several changes were proposed: among them being an increase in the number of pensioners, and the extension of the school by the addition of twenty-four foundation scholars in the upper school, and up to seventy-four in the lower.

As soon as the new plan was published Benjamin Webster wrote a letter to *The Times* suggesting that, in view of Alleyn's close connexion with the stage, a fourth of these increases should be reserved for actors and their children. His suggestion was not unfavourably received; and after communicating with the commissioners, he decided to call a meeting, representative of the whole dramatic profession, to press its claim on the college funds. It was held at the Adelphi Theatre, with Dickens in the Chair. On coming forward he was received with several rounds of applause, and said:

LADIES and Gentlemen, My part in the proceedings of today I apprehend will not be so much to talk myself, as to be the cause of talk—and I trust of action also—in others. I shall merely endeavour to present to you as plain and just a summary as I can possibly make of the circumstances under which we are assembled together, being as careful as I possibly can not to trench upon the part of this day's proceedings which has been assigned to those distinguished gentlemen and ornaments of the theatrical profession by whom I have the honour to find myself surrounded. [*Hear, hear.*]

The ideas which most people about London associate with Dulwich College are, probably, of the very vaguest kind. They associate it chiefly, I dare say, with a charming gallery of interesting pictures—very freely and laudably open to the public—which pictures are seen with an unusual absence of glare and bustle, with pleasant gardens outside and a beautiful country, rich in all the attractions of Surrey and Kent. They have, I dare say, certain indistinct associations with some musty old men, in black gowns, all bearing the name of Alleyn, and an embowered college where, without blame to anyone, I dare say a snug thing or two has been transacted in the way of a good place, which we should all be very happy to get if we were only fortunate enough, and were 'Alleyn' enough to obtain it. [*Cheers and laughter*.] They have probably no more distinct idea of the founder of Dulwich College than that he was rather an ancient personage, who lived many years ago, and who, somehow or other, bequeathed to posterity an excuse for passing an occasional pleasant holiday in a pretty country [*hear, hear*]; and I make so bold to say for myself, if he had only done that for this working time, I think he would have done better service to it than is rendered by many majestic and noble personages of much loftier pretensions.

But it becomes us, and the object for which we are here today, to look a little more closely into the history of Dulwich College, and in particular to ascertain whether he had any peculiar and close associations with the stage. He lived by the name of Edward Alleyn, and he lived too, in the days of a remarkable man who, though he died a commoner, who, though he was not honoured with a patent of nobility, nevertheless did the state some service—one William Shakespeare. [*Loud applause*.] His mother was the wife of an actor; he was himself bred to the stage; his brother engaged in theatrical pursuits; he married the daughter of the wife of an actor, who was herself an actress. He was himself a famous actor, and a great and prosperous theatrical manager. He was the manager of the Rose Theatre, and afterwards of the Fortune Theatre, and besides which he had a very large share—supposed to have been purchased from Shakespeare himself—in the Black-friars Theatre; he was also one of the two appointed Masters of the King's Games; and besides inheriting considerable property, he acquired by the actor's art and the manager's enterprise a great deal of money. Retiring from the stage before he was fifty years old, and being already Lord of the Manor of Dulwich, he founded there a college for the maintenance and support of one master, one warden, four fellows, six old men, and six old women, and twelve boys to be educated in good literature. To this college, after its completion, he himself retired, and there, wearing its habiliments and conducting himself in observance of its rules, he lived—and there he died, and there was buried in the year 1626, when he was sixty years of age. Now, when his ashes have lain under the chapel of that institution for more than two hundred years, a certain useful and very much needed public body—called the Charity Commission—discovered that the endowment of this college was extremely rich, and capable of great extension—which extension they recommended to the Legislature. [*Hear, hear*.]

Hereupon up rises, true to his art and true to his trust, a great theatrical manager of our own times, who prays—always keeping within the proposed extensions—prays that one fourth of the benefits may be extended to poor players of both sexes, and also to the children of poor players. [*Hear, hear.*] This appeal this gentleman makes in remembrance of the stage which Edward Alleyn embraced; in remembrance of the means by which he acquired fame and fortune; in remembrance of his unvarying interest in, and kindness to, poor actors during the whole course of his life; and in remembrance of the desire which such a man must in all reason be assumed to have had to benefit his own class, amongst others, when he devoted his munificent spirit to the foundation of Dulwich College. [*Loud applause.*]

Now, ladies and gentlemen, to array against the very moderate suspicion that the founder of Dulwich College, in the great act of his life, did not at once give the go-by to all the sympathies and associations of his whole existence, we have what the authors of romance in the present day might call one diabolical anecdote and one remarkable fact. [*Laughter.*] Now to dispose of this diabolical anecdote; in the first place it is sufficient to mention that as the tale goes it was how that once Alleyn played the Devil [*laughter*], and that thereupon he found upon the stage with him an original devil [*increased laughter*], which apparition so terrified him—as well it might—that he immediately retired from the theatre, and, as an expiation for ever having belonged to it and for the part he had played in it, founded this 'God's Gift', or Dulwich College. [*Much laughter.*] Now, as far as I have been able to learn, there is not the smallest reason to believe that Edward Alleyn even so much as played the Devil at all, indeed I find there is an angel's suit among the list of his wardrobe; and as this story is handed down to us by an old gentleman[1] who wrote charming stories about ghosts coming out of the wainscot and who went back again with a melodious twang, perhaps, under these circumstances, without disrespect to this particular devil, we might venture to dispose of him with a melodious twang of general consent. [*Loud laughter and cheers.*]

The remarkable fact is, however, of much greater importance. It is in the original gift that Edward Alleyn limited the benefits to inhabitants of certain particular parishes, including his own. These parishes, I should mention, expressly included the very districts

---

[1] John Aubrey (1626–97), antiquary and author of *Brief Lives*; the story of the ghost is told in his *Miscellanies*, 4th ed., 1857, p. 81, '*Anno* 1670, not far from Cirencester, was an Apparition: being demanded, whether a good spirit, or a bad? returned no answer, but disappeared with a curious perfume and a most melodious twang. Mr. W. Lilly believes it was a fairy.'

about the theatres in which the actors of that time habitually resided. Not to embarrass you with the names of persons, and places, and dates, it may be enough to say that the name of Edward Alleyn appears among the ratepayers of the liberty of the Clink, in Southwark; and, in addition we find the names of some ten thoroughly well-known actors rated to the relief of the poor—prominent amongst them appearing the names of Edward Alleyn and William Shakespeare.[1] [*Hear, hear.*] Surely we could hardly have a more striking corroboration of the intention that must have been in the mind of such a man than the express naming of those districts in which the players chiefly lived. Added to this, there is the fact that Edward Alleyn, himself an actor, was the first master of Dulwich College; and there is strong reason to believe—I say believe, because the spelling of the age renders the positive identification of names rather difficult—there is strong reason to believe, that two of the original officers of the College were also actors. Added to that, that at every period of his life, long after his retirement from the stage, and after his retirement to Dulwich, Edward Alleyn never forgot his brothers in the profession, nor ceased to be remembered by them as an actor; for we find on one occasion, a couple of years after he had built Dulwich College, he forgave a debt to a company of actors of £200 at a blow. [*Hear, hear.*] One actor writes to him in this style: 'I commend my love and humble duty to you, geving you thankes for your great bounty bestoed upon me in my sicknes, when I was in great want: god blese you for it.'[2] Lord Bacon writes of the College and of the founder—the actor—'I like well that Alleyn playeth the last act of his life so well.'[3] Alleyn himself writes to the former possessor of that ground on which the College now stands, and in which his ashes now repose, the following words in answer to such a taunt as a mean soul might be supposed to have thrown out upon his old profession:

That I was a player I can not deny, and I am sure I will not. My meanes of living were honest, and with the poore abilytyes wherewith god blesst me I was able to doe something for my selfe, my relatives, and my frendes, many of them now lyving at this day will not refuse to owne what they owght me. Therefore am I not ashamed.[4] [*Hear, hear.*]

Now, ladies and gentlemen, it would certainly be a grievous wrong to the writer of these noble words, and a great injury to the

---

[1] One of Collier's forgeries.

[2] John Payne Collier, *Memoirs of Edward Alleyn, Founder of Dulwich College*, Printed for the Shakespeare Society, 1841, p. 96, letter from Richard Tone.

[3] Ibid., p. 140.   [4] Ibid., p. 146, to Sir Francis Calton.

possessor of so manly a nature, to suppose him capable of having spurned the ladder by which he had risen, or to have set his face against the road by which he had come. I venture to say that in all biography there is not an instance of any man of honest self-reliance and self composure that was ever guilty of so base an action; accordingly Edward Alleyn never was. [*Hear, hear.*] The industry of my friend, Mr. John Payne Collier,[1] shows him to us in his habit as he lived; and it is easy, even in his secluded life at Dulwich, to trace many pleasant tenderings of his feet towards the old paths, and many delicate tenderings of his mind towards the old occupations. [*Hear, hear.*] When he goes upon an occasional visit from Dulwich to London on horseback his delight is to dine at the theatrical ordinary, and surround himself with the old familiar theatrical faces; and at the Twelfth Night parties at Dulwich, the boys have to play before the good old player. Late in life his theatre is burnt down, and forthwith he applies himself with energy to its reconstruction. One of his old parts, copied by the theatre copyist, is found amongst his papers ages after he is dead. Everything testifies to the truth and fidelity of his simple heart. [*Applause.*]

Gentle presences which I observe in the boxes, remind me that last night, when I was refreshing my memory with a reperusal of his good life, I found I had one uneasy doubt about him, and I built it upon his having stipulated that the fellows of his college should be single men. [*Laughter.*] This appeared to me uncomfortable. [*Great laughter.*] I soon found, however, his intention was to console them, and to recompense them for their miserable solitude, inasmuch as he had a wife of his own, to whom he was tenderly attached, and whom he was accustomed to address by the endearing epithet of 'Mouse' [*much laughter*], and when that grisly cat who is our common foe dispatched her he provided himself with another 'Mouse', with all convenient speed. [*Roars of laughter.*]

Now, ladies and gentlemen, it will be most conducive to the order and effect of our proceedings that you should hear from the lips which have the best right to relate it to you, what encouraging communication has been had with the Charity Commissioners. Therefore, venturing to express my great admiration of the man who has an honest respect for his calling and a generous and disinterested sympathy with the professors of his art, and who moreover does the great public service—by no means an unimportant

---

[1] John Payne Collier (1789–1883), Shakespearian scholar now best remembered for his forgeries; had begun his career as reporter for *The Times*, 1809–21, and, as member of the staff of the *Morning Chronicle*; recommended Dickens to the *Morning Chronicle* in 1833.

one in these times—of endeavouring to restore anything to its plain, original, truthful position, I beg to commend to your attention, Mr. Benjamin Webster. [*Loud and prolonged applause.*]

Webster explained what steps he had already taken, and that the Charity Commissioners had said they would consider seriously any petition for concessions to actors such as he had already outlined in his letter to *The Times*. Robert Keeley, seconded by J. B. Buckstone, proposed the first resolution in support of his proposals, stating that the meeting was of the opinion that they involved 'a just, reasonable, and moderate recognition of the claims of the poor players to participate in the great extension of Dulwich College proposed by the said Commissioners'. It was also resolved to present a memorial to the Home Secretary, and to appoint a committee to approach M.P.s, known to be interested in the Drama, in support of the actors' claims. A counter-proposal by an old scholar of the college is said to have been 'met with such a storm of disapprobation that the silly mover resumed his seat', and his seconder 'disappeared'.

The proceedings closed with a vote of thanks to the chairman, followed by three cheers for Dickens, and three for Webster.

ROYAL GENERAL THEATRICAL FUND

17 *March* 1856

THE eleventh anniversary festival was held at the London Tavern, with the Right Hon. Lord Tenterden[1] in the Chair. There were the usual loyal and patriotic toasts, the toast of the institution itself, and J. B. Buckstone's reply as treasurer on its behalf. He assured the company that 'the prosperity' of the fund was 'now confirmed'—

for which we have chiefly to thank our warmest, our oldest, and our best friend, Mr. Charles Dickens. Never on any occasion has he deserted us—never has he been absent but once from our eleven festivals, and which festivals, without *his* happy presence, would have been as the day without the sun.

The chairman then proposed 'The health of the Trustees and Mr. Charles Dickens'; and Dickens replied:

I WELL remember that when the opera of *Gustavus* was first produced at Covent Garden, the audience found something dangerously comic in that person referring to that which was the most momentous portion of his existence—whether he should or should not go to the ball where he received his death-wound—to the walking gentleman, Mr. Baker, who had never before opened his lips, or given any sign of his existence: I forget what Mr. Baker's opinion was, but the audience had no faith in him. [*Hear, hear.*]

---

[1] John Henry Abbott, 2nd Baron Tenterden (1796–1870).

And when Mr. Baker, who was dressed in a Court dress as the Court physician, replied to his royal master, the audience certainly were not so serious as they might have been. Now the Trustees are the Court Physicians and walking gentlemen in this place, inasmuch as we have nothing to do but to accept your thanks every year, and to acknowledge the same.

My interest in this society dates from the establishment of the Fund itself. I found it, at the beginning, a plain unpretending reality, designed by actors for the benefit of actors of all degrees, gratuitously administered by actors for actors, and supported by their small earnings from year to year and from month to month. [*Hear, hear.*] From that time to the present I find it the same, exactly what it claims and professes to be, with no kind of false pretence about it; and I do thoroughly believe it is one of the most deserving institutions in this country. [*Cheers.*]

I had, a few days ago, a communication from my friend and fellow Trustee, Mr. Macready, on the subject of this Fund. It arose out of that great change which has made Covent Garden a heap of ruins.[1] That event occasioned us to remember afresh that the English drama has no home or hope of a home in that waste spot. [*Hear, hear.*] That occasioned us to look afresh into the future,— whether there might be any claimants left on the Covent Garden Theatrical Fund [*hear, hear*]; for, while it will be impossible that any new members can be made, I do indulge a hope, amounting almost to a conviction, that the accumulated wealth of that institution must ultimately flow into the coffers of this society. [*Cheers.*] If it were possible, in the nature of things, that those distinguished professors of the dramatic art who are now most justly enjoying their annuities out of that fund as the result of their contributions to it,—even if it *were* possible to double, treble, and quadruple what they are now entitled to, we should all be delighted; but we cannot imagine, when all the purposes for which that fund was established are impossible of realization, what can become of its great capital, unless it finds its way to an institution founded for, and made accessible to, the whole dramatic profession through-out this kingdom. [*Cheers.*]

Having now thanked you on behalf of the Trustees for your favourable reception of their names, I will no longer stand in the way of the next toast, but thank you most gratefully for the hand-some, kind, and ready manner in which you were pleased to receive my name. [*Cheers.*]

---

[1] Burnt down on 5 Mar. 1856, after a Grand Carnival Gala and *bal masqué*. The theatre had been sub-let to John Henry Anderson, conjuror, 'The Wizard of the North'.

Dickens was followed by Lord Raynham, who proposed the health of the chairman, who briefly replied. The ladies, on this occasion, were particularly strongly represented in the galleries; and the next speaker, Charles Taylor,[1] flouted custom by addressing them at the beginning of his speech and deploring the lack of gallantry shown by Dickens and Buckstone who had ignored their presence. John Oxenford, Benjamin Webster, and E. T. Smith, all spoke in turn; and then, again, Dickens.

He would not follow, he said, the horrible example of his friend Mr. Taylor, who began by addressing the ladies, informing them that none of the other speakers had paid any regard to them, and having thus taken advantage of their unsuspecting nature [*laughter*] to gain their willing ear, forthwith abandoned them, addressed himself to the gentlemen, and never after alluded to the ladies throughout his speech. [*Laughter.*] The ladies and gentlemen present, or a large portion of them, would know that in order to make a performance go smoothly it was necessary to arrange a number of little points beforehand. Now, a little point had been arranged between Lord Tenterden and himself, which he would give the public the benefit of. Lord Tenterden had arranged for himself a speech which he had enjoined him (Mr. Dickens) not to entrench upon. It was enjoined to leave the chairman a little fat, and he was cautioned to keep to his toast. He would do so.

He was sure they were under deep obligations to the professional ladies and gentlemen who had contributed so much towards their enjoyment that evening, and he felt it a great honour to be allowed to propose their healths. [*Cheers.*]

The chairman then gave the final toast, which he had so carefully reserved for himself, and proposed 'The health of the Ladies, who had graced the company of that evening with their presence'.

ROYAL HOSPITAL FOR INCURABLES

5 *June* 1856

THE Royal Hospital for Incurables had been founded in 1854 by Dr. Andrew Reed,[2] who had already founded three orphanages and the Asylum for Idiots. He had been greatly heartened, when beginning his work, by reading an article in *Household Words* (20 August 1850), entitled 'No Hospital for Incurables': 'It is an extraordinary fact', it had said, 'that among . . . innumerable medical charities . . . there is not one for the help of those who of all others most require succour, and who

---

[1] Charles Taylor (1817–76), 2nd baronet 1857; at some time edited the *Court Journal*, and managed the Garrick Club.

[2] Dr. Andrew Reed (1787–1862), independent minister of Wycliffe Chapel.

must die . . . neglected and unaided. There are hospitals for the cure of every possible ailment and disease known to suffering humanity, but not one for the reception of persons past cure.'

The article had been written by the sub-editor, W. H. Wills, but it may well have owed something to Dickens. At the time Reed noted in his diary, 'While I am collecting statistics as my surest guide, I find a powerful pen preparing the way for me, and in such a fashion as few could do it.'[1]

Dickens, therefore, was an obvious choice for chairman at the first anniversary dinner, held at the London Tavern, at which he willingly consented to preside. After the usual loyal toasts, he rose to propose 'The Two Houses of Parliament', with which he associated the name of Lord Alfred Paget.[2] He alluded to Lord Alfred's escape the previous night when his yacht had been run down in the Channel by the Belgian Royal Mail packet-steamer *Diamant*.

IN proposing this toast, he said, he hoped it would not be at all supposed that he intended to hint that there was any connexion between a Hospital for Incurables, and the Houses of Lords and Commons. [*Laughter.*] Yet it must be admitted that these houses had given symptoms of labouring under a lingering disease, with intermittent fever—with this difference, that it appeared the cold fits were very long, and the hot fits very short. Yet under the influence of gentle stimulants, the Legislature had occasionally assumed an appearance of being possessed of a strong and vigorous constitution. [*Cheers and laughter.*] With the toast of the two Houses of Parliament he would couple the name of Lord Alfred Paget, who notwithstanding he had nearly met with a watery grave last night by his yacht being run down in the Channel, had been determined to be present that evening to support this great and noble charity. [*Cheers.*]

Lord Alfred Paget replied, and the chairman continued:

He approached the next toast, he said, with some trepidation, because he felt he could scarcely do justice to an institution which had for its object the finding a permanent home for a most deserving and afflicted class of the community. He had the high privilege to give a toast which recognized the immense social importance and the great Christian humanities of a hospital designed for the permanent care and comfort of those who, by disease, accident, or deformity, were hopelessly disqualified for the duties of life.

It was to be remembered at the outset that it was the distinguishing feature of this institution that it entered into competition with none of the existing hospitals, but came in aid of every one

---

[1] *Memoirs of Andrew Reed, D.D.*, ed. A. and C. Reed, 1863, 2nd ed., p. 429.
[2] Lord Henry Alfred Paget (1816–88), Chief Equerry to the Queen, and Clerk Marshal; M.P. for Lichfield, 1837–65; General, on the retired list, 1881.

of them. It did appear to him somewhat extraordinary that amongst
the innumerable and valuable charities of this metropolis it had
been so long without an institution for the relief of those who, in
their helplessness, could not be relieved by any other hospital.
There was no establishment for the treatment of the sick in this
city from the doors of which some unfortunate persons altogether
disqualified for the duties of life, were not driven away in consequence of the impossibility there was of rendering them that
assistance which their state of health required. The institution was
therefore no sooner in existence than, as might be expected, numbers of the most distinguished and experienced members of the
medical profession recorded their conviction of its immense usefulness; and certificates had since been signed which placed it wholly
and for ever beyond dispute.

There were very many cases of great distress; of persons who,
brought up in a respectable position, were cut down by hopeless
disease with no aid, no solace, in the dark hour of their affliction.
It was to afford such a home, it was to relieve such parties that this
charity was founded, and he trusted that it would grow, through
the fostering care of the public, into one of the greatest of
those benevolent institutions which did so much honour to the
country.

The Royal Hospital had scarcely achieved the second year of its
existence; but nevertheless it had obtained 'a local habitation and
a name', in one of the prettiest places in the environs of London.
There was nothing about the institution which partook of sec-
tarianism; its principle was to know no distinction in religion; and
there were now forty-four patients under its protective care. It
divided itself into two branches, affording, first, to those objects of
charity a home for life who had no other home; and, secondly,
assisting with regular donations and kind counsels such patients as
had friends to relieve them in part, and give them shelter, feeling
that they could not bear that sharpest pain—the separation from
those they loved. The necessity for such a hospital, which he could
not but observe with regret, was shown by the circumstance that
at the election within the last month, for ten recipients of the
advantages of the charity, there were no less than 87 candidates,
many of them having particular claims on the sympathy of the
benevolent.

He felt it was their duty to do everything that could be done
to give these poor creatures even a chance of recovery—or, if
not of recovery, of comfort in their closing days; and he trusted,
therefore, that the institution would be liberally supported. In
remembrance of those from whom they derived their birth; in

remembrance of Him who said to the afflicted, 'Take up thy bed and walk'; in remembrance of those whose pillows it might some day be their duty to smooth; in the name of those bright creatures upon whose breasts they hoped hereafter to rest their heads; for the love of God; for the love of man—which was one—he implored their aid on behalf of this infant institution, so that it might hereafter rank as a most beneficent giant. [*Cheers.*] In conclusion he had great pleasure in proposing 'Prosperity and Perpetuity to the Royal Hospital'.

ROYAL LITERARY FUND: ANNUAL GENERAL MEETING

11 *March* 1857

FOR the third year in succession the 'reformers', Dickens, Dilke, and Forster, made a public attack on the administration of the Literary Fund, at the Annual General Meeting. Lord Stanhope[1] was voted to the Chair; and, after the usual formal business had been dealt with, the annual report of the treasurers was read to the meeting. On the motion that it should be received and adopted, Dilke rose to move an amendment.

This year it was longer and more detailed than ever. Opening with the 'respectful request' that the General Committee should 'pledge themselves to reconsider the whole of the management and expenses', it went on to enumerate its reasons. They were: the usual unfavourable comparison with those of the Artists' General Benevolent Fund; the unnecessary expense of a paid secretary and a house of its own; the confused state of accounts, which had led to an official assurance at the last meeting that there was a separate 'House fund' when none actually existed; the form of application which required the signatures of 'two householders'; and, finally, the society's general lack of enterprise in spite of its ample endowments. Dilke was also concerned with the particular case of the widow and children of Joseph Haydn, the author of the *Dictionary of Dates*. His speech was rather too long, the members were impatient, and towards the end he was interrupted with cries of 'Come to the point!' 'Move, move!' 'Question!' 'Order!' and 'Chair!'. He finished all he had to say, however, and was seconded by Mark Lemon.

Robert Bell then replied at length, on behalf of the committee. All the speakers were concerned with the question of the 'House fund', and it

---

[1] Philip Henry Stanhope (1805–75), 5th Earl Stanhope, 1855, styled Viscount Mahon, 1816–55; historian, and biographer of Pitt; Under-secretary for Foreign Affairs, 1834–5; assisted Talfourd in promoting copyright legislation, 1841–2; President of Society of Antiquaries, and officer of various other learned societies; responsible for the formation of the National Gallery, 1856, and the Historical Manuscripts Commission, 1869; President of the Literary Fund, 1863–75.

formed a large part of what Dickens had to say. Without going into the question fully, it must be admitted that the reformers were quite correct in saying that there was no separate 'House fund', and that it was no more than an accountant's fiction. The question was of no importance in itself; but as the reformers had been silenced at the last meeting by the false assurance that there was a separate House fund to pay the rent, they were determined to show that the officers did not even understand how the society was run. Robert Bell was followed by Dickens:

As, he said, he should not speak seven minutes, he hoped he should not incur the sacred wrath of the gentlemen in the middle of the room who were so impatient of any waste of time when those opposed to the Committee spoke, but who did not feel the slightest annoyance however long the speeches of the honourable gentlemen at the table might be. He, however, wished it to be distinctly understood that if he were going to speak seven hours instead of seven minutes, although he did not represent Literature in the attitude in which it was there most favourably received—namely, in the person of a suppliant certified by two householders—he should most strenuously though respectfully maintain his claim to be heard in this place above all others; for, in whatever manner it was treated elsewhere, there, at all events, every other consideration should yield to its dignity.

As to the denial of Mr. Bell as to the analogy to be drawn between the Literary Fund and the Artists' Benevolent Fund, he at once took issue with him; he was very well acquainted with both funds, and protested that he knew of no difference between them, and of no reason whatever why this society should not be managed as cheaply as the other. With reference to the claims of Mr. Blewitt,[1] and Mr. Dilke's frequent acknowledgement of those claims, he impressed upon the meeting that there had been no change in the sentiments of his friend. All that they wanted was, that this society should avail themselves of the valuable services of Mr. Blewitt, in a wider and more efficient manner; and they had declared again and again that nothing would delight them more than to double or even treble Mr. Blewitt's salary, on the society's extending his sphere of operations. He passed over the somewhat lengthy case of Mr. Haydn, which, he submitted, with all due deference, had nothing whatever to do with the present discussion, and would endeavour to bring the attention of the meeting to the point at issue.

The question as to the existence or not of the House fund, was not a question of 1821,[2] but of last year; because, on the second Wednesday of last March, they—the conspiring reformers [*a laugh*]

[1] Secretary, see p. 7 n.
[2] The date of the amalgamation of the House fund with the General fund.

—were put down by the solemn assertion that there was a House fund of some £6,400. The subscription for that fund was a complete failure. He took it upon himself to say that it did not exceed £600. And the way in which this imaginary sum was got at was as follows:—the Prince Regent allowed two hundred guineas a year to pay the rent of the house inhabited by the society, paid yearly or half-yearly; but the sums paid for the rent had been put down as an accumulated fund, precisely as if they had it in hand at the present moment,—so the extraordinary statement made last year as to the existence of this sum, never had any real foundation. If statements were so rashly made in that expensive little room he thought it would not be long before the society itself would fall into disrepute.

He would, with their permission, give a short illustration of the mode in which this question had been dealt with. Let him suppose the case of a clerk in the receipt of one hundred pounds a year, paid half-yearly, and every farthing of which was anticipated before he received it. His having received that income twenty years, would not make him the possessor of £2,000. But he would carry the case further. Let them suppose a family picture representing an estimable old gentleman bestowing the hand of his only daughter upon the man of her heart, and saying to them, while tears of generosity coursed down his cheeks, 'My darling Emma, my dear Edward! take my blessing upon you each; and with my blessing accept my twenty years' receipts of my rent at £200 a year, which your filial affection will at once enable you to perceive are equal to £4,000 Consols, in perpetuity.' [*Loud laughter.*] Or let them, without any derogation of dignity, just fancy themselves for a moment upon an Old Bailey jury,—would they, or would they not decide that such a representation was a false one? His assertion was, most distinctly, that they (the reform party) were put out of court last year on an utterly false pretence; and that part of the resolution, at all events, every gentleman in the room was bound to consider before he decided. [*Hear, hear.*]

Dickens was followed by Monckton Milnes, who said that he thought the meeting took 'too archaeological a view of the case', and that the real question was what would be the best way of managing the present fund. Forster went over the same points as Dilke and Dickens, and wound up with a peroration on his favourite theme, saying that he was glad to see that the secretary had changed the style in which he recorded the patronage afforded by illustrious personages. He complained that the record of Prince Albert's part, at one of the past annual dinners, had been 'fawning, fulsome, and sycophantic', and thought that they should always bear in mind 'the dignity of literature'. The *Literary Gazette*, however, reported that though Forster was milder than usual, 'educated men cannot fail to resent the pretensions and bad taste of such speeches as those of Mr. Dickens and Mr. Forster'.[1]

When the amendment was put to the vote, it was defeated by 69 votes to 11. A few days later, Dickens wrote somewhat unguardedly to Macready: 'The annual fight at the Literary Fund came off last Wednesday. I am resolved to reform it or ruin it—one or the other.'[2]

ROYAL GENERAL THEATRICAL FUND

6 *April* 1857

THE anniversary was held at the Freemasons' Tavern, with Samuel Phelps[3] in the Chair. There was a large company, including 'a considerable number of elegantly attired ladies', who occupied raised benches covered with crimson cloth behind the upper table, while the opposite gallery 'was also filled with a large number of the fair sex, whose presence contributed in no small degree to enliven . . . the proceedings'.

There were the usual toasts. J. B. Buckstone, as Treasurer, replied for the society. In the course of his speech he referred to Dickens, as one of the trustees, saying:

I was really afraid when the dissolution of Parliament took place, that he would have to be away at this time electioneering, or a candidate perhaps this day for the representation of Middlesex.[4] However, we are all delighted to see him there, though of this I am convinced, should he ever contest an election anywhere he will be sure to be found at the head of the poll.

The chairman himself then proposed 'The Trustees of the Fund', and Dickens rose on their behalf to reply. He was enthusiastically cheered for some moments, and said:

GENTLEMEN, I have to acknowledge the toast which has been associated by our chairman with such flattering encomiums, and by you with so kind a welcome. Before I do so, I wish to offer a word of explanation in reference to the very startling remark which has fallen from my Right hon. friend the member for the Haymarket. [*Laughter and cheers.*] Gentlemen, God forbid that I should have any electioneering designs upon any constituency whatever. My way of life, my delight in life, my means of usefulness in life, such as they are, have long been chosen, and I assure you that I have no intention of canvassing any 'sex' whatever, except that

---

[1] 14 Mar. 1857, p. 255.   [2] 15 Mar. 1857, M.

[3] Samuel Phelps (1804–78) actor-manager; at the Sadlers' Wells Theatre 1844–62; at first in partnership with Mrs. Warner until 1847, and with Thomas Greenwood, 1844–60; well known to Dickens from the days when he acted under Macready.

[4] Parliament had been dissolved following a vote of censure on the Government's aggressive action in China. At the General Election on 31 March, the 'Peace party' was defeated, and Palmerston returned to office.

sex whose presence I feel behind me [*laughter*], of whose presence I have always a deep perception, appropriately seated in the clouds above me [*pointing to the gallery*], and that other sex whose presence I see before me. [*Renewed laughter.*]

Gentlemen, with this word of explanation, allow me, as one of your Trustees, to express the gratification that we feel, in which I have no doubt you participate, in the very prosperous budget which has been presented to us tonight by my Right Hon. friend, and allow me also to express our great satisfaction in finding him, notwithstanding the very frequent appeals he makes to his constituents, still holding the post of Chancellor of the Exchequer. [*Much laughter.*] If he should ever, in another phase of that office, as I have heard it whispered he has some deep prospective intention of doing—if he should ever relieve me of any portion of that income tax [*laughter*] which he nightly levies on the public [*increased laughter*], I hope, as I am sure you do, that in this and in all his enterprises he may be triumphantly successful. [*Cheers and laughter.*]

Gentlemen, as I have the honour in this institution to hold an official position, you will readily perceive that I should make a most interesting lengthy speech, but for the unfortunate circumstance that I am held in the bonds of official reserve [*laughter*], to which unhappy restraint, as the custom is in such cases, I the more gratefully submit, because I have no statement whatever to make, and nothing whatever to say. [*Laughter.*] I shall, therefore, content myself with thanking you on my own part, and on that of my fellow Trustees, for the toast you have just drunk, and with announcing that I shall beg the chairman's permission to propose another toast when the Toastmaster shall have called upon you, in due form, to charge your glasses. [*Much cheering.*]

The toastmaster having commanded the company to charge, and his order having been obeyed, Dickens promptly rose again and said:

Gentlemen, While I agreed with every part of the excellent address which was made by the chairman in proposing the Fund, I particularly sympathized with that portion of it in which he preferred a claim on the part of the stage to be regarded as a powerful and useful means towards the education of the people. [*Hear, hear.*] If there were ever a time when the Theatre could be considered to have a strong claim to consideration in that respect, it surely is the present. Gentlemen, we have schoolmasters going about like those horrible old women of whom we read in the public reports, perpetually flaying Whittington's cat alive; we have schoolmasters constantly demonstrating on blackboards to infant minds the utter impossibility of Puss in Boots; we have all the giants utterly dead and gone, with half the Jacks passing examinations every day in mental arithmetic; and with Tom Thumb[1] really only known in these times as the gallant general seeking kisses of the ladies at 6*d.* a head in the American market [*laughter*]; I say really, gentlemen, in these times, when we have torn so many leaves out of our dear old nursery books, I hold it to be more than ever essential to the character of a great people, that the imagination, with all its innumerable graces and charities, should be tenderly nourished; and foremost among the means of training it, I agree with the chairman, must always stand the stage, with its wonderful pictures of passion, with its magnificent illusions, and with its glorious literature. [*Loud cheers.*]

But, gentlemen, there is another aspect, to which the chairman could not with equal modesty advert, in which a thoroughly well-conducted theatre is of vast importance: that is, not only with reference to the public, who so greatly need it, but as a means of sustaining the honour and credit of the dramatic profession itself; as a means of presenting their usefulness to the public in its most striking colours; and as a means of always sustaining them against the reproaches which ignorance and malignity have showered upon them with the only liberality of which such qualities are capable. [*Cheers.*] Gentlemen, an ill-conducted theatre does a world of harm, no doubt. I will not go so far as to say, for that would be going very far indeed, that it does as much harm as a thoroughly ill-conducted school, or a thoroughly ill-conducted chapel; but it does harm enough, and a great deal more. A thoroughly well-conducted theatre, on the contrary, blots out the sins of a thousand bad ones, and will surely attract to itself the goodwill and respect of great numbers of well-meaning and virtuous people, previously objectors, and will conciliate them to understand that what they dreaded in the dramatic art arose not from its use, but from its abuse—not from its exertion, but from its perversion. [*Hear, hear.*]

Now, gentlemen, I perfectly well know that you will all agree with me that if ever a theatre attained these ends, it is the theatre Sadlers' Wells. [*Loud cheers.*] Gentlemen, that theatre, rescued from the wretchedest condition, from a condition so disgraceful that if on any night in the week the New River Company had poured in through its boxes, pit, and gallery[2] ['*No, no!*'] the Humane Society could have hardly done a worse thing at one time than have interfered. ['*No, no!*'] With a very bad audience—[*No, no!*'] I beg in reference to that gentleman's observation who says 'No,' to state

---

[1] Charles Sherwood Stratton (1838–83), Barnum's midget, known as General Tom Thumb; visited Europe, 1844–7, and England again in 1857.

[2] Water spectacles had been a speciality at that time.

that I have as accurate a knowledge of that theatre as any man in the kingdom, and I say, that with one of the most *vagabond* audiences that ever went into a theatre—utterly displaced from it, and with one of the most intelligent and attentive audiences ever seen, attracted to it and retained in it—I believe I am not very wrong in my rough calculation when I say, that that theatre has been opened under Mr. Phelps's management 3,000 nights, and that during 2,000 of those nights the author represented has been Shakespeare. [*Cheers.*] Gentlemen, add for the other thousand nights sterling old plays, tragedies and comedies, many new plays of great merit, accepted with a real sense of managerial responsibility, and paid for, as I have reason to know in the case of a friend, with a spirit and liberality that would have done honour to the old days of the two great theatres—add to that, that all these plays have been produced with the same beauty, with the same delicacy and taste, with the same sensible subservience of the scene-painter and the mechanist to the real meaning of the play [*cheers*], and with the same indebtedness to the creator of the whole for his admirable impersonation of a great variety of most opposite and diversified characters, and surely we must all agree, to say the very least, that the public is under a great debt to the profession, is under a great debt of obligation to Mr. Phelps, and that it has a strong legitimate interest in the continued success of his undertaking. [*Cheers.*]

Gentlemen, for the public I can only say that so far as I know it, I have never mixed with any grade or class of it by whom those exertions have failed to be held in the highest respect, or from whom they have failed to elicit the highest approval; and it may be worthy of remark, that I have found this feeling to exist quite as strongly among the intelligent artist classes of Paris as here in London. Gentlemen, on the other hand, for the profession, Mr. Phelps's position here tonight, and our recognition of him in it, are an ample and sufficient answer. He is here before you in a double capacity: firstly, as the mind[1] of the theatre in which the English drama has found a home, and in which graceful homage is rendered to the noblest of all dramatists—that he has there a body of students behind the curtain, and a body of students before the curtain, striving together to appreciate and extol him; Mr. Phelps is also here in the other capacity of one whose life and labour are a constant credit and a constant honour to, and a constant sustainer of, the dignity and credit of his art. [*Loud cheers.*]

Gentlemen, in this double capacity I am perfectly sure you are ready, for the second time, to give Mr. Phelps a double welcome. I am perfectly sure you will receive the toast, which is his health,

1 *mind*: 'manager'?

with a double acclamation, and that you will unite in a double expression of your best wishes for his success, health, happiness, and prosperity.

The toast was enthusiastically received, and Phelps briefly replied. In his speech he mentioned that one of his daughters had been asked to leave a school for young ladies, simply because one of the parents—who sent three daughters—objected to their being educated 'under the same roof with an actor's'.[1] He was succeeded by Buckstone who gained great applause by telling the company how, on Sabbatarian principles, he had had the pleasure of refusing to let the Haymarket to a reverend gentleman, 'for the purpose of preaching his peculiar doctrines', one Sunday evening.

A number of other speakers followed. Before the final toast of 'The Ladies', which was given by Mark Lemon, the chairman made an announcement which was received with great applause, that: 'My friend, Mr. Dickens, has just informed me that in the next anniversary festival which we hope to hold, Mr. Thackeray has promised, if he is in England, which he most likely will be, to take the Chair.'

ROYAL HOSPITAL FOR INCURABLES

21 *May* 1857

THE second anniversary dinner was held at the London Tavern with Dickens in the Chair. There were the usual loyal and patriotic toasts before the chairman rose to give the main speech of the evening, and said:

LADIES and Gentlemen, A few days ago I was called upon to fill up my proxy for the election of candidates to be admitted into the Royal Hospital—a Hospital established for the permanent care and comfort of those who by disease, accident, or deformity, are disqualified for the duties of life. Coming on that occasion to the perusal of the extended list of cases there set before me, I could not but feel—in common, I am sure, with many who are here—inexpressible pity for the vast number of persons who are in that forlorn condition. When I saw in that list no fewer than 121 cases, out of whom the subscribers to this charity at the next election can elect but ten, I thought, with a kind of despair, not only of the 111 who must suffer by rejection, but of the great crowd of incurables dispersed about this country of whom this society has never so much as heard, and who will never hear of it. Having that morning been busy about my own country rest and recreation, I could not but strongly feel

[1] It was a subject on which Dickens felt strongly. In connexion with another case he recommended it in a letter (of 6 Sept. 1858) to Wilkie Collins, also referring to Phelps; and Collins wrote about it under the title of 'Highly Proper', *Household Words*, 2 Oct. 1858.

the contrast between myself—then in the full enjoyment of health and the use of all my limbs—and that of so many of my fellow creatures, until I was glad to put this list aside, and make my escape from the reflections to which it gave rise.

In one of my recent walks, I found myself in a pretty village in Surrey,[1] which I had indeed often proposed to visit before, but had only paved the dusty road with good intentions—as I am sorry to say I have paved a worse place with a great deal of the same material —but on this morning I really found myself at the place. I inquired of a labourer for a house I wanted, and he told me, 'When you can't go any further, turn to your left, and there you'll see a house with some writing wrote on the outside, which they tell me is its name; but you'll know, because you can read, and I can't read.' At last I found it, and was shown into an agreeable sitting-room, which might be called a library. One sick man was lying on a sofa, and as soon as he saw me he opened the conversation, doing, as it were, the honours of the place. We spoke of the usual topics, talked of the weather, of our common enemy, the late wind, and of the progress of the crops, in the most pleasant and agreeable manner. He told me that that spot was above the cross of St. Paul's—a fact of which he seemed excessively proud—and was altogether quite as cheerful as I was, or as I am. As I went upstairs, I got pleasant glimpses of the grounds, and of persons walking about in them, and met another sick man, quite as anxious for the arrival of dinner time as any of us in the London Tavern, and insisting that the cook's clock must be ten minutes slow. [*Hear.*] I went upstairs into another sitting-room, where were a number of sick women of various ages grouped about on sofas and chairs, engaged in various feminine tasks, and all talking and smiling as they went on. There was one poor paralytic creature busy at her embroidery, delighted to have her work admired, and I could not help feeling great admiration that anything so orderly and straight could come out of a form so warped and cruelly afflicted. I very much doubt whether she was ever more contented in her whole life. Another woman, much older, having only a thumb and two fingers left to work with, was plodding away at her work, and very proud of what she was able to accomplish with such an imperfect complement of digits. She told me, that in her old healthy days she thought there was no greater pleasure than to sit and read all day, but that would not do now, and she had taken to this work for relief and comfort, and she had found relief and comfort here very much. One old lady, who said she had been awake all night, in great pain and trouble, was nevertheless wonderfully conversable and talkative. She said she was very

[1] Carshalton.

comfortable on the whole; but had a certain tendency to revert to the subject of rheumatism (and no wonder). In another and smaller room there was an old lady who said she was seventy-five years of age, but she was determined to persevere [*laughter*], which I told her I thought was a capital thing to do. Two other young women, evidently enduring much bodily suffering, had a pleasant consciousness of good looks, and showed a desire to make the most of them. I declare to you that in all these people—and all the inmates of this house whom I saw—there was not only a hopefulness of manner, but a serenity of face, a cheerfulness and social habit that perfectly amazed me. And this was the Royal Hospital, and these its incurable inmates.

Ladies and gentlemen, while I congratulated myself, as I need hardly tell you I did that morning most heartily, that this institution was able to give so much relief to sufferers in such very hopeless cases, I must not deceive you as to the Royal Hospital itself. It is not by any means what it ought to be. Its present temporary establishment is in a very inconvenient old house, by no means suitable, with rooms not half high enough, and not half ample enough. The beds are much too crowded together, and I [should] say ventilation is exceedingly difficult. The furniture is excessively inadequate to the requirements of the establishment; and a great number of appliances are needed which healthy people would, perhaps, call mawkish, but are of the gravest importance in the presence of sickness. In one comprehensive word, it wants money; and for that money, ladies and gentlemen, in the name of Christian charity, I have undertaken to appeal to you. I cannot possibly make this appeal sufficiently strong for my own satisfaction; but if I only rested it on this one consideration, that there is no hospital in London or throughout England to which this Royal Hospital is not a natural and necessary adjunct it would, I am sure, not be made in vain. The stronger the case for any of those excellent institutions which you may most favour, the stronger is this case. Every hospital knows what it is to be obliged to discharge incurable patients for whom it can do no more, and whom it cannot retain, and every member of the most generous and devoted of all professions—the medical profession—knows what it is to contemplate with pain the heartrending spectacle of those weary ones turning away from the friendly shelter of the infirmary, without any suitable resting-place, and in all probability to lay themselves down at the door of the poor-house. We know the goodness of the poor, and their readiness to help one another on all occasions. But if we do all we can to relieve them of the burden of incurable sufferers, we shall still leave them field enough for the exercise of their utmost virtues.

I will not distress you by imagining what must be the conditions of these unhappy sufferers, lodged in hot and crowded attics, or what must be the misery which their presence brings to others; I will only end, as I began, by referring you to the list of applicants for admission at the next election. We live in an age of elections—at one time or another we almost all apply to be elected into clubs for pleasure or for profit—into great corporations, the House of Commons, and what not; and three-fourths of us associate our ambition with an election of some sort or other. Within how small a compass lies the ambition of these 121 applicants! If one of this number could but make an audible address to you here at this table, instead of me, how touchingly might he say, 'Health has departed from us for ever—our place in the struggle for bread has been filled up by others, and we have faintly dropped out of the course. Give us only a quiet home, where we may endure what yet we have to undergo, and where, by our patient manner and our brightened faces, we may somewhat reward your kind interest on our behalf.' Once they were busy and strong, but now they are hopelessly disqualified for the duties of life; let us discharge the first of these, and provide for them a resting-place, where they may be sheltered and cared for in their irremovable afflictions. I am sure we shall not reject their prayers, and that the time will come when this Hospital shall be nobly and bountifully endowed, so that no other qualification will be needed to ensure entrance within its walls but the presence of incurable disease. [*Loud cheers.*] I call upon you to drink prosperity to the Royal Hospital.

Sir John Boileau[1] proposed the health of the chairman, to which he briefly replied.

Dickens then gave 'The President and the Vice-Presidents', coupled with the name of a distinguished gentleman who was not more remarkable for his talent than he was for possessing the kindest and tenderest heart. He proposed the health of Dr. Connolly.[2] [*Cheers.*]

Dr. Connolly returned thanks. The Hon. Edmund Phipps[3] proposed 'The City and Corporation of London', coupled with the name of Mr.

---

[1] Sir John Peter Boileau (1794–1869), archaeologist; vice-president of the Society of Antiquaries, and member of various other learned institutions.

[2] Dr. John Connolly (1794–1866), consultant physician of Hanwell Asylum, Middlesex; when resident, 1839–52, he had revolutionized treatment of the insane by insisting on the abolition of 'mechanical restraints'. Known personally to Dickens.

[3] Edmund Phipps (1808–57), third son of the Earl of Mulgrave and brother of 1st Marquis of Normanby; Recorder of Doncaster; author of various pamphlets on financial affairs, and the *Memoirs of Robert Plumer Ward*, 1850.

Sheriff Mechi,[1] the Sheriff of London and Middlesex; Mechi replied, some other speeches followed, and the total of subscriptions and donations was declared.

Finally, the chairman said that although he had been invited to take the Chair on the next occasion, he should recommend a change of diet. [*Laughter.*] But he would accept the office on one condition, that in the event of the City of London re-electing the best sheriff from the time of the great Whittington [*hear, hear*], he would preside over the next meeting; but if the City took anybody else he must claim his right to take his seat as a private individual.

The City of London did not carry out his wishes, and Dickens did not even attend the anniversary festival next year, on 10 June, when he was reading the story of *Little Dombey* at St. Martin's Hall.

Dickens had already expressed his misgivings about the accommodation at Carshalton privately, in a letter to the treasurer, Lord Raynham. A special meeting of the Board of Management was called as a result on 23 May, when he read out Dickens's letter, 'referring to the want of ventilation and other inconveniences which rendered the place in his view very undesirable for its present purpose'.[2] Dr. Reed himself undertook to reply explaining that they hoped that the house at Carshalton was only temporary, and that 'the points of his letter were under careful consideration'.[2]

Dr. Reed made a third appeal to Dickens to preside at the anniversary festival of 1862, which he was regretfully forced to refuse. The annual election remained his only association with the hospital, when he was called on to use his vote. He continued to find it equally painful, writing to Lady Rose Fane: 'It is terrible to observe what an interminable procession of incurable people want to get into this Hospital. I sometimes feel (unreasonably), as though it did more harm than good, in disappointing so many and sheltering so few.'[3]

ROYAL GEOGRAPHICAL SOCIETY

25 *May* 1857

THE annual meeting of the Royal Geographical Society was held at its house in Whitehall; and the same evening the anniversary was celebrated at the Freemasons' Tavern, with the president, Sir Roderick Murchison,[4] in the Chair. There were various appropriate toasts and

---

[1] John Joseph Mechi (1802–80), pioneer of improved methods of farming; Sheriff 1856–7; Alderman 1858; he might have become Lord Mayor in time, but having made a fortune, lost it, and resigned his aldermanship 1866.
[2] *Minutes*.   [3] 24 July 1863, DH.
[4] Sir Roderick Impey Murchison (1792–1871), geologist; president of the Geographical Society 1843–58; author of numerous papers and books on geological subjects.

speeches including 'Success to the final projected search for Sir John Franklin', to which Captain McClintock[1] replied, and 'The Healths of the Explorers of Distant Regions', which was responded to by Dr. Livingstone. There is apparently no record of Dickens's speech, except that he answered on behalf of 'Our Periodical Literature and the Press'.

It was the usual annual dinner, but Dickens's attendance may be accounted for by its being also regarded, as he wrote to Wilkie Collins, as 'to cheer on Lady Franklin's expedition'.[2] The search for Sir John Franklin's arctic expedition, which had set sail in May 1845, had already lasted ten years. Dickens had been in correspondence with Lady Franklin after his articles in *Household Words* in December 1854,[3] on 'The Lost Arctic Voyagers', in which he examined the evidence in Dr. Rae's Report which mentioned charges of cannibalism among some of the last survivors. The Admiralty had given up the search, but as a result of Lady Franklin's exertions the *Fox* yacht, under the command of Captain McClintock, had been fitted out to embark on a final quest. Further traces were found in 1859; Franklin's death was definitely established and the search was given up.

AFTER READING THE *CAROL* FOR THE JERROLD FUND: MANCHESTER
31 *July* 1857

DOUGLAS JERROLD[4] had died on 8 June, leaving his family insufficiently provided for. Dickens at once set about organizing a number of readings and lectures and a revival of *The Frozen Deep*, hoping to raise £2,000. The question of performing it at Manchester had already been considered, but not yet decided.

He was greeted with great applause on appearing on the platform, and again at the close of the reading. And when it had subsided, he said:

LADIES and Gentlemen, Between the two parts of my reading tonight, I have had the honour of receiving a visit from some of the gentlemen distinguished in England as being the leading men in this city, who have had the kindness to request that I would endeavour to bring my amateur company here [*loud applause and cries of 'Yes, yes!'*], in order that we might give a repetition in Manchester, for the same purpose as we have met tonight, of Mr.

---

[1] See p. 290.   [2] 22 May 1857.

[3] 2 and 9 Dec., x. 361–5 and 385–93; followed by a joint article by Dickens and Dr. Rae under the same title, 23 Dec., pp. 432–7; and a final contribution by Rae, 'Dr. Rae's Report', 30 Dec., pp. 457–9.

[4] Douglas Jerrold (1803–57), dramatist, novelist, miscellaneous writer; editor, in his time, of various magazines and finally of *Lloyd's Weekly Newspaper*; one of the founders of *Punch*; a strong radical and, notably, a wit. Apart from a difference over capital punishment, always a close friend of Dickens since 1835.

Wilkie Collins's *Frozen Deep*. [*Applause*.] I replied to those gentlemen, that we have no intention of going to any other place out of
London, our object now drawing to a close; but that we have too
lively a remembrance of the old generosity and encouragement
of Manchester in similar cases, and too affectionate a memory of
the happy nights we have passed here, to admit of our doubting for
a moment as to what we should do. I will make it my duty to go
into the necessary calculations and details; and if I find that with
any reasonable prospect of benefit to the object we have in view,
we can come here, we shall most certainly do it. [*Loud applause.*]

Cheered by the prospect, and I may say the hope, of seeing you
again before very long, allow me to thank you most heartily for
your cordial reception and kind welcome this evening. [*Loud
applause.*]

In fact the sum needed was not yet made up, and a decision was made
immediately. Three performances were given at the end of the next
month.

AFTER A PERFORMANCE OF *THE FROZEN DEEP*: MANCHESTER

24 *August* 1857

THE amateur players performed *The Frozen Deep* and Buckstone's farce,
Uncle John, in aid of the Jerrold Fund at the Free Trade Hall, on 21,
22, and 24 August. At the close of the final performance Dickens came
forward and said:

LADIES and Gentlemen, Will you allow me to say that on these
three occasions you have added three very bright flowers to the
garland of our happy and grateful recollections of this most hospitable and generous city? Permit me, in the name in remembrance
of which we have been banded together, and on behalf of my
companions in the company, and of the author, and of myself, to
tender you a most affectionate farewell.

WAREHOUSEMEN AND CLERKS' SCHOOLS

5 *November* 1857

THE fourth anniversary dinner was held at the London Tavern, with
Dickens in the Chair. The gallery was crowded with ladies. After the
cloth had been drawn, and grace had been sung, he rose and was received
with the most enthusiastic cheering which lasted several minutes. At
last Dickens said:

WHEN I have the honour to fill this or any similar place, I never lend my poor aid to uphold the preposterous fiction that the brightest part of creation are not present, and that the stars of the firmament on my right, which shine upon our waking and sleeping dreams, are not distinctly visible in the sky. [*Loud cheers.*] It seems to me the most inconsistent and ridiculous of all customs, when we come to propose the first lady of the land, to forget that ladies are present; and I, therefore, setting an example, trust and hope that you will follow that example, when I address you as ladies and gentlemen. [*Loud cheers.*]

Ladies and gentlemen, allow me to offer you a toast which includes a great deal more than the two syllabic words in themselves; which, whilst they express our loyalty towards the lady who rules England, hardly expresses its loyalty to the ladies who rule us. [*Great laughter.*] We most happily associate the institutions under which we live with the domestic virtues and happiness of a lady who is at once the boast of the country and of our homes, 'Her Majesty the Queen.' [*Loud cheers.*]

The chairman next gave 'The Prince Consort, Albert Prince of Wales, and the rest of the Royal Family', and then continued:

Ladies and Gentlemen, In this great commercial city, heaped up with riches on every side, to which hungry eyes are sometimes turned across the sea, those two great services the Army and Navy, even in times of profoundest peace, should never be forgotten. [*Cheers.*] But I am sure you will agree with me that in these so different times they should in our 'flowing cups', be freshly remembered [*cheers*]; remembered in connexion with the recent acts of gallantry that have won the admiration of the world [*cheers*]; remembered in intimate connexion with a manly composure in the face of pestilence, and a Christian resignation under the shadow of death, only to be equalled by the modesty, gentleness, and the perfect and profound self-command always attendant upon their great bravery.[1] [*Renewed cheers.*]

I understand that there happens to be no officer of either service here to acknowledge my toast. It occurs to me, however, that this matters very little, for throughout the civilized world the members of both are at this moment practically thanking us. [*Hear, hear.*] Wherever duty is to be done, they are thanking us; wherever fame and honour are to be gained, they are thanking us; wherever the sun shines they are thanking us; aye, even where the sun does

---

[1] The mutiny in India had broken out in May. Lucknow had been entered by Havelock on 25 Sept., but was not relieved by Sir Colin Campbell until 17 Nov. The news of the fall of Delhi had reached London on 26 Oct.

not shine—in the long night of a polar winter—one of those services at least is now thanking us with a most eloquent speech. Ladies and gentlemen, I beg to propose 'The Army and Navy'.

He then went on:

I must now solicit your attention for a few minutes to the cause of your assembling together—the main and real object of the evening's gathering; for I suppose we are all agreed that the motto of these tables is not 'Let us eat and drink, for tomorrow we die'; but, 'Let us eat and drink, for tomorrow we live'. [*Cheers.*] It is because a great and good work is to live 'tomorrow, and tomorrow, and tomorrow', and to live a greater and better life with every succeeding tomorrow, that we eat and drink here at all. [*Loud cheers.*]

Conspicuous on the card of admission for this dinner, and on the title-page of this little book descriptive of the institution, is the word 'Schools'. This set me thinking this morning, before I turned these pages about, what are the sorts of schools I don't like. I found them, on consideration, to be rather numerous. I don't like, to begin with—and to begin, as charity does, at home—I don't like the sort of school to which I once went myself, the respected proprietor of which was by far the most ignorant man I have ever had the pleasure to know [*laughter*], who was one of the worst-tempered men perhaps that ever lived, whose business it was to make as much out of us and to put as little into us as possible [*great laughter*], and who sold us at a figure which I remember we used to delight to estimate, as amounting to exactly £2. 4s. 6d. a head.[1] [*Laughter.*]

I don't like that sort of school, because I don't see what business the master had to be at the top of it instead of the bottom, and because I never could understand the wholesomeness of the moral preached by the abject appearance and degraded condition of the teachers who plainly said to us by their looks every day of their lives, 'Boys, never be learned; whatever you are, above all things, be warned from that in time by our sunken cheeks, by our poor pimply noses so cruelly eruptive in the frosty mornings [*laughter*], by our meagre diet, by our acid beer, and by our extraordinary suits of clothes [*roars of laughter*], of which no human being can say whether they are snuff-coloured turned black, or black turned snuff-coloured [*renewed laughter*], a point upon which we ourselves are perfectly unable to offer any ray of enlightenment, it is so very long since they were undarned and new'. [*Continued laughter.*] I do not like that sort of school, because I have never yet lost my ancient suspicion touching that curious coincidence that the boy with four

[1] Wellington House Academy, run by Mr. William Jones (1786?–1836).

brothers to come always got the prizes. [*Great laughter.*] In fact, and in short, I do not like that sort of school, which is a pernicious and abominable humbug altogether. [*Hear, hear.*]

Again, ladies and gentlemen, I don't like that sort of school—a ladies' school—with which the other school used to dance on Wednesdays, where the young ladies, as I look back upon them now, seem to me always to have been in new stays and disgrace—the disgrace chiefly concerning a place of which I know nothing at this day, that bounds Timbuctoo on the north-east [*laughter*]—and where memory always depicts the youthful enthraller of my first affection as for ever standing against a wall, in a curious machine of wood, which confined her innocent feet in the first dancing position,[1] while those arms, which should have encircled my jacket [*laughter*], those precious arms, I say, were pinioned behind her by an instrument of torture called a backboard, fixed in the manner of a double direction post. [*Hear.*]

Again, I don't like that sort of school, of which we have a notable example in Kent,[2] which was established ages ago by worthy scholars and good men long deceased, whose munificent endowments have been monstrously perverted from their original purpose, and which, in their distorted condition, are struggled for and fought over with the most indecent pertinacity. [*Hear, hear.*] Again, I don't like that sort of school—and I have seen a great many such in these latter times—where the bright childish imagination is utterly discouraged, and where those bright childish faces, which it is so very good for the wisest among us to remember in after life [*hear, hear*], when the world is too much with us early and late, are gloomily and grimly scared out of countenance; where I have never seen among the pupils, whether boys or girls, anything but little parrots and small calculating machines. [*Cheers.*]

Again, I don't by any means like schools in leather breeches, and with mortified straw baskets for bonnets, which file along the streets to churches in long melancholy rows under the escort of that surprising British monster, a beadle [*cheers and laughter*], whose system of instruction, I am afraid, but too often presents that happy union of sound with sense, of which a very remarkable instance is given in a grave report of a trustworthy school inspector, to the effect that a boy in great repute at school for his learning, presented on his slate, as one of the ten commandments, the perplexing prohibition, 'Thou shalt not commit doldrum'. [*Laughter.*]

---

[1] David Copperfield's 'Miss Shepherd', who no doubt represented someone Dickens knew while he was at school, was also rumoured to have been 'stood . . . in the stocks for turning in her toes'. (Ch. xviii.)

[2] Rochester, King's School.

Ladies and gentlemen, I confess, also, that I don't like those schools, even though the instruction given in them be gratuitous, where those sweet little voices which ought to be heard speaking in very different accents, anathematize by rote any human being who does not hold what is taught there. Lastly I do not like, and did not like some years ago, cheap distant schools, where neglected children pine from year to year under an amount of neglect, want, and youthful misery far too sad even to be glanced at in this cheerful assembly.[1] [*Hear, hear.*]

And now, ladies and gentlemen, perhaps you will permit me to sketch in a few words the sort of school that I do like. [*Hear, hear.*] It is a school established by the members of an industrious and useful order, which supplies the comforts and graces of life at every familiar turning in the road of our existence; it is a school established by them for the Orphan and Necessitous Children of their own brethren and sisterhood; it is a place of education where, while the beautiful history of the Christian religion is daily taught, and while the life of that Divine Teacher who Himself took little children on His knees is daily studied, no sectarian ill will nor narrow human dogma is permitted to darken the face of the clear heaven which they disclose. It is a children's school, which is at the same time no less a children's home, a home not to be confided to the care of cold or ignorant strangers, nor, by the nature of its foundation, in the course of ages to pass into hands that have as much natural right to deal with it as the peaks of the highest mountains or with the depths of the sea, but to be from generation to generation administered by men living in precisely such homes as those poor children have lost [*cheers*]; by men always bent upon making that replacement, such a home as their own dear children might find a happy refuge in if they themselves were taken early away. And I fearlessly ask you, is this a design which has any claim to your sympathy? Is this the sort of school which is deserving of your support.

This is the design, this is the school, whose strong and simple claim I have to lay before you tonight. I must particularly entreat you not to suppose that my fancy and unfortunate habit of fiction has anything to do with the picture I have just presented to you. [*Hear, hear.*] It is a sober matter of fact. The Warehousemen and Clerks' Schools, established for the maintaining, clothing, and educating of the Orphans and Necessitous Children of those employed

---

[1] These allusions to schools would have been more pointed for recent readers of his novels, who might remember Mr. McChoakumchild maiming his class's imagination in *Hard Times*, the fate of Mr. Toots at Dr. Blimber's, Rob the Grinder's charity school breeches in *Dombey*, and the Yorkshire schools of *Nicholas Nickleby*.

in the wholesale trades and manufactures of the United Kingdom, are, in fact, what I have just described. These schools for both sexes were originated only four years ago. In the first six weeks of the undertaking the young men themselves and quite unaided, subscribed the large sum of £3,000. The schools have been opened only three years, they have now on their foundation thirty-nine children, and in a few days they will have six more, making a total of forty-five. [*Cheers.*] They have been most munificently assisted by the heads of great mercantile houses, numerously represented, I am happy to say, around me, and they have a funded capital of almost £14,000. This is wonderful progress, but the aim must still be upwards, the motto always 'Excelsior'. [*Cheers.*]

You do not need to be told that five-and forty children can form but a very small proportion of the Orphan and Necessitous Children of those who have been entrusted with the wholesale trades and manufactures of the United Kingdom; you do not need to be informed that the house at New Cross, rented for a small term of years, in which the schools are at present established, can afford but most imperfect accommodation for such a breadth of design. To carry this good work through the two remaining degrees of better and best, there must be more work, more co-operation, more friends, more money. Then be the friends, and give the money. [*Cheers and laughter.*]

Before I conclude, there is one other feature in these schools which I would commend to your special attention and approval. Their benefits are reserved for the children of subscribers; that is to say, it is an essential principle of the institution that it must help those whose parents have helped them, and that the unfortunate children whose father has been so lax, or so criminal, as to withhold a subscription so exceedingly small that when divided by weeks it amounts to only threepence weekly, cannot, in justice, be allowed to jostle out and shoulder away the happier children, whose father has had that little forethought, or done that little kindness which was requisite to secure for them the benefits of the institution. [*Hear, hear.*] I really cannot believe that there will long be any such defaulting parents. [*Cheers.*] I cannot believe that any of the intelligent young men who are engaged in the wholesale houses will long neglect this obvious, this easy duty. [*Hear, hear.*] If they suppose that the objects of their love, born or unborn, will never want the benefits of the charity, that may be a fatal and blind mistake—it can never be an excuse, for supposing them to be right in their anticipation, they should do what is asked for the sake of their friends and comrades around them, assured that they will be the happier and the better for the deed. [*Cheers.*]

Ladies and gentlemen, this little 'labour of love' of mine is now done. I most heartily wish I could charm you now not to see me, not to think of me, not to hear me—I most heartily wish that I could make you see in my stead the multitude of innocent and bereaved children who are looking towards these schools, and entreating with uplifted hands to be let in. [*Cheers.*] A very famous advocate once said, in speaking of his fears of failure when he had first to speak in court, being very poor, that he felt his little children tugging at his skirts, and that recovered him. Will you think of the number of little children who are tugging at my skirts, when I ask you, in their names, on their behalf, and their little persons, and in no strength of my own, to encourage and assist this work? [*Cheers.*]

The toast was enthusiastically received, and the children belonging to the schools were paraded through the room. Sir James Duke then proposed the health of the chairman, and Dickens briefly replied:

This is the fifth of November—this is a very notorious and inauspicious a day to be publicly exhibited in a chair. [*Great laughter.*] And I must confess that I have several times this evening felt upon me an irresistible impulse to look about me on the table for my lantern and matches. [*Renewed laughter.*] I am, however, at this moment reassured by the circumstance that I have no mask to fall off [*cheers*]; that I am exactly what you see me, deeply penetrated by your great enthusiasm in my behalf; that I am heartily obliged to you for your great kindness, and that you are most cordially welcome to my small services. [*Cheers.*]

A toast to 'The Corporation and the Sheriffs of the City of London' was proposed and acknowledged; and Dickens then gave 'The President —the Right Honourable Lord John Russell'.[1]

He should, he said, do nothing so superfluous and so unnecessary as to descant upon his lordship's many faithful, long, and great public services [*cheers*], upon the honour and integrity with which he had pursued his straightforward public course through every difficulty, or upon the manly, gallant, and courageous character which rendered him certain, in the eyes alike of friends and opponents, to rise with every rising occasion, and which, like the seal of Solomon in the old Arabian story, enclosed in a not very large casket the soul of a giant. [*Loud cheers.*]—He felt perfectly certain

---

[1] Lord John Russell (1792–1878), 1st Earl Russell, 1866; Prime Minister 1846–52 and 1865–6. Having often reported Russell in the House of Commons, Dickens much later became well acquainted with him. *A Tale of Two Cities* was dedicated to him, 'In remembrance of many public services and private kindnesses', in Dec. 1859.

that that would be the response; for in no English assembly that he had ever seen was it necessary to do more than mention the name of Lord John Russell to ensure a manifestation of personal respect and grateful remembrance.

It being his pride and privilege to enroll the subject of the toast among his personal friends, he should take an early opportunity of telling him that he was not forgotten at the aniversary. [*Cheers.*]

The toast was drunk with great enthusiasm. Samuel Morley gave the health of the treasurer, who briefly replied; and Dickens then proposed 'The health of W. H. Russell[1] and the Press'.

He observed that under circumstances of the greatest difficulty, Mr. Russell had written descriptions of the Crimean campaign which rivalled in their brilliancy the greatest productions of the greatest novelists, and equalled in their fidelity and their regard for truth—as he had often heard testified by the best authorities— the most scholarly productions of the most deliberate historians. [*Cheers.*] In giving them the toast of the Press, he said, it was very much the same thing as if he had asked them to drink to his own family. He was almost born and bred to the Press, his earliest working years having been passed in the House of Commons, and he must be base indeed, or have a very much shorter memory than he believed he possessed, if anything that concerned its honour or reputation could be indifferent to him, or if it were not one of the foremost efforts of his life to do anything he could to uphold its character. [*Cheers.*]

The proceedings closed with a toast to 'The Ladies'.

AT A READING FOR THE ATHENAEUM: BRISTOL

19 *January* 1858

THE lecture-room was filled with a large and enthusiastic audience, who greeted Dickens's appearance with a burst of applause. To a local reporter, familiar only with the portraits that 'used to appear with some of his earlier works', he seemed greatly to have aged: 'His hair has been thinned upon his head, and the lines have been deepened upon his face which has become rather foreign-looking in its cast.'[2]

When the applause had died down, Dickens explained the course he intended to pursue.

[1] William Howard Russell (1820–1907), war-correspondent of *The Times* in the Crimea 1854–5; in India 1858; the United States 1861–2; and with the German army in 1870. Editor of the *Army and Navy Gazette*; knighted 1905; personal friend of Dickens.

[2] *Bristol Mirror and General Advertiser.*

ON occasions like the present, he said, there were always two remarks he addressed to his audience. First of all, he would inform them that he always allowed an interval of five minutes to elapse, as nearly as possible when half-way through the *Carol* as the natural divisions of the story would allow of. Secondly if, as they proceeded, any of his audience should feel disposed to give vent to any feeling of emotion, he would request them to do so in the most natural manner, without the slightest apprehension of disturbing him. Nothing could be more agreeable to him than the assurance of their being interested, and nothing would be more in accordance with his wishes than that they should all, for the next two hours, make themselves as much as possible like a group of friends, listening to a tale told by a winter fire, and forget all ceremony and forms in the manner of their coming together. [*Loud applause.*]

At the conclusion of the reading, the thanks of the Directors were expressed 'in acknowledgement of the great obligation under which he had placed the Athenaeum'.

Dickens briefly replied, that they had heard so much of his voice already that night, that in acknowledging their handsome tribute he would only inflict on them one more sentence. All he would say was, that he could have given them no pleasure that evening which they had not most fully and handsomely repaid to him. [*Loud cheers.*]

HOSPITAL FOR SICK CHILDREN
9 *February* 1858

THE Hospital for Sick Children had been started in a large house in Great Ormond Street in 1852. Dickens's attention was first called to it as editor of *Household Words* when it was opened, and he and Henry Morley collaborated in an article upon it called 'Drooping Buds'.[1] It was the only hospital of its kind in the country; and out of 50,000 people dying annually in London, 21,000 were children under ten years old. Yet even so, after six years, the hospital still had only 31 beds; and in spite of the announcement that Dickens would preside, the dinner at the Freemasons' Hall was very thinly attended.

The cloth having been removed, he rose to propose the health of Her Majesty the Queen.

IT was, he said, most appropriate that a hospital for children should be patronized by a mother; it was a most happy coincidence that

---

[1] 3 Apr. 1852, v. 45–48. Also published separately for the Hospital as a pamphlet.

her patronage should be extended just as she was about to part with her eldest child[1] [*cheers*]; and it was most important that the example of supporting such an institution should be set by a mother who was a Queen, and moreover a Queen whose example had always been for the advancement of charity, and exercised for the good of her people.

The healths of Prince Albert, and the rest of the royal family, were given without comment. The chairman then gave 'The Army and Navy'.

He hoped, he said, it would not be incompatible with the latest fashion, if he reminded the company that a large portion of the army were at this moment in India employed in punishing great treachery and great cruelty, and in upholding a government which, whatever its faults, had proved immeasurably superior to any Asiatic rule. [*Cheers.*] Of the army so employed he would say no more than to express his hope, in the words of the immortal Nelson applied to another service, that their humanity after the action might be as great as their valour in the field.[2] [*Hear.*] This was a peaceful country, and we wished to live on the best terms with all our neighbours, and he therefore hoped that a certain obstructive branch of our national defence might never find it necessary to throw itself in the way of those gay military spirits who had recently announced their intention 'to march far within the bowels of the land, without impediment.'[3] [*Cheers.*] For he had a strong misgiving that the naval capacity for understanding such practical jokes was none of the keenest, and that the gay spirits to whom he had alluded might, under certain possible contingencies, find themselves in a rather disagreeable dilemma. [*Cheers and laughter.*] He begged to couple with this toast the name of Colonel Hamley, who had distinguished himself no less in his literary than in his military capacity. [*Hear, hear.*]

Lieut.-Colonel Hamley[4] replied briefly, saying that he hoped England would always keep its army in a state of full efficiency, 'so as to be able,

[1] The Princess Royal had been married to Prince Frederick William of Prussia on 25 Jan.

[2] Cf. the prayer which was the last entry in Nelson's pocketbook before engaging the enemy at Trafalgar: '. . . may humanity after Victory be the predominant feature in the British Fleet.'

[3] A Naval siege train, under Captain Peel, had joined the Commander-in-Chief, and played an important part in the fighting in India and reoccupation of Lucknow next month.

[4] Lieut.-Colonel Edward Bruce Hamley (1824–93); he had seen active service in the Crimea; contributed to *Fraser's* and *Blackwood's* magazines; Professor of Military History, Sandhurst, 1859–64; Major-General 1877; General 1890.

at any moment, to put her foot on the neck of rebellion, or to listen with contempt to the vainglorious boasts of braggadocio Frenchmen'. [*Loud cheers.*] Dickens then rose to propose the toast of the evening, and said:

Ladies and Gentlemen, It is one of my rules in life not to believe a man who may happen to tell me that he feels no interest in children. I hold myself bound to this principle by all kind consideration, because I know, as we all must, that any heart which could really toughen its affections and sympathies against those dear little people must be wanting in so many humanizing experiences of innocence and tenderness, as to be quite an unsafe monstrosity among men. [*Hear, hear.*] Therefore I set the assertion down, whenever I happen to meet with it—which is sometimes, though not often—as an idle word, originating possibly in the genteel languor of the hour, and meaning about as much as that knowing social lassitude, which has used up the cardinal virtues and quite found out things in general, usually does mean. [*Cheers.*]

I suppose it may be taken for granted that we, who come together in the name of children, and for the sake of children, acknowledge that we have an interest in them; indeed, I have observed since we sat down here that we are quite in a childlike state altogether, representing an infant institution, and not even yet a grown-up company. [*Laughter.*] A few years are necessary to the increase of our strength and the expansion of our figure; and then these tables, which now have a few tucks in them, will be let out, and then this hall, which now sits so easily upon us, will be too tight and small for us. [*Cheers and laughter.*][1] Nevertheless, it is likely that even we are not without our experience now and then of spoilt children. I do not mean of our own spoilt children, because nobody's own children ever were spoilt [*laughter*], but I mean the disagreeable children of our particular friends. [*Laughter.*] We know by experience what it is to have them down after dinner, and across the rich perspective of a miscellaneous dessert, to see, as in a black dose darkly, the family doctor looming in the distance. [*Continued laughter.*] We know—I have no doubt we all know— what it is to assist at those little maternal anecdotes and table entertainments illustrated with imitations and descriptive dialogue which might not be inaptly called, after the manner of my friend Mr. Albert Smith,[2] the toilsome ascent of Miss Mary and the eruption (cutaneous) of Master Alexander. [*Great laughter.*] We know what it is when those children won't go to bed; we know

[1] 'The chairman's allusion being understood to apply to some empty chairs at the lower end of the room, the occupants of which had moved up the better to hear his observations.' (*Morning Post*, 11 Feb., p. 3.)
[2] See p. 170 n.

how they prop their eyelids open with their forefingers when they
will sit up; how, when they become fractious, they say aloud that
they don't like us, and our nose is too long, and why don't we go?
And we are perfectly acquainted with those kicking bundles which
are carried off at last protesting. [*Cheers and laughter.*] An eminent
eye-witness told me that he was one of a company of learned pundits
who assembled at the house of a very distinguished philosopher
of the last generation, to hear him expound his stringent views
concerning infant education and early mental development, and he
told me that, while the philosopher did this in very beautiful and
lucid language, the philosopher's little boy, for his part, edified
the assembled sages by dabbling up to the elbows in an apple pie
which had been provided for their entertainment, having previously
anointed his hair with syrup, combed it with his fork, and brushed
it with his spoon. [*Renewed laughter.*] It is probable that we also
have our similar experiences, sometimes, of principles that are not
quite practice, and we know people claiming to be very wise and
profound about nations of men who show themselves to be rather
weak and shallow about units of babies.

But, ladies and gentlemen, the spoilt children whom I have to
present to you after this dinner of today are not of this class. I
have glanced at these for the easier and lighter introduction of
another, a very different, a far more numerous, and a far more
serious class. The spoilt children whom I must show you are spoilt
children of the poor in this great city—the children who are, every
year, for ever and ever irrevocably spoilt out of this breathing life
of ours by tens of thousands, but who may in vast numbers be
preserved, if you, assisting and not contravening the ways of
Providence, will help to save them. [*Cheers.*] The two grim nurses,
Poverty and Sickness, who bring these children before you, preside
over their births, rock their wretched cradles, nail down their
little coffins, pile up the earth above their graves. Of the annual
deaths in this great town, their unnatural deaths form more than
one-third. [*Hear, hear.*] I shall not ask you, according to the custom
as to the other class—I shall not ask you on behalf of these
children, to observe how good they are, how pretty they are, how
clever they are, how promising they are, whose beauty they most
resemble—I shall only ask you to observe how weak they are, and
how like death they are! And I shall ask you, by the remembrance
of everything that lies between your own infancy and that so
miscalled second childhood when the child's graces are gone, and
nothing but its helplessness remains,—I shall ask you to turn your
thoughts to *these* spoilt children in the sacred names of Pity and
Compassion. [*Hear, hear.*]

Some years ago, being in Scotland, I went with one of the most humane members of the humane medical profession, on a morning tour among some of the worst-lodged inhabitants of the old town of Edinburgh. In the closes and wynds of that picturesque place—I am sorry to remind you what fast friends picturesqueness and typhus often are—we saw more poverty and sickness in an hour than many people would believe in a life. Our way lay from one to another of the most wretched dwellings—reeking with horrible odours—shut out from the sky—shut out from the air—mere pits and dens. In a room in one of these places, where there was an empty porridge-pot on the cold hearth, with a ragged woman and some ragged children crouching on the bare ground near it— where, I remember as I speak, that very light, reflected from a high damp-stained and time-stained house wall, came trembling in, as if the fever which had shaken everything else there had shaken even it—there lay, in an old egg-box which the mother had begged from a shop, a little feeble, wasted, wan, sick child. With his little wasted face, and his little hot worn hands folded over his breast, and his little bright attentive eyes, I can see him now, as I have seen him for several years, looking steadily at us. There he lay in his little frail box, which was not at all a bad emblem of the little body from which he was slowly parting—there he lay, quite quiet, quite patient, saying never a word. He seldom cried, the mother said; he seldom complained; 'he lay there, seeming to wonder what it was a' aboot'. God knows I thought, as I stood looking at him, he had his reasons for wondering—reasons for wondering how it could possibly come to be that he lay there, left alone, feeble and full of pain, when he ought to have been as bright and as brisk as the birds that never got near him—reasons for wondering how he came to be left there, a little decrepit old man, pining to death, quite a thing of course, as if there were no crowds of healthy and happy children playing on the grass under the summer's sun within a stone's throw of him, as if there were no bright moving sea on the other side of the great hill overhanging the city; as if there were no great clouds rushing over it; as if there were no life, and move- ment, and vigour anywhere in the world—nothing but stoppage and decay. There he lay looking at us, saying in his silence, more pathetically than I have ever heard anything said by any orator in my life, 'Will you please to tell us what this means, strange man? and if you can give me any good reason why I should be so soon, so far advanced on my way to Him who said that children were to come into His presence, and were not to be forbidden, but who scarcely meant, that they should come by this hard road by which I am travelling—pray give that reason to me, for I seek it very

earnestly and wonder about it very much'; and to my mind he has
been wondering about it ever since. Many a poor child, sick and
neglected, I have seen since that time in this London; many a poor
sick child have I seen most affectionately and kindly tended by
poor people, in an unwholesome house and under untoward circumstances, wherein its recovery was quite impossible; but at all such
times I have seen my poor little drooping friend in his egg-box, and
he has always addressed his dumb speech to me, and I have always
found him wondering what it meant, and why, in the name of a
gracious God, such things should be!

Now, ladies and gentlemen, such things need not be, and will
not be, if this company, which is a drop of the life-blood of the great
compassionate public heart, will only accept the means of rescue
and prevention which is mine to offer. Within a quarter of a mile
of this place where I speak, stands a courtly old house, where once,
no doubt, blooming children were born, and grew up to be men and
women, and married, and brought their own blooming children back
to patter up the old oak staircase which stood but the other day,
and to wonder at the old oak carvings on the chimney-pieces. In the
airy wards into which the old state drawing-rooms and family bed-
chambers of that house are now converted are such little patients
that the attendant nurses look like reclaimed giantesses, and the
kind medical practitioner like an amiable Christian ogre. Grouped
about the little low tables in the centre of the rooms are such tiny
convalescents that they seem to be playing at having been ill. On
the dolls' beds are such diminutive creatures, that each poor sufferer is supplied with its tray of toys; and, looking around, you
may see how the little tired, flushed cheek has toppled over half
the brute creation on its way into the ark; or how one little
dimpled arm has mowed down (as I saw myself) the whole tin
soldiery of Europe. On the walls of these rooms are graceful,
pleasant, bright, childish pictures. At the beds' heads, are pictures
of the figure which is the universal embodiment of all mercy and
compassion, the figure of Him who was once a child himself, and a
poor one.

Besides these little creatures on the beds, you may learn in that
place that the number of small Out-patients brought to that house
for relief is no fewer than ten thousand in the compass of a single
year. In the room in which these are received, you may see against
the wall a box, on which it is written, that it has been calculated,
that if every grateful mother who brings a child there will drop a
penny into it, the Hospital funds may possibly be increased in a
year by so large a sum as forty pounds. And you may read in the
Hospital report, with a glow of pleasure, that these poor women

are so respondent as to have made, even in a toiling year of difficulty and high prices, this estimated forty, fifty pounds. [*Cheers.*] In the printed papers of this same Hospital, you may read with what a generous earnestness the highest and wisest members of the medical profession testify to the great need of it; to the immense difficulty of treating children in the same hospitals with grown-up people, by reason of their different ailments and requirements; to the vast amount of pain that will be assuaged, and of the life that will be saved, through this Hospital—not only among the poor, observe, but among the prosperous too, by reason of the increased knowledge of children's illnesses, which cannot fail to arise from a more systematic mode of studying them. Lastly, gentlemen, and I am sorry to say, worst of all—(for I must present no rose-coloured picture of this place to you—I must not deceive you); lastly—the visitor to this Children's Hospital, reckoning up the number of its beds, will find himself perforce obliged to stop at very little over thirty; and will learn, with sorrow and surprise, that even that small number, so forlornly, so miserably diminutive, compared with this vast London, cannot possibly be maintained unless the Hospital be made better known; I limit myself to saying better known, because I will not believe that in a Christian community of fathers and mothers, and brothers and sisters, it can fail, being better known, to be well and richly endowed. [*Cheers.*]

Now, ladies and gentlemen, this, without a word of adornment—which I resolved when I got up not to allow myself—this is the simple case. This is the pathetic case which I have to put to you; not only on behalf of the thousands of children who annually die in this great city, but also on behalf of the thousands of children who live half-developed, racked with preventable pain, shorn of their natural capacity for health and enjoyment. If these innocent creatures cannot move you for themselves, how can I possibly hope to move you in their name?

The most delightful paper, the most charming essay, which the tender imagination of Charles Lamb conceived, represents him as sitting by his fireside on a winter night, telling stories to his own dear children, and delighting in their society, until he suddenly comes to his old, solitary, bachelor self, and finds that they were but dream-children, who might have been, but never were. 'We are nothing', they say to him; 'less than nothing, and dreams. We are only what might have been, and we must wait upon the tedious shore of Lethe, millions of ages, before we have existence and a name.' 'And immediately awakening', he says, 'I found myself in my arm-chair.'[1] The dream-children whom I would now raise, if I

---

[1] *Elia*, 'Dream-Children; a Reverie.'

could, before every one of you, according to your various circumstances, should be the dear child you love, the dearer child you
have lost, the child you might have had, the child you certainly
have been. Each of these dream-children should hold in its powerful
hand one of the little children now lying in the Child's Hospital,
or now shut out of it to perish. Each of these dream-children should
say to you, 'O help this little suppliant in my name; O, help it for
my sake!' [*Cheers.*] Well!—And immediately awakening, you should
find yourself in the Freemasons' Hall, happily arrived at the end of
a rather long speech, drinking 'Prosperity to the Hospital for Sick
Children', and thoroughly resolved that it shall flourish. [*Loud cheers.*]

The health of the chairman was then proposed, to which Dickens
briefly replied. The treasurer next read out the list of subscriptions
amounting to over £3,000, about £900 of which had been contributed by
the ladies in the gallery, one of whom gave £500, signing herself merely
'Mary Jane'. The final toast to 'The Ladies', was proposed by the chairman.

In doing so, he said, he coupled it with a special compliment to
'Mary Jane', and an emphatic good-night to all. Without the ladies
little good could be done in the world. He had once been reminded
of all Robinson Crusoe had done in a state of single blessedness, but
on careful investigation of the authorities he found that that worthy
had, in reality, had two wives.

It was one of Dickens's greatest triumphs as an orator. T. A. Reed,
the reporter, wrote: 'I never heard him, or reported him, with so much
pleasure. . . . His speech was magnificent, thoroughly characteristic, and
extremely telling.'[1] Macready read it, and sent his friend a subscription.
Dickens replied: 'You may be sure it is a good and kind charity. It is
amazing to me that it is not at this day ten times as large and rich as it is.'[2]

With the contributions resulting from this appeal the Hospital opened
an endowment fund and a building fund. Dickens was appointed an
Honorary Governor, and asked to give a public reading on its behalf.
Arrangements were made, and the reading—of the *Carol*—was given at
St. Martin's Hall, on 15 April.

ROYAL LITERARY FUND: ANNUAL GENERAL MEETING

10 *March* 1858

DICKENS, Forster, and Dilke still kept up their campaign against the
Literary Fund. This year they prepared for the Annual General Meeting
by issuing a pamphlet about a week beforehand called *The Case of The*

---

[1] F. G. Kitton, *Charles Dickens by Pen and Pencil, Supplement*, 1890, p. 46.
[2] 15 Mar. 1858.

Reformers in The Literary Fund.[1] They had lost all chance of winning a majority within the society, but still clung to the idea that somehow they could influence the committee by playing on public opinion. Copies of the pamphlet were sent to members, and to the leading newspapers and periodicals. It was a straightforward piece of pamphleteering, simply presenting the case for the reformers, and containing nothing new to anyone who had followed the controversy for the last three years. It stated the same demands for wider aims and narrower expenditure, ending with a final statement of reformist policy:

> Always in a minority, but always influencing, however slowly, the abuses of the Society, it is the intention of the Reformers steadily to persevere. They contend that its present expenditure is wholly unjustifiable. . . . They contend that Literature should be made the first consideration in the Literary Fund. They have said, and must always say, that it is not desirable to obtrude mere rank and station . . . into the governing body of the Institution. They have thought that the ground on which all men . . . should meet at the Literary Fund, is that of Literature only . . . and that any other course has the effect of putting prominently forward, those incidents of patronage which are simply humiliating, and which every man of rank, who is also a cultivator of letters, and a true gentleman, shrinks from seeing connected with his name.[2]

The meeting was held on 10 March, with Lord Stanhope in the Chair. He made a special appeal for 'as much good humour and courtesy as possible', and after disposing of other formal business, moved a vote of thanks to the registrars, treasurers, and auditors. Dickens then rose to propose an amendment, and said:

IN response to that very graceful appeal, will you allow me to say at once that I have not only the pleasure of assuring you that I am not going to make a speech, but I have also the pleasure of hoping that the course I am going to take will be equally satisfactory to both parties in the room. [*Hear, hear.*] This may appear, at first sight, rather a romantic expectation, but I will show you in half a dozen words what a practical expectation it is.

On the former occasions we have met here, the majority who supported the Committee in the existing state of things—of which majority the committee itself formed so influential, so satisfied, so laudatory, and so very large a part—have very strongly objected to drawing a comparison between this institution and any like institution in the known world. [*Laughter.*] Now, no such comparison shall be heard from me today. Upon former occasions I have observed that dry details which are utterly inseparable from questions of figures are extremely unpalatable here, and apt to be received with considerable resentment; and I hope my abstinence and resolve thereon will be quite agreeable to both parties. I will

---

[1] *The Case of The Reformers in The Literary Fund; stated by Charles W. Dilke, Charles Dickens, and John Forster.*

[2] pp. 14–15.

only plainly say on that head (if there be any member of the Literary Fund attending here for the first time) that if under any circumstances I were to venture to enter in detail into the last accounts, I am quite sensible that it would look like the wanderings of a lunatic if I were to point out in detail how a fund of this kind had drawn forty-one charitable drafts on the society's bankers, at a cost of £13 each—absolutely more, in three cases, than the sum drawn for; how upon these forty-one cases there was a cost of more than forty-five per cent; while only fifteen of those cases were new ones after all—all the others having already been relieved from once to eight times. [*Hear, hear, and laughter.*]

Well now, for that reason, and for the promotion of general good will amongst us, I will confine myself to the assertion of a principle. Before the public, who, as I said on a previous occasion, are indeed the real judges of this matter, I entertain the single wish to fasten upon myself, and those who act with me in this matter, the distinct assertion of a plain principle; and to fasten on the Committee, and those who support them, the distinct assertion of a principle equally plain and manifest. [*Hear, hear.*] Now, the very moderate amendment I have to move is this:

> That the accounts of the Literary Fund, showing a systematic expenditure of from 40 *l.* to 45 *l.* in the giving away of every 100 *l.* of grants, are not quite satisfactory; that such an appropriation of money, subscribed with a clearly defined charitable object, is not quite right; that its continuance as a distinctive feature of the Literary Fund is not so consistent with the professions of the Literary Fund as to tend to uphold that Institution in general confidence; that such continuance, therefore, ought not to be sanctioned from year to year, and is now protested against.

Very well; this resolution will, no doubt, be duly seconded, duly put from the Chair, and duly negatived. [*Hear, hear, and laughter.*] The majority will be glad to negative it, I shall be content to have it negatived, and we shall all be satisfied. It will then be distinctly proclaimed 'that the accounts of the Literary Fund, showing a systematic expenditure of from 40 *l.* to 45 *l.* in the giving away of every 100 *l.* of grants', are 'quite satisfactory'; and, further, that the continuance of 'such an appropriation of money, subscribed with a clearly defined charitable object', is 'quite right', that 'its continuance as a distinctive feature of the Literary Fund', is so consistent with its professions as 'to tend to uphold that institution in the general confidence'; and, 'that such continuance, therefore', should 'be sanctioned from year to year', and is *not* 'protested against.' [*Laughter.*]

Now, to the acceptance of this responsibility for myself, and to the putting of their responsibility on the Committee, I have steadily resolved to confine myself today. I am here wholly and solely for that purpose, and no consideration whatsoever shall induce me to swerve from it. In connexion with two friends who are now near me, I have written a letter[1] and caused it to be equally circulated amongst all members of this society without any distinction, and we have had it printed, in which we have set forth what seem to us to be very grave, self-evident objections to the administration and expenditure. If any champion of that administration and expenditure will impugn any one of those statements in writing, as we have done, upon his own personal honour, upon his personal responsibility, and with the fixed association of answer to assertion which belongs to productions in print, we will immediately answer him, and prove that case whatever it may be. But I wish it to be distinctly understood that I am not skirmishing to escape here from the one unqualified declaration that the present system of expenditure in the Literary Fund, as a charitable institution, is in principle and practice quite right, is calculated to attract public confidence, and does not require revision. We will not permit ourselves, under any circumstances whatsoever, to be led away from that, and therefore I can communicate to you, Lord Stanhope, the very comfortable intelligence, that after the resolution I have read has been put and disposed of, not one other word will be heard in this room from my lips, and not one from Mr. Dilke, and not one from Mr. Forster, until this time next year. [*Hear, hear, and laughter.*]

We assume, as we are bound in courtesy to assume, that our opponents have no greater desire to shrink from a broad open, manly acceptance of their responsibility, than we have desired to shrink from ours. Here in this resolution, read affirmatively and read negatively, are two responsibilities, for and against. Let each side please to take its own, and let both sides go on their way rejoicing. [*Laughter.*]

The amendment was seconded by John Forster.

[1] *The Case of The Reformers.* Both the *Daily News*, and the *Summary of Facts* issued by the committee, have 'in conjunction' for 'in connexion'. Whichever Dickens said, there is little doubt that *The Case of The Reformers* was almost entirely his work, although Dilke may have provided him with the facts and figures on which it was based. When Forster first suggested he should write it Dickens replied, in a letter of 13 May 1857, that he had 'so many matters pressing on [his] attention' that he could not turn to it at the time. *The Answer to The Committee's Summary of 'Facts'* was also certainly by Dickens, and in a letter to Wilkie Collins of 29 Apr. 1858 he writes of it as his own work: 'It is a facetious facer—which I have given to those solemn imposters, con amore.' [M.]

The tactics of the reformers were too obviously unfair to be convincing. Having issued a detailed pamphlet setting out all the arguments and statistics on their side of the case, it was impossible for anyone to accept Dickens's disclaimer of all interest in 'dry details' and 'questions of figures'. There had been no time to publish a reply to the pamphlet, but the committee-men had come to the meeting with carefully prepared speeches and they were not to be put off from reading them. In reply Milnes declared that 'the gentlemen who came forward as the reformers of the Literary Fund, were reformers in the sense that the insurgent Sepoys were reformers of the garrison at Lucknow'.

Dr. William Smith[1] made a sensible contribution, which was the more effective because he was clearly impartial. He thought some of the questions raised by the reformers were fair subjects for discussion, but that they were unjustified in stigmatizing members of the committee as 'patrons of abuse'. Other speakers followed, including Richard Blackmore and Robert Bell. Dickens challenged Blackmore's remark that the opposition of the reformers was partly due to being refused 'a slice of their funds' for the Guild; and Bell made a detailed official reply, much of which was later incorporated in the society's *Summary of Facts, . . . Issued In Answer to Allegations Contained in A Pamphlet Entitled 'The Case of the Reformers of The Literary Fund'*, which was published next month. Eventually, at the suggestion of the chairman, the vote of thanks to the officers was proposed and passed without opposition, and Dickens's amendment was put as a substantive motion. It was negatived by seventy votes to fourteen. After a further procedural wrangle, the meeting separated.

Next day Dickens wrote to Shirley Brooks:

Ah! You should have seen the virtuous grey hairs of Bentley,[2] in the foreground of a group of two score parson schoolmasters, he voting on their conservative side, and going direct to Heaven in their company. It was like the apotheosis of an evangelical (and drunken) butler.

Next month the official *Summary of Facts*, by Robert Bell, appeared; and Dickens countered almost immediately with *The Answer to The Committee's Summary of 'Facts'*.

In spite of his assurance of ceaseless opposition, he never spoke at an Annual General Meeting of the Society again. The reformers found the committee unmoved by publicity, which was even beginning to turn

[1] Dr. William Smith (1813–93), classical scholar and lexicographer; author of a *Dictionary of Greek and Roman Antiquities*, 1842, and many other works. Master at University College school. Assisted Dickens and Elwin in their negotiations with the General Committee, of which he was a member, in 1859–60. Succeeded Elwin in 1867 as editor of the *Quarterly Review*.

[2] Richard Bentley (1794–1871), publisher, for whom Dickens had written *Oliver Twist* and edited *Bentley's Miscellany*, 1837–9. As long as he had been bound to Bentley by contract there had been constant disputes between them. They were on better terms once they separated, but Forster was only smoothing things over when he wrote that 'certainly in later years there was no absence of friendly feeling' on the part of Dickens for his old publisher. (F, VIII. vi.)

against them. Next year, therefore, they tried diplomacy, and Dickens wrote to the registrars to say that an anonymous benefactor was prepared to bequeath his valuable library and collection of manuscripts to the society, with an endowment of £10,000 to maintain them, if they would agree to certain changes in the constitution.[1] The alterations asked for were slight, and were to be in accordance with the recommendations of the Special Charter Committee of 1855. After a protracted series of negotiations between the committee on the one hand, and Dickens and the Rev. Whitwell Elwin as representatives of the anonymous donor on the other, the offer was finally rejected.

As everyone knew, the mysterious benefactor was John Forster, whose library was later bequeathed to the Department of Science and Art, and is now in the Victoria and Albert Museum. Had his offer been accepted the manuscripts of Dickens's novels, and many of his letters, would now be in the keeping of the Royal Literary Fund. The proposal was sincere enough; but it was obvious that the committee were so exasperated that they were certain to reject it. None the less, it was a successful manœuvre since the committee was tricked into putting itself in the wrong by the way in which they refused it, while the reformers were able to break the deadlock without admitting their defeat.

AT A READING OF THE *CAROL* FOR THE PHILOSOPHICAL INSTITUTION: EDINBURGH

26 *March* 1858

For the past six months Dickens had been restlessly trying to make up his mind whether to give up his occasional readings for charity, and to begin them systematically on his own account. As early as April the previous year he had promised to give a reading for the Philosophical Institution, and he now approached it as a further test before making his decision.

As a 'burgess and guild brother' of the city since 1841, he was to be given an official reception. To Forster Dickens wrote, before leaving London:

You will be happy to hear that at one on Friday, the Lord Provost, Dean of Guild, Magistrates, and Council of the ancient city of Edinburgh will wait (in procession) on their brother freeman, at the Music Hall, to give him hospitable welcome. Their brother freeman has been cursing their stars and his own, ever since solemn notification to that effect.[2]

He was accompanied on his visit by W. H. Wills, the sub-editor of *Household Words*. Mrs. Wills had been Janet Chambers, and was the sister of William and Robert Chambers, the Edinburgh publishers. Writing to his wife the next day, Wills told her about their reception, and mentioned that the secretary of the Philosophical Institution had written to him to say 'that he had neither ate nor drank nor slept for

[1] Letter of 1 Mar. 1859, RLF.   [2] F, VIII. ii.

days, he has been so bullied for tickets. None but members could have them, so many made themselves members to come.'[1]

As Dickens entered the Music Hall, where the reading was to be given, he was greeted with prolonged applause.

HE began by saying that on the occasions when he had the honour of reading this little book to a public audience, he was accustomed to begin with two remarks: the first, that he would pause for a few minutes about half-way through; and second, that if as he proceeded they should feel disposed to give expression to any little emotion awakened by the story, he begged they would do so in the most natural way possible, and without the least apprehension of disturbing him. [*Laughter.*] Nothing could be more agreeable to him than to receive any assurance that they were interested, and nothing could be more in accordance with his wishes than that they should make themselves as like as possible to a small group of friends assembled to hear a tale told, and that they should at once forget everything ceremonious or formal in the manner of their coming together. [*Applause.*]

The reading itself was a great success. Wills reported a 'capital audience':

Wonderful unanimity. Wonderful happiness. Cheers and guffaws and pocket-handkerchiefs all in their right places. After it was over and Dickens was picking up his book, handkerchief, box of lozenges, &c., the Lord Provost came forward with a mahogany case. . . . Then he made a speech. Then he opened the case. It contained a magnificent chased and burnished wassail cup of great size with an inscription. The secretary told me privately it was meant to be an heirloom in the family. Dickens was delighted with it.[2]

Once more he was greeted with prolonged applause, as he came forward to return thanks, and said:

My Lord Provost, Ladies and Gentlemen, I beg to assure you that I am deeply sensible of your kind welcome and of this beautiful and great surprise, and I thank you for it cordially with all my heart. I have never forgotten, and I never can forget, that I have the honour to be a burgess and Guild brother of the Corporation of Edinburgh. [*Cheers.*] So long as sixteen or seventeen years ago, the first public recognition and encouragement I ever received was bestowed upon me in this generous and magnificent city—in this city so distinguished in letters and so distinguished in the arts. You will readily believe that I have carried to the various countries I have since traversed, and through all my subsequent career, the proud and affectionate remembrance of that eventful epoch of my

[1] Lady Priestley, *The Story of a Lifetime*, 1904, pp. 176–7.
[2] Ibid., p. 177.

life; and that coming back to Edinburgh is to me like coming back home. [*Loud cheers.*]

Ladies and gentlemen, you have heard so much of my voice tonight, that I will not inflict upon you the additional task of hearing any more from me. But I am the better reconciled to limiting myself to these very few words, because I know and feel full well that no amount of speech to which I could give utterance could formally express my sense of the honour and distinction you have conferred upon me, or the heartfelt gratification I have in its reception. [*Prolonged cheering.*]

Dickens was triumphant. 'It is an unspeakable satisfaction to me', he told Wills, 'to have left such an impression in Edinburgh.'[1] To Thomas Beard he wrote: 'It was a wonderful go', and 'certainly the most intelligent audience (2000 strong) I have ever had to do with.'[2] He felt sure that he was right: and a month later, after one more charity reading for the Child's Hospital, came the first for his own profit.

Forster heard of the success of the Edinburgh reading, and of his own failure in opposing Dickens's proposals, from his wife. Writing to Mrs. Forster Dickens announced:

The Reading was a tremendous success. Some two thousand people were crammed into the place; and nobody I know in Edinburgh could get admission on any terms. They gave me a gorgeous cup (tell Forster), and I made them a neat and appropriate.

All of which (please also tell Forster), I saw very faithfully and well described in The Scotsman yesterday morning. But of course I haven't got the Scotsman, or I would forward him to Montague Square.[3]

He told Forster himself soon after:

I had no opportunity of asking any one's advice in Edinburgh. The crowd was too enormous, and the excitement in it much too great. But my determination is all but taken. I must do *something*, or I shall wear my heart away. I can see no better thing to do that is half so hopeful in itself, or half so well suited to my restless state.[4]

ROYAL GENERAL THEATRICAL FUND

29 *March* 1858

As it had been announced towards the end of the dinner the previous year, the Chair on this occasion was filled by Thackeray. There were the usual loyal and patriotic toasts; following which the chairman rose to give the toast of the evening. He made a graceful reference to Dickens at the opening of his speech, regretting that he did not possess 'that happy genius and skill for the post which belongs to a friend of mine that I

[1] 3 Apr. 1858.   [2] 5 Apr. 1858 [DH].
[3] 28 Mar. 1858, from photograph, Dickens's birthplace museum, Portsmouth.
[4] F, VIII. ii.

think sits not very far from me'. Buckstone replied for the society, and
Dickens rose to propose the health of the chairman. He was received
with loud cheers, clapping, and waving of handkerchiefs by ladies in the
gallery, and said:

GENTLEMEN, In our theatrical experience as playgoers, we are all,
I have no doubt, pretty equally accustomed to predict from certain
little signs and tokens on the stage, what is going to happen there.
For example, when the young lady, the admiral's daughter, is left
alone to relieve her feelings with certain general observations not
particularly connected with the subject, and when a certain smart,
spiritual rapping is heard to proceed from the depths of the earth
immediately before her feet, we foretell that a song is intended.
[*Laughter.*] When two gentlemen enter for whom, by a happy
coincidence, exactly two chairs, and neither fewer nor more, are
waiting, we augur that a conversation will probably ensue, and that
it is far from impossible that that conversation will assume a
retrospectively biographical character. [*Laughter.*] In like manner
when two other gentlemen, particularly if they belong to the sea-
faring, the marauding, or smuggling professions, are observed to
have armed themselves since their last appearance with a very short
sword with a very large hilt, we predict with some confidence that
this cautious preparation will end in a combat. [*Laughter.*] Now
similarly, gentlemen, carrying out of the theatre those associations
of ideas which we so often carry into it, it may possibly have occurred
to you that when I just now asked permission of my old friend in
the Chair to propose a toast, I had my old friend himself in my eye,
and that I have him now on my lips.[1] [*Cheers and laughter.*]

Gentlemen, the duties of a Trustee of the General Theatrical Fund,
which office I have the honour to hold, are not so numerous as are his
privileges. He is, in short, a mere walking gentleman [*laughter*],
with the melancholy difference that he has no one to love. [*Laughter.*]
If his part could be a little revised in that particular, I could
answer that his character would be a much more agreeable one to
stage, and his forlorn condition would be very considerably ame-
liorated. The duties of this strange character consist in a half-
yearly call at the bank, when he signs his name in an extremely
large and extremely inconvenient volume, when he receives two
documents of which he knows nothing, which he immediately
delivers up to the property man, and makes his exit. [*Laughter.*]

His privileges, however, are great. He has the privilege of observing the steady growth and progress of the institution in which,
from its infancy, he has been interested; he has the privilege of

---

[1] The *Era*, and official pamphlet read: 'I have now you on my lips.' The
Morning Herald: 'I have him now', &c.

being invested with a kind of right on all proper occasions to bear his testimony to the providence, the goodness, the self-denial, and the self-respect of a class of people whom ignorance has a great deal too much depreciated, and to whom those virtues have long been denied out of the depths of a most mean, and ignorant, and stupid superstition. [*Loud cheers.*] And lastly, he has the privilege of being sometimes called upon to propose the health of the chairman at the annual dinner; and when that chairman is a man for whose genius he has a warm admiration and the most earnest respect [*cheers*], when that chairman is a gentleman who is an honour to literature, and in whom literature is honoured [*cheers*], when that is the case he feels that last privilege to be a great and high one. [*Renewed cheering.*] Gentlemen, from the earliest days of the institution I have ventured to impress upon its managers my individual opinion that they would best consult its credit and success by choosing its chairman as often as possible within the circle of literature and the arts. [*Hear, hear.*] I will venture to say that no similar establishment in existence can show itself to have been presided over by so many remarkable and distinguished men. [*Hear, hear.*] I am sure that it never has had, and that it never will have, simply because it never can have, a gentleman in that position shedding a greater lustre upon it than the noble English writer who fills this Chair tonight. [*Loud cheering.*]

Gentlemen, it is not for me at this time and place to take upon myself to flutter before you the well-thumbed pages of Mr. Thackeray's books, and to take upon myself to call upon you to observe how full of wit they are, how full of wisdom they are, how full of outspoken meaning—and yet, though out-speaking, how devoid of fear, and how devoid of favour. [*Hear, hear.*] But I may take leave to remark, in paying my little due of homage and respect to them, that I think it is a most appropriate and fit thing to have such a writer as my friend, and such an art as the dramatic brought face to face, as we see them here tonight. [*Cheers.*] Every good actor plays direct to every good author, and every writer of fiction, though he may not adopt the dramatic form, writes in effect for the stage. He may write novels always, and plays never, but the truth and wisdom that are in him must permeate the art of which truth and passion are the life, and must be more or less reflected in that great mirror which he holds up to nature. [*Cheers.*] Now, gentlemen, actors and managers and authors are all represented in this present company. We may, without any great effort of imagination, suppose that all of them have studied the mighty deep secrets of the human heart in many theatres of many kinds, great and small, but I am sure that none of them can have studied those mysterious workings in any theatre from the stage wagon of Thespis downwards, to greater advantage, to greater profit, and to greater contentment than in the airy booths of *Vanity Fair*. To this skilful showman, who has so much delighted us, and whose words have so charmed us tonight, we are now to express our gratitude and to convey our welcome; and in wishing him God speed through the many years and the many fairs which we earnestly hope are in store for him in which to exercise his potent art, we will now, if you please, join in drinking a bumper toast to the chairman's health, and God bless him!

The toast was drunk amid loud and protracted cheering. Thackeray, 'in a voice broken by emotion', briefly replied:

Gentlemen, your kind applause has lasted much longer than my speech will. You will agree with me, as you think over Mr. Dickens's speech, that I had best entirely leave my case in his hands. I cannot mend—I cannot come up to what he has said. If it is true, or if a part of it is true, I am sure I am most thankful, and I am thankful to find a friend and comrade at my right, and that two literary men are found who hold for one another such a sincere esteem.

He appeared to be so overcome with emotion that he was unable to proceed, and resumed his seat amid great cheering. A few other toasts followed before the proceedings came to an end.

AT THE FIRST READING FOR HIS OWN PROFIT

29 *April* 1858

AFTER some hesitation, and in spite of Forster's opposition, Dickens finally decided to begin readings in public for his own benefit. The first of a short series in London was given at St. Martin's Hall, where he had read two weeks earlier for the Hospital for Sick Children. The hall was crowded. There may have been some anxiety at first among his friends:

But the moment Dickens stepped on to the platform, walking rather stiffly, right shoulder well forward, as usual, bud in button-hole, and gloves in hand, all doubt was blown into the air. He was received with a roar of cheering which might have been heard at Charing Cross, and which was again and again renewed. Whatever he may have felt, Dickens showed no emotion. He took his place at his reading-desk, and made a short prefatory speech [1]

[1] Edmund Yates, *Recollections and Experiences*, 1884, ii. 98–99. Yates introduces this description with a circumstantially detailed account of the 'considerable amount of anxiety among Dickens's intimate friends lest the indignation caused by the publication of the "statement"', about the separation from his wife, and still existing among a section of the public, might find vent on his first appearance on the platform.' It could not 'still exist', since most of his closest friends were not told of the decision to separate until next month; the public did not begin to hear of it until after that; and the 'statement' was not published until 7 June in *The Times*, or in *Household Words*, for which it

LADIES and Gentlemen, It may perhaps be known to you that, for a few years past, I have been accustomed occasionally to read some of my shorter books to various audiences, in aid of a variety of good objects, and at some charge to myself, both in time and money. It having at length become impossible in any reason to comply with these always accumulating demands, I have had definitely to choose between now and then reading on my own account, as one of my recognized occupations, or not reading at all. I have had little or no difficulty in deciding on the former course. [*Cheers.*]

The reasons that have led me to it—besides the consideration that it necessitates no departure whatever from the chosen pursuits of my life—are threefold. Firstly, I have satisfied myself that it can involve no possible compromise of the credit and independence of literature. Secondly I have long held the opinion, and have long acted on the opinion, that in these times whatever brings a public man and his public face to face, on terms of mutual confidence and respect, is a good thing. [*Cheers.*] Thirdly, I have had a pretty large experience of the interest my hearers are so generous as to take in these occasions, and of the delight they give to me, as a tried means of strengthening those relations—I may almost say of personal friendship—which it is my great privilege and pride, as it is my great responsibility, to hold with a multitude of persons who will never hear my voice nor see my face. Thus it is that I come, quite naturally, to be here among you at this time; and thus it is that I proceed to read this little book, quite as composedly as I might proceed to write it, or to publish it in any other way. [*Loud cheers.*]

Dickens then went on to read the *Cricket on the Hearth*, which was listened to with deep attention interrupted only by applause. The reading was acclaimed an entire success.

ROYAL ACADEMY BANQUET
1 *May* 1858

THE annual dinner was held in the association's rooms in Trafalgar Square, with the president, Sir Charles Eastlake, in the Chair. The final toast was to Literature, to which both Dickens and Thackeray were called upon to reply. Dickens spoke first, and said:

FOLLOWING the order of your toast I have to take the first part

was written, until the 12th. His friends may have been doubtful, however, about the success of the reading for other reasons, and they were certainly anxious about Dickens's reception in the provinces because of public feeling about the separation when he began his tour in August. Yates was probably not so closely in Dickens's confidence at this time as he implies and as has been generally supposed.

in the duet to be performed in acknowledgement of the compliment you have paid to literature. In this home of art I feel it to be too much an interchange of compliments, as it were, between near relations, to enter into any lengthened expression of our thanks for the honour you have done us. I feel that it would be changing this splendid assembly into a sort of family party. [*A laugh.*] I may, however, take leave to say that your sister, whom I represent, is strong and healthy [*a laugh*], she has a great and an undying interest in you, and it is always a very great gratification to her to see herself so well remembered within these walls, and to know that she is an honoured guest at your hospitable board. [*Cheers and laughter.*]

He was immediately followed by Thackeray, who recalled his first meeting with Dickens. He told them how, when Dickens was writing *Pickwick*, he had 'wanted an artist to illustrate his writings; and I recollect walking up to his chambers with two or three drawings in my hand, which, strange to say, he did not find suitable. But for that unfortunate blight which came over my artistical existence, it would have been my pride and pleasure to have endeavoured one day to find a place on these walls for one of my performances.'[1]

The chairman then left the Chair, and the company dispersed to linger in the different rooms and continue their inspection of the exhibition.

ARTISTS' BENEVOLENT FUND

8 *May* 1858

THE forty-eighth anniversary festival was held at the Freemasons' Tavern with Dickens in the Chair. Among those who were also present were Sir Charles Eastlake, George A. Godwin, the editor of the *Builder*, and W. P. Frith whose 'Derby Day' was the sensation of this year's exhibition at the Royal Academy. The cloth having been removed, Dickens rose to propose the toast of 'The Queen'.

HE alluded to her Majesty's magnificent donation of 100 guineas. This fact in itself was no slight proof of the Queen's interest in the association. The art of the artist, coupled with the art of the Chancellor of the Exchequer, had rendered the Queen's head familiar to them at every hour of their daily lives. [*Hear, hear.*] And on that head they were now anxious, as loyal and devoted subjects, to invoke a blessing. [*Three times three loud cheers.*]

---

[1] Dickens had originally been engaged only to write the letterpress to accompany Robert Seymour's sketches; but between the publication of the first and second number of *Pickwick* Seymour shot himself, on 20 Apr. 1836. Thackeray's application was probably made soon after.

'The Prince Consort, the Prince of Wales, and the rest of the Royal Family' having been given from the Chair, Dickens continued with 'The Army and Navy'.

He alluded eloquently to their services. Although he was not one of those who feared or had the least apprehension of an invasion, or that the National Gallery in Trafalgar Square would be carried off —seeing, for instance, that it was a building that would not be worth the transport [*laughter and cheers*], yet at the same time it was well to be prepared for any emergency; and he was sure that should such arise, the services to which he had the honour to allude would be found—as ever—ready and willing to serve for the honour of their country. [*Cheers.*]

The chairman then rose amid loud and protracted cheering, and said:

Ladies and Gentlemen, There is an absurd theatrical story which was once told to me by a dear and valued friend, who has now passed from this sublunary stage,[1] and which is not without its moral as applied to myself, in my present presidential position. In a certain theatrical company was included a man, who on occasions of emergency was capable of taking part in the whole round of British drama, provided he was allowed to use his own language in getting through the dialogue. [*A laugh.*] It happened one night that Reginald, in *The Castle Spectre*, was taken ill, and this hardy veteran of a hundred characters was, of course, called up for the vacant part. He responded with his usual promptitude, although knowing nothing whatever of the character; but while they were getting him into the dress, he expressed a not unreasonable wish to know in some vague way what the part was about. [*Laughter.*] He was not particular as to details, but in order that he might properly portray his sufferings, he thought he should have some slight inkling as to what really had happened to him [*continued laughter*]; as, for example, what murders he had committed, whose father he was, of what misfortunes he was the victim,—in short, in a general way to know why he was in the place at all. [*Renewed laughter.*] They said to him, 'Here you are, chained in a dungeon, an unhappy father; you have been here for seventeen years, during which time you have never seen your daughter; you have lived upon bread and water, and, in consequence, are extremely weak, and suffer from occasional lowness of spirits'. [*Laughter.*] 'All right', said the actor of universal capabilities, 'Ring up.' [*Cheers and laughter.*]

When he was discovered to the audience, he presented an extremely miserable appearance, was very favourably received,

[1] Macready. Dickens had told his story before, see p. 125.

and gave every sign of going on well until, through some mental confusion as to his instructions, he opened the business of the act by stating in pathetic terms, that he had been confined in that dungeon seventeen years during which time he had not tasted a morsel of food, to which circumstance he was inclined to attribute the fact of his being at that moment very much out of condition. [*Renewed laughter.*] The audience, thinking this statement exceedingly improbable, declined to receive it, and the weight of that speech hung round him until the end of his performance.

Now I, too, have received instructions for the part I have the honour of performing before you, and it behoves both you and me to profit by the terrible warning I have detailed, while I endeavour to make the part I have undertaken as plain and intelligible as I possibly can.

As I am going to propose to you that we should now begin to connect the business with the pleasure of the evening, by drinking prosperity to the Artists' Benevolent Fund, it becomes important that we should know what that fund is. It is an association supported by the voluntary gifts of those who entertain a critical and admiring estimation of art, and has for its objects the granting of annuities to the widows and children of deceased artists—of artists who have been unable in their lives to make any provision for those dear objects of their love surviving themselves. [*Hear, hear.*] Now it is extremely important to observe that this institution of an Artists' Benevolent Fund, which I now call on you to pledge, has connected with it, and has arisen out of another artists' association, which does not ask you for help, which never did and never will ask you for help, which is self-supporting, and which is entirely maintained by the prudence and providence of its three hundred artist members. [*Cheers.*] That fund, which is called the Artists' Annuity Fund is, so to speak, a joint and mutual Assurance Company against infirmity, sickness, and old age. To the benefits it affords every one of its members has an absolute right, a right be it remembered produced by timely thrift and self denial, and not assisted by appeals to the charity or compassion of any human being. On that fund there are, if I remember aright, some seventeen annuitants who are in the receipt of eleven hundred a year, the proceeds of their own self-supporting institution. [*Hear, hear.*] In recommending to you this benevolent fund, which is not self-supporting, they address you, in effect, in these words: 'We ask you to help these widows and orphans, because we show you we have first helped ourselves. These widows and orphans may be ours or they may not be ours; but in any case we will prove to you to a certainty that we are not so many wagoners calling upon Hercules to do our work, because we do our own work, each has his shoulder to the wheel; each, from year to year, has had his shoulder set to the wheel; and the prayer we make to Hercules and all the gods at once is simply this—that this fact may be remembered when the wagon has stopped for ever, and the spent and worn-out wagoner lies lifeless by the roadside. [*Cheers.*]

Ladies and gentlemen, I most particularly wish to impress on you the strength of this appeal. I am a painter, a sculptor, or an engraver, of average success. I study hard, and work hard, with no immense return for my labour. Whilst I live in health, my hand and eye are mine. I prudently belong to the Annuity Fund, whose help whether in sickness or old age, I may or may not want, yet still I help to provide for some of my brethren who inevitably will want. [*Hear, hear.*] I thus do my duty to them and to myself by putting them and myself beyond the need of charity whilst life remains. But when life is gone from me; when this hand, once so skilful with the brush, the chisel, or the burin, has for ever lost its cunning; when this poor form, which for so many years bent patiently over the easel or the desk, is laid low, and the grass grows green above my grave, how consoling to my survivors that I had at least made some attempts at provision for them. [*Cheers.*]

This is the case with the Artists' Benevolent Fund, and in stating this I am only the mouthpiece of three hundred of the trade, who in truth stand as independent before you as if they were three hundred Cockers all regulated by the Gospel according to themselves. There is in existence a third Artists' fund, wholly unconnected with the two to which I have alluded—which must not be mentioned but with honour and respect.[1] It gives away sums of money in eleemosynary relief. I have the honour of being one of the honorary officers thereof. I know it to be a generous fund and a good fund. [*Hear, hear.*] But it addresses its appeal to you on behalf of those amongst the unfortunate or less provident men who have made no provision for themselves, or for those dependent on the contingencies of sickness or age. I address you on behalf of those professors of the fine arts who *have* made provision during life, and in submitting to you their claims I am only advocating principles which I myself have always maintained.

When I add that this Benevolent Fund makes no pretensions to gentility, squanders no treasure in keeping up appearances, that it considers that the money given for the widow and orphan, should really be held for the widow and orphan, I think I have exhausted the case, which I desire most strenuously to commend to you.

Perhaps you will allow me to say one last word. I will not consent to present to you the professors of Art as a set of helpless babies,

---

[1] Probably the Artists' General Benevolent Fund.

who are to be held up by the chin; I present them as an energetic and persevering class of men, whose income depends on their own faculties and personal exertions; and I also make so bold as to present them as men who in their vocation render good service to the community. I am strongly disposed to believe there are very few debates in Parliament so important to the public welfare as a really good picture. [*Cheers.*] I have also a notion that any number of bundles of the driest legal chaff that was ever chopped would be cheaply exchanged for one really accessible, really humanizing, really meritorious engraving. [*Cheers and laughter.*] At a highly interesting annual festival at which I have the honour to assist,[1] and which takes place behind two fountains, I sometimes observe that great ministers of state and other such exalted characters have a strange delight in rather ostentatiously declaring that they have no knowledge whatever of art [*cheers and laughter*], and particularly of impressing on the company that they have passed their lives in severe studies. [*Laughter.*] It strikes me when I hear these things as if these great men looked upon the arts as a sort of dancing dogs, or Punch's show, to be turned to for amusement when one has nothing else to do. Now I always take the opportunity on these occasions of entertaining my humble opinion that all this is complete 'bosh' [*renewed laughter*]; and of asserting to myself my strong belief that the neighbourhoods of Trafalgar Square, or Suffolk Street,[2] rightly understood, are quite as important to the welfare of the empire as those of Downing Street or Westminster Hall. [*Cheers and laughter.*] Ladies and gentlemen, on these grounds— upon grounds not one inch lower—and backed by the recommendation of three hundred artists in favour of the Benevolent Fund, I beg to propose its prosperity as a toast for your adoption.

The toast was received with enthusiastic cheers. The health of the chairman was then proposed by George Godwin, and briefly acknowledged.

PLAYGROUND AND GENERAL RECREATION SOCIETY

1 *June* 1858

THE first anniversary festival of this society was held at the London Tavern with Dickens in the Chair. On the cloth being removed, he rose to propose the health of 'Her Majesty the Queen':

IT was, he said, highly appropriate that the voice of a society whose chief object was the welfare of little children, and in promoting

[1] Royal Academy Banquet.
[2] Referring to the Royal Academy, and the British Artists' Society.

innocent amusements among them, should first be heard in proposing the health of a monarch endeared to them all, not only by the ties of loyalty, but by more graceful bonds of affection, as a devoted wife and tender mother.

Dickens then proposed 'The Prince Consort and the Royal Family', which was drunk with all the honours; followed by 'The Church':

The Society, he said, under whose auspices they met that evening, was established through the exertions of a very eminent, a very active, and a highly serviceable London incumbent, a gentleman then present—though his modesty had removed him from him— and who was now in his eye, as he doubted not he was in their remembrance.[1] The society was also very much indebted to other Christian ministers of all denominations for much of the success it had already attained; and, therefore, he had much pleasure in proposing 'The Church', coupling with it the name of the Rev. Dr. Irons,[2] and the Christian ministers of all denominations who truly exerted themselves for general instruction and general good.

Dr. Irons replied, contending that more time should be allowed to the poor for recreation. The chairman then proposed a toast to 'The two Houses of Parliament', with which he coupled the names of Mr. Sotheron Estcourt[3] and Mr. Slaney.[4]

He alluded, amidst much laughter, to the games sometimes performed in the political playground, which he said were not very improving or intelligent, and led to boys occasionally attempting 'over' posts which they had much better have left alone.

In proposing the toast of the evening, Dickens said:

Gentlemen, if you will allow me to recall the little train of familiar incidents through which I took a stroll from my own house within these last two or three hours, perhaps it will as aptly introduce the business we have in hand as a much more elaborate and a much more tiresome introduction.

You must know that I have still at home one very dear young child[5] who has not arrived at years of sufficient discretion to go to school in Germany or France with his brothers; who lives on terms

---

[1] Rev. David Laing, see p. 65.

[2] William Josiah Irons (1812–83), vicar of Brompton, and author of works on theology.

[3] Thomas Henry Sutton Sotheron Estcourt (1801–76), M.P. for North Wiltshire; appointed Privy Councillor 1858; Home Secretary Mar. to June 1859.

[4] Robert Aglionby Slaney (1792–1862), M.P. for Shrewsbury; Chairman of the House of Commons Committees on Education 1838, and the Health of Towns 1840; member of Royal Commission on Health of Towns 1843–6; High Sheriff of Shropshire 1854.

[5] Edward Bulwer Lytton Dickens, 'Plorn', then aged six.

of personal hostility towards all the cats in the neighbouring gardens, and who invents cats besides for the excitement of a Scotch terrier. These two—the English child and the Scotch dog—perpetually flying in and out of the garden-door in a sort of poetical rapture of cats, worry me very much more than I ever saw them worry any other living thing; for, indeed, they only seek a pretext for being constantly in motion, and are innocent of all harm. This very after-noon, a few hours ago, they were so strongly under the influence of this fury of cats, that I, sitting in my own room, endeavouring with a heavy heart to consider my present responsibilities, found myself unable to collect my senses by any means. So I resolved to go out for a short stroll.

The first thing I saw, when I went out of my own door, was a policeman hiding among the lilac trees apparently lying in wait for some burglar or murderer. After observing him with great dread and anxiety for a minute or two, I was much relieved to find that the object of his vigilance was nothing worse than a hoop, which he presently took into custody, and carried off to the station-house. [*Laughter.*]

Now, my way happened to lie through three of the leading squares. In the first square I encountered a company of seven little boys, each boy carrying a boy much larger than himself, an old pickle-bottle, and a very home-made fishing rod; with which impediments they were fagging up to Hampstead ponds, where I should judge that the party would scarcely arrive in time to tumble in before dark. I found the dignity of the second square, which is a highly genteel one, very much impaired by its having the game of hop-scotch chalked all over its pavement; and here too I found my own personal dignity suffered some little detriment through my becom-ing, without my own consent, the centre-point or pivot of a dodging game between two boys who evaded each other around me, and lunged at each other before me and made no more account of me than if I were a sort of moving post or pillar. [*Laughter.*] Coming to the long hackney-coach stand in that neighbourhood, I found the waterman in a state of red-heat and ire, because the children's shuttlecocks were flying about the horses' ears [*laughter*], and be-cause a train of little creatures, hailing an imaginary 'Bal—loon!' were filing in and out among his water-tubs. In the third square I arrived in time to dry the tears and relieve the distresses of two diminutive little creatures, the prey of a third diminutive little crea-ture, a size larger, who, in default of having anything else to play with, had taken off their caps, and thrown them down an area. [*Laughter.*]

And so I arrived in the course of time at Lincoln's Inn Fields,

where I positively seemed to find myself in an enemy's country;
prodigious and awful spikes being stuck into the posts of that
neighbourhood for the impalement of the youth of London [*Loud
laughter*]; and three distinct rushes taking place while I was there
on the part of an officer in a gold-laced hat, and armed with a
drawn cane, who drove before him a flying cloud of boys and girls,
and pursued them with horrible menaces. [*Laughter.*]

Thus I happily arrived at last in the haven where you now
behold me, meditating very much upon the great need there is,
in London and in all large towns, of places for the children to play
in; and considering with what a determined self-assertion nature
declares that play they must, and play they will, somewhere or
other, under whatsoever circumstances of difficulty.

Now, gentlemen, in the main, I quite agree with the reverend
doctor who just now so eloquently expressed himself; but I begin
with children, because we all began as children; and I confine myself to children tonight, because the child is the father of the man.
Some majestic minds out of doors may, for anything I know, and
certainly for anything I care, consider it a very humdrum and low
proceeding to stop, in a country full of steam-engines, power-looms,
big ships, monster mortars, and great guns of all sorts, to consider
where the children are to play. Nevertheless, I know that the
question is a very kind one, and a very necessary one. [*Hear, hear.*]
The surgeon and the recruiting sergeant will tell you with great
emphasis, that the children's play is of immense importance to a
community in the development of bodies; the clergyman, the
schoolmaster, and the moral philosopher, in all degrees, will tell
you with no less emphasis, that the children's play is of great
importance to a community in the development of minds. I
venture to assert that there can be no physical health without play;
and there can be no efficient and satisfactory work without play;
that there can be no sound and wholesome thought without play.
[*Hear, hear.*] A country full of dismal little old men and women
who had never played would be in a mighty bad way indeed; and
you may depend upon it that without play, and good play, too,
those powerful English cheers which have driven the sand of Asia
before them, and made the very ocean shake, would degenerate
into a puling whimper, that would be the most consolatory sound
that can possibly be conceived to all the tyrants on the face of the
earth. [*Cheers.*]

Now, gentlemen, great towns constantly increasing about us, as
the national trade and prosperity increase; houses constantly crowd-
ing together and continually accumulating; and the fields being
always put at an always increasing distance from the great mass

of the people; it becomes a very serious question where the children shall play, and how they shall grow up into men and women who must have played, or it would have been better for them and for all of us that they had never been born. The great importance of this question, in its many aspects both of humanity and policy, so strongly suggested itself to that gentleman who has been several times mentioned tonight—the Rev. Mr. Laing—so strongly suggested itself to him, not yet a year ago, that he conceived the idea of establishing a Playground Society; in other words a combination of certain ladies and gentlemen of some influence and position who, being agreed on the main question, should resolve to advance it by all means in their power. This infant society began by corresponding with the governing authorities in several large towns, and with other persons in position, with a view to ascertain their opinion. It also sought to elicit the opinion of that great mover of all opinion, the press. A cordial support of the principle, and an earnest approval of it, were, I believe, unanimously accorded. The Society then endeavoured, as Mr. Slaney has intimated, to impress upon the owners of lands the great benefit they would render to the country by sometimes conceding small gifts of open places for this benevolent purpose. Mr. Slaney himself, ever foremost in such good objects, brought in a Bill to facilitate the legal transfer of such lands, which Bill I have some reason to hope will pass without opposition. The Chief Commissioner of Public Works has further signified his approval that what are called 'School Treats' shall be allowed to be held in the easily accessible public parks, in certain parts of them set apart for that good purpose. The Society has also been in communication with the Government, and it hopes with some good effect, towards the reservation of Smithfield as a place of children's recreation. In a word, it has by every means in its power, during its brief existence of eight or nine months, cleared and paved the way for the distinct and plain proposal which I have to make to you. Everybody says, 'Begin this good and necessary work by all means'; but nobody begins it.

It is indeed extremely difficult to begin. We must remember that it is much more difficult in the present than it will be in the future, because the present finds the houses closely clustered together and the towns increased, whereas it is to be hoped that the future will find open spaces reserved, before the houses are agglomerated, and before the towns are so densely grown; and it is easy to understand that it is far more easy not to build houses up, than to find them built up, and have to pay for them and pull them down. The work, then, is very difficult to begin.

Yes. But how difficult is it to begin? Now, we happen to know that a playground in the populous Metropolitan district of St. Pancras, or in Marylebone Parish, somewhere in the close neighbourhood about Manchester Square, would cost perhaps £1,000. There are two earnest and munificent ladies known to this Society, one of whom will give towards the St. Pancras experiment £100, and one of whom will give towards the Marylebone experiment £100, if other people will be liberal in their degree, and according to the extent of their power, and subscribe the rest. This is, in fact, the Society's first report; and what I am to do tonight, is to entreat your help that the experiment may be made. There is no kind of castle-building, observe, in the case. The Society does not ask you for the vague and indefinite means of constructing fifty possible playgrounds or five hundred impossible playgrounds: it asks you for the clearly defined and ascertained means of proving the justice of their case by one experiment, and only one.

I will only trouble you by observing further, that of the success of the experiment, if practically and wisely carried out; of its being followed by innumerable imitations, and of its doing an incalculable amount of good; I myself have hardly a doubt. I believe, as Mr. Slaney has said, that the poor people would gladly even pay for a playground near to their own dwellings where they knew their children would be safe, under just so much supervision, and no more, as should exclude gross language, corrupting habits, and the demoralization and vagabondism of the streets. [*Cheers.*] We have made, as we all know, very great improvements in respect of our public parks; but they are obviously and unavoidably too far distant from many little legs and many little arms, encumbered with the weight of little brothers and sisters; and I think the domestic tenderness and household consideration evinced in this very idea of the playground would win over the parents who have experience of this truth every day, and would attract their confidence immediately.

I will not enter into the question whether the Playground Society shall aspire to add to its name the title of 'General Recreation Society', and to provide cheap *indoor* amusements for the young. I confess I am not myself quite clear upon that point. I have some individual doubt whether it might not become a little too wise, and whether, taking too deliberate an aim at these young birds, it might not blow them away with an overcharge of instruction. But that is no part of the question tonight. The question I have to put to you—leaving you to supply all its need of attendant considerations, of humanity, kindness, compassion, justice, and policy, for the present, and especially for the future—the question I have to put to you, and through you to the public, is, whether the case shall be proved or disproved, and whether this one experiment shall be tried or not tried ? I beg to propose you to drink, 'Prosperity to the Playground Society'.

The healths of the chairman, and of the ladies, were the two concluding toasts. The last was proposed by the chairman, who declared that he would not preside at another dinner unless the ladies dined with the gentlemen, an announcement which was received with enthusiastic cheers.

MEETING FOR THE FOUNDATION OF THE DRAMATIC COLLEGE

21 *July* 1858

IT was generally known in theatrical circles that a gift of five acres of land had recently been offered to the Royal General Theatrical Fund by a wealthy brickmaker and 'dust' contractor, Henry Dodd. After Charles Kean and other leading actors had been consulted, and Dickens's advice —as one of the fund's trustees—had also been asked, it had been agreed that the gift should be made the nucleus of an entirely new institution for retired actors and actresses, to be known as the Dramatic College. At Dickens's suggestion it was decided to hold a public meeting at one of the chief theatres ; and Kean consented to the use of the Princess's, where he was then appearing in the *Merchant of Venice*.

At the meeting the theatre was said to be as 'densely crowded as on the night of the most attractive revival'. Kean took the chair and explained why the meeting had been called. William Cullenford read a report of the Provisional Committee outlining a proposed constitution, the report was adopted, and the chairman then addressed the meeting for a second time.

He was followed by Dickens, who had to propose the first resolution. He was received with acclamation, and said:

LADIES and Gentlemen, I think I may venture to congratulate you beforehand on the pleasant circumstance that the movers and seconders of the resolutions which will be submitted to you will probably have very little to say. Through the Report which you have heard read, and through the comprehensive address of the chairman, the cause which brings us together has been so very clearly stated to you, that it can stand in need of very little, if of any further exposition. But, as I have the honour to move the first resolution which this handsome gift, and the vigorous action which must be taken upon it, necessitate, I think I shall only give expression to what is uppermost in the general mind here, if I venture to remark that, many as the parts are in which Mr. Kean has distinguished himself on these boards, he has never appeared in one in which the large spirit of an artist, the feeling of a man, and the grace of a gentleman [*hear, hear*], have been more admirably blended than in this day's faithful adherence to the calling of which he is a prosperous ornament, and in this day's manly advocacy of its cause. [*Cheers.*]

Ladies and gentlemen, the resolution entrusted to me is:

> That the Report of the Provisional Committee be adopted, and that this meeting joyfully accepts, and gratefully acknowledges, the gift of five acres of land referred to in the said Report.

It is manifest, I take it, that we are all agreed upon this acceptance and acknowledgement, and that we all know very well that this generous gift can inspire but one sentiment in the breast of every lover of the dramatic art. [*Hear, hear.*] As it is far too often forgotten by those who are indebted to it for many a restorative flight out of this working-day world, that the silks, and velvets, and elegant costumes of its professors must be every night exchanged for the hideous coats and waistcoats of the present day, in which we have now the honour and misfortune of appearing before you [*cheers and laughter*], so, when we do meet with a nature so considerably generous as this donor's, and we do find an interest in the real life and struggles of the people who have delighted it— so very spontaneous and so very liberal—we have nothing to do but to accept and to admire; we have no duty left but to 'take the goods the gods provide us', and to make the best and the most of them. Ladies and gentlemen, allow me to remark, that in this mode of turning a good gift to the highest account, lies the truest gratitude. [*Hear.*]

In reference to this, I could not but reflect, whilst Mr. Kean was speaking, that in an hour or two from this time, the spot upon which we are now assembled will be transformed into the scene of a crafty and cruel bond. I know that, in a few hours hence, the Grand Canal of Venice will flow, with picturesque fidelity, on the very spot I now stand dryshod, and that 'the quality of mercy' will be beautifully stated to the Venetian Council by a learned young Doctor from Padua, upon these very boards on which we now enlarge upon the quality of charity and sympathy. Knowing this, it came into my mind to consider how different the real bond of today from the ideal bond of tonight.—Now, all generosity, all forbearance, all forgetfulness of little jealousies and unworthy divisions, all united action for the general good; then, all selfishness, all malignity, all cruelty, all revenge, and all evil.—Now all good; then a bond to be broken within the compass of a few—three or four—swiftly passing hours; now a bond to be valid and of good effect generations hence. [*Great cheering.*]

Ladies and gentlemen, of the execution and delivery of this bond, between this generous gentleman on the one hand, and the united members of a too often and too long disunited art upon the other, be you the witnesses. Do you attest of everything that is liberal and free in spirit, that is 'so nominated in the bond', and of everything that is grudging, self-seeking, unjust, or unfair, that it is by no sophistry ever to be found there. I beg to move the resolution which I have already had the pleasure of reading. [*Loud and continued cheering.*]

Dickens's proposal was seconded, and the resolution was carried unanimously. Charles Kean, Webster, Dickens, and Thackeray were then elected trustees, and a number of other speakers followed.

In spite of Dickens's fine phrases a dispute shortly afterwards arose between Dodd and the Provisional Committee, over a number of quite reasonable stipulations the donor wished to make. Dickens was a member of the committee—a body of over a hundred—and at one time Dodd proposed that the affair should be submitted to his arbitration. Nothing came of the suggestion, and at a public meeting on 12 January 1859 his offer was rejected. Dickens held aloof, but he is later said to have told Mark Lemon 'that he never had occasion to repent but of two things, one being his conduct to Mr. Dodd'.[1] He is also said to have introduced him into *Our Mutual Friend* as Mr. Boffin, the Golden Dustman.

An attempt was made to enlarge the activities of the college by the addition of a school in 1864;[2] but it was a complete failure and came to an end in 1877. Public support had decreased, and it was found that retired actors, like the pensioners of the Guild, did not want to live outside London.

AT TWO READINGS IN EDINBURGH

27 *and* 28 *September* 1858

AFTER the success of his readings in London from April to July, Dickens set out on a long and strenuous tour of the country, including Scotland and Ireland.[3] He was due to read in Edinburgh at the end of September, where he was invited to a banquet of the Royal Scottish Academy on the 29th in honour of his old friends Clarkson Stansfield and David Roberts, but was compelled to decline: 'I read twice in Edinburgh on Wednesday—in the afternoon and in the evening—and I grieve to say that I can no more go to the Academy than the Academy can come to me.'[4]

[1] Henry Dodd, *Royal Dramatic College, Correspondence Respecting Proposed Gift of Land*, 2nd ed., 1859, p. 30.
[2] C. Roach Smith, *Retrospections*, 1886, ii. 99.
[3] For the Irish tour, see Jack Shaw, 'Dickens in Ireland', *Dickensian*, 1909, v. 33–41, where some of his prefatory remarks are given which anticipate those made at these readings in Edinburgh.   [4] *Edinburgh Courant*, 2 October 1858.

He opened the series of five readings, on the 27th, with *The Chimes*—prefacing it with the remark that he had written it in Italy, about twelve years ago, for the purpose of expressing his views on certain subjects then before the public mind.

On the following evening he read *Little Dombey*, which was much more popular. He again gave a short introduction, including a tribute to his old friend Lord Jeffrey, under whose auspices he had visited Edinburgh in 1841:

THE tale he had read, he explained, comprised all that part of his well-known novel *Dombey and Son* that related to the history of the short-lived junior partner of that house. He prayed the audience to be unreserved in their expressions, whether of mirth or sympathy, confessing that he too sometimes joined in the tears or laughter which the recital evoked. The little story he regarded as intimately associated with the city on account of a dear friend he had had there, now departed—one who had often pondered and dwelt on those few chapters, and shown a tender interest in the tale, which he could never forget.

The readings were a great success. 'I think I am better pleased with what was done at Edinburgh', Dickens wrote to Forster, 'than with what has been done anywhere, almost.'[1]

PRIZE-GIVING OF THE INSTITUTIONAL ASSOCIATION OF LANCASHIRE AND CHESHIRE: MANCHESTER

3 *December* 1858

A PUBLIC meeting of the association was held in the evening, in the Free Trade Hall, for the distribution of prizes and certificates to successful competitors in the examinations held in May. On taking the Chair, Dickens was greeted with acclamation. He said:

LADIES and Gentlemen, It has of late years become noticeable in England that the autumn season produces an immense amount of public speaking. I notice that no sooner do the leaves begin to fall from the trees, than pearls of great price begin to fall from the lips of the wise men of the east, and north, and west, and south; and anybody may have them by the bushel, for the picking up. [*Laughter.*] Now, whether the comet[2] has this year had a quickening influence on this crop, as it is by some supposed to have had upon the corn harvest and the vintage, I do not know; but I do know

---

[1] F, VIII. iv.

[2] Donati's comet had been brilliantly visible during the first ten days of October.

that I have never observed the columns of the newspapers to groan so heavily under a pressure of orations, each vieing with the other in the two qualities of having little or nothing to do with the matter in hand [*laughter*], and of being always addressed to any audience in the wide world rather than the audience to which it was delivered. [*Hear, hear.*]

The autumn being gone, and the winter come, I am so sanguine as to hope that we in our proceedings may break through this enchanted circle and deviate from this precedent; the rather as we have something real to do, and are come together, I am sure, in all plain fellowship and straightforwardness, to do it. We have no little straws of our own to throw up to show us which way any wind blows, and we have no oblique biddings of our own to make for anything outside this hall.

At the top of the public announcements of this meeting are the words 'Institutional Association of Lancashire and Cheshire'. Will you allow me, in reference to the meaning of those words, to present myself before you as the embodied spirit of ignorance recently enlightened, and to put myself through a short, voluntary examination as to the results of my studies? To begin with, the title did not suggest to me anything in the least like the truth. I have been for some years pretty familiar with the terms, 'Mechanics' Institutions', and 'Literary Societies', but they have, unfortunately, become too often associated in my mind with a body of great pretensions, lame as to some important member or other, which generally inhabits a new house much too large for it, and which is very seldom paid for [*hear, hear*], and which takes the name of mechanics most grievously in vain, for I have usually seen a mechanic and a dodo in that place together. [*Laughter.*]

I, therefore, began my education, in respect of the meaning of this title, very coldly indeed, saying to myself, 'Here is the old story'. But the perusal of a very few lines of my book soon gave me to understand that it was not by any means the old story; in short, that this association is expressly designed to correct the old story, and to prevent its defects from becoming perpetuated. I learnt that this Institutional Association is the union, in one central head, of one hundred and fourteen local Mechanics' Institutions and Mutual Improvement Societies, at an expense of no more than five shillings to each society; suggesting to them all how they can best communicate with and profit by the fountain-head and one another; keeping their best aims steadily before them; advising how those aims can be best attained; giving a direct end and object to what might otherwise easily become waste forces; and sending among them not only oral teachers, but, better still, boxes of excellent books, called 'Free Itinerating Libraries'. I learned that these books are constantly making the circuit of hundreds upon hundreds of miles, and are constantly being read with inexpressible relish by thousands upon thousands of toiling people, but that they are never damaged or defaced by one rude hand. [*Applause.*] These, and other like facts, lead me to consider the immense importance of the fact that no little cluster of working men's cottages can arise in any Lancashire or Cheshire valley, at the foot of any running stream which enterprise hunts out for water-power, but it has its educational friend and companion ready for it, willing for it, acquainted with its thoughts and ways and turns of speech even before it has come into existence.

Now, ladies and gentlemen, this is the main consideration that has brought me here. No central association at a distance could possibly do for those working men what this local association does. No central association at a distance could possibly understand them as this local association does. No central association at a distance could possibly put them in that familiar and easy communication with one another, as that I, man or boy, eager for knowledge in that valley seven miles off, should know of you, man or boy, eager for knowledge in that valley twelve miles off, and should occasionally trudge to meet you, that you may impart your learning in one branch of acquisition to me, whilst I impart mine in another to you. Yet this is distinctly a feature, and a most important feature, of this society.

On the other hand it is not to be supposed that these honest men, however zealous, could, as a rule, succeed in establishing and maintaining their own institutions of themselves. It is obvious that combination must materially diminish their cost, which is in itself a vital consideration; and it is equally obvious that experience, essential to the success of all combination, is especially so when its object is to diffuse the results of experience and reflection.

Well, ladies and gentlemen, the student of the present profitable history of this society does not stop here in his learning; when he has got so far, he finds with interest and pleasure that the parent society at certain stated periods invites the more eager and enterprising of the local societies to submit themselves to voluntary examination in various branches of useful knowledge, of which examination it takes the charge and arranges the details, and invites the successful candidates to come to Manchester to receive the prizes and certificates of merit which it impartially awards. The most successful of the competitors in the list of these examinations are now among us, and these little marks of recognition and encouragement I shall have the honour presently of giving them, as they come before you, one by one, for that purpose. [*Cheers.*]

I have looked over a few of those examination papers. They comprise history, geography, grammar, arithmetic, book-keeping, decimal coinage, mensuration, mathematics, social economy, the French language—in fact, they comprise all the keys that open all the locks of knowledge. I felt most devoutly grateful, as to many of them, that they had not been submitted to me to answer [*laughter*], for I am perfectly sure that if they had been, I should have had mighty little to bestow upon myself tonight. [*Laughter.*] And yet it is always to be observed and seriously remembered that these examinations are undergone by people whose lives have been passed in a continual fight for bread, and whose whole existence has been a constant wrestle with 'Those twin gaolers of the daring heart—low birth and iron fortune'.[1] [*Applause.*] I could not but consider, with extraordinary admiration, that these questions have been replied to, not by men like myself, the business of whose life is with writing and books, but by men, the business of whose life is with tools and machinery.

Let me endeavour to recall, as well as my memory will serve me, from among the most interesting cases of prize-holders and certificate-gainers who will appear before you, some two or three of the most conspicuous examples. There are two poor brothers from near Chorley, who work from morning to night in a coal-pit, and who, in all weathers, have walked eight miles a night, three nights a week, to attend the classes in which they have gained distinction. [*Loud applause.*] There are two poor boys from Bollington, who began life as piecers at one shilling or eighteen-pence a week, and the father of one of whom was cut to pieces by the machinery at which he worked, but not before he had himself founded the institution in which this son has since come to be taught. These two poor boys will appear before you tonight, to take the second-class prize in chemistry. [*Cheers.*] There is a plasterer from Bury, sixteen years of age, who took a third class certificate last year at the hands of Lord Brougham; he is this year again successful in a competition three times as severe. There is a wagon-maker from the same place, who knew little or absolutely nothing until he was a grown man, and who has learned all he knows, which is a great deal, in the local institution. There is a chain-maker, in very humble circumstances, and working hard all day, who walks six miles a night, three nights a week, to attend the classes in which he has won so famous a place. There is a moulder in an iron foundry who, whilst he was working twelve hours a day before the furnace, got up at four o'clock in the morning to learn drawing. [*Cheers.*] 'The thought of my lads', he writes in his modest account of himself, 'in their

[1] Lytton, *Lady of Lyons*, III. ii.

peaceful slumbers above me, gave me fresh courage, and I used to think that if I should never receive any personal benefit, I might instruct them when they came to be of an age to understand the mighty machines and engines which have made our country, England, pre-eminent in the world's history.' [*Applause.*] There is a piecer at mule-frames, who could not read at eighteen, who is now a man of little more than thirty, who is the sole support of an aged mother, who is arithmetical teacher in the institution in which he himself was taught, who writes of himself that he made the resolution never to take up a subject without keeping to it, and who has kept to it with such an astonishing will, that he is now well versed in Euclid and Algebra, and is the best French scholar in Stockport. The drawing classes in that same Stockport are taught by a working blacksmith; and the pupils of that working black-smith will receive the highest honours of tonight. [*Applause.*] Well may it be said of that good blacksmith, as it was written of another of his trade, by the American poet:

> Toiling—rejoicing—sorrowing,
> Onward through life he goes;
> Each morning sees some task begun,
> Each evening sees its close;
> Something attempted, something done,
> Has earned a night's repose.

Ladies and gentlemen—to pass from the successful candidates to the delegates from local societies now before me, and to content myself with one instance from amongst them. There is amongst their number a most remarkable man, whose history I have read with feelings I could not adequately express under any circumstances, and least of all when I know he hears me, who worked when he was a mere baby at hand-loom weaving until he dropped from fatigue; who began to teach himself as soon as he could earn five shillings a week; who is now a botanist, acquainted with every production of the Lancashire valleys; who is a naturalist, and has made and preserved a collection of the eggs of British birds, and stuffed the birds; who is now a conchologist, with a very curious and in some respects an original collection of fresh-water shells, and has also preserved and collected the mosses of fresh waters and the sea; who is worthily the president of his own local Literary Institution; and who was at his work this time last night as foreman in a mill. [*Prolonged applause.*]

So stimulating has been the influence of these bright examples, and many more, that I notice among the applications from Black-burn for preliminary test examination papers, one from an applicant who gravely fills up the printed form by describing himself as ten years of age, and who, with equal gravity, describes his occupation as 'nursing a little child'. [*Laughter and cheers.*] Nor are these things confined to the men. The women employed in factories, milliners' work, and domestic service, have begun to show, as it is fitting they should, a most decided determination not to be outdone by the men; and the women of Preston in particular, have so honourably distinguished themselves, and shown in their examination papers such an admirable knowledge of the science of household management and household economy, that if I were a working bachelor of Lancashire or Cheshire, or if I had not cast my eye or set my heart upon any lass in particular, I should positively get up at four o'clock in the morning with the determination of the iron-moulder himself, and should go to Preston in search of a wife. [*Hear, hear, and laughter.*]

Now, ladies and gentlemen, these instances, and many more, daily occurring, always accumulating, are surely better testimony to the working of this Association than any number of speakers could possibly present to you? Surely the presence among us of these indefatigable people is the Association's best and most effective triumph in the present and the past, and is its noblest stimulus to effort in the future? As its temporary mouth-piece I would beg to say to that portion of the company who attend to receive the prizes, that the institution can never hold itself apart from them— can never set itself above them; that their distinction and success must be its distinction and success; and that there can be but one heart beating between them and it. In particular, I would most especially entreat them to observe that nothing will ever be further from this Association's mind than the impertinence of patronage. [*Hear, hear, hear.*] The prizes that it gives, and the certificates that it gives, are mere admiring assurances of sympathy with so many striving brothers and sisters, and are only valuable for the spirit in which they are given, and in which they are received. The prizes are money prizes, simply because the institution does not presume to doubt that persons who have so well governed themselves, know best how to make a little money serviceable [*hear*], because it would be a shame to treat them like grown-up babies by laying it out for them, and because it knows that it is given, and knows it is taken, in perfect clearness of purpose, perfect trustfulness, and above all perfect independence. [*Cheers.*]

Ladies and gentlemen, reverting once more to the whole collective audience before me, I will, in another two minutes, release the hold which your favour has given me on your attention. Of the advantages of knowledge I have said, and I shall say, nothing. Of the certainty with which the man who grasps it under difficulties rises in his own respect and in usefulness to the community, I have said, and I shall say, nothing. In the City of Manchester, in the county of Lancaster, both of them remarkable for self-taught men, that were superfluous indeed. For the same reason I rigidly abstain from putting together any of the shattered fragments of that poor clay image of a parrot which was once always saying, without knowing why, that knowledge was a dangerous thing. I should as soon think of piecing together the mutilated remains of any wretched Hindoo who has been blown from an English gun. Both, creatures of the past, have been—as my friend Mr. Carlyle vigorously has it —'blasted into space'; and there, as to this world, is an end of them.

So I desire, in conclusion, only to sound two strings. In the first place let me congratulate you upon the progress which real mutual improvement societies are making at this time in your neighbour-hood, through the noble agency of individual employers and their families, whom you can never too much delight to honour. Else-where, through the agency of the great railway companies, some of which are bestirring themselves in this manner with a gallantry and generosity deserving of all praise. Secondly and lastly, let me say one word out of my own personal heart, which is always very dear to it in this connexion. Do not let us, in the midst of the visible objects of nature, whose workings we can tell off in figures, sur-rounded by machines that can be made to the thousandth part of an inch, acquiring every day knowledge which can be proved upon a slate or demonstrated by a microscope—do not let us, in the laudable pursuit of the facts that surround us, neglect the fancy and the imagination which equally surround us as part of the great scheme. [*Hear, hear.*] Let the child have its fables; let the man or woman into which it changes, always remember these fables tenderly. Let numerous graces and ornaments that cannot be weighed and measured, and that seem at first sight idle enough, con-tinue to have their places about us, be we never so wise. [*Applause.*] The hardest head may co-exist with the softest heart. [*Cheers.*] The union and just balance of those two is always a blessing to the possessor, and always a blessing to mankind. The Divine Teacher was as gentle and considerate as He was powerful and wise. You all know how He could still the raging of the sea, and could hush a little child. As the utmost results of the wisdom of men can only be at last to help to raise this earth to that condition to which His doctrine, untainted by the blindnesses and passions of men, would have exalted it long ago; so let us always remember that He set us the example of blending the understanding and the imagination, and that, following it ourselves, we tread in His steps, and help our race on to its better and best days. [*Applause.*] Knowledge, as all followers of it must know, has a very limited power indeed when it informs the head alone; but when it informs the head and heart too, it has a power over life and death, the body and the soul, and dominates the universe. [*Great applause.*]

The chairman then distributed the prizes to the successful candidates. After further business, and other speeches, a vote of thanks to Dickens was proposed, seconded, and carried by acclamation, the audience standing and loudly applauding. Dickens replied:

I am deeply obliged to you for your cordial reception. The honour of this presidency, believe me, is all mine; the pleasure attaching to it, I am sure, we shall divide between us. No man can have seen this scene tonight without having his heart touched with the most delightful emotions, and without feeling himself, as to the great mass of the community, a wiser, a better, a more helpful, a more happy man. But it is nothing new to me to receive satisfaction here; for I never come to Manchester without expecting pleasure, and I never leave it without taking pleasure away. [*Applause.*] I heartily assure you that you have been most cordially welcome to my poor services, and I most affectionately wish you good night. [*Applause.*]

PRESENTATION AND BANQUET IN HIS HONOUR: COVENTRY

4 *December* 1858

AFTER a reading for the Coventry Institute on 15 December 1857, a subscription was raised for presenting Dickens with a gold watch of local make. Sir Joseph Paxton, who was one of the local M.P.s, had persuaded Dickens to give the reading. He now wrote to thank him and to tell of the success of the subscription. Dickens replied to say that he was 'quite affected by the generosity of my friends at Coventry, but they shall not spoil me, if I can help it, and I will try to "go" as truly and staunchly as the repeater itself'.[1]

The presentation was made a year later, at a dinner given at the Castle Hotel, with C. Wren Hoskyns[2] in the Chair. The cloth having been removed there were the usual loyal toasts, after which the chairman rose to present the testimonial. The watch, he said, bore the inscrip-

---

[1] 23 Dec. 1857—'Dickens and Coventry', *Midland Daily Telegraph*, 14 Dec. 1922.

[2] Chandos Wren Hoskyns (1812–76), author of works on agriculture, including *Talpa: Or the Chronicle of a Clay Farm*, 1852; advocate of reform of land tenure.

tion, 'Presented to Charles Dickens Esq., by his friends in Coventry, as a grateful acknowledgement of his kindness to them, and of his eminent services in the interests of humanity.' Among other reasons which he gave for admiring Dickens was that he had 'done more than any other man living' to close the gulf between rich and poor.[1] The presentation was followed by an appropriate speech from a member of the committee; and, amid prolonged applause, Dickens rose to reply. He said:

MR. CHAIRMAN, Mr. Vice-Chairman, and Gentlemen, I hope your minds will be greatly relieved by my assuring you that it is one of the rules of my life never to make a speech about myself. If I knowingly did so, under any circumstances, it would be least of all under such circumstances as these, when its effect on my acknowledgement of your kind regard, and this pleasant proof of it, would be to give me a certain constrained air, which I fear would contrast badly with your greeting, so cordial, so unaffected, so earnest and so true. Furthermore, your Chairman has decorated the occasion with a little garland of good sense, good feeling, and good taste; so that I am sure that any attempt at additional ornament would be almost an impertinence.

Therefore I will at once say how earnestly, how fervently, and how deeply I feel your kindness. This watch with which you have presented me, shall be my companion in my hours of sedentary working at home, and in my restless wanderings abroad. It shall never be absent from my side, and it shall reckon off the labours of my future days; and I can assure you, gentlemen, that after this night the object of these labours will not less than before be to uphold the right and do good. [*Cheers.*] And when I have done with time and its measurement this watch shall belong to my children; and as I have seven boys, and as they have all begun to serve their country in various ways, and to elect into what distant regions they shall roam, it is not only possible, but very probable, that this little voice will be heard scores of years hence,—who knows?—in some yet unfounded city in the wilds of Australia, or communicating Greenwich time to Coventry Street, Japan. [*Laughter.*]

Once again, and finally, I thank you; and from my heart of hearts I can assure you that the memory of tonight, and of your picturesque and interesting city, will never be absent from my mind, and I can never more hear the slightest mention of the name of

---

[1] This opinion was echoed by another local speaker, who declared that in all Dickens had written there was not 'a single word that tended to irritate one class of society against another; but, on the contrary, his writings have tended to bind them together with the common sentiments of humanity and common feelings of Christian love'. They had had the very practical effect, too, he said, of promoting a conciliatory spirit which helped to prevent such strikes as that of the ribbon weavers, which they had recently suffered from.

Coventry without having inspired in my breast sentiments of unusual emotion and unusual attachment. [*Enthusiastic cheering.*].

A number of other speeches followed. Wills replied to a toast in his honour, as sub-editor of *Household Words*; and Dickens proposed the health of the chairman. He said:

Gentlemen, the chairman had wisely observed that it was a curious characteristic of the human mind, that it is almost always disposed to laugh when a thing is mentioned for the first time. That being the case, I am not in the least apprehensive of your laughter when I talk to you of the chairman himself, because his merits are so familiar to you that I should almost incline to suppose, according to the converse of the proposition, that you would cry. [*Laughter.*]

We all know that there are various systems for doing most things, each system claiming for itself the support of many friends, and encountering the opposition of various opponents. There may be a great variety of conflicting opinions in regard to farming, and especially with reference to the management of a clay farm; but however various opinions as to the merits of a clay farm may be, there can be but one opinion as to the merits of the clay farmer [*cheers*], and it is the health of that distinguished agriculturalist which I have to propose. [*Cheers.*]

In my ignorance of the subject, I am bound to say that it may be, for anything I know, indeed I am ready to admit that it *is* exceedingly important that a clay farm should go for a number of years to waste; but I claim some knowledge as to the management of a clay farmer, and I positively object to his ever lying fallow. [*Cheers and laughter.*] In the hope that this very rich and teeming individual may speedily be ploughed up [*laughter*], and that we shall gather into our barns and store-houses the admirable crop of wisdom, which must spring up wherever he is sown, I take leave to propose his health, begging to assure him that the kind manner in which he offered to me your very valuable present, I can never forget.

Other speakers followed, including George Eliot's friend, Charles Bray, who replied for the Press. He said that he was proud to tell Dickens 'that no man in the kingdom has been the means of doing me more good'.

Dickens was again loudly cheered when he rose and said:

It has been suggested to me that there is one concluding toast which we ought to drink; but I feel under some little difficulty, because I know the moment I touch the subject you will not unnaturally connect me with the great hero of this city[1] [*laughter*]; but many of you when you leave this place will have the privilege of going home to the softer and better sex. Heaven forbid that I should

---

[1] Presumably 'Peeping Tom'.

follow you,[1] but I think you ought to be able to tell your wives
that in our flowing cups they were freshly remembered. [*Cheers*]. It
would be ridiculous to say anything in praise of women—especially
here. We know that *she* was a woman.[2] [*Laughter*.] We know that the
Graces were all women [*renewed laughter*]; we know that the Muses
were women, and we know every day of our lives that the Fates are
women. [*Roars of laughter*.] I think that as we receive so much from
them, both in happiness and pain, we ought at least to drink their
healths. [*Cheers*.]

Dickens was pleased with the whole occasion. He wrote to Miss Burdett
Coutts: 'The Coventry people have given me a seventy-five Guinea
Watch, which is Chronometer, Repeater, and every other terrible machine
that a watch *can* be. It was very feelingly and pleasantly given, and I
prize it highly.'[3] The watch was not kept in the family, but was left by
Dickens to his 'dear and trusty friend John Forster', who bequeathed it
to Carlyle.

COMMERCIAL TRAVELLERS' SCHOOLS

22 *December* 1859

FOR the second time Dickens took the Chair at the anniversary festival
of the society. Not being well, with much writing and administrative
work to do for *All the Year Round*, and public readings to be given, he
was at first unwilling to preside. He consented only after a second appeal
from George Moore, to which he replied that 'I believe nothing less than
your note would have induced me to undertake a Chairmanship; but I
have a great respect for you, and I know what a good and well-ordered
Society that is in whose behalf you exert yourself. So I am at its and your
disposal'.[4]

The dinner was held at the London Tavern. After giving the usual
toasts to the royal family, Dickens then proposed 'The Army and
Navy':

THEY were sometimes told, he said, as if it were a new discovery,
that war was the greatest of all evils. Now, he thought he preferred
no high claim on the intelligence of this company when he said they
all knew it to be so. [*Hear, hear*.] Common humanity taught them
to regard war as an unparalleled calamity. So strongly rooted was
this feeling in the English mind, that it might truly be said that the
popular voice was almost always for peace, and always attached
enormous responsibility to any men in power who, for selfish ends,
should be the first to 'cry havoc, and let slip the dogs of war'. But

---

[1] A significant and uncharacteristic remark in view of the separation from
his wife; Dickens was usually much more guarded.   [2] Lady Godiva.
[3] 13 Dec. 1858.   [4] 31 Oct. 1859, from the society's *Minutes*, 7 Nov.

the next greatest sin to such an act was that of any men who accepted the responsibility of government and left the people ill prepared to resist aggressive war. [*Hear, hear.*] It was because they who sat there were devoted to the arts and ways of peace, and because they exhibited all the signs of outward prosperity, that he congratulated them upon the manly and national spirit which was then stirring amongst them as well as amongst our professed defenders by sea and land.[1] [*Loud cheers.*]

We Englishmen uttered no defiance, no braggart boast, against any nation on the face of the earth, but wished quietly to keep our own; and, with the blessing of heaven, which helped those who helped themselves, they would most assuredly do it. [*Loud cheers.*] The plain meaning of the Rifle movement was but the revival of the old brave spirit of our forefathers, and a proof that all who had a stake in the country—and who that had life in it had not?—were ready if occasion required to fight and die in its defence. On that account, he would, with their permission, slightly alter the toast about to be proposed, and give 'The Army and Navy, and the Volunteers'. [*Loud cheers.*]

After this toast the children, neatly attired, were introduced into the gallery. The chairman then rose to propose the toast of the evening.

He was told, he said, that it was once observed by a lady who kept a commercial boarding-house in the neighbourhood of the Monument, named Mrs. Todgers [*loud laughter*], that no such strong passion existed in the human breast as that of commercial gentlemen for gravy.[2] [*Continued laughter.*] She said, as he had been informed, and had reason to believe true, that it was her opinion that no animal known to butchers or experienced housekeepers would yield from any of its joints the amount of gravy that was called for by the peculiarity of the commercial palate. [*Renewed laughter.*] The anxiety, and mental agony that this most estimable lady had undergone from this single cause was sufficient to undermine the strongest constitution. [*Great laughter.*] With this lady's experience and responsibilities heavy on his soul, he was thrown into a gloomy state of feeling when the duties and responsibilities of this eventful day loomed and darkened upon him. He was disturbed by the amount of oratorical gravy which he knew would be expected from the head of the table, and his sorrows were aggravated by his own personal knowledge of the inadequacy of the supply. [*Cheers.*] It was

---

[1] In May 1859 the War Office had sanctioned the formation of Volunteer Rifle Corps under the old Militia Act; and, in alarm at the danger of war with France and invasion, there were soon 180,000 volunteers.

[2] *Martin Chuzzlewit*, ch. ix.

very small comfort for him to remember that the last time he had the honour to fill that place the guests were most kind and considerate. He could not banish the shadow of 'Todgers's', nor get rid of the horrors of that lady's experience of what gravy was to a commercial man. In short he was dreadfully perplexed to know how he should act upon the present occasion. [*Laughter.*]

In this disturbed state of mind he had made several forlorn attempts to get material for a speech. He had looked through the advertisement pages of *Bradshaw* [*laughter*], and asked himself whether anything could be done with those inviting advertisements of hotels in which were offered, at fixed charges, bed, breakfast, and attendance, with the additional advantages of perfect solitude and an Italian atmosphere. [*Laughter.*] He had asked himself, despondingly, the question whether anything apropos might be got out of the unfortunate porter who sat up all night, and who never went to bed in the day time. [*Great laughter.*] He had then started off by express train of remembrances to another and much larger hotel at Leeds, where he had happened to be staying about seven weeks before, where the chamber appurtenances belonged to a period far anterior to the present, and where the night candles were nothing less than mutton truncheons of most exaggerated proportions [*roars of laughter*], and could not by any possibility be blown out. [*Great laughter.*]

In that hotel I had seen many members of the present company, next morning, brushing their coats in the hall, and I then considered whether anything could be done with the word Travellers; and I thought whether any fanciful analogy could be drawn between those travellers who diffuse the luxuries and necessities of existence, and those who carry into desert places the waters of life, such as Dr. Livingstone,[1] or Captain McClintock[2] and his bold companions, who have graved the record of English modesty, gallantry, and perseverance in the everlasting ice surrounding the North Pole. [*Cheers.*] This put into my mind the fact that the best and greatest of these travellers have usually been amongst the gentlest and mildest of men. I then asked myself whether I could make any fanciful parallel between my friend Mr. Layard,[3] who brought to

[1] David Livingstone (1813–73), explorer; after sixteen years in Africa, 1840–56, he had returned to England, published his *Missionary Travels*, 1857, and set out again in command of an expedition to explore Eastern and Central Africa, 1858.

[2] Francis Leopold McClintock (1819–1907), Captain in Royal Navy, and Arctic explorer; had recently returned from the expedition sent out by Lady Franklin, and published his account, *The Voyage of the Fox in the Arctic Seas*, see pp. 236–7.

[3] See p. 191 n.

light the hidden memorials of a long extinct people, and my friend
Mr. George Moore, who sits beside me, who has brought to light
the hidden capabilities of a great trade.

Not deriving any comfort from these ingenious speculations, I
resolved, like the heroes in the fairy tales, to go out to seek my
fortune; and I resorted to a friendly giant—a commercial giant—
and we sallied out together only yesterday. We travelled on and on,
very like the people in the fairy tales, until we came to a great
castle of a bright red colour, looking perfectly glorious in the cold
sunlight of a winter afternoon. We were received, not by one of
those conventional monsters with a great eye in his forehead as
large as six, but by a man with an extremely humorous expression
of countenance and two bright eyes, under whose guidance we
inspected the livestock and eatables of the establishment, which
suggested to us nothing but an abundance of milk and pork.

We then entered the castle, and found it within, a noble structure,
with a cheerful lofty hall, large airy corridors, dormitories and
bathrooms, and admirable banqueting-hall—not at all a matter of
form, as I found on perusing the dietary table hanging on the wall;
for I perceived that the most agreeable weekly exercises were
practised, varying from roast beef and plum pudding, to boiled
mutton and hashes, with cold meat as an exceptional mortification
[*laughter*], until the weekly circle was completed, and the roast beef
of old England with its pleasing concomitant of plum pudding—by
the by, suggestive of the season—made their pleasing appearance
on the table before the happy and cheerful faces of the recipients of
your bounty. [*Cheers.*]

My attention was called to the circumstance that one hundred
young male giants, and fifty young female giants, were the partakers of this magnificent diurnal hospitality, and that they were at
the same time receiving an excellent education in this spacious edifice.
I looked over some of the examination papers, and I found them
remarkable for a prevailing good sense and adaptation to the solid
business and solid virtues of life, which I had not seen—no verily—
in some colleges and ancient foundations. [*Loud cheers.*] I looked
at these young people—the male creatures—and I saw that they
were healthy, cheerful, easy, and rational, under a system of moral
restraint far better than all the physical force that ever crushed a
timid nature and never bent a stubborn one. [*Applause.*] I found
other of these young people walking under their own control in the
lanes outside the establishment, and coming home in the frosty air
with cheery faces that were worthy of the season and of the weather.
I spoke to many of them, and I found that they answered truly and
fearlessly. I observed that they had an excellent way of looking

those in authority full in the face. [*Loud cheers.*] I did not see the sisterhood, and was very glad not to see them, because they were out for a long walk and had not yet come home. Gentlemen, I am told that these young people of both sexes are instructed, lodged, clothed, and boarded until they are fifteen years of age, when they are sent into the world, to the region of gold and silver which is the dream of aspiring youth. Some of the children were preparing themselves for this great world, in which many of them will no doubt hereafter distinguish themselves, by studying a number of cardboard locomotive engines and trains, admirably made, and closely resembling those which by day and night pass before the windows of their school at Pinner. [*Cheers.*] Finally, I made two discoveries of considerable importance to me; firstly that this was indeed, a most rare magical castle, by reason that it cost some £20,000, and belongs to a public body, and is paid for [*loud applause*]; secondly, and lastly, I found that I had gone out to seek my fortune not in vain, for in this castle I discovered my speech. [*Loud cheers.*]

Gentlemen, this castle is your own, and I assure you that its solid timbers, bricks, and stones are not more solid than the effects which I have fancifully set before you. This castle is the Commercial Travellers' Schools; and, in the endowing and maintaining of such an institution, the Commercial Travellers must raise themselves both in their own esteem and in the public regard. [*Hear, hear.*] In this place any individual here can establish an individual right and title by the humble contribution of one guinea, and it could be handsomely maintained if every commercial traveller in the world would give it one half crown on a given day in every year. [*Hear, hear.*] Gentlemen, I wish I could say of my order, or of others of greater pretensions, that its members were united in following such an example. I can say that there is no other order of men in this kingdom who, in their selection of men in whom to repose educational trust, do greater honour to themselves or to the cause of education than the board of management of this institution. [*Cheers.*] I hope then, sincerely, that the time is not far distant when the Commercial Traveller who does not belong to this institution will be a rare and isolated case. [*Cheers.*] I do hope this with some confidence, because I cannot believe that it is possible that many Commercial Travellers can look upon their own dear children and not feel they would be better and lighter hearted for being sharers in this institution. [*Cheers.*]

Gentlemen, we should remember tonight that we are all Travellers, and that every round we take converges nearer and nearer to our home; that all our little journeyings bring us together to one certain end; and that the good that we do, and the virtues that we show, and particularly the children that we rear, survive us through the long and unknown perspective of time. [*Cheers.*] When those children who now contemplate our proceedings pass around us presently, it can scarcely be but that some of this company will recognize in some little face the likeness of some friend or companion. [*Hear, hear.*] Any one of us may read the affecting words of tenderness which were spoken by Him who was once a child, and who loved little children. Let those words, not mine, speak eloquently for those Schools. [*Applause.*]

And now I will not detain you longer; I feel that I have put the case of this invaluable institution on its own merits, and having done so feel called upon to propose the toast of the evening, namely 'Prosperity to the Commercial Travellers' Schools'. [*Cheers.*] In half a century to come, the boys of today will remember what has occurred this evening and, at a meeting like the present, evince by their conduct how they appreciate the good performed by those who had gone before them. [*Cheers.*]

The toast having been drunk with immense enthusiasm the children were paraded round the room, when their clean and neat appearance, and their happy faces, are said to have 'excited the deepest interest'. They sang several part songs, 'with much taste and precision'. The Rev. J. Bellew[1] then proposed the health of the chairman, referring to the immense good that his books had effected. 'He was one', he said, 'who had been specially appointed to break down with a sledge-hammer, the anointed iniquity of high places.'

The chairman, who appeared overcome by the manner in which his health was received, briefly returned thanks.

He went on to ask permission to propose the health of a gentleman to whom the institution, the progress of which they were met to celebrate, was more indebted than to any other creature, and to whose zeal and liberality much of its success was owing. He proposed 'The health of Mr. George Moore, the Treasurer'. [*Loud cheers.*] He must say, in passing, that he was the commercial giant who had accompanied him on the occasion to which he had referred, but he himself could never be Jack, for he could neither deceive or kill such a giant on any account.

George Moore replied appropriately, recalling the chairman's previous presidency at the anniversary of 1859, and those of Sir Edward Bulwer Lytton and Thackeray since then. Several further complimentary toasts followed.

[1] John Chippendall Montesquieu Bellew (1823–74), Assistant-minister of St. Mark's, St. John's Wood; popular preacher, and successful public reader.

ROYAL SOCIETY OF MUSICIANS
8 *March* 1860

THE hundred-and-twenty-second anniversary of the society was held in the Freemasons' Hall, with Dickens in the Chair. When the Grace had been sung, there were the usual loyal toasts; after which the chairman continued:

LADIES and Gentlemen, I suppose I may venture to say that it is pretty well known to everybody that all people, whenever they are brought together at dinner in private society for the declared purpose of discussing any particular matter or business, it invariably happens that they never can by any ingenuity be brought to approach that business, and that they invariably make it the one sole object and ground on which they cannot be trapped into the utterance of a syllable. This being the curious concurrent experience of all mankind, it is the cautious custom of this particular dinner to place its business in the very front of the evening's engagements. It commits it to paper, and places it in black and white before the unhappy chairman whilst he speaks. [*Laughter.*] It guards him with a long row of distinguished gentlemen on either hand to keep him up to the mark and force him to approach the thing from which everybody knows he has a secret tendency to retreat; and there is a voice at his ear—a sonorous voice—which, like the warning voice of the slave of old, reminds him in all stages of the pageant that he is but a mortal chairman, and that it is the common lot of all his race to 'speak and to die'.

This, ladies and gentlemen, is the one hundred and twenty-second anniversary festival of the Royal Society of Musicians. [*Loud cheers.*] One hundred and twenty years have passed since the casual contemplation by two gentlemen standing at a coffee-house door of two poor boys driving a pair of milch asses through the London streets within half a mile of the place where we are now assembled, led to its establishment.[1] These two boys were the sons of a deceased musician; and the two rich hearts that took pity on them were the hearts of two deceased musicians; and the noble soul that came spontaneously to their aid was the soul of a deceased musician, known among the natural nobility of the art by but one 'Handel' to his name[2] [*great cheering*], and that a very glorious one,

[1] The two boys were the sons of Kytch, an oboe soloist; and the *three* musicians, who saw them from the door of the Orange Coffee House in the Haymarket, were Festing, the leader at the Opera, Wiedeman, a flautist, and Vincent, a bassoon player in the Guards. After they had called together other musicians, the society had been started in 1738.

[2] Handel was one of the society's most generous benefactors. Recording his recollection of this dreadful pun for F. G. Kitton, Francesco Berger wrote:

and derived—as I take it—directly from God. [*Hear, hear, hear.*] Now, ladies and gentlemen, that 'Harmonious Blacksmith' hammered so soundly upon the iron of his order while it was hot, that he struck out of it the sound of self-respect, independence, and prosperity, which are present in this society at the moment while I speak. During the remaining nineteen years of his life he wrought for it at the forge of his art with a true faith and vigour; and, when he died, he left it the princely bequest of £1,000. [*Loud cheers.*] We see now what good seed is, and what good music is. One hundred and twenty-two years have gone; the ruffles and powder have gone; the white capes, great coats, and huge cravats and top boots have gone; but the good seed is here in the shady and flourishing tree under which we sit tonight; and the good music is here, ever young in the young ears, and on the young lips and fingers, of every new generation. [*Cheers.*]

Ladies and gentlemen, it is my custom when I have the honour to hold such a position as this, to offer to those amongst the company who may not be personally acquainted with the society under consideration, those recommendations in its behalf which have been most powerful with myself. Will you allow me to sum up under a few heads the reasons that I have for regarding with particular sympathy and respect this Royal Society of Musicians?

First, because it is a real thing [*hear, hear*]—it is in fact as well as in name a society of musicians: not a heterogeneous concourse of nondescripts with here and there a musician smuggled in to justify the misuse of an art, but a society of professional men bound together in the love of their common art, and with the objects important to their art. [*Cheers.*] Because these gentlemen come together, as they only usefully and independently could come together as a benefit society [*hear, hear*] making timely provision if not for their own old age, distress or infirmity, certainly for those casualties in the lives of their brethren, and for their widows, and their orphan children. Because it not only grants money for the education and apprenticeship of those poor children, but afterwards preserves a parental care over them in this way—that when they have done well in their apprenticeship, it encourages them to come back and to be rewarded for having done well, and to stimulate them to continue to tread the paths of truth and duty. [*Applause.*] Because it is not an exclusive society, but concedes to its newest members the privileges of its oldest, and freely admits foreigners as members who are really domiciled in England as practitioners of music. Because it manages its own affairs [*hear,*

'I remember I felt it was unworthy of so great a man and so ready a wit.' (*Charles Dickens by Pen and Pencil, Supplement,* 1890, p. 18.)

hear], and manages them in a manner so excessively irrational and unpopular that it pays only two small salaries for real services, while the governors actually pay the expenses of their meetings out of their own pockets. [*Loud applause.*] Ladies and gentlemen, you have no notion of what confusion would be carried into a certain literary society[1] if the ferocious person who addresses you in his own plain way, were to get up there and to propose the Musicians in these respects as an example for imitation. [*Laughter and cheers.*] Lastly, ladies and gentlemen, I recommend the society to such of this assembly as do not know it, because it is a society of artists who begin by putting their own shoulders to their own wheel. Every member of this body stands pledged to every other to exercise his talents gratuitously at any performance whatsoever given in aid of the society's objects. Every member is formally and distinctly reminded on his enrolment that he accepts the responsibility of a great work connected with the labour of his art, and to that he is understood to pledge himself thenceforth. Now these, ladies and gentlemen, are the main features of the body of professional men that pass tonight the one hundred and twenty-second milestone on the road of its life—the main features except one, and that is that the annual income derived from one source, the annual subscription of its members, is not much more than a tithe of the money annually expended in the execution of its excellent objects.[2]

Turning over the book just now, with the words 'One hundred and twenty-second night' printed on its outside, I feel in a half kind of fancy, remembering the wonderful things which music has of course suggested to me from my earliest childhood. I feel a kind of fancy that I might have gone back to the one hundred and twenty-second night of the great *Arabian Nights*, and have heard Dinarzade saying, about half an hour before daybreak, 'Sister Scheherazade, if you are still awake, and my lord the Sultan will permit, I beg you to finish the story of—the British musicians.' [*Laughter and cheers.*] To which Scheherazade replies that she would willingly proceed, but that to the best of her belief it was a story without an end [*cheers*], because she considered that as long as mankind lived, and loved, and hoped, so long music, which draws them upward in all their varying and erring moods, could never cease out of the world. [*Cheers.*] So the Sultan, who changed his name for the purpose for the time, girded on, not his scimitar, but

[1] Royal Literary Fund.

[2] Dickens probably said that the expenses of administration were little more than a tithe of the annual income from subscriptions. See 'Notes on Text and Sources', p. 437.

a scythe, and went out graciously resolving that the story should have its one hundred and twenty-second night, and that the brother-hood should live for ever. [*Loud applause.*]

Ladies and gentlemen, these may appear to you vagrant ideas, but music is suggestive of all fancies. You know it can give back the dead; it can place at your side the congenial creature dear to you who never lived. You know that the blind see in it; the bed-ridden have hope in it; the dead hear it. We all hear it from the sound of the varying seasons, to the beating of the waters upon which our Saviour walked. Let me, in conclusion, entreat you to listen also to one strain which will certainly be heard through all the sweet sounds of tonight, and which will be simply this—no less, no more. The hand cannot always keep its hold upon the bow, the string, the keys; the breath will sometimes fail. It is the in-evitable result of the skilful combination of many instruments that there must be some players who can never hope to attain a great success or great reward, but who are nevertheless quite inseparable from, and necessary to your delight. And so, if you listen to it, the strain will say: 'I am one of those; I have been young and now am old; my hand has lost its mastery; my breath has failed. Now for the love of the much that music has done for you, do that little for me.'

I beg to propose to you to drink 'Prosperity to the Royal Society of Musicians'. [*Loud applause.*]

The health of the chairman was then proposed, and he briefly re-turned thanks, 'in a few honest hearty words', which, according to the *Morning Post*, 'produced as great an effect as if it were a speech as long as the oration of Cicero against Milo, or Burke against Warren Hastings'. Among the other speakers was Wilkie Collins.

In proposing the toast of 'The Ladies', Dickens made his usual protest against their segregation:

Why, he asked, should the gentlemen be ensconced before their smoking edibles and glittering decanters, and the ladies be compelled to sit above, behind that 'blistering screen', and look on con-tentedly all the while? Even in the Sandwich Isles or Otaheite the savages would not expel the fair sex from their banquets. Why should not these things be altered? For his part, if the committee would promise to introduce ladies next year, or the year after, to the dinner-table at the annual festival, and place one on each side of the Chair, he would not have the least objection to act as presi-dent. [*Cheers.*]

According to the reporter of *The Times*, Dickens's remarks 'created such a sensation . . . as to encourage the hope that an union between the Royal Society of Musicians, and the Royal Society of Female Musicians, might eventually be brought about'. They were amalgamated in 1866.

LECTURE BY A. H. LAYARD FOR THE MECHANICS' INSTITUTE: CHATHAM

17 *April* 1860

AUSTEN HENRY LAYARD had agreed to give a talk for the Institute on 'Recent Discoveries in Assyria and in the Ruins of Nineveh'; and Dickens, as a friend of the speaker, and President of the Institution, had been invited to take the Chair. He first introduced Layard to the meeting:

BUT for his position that evening, he said, it would be impertinent for him to interpose between them and the lecturer, for wherever an enterprising and bold spirit was held in esteem, there the name of Mr. Layard needed no introduction. [*Applause.*] But, very much as the Sovereign cannot enter the City of London without a flourish of trumpets, so it appeared that a most remarkable traveller could not proceed to his lecture without a little blast from the trumpet of the appointed officer. In obedience to this custom, and with a lively sense of its absurdity, would they allow him to introduce his distinguished friend, the lecturer of that evening?

In reply to a vote of thanks, moved by a speaker who referred to 'the large placards of neutral tint' which had announced the names of the chairman and lecturer, Dickens replied briefly.

If those placards of 'neutral tint', he said, to which Mr. Otway had alluded, could have sympathized with him, they would have turned to burning red for the prominence given to his name in connexion with an event in which he had so small a part. The institution was always cordially welcome to his small services. [*Ap plause.*]

READING FOR THE MECHANICS' INSTITUTE: CHATHAM

18 *December* 1860

AFTER giving a reading for the benefit of the Institute, Dickens replied briefly to a vote of thanks.

HE hoped, he said, that a time would come when a few mechanics would be found in a Mechanics' Institute. He was happy to aid the institution. He wished them all the good wishes of the coming season: he might be rather premature as to the time of uttering these, but they were surely not out of season, for good wishes were never out of season. [*Cheers.*]

Dickens repeated his remarks in 'Dullborough Town' (meaning Chatham) when as the Uncommercial Traveller he visited the Mechanics' Institution, which he found 'flourishing . . . and of the highest benefit to the town: two triumphs which I was glad to understand were not at all impaired by the seeming drawbacks that no mechanics belonged to it, and that it was steeped in debt to the chimney-pots'.

BANQUET AT THE MANSION HOUSE

1 *April* 1861

THE customary Easter banquet was given in the Egyptian Hall of the Mansion House, by the lord mayor, William Cubitt.[1] He was well known to Dickens, who was also a friend of his daughter, Lady Olliffe, wife of Sir Joseph Olliffe, physician to the British Embassy at Paris. She acted as lady mayoress during her father's double term of office. After the usual loyal toasts, therefore, Dickens was called upon to propose the health of the lady mayoress. On rising he was received with loud applause, and said:

MY Lord Mayor, Ladies and Gentlemen, being honoured with your permission to propose a toast, I would venture to remark that since I have been seated at this table I have found it pleasant to consider (reverting, as men naturally do, to their own pursuits) how ill English literature could afford to part with its Lord Mayors of London. [*Cheers and laughter.*] The literature of English history, losing its Lord Mayors, would lose, I find on consideration, some of its most notable instances of the public spirit, the munificence, the personal bravery, and the prowess of the good old citizens on this side Temple Bar. [*Cheers.*] The literature of English romance, losing its Lord Mayors, would lose at one blow its wealthiest of London merchants, and its most beautiful merchant's daughter, its crossest cook [*laughter*], its best known foreign adventurer, its most profitable investment on record, and its most wonderful cat. [*Great laughter and cheers.*] Similarly English biography, losing its Lord Mayors, would lose some of its most notable examples of rewarded perseverance and integrity, and some of its highest illustrations of the nobility of self-made men. [*Loud applause.*] I find that even the greatest of English satirists, of whom it is well said that his pictures require to be read like books—I find that even he could no more dispense with his Lord Mayors than any of the rest; for without them he could neither have committed his 'idle apprentice' for trial, nor, under circumstances of very touching and

[1] William Cubitt (1791–1863) building contractor; Lord Mayor 1860–2, M.P. 1847–62.

powerful contrast, have rewarded his 'industrious apprentice' by presenting him at the height of his fame and fortune.

Now these considerations suggest to me and to all here that a Lord Mayor never is, never was, and never can be, considered complete without a Lady Mayoress; and the Lady Mayoress is the theme of the very few words I have to add. [*Loud cheers.*] My lord, among the respects in which the City of London has set a highly civilized and most admirable example, is the one that it steadily disassociates itself on occasions like the present, from the absurd English custom of separating the lords of creation from the ladies. [*Hear.*] As to which custom, I think that if the male sex were fairly polled, they would arrive at an almost unanimous conclusion that we men were never so wearisome to ourselves, never so exceedingly uninteresting to each other, as when conventionally we were supposed to be left entirely at our ease. [*Laughter and cheers.*] Yet this abrogation of a bad usage on the part of the City, although no doubt it has its roots in social gallantry and good sense, is attended with the one inconvenience that it necessitates the proposing the Lady Mayoress's health in the Lady Mayoress's presence. And this renders exceedingly difficult a task which, from its very acceptable and its obvious nature, would otherwise have been almost easy. On the other hand, according to the great law of compensation which pervades the universe, it is to be observed that that silent presence is in itself the most eloquent speech that could be made in offering the toast, and the best illustration of the virtues and graces of its subjects. [*Loud applause.*]

And if I may venture to depart from a mere state and ceremony, it is to tell you that I have had the honour of an intimate personal friendship with the Lady Mayoress, and that it has been my personal privilege to see her widely diffusing her excellent influence in another capital than this. And let me add that, as the liberality and princely hospitality of the chief magistrate of London could find no fitter female representative than her, so the wholesome influence of an English lady could certainly find no better representative there [*Applause.*] With the permission of his lordship, I beg to propose 'The health of the Lady Mayoress'. [*Renewed applause.*]

The toast was received with loud acclamation, and the lord mayor briefly returned thanks on his daughter's behalf.

READING FOR THE MECHANICS' INSTITUTE: CHATHAM

16 *January* 1862

AFTER a reading of *David Copperfield* for the benefit of the institution there was the usual vote of thanks. In seconding the motion, H. G. Adams, the secretary, referred to the scene in the *Uncommercial Traveller* in which the writer takes up a small boy from Chatham who points out the house at Gad's Hill.[1] Dickens briefly replied.

HE was always, he said, happy to assist the Institute. With reference to the allusion by Mr. Adams to his early connexion with that locality, he could only say that during the evening he had found it difficult to disassociate the characters he had to represent from the very stones of Chatham. [*Loud cheers.*]

As the reading version of *David Copperfield* was concerned only with the story of Little Emily and the courtship of Dora, Dickens's remarks confirm that the east-coast fishermen of the novel were actually more closely associated in his mind with Chatham than Great Yarmouth.

ARTISTS' GENERAL BENEVOLENT FUND

28 *March* 1862

THE forty-seventh anniversary was held at the Freemasons' Tavern with Dickens in the Chair. A greater company assembled than had ever attended a similar occasion on the society's behalf before. 'The gallery', it was reported, 'was again filled with ladies, whose presence lent its usual happy lustre; and rarely has the magnificent Hall . . . looked more attractive'.[2] Grace having been sung, Dickens gave the usual loyal and patriotic toasts in a terse yet eloquent manner. The health of 'The Queen', was given briefly and impressively, and received in profound silence, the chairman gracefully referring to the recent death of the Prince Consort.[3]

Having given 'The Army and Navy', coupled with 'The Volunteers', which was acknowledged by Ensign Edmund Yates,[4] the chairman rose to give the toast of the evening.

[1] 'The German Chariot', *All the Year Round*, 7 Apr. 1860, ii. 557–62; in the collected *Uncommercial Traveller*, renamed 'Travelling Abroad'.
[2] *Era*.   [3] 14 Dec. 1861.
[4] Edmund Yates (1831–94), journalist, novelist, miscellaneous writer, and post-office official; son of Frederick Yates, the actor; contributor to *Household Words* and *All the Year Round;* close friend of Dickens, who advised him in his dispute with the Garrick Club following his article on Thackeray in *Town Talk*, as a result of which Yates was dismissed the Club, and Dickens resigned, 1858. Later, he was successively editor of *Temple Bar*, *Time*, and *The World*. He described his association with Dickens in his *Recollections and Experiences*, 1884.

HE believed, he said, that it was pretty generally understood that there was probably nothing more easily done in this world than to spend one's money, excepting it was to spend the money of other people. [*Laughter.*] However, he was happy, so far as the institution for which he had the honour and satisfaction to appeal, to say that as far as *it* was concerned, it had attained such a degree of perfection that its promoters and supporters deemed the spending properly the money placed at their disposal an object of the highest importance. [*Hear, hear.*] It was also an object of the first importance, looking at any institution, to know what were the costs of its administration. [*Hear, hear.*] When such an institution was founded in the great name of Benevolence; and when men had to deal with the large sums of money so often contributed with such ready hands, and with such unlimited generosity, towards the relief of distress—and oftentimes, mayhap, of misery—it became more than ever essential to be assured that such money was faithfully expended, and not diverted into other channels than those for which it was legitimately designed. [*Applause.*] In any other case, though flowing knee-deep with all the cardinal virtues, and chin-deep with all the gentilities and respectabilities [*laughter*], and with all the red and blue books that were ever published [*increased laughter*], it would but be like the unhappy man on whom a verdict was delivered, 'found drowned'. [*More laughter.*]

Six or seven years ago when he had occasion on certain and sufficient grounds consistent with the dignity and independence of what he might term his own art, to look about for encouragement and example among institutions connected with the sister arts (yet with no possible reference to this order—having no glance whatever towards this occasion—no conceivable motive for giving on other than just grounds one a preference over the other) he must say that he pointed out as a model this institution.[1] [*Loud applause.*] He had shown how modestly, how sincerely, how economically it was managed—how well its conductors dealt with the trusts admitted to their hands, and how in every way honourably they discharged their responsibilities. [*Hear, hear.*]

The chairman then, at some length, went into the details of the operations of the institution, contrasting its position in 1854 and 1861, and saying that he stood firm by his model with unshaken steadfastness and unabated confidence. [*Loud applause.*] In the past year the institution had administered, in round figures, £2,000, and distributed £1,126 among the recipients of the bounty of the charity, at a cost of something like £100 [*hear, hear*]; and this small sum of £100 included salaries, commissions, and a lot of other items.

---

[1] During the dispute with the Royal Literary Fund, see pp. 225 ff.

[*Hear, hear.*] He had further found that, at this moderate cost, the institution had relieved no fewer than seventy-two applicants. He would only ask them for a moment to picture to themselves what worldly reverses, what overwhelming cases of domestic distress, what affliction, what home sorrows might not have been alleviated and assuaged in such cases as those which stood marked in the records of the institution. [*Hear, hear.*] The chairman then enumerated a list of cases in point, without mentioning names, which fully bore out his remarks.

Such, he went on, were the merits of the institution to which, in the forty-seventh year of its age, he had to ask them to drink health, wealth, and length of life—an institution having no other recorded fame than that which appeared in noble characters in its printed descriptions of itself—*Mercy and Distress constituting the claims on its Benevolence.* [*Cheers.*]

He then went on to address, as he said, the two classes present—those who were artists, and those who were not—and he did so in the name and for the sake of Art. For being, if he might be permitted to say so, somewhat of an artist himself, he had some claim to be related to the family, and certainly had always very sensitive feelings in reference to the honour of the family name. [*Laughter and applause.*] To those gentlemen present who were not artists he must beg respectfully to say—addressing them in the name of Art —he could not, and did not, stoop to ask for charity. [*Hear, hear.*] In the ordinary and popular signification of that word in England —where it was almost as strongly illustrated as the term Art itself —he could, in the place where he was addressing them, have nothing whatever to do; but in its broader and wider signification he thought it might most aptly and fitly be associated indeed with Art. [*Applause.*]

There had been, and perhaps were, those of certain conventional ideas, who present Art as a mere child: a poor moon-striken creature unable to take care of itself waiting as it were, to be safely conducted over the great crossings of life by some professional sweepers [*laughter*]; as a miserable, slovenly slattern, down-at-heel and out-at-elbows, with no appreciation of the value of a home, no knowledge whatever of the value of money—and so on; but with these popular and still lingering hallucinations he had nothing whatever to do. [*Hear, hear.*] He altogether renounced them. [*Hear, hear.*] He represented the artist in a widely different light. Yes! as a reasonable creature; a sensible, practical, responsible gentlemen [*hear, hear, and laughter*]; as one quite as well acquainted with the value of his own time and money as though he were 'on high "Change"' every day [*hear, hear, and laughter*]; as steadfast and methodical as if he had even a Bank or Life-office of his own to attend to; who lived in a house as well as others who were not artists; who enjoyed the pleasures of his wife, and home, and children, as other men; the former of whom not only attended properly to the ordinary matters of dress and curling of hair but, in short, was usually to be found marked by an association with a decorous amount of drapery. [*Laughter and applause.*] On the other hand he presented the artist as one to whom the finest and frailest of the five senses was essential to the achievement of every business of his life. He could not gain wealth or fame by buying something he never touched or saw, or selling to another man something he might never touch or see. No! he must strike out of himself every spark of the fire which warmed and lighted—aye, and perhaps consumed him. He must win the great battle of life with his own hands and by his own eyes, and he could not choose but be in the hot encounter, General Commander-in-Chief, Captain, Ensign, non-commissioned-officer, private, drummer, all, in one short word, in his own unaided self. [*Loud and continued applause.*]

This, was the artist. But he might be at times a self-deluded man, a man mistaken in his own views and judgements, and he might at times be pursuing some phantom which lured him to unsuccessful ends. Or he might be an unfortunate man simply in being in a position in which he was unable to adapt himself to the prevailing taste of his times. Or, for instance, he might be an engraver, whose work for popular approval was necessarily hard and slow—and for which, by the way, he was not always munificently paid—and which was not usually recommended by the faculty either for improving the eye or opening the chest. [*Loud laughter and applause.*] Or again, it might be that he was merely but a humble teacher of drawing, whose business it was to infuse into the rising generation a better appreciation of the labours of more richly gifted men; or one of those merely manual workers in the lower walks of Art, whose existence was necessary still, in a greater or less degree, to the furtherance of that Art, albeit he might only be a little rill, tributary—as it were—to the great broad ocean of genius. [*Loud applause.*] Still he presented him as the Artist, and still he could not be led to lay his honour or his calling at the foot of any man. [*Applause.*] He asked for help from without for the fund not as alms-giving, not as propping up a mere cripple: he asked it as part payment of a debt which all civilized men owed to Art. [*Prolonged applause.*] He asked it as a mark of respect, as a decoration not a badge [*reiterated cheering*], as a remembrance of what this land would be without Art, and its inseparability from the best and purest enjoyments, all along the journey down to the fast-flowing river that had brought them all there, a very long way from those well remembered pictures in their childhoods' story-books, which none of them, as children, could ever read again. [*Loud and continued applause for some minutes.*]

The chairman next addressed a few words to those who were Artists. He said that it must be to them a very gratifying and cheering fact that the institution, in which they were undoubtedly so much interested, was so nobly supported by men who were themselves distinguished Artists. [*Hear, hear.*] Having mentioned the name of Mr. Jones[1] in connexion with this point, the chairman also referred to the published statistics of the institution, and remarked in eulogistic terms on the liberal and generous manner in which its patrons had supported it. The presence of the distinguished and experienced gentlemen who sat around him, as well as others who were present in that room, was indeed an encouragement to artists never to be ashamed of the honest struggles which belonged to their calling; while at the same time it most emphatically, and even affectionately, entreated them to forget the station of others. It was no small satisfaction to him to be able to direct their attention to this gratifying circumstance—that even some of those who had once accepted help from its funds now held up their heads with pride, because they were enrolled among the subscribers to its funds. [*Hear, hear.*]

In conclusion he would say one word to the more young artists; and that was to counsel them not to deceive themselves in the first flush of youth and hope by the notion that they should never want help. They might; and their great duty would be to provide for such a contingency during the days of their competency. [*Loud cheers.*]

Dickens also proposed 'The Royal Academy and Other Institutions', and other toasts followed including the health of the chairman.

NEWSVENDORS' BENEVOLENT INSTITUTION

20 *May* 1862

DICKENS had been asked to preside at the anniversary festival the previous year, and had consented to take the Chair; but, at the last

---

[1] George Jones (1786–1869), painter, chiefly of battle-scenes and official ceremonies; R.A., 1824; Librarian, 1834–40; Keeper, 1840–50; and acting President of the Royal Academy, 1845–50.

minute, he had been so ill that he had had to arrange for Wilkie Collins[1] to take his place.[2]

This year the anniversary festival was again held at the Freemasons' Hall, and, this time, Dickens took the Chair. For the first time, instead of the ladies being left to watch from the gallery, they were invited to sit down to dinner with the gentlemen. Several of his family, friends and acquaintances were present, including Miss Georgina Hogarth, Mamie and Frank Dickens, Mrs. W. H. Wills, and Frederick Lehmann with his wife and daughter.

After the usual toasts, Dickens rose and said:

LADIES and Gentlemen, When I had the honour of being asked to preside over the anniversary dinner of the society last year, I was prevented from doing so by indisposition. I requested my friend Wilkie Collins to reign in my stead. He very kindly complied, to my great relief, and he made an excellent speech. [*Hear, hear.*] Indeed, to tell you the truth, I read the account at the time with considerable uneasiness, for it inspired me with a strong misgiving that I might have done better to have presided last year with neuralgia in my face and my subject in my head, rather than preside this year with my neuralgia all gone, and my subject anticipated. [*Laughter.*] Therefore I shall preface the toast of the evening by making the managers of this institution one very solemn and repentant promise, and it is this—if ever I have to find them a substitute again, they may implicitly rely upon my sending them the most speechless man in my circle of acquaintance. [*Laughter.*]

The chairman of last year presented you with an admirable view of the universality of a newsman's calling, and the great variety of people who look to him each day, and the diversity of interest with which his burden is expected. Now nothing I can think of seems to be left for me, but to imagine the newsman's burden itself, to unfold one of those wonderful sheets which he every day disseminates, and to take a glance over his shoulder—a bird's-eye view of the general character of its contents. [*Hear, hear.*] So, if you please, choosing my own time—as the newsman cannot, as he must be equally active in all weathers, in winter as in summer, in sunshine and snow, in light and darkness, early and late—I say, choosing my

---

[1] William Wilkie Collins (1824–89), novelist, author of *The Woman in White* (1860), *The Moonstone* (1868), &c. He was introduced to Dickens as a recruit for the amateur players in 1851, and thereafter, with some intermissions, they were close friends. Collins contributed to *Household Words*, and *All the Year Round;* and they collaborated in the *Lazy Tour of Two Idle Apprentices*, and the *Perils of Certain English Prisoners*, in 1857, and *No Thoroughfare*, 1867. Collins wrote the *Lighthouse*, 1855, and the *Frozen Deep*, 1857, for Dickens's amateur theatricals. His brother Charles Alston Collins (1828–73), married Dickens's second daughter, Kate.   [2] *Daily News*, 24 May 1861.

weather, as an amateur can but as he cannot, I will for two or three moments start off with my newsman on a fine May morning, and take a peep over his shoulder at one of the wonderful broadsheets which he every day scatters broadcast over the country.

Well, the first thing that occurs to me in taking up the newspaper every morning is that we are born every day, that every day we—or, at least, some of us—are married, and that every day we die. Consequently my first glimpse over the newsman's shoulder instructs me that Atkins is born, Catkins is married, and that Datkins is dead. [*Laughter.*] But one of the most remarkable circumstances connected with the sheet is, that Atkin's infancy seems to be surprisingly brief, for I immediately discover in the very next column that he has grown up to be seventeen years old, and has run away from his mother. At least I see that, 'if W. A.', which stands for William Atkins, 'who is seventeen years old, in a dress suit, with one front tooth missing, will only return to his disconsolate parents, everything will be arranged to the satisfaction of everyone'. [*Hear, hear, and laughter.*] I am afraid he never will return, for the reason, amongst others perhaps, that if he had ever meant to have come back he never would have gone away. [*Laughter.*] Immediately below, I find a mysterious character, in a position of such mysterious difficulty, that it is only to be expressed by several disjointed letters, several figures, several stars, and some such adjuration as, 'Amelia write instantly. Destruction, all is lost! The canary bird has made over his property to his uncle. The elephant is on the wing.'

Then, still glancing over the shoulder of my industrious friend the newsman, there pass by fleets of ships bound to all parts of the earth, all going to have immediate dispatch, all with a little more stowage for a little more cargo, and a few more berths for a few more passengers, that they all have the most spacious cabins, all teak-built and copper-fastened, all carrying surgeons of experience, and having elevated space between decks—all, in short, A.1. at Lloyd's and everywhere else. [*Laughter.*] Still glancing over the shoulder of my industrious friend, I find I am offered every kind of house, lodging, clerk, servant, situation, that I can possibly or impossibly want, with everything to eat, drink, wear, and use. I learn, to my intense gratification—for I begin to have some doubts upon the subject myself—that I need never grow old; that I may preserve the juvenile bloom of my complexion to any period of life; that I need never more have any grey hairs; that if I ever cough again it is entirely my own fault; that I need never be ill of any complaint; that if I want brown cod liver oil I know where to find it; that if I want a Turkish bath I know where to get it; and that if I want an income of seven pounds a week for life for 2s. 6d. down, I have only to send the postage stamps and there it is. [*Great laughter.*]

Still glancing over the newsman's shoulder, my eye rests on the Imperial Parliament, and there I read among other stereotyped passages, which I am always sure to find there, how the hon. member for somewhere, asked the Right hon. gentlemen the Secretary of State for the Home Department, whether he had any intelligence to communicate respecting that last outrage, or that last railway accident, or that last mine explosion, or that last case of police justice; and I always read how the Right hon. gentleman said in reply, rather magnificently, that 'he knew nothing whatever about the matter except what he had read in the newspapers'. [*Laughter.*] Which stereotyped reply I observe to be received universally with a 'Hear, hear', which is, to me, perfectly incomprehensible; because I can read such things in a paper without drawing a salary for doing it. [*Great laughter.*]

Well then I look to the Police Intelligence, and that teaches me that if I want to bite off a woman's nose I can do it very cheap [*hear, hear, and laughter*], but if I want surreptitiously to make off with the salted nose of a pig or calf from a shop window, it will cost me exceedingly dear. [*Laughter.*] And, also, that if I allow myself to be betrayed into the folly, say, of killing an inoffensive tradesman on his own doorstep, that little act of indiscretion will not in the least interfere with my triumphant production of testimonials to character as a most amiable young man, particularly to be esteemed in all respects, but above all things remarkable for the singular inoffensiveness of my character and disposition. [*Laughter.*]

So, also looking over the shoulder of my friend the newsman of the day, I pass to the theatrical intelligence; and there, perhaps, I read the gratifying announcement, which is no news to anyone, that the true spirit of a picturesque artist has again been displayed by Mr. Benjamin Webster [*laughter*], and that another most subtle and delicate piece of genuine comedy has been achieved by my friend Mr. Alfred Wigan.[1] [*Cheers.*] Then, turning my eye to the Fine Arts, under that head I find the latest intelligence to be that a certain 'J. O.' has most triumphantly exposed a certain 'J.O.B.', which 'J.O.B.' is remarkable for this singular and particularly novel feature, that I was required to make the sacrifice of depriving myself of the best of my pictures for six months; that for that time they were to be hung upon wet walls; and that I was to be requited

[1] Alfred Sydney Wigan (1814–78), actor, manager, and dramatist; had appeared as the original John Johnson, in Dickens's *Strange Gentleman*, at the St. James's Theatre, in 1836.

for my courtesy by having them impertinently covered with a wet blanket.[1] [*Laughter.*]

Now, ladies and gentlemen, summing up in short, this one glance over my newsman's shoulder gives me the comprehensive knowledge of what is going on over the great continent of Europe, over the great continent of America to boot, to say nothing of such little-known geographical regions as India and China; for Reuter's telegrams come straight to me. Under the heading of Military Intelligence, I read the last news of my boy in the Army, and under the head of Naval Intelligence, I read the last news concerning my boy in the Navy. All these topics are ready sifted for me in sharp, terse, pointed, leading articles. In a word, every morning before my breakfast is done, I can put a girdle round the earth, like Ariel, and come up to the time of high water at London Bridge, and the arrival of the Japanese ambassadors.[2] [*Laughter.*] By the by, the Japanese ambassadors ought of all things to be here tonight. [*Hear, hear.*] They could not be shown anything in England so astonishing as a newsvendors' dinner, seeing that it is the usage and policy of their country, as described by travellers, to forbid the circulation of news of any kind, on pain of instant death, and to cut the newsman in half the moment he shows himself. [*Laughter.*]

Now, my friends, this is the glance over the newsman's shoulder from the whimsical point of view, which is the point, I believe, that most promotes digestion. The newsman is to be met with at every turn, on steamboats, and in railway stations. His profits are small,

---

[1] Referring to a heated controversy recently conducted through letters to *The Times*. The International Exhibition at South Kensington, which had been opened on 1 May, included a gallery of pictures and sculpture. The commissioners had invited owners and artists to lend their pictures, and Francis Turner Palgrave to write a *Handbook* to the collection. An anonymous correspondent, who wrote over the initials 'J.O.', opened the attack on the *Handbook* and its author in a letter of 15 May. Palgrave had outspokenly condemned a number of pictures selected by the Commissioners and extravagantly praised others, especially those by Arthur Hughes and Holman Hunt, while he wrote of the sculpture of Thomas Woolner as almost beyond praise. 'J.O.' objected to personal criticism of borrowed pictures in an official publication on principle; he showed that Palgrave and Woolner were close friends sharing the same house; and that the commissioners had not read their own *Handbook*. It was generally agreed that those responsible had acted unwisely, although in good faith, and the book was withdrawn. Palgrave was particularly contemptuous of G. G. Adams's busts of Sir Francis Burdett and the Duke of Wellington, of which Dickens rather approved. G. Leslie wrote in defence of his father's work; Holman Hunt in support of Woolner; and Millais and Watts in protest at personal criticism being given official sanction.

[2] The first Japanese embassy to Europe had arrived in England from France on 30 Apr. Its members were more interested in Woolwich Arsenal, than the free press.

he has a great amount of anxiety and care, and no little amount of personal wear and tear. He is indispensable to civilization and freedom, and he is looked for with pleasurable excitement every day, except when he lends the paper for an hour, and then his punctuality in calling for it is anything but agreeable. [*Hear, hear, and laughter.*] I think the lesson we can learn from the newsman is some new illustration of the uncertainty of life, some illustration of its vicissitudes and fluctuations. Mindful of this permanent lesson, some members of the trade founded this society, which would afford them assistance in time of sickness and indigence in return for their subscription—a subscription which is infinitesimal. It amounts to five shillings per annum. Looking at the returns before me, the progress of the society would seem to be slow, but it has only been slow for the best of all reasons, that it has been sure. The pensions granted by the society are all drawn out of the interest on the funded capital [*hear, hear*], and, therefore, the institution is literally as safe as the Bank. It is stated that there are several newsvendors who are not members of this society; but that is equally the case in all institutions which have come under my experience. The very persons who are most likely to stand in need of the benefits which an institution of this kind confers, are usually the persons to keep away until bitter experience comes to them too late, and shows that men have much to lose in keeping apart from it.

In asking you to drink this toast I have to congratulate you on the success which has followed this institution, and I must also congratulate you on the fact that a rare article of intelligence will appear in the public prints tomorrow, and give employment to the newsvendors—the fact, namely, that ladies have dined at a public dinner table. I respect the gallantry and good sense of the committee in abolishing, so far as they have been concerned, the barbarous and preposterous custom which condemned the ladies to a distinct place while the other sex were eating and drinking—which is the custom of all savage tribes. [*Cheers, and laughter.*]

The chairman concluded by proposing 'Prosperity to the Newsvendors' Provident and Benevolent Institution', which was drunk with great enthusiasm.

ROYAL GENERAL THEATRICAL FUND

4 *April* 1863

THE anniversary festival was held, as usual, at the Freemasons' Tavern. Wilkie Collins was to have been chairman, but at the last moment he was prevented by severe illness, and Dickens undertook to take his place. After grace was sung, he rose amid loud and general applause, and said:

LADIES and Gentlemen, I am aware that nothing I may say can add to the enthusiasm with which the toast will be received, but in proposing to you to drink the loyal toast, 'The Queen', I have the gratification of informing you that Her Majesty has again repeated her munificent annual donation of one hundred pounds in aid of the Royal General Theatrical Fund. [*Cheers.*]

The toast was drunk with every demonstration of loyalty. The chairman then said:

Ladies and Gentlemen, It is not the least notable circumstance in the young lives of the two exalted persons who have lately engrossed so much general attention, that as each is the deserving object of the other's free choice, so the future career of both must henceforth for ever be inseparable from that of a free people deserving to be free.[1] Surely no old poet, or painter, or sculptor ever conceived a more graceful or beautiful marriage procession than that of the other day, where all ages, all classes, all conditions of the fruition of hope or the disappointment of hope joined together in one great equal, generous enthusiasm in behalf of those two young people in the flush of life and fortune, and governed themselves and governed their tempers in honour of the interesting scene. [*Cheers.*] I am sure you will agree with me in saying: never may that young Prince and Princess, and the great true-hearted English people, be less worthy of one another, or less at peace with one another, than they were that day. [*Cheers.*] I beg to propose to you to drink, 'Their Royal Highnesses the Prince and Princess of Wales, and the rest of the Royal Family.'

The toast was drunk with great enthusiasm. The chairman then said:

Ladies and Gentlemen, It is equally the characteristic of the Army and of the Navy that the members of those two brave services very seldom talk about their duty, and always do it. I cannot better testify my respect for that noble model than by adopting it. I therefore beg to propose to you, 'The Army and Navy and the Volunteers', with which toast I will connect the name of Captain Ward of the Army who sits upon my right. [*Cheers.*]

The toast having been drunk and briefly acknowledged, the toast-master then commanded the company to charge their glasses for a bumper toast. On rising once more, the chairman was most enthusiastically greeted, and said:

Ladies and Gentlemen, With my present responsibilities impending over me, I happened the other night, as I sat alone, to be reading

[1] The Prince of Wales, and Princess Alexandra of Denmark, had been married at Windsor on 10 Mar.

a paper in *The Tatler*[1] referring to the time when Mr. Powell's company of performing puppets was in high vogue with persons of quality. In that number of *The Tatler* the brilliant essayist gives a humorous description of a contest then raging between two ladies at Bath—Prudentia and Florimel—as to which of them should set the fashion to the greatest number of imitators. In the course of this noble struggle Florimel bespoke *Alexander the Great* to be acted by the players, and Prudentia bespoke *The Creation of the World*, to be acted by the puppets: at the same time darkly putting it about, for the confusion and ridicule of her rival, that the puppet Eve, whom I suppose to have been but indifferently modelled, would be found in figure 'the most like Florimel that ever was seen'. [*Laughter.*] Now what were the missing charms, what were the defective points in this wooden lady's anatomy does not appear, otherwise I should have the honour of delicately stating them to this company; but it does appear that his Worship the Mayor inclined to the wooden side of the question, and that on high moral grounds he greatly preferred those innocent creatures, the puppets, to those wicked players. [*Laughter.*]

Now, ladies and gentlemen, as I have a profound veneration for Mayors and such like [*laughter*], this sentiment caused me to close the book and to consider how much we should gain if there were no manager now but Mr. Powell, and if there were no actors now but puppets. [*Laughter.*] In the first place—and on the immense advantage to be reaped here, I have no doubt we shall be all agreed—there would be no Fund, no dinner, no chairman, and no speech. [*Laughter.*] Then on Saturdays there would be no treasury, although I am told that that great point has occasionally been gained even under the existing system [*laughter*]; there would never be any throwing up of parts, there would never be any colds, there would never be any little jealousies or dissensions; the two leading ladies might dress for any length of time in the same room without the remotest danger of ever coming to words, and the loftiest tragedian that ever was or ever will be, might be doubled up with his legs round his neck, and put away in the same box with the reddest-nosed and most flowered waistcoated of comic countrymen. [*Laughter.*] Now these, I considered to myself, were the points to be gained. On the other hand there would be human interest to be lost, there would be the human face to be lost—which after all does stand for a little —and last, not least, there would be that immense amount of comfort and satisfaction to be lost by a large number of well-meaning persons, which they constitutionally derive from slightly disparaging those who entertain them. [*Cheers and laughter.*] This last high

[1] No. 16.

moral gratification, this cheap, this complacent self-assertion I felt
could not possibly be parted with; and, therefore, I quickly came
to the conclusion that we must have those wicked players after all.
[*Cheers and laughter.*]

Ladies and gentlemen, it is an astonishing thing to me, but
within my limited range of observation and experience it is nevertheless true, that there should be, and that there is, in a part of
what we call the world—which certainly is in the main a kind, good-
natured, always-steadily-improving world—this curious propensity
to run up a little score against, and as it were to be even with, those
who amuse and beguile them. 'That man in the farce last night,
made me laugh so much', says Portman Square, Esq., at breakfast,
'that I hope there may be nothing absolutely wrong about him, but
I begin to think this morning there must be.' [*Laughter.*] 'My Dear',
says Mr. Balham Hill to Mrs. Balham Hill, 'I was so profoundly
affected at the theatre last night, and I felt it so very difficult to
repress my sobs when the poor mad King listened in vain for the
breathing of his dead daughter, that I really felt it due to myself
to patronize that gentleman this morning. I felt a kind of compensation to myself to regard him as an extraordinary man, having no
recognized business that can be found in the Post Office Directory.
[*Laughter.*] I feel it necessary to put up with him, as it were, as a
kind of unaccountable creature who has no counting-house anywhere; in short, to bear with him as a sort of marvellous child in a
Shakespearian go-cart.' [*Roars of laughter.*]

Ladies and gentlemen, this is quite true in a greater or less degree,
I think, of all artists; but it is particularly true of the Dramatic
artist, and it is so strange to me. Surely it cannot be because he
dresses himself up for his part, for, as you all know very well, there
is an enormous amount of dressing and making-up going on in high
stations all around us. I never saw a worse make-up in the poorest
country theatre than I can see in the House of Commons any night
when there is a message from the Lords [*laughter*]; and I assure you,
on my personal veracity, that I have known a Lord High Chancellor at twenty-five shillings a week who, in his wigs and robes, looked
the part infinitely better than the real article at fifteen thousand a
year. [*Much laughter.*] Ladies and gentlemen, I think the secret
cannot lie here; I think the truth is that this little harmless disposition occupies a little quiet, out-of-the-way corner of our nature, and
as I think it a little ungracious, and a little ungenerous, and certainly more so than it is meant to be, I always, whether in public
or in private, on principle steadily oppose myself to it for this
reason which I have endeavoured to explain to you. Although I am
now going to urge upon you the case of, and am going to entreat

your active sympathy with, this General Theatrical Fund on this
eighteenth anniversary, you will hear from me nothing conventional
about the

Poor player
Who struts and frets his hour upon the stage,[1]

which shall in any way separate him otherwise than favourably
from the great community of us poor players, who all strut and fret
our little hours upon this stage of life. His work, if he be worth
anything to himself or to any other man, is at least as real and as
hard to him as the banker's is to him, or the broker's is to him, or
the professional man's to him, or the merchant's to him. His Fund
is a business Fund, and is conducted on sound, business, honourable,
independent principles. [*Hear, hear.*] It is a Fund, as many here
already know, for granting annuities to such members as may be
disqualified by age, sickness or infirmity from pursuing the Theatrical Profession, and also for extending aid to the sick, I think in
some cases even when they are not members, and to the bereaved
survivors of the dead. It is a Fund to which the members contribute
periodically according to certain carefully calculated scales, very
often out of very imperfect and very uncertain earnings. It is a
Fund which knows no distinction whatever of Theatre, and knows
no grade whatever of actors. I have had the honour of being one of
its Trustees from the hour of its first establishment [*cheers*], and I
bear testimony with admiration to the extraordinary patience,
steadiness, and perseverance with which those payments are made.
[*Cheers.*] Therefore, ladies and gentlemen, you will see that I occupy
here the vantage ground of entreating you to help those who do
really and truly help themselves, who do not come here tonight for
a mere field-night and theatrical display, but who as it were rise to
the surface once in every twelve months to assure you of their constancy and good faith and then burrow down to work again, many
of them surrounded by innumerable obstacles, many of them working under great difficulties, and, believe me, with little cheer and
encouragement throughout the whole toiling year, and in obscurity
enough. [*Hear, hear.*]

Now, ladies and gentlemen, in defiance of all these heavy blows
and great discouragement in the Actor's life, I fearlessly add these
words—If there be any creature here knowing a theatre well who
knows any kind of place, no matter what, cathedral, church, chapel,
tabernacle, high cross, market, change, where there is a more sacred
bond of charitable brotherhood, where there is a more certain
reliance to be placed on sympathy with affliction, where there is a

[1] *Macbeth*, v. vi.

greater generosity in ready giving, where there is a higher and more sacred respect for family ties, where there is habitually a more cheerful, voluntary bearing of burthens on already heavily burthened backs, then let him take his money to that place, to me unknown, and not produce it here. [*Cheers.*] But if he altogether fails in such knowledge, then let him communicate with Mr. Cullenford [*laughter*], now sitting expectant at a card table, and let him communicate to Mr. Cullenford something to this Fund's advantage, as he respects all the true saints in the calendar, and as he defies and despises all the sham saints out of it. [*Cheers and laughter.*]

Now gentlemen, as I have taken upon myself to say what a good corporation the Players are among themselves, and how cheerily and readily they invariably help one another, I may not unreasonably be asked by an outsider why he should help them. If it were the claims of an individual that I was advocating here in these days, I should be met, and very properly met, by the question, 'What is his case? What has he done?' Moreover, as to that agglomeration of individuals, the Theatrical Profession, we are most of us constantly met with by a reference to the times when there were better actors, and when there was a better stage literature, and with a mournful shrugging of shoulders over the present state of things. Now, accepting the theatrical times exactly as they stand, and seeking to make them no better than they are, but always protesting against anybody's seeking to make them worse, the difficulty with me standing before you is not to say what the Actor has done, but to say what he has not done, and is not doing every night. [*Hear, hear.*] I am very fond of the play, and herein lies one of the charms of the play to me; for example, when I am in front—and when I discharge for the moment all my personal likings and friendships for those behind—when I am in front any night, and when I see, say, my friend Mr. Buckstone's eye roll into the middle of the pit with that fine expression in it of a comically suspended opinion which I like so much, how do I know on whom it alights, or what good it does that man? Here is some surly morose creature come into the theatre bent upon the morrow on executing some uncharitable intention, and the eye of Mr. Buckstone dives into his right-hand trousers pocket where his angry hand is clenched, and opens his hand and mellows it, and shakes it in quite a philanthropic manner. I hear a laugh there from my left. [*From Mr. T. P. Cooke.*[1]] How do I know how many a lout has been quickened into activity by Mr. T. P. Cooke's

[1] Thomas Potter Cooke (1786–1864), actor; saw active service in the Navy, 1796–1802; which was followed by successful stage career, especially in nautical parts, the best known being William, in Jerrold's *Black Eyed Susan*, and Long Tom Coffin, in Fitzball's *The Pilot*; steady supporter of theatrical charities.

hornpipe? [*Cheers.*] How do I know on how many a stale face and heart Long Tom Coffin, and Nelson's coxwain, and Black-Eyed Susan's William, have come healthily dashing like the spray of the sea? Over and over again it is my delight to take my place in the theatre next to some grim person who comes in a mere figure of snow, but who gradually softens and mellows until I am also led to bless the face that creases with satisfaction until it realizes Falstaff's wonderful simile of being 'like a wet cloak ill laid up'. It is a joke in my home that generosity on the stage always unmans me, and that I invariably begin to cry whenever anybody on the stage forgives an enemy or gives away a pocket book. [*Laughter.*] This is only another and droller way of experiencing and saying that it is good to be generous, and good to be open-handed, and that it is a right good thing for society, through its various gradations of stalls, boxes, pit, and gallery, when they come together with but one great, beating, responsive heart among them, to learn such a truth together. [*Cheers.*] Depend upon it the very best among us are often bad company for ourselves (I know I am very often); and in bringing us out of that, and in keeping us company, and in showing us ourselves and our kind in a thousand changing forms of humour and fancy, the actor—all the solemn humbugs on the earth to the contrary notwithstanding—renders a high and inestimable service to the community every night of his life. [*Hear, hear.*]

I dare say the feeling peculiar to a theatre is as well known to everybody here as it is to me, of having for an hour or two quite forgotten the real world, and of coming out into the street with a kind of wonder that it should be so wet, and dark, and cold, and full of jostling people and irreconcilable cabs. [*Laughter.*] By the remembrance of that delightful dream and waking; by all your remembrance of it from your childhood until now; and by your remembrance of that long glorious row of wonderful lamps; and by the remembrance of that great mysterious curtain behind it; and by the remembrance of those enchanted people behind that, who are disenchanted every night and go out into the wet and worry; by all these things I entreat you not to go out into Great Queen Street by-and-by, without saying that you have done something for this fleeting fairy-land which has done so much for us. [*Loud cheering.*] Ladies and gentlemen, I beg to propose to you, 'The General Theatrical Fund'.

The toast was drunk upstanding with three times three. Buckstone made an amusing speech, on behalf of the society, in reply. Among much else he mentioned that he had promised to take the Chair, next Ash Wednesday, at another Dramatic Fund Dinner,[1] where the ladies were

[1] Dramatic, Equestrian, and Musical Fund, for which Dickens presided in 1866, see pp. 353 ff.

not segregated in the gallery; and that if he found it 'very comfortable', he would recommend to the directors of their own fund, to do the same thing.

The chairman then rose, and said:

Ladies and gentlemen, It now becomes me, like a well graced actor, to retire from the scene, and make place for a better graced actor. I have next to propose to you 'The Drama'. Looking round the table upon my left to see whom I should call upon to return thanks for that toast, my eye lightened upon the face of a valued and esteemed friend of mine whom I last heard of at a considerable distance, in Nice,[1] and whom I am surprised and gratified to find has graced this board tonight. Allow me to propose 'The Drama', and to connect with that toast the respected name of Mr. Alfred Wigan. [*Loud cheering.*]

Wigan replied; and Edmund Yates then proposed the health of the chairman, who rose and said:

Ladies and gentlemen, I will only assure you on behalf of myself that I am deeply indebted to you, as I always am, for your kind reception, and that I am also deeply indebted to my friend on my right for the kind and feeling terms in which he proposed my health, during which impressive speech my excellent friend Buckstone whispered in my ear that he had often nursed that young man on his knee [*laughter*], which I don't believe. [*Increased laughter.*]

As I am on my legs, as the Parliamentary phrase is, I will not be off my legs without proposing to you another toast. 'Coming events cast their shadows before', and coming events cast their lights before also, and as we have among us tonight a gentleman highly esteemed in the City, and by all who know him, who will shortly become Lord Mayor and who has passed through the important preliminary office of Sherriff,—as to which, we were once assured by a Sheriff at this Dinner that he knew of no actor who had ever been hanged [*laughter*], in reply to which I had the pleasure of informing him, on the part of the Dramatic Profession, that I knew of no Sheriff who had ever been hanged[2] [*increased laughter*]—I say, that as we have among us a gentleman whom we are disposed to make so welcome, I will, if you please, propose his health in connexion with the City. Allow me to propose 'The City of London and Alderman Phillips'.[3]

---

[1] At the Olympic, in *Taming the Truant*, adapted from the French by his brother, Horace Wigan.

[2] See p. 93.

[3] Benjamin Samuel Phillips (1811–89), city merchant; alderman, 1857–88; sheriff, 1859–60; Lord Mayor, 1865–6; knighted, Dec. 1866. See pp. 352 ff. and 358 ff.

The toast was drunk with much enthusiasm, and Alderman Phillips replied. The chairman then said:

You know what the last toast always is; it is 'The Ladies', and upon this subject I have a very considerable crow to pick with my friend Mr. Buckstone, who has taken great credit to himself tonight for a certainly new-mooted idea in abeyance here as to whether ladies shall dine at this table. I did enunciate against this Fund the terrific threat ten years ago, that if the ladies did not dine here I never would come here again. [*Laughter.*] Unless next Ash Wednesday's experience satisfies Mr. Buckstone that the ladies ought to dine here, I shall invite the ladies to a General Theatrical Fund Supper-Dinner at the Freemasons' Tavern, on which occasion, if they will do me the honour to allow me to receive them as their chairman, they will hear something to Mr. Buckstone's disadvantage, which he would much rather not hear himself. [*Much laughter.*] We are always delighted to see the ladies anywhere, but particularly here. I have been delighted myself to see them under all manner of circumstances, and I have felt the want of them particularly. [*Laughter.*]

Upon a certain occasion some years ago, I was acting in Canada with some of our officers, when no ladies were to be found, and it was absolutely necessary that young and newly caught officers should supply their places; upon which occasion, in order that they might acquire something of the feminine walk it was found absolutely necessary to tie their legs. Upon another occasion I witnessed the representation of *Black Eyed Susan* at a country theatre, when I was delighted to find the court-martial composed of, I think, eight young ladies, with very perceptible back-hair, and very perceptible combs, who had put on the conventional notaries' gowns and sat down at a table and represented themselves to the public as midshipmen. Still it was charming to see them, and I never was so delighted in my life to see a real midshipman as I was to see those false midshipmen. [*Laughter.*]

Now I have one other crow to pick with Mr. Buckstone. I particularly object to the arrangement of these tables, and I particularly object to it for two reasons. In the first place, when I preside at, or when I attend one of these dinners, I am always in the most tantalizing position possible, inasmuch as I always want to look this way [*turning to face the ladies*], and I am obliged to look this. [*Facing the gentlemen.*] Also I never have so painful a sense that my hair is a little going behind. [*Laughter.*] So that on this occasion—if you will take my word for it—I assure you I have overheard tonight one or two very distressing expressions upon the subject. [*Laughter.*] Nay more, ladies and gentlemen, although I am always delighted to see the ladies, I really would rather see them in front of me [*laughter*]; but here, or there, or anywhere, or everywhere, we are always delighted to see them and let us drink their health.

The toast was drunk upstanding, with three times three, and 'one fire more'. The company then separated.

ROYAL FREE HOSPITAL

6 *May* 1863

THE thirty-fifth anniversary took place at the Freemasons' Tavern, with Dickens in the Chair. The cloth having been removed, the gallery was speedily crowded with ladies.

The chairman gave in quick succession, 'The Queen', 'The Prince and Princess of Wales and the rest of the Royal Family', and 'The Army, the Navy, and the Volunteers'—remarking that the services unfortunately contributed a full share of the sick and wounded to the practice of hospitals, and exhibited a still larger share of heroic fortitude and noble endurance. He then proposed the toast of the evening, and said:

I ADDRESS you, Gentlemen, I hope, in that phraseology for the last time tonight, because I intend to dispense with so savage and unmeaning a conventionality, and shall commence with what I have to say concerning the great object which has called us together by using the phrase, Ladies and Gentlemen. [*Loud cheers*.]

Ladies and Gentlemen, then, it happened some years ago, immediately after the close of the great Crimean War, that I was walking in the neighbourhood of Blackheath with a civilian just come home, who had greatly distinguished himself in connexion with that event.[1] The conversation naturally turned on the incidents he had lately witnessed, and my companion remarked that the ground upon which we happened to be standing was sufficiently like the ground on which one of the most memorable of the Crimean battles was fought to give me a very good idea of the field.

'Put behind every one, even of the least of the furze-bushes on that heath', said he,—'put behind every patch of shelter before us which could possibly conceal a crouching human form, one—at least one—wounded soldier, and you will have a very clear idea of the field, supposing that soldier dead, as I saw it myself on the morning after the fight.'

'I suppose', said I, 'that the badly wounded men crept behind those bushes when they were struck to get out of fire?' 'Well, in part for that reason', he said, 'but I think only for a very small part, because I have noticed that it became a kind of instinct in a

[1] Almost certainly W. H. Russell, correspondent of *The Times*, see p. 245 n.

badly wounded man to creep away and crawl behind any little bit of shelter, and crouch, and die alone, like some of the lower animals.'

Gentlemen—Ladies and Gentlemen—that picture impressed my fancy very much at the time, and since then, when I have passed through any of the crowded byways of this vast London, or of any other great town or city, I have hoped within myself that it may not be in peace as it is in war, and that many of the striken among us may not retire to their miserable places of refuge—may not coil themselves up in their wretched places of shelter—and die in the midst of us, untended and alone. [*Cheers.*]

Now, ladies and gentlemen, the most prosperous and best cared for among men and women know full well that whosoever is hit in this great and continuing battle of life, howsoever vast the gap may be that is made, howsoever dear the companion may be that is down, we must close up the ranks, and march on, and fight out the fight. But it happens that the rank and file are many in number, and the chances against them are many and hard, and they necessarily die by thousands, when the captains and standard-bearers only die by ones and twos. [*Cheers.*]

How those privates live, and how they fight, and how they die, are questions of immense moment to the whole social army. [*Hear, hear.*] If they were not felt so in these later times—if they were not felt honestly and thoroughly to be so—there can be no doubt that our own ranks would contain within themselves the certain elements of swift destruction and dissolution, and that we should need no enemy to ruin us, but our own misdeeds. Accordingly, ladies and gentlemen, and because people in general are, thank God! disposed to be humane, and to do right and to do good, this great capital teems with institutions for the relief of the indigent sick. They are not, it is true, by any means equal in number to the dire need —they are not equal in capacity to the heavy demands made upon them—but they are great institutions, nevertheless, many of them richly endowed, all of them nobly remarkable for the great medical science and skill which is freely placed at their command. [*Cheers.*] Now, as I have to entreat your active interest in behalf of one of these, it may be right that I should try, always without depreciation or the shadow of disparagement of any of the others, to show in what its peculiar claims consist.

Happily for me, ladies and gentlemen, the task is an easy one. The distinguishing character of the Royal Free Hospital is amply expressed in its simple name. It *is* a free hospital [*hear, hear*], no recommendation is needed by the suffering creature who seeks admission; no letter from a governor or a subscriber has with difficulty to be hunted out. [*Hear, hear.*] 'Look at me, look at me;

I am sick, I am poor, I am helpless, I am forlorn.' Those are the patient's credentials. Is there anybody here—is there anybody anywhere knowing that fact, whose fireside on a bleak winter night would not be the brighter and warmer for the reflection that he had done something towards the maintenance of that hospital which afforded such an easy and accessible refuge ? [*Hear.*] Is there a single court or alley in that great maze of courts and alleys which now intervenes between us and the hospital itself, that does not contain at this moment some pain-worn creature to whom, as we are sitting at these abundant tables, that hospital would be a haven of refuge and a dawn of hope ? Yes ; but consider how many pain-worn creatures there are within that space—consider how many crowded courts and alleys—consider how much wretchedness, distress, disease, and accident ; and yet this hospital, which might be made to prove so extensively serviceable, has this night not quite 100 beds to meet the whole of this demand. [*Hear, hear.*] Ladies and gentlemen, though its sphere of action is so large, and though the demands upon its resources are so enormous, that its in- and out-patients amounted last year, I think, to no fewer than 30,000, it has at this moment not quite 100 beds.

That is the worst of the case looked steadily in the face. And it is at first sight so disheartening and so dismaying, that I admit it would justify the despondent in saying, 'This is a hopeless case, beyond our reach', if it were not for the very encouraging statement that I can set against it. And it is briefly this.

The hospital has for some years past been paying for its unusually commodious premises an annual rental of £200. Now, it occurred to one of its most valuable supporters [*prolonged cheering*], a gentleman who is present, and who I am proud to call my friend, a gentleman of great business knowledge, of great influence, of great charity, and of great energy—Mr. George Moore[1] [*loud cheers*], that by an appeal to the munificence and liberality of the bankers and merchants of the city of London, a sufficient sum might be raised to purchase these premises.

Well, ladies and gentlemen, although this appeal was made at the time of the prevalence of the Lancashire distress, and although many other circumstances combined against success attending such an effort—although the sum of money was so large that it had to be counted not by hundreds, but by thousands of pounds—although in simple numbers it amounted to £6,000, that gentleman's efforts have already produced £4,000, and I most sincerely and earnestly hope that when the results of this night's proceedings shall be declared by the treasurer, this meeting will be able to regard the

[1] See p. 170 n.

hospital as henceforth and for ever saved that annual rent-charge, and as established on its own unencumbered property.[1] The meeting may rest satisfied that the hospital is otherwise unencumbered and free from debt, and consequently this meeting will dissolve with the assurance that every shilling subscribed to the hospital fund will go straight to the advancement of its objects, and to the alleviation of pain and misery.

But the hopefulness of the case, ladies and gentlemen, does not stop here. I have spoken of the hospital being a commodious building. I have made it my business to see that building, and to go over, I believe, every foot of it. It contains at this moment 130 beds, all of which could be filled if the income admitted that extension; and not only this, but it contains ample area, excellent light, cheerful galleries, capable of holding many more beds. [*Cheers.*] And it is to be particularly observed that the more the capabilities of the house are brought into action, the less will be the expense attendant upon them, as the staff and plant would not need to be increased in anything like the proportion of patients; and as the building would not need to be increased at all, it indubitably follows that the larger the number received and relieved, the smaller must be the individual cost. [*Hear, hear.*]

Now, ladies and gentlemen, if I were to speak for an hour by the clock—which, happily for you, I have not the slightest intention to do—I should only weaken this strong, plain statement of facts: I could but surround it with flourishes, which, like the writing-master's flourishes, would only obscure the text. Ladies and gentlemen, it is a sad reflection to know that in this densely-crowded city, rife with diseases, and with every casualty that can possibly befall the labouring man, this hospital has only an income sufficient to shelter and relieve 100 in-patients.

This is no case of a Château en Espagne—a castle in the air— a hospital of good intentions that may or may not be built some day of fragments rescued from the infernal pavement. There it stands in solid bricks and mortar. It is as real as the poor suffering creature who lies at your feet at the door-step, as you pass home in the dark. The means of assuaging the suffering is at hand if the public will only supply the requisite funds.

There was never so strong or so hopeful a cause. I believe that there are in this great town hundreds of well-disposed people so struck to the heart by the spectacles which the streets of this great city present, and still more by the dreadful spectacles they hide— they would gladly do anything to set those things right if they knew how. [*Hear, hear.*] In its extent and degree this is how. Set up and

[1] £6,000 was subscribed; and the freehold was purchased shortly afterwards.

maintain 500 beds, and it is positively certain that five times 5,000 human creatures will have laid their wretched heads upon them to recover or to die, within five years.

Oh! ladies and gentlemen. I cannot but think, in speaking of this hospital today, how little the poor need to be done for them, when all is said and done. I have spoken of beds. When we talk of beds we think of a well-appointed and long-established home—we think of a luxurious room, grown to be an old and dear companion—we think, perhaps, of a number of pretty rooms surrounding it, where we have watched our children sleeping from their cradles upward. The hospital bed is a poor little frame of iron, some four feet wide, in a great bare ward the patients never saw before—a little space not much larger than a grave, in a long perspective of unrest and pain.

But to the body stretched upon that little bed, come the ready hand, the soothing touch, the knowledge that can relieve pain within that suffering body; and to the softened mind within it come, at the best time, the words of the Great Friend of the sick in body, and the sick in spirit, who never raised His hand upon earth except to heal. [*Cheers.*]

Ladies and gentlemen, for His sake remember—for God's sake remember—these are the things that evoke the gratitude of the sick poor; these are the things which do men lasting good—these are the blessings we can bestow upon them, at so little cost to ourselves, and by which, after all, we bridge across that great gulf between their beds and ours as we all tend to that common road on which we must be equal travellers at last. Ladies and gentlemen, I beg to propose to you to drink,'Prosperity to the Royal Free Hospital'.

PRINTERS' PENSION SOCIETY

6 *April* 1864

THE anniversary festival was held at the London Tavern with Dickens in the Chair. There is apparently no report of the occasion except for an account of Dickens's main speech in which he said:

I DO not know whether my feelings are exceptional, but I have a distinct recollection (in my early days at school, when under the dominion of an old lady, who to my mind ruled the world with the birch) of feeling an intense disgust with printers and printing. I thought the letters were printed and sent there to plague me, and I looked upon the printer as my enemy. When I was taught to say my prayers I was told to pray for my enemies, and I distinctly remember praying especially for the printer as my greatest enemy. I never now see a row of large, black, fat, staring Roman capitals, but this reminiscence rises up before me. As time wore on, however, and I became interested in *Jack the Giant Killer*, and other story-books, this feeling of disgust became somewhat mitigated; and was still further removed when I became old enough to read *The Arabian Nights*, and *Robinson Crusoe* with his man Friday; in fact, from the savages enjoying their feast upon the beach, I believe I might trace my first impressions of a public dinner!

But this feeling of dislike to the printer altogether disappeared from the time I saw my own name in print. I now feel gratified at looking at the jolly letter O, the crooked S, with its full benevolent turns, the curious G, and the Q with its comical tail, that first awoke in me a sense of the humourous. The printer and myself are, and have been for some time, inseparable companions.

I have served three apprenticeships to life since I last presided over one of the festivals of this Society. It is twenty-one years since I have taken this chair. How many chairs have I taken since then? —In fact, I might say, a whole pantechnicon of chairs; and, in having worked my way round, I feel that I have come home again. My interest in the prosperity of the Society remains unabated. It has not been in existence forty years,[1] and it has accumulated a fund of £11,000, and has now seventy-six pensioners—male and female—on its funds, at an annual outlay of £850. It has done and is doing great good, and it is only to be regretted that the whole of the claimants on the charity cannot be taken under its charge.

The printer is a faithful servant, not only of those connected with the business, but of the public at large, and has, therefore, when labouring under infirmity or disease, an especial claim on all for support. Without claiming for him the whole merit of the work produced by his skill, labour, endurance, and intelligence; without it what would be the state of the world at large? Why, tyrants and humbugs in all countries would have everything their own way! I am certain there are not in any branch of manual dexterity so many remarkable men as might be found in the printing trade. For quickness of perception, amount of endurance, and willingness to oblige, I have ever found the compositor pre-eminent. His labour is of a nature calling for the sympathy of all. Often labouring under an avalanche of work, carried through half the night—often through the whole night—working in an unnatural and unwholesome atmosphere produced by artificial light, and exposed to sudden changes from heat to cold, the journeyman printer is rendered peculiarly liable to pulmonary complaints, blindness, and other serious dis-

[1] Founded 1827.

eases. The afflicted printer who has lost his sight in the service, sitting through long days in his one room, the pleasures of reading —his great source of entertainment—being denied him, his daughter or wife might read to him: but the cause of his misfortune would invade even that small solace of his dark seclusion, for the types from which that very book was printed, he might have assisted to set up. Is this an imaginary case? Nearly every printing office in London of any consideration has turned out numbers such. The public, therefore, in whose interest and for whose instruction and amusement the work was executed, are bound to support the Printers' Pension Society!

In connexion with this part of the subject I may mention two pleasing facts: my good friend Mr. Banting[1] who has incurred a certain amount of public ridicule for writing a pamphlet on the cure of corpulency, has presented the society with £52. 10s., being the present amount of profit received from the sale of this pamphlet. I can only say, if the society could find many friends like that, it would soon get fat. A Mr. Vincent, who had published some works, and whose interest in the welfare of the printer had originated entirely from the kind and ready assistance, the civility, and courtesy he had received during his business engagements at the office where his printing had been done, has signified his intention of bestowing upon the society house property in Liverpool of the annual rental of £150, from which there are to be created five pensions of £20, and the residue to go to the capital fund of the Society.

The chairman then went on to urge, in eloquent terms, the claims of the society, concluding as follows:

The tyrants and humbugs before referred to—and many tyrants and humbugs there were in Europe—would gladly pension off all the printers throughout the world and have done with them; but let the friends of education and progress unite in pensioning off the worn out and afflicted printers, and the remainder would ultimately press the tyrants and humbugs off the face of the earth. For if ever they were to be pressed out, the printer's is the press that will do it. The printer is the friend of intelligence, of thought; he is the friend of liberty, of freedom, of law; indeed, the printer is the friend of every man who is the friend of order; the friend of every man who can read. Of all inventions, of all the discoveries in science or art, of all the great results in the wonderful progress of mechanical energy and skill, the printer is the only product of civilization necessary to the existence of free man.

---

[1] William Banting (1797–1878), undertaker and author of *A Letter on Corpulency, addressed to the Public*, 1863, a highly successful treatise on slimming, written from personal experience. 'To bant' became a popular term.

UNIVERSITY COLLEGE HOSPITAL

12 *April* 1864

THE anniversary dinner was held at Willis's Rooms with Dickens in the Chair. The healths of the Queen, the Prince and Princess of Wales, and the rest of the royal family having been duly honoured, he said:

GENTLEMEN, On all other occasions of this nature 'The Army and Navy' have but to be named, and they are sure of evoking the general admiration and respect. But they have a special interest for a school of medicine, inasmuch as the medical officers of those two services, representing equally, as they do, the noblest studies of peace and the noblest humanities of war, are among their brightest ornaments. Further it may be observed that the better our public institutions for the recovery of the sick, so much the better and stouter is the stock of which our soldiers and sailors are made. This latter remark will apply with equal strength, though in a less degree, to that fine-spirited body, the Volunteers, of whose Muscular Christianity I avow myself a devoted admirer—holding, as I do, that muscular development of anything that is good is strong presumptive proof of soundness of condition. If the various corps of Volunteers had been enrolled in the 'school-days' of a certain youth with whom I believe we have all made acquaintance, I have little doubt that I should have found at the head of their list the name and title of Lieut.-Col. Tom Brown. As I have searched the list in vain for that name and title, and as I cannot, therefore, have the pleasure of coupling that name with the toast, I will, with your permission, substitute the name of Lieut.-Col. Thomas Hughes.[1] [*Loud cheers.*]

Hughes made an appropriate speech in reply; and Dickens went on to give the toast of the evening:

Gentlemen, My first remembrance of a certain spot in north-western London, which I have reason for recalling, is of a very un-inviting piece of wet waste ground, and a miserable pool of water; it looked rather like a barbarous place of execution, with its poles and cross-poles erected for the beating of carpets; and it was over-run with nettles and dock-weed. Associated with this place was a story, captivating enough to my boyish imagination, concerning the 'Field of the Forty Footsteps'; a part of the rank place so called, as I remember—and I remember it very distinctly now—because of a duel that was traditionally supposed to have been

---

[1] Thomas Hughes (1822–96), author of *Tom Brown's Schooldays*, 1857; barrister; and M.P., 1865–74; associate of F. D. Maurice and Charles Kingsley, in Christian socialist movement.

fought there between two brothers, one of whom, advancing upon
the other certain paces as he retreated, to wound him mortally, the
grass got trodden down by forty dreadful footsteps, upon which the
grass grew never more.[1] I remember to have gone, accompanied by
an adventurous young Englishman of my own age, about eleven,
with whom I had certain designs to seek my fortune in the neighbourhood of the Spanish Main, as soon as we should have accumulated forty shillings each and a rifle, which we never did [*laughter*],
I remember to have gone, accompanied by this young pirate, to
inspect this ground. I also remember to have counted forty places
on which the grass indubitably did not grow—though whether grass
grew anywhere thereabouts for a few feet together, without being
chequered with bald patches I will not say. [*Cheers and laughter.*]
This 'Field of Forty Footsteps' was close to the site on which was
afterwards built University College, and formed, generally, a part
of the open space of ground on which now stands University College
Hospital.

On looking over the papers this morning issued by this society
in illustration of the usefulness of its charity, I found the old story
so strangely changed, and yet with so odd a preservation of the
number four in it, that this field has become the field of 440,000 odd
footsteps. For I found that it is recorded here that 440,000 odd sick
and weary creatures—brothers too [*cheers*]—had taken refuge in
the hospital since its first foundation, thirty years ago. And so
humanely has the old unnatural story become transformed—much
as the brutes in other stories become transformed into men—that
the struggle through all those years has been against death, and
for the restoration of all those many brethren to life, enjoyment,
industry, and usefulness. [*Prolonged cheers.*]

Gentlemen, you already know, as well as I do, that it is the
cause of this Hospital that I have now to present to you, and that
it is its claim upon the gratitude and pride of all London—I will go
so far as to say of all England—that I have to urge upon your
generosity. That it is much in want, sorely in need of help, I think
I can make plain by the aid of as few figures as I have ever had to
deal with on an occasion of this nature. The annual expenditure of
the hospital is £6,000. Its annual income is not nearly half the

---

[1] The tale was traditional. A novel by Jane Porter was founded on it, *The
Field of Forty Footsteps*, 1828, which was also adapted, in more than one
version, for the stage. Authorities vary as to the exact site, but it was generally
described as 'in the fields behind Montague House'—the British Museum—
which were open ground up to the beginning of the nineteenth century.
Southey visited the field (*Common Place Book*, 2nd series, 1849, p. 20). The
Dickens family was then living in Camden Town, or a little later, in Gower St.,
which was nearer still.

money. And even of that insufficient income, almost one-half is derived from the noble generosity of its medical staff, who relinquish every year to the charity all the fees paid by the students for clinical instruction. [*Cheers.*] Thus there has to be got together every year, by the zealous administrators of the Hospital, no less a sum than £4,000 to supply the deficiency; and, emphatically, God knows how they do it! [*Cheers.*] But that it would seem that well-gotten money must sometimes come in, as people say ill-gotten money always goes out—no man can tell how—it would be absolutely impossible that this charity should continue to exist. [*Loud cheers.*] Add that there is a debt upon it, amounting in round numbers to the whole of a year's expenditure, and I believe that I have stated the case of its need quite as fully as if I had taken the whole night to state it in. Of course I know very well that the mere statement of need in such a case is no claim upon the public help. I know very well, as you all do here, and as the public outside do, that a very bad institution may be in want. [*Hear, hear, and laughter.*] Therefore I will proceed, as the main part of my duty, to the question of desert.

I will assume that everybody here has sufficiently considered what an immense amount of good may be done through such a means with a little money. I will assume that everybody here has reflected how narrow, how small, how insignificant is the space occupied by a single hospital-bed, yet over what a breadth of misery its relief and rest extend. So, passing at once to the claims of this institution, in its specialities on public support and aid, I think we may take them, for our present purpose, to be three.

The first is the least, because comprised within the narrowest limits, but it is, nevertheless, of immense importance to the charity. The Hospital is founded in a poor district, where no such institution previously existed, and which suddenly received a great access of population. That it is of unspeakable advantage to such a population cannot be doubted, as the local clergy and others best acquainted with the people there abundantly testify. But it is to be observed, that it is not founded in a specially and exclusively poor neighbourhood such as we may find in the eastern districts of London, but exists in a quarter in which there are many large houses, which are inhabited by people who are extremely well-to-do. If the occupants of those houses would subscribe only one guinea a year each to the Hospital, they would render to it incalculable assistance. And, surely, it has this special claim upon them, that if any workman or servant in their employment received an injury, the sufferer would be carried to this Hospital straight, as a matter of course, and would there have the best assistance; while the restoration of such sufferers to their suspended labour as speedily as possible must diminish the local rates.

The second speciality is a different one, because it appeals not only to the gratitude and support of north-western London, but to that of the whole country. I may take it for granted, for it is undoubted, that the establishment of the University College school of medicine has been of immense service to the cause of medical education all over England. [*Hear, hear.*] I may venture to say that this Hospital has been in its time a school for schools, and a hospital for hospitals, and that it has discharged cured many obstinate cases of almost chronic obstruction and general debility. That herein it has conferred immense benefit upon the community, and that the community in supporting it are only supporting their best interests, I suppose no reasonable creature can doubt.

The third speciality is a wider one still, and on that I lay even higher stress. And it is this—highly important in this time, and in all times. University College Hospital represents, if I understand it, the largest liberality of opinion. [*Cheers.*] It excludes no one— patient, student, doctor, surgeon, nurse—because of religious creed. It represents the completest relinquishment of claims to coerce the judgement or conscience of any human being. [*Cheers.*] It exacts professions from no one. It may hold, for anything I know, that the Lady Britannia, like the Lady Desdemona, 'doth protest too much'.[1] [*Cheers and laughter.*] But, in any case, it gives all that to the winds, to be blown whithersoever it may; perhaps to take refuge at last in the Hospital for Incurables. I say that, in consistently doing this, it renders, and has always rendered, an unspeakable service, by its influence and example, not only to the cause of medical education, but to the cause of general education. I feel perfectly convinced that the high reputation attained by this Hospital has been of immense service in calling public attention to University College. I cannot separate it in my own mind from the establishment of the London University, and the granting of degrees there. I will go further, and say that I think it no great stress of imagination to pursue the wholesome influences of this place even away into the Queen's Colleges of Ireland,[2] and at home again into the rubbed eyes and quickened steps of those famous old universities that we all admire.[3] [*Loud cheers.*]

[1] *Hamlet*, III. ii, the Player Queen not Desdemona.

[2] Belfast, Cork, and Galway, the secular 'Godless colleges', established 1845.

[3] There was a general movement for reform after the Royal Commision of 1850, and Act of 1854. More specifically, a Bill to abolish religious tests for those taking degrees at Oxford, was to pass its second reading on 16 Apr. 1864, only to be lost by two votes on the third reading on 1 July; they were not abolished until 1871.

Gentlemen, for all these reasons combined, I confidently submit to you that this University College Hospital holds a distinguished and exceptional position, and one that has been obtained in an equal degree by no other similar institution, however unimpeachable its benevolence. And I would beg to remind you of this fact, that it would not be easy to draw a line anywhere across the map of the world, and say, 'This is the geographical line beyond which this influence has not been extended.' Among the students of University College, there have been Parsees, and other native youths from the far East, who have been enabled to obtain medical education there owing to the absence of religious tests, and who have carried home to their countrymen the blessings derivable from their skill and knowledge. This liberality has been so appreciated by their own countrymen, that in one instance, a great Parsee merchant[1] presented the Hospital with a liberal donation, expressly to mark his high estimation of that liberality. [*Cheers.*] Also, among the students of University College there have been, as I perceive by looking at its records, men now distinguished in Calcutta, in Bombay, and elsewhere, for their attainments in botanical science, in medical science, and in natural science of all kinds. Also, I am delighted to find that there has been among the students of the University College Hospital, one gentlemen, at all events, who has wandered so far afield as the Celestial Empire, and has established there a hospital for the succour of the native Chinese. [*Cheers.*] Now, surely it is impossible to suppose that this seed can ever have fallen upon absolutely barren ground. Surely it is impossible to suppose that those things can fail to have suggested to the man a little above the average—the man everywhere to be found, however high his cheek-bones, however long his pigtail, however lithe his figure, however brown his colour, however complicated the folds of his turban, however sacred his river, of however intolerant his caste—it is impossible to suppose that those things can have failed to have suggested to such a man, that there must be something good in the Liberty which secures such results, and in that comprehensive religion, which, without distinction of creed or faith, permits this to be done.

Hence, gentlemen, it is that I present to you this Hospital for your serious consideration and your liberal support, as a Hospital whose salutary influences extend, and always have extended, far beyond its walls; as a Hospital that does good to the sound, no less than to the sick; as an institution that consistently enforces—alike in the public principles on which it takes its quiet stand, and in its daily practice at the bedsides of its poor patients—that practice is

[1] Sir Jamsetjee Jeejebhoy (1783–1859), merchant and philanthropist.

infinitely better than any amount of professions, and that those who have good gifts in charge cannot possibly make a better use of them, than by diffusing them unconditionally among the whole human family. Gentlemen, I beg to propose to you to drink 'Prosperity to University College Hospital'. [*Loud cheers.*]

The health of the chairman was proposed by John Marshall, F.R.S., and briefly acknowledged. Shirley Brooks[1] gave 'The President, Treasurer, Committee, and Auditors of University College Hospital', to which A. W. Jaffray, a member of the House Committee, replied. He spoke of the difficulty of tapping the 'great spring of benevolence', of the metropolis, which he likened to the 'vast bed of water which we are told underlies the whole of London. Pierce deep enough and it gushes forth in refreshing streams, mounts high into the air, and falls in fertilizing showers on the ground. In other instances, though the spring is tapped, it requires a powerful pump to bring it to the surface'. A general hospital, he thought, seemed to have less claim upon the public than a special one, though it was open to everyone, at all times, without restriction. Dickens replied:

Before I propose the toast which I have now in charge, allow me to say that I listened with great pleasure to Mr. Jaffray's excellent speech, until my mind seemed to misgive me that he was disposed to include me in his catalogue of 'powerful pumps'. I sincerely hope that you will bear testimony to this not being the case, and that you will prove it by coming to the surface with your money without this species of persuasion.

Now gentlemen, if anyone expressed a doubt to me about the high position of University College Hospital, or hesitated to place unbounded confidence in its treatment of the sick, I should content myself by simply referring him to its list of medical officers. Of the disinterestedness and generosity of those medical gentlemen I have already spoken. To their patience, to their unwearied attention, skill, humanity, and kindness, there are better witnesses than I am, and their name is Legion. No patient passes through this Hospital but carries out of doors his or her tale of pain relieved, disease cured, or casualty remedied, through the agency of these gentlemen. I need not remark to this company that these services, rendered without price, are above all price; and that these gentlemen are not only distinguished in the foremost ranks of their calling, but are foremost among the most generous members of the most generous profession known to civilization.

I have been requested by the managers of this dinner to couple with the toast of the medical officers, that benevolent body of

---

[1] Charles William Shirley Brooks (1816–74), journalist, dramatist, and miscellaneous writer; contributor to *Punch* from 1851, and editor, 1870-4; friend of Dickens.

Ladies who now act as nurses in the Hospital; and I have particularly been requested to convey to you the earnest assurance of the managers, that the vigilance, patience, and tenderness of those Ladies, combined with their undoubted qualification for the duties they have undertaken, have given to those who have had the best opportunity of observing them, the warmest satisfaction. Also, that they have in all things most honourably observed their pledge never in the least to interfere with the religious opinions of the patients. Gentlemen, I propose to you to drink 'The Medical Officers of the Hospital, and the Ladies of All Saints' Home, coupled with the name of Dr. Reynolds'.

Professor J. Russell Reynolds[1] acknowledged the toast on behalf of his colleagues and himself, and then of the Ladies of All Saints' Home, saying 'I remember the "Sairey Gamp" epoch of nursing that existed some years ago; the gin bottle was then in faithful attendance, and the night nurse sometimes managed her own pillows more comfortably than those of her patients. I know what we are blessed with now'. Dickens then said:

I have next to propose 'The health of the Chaplain of the Hospital, the Rev. Dr. Stebbing'.[2] I hope that I may be excused for saying that it is personally interesting to me to have an old fellow labourer in literature in so distinguished and responsible a position. Through more years than one cares to count at a festival, I have known Dr. Stebbing to have enriched the sounder literature of the time, with various contributions strongly expressive of his ability, his industry, and his learning. And so various has he been, that I should bestow here a word of eulogy upon his verse if I were not immediately jostled by the recollection of his prose papers in the *Cabinet Cyclopaedia*, and should recall the merits of his continuation of the *History of the Church*, if I were not divided between that and the merits of his *Italian Poets*. But sure I am, gentlemen, that the influence of these attainments upon so modest a nature and so good a man, must always tend to the advantage of his charges in the Hospital, and as I observe the wards themselves to have been recently brightened and humanized by some infusion of the arts, so I feel convinced that their occupants, who are the subjects of the Chaplain's gentle ministration, never find

---

[1] John Russell Reynolds (1828–96), Professor of the Principles and Practice of Medicine; President of the Royal College of Physicians, 1893–5; created baronet, 1895.

[2] Henry Stebbing (1799–1883), Rector of St. Mary Somerset and other city parishes; chaplain to the Hospital, 1834–79; poet, historian, and miscellaneous writer; author of the *Lives of the Italian Poets*, 1831, a *History of the Christian Church*, and many other works; contributor to, and for a time acting-editor of, the *Athenaeum*; knew Dickens.

it the less persuasive or the less consolatory, because of the graces of his mind.

Dr. Stebbing replied, paying a eulogistic tribute to the chairman, and going to speak in praise of the students of the hospital, adding that he hoped some gentleman at the head of the table would propose their health. Dickens at once rose, and said:

I immediately accept the duty suggested by my reverend friend, as one who has been a student, as one who knows the aspirations of a young and striving man, as one who has felt them, accompanied with that poverty which is the lot of many young men, as one who has attained to that success which is the lot of few. I beg to propose to you the health of the young and striving body, 'The Students of the University College Hospital'.

The chairman finally proposed the toast of 'The Ladies', which was duly honoured, and the proceedings were brought to a close.

MEETING FOR THE ESTABLISHMENT OF THE SHAKESPEARE FOUNDATION SCHOOLS

11 *May* 1864

A PUBLIC meeting in aid of the establishment of the Shakespeare Foundation Schools, in connexion with the Royal Dramatic College,[1] was held at the New Adelphi Theatre, with Dickens in the Chair. On coming forward he was loudly cheered, and said:

LADIES and Gentlemen, Fortunately for me, and fortunately for you, it is the duty of the chairman on an occasion of this nature, to be very careful that he does not anticipate those speakers who come after him. Like Falstaff, with a considerable difference, he has to be the cause of speaking in others. [*Laughter.*] It is rather his duty to sit and hear speeches with exemplary attention than to stand up and make them; so I shall confine myself, in opening these proceedings as your business official, to as plain and short an exposition as I can possibly give you of the reasons why we come together.

First of all I will take leave to remark that we do not come together in commemoration of Shakespeare. [*Hear, hear.*] We have nothing to do with any commemoration, except that we are of course humble worshippers of that mighty genius, and that we propose by-and-by to take his name, but by no means to take it in vain. [*Hear, hear.*] If, however, the Tercentenary celebration were a hundred years hence, or a hundred years past, we should

[1] See pp. 275 ff.

still be pursuing precisely the same object, though we could not pursue it under precisely the same circumstances. [*Hear.*] Well, then, the facts are these.—There is, as you know, in existence an admirable institution called the Royal Dramatic College, which is a place of honourable rest and repose for veterans in the dramatic art. The charter of this college, which dates some five or six years back, expressly provides for the establishment of schools in connexion with it; and I may venture to add that this feature of the scheme, when it was explained to him, was especially interesting to his Royal Highness the late Prince Consort, who hailed it as evidence of the desire of the promoters to look forward as well as to look back; to found educational establishments for the rising generation, as well as to establish a harbour of refuge for the generation going out, or at least having their faces turned towards the setting sun. [*Cheers.*] The leading members of the dramatic art, applying themselves first to the more pressing necessity of the two, set themselves to work on the construction of their harbour of refuge, and this they did with the zeal, energy, good-will, and good faith that always honourably distinguish them in their efforts to help one another. [*Hear, hear.*] Those efforts were very powerfully aided by the respected gentleman under whose roof we are assembled [*cheers*], and who, I hope, may be only half as glad of seeing me on these boards as I always am to see him there. [*Cheers.*] With such energy and determination did Mr. Webster and his brothers and sisters in art proceed with their work, that at this present time all the dwelling-houses of the Royal Dramatic College are built, completely furnished, fitted with every appliance, and many of them inhabited. The central hall of the College is built, the grounds are beautifully planned and laid out, and the estate has become the nucleus of a prosperous neighbourhood.

This much achieved, Mr. Webster was revolving in his mind how he should next proceed towards the establishment of the schools when, this Tercentenary celebration being in hand, it occurred to him to represent to the National Shakespeare Committee their just and reasonable claim to participate in the results of any subscription for a monument to Shakespeare. He represented to the committee that the social recognition and elevation of the followers of Shakespeare's own art, through the education of their children, was surely a monument worthy even of that great name. He urged upon the committee that it was certainly a sensible, tangible project, which the public good sense would immediately appreciate and approve. This claim the committee at once acknowledged; but I wish you distinctly to understand that if the committee had never been in existence, if the Tercentenary celebration had never been attempted, those schools, as a design anterior to both, would still have solicited public support.

Now, ladies and gentlemen, what it is proposed to do is, in fact, to found a new self-supporting public school; with this additional feature, that it is to be available for both sexes. This, of course, pre-supposes two separate distinct schools. As these schools are to be built on land belonging to the Dramatic College, there will be from the first no charge, no debt, no incumbrance of any kind under that important head. It is, in short, proposed simply to establish a new self-supporting public school, in a rapidly increasing neighbour-hood, where there is a large and fast accumulating middle-class population, and where property in land is fast rising in value. But, inasmuch as the project is a project of the Royal Dramatic College, and inasmuch as the schools are to be built on their estate, it is pro-posed evermore to give the followers of Shakespeare's art a prominent place in them. [*Cheers.*] With this view, it is confidently believed that the public will endow a foundation, say, for forty foundation scholars—say, twenty girls and twenty boys—who shall always receive their education gratuitously, and who shall always be the children of actors, actresses, or dramatic writers. This school, you will understand, is to be equal to the best existing public school. It is to be made to impart a sound, liberal, comprehensive educa-tion, and it is to address the whole great middle class at least as freely, as widely, and as cheaply as any existing public school.

Broadly, ladies and gentlemen, this is the whole design. There are foundation scholars at Eton, foundation scholars at most or all our old schools, and if the public, in remembrance of a noble part of our standard national literature, and in remembrance of a great human-izing art, will do this thing for these children, it will at the same time be doing a wise and good thing for itself, and will unquestion-ably find its account in it. Taking this view of the case—and I cannot be satisfied to take any lower one—I cannot make a sorry face about 'the poor player'. I think it is a term very much misused and very little understood, being I venture to say appropriated in a wrong sense by the players themselves. Therefore, ladies and gentlemen, I can only present the player to you exceptionally in this wise: that he follows a peculiar and precarious vocation, a vocation very rarely affording the means of accumulating money; that that vocation must, from the nature of things, have in it many undistinguished men and women to one distinguished one; that it is not a vocation the exerciser of which can profit by the labours of others, but in which he must earn every loaf of his bread in his own person, with the aid of his own face, his own limbs, his own voice, his own memory, and his own life and spirits; and these failing, he fails. [*Hear.*] Surely this is reason enough to render him some little help in opening for his children their paths through life. I say their paths advisedly, because it is not often found, except under the pressure of necessity, or where there is strong hereditary talent—which is always an exceptional case—that the children of actors and actresses take to the stage. Persons, therefore, need not in the least fear that by helping to endow these schools they would help to overstock the dramatic market. They would do directly the reverse, for they would divert into channels of public distinction and usefulness those good qualities which would otherwise languish in that market's over rich superabundance.

This project has received the support of the head of the most popular of our English public schools. On the committee stands the name of that eminent scholar and gentleman, the Provost of Eton. [*Cheers.*] You justly admire this liberal spirit, and your admiration—which I cordially share—brings me naturally to what I wish to say, that I believe there is not in England any institution so socially liberal as a public school. [*Hear.*] It has been called a little cosmos of life outside, and I think it is so, with the exception of one of life's worst foibles—for, as far as I know, nowhere in this country is there so complete an absence of servility to mere rank, to mere position, to mere riches as in a public school. A boy there is always what his abilities or his personal qualities make him. We may differ about the curriculum and other matters, but of the frank, free, manly, independent spirit preserved in our public schools, I apprehend there can be no kind of question. It has happened in these latter times that objection has been made to children of dramatic artists in certain little snivelling private schools [*laughter*], but in public schools never. [*Cheers.*] Therefore, I hold that the actors are wise, and gratefully wise, in recognizing the capacious liberality of a public school, in seeking not a little hole-and-corner place of education for their children exclusively, but in addressing the whole of the great middle class, and proposing to them to come and join them, the actors, on their own property, in a public school, in a part of the country where no such advantage is now to be found. [*Hear.*]

I have now done. The attempt has been a very timid one. I have endeavoured to confine myself within my means, or, rather, like the possessor of an extended estate, to hand it down in an unembarrassed condition. [*Cheers.*] I have laid a trifle of timber here and there, and grubbed up a little brushwood, but merely to open the view, and I think I can descry in the eye of the gentleman who is to move the first resolution that he distinctly sees his way. Thanking you for the courtesy with which you have heard me, and not at all doubting that we shall lay a strong foundation of these schools today, I will call, as the mover of the first resolution, on Mr. Robert Bell. [*Cheers.*]

Various resolutions were passed, and various other speakers followed including Anthony Trollope, Tom Taylor, J. B. Buckstone, and Benjamin Webster. Webster was elected treasurer, and members of a committee were appointed which included Dickens and the Rev. Dr. Godfrey, Provost of Eton.

The proceedings closed with a vote of thanks to the chairman, moved by Edmund Yates. Dickens replied:

As master of the school now breaking up, I am very happy to dismiss you for a holiday. I beg to assure my young friends that their patient and unremitting attention to their studies has afforded me the liveliest satisfaction. [*Cheers.*]

How far these plans were carried into effect is obscure. The Dramatic College itself was officially opened by the Prince of Wales on 5 June 1865, and was dissolved in 1877.

NEWSVENDORS' BENEVOLENT INSTITUTION

9 *May* 1865

THE dinner was held at the Freemasons' Tavern, with Dickens in the Chair. Also present were W. H. Wills, Edmund Yates, and James Grant, editor of the *Morning Advertiser*. The cloth having been removed, the chairman proposed the health of Her Majesty the Queen. In doing so he congratulated the company on having abolished the absurd Salic law which prohibited the presence of ladies on occasions like the present, when it was particularly acceptable as tending to exert a beneficial influence in favour of the objects of the gathering. The toast was received with enthusiastic applause; after which others briefly followed to the 'Prince and Princess of Wales and the rest of the Royal Family', and the 'Army, Navy, and Volunteers'. The chairman then rose, and said:

LADIES and Gentlemen, Dr. Johnson's experience of that club, the members of which had travelled over one another's minds in every direction,[1] is not to be compared with the experience of the perpetual President of a society like this [*cheers and laughter*], who, having on previous occasions said everything about it that he could possibly find to say, is again produced, with the usual awful

[1] James Boswell, *Life*, ed. A. B. Hill rev. L. F. Powell, 1934, IV, 183, 'Dr. Goldsmith once said to Dr. Johnson, that he wished for some additional members to the LITERARY CLUB, to give it an agreeable variety; for (said he), there can be nothing new among us: we have travelled over one another's minds. Johnson seemed a little angry, and said, "Sir, you have not travelled over *my* mind, I promise you." '

solemnities, to say anything about it that he can *not* possibly find
to say. It struck me, when Dr. Frederick Jones[1] was referring just now
to Easter Monday, that the case of such an ill-starred President is
very like that of the stag at the Epping Hunt on Easter Monday.
The unfortunate animal, when he is uncarted at the tavern where
the meet comes off, generally makes away, I am told, at a cool trot,
venturesomely followed by the whole field, to the yard where he
lives, and there subsides into a quiet inoffensive existence, until
he is again brought out, to be again followed by exactly the same
field, over exactly the same ground, under exactly the same circumstances, next Easter Monday. [*Laughter.*]

Ladies and gentlemen, the difficulties of the situation—and here
I mean the President's and not the stag's—are greatly increased in
such an instance as this by the peculiar nature of the institution.
In its unpretending solidity, reality, and usefulness, believe me—
for I have carefully considered the point—it presents no opening
whatever of an oratorical nature. If it were one of those costly
charities, so-called, whose yield of wool bears no sort of proportion
to their cry for cash, I very likely might have a word or two to say
on the subject. If its funds were lavished on patronage and show,
instead of being honestly expended in providing small annuities
for hard-working people who have themselves contributed to its
funds; if its management were entrusted to people who could by
no possibility know anything about it, instead of being invested in
plain, practical, business hands; if it hoarded when it ought to spend,
and if it got by cringing and fawning what it never deserved, I might
possibly impress you with my indignation. If the managers could
tell me that it was insolvent, that it was in a hopeless condition,
that its accounts had been kept by Mr. Edmunds [*roars of laughter*],
or by 'Tom'[2] [*renewed laughter*], or if its treasurer had only done
me the favour of running away with the money-box, then I might
have made a pathetic appeal to your feelings. But I have no such
chance. And just as the nation is happy whose records are barren,
so is the society fortunate that has no history, and its President
unfortunate. I can only assure you that our institution continues
its plain, unobtrusive, useful career, and that the objects of its care
and the bulk of its members are faithful hard-working servants of
the public, who minister to their wants at untimely hours, in all
seasons, and in all weathers; at their own doors, at the street corners,

---

[1] He had replied to the toast of the 'Army, Navy, and Volunteers'.

[2] 'The Edmunds case', which concerned a member of the Patent Office who
had embezzled a large sum—with the help of Thomas Ruscoe a clerk—was a
recent official scandal. Lord Brougham, and the Lord Chancellor, were both
implicated, and a Committee of Peers had been appointed to consider the case,
which had just issued a report.

at every railway train, at every steam-boat; equally through the agency of enormous establishments and the tiniest little shops; and that whether regarded as master or regarded as man, their profits are very modest and their risks numerous, while their trouble and responsibility are very great.

The newsvendors and newsmen are no doubt a very subordinate part of that wonderful engine, the Newspaper Press; but I think we all know very well that they are to the fountain-head what a good service of water pipes is to a good water-supply. Just as a goodly store of water, say at Watford, would be a mere tantilization to thirsty London if it were not brought hither and skilfully laid on, so would any amount of news accumulated at Printing House Square, or Fleet Street, or the Strand, be a mere mockery of the public impatience if there were no skill and enterprise engaged in its dissemination. [*Hear, hear.*]

We are all of us in the habit of saying in our everyday life, that 'we never know the value of anything until we lose it'. Try the newsvendors by that test. A few years ago we discovered one morning that there was a strike of cab-drivers in London. Now, let us imagine a similar strike of newsmen. [*Hear, hear, and laughter.*] Imagine all the morning trains waiting in vain for all the newspapers. Imagine all sorts and conditions of men dying to know the shipping news, the commercial news, the legal news, the criminal news, the foreign news and domestic news [*hear, hear*]—paralysis on all the provincial exchanges, the silence and desertion on the newsmen's exchange in London, the circulation of the blood of the country standing still, the clock of the world stopped! Why, even Mr. Reuter, the great Reuter whom I am always glad to imagine slumbering at night by the side of Mrs. Reuter, with a galvanic battery under the bolster, telegraph wires to the head of his bed, and an electric bell at each ear [*roars of laughter*] even he would click and flash those wondrous dispatches of his to little purpose, if it were not for the humble, and by comparison, slow activity, which gathers up the stitches of the electric needle, and scatters them over the land. [*Cheers.*]

It is curious to consider—and the thought occurred to me today, when I was out for a stroll pondering over the duties of this evening, then looming in the distance, and, to confess the honest truth, not half so far off in the distance as I could have desired—I found it very curious to consider that though the newsman must be allowed to be a very unpicturesque rendering of Mercury, or Fame, or whatnot conventional messenger from the clouds, and although we must allow that he is of this earth, and often has a great deal of it on his boots, poor fellow [*laughter*], still that he has two very remarkable characteristics to which none of his celestial predecessors can lay the slightest claims. One is that he is always the messenger of civilization; the other, that he is at least equally so not only in what he brings, but in what he ceases to bring. The time was, and not so many years ago either, when the newsman constantly brought home to our doors (though I am afraid not to our hearts, which were custom-hardened then) the most terrific accounts of numbers of our fellow creatures being publicly put to death for what we should now call trivial offences, in the very heart of London, regularly every Monday morning. In the same times the newsmen regularly brought to us accounts of other savage punishments, which were demoralizing to the innocent parts of the community, while they did not operate as punishments in deterring offenders from the perpetration of crime. In the same times also, the newsman brought to us daily accounts of a regularly accepted and received system of loading the unfortunate insane with chains, littering them down on straw, starving them on bread and water, denying them their clothes, soothing them under their tremendous affliction with the whip, and making periodical exhibitions of them at a small charge, rendering our public asylums a kind of demoniacal Zoological Gardens. He brought us constant accounts of the destruction of machinery which was destined to supply unborn millions with employment. In the same times he brought us accounts of riots for bread, which were constantly occurring and undermining the State, of the most terrible animosity of class against class, and of the habitual employment of spies for the discovery, if not for the organization of plots, in which that animosity on both sides found in those days some relief. In the same times the same newsmen were apprising us of the state of society all around us in which the grossest sensuality and intemperance were the rule, and not as now the ignorant, the wicked, or inexcusably vicious exception—a state of society in which the professional bully was rampant, and in which the deadliest of duels were daily fought for the absurdest and most disgraceful causes. All this the newsman has ceased to tell us. This state of society has discontinued in England for ever. And when we remember the undoubted truth, that the change could never, never, never have been effected without the aid of the load the newsman bears, surely it is not very romantic to claim for him from the public some little token of that sympathetic remembrance which we are all of us so glad to bestow on the messengers of good news and the bearers of blessed tidings. [*Cheers.*]

Now, ladies and gentlemen, you will be glad to hear that I am coming to a conclusion; and for the conclusion I have a familiar precedent. You all of you know how often it happens when you have been away from home for a short excursion, that you find on your return a delicate intimation that 'the collector has called'. Well, ladies and gentlemen, I am the collector for this district, and I hope that you will bear in mind, coming back from the excursion into which I have betrayed you, that I have respectfully called. [*Hear, and laughter.*]

Regarding the institution on whose behalf I have presented myself, I need only say technically two things. First, that its annuities are granted out of the interest on its funded capital, and that therefore it is literally as safe as the Bank; and, secondly, they are attainable by such a slight exercise of prudence and foresight, that a payment of twenty-five shillings extending over a period of five years, entitles a subscriber if a male to an annuity of sixteen pounds a year, and if a female to one of twelve pounds. Pray bear in mind that this is the plain, practical institution on behalf of which the collector has called, leaving behind him the assurance that what you can give to one of the most faithful of your servants, will be thoroughly well bestowed, and faithfully applied to the purposes which you intend to further, and to those purposes alone. [*Loud cheers.*]

Dickens was followed by James Grant,[1] speaking in reply to the toast of 'The Press', who mentioned his pleasure at the presence of the chairman:

They had commenced their careers in connection with the Press at the same time, many years ago—how many he, for his own sake, would not like to mention. They had also some time after commenced their careers as authors, though Mr. Dickens had in the course of a few years so far outdistanced him . . . as to be entirely out of sight.

There were a few remaining toasts to follow, including one to Dickens, as the president, proposed by Edmund Yates, when Dickens showed his great presence of mind. Although the reporters took no notice of it, Yates recalled the occasion in his *Recollections*:

. . . I was so much in the habit of going with him to public dinners, and the managers of those entertainments so frequently begged me to propose his health as chairman, that it became a joke . . . as to whether I could possibly find anything new to say. On one occasion—it was at one of the Newsvendors' dinners—I said nothing at all. I duly rose, but, after a few words, my thoughts entirely deserted me, I entirely lost the thread of what I had intended saying, I felt as though a black veil were dropped over my head; all I could do was to mutter 'health,' 'chairman,' and to sit down. I was tolerably well known to the guests at these dinners and they were evidently much astonished. They cheered the toast, as in duty bound, and Dickens was on on his feet in a

---

[1] James Grant (1802–79), editor of the *Morning Advertiser*, 1850–71; he had left the reporting staff of the *Morning Chronicle* just as Dickens joined it, in Aug. 1834, and as editor of the *Monthly Magazine*, in 1836, had unsuccessfully tried to get Dickens to contribute further 'Sketches',

moment. 'Often,' he said, 'often as I have had the pleasure of having my health proposed by my friend, who has just sat down, I have never yet seen him so overcome by his affection and generous emotion as on the present occasion.' These words turned what would have been a fiasco into a triumph. 'I saved you that time, I think, sir!' he said to me as I walked away with him. 'Serves you well right for being over-confident.'[1]

THE NEWSPAPER PRESS FUND

20 *May* 1865

THE Newspaper Press Fund had been originated by the Parliamentary reporters of the London Press, at a meeting of 25 June 1858, but had failed to prosper as a self-supporting body. It was reconstituted in 1864, and held its first anniversary festival on 21 May under the presidency of Lord Houghton. It was then announced that, among many others, a letter of apology regretting his inability to attend had been received from Charles Dickens. His was, however, one of a distinguished collection of Vice-Presidents including Disraeli, Froude, Charles Reade, Tennyson, Trollope, and Tupper.

Several of these were present at the second anniversary dinner of the society, which was held next year at the Freemasons' Tavern, with Dickens in the Chair. After its initial difficulties, and in spite of the continued opposition of *The Times*, it was clear that the institution was now fairly established.

When the cloth had been removed, the chairman briefly gave the usual loyal toasts, which were duly honoured, and then rose to propose the 'Army, Navy, and Volunteers', and said:

IT is one of the characteristics of our English army and navy that we never hear of great deeds done in those famous services from the lips of the doers. [*Cheers.*] But happily the great independence and enterprise of our newspaper press, and the bolder and more brilliant the describers who write in it, the better the country learns what her heroes deserve, and the prouder she becomes to hold them in her love and honour. I cannot offer you the toast now in my hands, without begging your serious attention to a suppositious case in the French army. It is the case of a young man who enlisted in the ranks of what we would call the Scots Fusilier Guards. He was a sergeant in the Crimea, and at Inkerman displayed such notable gallantry that he received at the hands of his sovereign a commission in what we would call the Rifle Brigade, as what we should call a lieutenant in that distinguished corps. He volunteered to lead the ladder party in that famous unsuccessful attack on the Redan. While binding up a fellow officer's wounds he was so severely shot in the left arm that the surgeon found it necessary immediately

---

[1] *Recollections and Experiences*, 1884, ii, 111-12.

to remove it from the socket. He was so little discomposed or disabled by its loss, that he presently took what we should call a first-class certificate as instructor of musketry at Hythe. He was afterwards nominated to a company by what we should call the Prince Consort [*hear, hear*], and received a staff appointment abroad from what we should call the Duke of Cambridge. [*A laugh.*] And all these things took place in fifteen years.

Now I am proud to tell you that this is not a suppositious case in the French army, but a real case in the English army. [*Cheers.*] That British officer wears the Victoria Cross, and he is seated at this board today.[1] The toast I propose is 'The Army, Navy, and Volunteers'; with the first clause of it I beg to couple the distinguished name of Sir John Boileau,[2] with the second Admiral Burney, and with the third Lord Truro.

The toast was drunk with loud cheering; and having been acknowledged, Dickens rose and said:

Ladies and Gentlemen, When a young child is produced after dinner to be shown to a circle of admiring relations and friends, it may generally be observed that their conversation—I suppose in an instinctive remembrance of the uncertainty of infant life—takes a retrospective turn. As how much the child has grown since the last dinner; what a remarkably fine child it is, to have been born only two or three years ago, how much stronger it looks now than before it had the measles, and so forth. When a young institution is produced after dinner, there is not the same uncertainty or delicacy as in the case of the child, and it may be confidently predicted of it that if it deserve to live it will surely live, and that if it deserve to die it will surely die. The proof of desert in such a case as this must be mainly sought, I suppose, firstly, in what the society means to do with its money; secondly, in the extent to which it is supported by the class with whom it originated, and for whose benefit it is designed; and lastly, in the power of its hold upon the public. [*Hear, hear.*] I add this, lastly, because no such institution that I ever heard of ever yet dreamed of existing apart from the public, or ever yet considered it a degradation to accept the public support. [*Hear, hear, and cheers.*]

Now, what the Newspaper Press Fund proposes to do with its money is to grant relief to members in want or distress, and to the widows, families, parents, or other near relatives of deceased members, in right of a certain moderate annual subscription—commutable, I observe, for a moderate provident life subscription—and

---

[1] Major John Simpson Knox.
[2] Major-General Sir John Theophilus Boileau (1805–86).

its members comprise the whole paid class of literary contributors to the Press of the United Kingdom, and every class of reporters. The number of its members at this time last year was something below 100. At the present time it is somewhat above 170, not including 30 members of the Press who are regular subscribers, but have not as yet qualified as regular members. This number is steadily on the increase, not only as regards the metropolitan Press, but also as regards the provincial throughout the country. I have observed within these few days that many members of the Press at Manchester have lately at a meeting expressed a strong brotherly interest in this institution, and a great desire to extend its operations, and to strengthen its hands, provided that something in the independent nature of life assurance and the purchase of deferred annuities could be introduced into its details, and always assuming that in it the metropolis and the provinces stand on perfectly equal ground. [*Hear, hear, and cheers.*] This appears to me to be a demand so very moderate, that I can hardly have a doubt of a response on the part of the managers, or of the beneficial and harmonious results. [*Hear, hear.*] It only remains to add, on this head of desert, the agreeable circumstance that out of all the money collected in aid of the society during the last year more than one third came exclusively from the Press. [*Hear, hear, and cheers.*]

Now, ladies and gentlemen, in regard to the last claim—the last point of desert, the hold upon the public—I think I may say that probably not one single individual in this great company has failed today to see a newspaper, or has failed today to hear something derived from a newspaper which was quite unknown to him or her yesterday. [*Hear, hear.*] Of all those restless crowds that have this day thronged through the streets of this enormous city, the same may be said as the general gigantic rule. [*Hear, hear.*] It may be said almost equally of the brightest and the dullest, the largest and the least provincial town in the empire; and this, observe, not only as to the active, the industrious, and the healthy among the population, but also to the bedridden, the idle, the blind, and the deaf and dumb. [*Hear, hear.*] Now, if the men who provide this all-pervading presence, this wonderful ubiquitous newspaper, with every description of intelligence on every subject of human interest, collected with immense pains and immense patience, often by the exercise of a laboriously acquired faculty united to a natural aptitude, much of the work done in the night at the sacrifice of rest and sleep, and (quite apart from the mental strain) by the constant overtasking of the two most delicate of the senses, sight and hearing—I say, if the men who, through the newspapers, from day to day, or from night to night, or from week to week, furnish the public with so much to remember, have not a righteous claim to be remembered by the public in return, then I declare before God I know no working class of the community who have. [*Loud cheers.*]

It would be absurd, it would be actually impertinent in such an assembly as this, if I were to attempt to expatiate upon the extraordinary combination of remarkable qualities involved in the production of any newspaper. But assuming the majority of this associated body to be composed of reporters, because reporters, of one kind or another, compose the majority of the literary staff of almost every newspaper that is not a compilation. I would venture to remind you, if I delicately may, in the august presence of members of Parliament, how much we, the public, owe to the reporters, if it were only for their skill in the two great successes of condensation and rejection. [*Laughter and loud cheering.*] Conceive what our sufferings, under an Imperial Parliament however popularly constituted, under however glorious a constitution, would be if the reporters could not skip. [*Much laughter.*] Dr. Johnson, in one of his violent assertions, declared that 'the man who was afraid of anything must be a scoundrel, sir'. By no means binding myself to this opinion—though admitting that the man who is afraid of a newspaper will generally be found to be something like it—I still must freely own that I should approach my Parliamentary debate with infinite fear and trembling if it were so unskilfully served up for my breakfast. [*Laughter.*] Ever since the time when the old man and his son took their donkey home, which were the old Greek days, I believe, and probably ever since the time when the donkey went into the ark (perhaps he did not like the accommodation there), but certainly from that time downwards, he has objected to go in any direction required of him [*laughter*]—from the remotest periods it has been found impossible to please everybody. [*Hear, hear.*]

I do not for a moment seek to conceal that I know this institution has been objected to. As an open fact challenging the freest discussion and inquiry, and seeking no sort of shelter or favour but what it can win, it has nothing, I apprehend, but itself to urge against objection. No institution conceived in perfect honesty and good faith has a right to object to being questioned to any extent, and any institution so based must in the end be the better for it. [*Hear, hear.*] Moreover that this society has been questioned in quarters deserving of the most respectful attention, I take to be an indisputable fact. Now, I for one have given that respectful attention, and I have come out of the discussion to where you see me. [*Cheers.*] The whole circle of arts is pervaded by institutions between which and this I can descry no difference. The painter's art has four or five such institutions. The musician's art, so generously and so charmingly represented here, has likewise several such institutions. In my own art there is one, concerning the details of which my noble friend the President of the society and myself have torn each other's hair to a considerable extent, and which I would, if I could, assimilate more nearly to this. [*Laughter.*] In the dramatic art there are four, and I never heard of any objection to their principle, except, indeed, in the cases of some famous actors of large gains, who having through the whole period of their successes positively refused to establish a right in them, became, in their old age and decline, repentant suppliants for their bounty. [*Hear, hear.*]

Is it urged against this particular institution that it is objectionable because a parliamentary reporter, for instance, might report a subscribing M.P. in large, and a non-subscribing M.P. in little? [*Laughter.*] Apart from the sweeping nature of this charge, which it is to be observed lays the unfortunate member and the unfortunate reporter under pretty much the same suspicion—apart from this consideration, I reply that it is notorious in all newspaper offices that every such man is reported according to the position he can gain in the public eye, and according to the force and weight of what he has to say. [*Cheers.*] And if there were ever to be among the members of this society one so very foolish to his brethren, and so very dishonourable to himself, as venally to abuse his trust, I confidently ask those here, the best acquainted with journalism, whether they believe it possible that any newspaper so ill conducted as to fail instantly to detect him could possibly exist as a thriving enterprise for one single twelvemonth? [*Loud cheers.*] No, ladies and gentlemen, the blundering stupidity of such an offence would have no chance against the acute sagacity of newspaper editors. But I will go further, and submit to you that its commission, if it be to be dreaded at all, is far more likely on the part of some recreant camp-follower of a scattered, disunited, and half-recognized profession, than where there is a public opinion established in it, by the union of all classes of its members for the common good: the tendency of which union must in the nature of things be to raise the lower members of the Press towards the higher, and never to bring the higher members to the lower level. [*Cheers.*]

I hope I may be allowed, in the very few closing words that I feel a desire to say in remembrance of some circumstances rather special attending my present occupation of this chair, to give these words something of a personal tone. I am not here advocating the case of a mere ordinary client of whom I have little or no knowledge. I hold a brief tonight for my brothers. [*Loud and continued cheering.*] I went into the gallery of the House of Commons as a Parliamentary

¹ Royal Literary Fund.

reporter when I was a boy not eighteen, and I left it—I can hardly
believe the inexorable truth—nigh thirty years ago.[1] I have pursued the calling of a reporter under circumstances of which many of
my brethren at home in England here, many of my modern succes-
sors, can form no adequate conception. I have often transcribed for
the printer from my shorthand notes, important public speeches in
which the strictest accuracy was required, and a mistake in which
would have been to a young man severely compromising, writing on
the palm of my hand, by the light of a dark lantern, in a post chaise
and four, galloping through a wild country, all through the dead of
night, at the then surprising rate of fifteen miles an hour. The very
last time I was at Exeter, I strolled into the Castle Yard there to
identify, for the amusement of a friend, the spot on which I once
'took', as we used to call it, an election speech of my noble friend
Lord Russell,[2] in the midst of a lively fight maintained by all the
vagabonds in that division of the county, and under such a pelting
rain, that I remember two good-natured colleagues, who chanced to
be at leisure, held a pocket handkerchief over my notebook after the
manner of a state canopy in an ecclesiastical procession. [*Laughter.*]
I have worn my knees by writing on them on the old back row of the
old gallery of the old House of Commons; and I have worn my feet
by standing to write in a preposterous pen in the old House of Lords,
where we used to be huddled together like so many sheep [*laughter*],
kept in waiting, say, until the woolsack might want re-stuffing. [*A
laugh.*] I have been, in my time, belated on miry by-roads, towards
the small hours, in a wheelless carriage, with exhausted horses and
drunken postboys, and have got back in time for publication, to be
received with never-forgotten compliments by the late Mr. Black,[3]
coming in the broadest of Scotch from the broadest of hearts I ever
knew. [*Hear, hear.*]

Ladies and gentlemen, I mention these trivial things as an assurance to you that I have never forgotten the fascination of that old
pursuit. [*Cheers.*] The pleasure that I used to feel in the rapidity and
dexterity of its exercise has never faded out of my breast. Whatever
little cunning of hand or head I took to it, or acquired in it, I have so
retained as that I fully believe I could resume it tomorrow, very

[1] Precisely when Dickens began reporting in the gallery is unknown, but he
seems quite certain himself that it was some time before Feb. 1830. His
reporting in the country was undertaken when he was on the staff of the
Morning Chronicle, to which he belonged from Aug. 1834 to Nov. 1836.

[2] 1 May 1835.

[3] John Black (1783–1855), editor of the *Morning Chronicle*, 1817–40; he
encouraged Dickens to be an author, as well as a reporter—Dickens called
Black, 'my first hearty out-and-out appreciator', while Black said of Dickens,
'Keep "Boz" in reserve for great occasions. He will *aye* be ready for them.'

little the worse from long disuse. [*Cheers.*] To this present year of my life, when I sit in this hall, or where not, hearing a dull speech—the phenomenon does occur—I sometimes beguile the tedium of the moment by mentally following the speaker in the old way; and sometimes, if you can believe me, I even find my hand going on the table cloth, taking an imaginary note of it all. [*Laughter.*] Accept these little truths as a confirmation of what I know; as a confirmation of my undying interest in this old calling. Accept them as a proof that my feeling for the vocation of my youth is not a sentiment taken up tonight to be thrown away tomorrow [*hear, hear*], but is a faithful sympathy which is a part of myself. [*Cheers.*] I verily believe—I am sure—that if I had never quitted my old calling I should have been foremost and zealous in the interests of this institution, believing it to be a sound, a wholesome, and a good one. Ladies and gentlemen, I am to propose to you to drink 'Prosperity to the Newspaper Press Fund', with which toast I will connect, as to its acknowledgement, a name that has shed new brilliancy on even the foremost newspaper in the world—the illustrious name of Mr. Russell.[1] [*Loud cheers.*]

Russell then replied. In spite of his connexion with *The Times*, he was a keen supporter of the Fund. He briefly referred to its opposition, saying 'you may be aware that a voice of support and encouragement may not be expected to come from the resorts to which I have been accustomed'. He went on to propose the health of the chairman, and said:

. . . I find I have no words in which I could express the regard which I feel for Mr. Dickens personally, and the admiration which everyone who reads the English language must entertain for his genius. [*Cheers.*] But we can all appreciate the incessant and untiring diligence with which, in hours stolen from labours which are to delight every reader of the English tongue, he devotes himself to the cause of philanthropy and the advancement of every society which deserves the assistance of humane and honest men. [*Renewed cheers.*]

Dickens spoke briefly in acknowledgement. Other speakers who followed, included Lord Truro and Spencer Walpole, who responded to the toast of 'The Houses of Parliament'. After proposing the healths of 'The Vocalists', and 'The Ladies', Dickens left the Chair and the company separated.

Writing to Russell, a few days later, he referred to the dinner and an incident which occurred towards the end of the evening:

The dirty-faced man (it must have been the same, because there cannot have been two men, each so dirty-faced) was beset by an idea, after I vacated the chair, that I had lost something. He tried to articulate a sentence to the effect that whatever I had lost, should be instantly found. At that period he was supported by an angle between two doors, and his shirt-front had the appearance of having been clutched by waiters in personal strife. I think he must have confounded me with himself, and that he had lost his senses in making the preliminary arrangements.[2]

The dinner seems to have been, in every way, a great success.

[1] See p. 245 n.　　　　　　　　　　　　　　[2] 26 May 1865.

AFTER THE OPENING OF THE GUILD HOUSES: KNEBWORTH

29 *July* 1865

AFTER having raised a fund of about £4,000, the members of the Guild found that according to the Act of Parliament by which they were incorporated in 1854 they were unable to make any use of the money for seven years. The society never really recovered from the blow. But in 1861 interest revived again, the constitution was revised, and on renewal of Sir Edward Bulwer Lytton's offer of a few acres of land on his estate in Hertfordshire, it was decided to proceed with the plan of erecting houses for retired artists and authors which they might be granted free of rent. The houses were duly built; and it was arranged that there should be an excursion to inspect them, by members of the Guild, combined with a visit to Knebworth at the invitation of Sir Edward Bulwer Lytton.

The party, including Dickens, Charles Reade, W. H. Wills, Forster, Frederic Ouvry, Yates, Peter Cunningham, Charles Knight, Charles Kent, Buckstone, Webster, and various other members of the Guild, all travelled down together. On arrival they conscientiously inspected the Guild houses, and no less closely investigated a new public house which had sprung up practically opposite, named 'Our Mutual Friend'. They then drove on to Knebworth, where they were welcomed by their host, and introduced to a large party of the county gentry.

It was a memorable occasion, both for the visitors who were delighted with the old house and beautiful gardens, and for the local guests who were rather surprised at the appearance of some of the celebrities. Percy Fitzgerald recalled 'Forster pacing along in great state and dignity, full of importance', and 'Boz in the highest spirits, gay as a bridegroom with his flower, bright costume', and 'hat set a *little* on one side'.[1] Lunch was served in the old Hall; and, as it drew to an end, Lytton climbed on his chair to address the company. He recalled the occasion fifteen years before, when the amateur players had visited Knebworth, and had acted *Every Man In His Humour* in the Hall in which they were seated; and that it was then that 'the idea was started of establishing a sort of literary Guild or brotherhood'. He went on to propose the toast of 'Prosperity to the Guild of Literature and Art'—

---

[1] P. H. Fitzgerald, *Memories of Charles Dickens*, 1913, pp. 21–22. It is only fair to say, however, that quite apart from the fact that he was staying at the house, Forster was on a very different footing from the other guests. For almost the past thirty-five years he had been as staunch an ally of Lytton as he had been of Dickens. He was the deservedly, well-loved god-parent of Robert Lytton, the eldest son; to Robert's wife, Edith Lytton, he was never anything but 'dear Forster'; and to them both, as she said, 'he was nearer a Father . . . than anyone else' either had ever known. If Forster often showed a different side of his nature to Fitzgerald, who claimed to be his 'friend', it was because he knew him only too well.

. . . coupled with the name of the man who has taken a most effective part in its formation, . . . the name of a man whose writings are equally the delight of the scholar and of the artisan, whose creations dwell in our hearts as familiarly and fondly as if they were our own kinsfolk, and who has united unrivalled mastery over the laughter and tears of millions, with as gentle and sweet a philosophy as ever made the passions move at the command of virtue.

The toast was received with great enthusiasm, and Dickens mounted the same chair to reply, in 'singular dramatic and incisive tones'.[1] He said:

LADIES and Gentlemen, It was said by a very sagacious person, whose authority I am quite sure my friend of many years will not impugn, notwithstanding he was named Augustus Tomlinson, and was the guide, philosopher, and friend of Paul Clifford—it was said by that remarkable man. 'Life is short, and why should speeches be long?'[2] [*Laughter.*] An aphorism so sensible under all circumstances, and particularly in these circumstances, with this delicious weather and such charming gardens near at hand, and the rather because my friend's remarks have been, as his speeches always are, quite exhaustive of the subject in hand, and not the least exhaustive of his audience. [*Cheers.*] In thanking him for the toast which he has done me the honour—an honour I very much prize—of associating my name, allow me to correct an omission which my friend has fallen into, and to assure you that these houses in question would never have been built, or could never have been built, but by his zealous and invaluable co-operation [*cheers*], and also that the pleasant labour out of which they arose would certainly have lost one of its greatest charms and one of its strongest impulses, if it had lost his ever ready sympathy with that class in which he has risen to the foremost rank, and of which he is the brightest ornament. [*Cheers.*]

Having said this much as simply due to my friend, I can only say on behalf of my associates, that the ladies and gentlemen whom we shall invite to occupy these houses, will never be placed in them as being under any social disadvantage. They will be invited to accept them as artists receiving a mark of respect, and assurance of high consideration, from some of their fellow workers. They will be invited to occupy them as artists who, we hope, will often exercise their calling within those walls for the general advantage; and they will also claim, on equal terms, the hospitality of their generous neighbour. [*Cheers.*]

Having thanked you on behalf of my brothers and sisters—for ladies became members of the Guild [*hear, hear*]—and myself, I am sure I may take the liberty of giving utterance to your feelings not less than to my own in proposing the health, long life, and prosperity

---

[1] P. H. Fitzgerald, *Recreations of a Literary Man*, 1882, i. 126.
[2] Lytton, *Paul Clifford*, ch. xvi.

of our distinguished host. [*Cheers.*] You all know very well that when the health, life, and beauty now overflowing this hall shall have fled out of it, and out of existence, crowds of people not yet born will come here to see where he lived and wrote. [*Cheers.*] Setting aside the orator and statesman—for happily we have no party here but this agreeable party [*laughter*]—setting aside all this, you know very well that this is the home of a very great man whose connexion with Hertfordshire every other county in England will envy for many long years to come. [*Cheers.*] You know very well that when this house is at its darkest and emptiest, you can make it when you please brightest and fullest by peopling it with the creatures of his brilliant fancy. Let us all wish together that there may be many more of them —the more there are the better we shall be, and, as he always excels himself, the better they will be. Now ladies and gentlemen, pray listen to their praises and not mine, and let them, and not we, propose his health. [*Loud cheers.*]

The toast was enthusiastically received. Fitzgerald noted in his diary:

It is impossible to describe the effect of these well-chosen words, delivered with every grace that fitted the scene, the gala dresses, the sunlight through the stained glass, and the cheerful board. I know I found myself, with many others, shouting at its close with enraptured delight.[1]

At their host's invitation the guests then dispersed, to explore the house and gardens, or for open-air dancing to a band of the Coldstream Guards. Edith Lytton, Lord Lytton's daughter-in-law and wife of his eldest son, described the affair for her husband. The day, she wrote, 'was a great success', and 'Sir Edward made the most perfect little speech, and I was so delighted to hear him, his language is so eloquent and well chosen and his voice quite beautiful. . . . Dickens's speech was most touching also, speaking in praise of your Father; it really made the tears come into my eyes, when he talked of the yet 'unborn' who would come into that Hall and speak of that *great man*.'[2]

In the evening the members of the Guild left for the station to return. Some of them, however, are said to have already made their way as far as 'Our Mutual Friend', where they felt more at ease, and were seated on the benches by the road. As Dickens drove by they 'all rose, and with uplifted goblets gave stentorian cheers'.[3]

The whole plan turned out a complete failure. No one would take advantage of the Guild's life insurance, and nobody wanted to live in its houses. Although it was not dissolved until 1897, Dickens lived to recognize his mistakes. He took part in meetings of the council in 1869–70 when it was decided to sell the houses and apply the funds to a scholarship in Literature and Art; but even that fell through. The scheme

[1] *Recreations of a Literary Man*, i. 126.
[2] Lady Emily Lutyens, *The Birth of Rowland*, 1956, p. 101.
[3] *Recreations of a Literary Man*, i. 127.

which had been begun in the belief that it would 'entirely change the status of the literary man in England, and make a revolution in his position, which no Government, no power on earth but his own, could ever effect',[1] was at last quietly ended, in 1897, by an 'Act to Provide for the Winding-up and Dissolution of the Guild of Literature and Art', by which its funds were divided between the Artists' General Benevolent Institution and the Royal Literary Fund.

BANQUET AT THE MANSION HOUSE

16 *January* 1866

THE members of the Court of Aldermen, and various distinguished guests, were entertained at a banquet at the Mansion House by the lord mayor, Sir Benjamin Phillips.[2] There were the usual loyal toasts. Sir James Duke replied for the Court of Aldermen, and Mr. Justice Shee[3] spoke for the judges.

The lord mayor then proposed 'The House of Commons', saying that the last time he gave that toast he had called it 'an august assembly'— a term which was afterwards commented on severely. He would not only call it 'an august assembly', however, but a noble institution of which the people of this country were justly proud. He concluded by calling on the Right Hon. George Goschen, Vice-President of the Board of Trade, and Chancellor of the Duchy of Lancaster,[4] to reply. He did so, as required, in much the same strain.

A number of other toasts followed, before Dickens proposed 'The Health of the Lady Mayoress'—'with characteristic grace'—and the company separated.

There is no record of what Dickens actually said; but, two days later, he expressed a forcible opinion of the other speakers in a letter to Charles Kent. He declared that he had sat 'pining under the imbecility of constitutional and corporational idiots'. Yet, in proposing the lady mayoress, he had succeeded in making certain remarks which had brought him 'some faint consolation from the company's response'. The lord mayor's tribute to Parliament must have been particularly exasperating, and Dickens appears to have found Goschen 'almost the worst speaker I ever heard in my life'. His daughter Mary, and his sister-in-law, seated either side of him, had urged him to look pleasant: 'I replied in expressions not to be repeated. Shee (the judge) was just as good and graceful, as he (the member) was bad and gawky.'

---

[1] Letter to Lytton, 5 Jan. 1851.   [2] See p. 317 n.
[3] Sir William Shee (1804–84), justice of the Court of the Queen's Bench.
[4] George Joachim Goschen (1831–1907).

DRAMATIC, EQUESTRIAN, AND MUSICAL SICK FUND ASSOCIATION

14 *February* 1866

THE tenth anniversary of this society was held at Willis's Rooms, with Dickens in the Chair. Ladies and gentlemen occupied alternate seats. On his right and left were Mrs. Stirling and Miss E. Howard.

Above the head of the Chairman (reported the *Era*) hung bannerets on which details relating to former banquets of the Association were blazoned in chronological order, together with two inscriptions, in letters visible at the furthest end of the hall, 'Charles Dickens Esq.,' and 'St. Valentine's Day', apparently intended for the information of those supporters of the Association who might have forgotten the auspicious occurrence of the double event.

On first rising Dickens was received with loud and long continued cheering. He went briefly through the usual loyal and patriotic preliminaries, which were enthusiastically received, and then, in proposing the toast of the evening, said:

LADIES, before I couple you with the gentlemen, which will be at least proper to the inscription over my head [*laughter*], before I do so, allow me, on behalf of my grateful sex here represented, to thank you for the great pleasure and interest with which your gracious presence at these festivals never fails to inspire us. [*Cheers.*] There is no English custom which is so manifestly a relic of savage life as that custom which usually excludes you from participation in similar gatherings. [*Hear.*] And although the crime carries its own heavy punishment along with it, in respect that it divests a public dinner of its most beautiful ornament and of its most fascinating charm, still the offence is none the less to be severely reprehended on every possible occasion, as outraging equally nature and art. [*Cheers and laughter.*]

I believe that as little is known of the saint whose name is written here as can well be known of any saint or sinner. [*Laughter.*] We, your loyal servants, are deeply thankful to him for having somehow gained possession of one day in the year—for having, as no doubt he has, arranged the almanac for 1866 expressly to delight us with the enchanting fiction that we have some tender proprietorship in you which we should scarcely dare to claim on a less auspicious occasion. [*Cheers.*] Ladies, the utmost devotion sanctioned by the saint we beg to lay at your feet, and any little innocent privileges [*laughter*] to which we may be entitled by the same authority we beg respectfully but firmly to claim at your hands. [*Cheers.*]

Now, ladies and gentlemen, you need no ghost to inform you that

I am going to propose 'Prosperity to the Dramatic, Musical, and Equestrian Sick Fund Association' [*hear, hear*], and, further, that I should be going to ask you actively to promote that prosperity by liberally contributing to its funds, if that task were not reserved for a much more persuasive speaker. But I rest the strong claim of the society for its useful existence and its truly charitable functions on a very few words, though, as well as I can recollect, upon something like six grounds. First, it relieves the sick; secondly, it buries the dead; thirdly, it enables the poor members of the profession to journey to accept new engagements whenever they find themselves stranded in some remote inhospitable place, or when, from other circumstances, they find themselves perfectly crippled as to locomotion for want of money; fourthly, it often finds such engagements for them by acting as their honest, disinterested agent; fifthly, it is its principle to act humanely upon the instant, and never, as is too often the case within my experience, to beat about the bush till the bush is withered and dead [*cheers*]; lastly, the society is not in the least degree exclusive, but takes under its comprehensive care the whole range of the Theatre and the Concert Room, from the Manager in his room of state, or at the drum-head [*laughter*], down to the theatrical housekeeper who is usually to be found amongst the cobwebs in the 'flies', or down to the hall porter who passes his life in a thorough 'draft' [*laughter*], and, to the best of my observation, in perpetually interrupted endeavours to eat something with a knife and fork out of a basin, by a dusty fire, in that extraordinary little gritty room, upon which the sun never shines, and on the portals of which are inscribed the magic words, 'Stage Door'. [*Laughter.*]

Now, ladies and gentlemen, this society administers its benefits sometimes by way of loan; sometimes by way of gift; sometimes by way of assurance at very low premiums; sometimes to members, oftener to non-members; always, expressly, remember, through the hands of a secretary or committee well acquainted with the wants of the applicants, and thoroughly well versed, if not by hard experience at least by sympathy, in the calamities and uncertainties incidental to the general calling. One must know something of the general calling to know what those afflictions are. A lady who had been upon the stage from her earliest childhood till she was a blooming woman, and who came from a long line of provincial actors and actresses, once said to me when she was happily married; when she was rich, beloved, courted; when she was mistress of a fine house—once said to me at the head of her own table, surrounded by distinguished guests of every degree, 'Oh, but I have never forgotten the hard time when I was on the stage, and when my baby brother died, and when my poor mother and I brought the little baby from Ireland to

England, and acted three nights in England, as we had acted three nights in Ireland, with the pretty creature lying upon the only bed in our lodging before we got the money to pay for its funeral.'

Ladies and gentlemen, such things are every day, to this hour; but happily, at this day and in this hour, this Association has arisen to be the timely friend of such great distress. [*Cheers.*]

It is not often the fault of the sufferers that they fall into these straits. Struggling artists must necessarily change from place to place, and thus it frequently happens that they become, as it were, strangers in every place, and very slight circumstances—a passing illness, the sickness of the husband, wife or child, a serious town [*laughter*], an anathematising expounder of the gospel of gentleness and forbearance—any one of these causes may often in a few hours wreck them upon a rock in a barren ocean; and then, happily, this society, with the swift alacrity of the lifeboat, dashes to the rescue and takes them off. [*Cheers.*] Looking just now over the last report issued by this society, and confining my scrutiny to the head of illness alone, I find that in one year, I think, 672 days of sickness had been assuaged by its means: in nine years, which then formed the term of its existence, as many as 5,500 and odd. Well, I thought when I saw 5,500 and odd days of sickness, this is a very serious sum, but add the nights! Add the nights, those long dreary hours in the twenty-four, when the shadow of death is darkest, when despondency is strongest, and when hope is weakest, before you gauge the good that is done by this institution, and before you gauge the good that really will be done by every shilling that you bestow here tonight. [*Cheers.*] Add, more than all, that the improvidence, the recklessness of the general multitude of poor members of this profession, I should say is a cruel, conventional fable. [*Cheers.*] Add that there is no class of society the members of which so well help themselves or so well help each other. [*Hear, hear.*] Not in the whole grand chapters of Westminster Abbey and York Minster, not in the whole quadrangle of the Royal Exchange, not in the whole list of members of the Stock Exchange, not in the Inns of Court, not in the College of Physicians, not in the College of Surgeons, can there possibly be found more remarkable instances of uncomplaining poverty, of cheerful, constant self-denial, or the generous remembrance of the claims of kindred and professional brotherhood, than will certainly be found in the dingiest and dirtiest concert room, in the least lucid theatre, even in the raggedest tent circus that was ever stained by weather. [*Cheers.*]

I have been twitted in print before now with rather flattering actors when I address them as one of the Trustees at their General Fund dinner. Believe me, I flatter nobody, unless it be sometimes myself;

but, in such company as the present, I always feel it to be my manful duty to bear my testimony to this fact: first, because it is opposed to a stupid, unfeeling libel; secondly, because my doing so may afford some slight encouragement to the persons who are unjustly depreciated; and lastly, and most of all, because I know it is the truth. [*Cheers.*]

Now, ladies and gentlemen, it is time we should what we professionally call 'ring down' on these remarks. If you, such members of the general public as are here, will only think the great theatrical curtain has really fallen, and been taken up again for the night on that dull, dark vault which many of us know so well. If you will only think of the Theatre or other place of entertainment as empty. If you will only think of the 'float' or other gas fittings, as extinguished. If you will only think of the people who have beguiled you of an evening's care, whose little vanities and almost childish foibles are engendered in their competing face to face with you for their favour— surely it may be said their failings are partly of your making, while their virtues are all their own? If you will only do this, and follow them out of that sham place into the world, where it rains real rain, snows real snow, and blows real wind; where people sustain themselves by real money, which is much harder to get, much harder to make, and very much harder to give away than the pieces of tobacco-pipe in property bags [*laughter*]; if you will only do this, and do it in a really kind, considerate spirit, this society, then certain of the result of the night's proceedings, can ask no more. I beg to propose to you to drink ' Prosperity to the Dramatic, Equestrian, and Musical Sick Fund Association'. [*Cheers.*]

The toast was drunk with three times three. In proposing the next toast Dickens said:

Gentlemen, as I addressed myself to the ladies last time, so I address you this time, and I give you the delightful assurance that it is positively my last appearance but one on the present occasion. A certain Mr. Pepys, who was Secretary for the Admiralty in the days of Charles II, who kept a diary well in shorthand, which he supposed no one could read, and which consequently remains to this day the most honest diary known to print—Mr. Pepys had two special and very strong likings, the ladies and the Theatres. But Mr. Pepys, whenever he committed any slight act of remissness, or any little peccadillo which was utterly and wholly untheatrical, used to comfort his conscience by recording a vow that he would abstain from the Theatres for a certain time. In the first part of Mr. Pepys' character I have no doubt we fully agree with him; in the second I have no doubt we do not.

I learn this experience of Mr. Pepys from remembrance of a passage in his diary that I was reading the other night, from which it appears that he was not only curious in plays, but curious in sermons; and then one night when he happened to be walking past St. Dunstan's Church, he turned, went in, and heard what he calls 'a very edifying discourse'; during the delivery of which discourse, he notes in his diary, 'I stood by a pretty young maid, whom I did attempt to take by the hand.' [*Laughter.*] But, he adds, 'She would not; and I did perceive that she had pins in her pocket with which to prick me if I should touch her again [*laughter*], and was glad that I spied her design.'[1] Afterwards about the close of the same edifying discourse, Mr. Pepys found himself near another pretty fair young maid, who would seem upon the whole to have had no pins, and to have been more impressible.

Now, the moral of this story which I wish to suggest to you is, that we have been this evening in St. James's much more timid than Mr. Pepys was in St. Dunstan's, and that we have conducted ourselves very much better.[2] [*Laughter.*] As a slight recompense to us for our highly meritorious conduct, and as a little relief to our over-charged hearts, I beg to propose that we devote this bumper to invoking a blessing on the ladies. [*Cheers.*] It is the privilege of this society annually to hear a lady speak for her own sex. [*Cheers.*] Who so competent to do this as Mrs. Stirling? [*Renewed cheering.*] Surely one who has so gracefully and captivatingly, with such an exquisite mixture of art and fancy and fidelity, represented her own sex in innumerable charities, under an infinite variety of phases, cannot fail to represent them well in her own character, especially when it is, amidst her many triumphs, the most agreeable of all. [*Cheers.*] I beg to propose to you 'The Ladies', and I will couple with that toast the name of 'Mrs. Stirling.'[3]

The toast was received enthusiastically; and Mrs. Stirling made a graceful and amusing speech in reply. The next, and final toast was 'The Health of the Chairman', proposed by Serjeant Ballantine, and briefly acknowledged by Dickens. The speaking was cut short to give time for 'a varied programme of dancing—an innovation which was fully appreciated by the fairer portion of the guests'.

[1] Samuel Pepys, *Diary*, ed. Lord Braybrooke, 1885, iii. 222.
[2] Surely the unreported (or forgotten) point of the contrast was that, unlike Pepys, they were to put their hands into their *own* pockets?
[3] Fanny Stirling (1815–95), actress, born Mary Anne Kehl, wife of Edward Stirling, a minor dramatist and actor; married Sir Charles Gregory, 1894. Dickens would have known her as a member of Macready's companies in the eighteen-forties, if not earlier.

ROYAL GENERAL THEATRICAL FUND

28 *March* 1866

THE anniversary festival was held at the Freemasons' Tavern, with the lord mayor, Sir Benjamin Phillips, in the Chair. There were the usual loyal and patriotic toasts and the usual programme of speeches. Dickens was preceded by Buckstone, who mentioned in his speech that the presence of the lord mayor was due to Dickens, 'for it was he who asked the Lord Mayor to come, and it was the Lord Mayor who said to me that the wishes of Mr. Dickens were his commands'. On rising to propose the health of the chairman, Dickens was warmly received, and said:

GENTLEMEN, in my childish days I remember to have had a vague but profound admiration for a certain legendary person called the Lord Mayor's Fool. I had the highest opinion of the intellectual capacity of that suppositious retainer of the Mansion House, and I really regarded him with feeling approaching to absolute veneration, because my nurse informed me on every gastronomic occasion that the Lord Mayor's Fool liked everything that was good. [*Laughter.*] You will agree with me, I have no doubt, that if this discriminating jester had existed at the present time he could not fail to have liked his master very much [*cheers*], seeing that so good a Lord Mayor is very rarely to be found, and that a better Lord Mayor could not possibly be. [*Renewed cheering.*]

You have already divined, gentlemen, that I am about to propose to you to drink the health of the right honourable gentleman in the Chair. [*Loud and prolonged cheering.*] As one of the Trustees of the General Theatrical Fund, I beg officially to tender him my best thanks for lending the very powerful aid of his presence, his influence, and his personal character to this very deserving institution. [*Hear, hear.*] As his private friends we ventured to urge upon him to do this gracious act, and I beg to assure you that the perfect simplicity, modesty, cordiality, and frankness with which he assented, enhanced the gift one thousandfold. [*Prolonged cheering.*] I think it must be very agreeable to a company like this to know that the President of the night is not ceremoniously pretending, 'positively for this night only', to have an interest in the drama, but that he has an unusual and thorough acquaintance with it, and that he has a living and discerning knowledge of the merits of the great old actors. It is very pleasant for me to remember that the Lord Mayor and I once beguiled the tedium of a journey by exchanging our experiences upon this subject. I rather prided myself on being something of an old stager, but I found the Lord Mayor so thoroughly up in all the stock pieces, and so knowing and yet so fresh about the merits of those who are most and best identified with them, that I readily recognized in him what would be called in fistic language, a very ugly customer—one, I assure you, by no means to be settled by any novice not in thorough good theatrical training. [*Laughter.*]

Gentlemen, we have all known from our earliest infancy that when the giants in Guildhall hear the clock strike one, they come down to dinner. Similarly, when the City of London shall hear but one single word in just disparagement of its present Lord Mayor, whether as its enlightened chief magistrate, or as one of its merchants, or as one of its true gentlemen, he will then descend from the high personal place which he holds in the general honour and esteem. Until then he will remain upon his pedestal, and my private opinion, between our-selves, is that the giants will come down long before him. [*Cheers and laughter.*]

Gentlemen, in conclusion, I would remark that when the Lord Mayor made his truly remarkable, and truly manly, and unaffected speech, I could not but be struck by the odd reversal of the usual circumstances at the Mansion House, which he presented to our view; for whereas it is a very common thing for persons to be brought tremblingly before the Lord Mayor, the Lord Mayor presented him-self as being brought tremblingly before us. [*Laughter.*] I hope that the result may hold still further; for whereas it is a common thing for the Lord Mayor to say to a repentant criminal who does not seem to have much harm in him, 'Let me never see you here again', so I would propose that we all with one accord say to the Lord Mayor, 'Let us by all means see you here again on the first opportunity.' [*Much laughter.*] Gentlemen, I beg to propose to you to drink, with all the honours, 'The health of the Right Honourable the Lord Mayor'.

The toast was drunk upstanding, with three times three cheers. A number of other speakers followed, including Robert Keeley, Leicester Buckingham, and Benjamin Webster.

This was the last time Dickens spoke for the fund. He agreed to reply for the Trustees at the anniversary held on 16 May 1870, when the Prince of Wales presided, but had to excuse himself at the very last moment, finding his foot so painful that, he explained, 'I could no more walk into St. James's Hall than I could fly in the air.'[1]

METROPOLITAN ROWING CLUBS

7 *May* 1866

THE rowing season had been opened the previous Saturday by a grand procession of the amateur clubs on the Thames; and on the following Monday a dinner of the Metropolitan Rowing Clubs was held at the

[1] Letter to J. B. Buckstone, 15 May 1870.

London Tavern, with Charles Dickens, as President of the Nautilus Rowing Club, in the Chair. Charles Dickens, Junior, was also present; and probably it was his interest in rowing, which had led to the invitation to his father to preside.

On conclusion of the dinner the chairman gave the usual loyal toasts; after which he proposed the toast of the evening, 'Prosperity to the Rowing Clubs of London'.

HAVING asked the indulgence of those present, as he was labouring under a bad cold, he went on to remark that he could not avoid the remembrance of what very poor things the amateur rowing clubs on the Thames were in the early days of his noviciate; not to mention the difference in the build of the boats. He could not get on in the beginning without being a pupil under an anomalous creature called a 'fireman-waterman' [*laughter*], who wore an eminently tall hat, and a perfectly unaccountable uniform, of which it might be said that if it were less adapted for one thing than another, that thing was fire. He recollected that this gentleman had on some former day won a King's prize wherry; and they used to go about in this accursed wherry, he and a partner, doing all the hard work, while the fireman drank all the beer. [*Laughter.*]

The river was very much clearer, freer, and cleaner in those days than these; but he was persuaded that this philosophical old boatman could no more have dreamt of seeing the spectacle which had taken place on Saturday, or of seeing these clubs matched for skill and speed, than he [*the chairman*] should dare to announce through the usual authentic channels that he was to be heard of at the bar below, and that he was perfectly prepared to accommodate Mr. James Mace if he meant business. [*Laughter.*] Nevertheless, he could recollect that he had turned out for a spurt a few years ago on the River Thames with an occasional Secretary, who should be nameless[1] [*a laugh*], and some other Eton boys, and that he could hold his own against them. [*Hear, hear.*] More recently still, the last time that he rowed down from Oxford he was supposed to have covered himself with honour [*cheers and laughter*], though he must admit that he found the locks so picturesque as to require much examination for the discovery of their beauty. [*Renewed laughter.*]

But what he wanted to say was this: that though his 'fireman-waterman' was one of the greatest humbugs that ever existed, he yet taught him what an honest, healthy, manly sport this was. [*Cheers.*] Their waterman would bid them pull away, and assure them that they were certain of winning in some race. And he would remark that aquatic sports never entailed a moment's cruelty, or a moment's pain, upon any living creature. Rowing men pursued recreation

[1] Charles Dickens, Junior.

under circumstances which braced their muscles, and cleared the cobwebs from their minds. He assured them that he regarded such clubs as these as a 'national blessing'. [*Cheers.*] They owed, it was true, a vast deal to steam power—as was sometimes proved at matches on the Thames [*a laugh*]—but, at the same time, they were greatly indebted to all that tended to keep up a healthy, manly tone. [*Hear, hear.*] He understood that there had been a committee selected for the purpose of arranging a great amateur regatta, which was to take place off Putney in the course of the season that was just begun. [*Hear, hear.*] He could not abstain from availing himself of this occasion to express a hope that the committee would successfully carry on its labours to a triumphant result [*cheers*], and that they should see upon the Thames, in the course of this summer, such a brilliant sight as had never been seen there before. To secure this there must be some hard work, skilful combinations, and rather large subscriptions. But although the aggregate result must be great, it by no means followed that it need be at all large in its individual details.

In conclusion Dickens went on to make a laughable comparison between the paying off or purification of the National Debt, just advocated by Mr. Gladstone in his budget speech, and the purification of the river Thames.

Among the other toasts which followed, was one to the chairman, which was received with loud cheers.

RAILWAY BENEVOLENT INSTITUTION

5 *June* 1867

AFTER the success of the *All the Year Round* Christmas number, *Mugby Junction*, in 1866, Dickens was asked and consented to preside at the ninth anniversary festival of the Railway Benevolent Institution, next year. The dinner was held at Willis's Rooms. The usual loyal and patriotic toasts were given and received. Sir Daniel Gooch, the Chairman of the Great Western Railway, briefly replied for the House of Commons; and Dickens then rose to propose the toast of the evening, and said:

GENTLEMEN, Although we have not yet left behind us by the distance of quite fifty years the time when one of the first literary authorities of this country insisted upon the speed of the fastest railway train that the legislature might disastrously sanction being expressly limited by Act of Parliament to ten miles an hour, yet it does somehow happen that this evening, and every evening, there are railway trains running pretty smoothly to Ireland and to Scotland at the rate of fifty miles an hour. [*Hear, hear.*] Much as it was objected in its time, to vaccination, that it must have a tendency to impart to human children something of the nature of the cow [*laughter*], whereas I believe to this very time vaccinated children are found to be as easily defined from calves as they ever were [*laughter*], and certainly they have no cheapening influence on the price of veal [*renewed laughter*]; much as it was objected that chloroform was a contravention of the will of Providence, because it lessened providentially inflicted pain—which would be a reason for not rubbing your face if you had the toothache, or not rubbing your nose if it itched [*a laugh*]: so it was confidently predicted that the railway system, if anything so absurd could be productive of any result, would infallibly throw half the nation out of employment; whereas, you observe that the very cause and occasion of our coming here together tonight is, apart from the various tributary channels of occupation which it has opened up, that it has called into existence a specially and directly employed population of upwards of 200,000 persons. [*Cheers.*]

Now, gentlemen, it is pretty clear and obvious that upwards of 200,000 people engaged upon the various railways of the United Kingdom cannot be rich. [*Hear, hear.*] Although their duties require great care and exactness, and although our lives are every day, humanly speaking, in the hands of many of them, still for the mass of those places there will always be great competition, because they are not posts which require skilled workmen to hold. Wages, as you know very well, cannot be high where competition is great, and you also know very well that railway directors, in the bargains they make, and the salaries they pay, have to deal with the money of shareholders, to whom they are accountable. [*Hear, hear.*] Thus it necessarily happens, that railway officers and servants are not remunerated, on the whole, by any means splendidly [*hear, hear, and laughter*], and that they cannot hope in the ordinary course of things to do more than meet the ordinary wants and hazards of life. But it is to be observed that the hazards of life are in their case, by reason of the dangerous nature of their avocations, exceptionally great; so very great, I find, as to be stateable, on the authority of a Parliamentary paper, in the very startling round figures, that, whereas one railway traveller is killed in 8,000,000 of passengers, one railway servant is killed in every 2,000 employed.[1] [*Hear, hear.*]

[1] Probably from W. F. Mills, *The Railway Service*, 1867, pp. 41–49: Mills was secretary of the Railway Benevolent Institution. His figures were based on Board of Trade returns for the whole period 1841–65, according to which an average of 105 railway employees were killed, and about 70 seriously injured every year; and this was certainly an understatement, particularly of injuries. Stokers and guards ran greater risks than coal miners, and engine-drivers little less. On the other hand, only one passenger was killed in every 6,998,885 travellers.

Hence, from general, special, as well no doubt from prudential and benevolent considerations, there came to be established among railway officers and servants, nine years ago, this Railway Benevolent Institution. [*Cheers.*] I may suppose, therefore, gentlemen, as it was established nine years ago, that this is the ninth occasion of publishing from this chair the banns between this institution and the public. [*Cheers.*] Nevertheless, I feel bound individually to do my duty the same as if it had never been done before, in stating to you briefly what the institution is, before asking you whether there is any just cause or impediment why these two parties—the institution and the public—should not be joined together in holy charity. [*Cheers.*] As I understand the society, after having read its papers, its objects are fivefold. Firstly, to grant annuities, which, it is always to be observed, are paid out of the interest of invested capital, so that they may be always secure and safe—annual pensions of from £10 to £25, to distressed railway officers and servants incapacitated through age, sickness, or accident; secondly, to grant similar pensions to distressed widows; thirdly to educate and maintain orphan children; fourthly to provide temporary relief for all classes until lasting relief can be guaranteed out of funds sufficiently large for the purpose; and lastly, to induce railway officers and servants to insure their lives in some well-established office, by subdividing the payments of premiums into small periodical sums, and also by granting a reversionary bonus of ten per cent. on the amount insured, from the funds of the institution.

Now this is the society that we are met to assist—simple, sympathetic, practical, easy, sensible, unpretending. The number of its members, as I believe, largely and rapidly on the increase, is 12,000; the amount of its invested capital very nearly £15,000. [*Cheers.*] It has done a world of good and a world of work in these first nine years of its life, and yet I am proud to say that the annual cost of its management to the institution is less than ten per cent. [*Cheers.*] And now, if you do not know all about it in a small compass, either I don't know all about it myself, or the fault must be in my 'packing'.

One naturally passes from what the institution is and has done, to what it wants. Well, gentlemen, it wants to do more good, and it cannot possibly do more good until it has more money. It cannot safely, and therefore it cannot honourably, grant more pensions to deserving applicants until it grows richer, and it cannot grow rich enough for its laudable purpose of its own unaided self. The thing is absolutely impossible. The means of these railway officers and servants are far too limited. Even if they were helped to the utmost by the great railway companies, their means would still be too limited. Even if they were helped—as I hope they shortly will be—by some of the great corporations of this country, whom railways have done so much to enrich,[1] their means would still be too limited. In a word, these railway officers and servants, on their road to a very humble and modest superannuation, can no more do without the help of the great public, than the great public, on their road from Torquay to Aberdeen, could do without them. [*Cheers.*] Therefore, I desire to ask the public whether the servants of the great railways are not in fact their servants; whether they are not every day their ready, zealous, faithful, hard-working servants; and whether they have not established, and whether they do not every day establish, a reasonable claim upon the public's liberal remembrance. [*Cheers.*]

Now, gentlemen, upon this point of the case there is a story once told me by a friend of mine, which seems to my mind to have a certain application.[2] My friend was an American Sea Captain, and therefore it is quite unnecessary to say his story was a true one. [*Laughter.*] He was Captain and part owner of a large American liner. On a certain voyage out, in exquisite summer weather, he had for cabin passengers one beautiful young lady, and ten more or less beautiful young gentlemen. Light winds or dead calms prevailing, the voyage was slow, and before they had made half their distance, the ten young gentlemen were all madly in love with the beautiful young lady. They had all proposed to her, and bloodshed among the rivals seemed imminent, pending the young lady's decision. [*Laughter.*] In this extremity the beautiful young lady confided in my friend the Captain, who gave her this very discreet advice:'If your affections are disengaged, take the one whom you like the best, and settle the question.' [*Laughter.*] To which the beautiful young lady replied, 'I cannot do that, because I like them all equally well.' My friend the Captain, who was a man of resource, hit upon this ingenious expedient. Said he, 'Tomorrow morning, at mid-day, when lunch is announced and they are all on deck, do you plunge bodily overboard, head foremost. I will be alongside in a boat to pick you up, and take the one of the ten who dashes to the rescue.' The young lady highly approved of this, and did accordingly. But after she plunged in, nine of the ten more or less beautiful young gentlemen immediately plunged in after her. The tenth shed tears [*great laughter*], and looked over the side, but remained on deck. They were all picked up together. When they mustered dripping, on the deck, and stood there in a limp row, the beautiful young lady said to the Captain: 'What am I to do now? See what a state they are in. How can I possibly choose one of the nine, when they are all equally wet?' Then, with sudden inspiration, my friend

---

[1] About this time the Corporation of London rejected an appeal for help from the institution, because of the strike on the Brighton line in March.

[2] Dickens had told the same story, in his speeches, before: see p. 112.

the Captain said, 'My dear, take the dry one!' [*Loud laughter.*] I am sorry to say she did so, and they lived happily ever after.

Now gentlemen, in my application of this story, I would exactly reverse my friend the Captain's anecdote, and entreat the public in looking about to consider who are fit subjects for their bounty, to give their hands, with something in them, not to the dry but the wet ones, to the ready and dextrous servants constantly at their beck and call. And I would ask anyone with a doubt upon this subject, to consider what his experience of the railway servant is, from the time of his driving up to the departure platform, to the end of his journey. I know what mine is. Here he is, in velveteen or in a policeman's dress, scaling cabs, storming carriages, finding lost articles by a kind of instinct, binding up lost umbrellas and walking sticks, wheeling trucks, counselling old ladies, with a wonderful interest in their affairs—mostly very complicated—and sticking labels upon all sorts of articles. I look around me. There he is again, in a station-master's uniform, directing and overseeing, with the head of a general, and the manners of a courteous host. There he is again in a guard's belt and buckle, with a handsome figure, inspiring confidence in timid passengers. He is as gentle to the weak people as he is bold to the strong, and he has not a single hair in his beard that is not up to its work.

I glide out of the station, there he is again, with flags in his hands. There he is again, in the open country, at a level crossing. There he is again at the entrance to the tunnel. At every station that I stop at, there he is again as alert as usual. There he is again at the arrival platform, getting me out of the carriage as if I was his only charge upon earth. Now, is there not something in the alacrity, in the ready zeal, in the interest of these men that is not acknowledged, that is not expressed in their mere wages? May it not be agreeable to the public to consider that this institution gives them the means of enjoying that something not only without compromise of their independence, but greatly to their permanent advantage? And if your experience coincides with mine, and enables you to have this good feeling for, and to say a good word in regard of, railway servants with whom we do come into contact, surely it may induce us to have some little sympathy with those whom we do not—those signalmen for instance whom we rush past and do not distinctly see? And there are two sides to these points. If we take a human interest in them, will they not take a human interest in us? [*Cheers.*] We shall not be merely the 9.30 or the 10.30 rushing by, but we shall be an instalment of the considerate public that is ready to lend a hand to the poor fellows in their risk of their lives; and we cannot fail to derive a benefit from the interest they will consequently take in us.

I have, unconsciously, given you rather a long run, but I assure you that if you had done less on your part to get my steam up, I should have shut it off much sooner. Gentlemen, with a very hearty and real interest in the cause, and in the men, I beg you to drink 'Prosperity to the Railway Benevolent Institution'. [*Loud and prolonged cheering.*]

Sir Daniel Gooch proposed the health of the chairman; and in reply Dickens thanked the company heartily, saying that they were exceedingly welcome to his poor services, and that he could not better express his thanks than by giving way to the next speaker.

A number of other toasts followed, to officers of the society and guests.

PRINTERS' READERS' ASSOCIATION

17 *September* 1867

THE public meeting of the Printers' Readers' Association, at which Dickens had been invited to take the Chair, was held at the Salisbury Hotel, Salisbury Square. Its purpose was to adopt a memorial to their employers asking either for a reduction in the number of hours they worked, or for an increase in salary. A circular had already been privately sent to members of the association outlining their case; which was, principally, that an average wage of £2. 0s. 5½d, was not enough for a 53 hour week, with only 9½d. an hour for overtime.

One of the members who was present has left a sketch of Dickens's appearance that evening:

As he threw aside his large cloak, he shook hands with all who sought that honour with the utmost warmth. Even now I fancy I can feel that firm grip, and see his cheery smile. He was dressed with the greatest care and elegance, as if for an evening party or state ball. His florid complexion, dark glittering eye, and grizzled beard, were very striking; but, above all, the loftiness of his massive brow—denoting 'the mighty brain within'—inspired the beholder with reverence.[1]

In opening the proceedings, Dickens said:

GENTLEMEN, as this society is convened not to hear a speech from me, but to hear a statement of facts and figures very nearly affecting the personal interests of, at all events, the great majority of those who compose it, I feel that my preface need be but very brief. Of the details of the question at issue I know, of myself, absolutely nothing. I have consented to occupy the chair at the request of the London Association of the Correctors of The Press for two reasons. Firstly, because I think that openness and publicity in such a case is a very wholesome example, very much needed at this time and highly becoming a body of men associated with the great public

---

[1] F. G. Kitton, *Charles Dickens by Pen and Pencil*, 1890, p. 84.

safeguard, the Press. [*Cheers.*] Secondly, because I know from some slight practical experience, what the duties of the correctors of the press are, and how those duties are usually performed; and I can testify, and do testify here, that they are not mechanical, that they are not mere matters of manipulation and routine, but that they require from those who perform them much natural intelligence, much superadded cultivation, considerable readiness of reference, quickness of resource, an excellent memory, and a clear understanding. [*Loud cheers.*] And I most grate-fully acknowledge that I have never gone through the sheets of any book that I have written without having had presented to me by the corrector of the press, some slight misunderstanding into which I have fallen, some little lapse I have made; in short, without having set down in black and white some unquestionable indication that I have been closely followed through my work by a patient and trained mind [*hear, hear*], and not merely by a skilful eye. [*Hear, hear.*] In this declaration I have not the slightest doubt that the great body of my brother and sister writers would, as a plain act of justice, heartily concur. [*Hear, hear.*]

For these plain and short reasons, briefly stated, I am here; and being here I beg to assure you that if anyone is present who is in any way associated with the printing press, and should desire to address you, he shall receive from me, whatever his opinions, the readiest attention and the amplest opportunity. [*Loud cheers.*]

Various speakers followed, and two resolutions were passed: one expressing the opinion of the meeting that 'the services of the London readers were inadequately remunerated', and the other adopting a mem-orial to the master printers asking for a 10 per cent. rise in wages. A Mr. Challoner carefully explained that the association 'was not at all in the nature of a trade union', and that they simply desired to lay their case fully and fairly before their employers, having no intention to force them by combination. A committee was appointed to present the memorial, and the proceedings concluded with a vote of thanks to the chairman. On rising to reply he was received with several hearty cheers, and said:

I beg to thank you very cordially for the hearty reception which you have given me. I can assure you that you are most fully wel-come to the small service, and I sincerely trust, and do believe, that your very calm and temperate proceedings will finally result in the establishment of relations perfectly amicable between employers and employed, and consequently to the general welfare. Good night. [*Cheers.*]

FAREWELL BANQUET BEFORE VISIT TO THE UNITED STATES

2 *November* 1867

DICKENS'S departure for the United States had already been fixed for 9 November when it was decided, at short notice, that a farewell banquet should be given in his honour. A committee was formed consisting of S. Arthur Chappell, Thomas Chappell, Wilkie Collins, Charles Fechter, Charles Kent,[1] Edward Levy,[2] Sir Charles Russell, George Russell, W. H. Wills, and Edmund Yates. The arrangements were left to Charles Kent, Levy and Yates.

Kent's secretarial correspondence gives an idea of the way in which such affairs were organized. There was a greater demand for places than there was room to supply them; but most of Dickens's old friends managed to secure tickets by inviting themselves and prompt payment. His more eminent friends and acquaintances had their names included in a printed List of Stewards, which was drawn up by the committee. A rough proof of this was then sent out to each of them, with a circular asking permission to retain their names even if they were unable to attend. Few liked to refuse.

Most of the replies were merely formal; a few were characteristic. Gladstone felt 'some scruple at paying to Mr. Dickens . . . a compliment which must be merely nominal';[3] while Disraeli asked through his secretary, 'with every feeling of respect', for his name to be withdrawn.[4] Ruskin wrote:

No one has a deeper respect for a genius, and the practical goodness, and limitless good service of Mr. Dickens than I have. But just because it *is* deep, I have not the least mind to express it Dinnerwise.[5]

While Tennyson replied to say, 'I have never yet attended any public dinner . . . but if you merely wish my name to appear . . . as a mark of respect to my old friend Charles Dickens, I am very willing that it should.'[6]

John Forster was unable to attend, being seriously ill, but he fired off a long letter of advice and protest on seeing how the stewards with titles were listed separately from those without:

The names of your Stewards are unobjectionable—but I have a *most earnest* request to make to you in connexion with the manner in which they are set forth. . . .

---

[1] William Charles Mark Kent (1823–1902), author and journalist; editor of the *Sun*, 1845–71; personal friend of Dickens.

[2] Edward Levy (1833–1916) took additional name of Lawson, 1875; 1st Baron Burnham, 1903; editor of *Daily Telegraph*, which was owned by his father Joseph Moses Levy, 1855–1903.

[3] *A Souvenir of Charles Dickens' Last Visit to America*, album in 2 vols. 'containing a complete collection of autograph letters from all the distinguished men who were invited to accept the office of steward.'—To Charles Kent, 30 Oct. 1867. H.   [4] Ibid. from C. Rivers Wilson to Kent, 18 Oct. 1867.

[5] Ibid., 1 Nov. 1867.   [6] Ibid. no date.

We all give our names is testimony of our regard and respect for our friend. . . . Who in such a case is to assume the right of bracketing off in solitary dignity any such names leaving the rest to alphabetical sequence? I really cannot trust myself to speak of it as I think—and *as* I think . . . so has Mr. Dickens himself thought in all the years I have known him. . . . I make the most urgent appeal to you to recast the names, putting Lord Shaftesbury with the S's, and so on, and allowing Mr. Tennyson equal dignity with Sir Benjamin Phillips, and mounting Mr. Carlyle to the level of Mr. Gleig.[1]

However it was expressed, Dickens was deeply moved by this tribute from his friends and admirers. He also saw it as an admirable opportunity for publicly announcing his change of heart towards America since 1842.

The dinner was held at the Freemasons' Hall, with Lord Lytton in the Chair. 'A Great Author', wrote Charles Kent, 'certainly never had any more magnificent demonstration than that which was afforded Charles Dickens.' Nearly 450 guests sat down to the banquet in the hall, 'while more than 100 fair spectators were ranged in the ladies' gallery'. In his published account, Kent went on to quote the *Observer*, in his own praise:

It was a happy thought of the Honorary Secretary . . . that the walls of the dining-hall should suggest the presence of those other friends, scarcely less real . . . from our dear old acquaintance Mr. Pickwick, to our dear new acquaintance, Dr. Marigold. . . . The walls of the hall consisted of twenty large blank panels with arched tops . . . borders of laurel leaves on a deep red ground were run round the panels, and in the arched top of each the name of one of Mr. Dickens's works was introduced in gold letters. . . . The noble room had all the semblance of a temple especially erected to the honour and for the glorification of England's favourite author.[2]

The American press was equally excited. The *New York Tribune* hailed it as 'a high historical event'.[3]—'Nothing like it', declared its special reporter, 'has ever before occurred in London. . . . The company that assembled to honor Dickens, represented humanity.' Artists, actors, writers, eminent lawyers, peers, merchants, bankers, and even reporters, were seated side by side:

At length the doors were thrown open, and the well-known faces of Dickens and Bulwer appeared at it. They were arm-in-arm. A cry rang through the room, handkerchiefs were waved on the floor and in the galleries, . . . and the band struck up a full march. As Dickens passed up the aisle his cheeks were on fire, his eyes flamed. He glanced around the room, on whose walls all around were written in great gold letters the names of his works. Ahead he saw the English flag knit with the Stars and Stripes, and above them the word 'Pickwick'. There was a serious look on the face of Lord Lytton, and it seemed to me to say, 'How gladly would I give up my title and my estates to have this enthusiasm surging up to me from the Anglo-Saxon heart.'[4]

---

[1] Ibid. 20 Oct. 1867.
[2] Charles Kent, *The Charles Dickens Dinner*, 1867, pp. 7–8.
[3] 18 Nov. 1867.
[4] Ibid.

B b

The dinner, according to some reports, was 'all that could be desired', but the London correspondent of the *Nation*, 'refrained' from giving his opinion: 'What use is it to speak of drunken waiters, of hopeless scrambles for greasy fragments of tepid dishes, of cold plates with the soup, and hot plates with the ice pudding, and other petty miseries far too insignificant to cross a thousand leagues of salt water?'[1]

After grace was sung there were the usual loyal and patriotic speeches, before Lytton rose to give the toast of the evening. He dwelt, rather obviously, on the theme of the common language of England and America. But though his speech was dull, he kept the attention of his hearers by his peculiar manner:

> Lord Lytton, the Chairman rises. He is excessively made up, and cannot suppress his vanity. . . . His speaking is ingeniously bad. It is the ideal of the hard-shell Baptist preacher from far-away in Old Virginia. A hard convulsive word or two—a long drawl—terminated by a jerk at which the forehead is thrown down until the audience sees the back of the head—this is the history of one of Bulwer's rasping sentences. He throws his hand (with faultless cuffs) straight out; clasps it in under his arm, as a man would pulling in a gudgeon—and this is his gesture. He should appear only in print.[2]

His speech was, nevertheless, repeatedly interrupted by ringing cheers.

Then, when Dickens rose to acknowledge the toast he was, for some time, quite unable to make himself heard. As soon as he got up the whole company rose in their seats, and cheered again and again; those at the lower tables forced their way up the aisles until he was surrounded by a living wall of friends; others 'leaped upon chairs. Tossed up napkins, waved not only glasses, but decanters and half-emptied champagne bottles, over their heads—not without baptizing sundry persons under them'[3]; while the ladies fluttered fans and handkerchiefs from the gallery. 'Twice his throat faltered as he began,' wrote one reporter, 'the glow of his face came before the words, and all felt that it was a sacred moment with him.'[4]—'When I got up to speak', Dickens wrote to Wills next day, 'but for taking a desperate hold of myself, I should have lost my sight and voice and sat down again.' At last he said:

My Lords, Ladies, and Gentlemen, No thanks that I can offer you can express my sense of my reception by this great assemblage, or can in the least suggest to you how deep the glowing words of my friend the chairman, and your acceptance of them, have sunk into my heart. [*Cheers.*] But both combined have so greatly shaken the composure I am used to command in the presence of an audience, that I hope you may observe in me some traces of an eloquence more expressive than the richest words. [*Loud cheers.*] To say that I am fervently grateful to you, is to say—nothing; to say that I can never forget this beautiful sight is to say—nothing. To say that it brings upon me a rush of emotion, not only in its present pride and

[1] *Nation*, New York, 28 Nov. 1867, 'England', pp. 435–6.
[2] *New York Tribune*.   [3] Ibid.   [4] Ibid.

honour, but in the thoughts of its remembrance in the future by those who are dearest to me, is to say—nothing. To feel all this, however, for the moment even almost to pain, is very much indeed. Mercutio says of the wound in his breast, dealt him by the hand of a foe, that—' 'Tis not so deep as a well nor so wide as a church door; but 'tis enough, 'twill serve.' I may say of the wound in my breast, newly dealt by the hands of my friends, that it is deeper than the soundless sea, and wider than the whole Catholic Church. [*Cheers, and a laugh.*] And I may safely add, that it has for the moment almost stricken me dumb.

My Lords, ladies and gentlemen, I should be more than human— and I am very human indeed [*cheers*]—if I could look upon this brilliant representative company and not feel greatly thrilled and stirred by the presence of so many of my brother artists, not only in literature but also in the sister arts, especially painting, among whose professors living, and, unhappily, dead, are many of my oldest and best friends. I hope that I may regard this thronging of my brothers round me as a testimony on their part that they believe that the cause of art generally has been safe in my keeping [*cheers*], and that they think it has never been falsely dealt with by me. [*Renewed cheering.*] Your resounding cheers just now would have been but so many cruel reproaches to me if I could not here declare that, from the earliest days of my career down to this proud night, I have always tried to be true to my calling. [*Great cheering.*] Never unduly to assert it on the one hand, and never on any pretence or consideration, to permit it to be patronized in my person on the other, has been the steady endeavour of my life; and I have occasionally been vain enough to hope that I may leave its social position in England something better than I found it. Similarly, and equally, I hope, without presumption, I trust that I may take this general representation of the public here, through so many orders, pursuits, and degrees, as a token that the public believe, that with a host of imperfections and shortcomings upon my head, I have as a writer, in my soul and conscience, tried to be as true to them as they have ever been to me. [*Loud cheers.*]

And here, in reference to the inner circle of the arts, and the outer circle of the public, I feel it a duty tonight to offer two remarks. I have in my day at odd times heard a great deal about literary sets, and cliques, and coteries, and barriers, and about keeping this man up, and keeping that man down, and about sworn disciples, and sworn unbelievers, and mutual admiration societies, and I know not what other dragons in the upward path. I began to tread it when I was very young, without influence, without money, without companion, introducer, or adviser, and I am bound to put in evidence in this place that I have never lighted on those dragons yet. [*Cheers.*]

So have I heard in my day, at divers other odd times, much generally to the effect that the English people have little or no love of art for its own sake, and that they do not greatly care to acknowledge or do honour to the artist. My own experience has uniformly been exactly the reverse. [*Renewed cheering.*] I *can* say that of my countrymen, although I cannot say that of my country.

And now, ladies and gentlemen, passing to the immediate occasion of your doing me this great honour, the story of my going again to America is very easily and briefly told. Since I was there before, a vast entirely new generation has arisen in the United States. Since I was there before most of the best known of my books have been written and published. The new generation and the books have come together, until, at last, numbers of those who have so widely and constantly read me, have expressed a strong wish that I should read myself. This wish, at first conveyed to me through public channels and business channels, has gradually become enforced by an immense accumulation of letters from individuals, and associations of individuals, all expressing in the same hearty, homely, cordial, unaffected way, a kind of personal interest in me, I had almost said a kind of personal affection for me [*cheers*], which, I am sure you will agree with me, it would be dull insensibility on my part not to prize. Little by little this pressure has become so great that although, as Charles Lamb says, 'My household gods strike a terribly deep root',[1] I have torn them from their places, and this day week, at this hour, shall be upon the sea. You will readily conceive that I am inspired besides by a natural desire to see for myself the astonishing change and progress of a quarter of a century over there, to grasp the hands of many faithful friends whom I left upon those shores, to see the faces of a multitude of new friends upon whom I have never looked, and last, not least, to use my best endeavour to lay down a third cable[2] [*great cheering*] of intercommunication and alliance between the old world and the new. Twelve years ago, when, Heaven knows, I little thought I should ever be bound upon the voyage which now lies before me, I wrote, in that form of my writings which obtains by far the most extensive circulation, these words of the American nation:—'I know full well, whatever little motes my beamy eyes may have descried in theirs, that they are a kind, large-hearted, generous, and great people.'[3] [*Cheers.*] In

[1] *Elia*, 'New Year's Eve'—'My household-gods plant a terrible fixed foot.'
[2] There were two in operation, laid in 1865 and 1866.
[3] From *The Holly-Tree* (Christmas number of *Household Words*, for 1855), 'First Branch: Myself', '. . . full well knowing that, whatever little motes my

that faith I am going to see them again. In that faith I shall, please God, return from them in the spring; in that same faith to live and to die! [*Loud and continued cheering.*]

My Lords, ladies and gentlemen, I told you in the beginning that I could not thank you enough, and Heaven knows I have most thoroughly kept my word. If I may quote one other short sentence from myself, let it imply all that I have left unsaid, and yet most deeply feel; let it, putting a girdle round the earth, comprehend both sides of the Atlantic at once in this moment. 'And so,' as Tiny Tim observed. 'God bless us every one!'

Dickens resumed his seat amids rounds of repeated cheering. Edmund Yates, for some reason, thought he had never 'heard him speak to less advantage' than on this occasion 'when most was expected of him';[1] but everyone else was greatly impressed. Even the rather sour correspondent of the *Nation*, 'went home content that the most important speech of the evening, at any rate, had not missed fire'. According to the reporter of the *Tribune*:

The scene at various passages of this address was indescribable. I do not allude so much to the wild burst of applause which attended it as to the profounder sensations produced by the allusions contained in it—allusions that may be more fully understood here than in America. When, for example, he spoke with much feeling of his never having permitted his calling, on any pretence or consideration, to be patronised in his person, it was appreciated by those who knew that not only had the aristocrats who sought him in success whom they had snubbed in earlier days been snubbed in their turn, but that when a still higher personage than any aristocrat desired to have Mr. Dickens to act a theatrical part in an exalted drawing room, he had returned the simple answer: 'Mr Dickens declines to appear as an artist in any place where he could not appear as a man.'[2]

beamy eyes may have descried in theirs, they belong to a kind, generous, large-hearted, and great people'.

[1] *Recollections and Experiences*, 1884, ii. 113.

[2] The same story was frequently told, with variations, and was introduced into his speech by George William Curtis at the dinner given in Dickens's honour by the New York Press, on 18 Apr. 1868, see p. 383. Immediately afterwards James T. Fields asked Dickens 'if Curtis was quite right in the facts', and Mrs. Fields noted Dickens's reply in her diary.

He answered, 'Not altogether.' It was true that he had rejected a suggestion to perform the *Frozen Deep* at Buckingham Palace, since each of his daughters had a part in the play; and, as neither he nor they had ever been presented at Court, 'of course they could not go as amateur performers where they had never been as visitors'. It was given instead at the Gallery of Illustration, where all went well until after the *Frozen Deep* was over, when Dickens was sent for by the Queen. 'This was considered an act of immense condescension and kindness on her part, and the little party behind the scenes were delighted. Unfortunately, I had just prepared myself for the farce which was to follow and was already standing in motley dress with a red nose. I knew I could not appear in that plight, so I begged leave to be excused on that ground. However, that was forgiven and all passed off well.' The performance cost him £150 to £200, and at the Queen's request she was presented with two beautifully

Other speakers who followed included Sir Charles Wentworth Dilke, Sir Thomas Gabriel, Lord Mayor of London, and A. H. Layard. Sir Edwin Landseer, and Sir Francis Grant, President of the Royal Academy, are said to have 'provided an interlude of dullness'; Ben Webster replied for the Drama; while Trollope made a vigorous speech in defence of fiction in reply to the toast of 'Literature'. He defended it, in a forthright manner, against the prophetic lamentations of Carlyle: 'Oh my friend, you will have to think how perilous and close a cousinship it has with lying.'—Trollope countered by affirming that 'we who write fiction have taught purity of life, nobility of action, and self denial, and have taught those lessons with allurements to both the old and the young which no other teacher of the present day can reach, and which no prophet can teach'.

The Lord Chief Justice, Sir Alexander Cockburn, who had been Lytton's companion at college, proposed the health of the chairman, in an elegant style. Lytton responded, and then went on to give the final toast to 'The Ladies', to which J. B. Buckstone replied:

Mr. Dickens has exhausted the Old World, and is going to the New. I really don't know why I have been selected to return thanks for the Ladies, because I am not particularly, that I am aware of, a ladies' man. [*Much laughter.*] I must acknowledge though, that there are some ladies of my acquaintance with whom I have passed many happy nights [*cries of 'Oh! oh!' and roars of laughter*]—in fact, I mean to say, many happy evenings. [*Much laughter.*] I feel inclined to mention their names, though perhaps hardly etiquette to do so. But I am sure that you will be charmed to know that I mean Mrs. Gamp [*great laughter*], Betsy Prig [*laughter*], Mrs. Nickleby, and not forgetting Mrs. Harris [*laughter*], and I am inclined to add our 'dear little mother'. [*Cheers.*]

The occasion left some Americans unmollified. The *Northern Monthly Magazine* was particularly disgusted at Buckstone's 'indecent utterance', and condemned the whole affair as a 'Sardanapulian scene' or drunken 'orgie'.[1]

The proceedings ended shortly before half past eleven, but Dickens had to shake hands and say good-bye to so many friends, that it was long before he was able to leave. As he appeared, a crowd which had gathered outside, in Great Queen Street, 'gave him a last ringing cheer by way of—Farewell!'[2] He sailed from Liverpool on 9 November, and arrived at Boston ten days later.

---

bound, manuscript copies of the play; since when she had shown no signs of gratitude. 'Good Mr. Dolby said quietly, "You know in England we call her 'Her Ungracious Majesty.'"' (M. A. DeWolfe Howe, *Memories of A Hostess . . . Drawn Chiefly from the Diaries of Mrs. James T. Fields*, 1923, pp. 188–9.)

[1] 'Plain Words Concerning Mr. Charles Dickens', *Northern Monthly Magazine*, Newark, N.J., Jan. 1868, ii. 244–5.

[2] Charles Kent, *The Charles Dickens Dinner*, 1867, p. 32.

FIRST AND FAREWELL READINGS: WASHINGTON

3 *and* 7 *February* 1868

AFTER all the doubts and discussions that had preceded his decision to go on tour in the United States, Dickens's readings turned out a brilliant success. By the time he reached Washington he was half-way through them; and magnificent profits were assured, although he was already beginning to feel the strain.

On 3 February, he gave his first reading in the capital, from the *Carol* and the *Trial from Pickwick*, to an audience which included the President, the chief members of the cabinet, and 'all the foremost men and their families';[1] and on the 7th, on his birthday, he gave the last, from *Nickleby*, and *Boots at the Holly Tree Inn*. In writing home to his daughter he mentioned 'speeches' on both these occasions, although they were really no more than brief remarks.

On 4 February, he wrote, 'the gas was very defective indeed last night, and I began with a small speech to the effect that I must trust to the brightness of their faces for the illumination of mine; this was taken greatly'.[2]

The final reading was at least equally successful, and the audience even more enthusiastic. 'After Boots, at night,' Dickens wrote, 'the whole audience rose and remained (Secretaries of State, President's family, Judges of Supreme Court, and so forth) standing and cheering until I went back to the table and made them a little speech.'[3] He simply said:

LADIES and Gentlemen, In all probability I shall never see your faces again, but I can assure you that yours have yielded me as much pleasure as I have given you.

This was also warmly acknowledged, and the audience then slowly dispersed.

The newspaper reports are more interesting for their general comments on his appearance, and his style of reading. Inevitably they contradict each other. One reporter describes his 'faultlessly neat and white shirt bosom, from which flashes the light of several diamonds, with ditto from a ring upon a left hand finger',[4] while another, on the same night, saw 'not a trace of the old foppery', and 'nothing more pretending than a plain gold stud'.[5] Some of the audience had expected too much from the readings and were rather disappointed, but none the less everyone enjoyed them. All thought the *Trial*, and *Boots* the best, 'better than a picture, and equal to a play'.[6] The reporters agreed in finding Dickens's general style precise, and his rising inflection—more suitable to larger halls—particularly remarkable, though somewhat monotonous.

[1] F, x. ii.
[2] To Mary Dickens, 4 Feb. 1868.
[3] To Mary Dickens, 11 Feb. 1868.
[4] *Daily National Intelligencer.*
[5] *National Republican.*
[6] *Daily Morning Chronicle,* 8 Feb.

The success of the first reading, according to the *National Republican*, was evident from the opening sentence:

From first to last there is no trickery in it—full of action, abounding in gesture, with a voice for every character in every mood; with a face for every man, woman, and child, reflecting every feeling. There is no straining for stage effect, no attitudinizing, no affectation. The most effective reading we ever listened to, it was the most beautifully simple, straightforward, hearty piece of painting from life.

... But, on the whole, his accent and pronounciation are not what we call English. The great difference between his delivery and that of our best Americans is in its slow, deliberate, clear-cut distinctness. This is in the descriptive parts. Where it suits the occasion, his delivery takes every shape, and is good for all needs. Scrooge's growl—Bob Cratchit's trembling appeal—the pompous bluster of Buzfuz—Mrs. Cluppin's maundering whine—and Sam Weller's manly yeoman's shout, and all echoed by that magical voice.

'Mr. Dickens's voice', reported the *Evening Express*, 'is not of the best, but it is wonderful to see how accurately he portrays the different phases of character and shades of feeling.'[1] To his sister-in-law Dickens wrote, 'This is considered the dullest and most apathetic place in America. *My* audiences have been superb';[2] to Lytton, a few days later, 'I am going on in the same splendid way as at first';[3] but to Forster, 'Alas! alas! my cold worse than ever.'[4]

BEFORE A READING: PROVIDENCE, R.I.

DICKENS was worried by ticket-speculators throughout his tour, but serious trouble arose when one of the assistants of George Dolby, his Reading manager, was also found to have been speculating. A reading at New Haven had to be cancelled and at Providence Dickens briefly addressed the audience before he began. He said.

LADIES and Gentlemen, Before I begin my reading, I beg your permission to depart from my usual custom and to interpose a very few not very agreeable words. An hour or two ago I learnt, with an astonishment only to be equalled by my indignation, that a subordinate person in my employment, sent forward here to transact the preliminary business—to which he is well accustomed—had hazarded the amazing statement that his instructions were to sell no fewer than six tickets to one purchaser. Allow me to assure you, on my personal faith and honour, that this statement has no foundation whatever; that the absurd injustice it would involve, if true, is opposed to the invariable practice on my readings both on your side of the Atlantic and on mine; and that I have instantly called this offender to a very strict account indeed.

[1] 4 Feb.
[2] 7 Feb. 1868.
[3] 10 Feb. 1868.
[4] F, x. ii.

Rather curiously, after all this, though Dickens was at first determined to discharge the agent, whose malpractices had cost him £300 at Providence alone, it was later decided to keep him on.

FAREWELL READING: BOSTON
8 *April* 1868

JUST before he began his final series of readings in Boston and New York, Dickens wrote to Forster, on 30 March, and confessed 'I am nearly used up. Climate, distance, catarrh, travelling, and hard work, have begun (I may say so, now they are nearly over) to tell heavily upon me. Sleeplessness besets me.'[1] Half-way through the readings at Boston he was almost in a state of collapse, for 'up to four o'clock in the afternoon' of 3 April, according to Dolby, 'it became a matter of grave doubt whether he would be able to read or not'.[2] But this was the turning-point: at the reading that evening he was reported 'to be in the best of spirits',[3] and to have thrown 'great life and vigor into his work, and appeared at his best'.[4] To his daughter he wrote a few days later, 'I not only read on Friday, when I was doubtful of being able to do so, but read as I never did before, and astonished the audience quite as much as I did myself. You never heard or saw such a scene of excitement.'[5]

The final reading was given on the 8th. The audience was larger than ever, 'numbering the culture and intelligence, and the fashion and influence of the city'.[6] On appearing on the stage, where he was greeted with immense applause, Dickens found that his reading-table had been decorated with flowers, the gift of friends, 'rare and beautiful as they were abundant'.[7] He acknowledged the compliment, and said:

LADIES and Gentlemen, Before allowing Doctor Marigold to tell his story in his own peculiar way, I kiss the kind fair hands unknown which have so beautifully decorated my table this evening.[8] [*Applause.*]

He then went on to read *Doctor Marigold* and *Mrs. Gamp.* The pathetic passages in the first were thought to have been given more tenderly than before, while the humour was 'as lively and brilliant as ever'.[9]

The prolonged and enthusiastic applause, on their conclusion, drew him back as he was leaving the platform, to make a final speech of farewell:

[1] F, x. ii.   [2] *Charles Dickens as I Knew Him*, 1885, p. 296.
[3] *Boston Daily Evening Transcript*, 9 Apr. 1868.
[4] *Boston Daily Advertiser*, 9 Apr. 1868.
[5] To Mary Dickens, 7 Apr. 1868.   [6] *Boston Post*, 9 Apr. 1868.
[7] *Boston Daily Evening Transcript*, 9 Apr. 1868.
[8] As told by Dolby, pp. 296–303, these remarks were made at the reading on the 3rd. There is no doubt that he was wrong: they are not mentioned in any of the reports consulted of the earlier reading, while they are included in all those of the farewell reading. He is also wrong in giving the *Carol* and the *Trial from Pickwick*, in place of *Doctor Marigold* and *Mrs. Gamp.* See also 'Notes on Text and Sources', pp. 441–2.   [9] *Boston Daily Advertiser*, 9 Apr. 1868.

Ladies and Gentlemen, My gracious and generous welcome in America, which can never be obliterated from my remembrance, began here. [*Applause.*] My departure begins here, too; for I assure you that I have never until this moment really felt that I am going away. In this brief life of ours it is sad to do almost anything for the last time, and I cannot conceal from you, although my face will so soon be turned towards my native land, and to all that makes it dear, that it is a sad consideration with me that in a very few moments from this time, this brilliant hall and all that it contains, will fade from my view—for evermore. But it is my consolation that the spirit of the bright faces, the quick perception, the ready response, the generous and the cheering sounds that have made this place delightful to me, will remain; and you may rely upon it that that spirit will abide with me as long as I have sense and sentiment. [*Applause.*]

I do not say this with any limited reference to the private friendships that have for years upon years made Boston a memorable and beloved spot to me, for such private references have no business in this public place. I say it purely in remembrance of, and in homage to, the great public heart before me.

Ladies and gentlemen, I beg most earnestly, most gratefully, and most affectionately, to bid you, each and all, farewell. [*Overwhelming applause.*]

He spoke with great emotion: 'not only were the tears visible in his eyes, but they communicated themselves to his voice'.[1] At the word 'farewell', the audience rose 'amid shouts and cheers, and waving of hats and handkerchiefs',[2] as he left the stage at Boston for the last time.

BANQUET IN HIS HONOUR: NEW YORK

18 *April* 1868

DICKENS had gladly accepted the invitation of the New York Press early in February; but by the time he was nearing the end of the tour, he was quite unfit for any further public appearance. He wrote to W. H. Wills, on the 14th, 'I wish it were over.'[3] On the day of the banquet his right foot was swollen and giving him great pain and 'all hope of getting a boot on was out of the question'.[4] Dolby drove all round New York looking for a gout-stocking to draw over the bandages; and ended by borrowing one from an English gentleman, since no true republican would admit to suffering from such a ludicrously undemocratic complaint.

By the time Dickens was ready, he was over an hour late, and his hosts were getting anxious. The news that he was coming, was received

---

[1] Dolby, p. 301.   [2] *Boston Daily Advertiser*, 9 Apr. 1868.
[3] H.   [4] George Dolby, *Charles Dickens As I Knew Him*, 1885, p. 310.

with tremendous cheers. He was met by the committee at the door of Delmonico's, where the dinner was being held, and wearily limped up stairs, leaning on the arm of Horace Greeley.[1] He was in great pain, but none the less pleased at his welcome; and, thereafter, all went according to plan.

A fine band of music in attendance in an adjoining room favored the company with choice selections and the National airs of the two countries represented by the distinguished guest and his entertainers. The decoration of the tables and the room was in exceedingly good taste, and the rare flowers that graced the board filled the room with the genial breath of Spring.[2]

Greeley was in the Chair. About nine o'clock he rose amid loud applause, to propose the toast of the evening. He recalled how thirty years before, as a young printer in New York he had had 'the audacity to undertake the editing and publishing a weekly newspaper for the first time'. Among the contributions included in the first number of this first journal with which his name was ever connected, had been a sketch entitled 'Delicate Attentions', from the old *Monthly Magazine*, better known in its later form as 'Mr. Watkins Tottle'. It was 'by a then unknown writer—known to us only by the quaint designation of "Boz".' He concluded by giving them the sentiment of 'Health and happiness, honour and generous (because just) recompense, to our friend and guest, Charles Dickens'. It was received with tremendous applause, and three hearty cheers.

Dickens rose and, said:

Gentlemen, I cannot do better than take my cue from your distinguished President, and to refer in my first remarks to his remarks in connexion with the old natural association between you and me. When I received an invitation from a private association of working members of the Press of New York to dine with them today, I accepted that compliment in grateful remembrance of a calling that was once my own, and in loyal sympathy towards a brotherhood which, in the spirit, I have never quitted. ['*Good*', '*Good*', *and applause.*] To the wholesome training of severe newspaper work, when I was a very young man, I constantly refer my first successes; and my sons will hereafter testify of their father that he was always steadily proud of that ladder by which he rose. [*Great applause.*] If it were otherwise I should have but a very poor opinion of their father—which, perhaps, upon the whole, I have not. [*Laughter and cheers.*] Hence, gentlemen, under any circumstances, this company would have been exceptionally interesting and gratifying to me. But whereas I supposed that, like the fairies'

---

[1] Horace Greeley (1811–72), editor of the *New York Tribune*, 1841; social and moral crusader; almost uniformly failed in his candidacy for political office, culminating in his defeat in a campaign for the Presidency in 1872.

[2] *New York Tribune*, 20 Apr. 1868.

pavilion in the *Arabian Nights*, it would be but a mere handful, and I find it to turn out, like the same elastic pavilion, capable of comprehending a multitude, so much the more proud am I of the honour of being your guest; for you will readily believe that the more widely representative of the Press in America my entertainers are, the more I must feel the good-will and the kindly sentiments towards me of that vast institution. [*Applause.*]

Gentlemen, so much of my voice has lately been heard in the land, and I have for upwards of four hard winter months so contended against what I have been sometimes quite admiringly assured was 'a true American catarrh' [*laughter*]—a possession which I have throughout highly appreciated, though I might have preferred to be naturalized by any other outward and visible means. [*Shouts of laughter.*] I say, gentlemen, so much of my voice has lately been heard, that I might have been contented with troubling you no further from my present standing-point, were it not a duty with which I henceforth charge myself, not only here but on every suitable occasion, whatsoever and wheresoever, to express my high and grateful sense of my second reception in America, and to bear my honest testimony to the national generosity and magnaminity. [*Great applause.*] Also, to declare how astounded I have been by the amazing changes that I have seen around me on every side—changes moral, changes physical, changes in the amount of land subdued and peopled, changes in the rise of vast new cities, changes in the growth of older cities almost out of recognition, changes in the graces and amenities of life, changes in the Press, without whose advancement no advancement can be made anywhere. [*Applause.*] Nor am I, believe me, so arrogant as to suppose that in five-and-twenty years there have been no changes in me, and that I have nothing to learn, and that I had nothing to learn and no extreme impressions to correct from when I was here first. [*A voice—'Noble,' and applause.*]

And, gentlemen, this brings me to a point on which I have, ever since I landed here last November, observed a strict silence, though sometimes tempted to break it, but in reference to which I will, with your permission, beg leave to take you now into my confidence. [*Laughter and applause—cries of 'Silence'.*] Even the Press, being human [*laughter*], may be sometimes mistaken or misinformed, and I rather think that I have myself, on one or two occasions, in some rare instances, known its information to be not perfectly accurate with reference to myself. [*Laughter and applause.*] Indeed, I have now and again been more surprised by printed news that I have read of myself, than by any printed news that I have ever read in my present state of existence. [*Laughter.*] Thus, the vigour and perseverance with which I have for some months past been collecting materials and hammering away at a new book on America have much astonished me [*renewed laughter*]; seeing that all that time it has been perfectly well known to my publishers on both sides of the Atlantic, that I positively declared that no consideration on earth should induce me to write one. But what I have intended, what I have resolved upon (and this is the confidence I seek to place in you) is, on my return to England, in my own person to bear, for the behoof of my countrymen, such testimony to the gigantic changes in this country as I have hinted at tonight. [*Immense applause.*] Also, to record that wherever I have been, in the smallest places equally with the largest, I have been received with unsurpassable politeness, delicacy, sweet temper, hospitality, consideration, and with unsurpassable respect for the privacy daily enforced upon me by the nature of my avocation here, and the state of my health. [*Applause.*] This testimony, so long as I live, and so long as my descendants have any legal right in my books, I shall cause to be republished, as an appendix to every copy of those two books of mine in which I have referred to America. [*Tremendous applause.*] And this I will do and cause to be done, not in mere love and thankfulness, but because I regard it as an act of plain justice and honour. [*'Bravo!' and cheers.*]

Gentlemen, the transition from my own feelings towards and interest in America to those of the mass of my countrymen seems to be a natural one; but, whether or no, I make it with an express object. I was asked in this very city, about last Christmas time, whether an American was not at some disadvantage in England as a foreigner. The notion of an American being regarded in England as a foreigner at all, of his ever being thought of or spoken of in that character, was so uncommonly incongruous and absurd to me, that my gravity was for the moment quite overpowered. [*Laughter.*] As soon as it was restored, I said that for years and years past I hoped I had had as many American friends and had received as many American visitors as almost any Englishman living, and that my unvarying experience, fortified by theirs, was that it was enough in England to be an American to be received with the readiest respect and recognition anywhere. [*Applause.*] Hereupon, out of half a dozen people, suddenly spoke out two, one an American gentleman, with a cultivated taste for art, who, finding himself on a certain Sunday outside the walls of a certain historical English castle, famous for its pictures, was refused admission there, according to the strict rules of the establishment on that day, but who, on merely representing that he was an American gentleman on his travels, had, not to say the picture gallery, but the whole castle, placed at his immediate disposal. [*Laughter.*] The other was a lady who, being in London, and having a great desire to see the famous reading-room of the British Museum, was assured by the English family with whom she stayed that it was unfortunately impossible, because the place was closed for a week, and she had only three days there. Upon that lady's going to the Museum, as she assured me, alone to the gate, self-introduced as an American lady, the gate flew open, as it were magically. [*Laughter and applause.*] I am unwillingly bound to add that she certainly was young and exceedingly pretty. [*Laughter.*] Still, the porter of that institution is of an obese habit [*laughter*], and, according to the best of my observation of him, not very impressible. [*Great laughter and cheering.*]

Now, gentlemen, I refer to these trifles as a collateral assurance to you that the Englishman who shall humbly strive, as I hope to do, to be in England as faithful to America as to England herself, has no previous conceptions to contend against. [*'Good!' 'Good!' and cheers.*] Points of difference there have been, points of difference there are, points of difference there probably always will be between the two great peoples. But broadcast in England is sown the sentiment that those two peoples are essentially one [*great applause*], and that it rests with them jointly to uphold the great Anglo-Saxon race, to which our President has referred, and all its great achievements before the world. [*'Bravo!' and applause.*] And if I know anything of my countrymen—and they give me credit for knowing something—if I know anything of my countrymen, gentlemen, the English heart is stirred by the fluttering of those Stars and Stripes, as it is stirred by no other flag that flies except its own. [*Tremendous applause, and three cheers.*] If I know my countrymen, in any and every relation towards America, they begin, not as Sir Anthony Absolute recommended that lovers should begin, with 'a little aversion', but with a great liking and profound respect [*applause*]; and whatever the little sensitiveness of the moment, or the little official passion, or the little official policy now, or then, or here, or there, may be, take my word for it, that the first enduring, great popular consideration in England is a generous construction of justice. [*'Bravo!' and cheers.*]

Finally, gentlemen, and I say this subject to your correction, I do believe that from the great majority of honest minds on both sides, there cannot be absent the conviction that it would be better for this globe to be riven by an earthquake, fired by a comet, overrun by an iceberg, and abandoned to the Arctic fox and bear, than that it should present the spectacle of these two great nations each of which has, in its own way and hour, striven so hard and so successfully for freedom, ever again being arrayed the one against

the other. [*Tumultuous applause, the company rising and cheering.*]
Gentlemen, I cannot thank your President enough, or you enough,
for your kind reception of my health and of my poor remarks; but,
believe me, I do thank you with the utmost fervour of which my soul
is capable. [*Great applause.*]

The band played 'God Save the Queen', in singing which the company
joined. The chairman then proposed 'The New York Press', to which
Henry J. Raymond replied; and the band played the 'Star-spangled
Banner'. George William Curtis responded on behalf of 'The Weekly
Press', in a speech which, after his return to England, Dickens declared
the best he had ever heard. A succession of other toasts followed, to the
Monthly Press, the Press of Boston, of New England, of Philadelphia, of
the north, the west, the south, the south-west, and to the Scientific Press.

Dickens was still in pain and left the hall, to the cheers of his hosts,
before the speech-making was over. Mrs. James T. Fields noted in her
diary, that 'he returned with his foot feeling better.'[1] But the improvement was not to last for long.

FAREWELL READING: NEW YORK

20 *April* 1868

ALTHOUGH he seemed stronger immediately after the banquet, the
old illness soon reasserted itself, and he had to face the final reading in
America as an ordeal. On the night itself, a printed certificate by his
doctor was distributed throughout the hall to explain that he was 'suffering from a neuralgic affection of the right foot', but that it was thought
that he would be able to read 'without much pain or inconvenience'.
The *Carol* and the *Trial from Pickwick* were given without mishap; and,
on conclusion, Dickens said:

LADIES and gentlemen, The shadow of one word has impended
over me all this evening, and the time has come at last when the
shadow must fall. It is but a very short one, but the weight of such
things is not measurable by their length, and two much shorter
words express the whole round of our human existence. When I
was reading *David Copperfield* here last Thursday night, I felt there
was more than usual significance for me in Mr. Peggotty's
declaration, 'My future life lies over the sea.' And when I closed this
book just now, I felt most keenly that I was shortly to establish such
an *alibi* as would have satisfied even the elder Mr. Weller. [*Laughter.*]

The relations that have been set up between us in this place—
relations sustained, on my side at least, by the most earnest devotion of myself to my task: sustained by yourselves, on your side,
by the readiest sympathy and kindest acknowledgement—must

[1] *Memories of a Hostess*, ed. Mark A. DeWolfe Howe, 1923, p. 184.

now be broken, for ever. But I entreat you to believe that in passing from my sight, you will not pass from my memory. I shall often, often recall you as I see you now, equally by my winter fire and in the green English summer weather. I shall never recall you as a mere public audience, but rather as a host of personal friends, and ever with the greatest gratitude, tenderness, and consideration. Ladies and gentlemen, I beg to bid you farewell—and I pray God bless you, and God bless the land in which I leave you. [*Great applause.*]

'This little speech', wrote Dolby, 'was listened to with rapt attention, and after many recalls, and much shouting, cheering, and waving of handkerchiefs, Mr. Dickens retired from the platform, never any more to appear in public in America.'[1] They embarked in the *Russia* on the 22nd, and were in Liverpool by 1 May.

BANQUET IN HIS HONOUR AT SAINT GEORGE'S HALL: LIVERPOOL

10 *April* 1869

IT was proposed at a meeting of the City Council, early in December, that a civic banquet should be given in Dickens's honour, when he visited Liverpool on his farewell tour. Dickens accepted,[2] and arrangements were made for the first provincial celebration in his honour since his reception at Edinburgh in 1841.

The banquet was organized on a grand scale. Over 650 guests were to sit down to dine, and as many more to be present as spectators in the gallery and orchestra. On his arrival Dickens was appalled at the size of the hall and the arrangements that had been made. He borrowed some flags from the Navy, and had them hung up all over the place 'with some hope of stopping echoes'.[3] A detachment of seamen was detailed to carry out his orders the day before the banquet; and Dickens wrote to James T. Fields that 'they were all hanging on aloft upside down, holding to the gigantically high roof by nothing, this morning, in the most wonderfully cheerful manner'.[4]—'Seriously,' he wrote, 'it is less adapted to speaking than Westminster Abbey, and is as large';[4] and, 'my only consolation is that if anybody can be heard, *I* probably can be'.[3]

The scene in the hall was said to be magnificent. The *Courier* might grumble that the dingy flags had 'seen a good deal of service', and that 'the lowered lights . . . had a sort of dim cathedral effect, more suggestive of funeral baked meats than of festivities[5]; but others could 'only write in terms of praise and approbation'.[6]

---

[1] *Charles Dickens As I Knew Him*, 1885, pp. 320–1.

[2] To Thomas Dover, 22 Dec. 1868—MS. Hornby Collection, Picton Library, Liverpool.   [3] To Georgina Hogarth, 4 Apr. 1869.

[4] 9 Apr. 1869.   [5] *Daily Courier*, leader.

[6] *The Porcupine*, Liverpool, 17 Apr. 1869, pp. 16–17.

It was not, however, until after the dinner, when the orchestra and galleries began to fill, and the lights were turned full on, that the scene assumed its most brilliant aspect; . . . we doubt whether ever a banquet in Liverpool was graced with so much beauty and fashion. The principal tables were laden with flowers and plants, and sparkling with rich silver candelabra and specimens of fine art work. A silver gilt fountain, . . . which dispensed refreshing streams of rose water, was placed in front of the chairman's seat. The band of the police force was placed in the vestibule, and played during the arrival of the guests, and during the dinner the band of the Orphan Asylums . . . performed in the gallery of the hall.

At half-past five o'clock the distinguished guests entered the hall and took their places, the whole audience rising and cheering vociferously. Messrs. Charles Dickens and the Mayor of Liverpool led the way, his worship taking the chair, with Mr. Dickens upon the right.

The banquet . . . was of the most sumptuous and recherché character.[1]

As soon as the tables had been cleared, the mayor rose and proposed the usual loyal toasts, which were enthusiastically received. Vice-Admiral Evans, replying for the Navy paid a special tribute to Captain Cuttle; which 'seemed to please Mr. Dickens hugely'.[1]

The Right Hon. Lord Dufferin,[2] Chancellor of the Exchequer, responded on behalf of 'Her Majesty's Ministers'; and then the Rev. Dr. Bateson, Master of Trinity College, Cambridge proposed 'The Houses of Parliament' to which Lord Houghton[3] replied. Speaking with entire good humour, he took the opportunity to defend the House of Lords, and to express his regret that Dickens had never taken an active part in political affairs:

I may say that it has struck the members of that assembly which I represent with occasional pain and regret, that amidst the life-like and admirable portraitures of every class of society in Mr. Dickens's works, the members of the House of Lords appear in a not very frequent or flattering character. [*Laughter.*] In fact, ladies and gentlemen, I can hardly speak aloud the designation which Mr. Dickens has bestowed upon us. [*Mr. Dickens: 'Oh! do.'*] Well, I really cannot. [*Laughter.*] . . .

My friend, Mr. Dickens, has shown little or no interest in the matter of our political life. Why has he not taken part in the civic rights of his friends? [*Hear, hear, and a laugh.*] . . . I regret that Mr. Dickens has not been our comrade in this matter, because I know that those wonderful powers of expression, to the utterance of which you yourselves have lately been witness, and with his large heart and deep sympathy and insight into the wants and wishes and ways of the people of this country, he would have been a great power in our great national assembly. [*Hear, hear, and cheers.*] And if he had chosen, or, perhaps, condescended so far, he might have succeeded to the honours of Lord Macaulay or Lord Lytton. [*Renewed cheering.*] It may seem somewhat ungenerous to say that any one man who has done so much, could have been asked to do anything more; therefore I feel we have here to express

---

[1] *Daily Courier*, report.

[2] Frederick Temple Blackwood, Lord Dufferin (1826–1902), diplomatist; Liberal; author of *Letters from High Latitudes*, 1856.

[3] Richard Monckton Milnes, see p. 194 n.; he had been created Baron Houghton in 1863.

but the deepest gratitude which we owe to Mr. Dickens. Gratitude is the genius of this meeting, and to it I give my entire homage. [*Cheers.*]

Lord Dufferin then proposed the toast of the evening; saying, in the course of his speech, with the farewell readings in mind:

He has so penetrated our very hearts and our very natures with the inspiration of his genius that he has established between us something of a domestic tie, and we are naturally anxious to grant the freedom of our hearts to him who has added a tenfold grace to all our social intercourse. [*Cheers.*] This feeling has been universal amongst Mr. Dickens's own countrymen, and he has been good enough of late to gratify it, at much inconvenience to himself, by his public readings in several great towns in Great Britain and Ireland.

On rising to reply, Dickens was received with loud cheering, and said:

MR. MAYOR, Ladies and Gentlemen, Although I have become so well accustomed of late to the sound of my own voice in this neighbourhood as to hear it with perfect composure [*laughter*], the occasion is, believe me, very very different in respect of those overwhelming voices of yours. As Professor Wilson[1] once confided to me in Edinburgh that I had not the least idea from hearing him in public, what a magnificent speaker he found himself to be when quite alone [*laughter*], so you can form no conception, from the specimen before you, of the eloquence with which I shall thank you again and again in some of the innermost moments of my future life. [*Loud cheers.*] Often and often then, God willing, my memory will recall this brilliant scene, and will reilluminate this:

> —banquet hall deserted,
> Whose lights are fled
> Whose garlands dead
> And all but I departed:[2]

and, faithful to this place in its present aspect, I will mark and observe it exactly as it stands—not one man's seat empty, not one woman's fair face absent—while life and memory abide by me. [*Cheers.*]

Mr. Mayor, Lord Dufferin in his speech so affecting to me, so eloquently uttered, and so rapturously received, made a graceful and gracious allusion to the immediate occasion of my present visit to your noble city. It is no homage to Liverpool, based upon a moment's untrustworthy enthusiasm, but it is a solid fact built upon the rock of experience that when I first made up my mind, after considerable deliberation, systematically to meet my readers in large numbers, face to face, and to try to express myself to them through the breath of life, Liverpool stood foremost among the great places outside London to which I looked with eager confidence and pleasure. [*Cheers.*] And why was this? Not merely

---

[1] See p. 8 n.   [2] Thomas Moore, 'Oft in The Stilly Night'.

because of the reputation of its citizens for generous estimation of the arts; not merely because I had unworthily filled the chair of its great self-educational institution long ago [*hear, hear*]; not merely because the place had been a home to me since the well-remembered day when its blessed roofs and steeples dipped into the Mersey behind me on the occasion of my first sailing away to see my generous friends across the Atlantic [*hear, and applause*] seven-and-twenty years ago. Not for one of those considerations; but because it had been my happiness to have a public opportunity of testing the spirit of its people. I had asked Liverpool for help towards the worthy preservation of Shakespeare's house. [*Applause.*] On another occasion I had ventured to address Liverpool in the names of Leigh Hunt and Sheridan Knowles. [*Applause.*] On still another occasion I had addressed it in the cause of the brotherhood and sisterhood of letters and the kindred arts.[1] And on each and all the response had been unsurpassably spontaneous, open-handed, and munificent. [*Hear, hear.*]

Mr. Mayor, and ladies and gentlemen, if I may venture to take a small illustration of my present position from my own peculiar craft, I would say that there is this objection, in writing fiction, to giving the story an autobiographical form: that through whatever dangers the narrator may pass, it is clear unfortunately to the reader beforehand that he must come through them somehow [*laughter*], else he could not have lived to tell the tale. [*Renewed laughter and applause.*] Now in speaking fact, when the fact is associated with such honours as those with which you have enriched me, there is this singular difficulty in returning thanks, that the speaker must infallibly come back to himself through whatever oratorical disasters he may languish on the road. [*Laughter.*] Let me, therefore,—let me, then, take the plainer and simpler middle course of dividing my subject equally between myself and you. [*Applause.*] Let me assure you that whatever you have accepted with pleasure, either by word of pen or by word of mouth, from me, you have greatly improved in the acceptance. [*Cheers.*] As the gold is said to be doubly and trebly refined which has seven times passed the furnace, so a fancy may be said to become more and more refined each time it passes through the human heart. [*Loud applause.*] You have, and you know you have, brought to the consideration of me that quality in yourselves without which I should have beaten the air. Your earnestness has stimulated mine, your

---

[1] In July 1847 the Amateur Players had performed at Liverpool in aid of Leigh Hunt, in June 1848 for the endowment of the curatorship of Shakespeare's house at Stratford—the proceeds were eventually diverted to Knowles; and, in Feb. 1852, for the Guild of Literature and Art.

laughter has made me laugh, and your tears have overflowed my eyes. [*Loud applause.*] All that I claim for myself, in establishing the relations which exist between us, is constant fidelity to hard work. My literary brethren about me, of whom I am proud to see so many [*applause*], know very well how true it is, of all art, that what seems the easiest done is oftentimes the most difficult to do, and that the smallest truth may come of the greatest pains,— much, as it occurred to me at Manchester, the other day, the sensitive touch of Mr. Whitworth's[1] wonderful measuring machine comes at last, though Heaven, Manchester, and its maker only knew how much previous hammering and firing were required to bring it out. [*Hear, hear.*] And my companions-in-arms know thoroughly well, and I think it is right that the public should know too, that in our careful toil and trouble, and in our steady striving for excellence— not in any little gifts, misused by fits and starts—lies our highest duty at once to our calling, to one another, to ourselves and to you. [*Applause.*]

Ladies and gentlemen, before sitting down I find that I have to clear myself of two very unexpected accusations. [*Hear, hear.*] The first is a most singular charge preferred against me by my old friend Lord Houghton: that I have been somewhat unconscious of the merits of the House of Lords. [*Laughter.*] Now, ladies and gentlemen, seeing that I have had some not altogether obscure or unknown personal friends in that assembly; seeing that I had some little association with, and knowledge of, a certain obscure peer lately[2] known in England by the name of Lord Brougham[3] [*renewed laughter*]; seeing that I regard with some admiration and affection another obscure peer wholly unknown in literary circles, called Lord Lytton [*continued laughter*]; seeing also that I have had for some years some slight admiration of the extraordinary judicial properties and amazingly acute mind of a certain Lord Chief Justice popularly known by the name of Lord Cockburn; and also seeing that there is no man in England whom I more respect in his public capacity, whom I love more in his private capacity, or from whom

---

[1] Joseph Whitworth (1803–87), mechanical engineer; constructed famous measuring-machine; established system of standard measures and gauges, and a uniform system of screw threads; from 1855 began the design and manufacture of armaments, which were consistently superior to those favoured by the War Office, but which for some time were systematically rejected by 'circumlocutionary' officials; created baronet, 1 Nov. 1869.

[2] *Lately*: alternatively 'little'.

[3] Henry Peter Brougham, Baron Brougham and Vaux (1778–1868), Lord Chancellor 1830–4; Edinburgh Reviewer; advocate of law reform, abolition of slavery, and popular education; founder of Society for the Diffusion of Useful Knowledge, 1825, and London University, 1828. Well acquainted with Dickens, especially about 1840–3.

I have received more remarkable proofs of his honour and love of literature, than another obscure nobleman called Lord Russell [*renewed laughter and applause*]; taking all these circumstances into consideration, I was rather amazed by my noble friend's accusation. When I asked him, on his sitting down, what amazing devil possessed him to make this charge, he replied that he had never forgotten the days of Lord Verisopht.[1] [*Laughter.*] Then, ladies and gentlemen, I understood it all; because it is a remarkable fact, that in the days when that depreciative and profoundly unnatural character was invented, there was no Lord Houghton in the House of Lords. [*Loud laughter and applause.*] And there was in the House of Commons, a rather indifferent member called Richard Monckton Milnes. [*Laughter.*]

Ladies and gentlemen, to conclude [*cries of 'No,' and 'Go on'*] —for the present [*laughter*]; to conclude, I close with the other charge of my noble friend, and here I am more serious, and I may be allowed perhaps to express my seriousness in half a dozen plain words. When I first took Literature as my profession in England, I calmly resolved within myself that whether I succeeded or whether I failed, Literature should be my sole profession. [*Hear, hear, and applause.*] It appeared to me at that time that it was not so well understood in England as it was in other countries that Literature was a dignified profession [*hear, hear*], by which any man might stand or fall. [*Applause.*] I made a compact with myself that in my person Literature should stand, and by itself, of itself, and for itself [*hear, hear*]; and there is no consideration on earth that would induce me to break that bargain. [*Loud applause.*]

Ladies and gentlemen, finally allow me to thank you for your great kindness, and for the touching earnestness with which you have drunk my health. I should have thanked you with all my heart if it had not so unfortunately happened that, for many sufficient reasons, I lost my heart, at between half-past six and half-past seven o'clock tonight.[2] [*Loud and prolonged cheering.*]

The next toast was to 'Modern Literature', which was associated with the names of Anthony Trollope, and William Hepworth Dixon, the editor of the *Athenaeum*. Trollope began by saying that he would speak on light literature, while leaving the 'heavy part' to Dixon; and that:

You have in this room the man who, of all others in England, and, I firmly believe, in the world, would be the most fit to make that short speech which

---

[1] *Nicholas Nickleby*, 1838–9; Verisopht was one of the very few honest and likeable members of the nobility in the novels, and far more admirable for example than Lord Coodle, Lord Decimus Tite Barnacle, and Lord Snigsworth, in *Bleak House*, *Little Dorrit*, and *Our Mutual Friend*.

[2] When the ladies were admitted to the gallery.

I have now to make to you. That man is Mr. Dickens. [*Applause.*] In the ranks of light literature he is *facile princeps*.

He went on, characteristically, to speak in defence of writers of fiction, taking as his text some recent words of Froude in an inaugural address to the students of Saint Andrews: 'Without taking more than a simple view of the matter, literature happens to be the only occupation in which wages are not given in proportion to the goodness of the work done'.

I think you will agree with me—and I am quite sure that those who are connected with me in my profession will agree with me—that the people of England are not so stupid, are not so bad, and are not so vain, as not to give bad wages for bad work, or so blind as not to give good wages for good work. [*Hear, hear.*] We work hard, and do our best to please you; and I believe that as far as we work well you will accept our work, and when we work ill you will reject our work. [*Hear, hear.*] If we can so amuse you without making the purity of woman less pure, without making the manliness of man less manly— then, I say, we do a great and good work.

Trollope had spoken in defence of light literature; but Hepworth Dixon made an ill-advised attack on 'official formalism', the 'circumlocution office', and 'red-tapeism which belongs to the past' which denied an adequate recognition of Modern Literature by the state.

The *Courier* was outspoken:

Mr. Anthony Trollope has not an agreeable voice, but his short speech was marked by manliness, good sense, and a touch of quiet humour. . . . Mr. Hepworth Dixon has an even more unsympathetic voice than Mr. Trollope . . . and . . . his well-meant vindication of the rights of literature was so cumbrously conceived and so offensively expressed, that he scored the distinction of being one of the triumvirate of speakers who were 'put down' by general consent.[1]

He referred to the expected appointment of J. L. Motley as the American minister in England, and to Washington Irving who had been American ambassador to Spain. He went on to say that Dickens was 'the English Washington Irving and a great deal more'; yet it would be thought 'a joke' if he were appointed English ambassador to the United States. 'Well, now', he asked, 'why should this be?'

Alphonse Esquiros, of the *Revue des Deux Mondes*, Andrew Halliday, dramatist and contributor to *All the Year Round*, and the Mayor of Manchester spoke next, replying to the toast to 'distinguished visitors'. Halliday distinguished himself still further by making a speech 'neither eloquent, nor witty, but simply impertinent', and which was not well received, in which he complained at the 'Drama' having been omitted from the toast-list when the 'Newspaper Press' was included. The toast to the latter, which had a special association with the principal guest, was given by Lord Houghton. His speech 'became curiously hazy towards

---

[1] *Daily Courier*, leader. The 'triumvirate' were the Principal of Liverpool College, who had replied for the clergy; Dixon himself; and Lord Houghton, on later proposing the 'Newspaper Press'. There were several interruptions during Dixon's speech.

its close, and consequently was received with good-natured impatience'.
'How much more potent a fluid is champagne', said the *Courier*, 'than
nepenthe'.

G. A. Sala, who replied for the Press, evidently had a stronger head.
Dickens had had his doubts. 'As he is certain to be drunk', he had
written to Miss Hogarth, 'I am in great hesitation whether or no I
should warn the innocent committee'. He was thought, however, to
have made 'a modest, sensible, but most effective speech'.

Dickens then rose, and was again received with great applause. He said:

Gentlemen—for I address myself solely to you—the nature of
the toast I am about to propose cannot, I think, be better or more
briefly expressed than in a short quotation from Shakespeare,
slightly altered:

> Scene: A banqueting hall. Thunder—of admiration. Light-
> ning—of eyes. Enter Macbeth and Banquo:
> Banquo: Who are these,
>   So sparkling and so bright in their attire,
> [*laughter*]   That look not like the inhabitants o' the earth
>   And yet are on't?
> [*Loud laughter and applause.*] Reply:
>   Sir, these are the Lancashire Witches.[2]

[*Applause.*]

Pondering this turn in my mind just now, and looking round this
magnificent hall, I naturally pondered also on the legend of its
patron saint. It is recorded of Saint George that he was even more
devoted to love and beauty than the other six Champions of Chris-
tendom. [*Laughter and applause.*] And I, his loyal imitator and disciple, have moulded myself completely upon him in looking around
me here.

> How happy could I be with either,
> Were t'other dear charmer away,[3]

[*laughter*] is a sentiment that was first put into writing some few
ages after Saint George's time; but I have a profound conviction
that he would have originated it if he could have projected himself
into this occasion. [*Laughter.*] However, he was much better employed in killing the Dragon. [*Cries of 'Oh!'*] Oh yes!—much better
employed in killing the Dragon, who would have devoured the lady.
And he was much better employed still, in marrying the lady, and
enslaving himself by freeing her. The legend, as I remember, goes
on to relate that the accursed brood of dragons after that time
retired into inaccessible solitudes, and was seen no more—except

---

[1] 4 Apr. 1869.   [2] See p. 51 n.   [3] Gay, *The Beggar's Opera*, II. xiii.

on very special occasions. [*Laughter.*] Now, it occurs to me, that if any of those dragons should yet be lingering in retirement, and if they should have, in virtue of any bewitched sixth sense, the slightest notion of the havoc that will be wrought amongst Saint George's descendants by this assembly of glowing beauty here tonight, then the dragon race is even with Saint George at last, and is most terribly avenged. [*Laughter and applause.*] Gentlemen, I give you 'The Ladies'. [*Cheers.*]

Mr. George Segar, a young local barrister, replied for the Ladies. He complained that in saying that 'were t'other dear charmer away', Dickens implied that his affections were confined to a single lady, 'which was not exactly the thing which they, as ladies, had expected from Mr. Dickens'. He spoke fluently, but made a fatal slip. 'Speaking for the ladies,' he said, 'and for myself as one of them——.' —'There was a titter', noted one of the audience, 'and I caught a gleam from Dickens's wonderful eyes.'[1]

For the last time he rose, to propose the final toast of the evening, 'The Mayor and Corporation', saying:

Ladies and gentlemen, the learned lady who has just sat down [*laughter*[2]] has completely mistaken me. I referred not to my having been enslaved tonight by one lady, or two, but by all present [*laughter*]; and when I made the quotation from Captain Macheath, I made a quotation from a gentleman who, though he happened at the moment to be attended by only two ladies, was notoriously the slave, as I am, of the whole sex. [*Laughter and applause.*]

I have now, ladies and gentlemen, to propose to you a toast inseparable from the enterprise of Liverpool—from the public honour and public spirit of Liverpool; equally inseparable from the stately streets and buildings around us, and from the hospitals, schools, and free libraries, and those great monuments of consideration for the many which have made this place an example to England. [*Great cheering.*] I have to propose to you to drink 'His Worship the Mayor and the Corporation of this Town'.

Dickens resumed his seat amid the most enthusiastic cheering; and the mayor having briefly acknowledged the toast, the company separated.

The arrangements for the banquet had gone well, and they were marred only after they were practically over by what the *Courier* subtitled 'Disgraceful Row at the Cloakroom'. The attendants were slow in giving out the hats and coats, and 'gentlemen began to get rather impatient and to use high words'; they started pushing each other about, 'and blows were exchanged pretty freely'. A file of police constables then had to be called in, who, 'after a great amount of trouble,

[1] L. F. Austin, *Points of View*, 1908, p. 164.
[2] Ibid. 'The shout that stormed through the hall still rings in my ears.'

managed to restore order but not quietness, and compelled the "gentle-men" to go up to the cloakroom one at a time'.

The Press at once took up the more controversial points introduced by some of the speakers. The *Pall Mall Gazette*[1] suggested there was personal hostility behind Dickens's exchanges with Lord Houghton, which the *Porcupine* quite justly declared 'an unworthy and untruthful attempt to give the colour of a squabble to the good humoured chaff that passed between [them]. . . . It is enough to say that all who heard this little mock passage-at-arms regarded it in its true light; and no one believed that there was the slightest loss of temper in it'.[2]

The *Saturday Review* was contemptuous of the whole affair, ridiculing the speakers as utterly unrepresentative of Literature: 'With the Liver-pool estimate of letters accepted, there is a chance of our forgetting that we have, or recently had, a Hallam and a Milman and a Grote, a Thirl-wall and a Merivale, a Tennyson and a Browning, a Darwin and an Owen, and a Newman and a Mill among us.' *The Times*[3] quite seriously put forward the suggestion that not only might Dickens have done well to enter politics, but that he should be considered in connexion with Earl Russell's new Bill for creating Life-Peerages. This only gave the *Review* a further opportunity for expressing its usual scorn for all fiction and writers of fiction, of which it took full advantage.

The weekly reviews could no longer ignore him; but the greater Dickens's popularity, the less acceptable was his success. The *Spectator* refused to consider him a writer 'of absolute sincerity and realism'— which few ever supposed he was—but thought that:

. . . half the geniality which is supposed to be Mr. Dickens's great merit is in the most vulgar good humour of temperament—a strong disposition to approve the distribution of punch and plum-pudding, slap men heartily on the back, and kiss pretty women behind doors. . . . His picture of domestic affections, which Lord Dufferin calls the strong point of his teaching, seems to us very defective in simplicity and reserve. It is not really English and tends to modify English family feeling in the direction of theatric tenderness and an impulsive-ness wholly wanting in self-control.[4]

The authentic Podsnap, when he disapproved of anything, 'would con-clusively observe, "Not English!"' when PRESTO! with a flourish of the arm, and a flush of the face', it was swept away. Yet as Dickens was walking to the station next day, he was stopped again and again, 'by persons of the working classes wanting to shake hands with him; and all of them eager to thank him for the pleasure his books had afforded them'.[5]

[1] 12 Apr., p. 8.
[2] 17 Apr., pp. 16–17.
[3] 14 Apr., p. 9.
[4] 17 Apr., 'Mr. Dickens's Moral Services to Literature', pp. 474–5.
[5] George Dolby, *Charles Dickens as I Knew Him*, 1885, p. 400.

BANQUET TO THE OXFORD AND HARVARD CREWS

30 *August* 1869

THE long-awaited match between Oxford and Harvard took place on 27 August. Harvard were the challengers of the all-conquering Oxford four, and the race was rowed from Putney to Mortlake. The keenest interest was excited, and it was treated as an international event. The two crews were closely matched, although Oxford were, if anything, the favourites; but Harvard made an excellent start, and were soon over a length in front. Oxford only began to overhaul them, 'inch by inch, and stroke by stroke', as they came in sight of Hammersmith Bridge; they drew abreast on rounding the bend just below Chiswick Eyot, and the Oxford crew rowed home the winners by about three-quarters of a length.

The London Rowing Club invited both crews to a dinner at the Crystal Palace. Immediately after dinner, the whole company adjourned to see a firework-display, in the grounds, where there was a crowd of over 20,000. One of the set-pieces was a device 'in which the words "Harvard" and "Oxford" appeared in their appropriate colours . . . the whole being encircled with a laurel wreath of fire. The band also played "Yankee Doodle" and "See the Conquering Hero Comes" '.[1]

On returning to the dining-room, the chairman proposed the healths of 'The Queen and the rest of the Royal Family', and 'The President of the United States'. He then called on Dickens to give the next toast. He was greeted with loud cheers, and said:

GENTLEMEN, flushed with fireworks, I can warrant myself to you as about to imitate those gorgeous illusions by making a brief spurt and then dying out. [*Laughter.*] And, first of all, as an invited visitor of the London Rowing Club to this most interesting occasion, I will beg, in the name of the other invited visitors present— always excepting the distinguished guests who are the cause of our meeting—to thank the President for the modesty and courtesy with which he has deputed to one of us the most agreeable part of his evening's duty. It is the more graceful in him to do this because he can hardly fail to see that he might very easily do it himself; as this is the case, of all others, in which it is according to good taste and the very principles of that great social vice, speech-making, should hide its diminished head before the great social virtue, action. [*Loud cheers.*] However, there is an ancient story of a lady who threw her glove into an arena full of wild beasts to tempt her attendant lover to climb down and reclaim it.[2] The lover, rightly inferring from the action the worth of the lady, risked his life for the glove,

---

[1] *Daily News*, 31 Aug., p. 3.
[2] Told by Leigh Hunt in 'The Glove and the Lions'; and by Browning, with a different interpretation, as 'The Glove'.

and then threw it lightly in her face as a token of his eternal adieu.
[*Laughter.*] I take up the President's glove, on the contrary, as a
proof of his much higher worth, and of my real interest in the cause
in which it was thrown down, and I now profess my readiness to do
even an injustice to the duty which he has assigned me. [*Cheers.*]

Gentlemen, a very remarkable and affecting volume[1] was published in the United States within a short time before my last visit
to that hospitable land, containing ninety-five biographies of young
men, for the most part well born and well nurtured, and trained in
various peaceful pursuits of life, who, when the flag of their country
waved them from those quiet paths in which they were seeking
distinction of various kinds, took arms in the dread civil war which
elicited so much bravery upon both sides, and died in defence of
their country. [*Cheers.*] These great spirits displayed extraordinary
aptitude in the acquisition, even in the invention, of military
tactics, in the combining and commanding of great masses of men,
in surprising readiness of self-resource for the general good, in
humanely treating the sick and wounded, and in winning to themselves a very rare amount of personal confidence and trust. [*Cheers.*]
They had all risen to be distinguished soldiers; they had all done
deeds of great heroism; they had all combined with their valour
and self-devotion a serene cheerfulness, a quiet modesty, and a
truly Christian spirit; and they had all been educated in one school
—Harvard University. [*Great cheering.*]

Gentlemen, nothing was more remarkable in these fine descendants of our forefathers than the invincible determination with
which they fought against odds, and the undauntable spirit with
which they resisted defeat. I ask you, who will say after last Friday
that Harvard University is less true to herself in peace than she
was in war? [*Immense cheering.*] I ask you, who will not recognize
in her boat's crew the leaven of her soldiers, and who does not feel
that she has now a greater right than ever to be proud of her sons,
and take these sons to her breast when they return with resounding
acclamations? It is related of the Duke of Wellington that he once
told a lady who foolishly protested that she would like to see a
great victory, that there was only one thing worse than a victory,
and that was a great defeat.

But, gentlemen, there is another sense in which to use the term,
a great defeat. Such is the defeat of a handful of daring fellows who
make a preliminary dash of three or four thousand stormy miles to
meet great conquerors on their own domain [*cheers*], who do not
want the stimulus of friends and home, but who sufficiently hear

---

[1] Thomas Wentworth Higginson, *Harvard Memorial Biographies*, Cambridge,
Mass., 1867.

and feel their own dear land in the shouts and cheers of another [*renewed cheers*], and who strive to the last with a desperate tenacity that makes the beating of them a new feather in the proudest cap. [*Great cheers.*] Gentlemen, you agree with me that such a defeat is a great, a noble, part of a manly wholesome action; and I say that it is in the essence and life-blood of such a defeat to become at last a sure victory. [*Hear, hear, and cheers.*]

Now, gentlemen, you know perfectly well the toast I am going to propose, and you know equally well that in thus glancing first towards our friends of the white stripes, I merely anticipate and respond to the instinctive courtesy of Oxford towards our brothers from a distance—a courtesy extending, I hope, and I do not doubt, to any imaginable limits except allowing them to take first place in last Friday's match, if they could by any human or honourable means be kept in the second. [*Laughter.*] I will not avail myself of the opportunity provided for me by the absence of the greater part of the Oxford crew—indeed, of all but one, and that its most modest and devoted member [*cheers*]—I will not avail myself of the golden opportunity considerately provided for me, to say a great deal in honour of the Oxford crew. I know that the gentleman who attends here attends under unusual anxieties and difficulties, and that if he were less in earnest his filial affection could not possibly allow him to be here. [*Hear, hear.*]

It is therefore enough for me, gentlemen, and enough for you that I should say, here and now, that we all unite with one accord in regarding the Oxford crew as the pride and flower of England [*cheers*], and that we should consider it very weak indeed to set anything short of England's very best in opposition to, or competition with, America; though it certainly must be confessed—I am bound in common justice to admit it—it must be confessed in disparagement of the Oxford men, as I heard a discontented gentleman remark last Friday night, about ten o'clock, when he was baiting a very small horse in the Strand—he was one of eleven with pipes in a chaise cart [*laughter*]—I say it must be admitted in disparagement of the Oxford men on the authority of this gentleman, that they have won so often that they could afford to lose a little now, and that 'they ought to do it, but they won't'. [*Great laughter.*]

Gentlemen, in drinking to both crews, and in offering the poor testimony of our thanks in acknowledgement of the gallant spectacle which they presented to countless thousands last Friday, I am sure I express not only your feeling and my feeling, but also the feeling of the whole people of England, when I cordially give them welcome to our English waters and English ground, and also bid them 'God speed' in their voyage home. [*Prolonged cheers.*] As the greater includes the less, and the sea holds the river, so I think it is no very bold augury to predict that in the friendly contests yet to come and to take place, I hope, on both sides of the Atlantic [*much cheering*], there are great river triumphs for Harvard University yet in store. [*Cheers.*] Gentlemen, I warn the English portion of this audience that these are very dangerous men. [*Laughter and cheers.*] Remember that it was an undergraduate of Harvard University who served as a common seaman 'Two Years Before the Mast', and who wrote about the best sea book in the English tongue.[1] [*Cheers.*] Remember that it was one of those American gentlemen who sailed his mite of a yacht across the Atlantic in mid-winter, and who sailed in her to sink or swim with the men who believed in him.[2] [*Hear, hear.*]

And now, gentlemen, in conclusion, animated by your cordial acquiescence, I will take upon myself to assure our brothers from a distance that the utmost enthusiasm with which they can be received on their return home will find a ready echo in every corner of England [*enthusiastic cheers*], and, further, that none of their immediate countrymen—I use the qualifying term 'immediate', for we are, as our President said, fellow-countrymen, thank God [*cheers*]—that none of their compatriots who saw, or who will read of, what they did in this great race, can be more thoroughly imbued with a sense of their indomitable courage, and their high deserts, than are their rivals and their hosts tonight. [*Hear, hear, and cheers.*] Gentlemen, I beg to propose to you to drink 'The Crews of Harvard and Oxford University', and I beg to couple with that toast the names of Mr. Simmons and Mr. Willan. [*Continued cheering.*]

W. H. Simmons representing Harvard, and F. Willan on behalf of Oxford, then appropriately replied. Other speakers followed, including Thomas Hughes, author of *Tom Brown's Schooldays*, and *Tom Brown at Oxford*, who had himself stroked the Oxford crew in 1843.

BIRMINGHAM AND MIDLAND INSTITUTE: ANNUAL INAUGURAL MEETING: BIRMINGHAM

27 *September* 1869

EARLY in January 1869 Dickens was unanimously elected President of the Birmingham and Midland Institute for the following year. He replied to the secretary, John Henry Chamberlain, on 23 January, to

[1] Richard Henry Dana (1815–82), author of *Two Years Before the Mast*, 1840; graduate of Harvard, and lecturer in Law School, 1866–8. Dickens had met him at Boston, in 1842.

[2] The first transatlantic yacht race had been held between three American schooners, *Henrietta*, *Vesta*, and *Fleetwing*, from 11 to 25 Dec. 1866; it was won by the first-named in just under fourteen days.

say 'I accept the distinction thus conferred upon me, and am proud of it'.[1] The annual inaugural meeting, at which he had been invited to speak, was held in the Town Hall: the galleries as well as the floor were crowded, and it presented a brilliant appearance. As Dickens appeared on the platform, accompanied by the chairman, George Dixon,[2] he was greeted with hearty and repeated cheers, which were renewed when he rose to address the meeting. He said:

LADIES and Gentlemen, We often hear of our own country that it is an over-populated one, that it is an over-pauperized one, and that it is an over-taxed one. Now I entertain, especially of late time, the heretical belief that it is an over-talked one [*laughter*], and that there is a deal of public speech-making going about in various directions which might be advantageously dispensed with. If I were free to act upon this conviction, as president for the time being of the great Institution so numerously represented here, I should at once subside into a golden silence, which would be of a highly edifying, because of a very exemplary, character. [*Hear, hear, and laughter.*] But I happen to be the Institution's willing servant: not its imperious master; and it exacts tribute of mere silver or copper speech—not to say brazen [*laughter*]—from whomsoever it exalts to my high office. So, some African tribes—not to draw the comparison disrespectfully—some savage African tribes, when they make a king, require him perhaps to achieve an exciting foot-race under the stimulus of considerable prodding and goading, or perhaps to be severely and experimentally knocked about the head by his privy council, or perhaps to be dipped in a river full of crocodiles, or perhaps to drink immense quantities of something nasty out of a calabash—at all events to undergo some purifying ordeal in the presence of his admiring subjects.

I must confess that I became rather alarmed when I was duly warned by your constituted authorities that whatever I might happen to say here tonight would be termed an inaugural address on the entrance upon a new term of study by the members of your various classes; for besides that the phrase is something high-sounding for my taste, I avow that I do look forward to that blessed time when every man shall inaugurate his own work for himself, and do it. I believe that we shall then have inaugurated a new era indeed, and one in which the Lord's Prayer will be a fulfilled prophecy upon this earth. Remembering, however, that you may call anything by any name without in the least changing its nature—bethinking

---

[1] MS. Birmingham and Midland Institute.

[2] George Dixon (1820–98), business man and educational reformer; Mayor of Birmingham, 1866; advanced liberal M.P., 1867–76, and 1885–98; one of the founders of the National Education League, and president of its first conference, held at Birmingham, in Oct. 1869.

myself that you may, if you be so minded, call a butterfly a buffalo, without advancing a hair's breadth towards making it one—I became composed in my mind, and resolved to stick to the very homely intention I had previously formed. This was merely to tell you, the members, students, and friends, of the Birmingham and Midland Institute; firstly, what you cannot possibly want to know (this is a very popular oratorical theme); secondly, what your Institution has done; thirdly, what, in the poor opinion of its president for the time being, remains for it to do, and not to do.

Now, first, as to what you cannot possibly want to know. You cannot need from me any oratorical declamation concerning the abstract advantages of knowledge, or the beauties of self-improvement. If you had any such requirement, you would not be here. I conceive that you are here, because you have become thoroughly penetrated with such truths, either in your own persons or in the persons of some striving fellow creatures, on whom you have looked with interest and sympathy. I conceive that you are here because you conceive the welfare of a great chiefly adult educational establishment, whose doors stand really open to all sorts and conditions of people, to be inseparable from the best welfare of your great town and its neighbourhood. Nay, if I take a much wider range than that, and say that we all—every one of us—perfectly well know that the benefits of such an establishment must extend far beyond the limits of this midland county fires and smoke, and must comprehend, in some sort, the whole community, I do not strain the truth. [*Applause.*] It was suggested by Mr. Babbage,[1] in his *Ninth Bridgewater Treatise*,[2] that a mere spoken word—a mere syllable thrown into the air—may go on reverberating through illimitable space for ever and for ever, seeing that there is no rim against which it can strike: no boundary at which it can possibly arrive. Similarly it may be said—not as an ingenious speculation, but as a steadfast and absolute fact—that human calculation cannot limit the influence of one atom of wholesome knowledge patiently acquired, modestly possessed, and faithfully used. [*Applause.*]

As astronomers tell us that it is probable there are in the universe innumerable solar systems besides ours, to each of which myriads

[1] Charles Babbage (1792–1871), mathematician, and inventor of a celebrated calculating-machine; well acquainted with Dickens.

[2] *The Ninth Bridgewater Treatise, A Fragment*, 1837, p. 110. It was not one of the original series 'On the Power, Wisdom, and Goodness of God as manifested in the Creation', commissioned and paid for, according to a bequest by the Earl of Bridgewater, but was published separately as an attempt to reconcile the evidence of men of science with religion. This was clearly a theme Dickens had particularly in mind in his address, see pp. 403–4, but he treated it with excessive caution.

of utterly unknown and unseen stars belong,[1] so it is certain that every man, however obscure, however far removed from the general recognition, is one of a group of men impressible for good and impressible for evil, and that it is in the eternal nature of things that he cannot really improve himself without in some degree improving other men. [*Hear, hear.*] And observe: this is especially the case when he has improved himself in the teeth of adverse circumstances, as in a maturity succeeding to a neglected or an ill-taught youth, in the few daily hours remaining to him after ten or twelve hours of labour, in the few pauses and intervals of a life of toil; for then his fellow creatures and companions have assurance that he can have known no favouring conditions, and that they can do what he has done, in wresting some enlightenment and self-respect from what Lord Lytton finely calls—

> Those twin gaolers of the daring heart,
> Low birth and iron fortune.[2]

As you have proved these truths in your own experience or in your own observation, and as it may be safely assumed that there can be very few persons in Birmingham, of all places under heaven, who would contest the position that the more cultivated the employed the better for the employer, and the more cultivated the employer the better for the employed; therefore, my reference to what you do not want to know shall here cease and determine. [*Laughter and applause.*]

Next, with reference to what your Institution has done; on my summary, which shall be as concise and as correct as my information and my remembrance of it may render possible, I desire to lay emphatic stress. Your Institution, sixteen years old, and in which masters and workmen study together, has outgrown the ample edifice in which it receives its 2,500 or 2,600 members and students. It is a most cheering sign of its vigorous vitality that of its industrial students almost one-half are artisans in the receipt of weekly wages. I think I am correct in saying that 400 others are clerks, apprentices, tradesmen, or tradesmen's sons. I note with particular pleasure the adherence of a goodly number of the gentler sex, without whom no Institution whatever can truly claim to be either a civilizing or a civilized one. [*Applause.*] The increased attendance at your educational classes is always greatest on the

---

[1] Dickens was almost certainly thinking of Sir David Brewster's *More Worlds than One*, 1854, written in reply to Dr. William Whewell's *On the Plurality of Worlds*, 1853, in both of which he had been greatly interested when they first appeared. They were both attempts to discuss the question in a manner analogous to the geological controversies. Whewell had written the first *Bridgewater Treatise*.   [2] *Lady of Lyons*, III. ii.

part of the artisans—the class within my experience the least
reached in similar institutions elsewhere, and whose name is oftenest and most constantly taken in vain. [*Laughter and applause.*]
But it is especially reached here, not improbably because it is, as it
should be, specially addressed; in the foundation of the industrial
department, in the allotment of the direction of the society's affairs,
and in the establishment of what are called its penny classes—a
bold and, I am happy to say, a triumphantly successful experiment, which enables the artisan to obtain sound evening instruction
in subjects directly bearing on his daily usefulness or on his daily
happiness: as arithmetic (elementary and advanced), chemistry,
physical geography, and singing: on payment of the astounding
low fee of a single penny every time he attends a class. [*Loud
applause.*] I beg emphatically to say that I look on this as one of the
most remarkable schemes ever devised for the educational behoof
of the artisan, and if your Institution has done nothing else in all
its life, I would take my stand by it on its having done this. [*Loud
applause.*]

Apart, however, from the industrial department, it has its general department, offering all the advantages of a first-class literary
Institution. It has its reading rooms, its library, its chemical laboratory, its museum, its art department, its lecture hall, and its long
list of lectures on subjects of various and comprehensive interest,
delivered by lecturers of the highest qualifications. Very well. But
it may be asked, what are the practical results of these appliances?
Now, let us suppose a few. Suppose that your Institution should
have educated those who are now its teachers. That would be a
remarkable fact. Supposing besides, that it should, so to speak, have
educated education, all around it, by sending forth numerous and
efficient teachers into many and divers schools. Supposing the
young student, reared exclusively in its own laboratory, should be
presently snapped up by the laboratory of a great and famous
hospital. Suppose that in nine years its industrial students should
have carried off a round dozen of the much-competed-for prizes
awarded by the Society of Arts and Government departments,
besides two local prizes originating in the generosity of a Birmingham man. Suppose that the Town Council, having it in trust to find
an artisan well fit to receive the Whitworth prizes, should find him
here. Suppose that one of your industrial students should turn his
chemical studies to the practical account of extracting gold from
waste colour water, and of taking it into custody, in the very act
of running away by the thousand pounds worth, down the town
drains. Suppose another should perceive in his books, in his
studious evenings, what was amiss with his master's until then

inscrutably defective furnace, and should go straight at it—to the great annual saving of that master—and put it right. Suppose another should puzzle out the means, until then quite unknown in England, of making a certain description of coloured glass. Suppose another should qualify himself to vanquish one by one, as they daily arose, all the little difficulties incidental to his calling as an electroplater, and should be applied to by his companions in the shop, in all emergencies, under the name of the 'Encyclopædia'. [*Laughter and applause.*] Suppose a long procession of such cases, and then consider that these are not suppositions at all, but are plain unvarnished facts [*loud applause*], culminating in the one special and significant fact that, with a single solitary exception, every one of the Institution's industrial students who have taken its prizes within ten years, has since climbed to a higher station in his way of life. [*Applause.*]

As to the extent to which the Institution encourages the artisan to think, and so, for instance, to rise superior to little shackling prejudices perchance existing in his trade when they will not bear the test of inquiry, that is only to be equalled by the extent to which it encourages him to feel. There is a certain tone of modest manliness pervading all the little facts I have looked through which I found remarkably impressive. The decided objection on the part of the industrial students to attend the classes in their working clothes breathes this tone, as being a graceful and yet at the same time perfectly independent recognition of the place and of one another. And this tone is admirably illustrated in the case of a poor bricklayer, who, being in temporary reverses through illness in his family, had consequently been obliged to part with his best clothes; and who, being therefore missed from the classes in which he had been noticed as a very hard worker, was entreated to attend them in his working clothes. He replied, 'No, it was not possible. It must not be thought of. It must not come into question for a moment. It might be supposed that he did it to attract attention.' And the same man being offered by one of the officers a loan of money to enable him to rehabilitate his appearance, positively declined it, on the ground that he came to the Institution to learn, and to know better how to help himself [*applause*]: not otherwise to ask help, or to receive help, from any man. [*Loud applause.*] Now, I am justified in calling this the tone of the Institution, because it is no isolated instance, but it is a fair and honourable sample of the spirit of this place, and as such I put it at the conclusion—though last, certainly not least—of my reference to what your Institution has indisputably done.

Well, ladies and gentlemen, I come at length to what, in the humble opinion of its evanescent officer before you, remains for the Institution to do, and not to do. As Mr. Carlyle has it, towards the closing pages of his grand history of the French Revolution, 'This with due brevity disposed of, then courage, oh, listener, I see land!'[1] I earnestly hope—and I firmly believe—that your Institution will do henceforth as it has done hitherto: it can hardly do better. I hope and believe that it will know amongst its members no distinction of person [*hear*], creed [*hear*], or party [*hear, hear*]; but that it will conserve its place of assemblage as a high and pure ground, on which all such considerations shall merge into the one universal, heaven-sent aspiration of the human soul to be wiser and better. [*Applause.*] I hope and believe that it will always be expansive and elastic; for ever seeking to devise new means of enlarging the circle of its members, and of attracting to itself the confidence of still greater and greater numbers, and never more evincing any more disposition to stand still than time does, or life does, or the seasons do. And above all this, I hope, and I feel confident from its antecedents, that it will never allow any consideration on the face of the earth to induce it to patronize or to be patronized [*applause*], for I verily believe that the bestowal and receipt of patronage in such wise has been a curse in England, and that it has done more to prevent really good objects, and to lower really high character, than the utmost efforts of the narrowest antagonism could have effected in twice the time. [*Applause.*]

I have no fear that the walls of the Birmingham and Midland Institute will ever tremble responsive to the croakings of the timid opponents of intellectual progress [*hear, hear*]; but in this connexion generally I cannot forbear from offering a remark which is much upon my mind. It is commonly assumed—much too commonly —that this age is a material age, and that a material age is an irreligious age. I have been pained lately to see this assumption repeated in certain influential quarters for which I have a high respect, and desire to have a higher.[2] I am afraid that by dint of constantly being reiterated and reiterated, without protest, this assumption— which I take leave altogether to deny—may be accepted by the

---

[1] vii. i, 'and then—O Reader!—Courage, I see land!'

[2] Referring to Dr. Francis Close, Dean of Carlisle, who was recently reported to have preached a sermon in which he said: 'There is no question that there is in the present day an evil spirit of the "bottomless pit" rising up among us, . . . and he was bound to say he laid a large portion of it at the door of science. Did not philosophers at the present day dig out of the bowels of the earth evidences against God? How fearful and how humbling a thing it was that there were those who would . . . prefer any dream, however foolish or vain, to the testimony of God respecting the origin of our species!'—and much more. *The Times*, 22 Sept., p. 8.

more unthinking part of the public as unquestionably true; just as certain caricaturists and painters professedly making a portrait of some public man, which was not in the least like him, to begin with [*laughter*], have gone on repeating it and repeating it, until the public came to believe that it must be exactly like him, simply because it was *like itself* [*laughter*], and really have at last, in the fullness of time, grown almost to resent upon him their tardy discovery [*laughter*] that he was not *like it*. [*Renewed laughter.*] I confess, standing here in this responsible situation, that I do not understand this much-used and much-abused phrase, a 'material age', I cannot comprehend—if anybody can: which I very much doubt—its logical signification. For instance: has electricity become more material in the mind of any sane, or moderately insane [*laughter*] man, woman, or child, because of the discovery that in the good providence of God it was made available for the service and use of man to an immeasurably greater extent than for his destruction? Do I make a more material journey to the bedside of my dying parents or my dying child, when I travel there at the rate of sixty miles an hour, than when I travel thither at the rate of six? Rather, in the swift case, does not my agonized heart become overfraught with gratitude to that Supreme Beneficence from whom alone can have proceeded the wonderful means of shortening my suspense? What is the materiality of the cable or the wire, compared with the immateriality of the spark? What is the materiality of certain chemical substances that we can weigh or measure, imprison or release, compared with the immateriality of their appointed affinities and repulsions, prescribed to them from the instant of their creation to the day of judgement? When did this so-called material age begin? With the invention of the art of printing? Surely it has been a long time about; and which is the more material object, the farthing tallow candle that will not give me light, or that flame of gas that will? [*Laughter and applause.*]

No, ladies and gentlemen, do not let us be discouraged or deceived by vapid, empty words. The true material age is the stupid Chinese age [*hear, hear*], in which no new grand revelation of nature is granted, because such revelations are ignorantly and insolently repelled, instead of being diligently and humbly sought. The difference between the ancient fiction of the mad braggart defying the lightning, and the modern historical picture of Franklin drawing it towards his kite, in order that he might the more profoundly study what was set before him to be studied (or it would not have been there), happily expresses to my mind the distinction between the much maligned material sages, and the—I suppose immaterial, but certainly in one sense very much so—sages of the Celestial Empire school. [*Laughter.*] And consider: whether is it likely or unlikely, natural or unnatural, reasonable or unreasonable, that I, a being capable of thought, and finding myself surrounded by such diversified wonders on every hand, should sometimes ask myself the solemn question—should be disposed to put to myself the solemn consideration—Can these things be among those things which might have been disclosed by Divine lips nigh upon two thousand years ago, but that the people of that time could not bear them? And whether this be so or no, I, finding myself so surrounded on every hand, is not my moral responsibility tremendously increased thereby, and with it my intelligent submission of myself as a child of Adam and the dust, before that Shining Source equally of all that is granted and of all that is withheld, who holds in His mighty hands the unapproachable mysteries of life and death?

To the students of your industrial classes generally, I have had it in my mind, first, to commend the short motto, in two words, 'Courage, Persevere'. [*Applause.*] This is the motto of a friend and worker. Not because the eyes of Europe are upon them, for I don't in the least believe it [*laughter*]; nor because the eyes of even England are upon them, for I don't in the least believe it; not because their doings will be proclaimed with blast of trumpet at the street corners, for no such musical performance will take place [*much laughter*]; not because self-improvement is at all certain to lead to worldly success, but because it is good and right of itself [*hear, hear*]; and because, being so, it does assuredly bring with it, its own resources and its own rewards. I would further commend to them a very wise and witty piece of advice on the conduct of the understanding, which was given more than half a century ago by the Reverend Sydney Smith—wisest and wittiest of the friends I have lost. He says—and he is speaking, you will please understand, as I speak, to a school of voluntary students—he says:

> There is a piece of foppery which is to be cautiously guarded against, the foppery of universality, of knowing all sciences and excelling in all arts: chemistry, mathematics, algebra, dancing, history, reasoning, riding, fencing, Low Dutch, High Dutch, and natural philosophy. In short, the modern precept of education very often is, 'Take the Admirable Crichton for your model, I would have you ignorant of nothing.' Now—said he—my advice, on the contrary, is to have the courage to be ignorant of a great number of things, in order that you may avoid the calamity of being ignorant of everything. [*Laughter.*]

To this I would superadd a little truth, which holds equally good of my own life, and the life of every eminent man I have ever known.

The one serviceable, safe, certain, remunerative, attainable quality in every study and in every pursuit is the quality of attention. My own invention or imagination, such as it is, I can most truthfully assure you, would never have served me as it has, but for the habit of commonplace, humble, patient, daily, toiling, drudging attention. [*Applause.*] Genius, vivacity, quickness of penetration, brilliancy in association of ideas—such mental qualities, like the qualities of the apparition of the externally armed head in *Macbeth* will not be commanded; but attention, after due term of submissive service, always will. Like certain plants which the poorest peasant may grow in the poorest soil, it can be cultivated by anyone, and it is certain in its own good season to bring forth flowers and fruit.—I can most truthfully assure you, by the by, that this eulogium on attention is so far quite disinterested on my part, as that it has not the least reference whatever to the attention with which you have honoured me. [*Laughter.*]

Well, ladies and gentlemen, I have done. I cannot but reflect how often you have probably heard within these walls one of the foremost men, and certainly one of the best speakers, if not the very best, in England. [*Applause.*] I could not say to myself when I began just now, in Shakespeare's line:

I will be Bright and shine in gold.[1] [*Applause.*]

But I could say to myself, and I did say to myself, 'I will be as natural and easy as I possibly can, because my heart has long been in my subject, and I bear an old love towards Birmingham [*hear, hear*] and Birmingham men.' [*Cheers.*] I have said that I bear an old love towards Birmingham and Birmingham men; let me amend a small omission, and add 'and Birmingham women'. [*Cheers and laughter.*] This ring I wear on my finger now is an old Birmingham gift[2] [*hear*], and if, by rubbing it I could raise the spirit that was obedient to Aladdin's ring, I heartily assure you that my first instruction to that Genie on the spot should be to place himself at Birmingham's disposal in the best of causes. [*Loud applause.*]

---

[1] *Titus Andronicus*, II. i, 'I will be bright and shine in pearl and gold.' Sir Henry Fielding Dickens particularly recalled in his *Recollections*, 1934, p. 60, how at this reference to Bright, 'the people rose in a body and cheered until they were hoarse'.

John Bright (1811–1889), statesman; outstanding advocate of Free Trade; M.P. for Durham, 1843–6, and for Manchester, 1847–57; lost his seat through opposition to war with Russia, and thereafter represented Birmingham from 1857 to 1885. Appointed President of the Board of Trade, 1868–70, and member of the cabinet and privy council, 1868. He spoke in the Town Hall the following week, when his speech was referred to—quite wrongly—by some of the local press, as a reply to Dickens.

[2] Presented to him in Jan. 1853, see pp. 154 ff.

The treasurer of the institute then took the place of the chairman, and Mr. G. Dixon, M.P., proposed a vote of thanks, reminding the assembly of the part Dickens had played when the institution was started, by giving the Christmas readings on their behalf, in 1853, which resulted in the largest contribution it had ever received. Since then, he went on, their numbers had greatly expanded, but they could still obtain no help whatsoever from the Government:

The ignorant and poor, who wanted education, and who came to the doors of that institution ... had to be turned away. ... When he saw that voluntaryists were unable to perform the duty, and yet that the State did not come forward, and would not supply deficiencies, he said that the Government of this country did not yet understand its highest functions, and that it was the duty of the people to teach even the highest and chiefest members of the Government to educate, not only the children in the gutters, but to educate themselves. [*Cheers.*]

The motion was seconded, put by the chairman, and carried with acclamation. The chairman mentioned that Dickens might be able to distribute the prizes in January; and Dickens replied:

Ladies and Gentlemen, as I hope that it is more than possible that I shall have the pleasure [*applause*] of meeting you again before Christmas is out, and shall have the great interest of seeing the faces, and touching the hands, of the successful competitors in your lists [*loud applause*], I will not cast upon that anticipated meeting the terrible foreshadowing of dread which must inevitably result from a second speech. I thank you most heartily, and I most sincerely and fervently say to you, Good night, and God bless you! In reference to the appropriate and excellent remarks of Mr. Dixon, I will now discharge my conscience of my political creed, which is contained in two articles, and has no reference to any party or persons. My faith in the people governing, is, on the whole, infinitesimal; my faith in The People governed, is, on the whole illimitable. [*Loud applause.*]

There, the proceedings for the evening concluded; but neither local readers, nor the national press, were slow to comment on Dickens's final remarks. It is easy enough to see how they were misunderstood when taken apart from their reference to the preceding speech, and without the careful distinction between capital Ps, and small ones, which Dickens added later. The correspondents of the *Birmingham Daily Post*, for example, expressed typical doubts. 'A.R.' began by modestly hoping that someone would be kind enough to explain what had been meant, and querying, 'Would it be fair, "on the whole", to take America and Austria as illustrations of the great novelist's two faiths?' 'A LIBERAL' was deeply concerned to think that Dickens might have become another lost leader:

I thought Mr. Charles Dickens was in politics a liberal, but the few last words he uttered in the Town Hall on Monday night, would seem to indicate the reverse. . . . The distinguishing feature in the Tories' creed being the same, namely that the people should not govern, but be governed, surely his political principles must be identified with theirs?

Can you, or any of your readers, help me out of this dilemma?

The editor replied:

We don't think Mr. Dickens *can* be a Tory; but we suspect his politics do not soar above the level of epigram.

'E.' wrote to say, 'Let your Liberal readers take comfort, Mr. Dickens is no Tory'. But there was good reason for asking the question, since if 'the people governing' was taken to apply to party, it referred to the Liberal administration under Gladstone, which included Bright, whom Dickens had just gone out of his way to praise; and the Conservative press was delighted to have the chance of quoting Dickens against the Liberals, whatever he may have meant.

By the next number several correspondents had come forward to give the same explanation that Dickens later authorized himself. Yet the London Correspondent's letter was still to appear (though dated 30 September) giving a further reason for the misunderstanding, and saying of the same epigram, that 'it was remarkable as showing his ambition to be a disciple of Carlyle in his worst phase'.

Of the national press, *The Times* avoided committing itself to any interpretation, but nevertheless protested that 'sentiments like these might be justifiable in the latitude of St. Petersburg or Pekin, but then they would not be likely to get a hearing there'.[1] The *Morning Star* agreed with Dickens that, to be consistent, the Dean of Carlisle 'should be officiating in a joss house and not in a cathedral',[2] and the *Daily News* felt that Dickens, himself, is 'a living proof that the age is not as "material" as it seems'.[3]

The question of the people governing, and The People, was taken up again when Dickens spoke at the prize-giving early in January. Meanwhile, he wrote to a lecturer at the institute to explain what he meant:

You are perfectly right in your construction of my meaning in Birmingham. If a capital P. be put to the word People in its second use in the sentence and not in the first, I should suppose the passage next to impossible to be mistaken, even if it were read without any reference to the whole spirit of my speech and the whole tenor of my writings.[4]

He replied to the same effect on returning the corrected proofs of his speech to the secretary, carefully correcting the capitalization and punctuation so that there should be no further doubt.

[1] 30 Sept., p. 7.   [2] 29 Sept., p. 4.   [3] 29 Sept., pp. 4–5.
[4] To H. G. Pearson, 6 Oct. 1869.

BIRMINGHAM AND MIDLAND INSTITUTE PRIZE-GIVING: BIRMINGHAM

6 *January* 1870

IT was Dickens's last visit to Birmingham. A large and brilliant audience had assembled in the Town Hall to hear him. 'I could not help noticing', wrote W. R. Hughes, 'the great change that excitement, worry, and the American Readings had wrought. His face wore a hectic flush, his hair was greyer and thinner; but the eloquent voice and the bright eyes remained unaltered.'[1]

As he rose, to present the prizes, he was greeted with loud applause, and said:

LADIES and Gentlemen, When I last had the honour of presiding over the institution which again brings us together, I took occasion to remark upon a certain super-abundance of public speaking which seems to me to distinguish the present time. It will require very little self denial on my part to practise now what I preached then; firstly, because I said my little say that night; and secondly because we have a definite and highly interesting action before us tonight. We have now to bestow the rewards which have been brilliantly won by the most successful competitors in the society's lists. I say the 'most successful', because tonight we should particularly observe, I think, that there is success in all honest endeavour, and that there is some victory gained in every gallant struggle that is made. To strive at all involves a victory achieved over sloth, inertness, and indifference; and competition for these prizes involves besides, in the vast majority of cases, competition with and mastery asserted over circumstances adverse to the effort made. Therefore, every losing competitor among my hearers may be certain that he has still won much—very much—and that he can well afford to swell the triumph of his rivals who have passed him in the race. [*Applause.*]

I have applied the word 'rewards' to these prizes, and I do so, not because they represent any great intrinsic worth in silver or gold, but precisely because they do not. They represent what is above all price, what can be stated in no arithmetical figures, and what is one of the needs of the human soul—encouraging sympathy. They are an assurance to every student present or to come in your institution, that he does not work there neglected or unbefriended, but that he is watched, felt for, stimulated, and appreciated. Such an assurance, conveyed in the presence of this large assembly, and striking to the breasts of the recipients that thrill which is

---

[1] F. G. Kitton, *Charles Dickens By Pen and Pencil*, Supplement, 1890, p. 44.

inseparable from any great united utterance of feeling, is a reward, to my thinking, as purely worthy of the labour as the labour itself is worthy of the reward; and by a sensitive spirit can never be forgotten. [*Applause.*]

Now, ladies and gentlemen, with your permission, I will at once proceed to the discharge of the delightful duty you have entrusted to me—the distribution of the prizes and certificates. [*Loud applause.*]

The first prize-winner was Charles Caswell, who had carried off all the honours in chemistry:

He had also, the President announced, taken the Evans prize, of twenty pounds, founded, as they knew, by a manufacturer of Birmingham; and he noticed three circumstances in Mr. Caswell's career with great pleasure. The first was that he was not yet twenty-one; the second was that in the right of taking the Evans prize he had received the appointment of analytical chemist in the Messrs. Chances's great works; and the third was that he had done him the honour of affixing to his examination papers the motto he had himself suggested when he was in Birmingham the last time, 'Courage, Persevere'.

Dickens shook each of the successful students warmly by the hand, published their honours, and stated the subjects for which they were given. The announcement of Miss Winkle as a prize-winner was received with laughter. He spoke to her in an undertone, and, when she had retired, observed to the audience, 'I have recommended Miss Winkle to change her name.' Having gone through the list, he went on:

The prizes are now all distributed, and I have discharged myself of the delightful task you have entrusted to me; and if the recipients of these prizes and certificates who have come upon this platform have had the genuine pleasure in receiving their acknowledgements from my hands that I have had in placing them in theirs, they are in a true Christmas[1] temper tonight. [*Applause.*] I have the painful sense upon me that it is reserved for someone else to enjoy this great satisfaction of mind next time. It would be useless for the few short moments longer to disguise the fact that I happen to have drawn King this Twelfth Night, but that another sovereign will soon sit on my inconstant throne. Tonight I abdicate, or, what is much the same thing in the modern annals of royalty, I am politely dethroned. [*Laughter.*] This melancholy reflection, ladies and gentlemen, brings me to a very small point, personal to myself, upon which I will beg your permission to say a closing word. When I was here last autumn I made, in reference to some remarks

---

[1] *Christmas:* alternatively 'Christian'.

of your respected member, Mr. Dixon, a short confession of my political faith [*applause*], or perhaps I should better say, want of faith. [*Laughter*.] It imported that I have very little faith in the people who govern us—please to observe 'people' there will be with a small 'p' [*laughter*], but that I have great confidence in the People whom they govern: please to observe 'People' there with a large 'P'. [*Renewed laughter*.] This was shortly and elliptically stated; and was, with no evil intention I am absolutely sure, in some quarters inversely explained. Perhaps as the inventor of a certain extravagant fiction, but one which I do see rather frequently quoted as if there were grains of truth at the bottom of it, a fiction called 'The Circumlocution Office' [*laughter*], and perhaps also as the writer of an idle book or two, whose public opinions are not obscurely stated—perhaps in these respects I do not sufficiently bear in mind Hamlet's caution to speak by the card lest equivocation should undo me. [*Laughter and applause*.]

Anyhow I complain of nobody, but simply in order that there may be no mistake as to what I did mean, and as to what I do mean, I will restate my meaning, and I will do so in the words of a great thinker, a great writer, and a great scholar—whose life, unfortunately for mankind, was cut short—in his *History of Civilization in England*:

> They . . . may talk as they will about the reforms which government has introduced, and the improvements to be expected from legislation. But whoever will take a wider and more commanding view of affairs, will soon discover that such hopes are chimerical. They will learn that lawgivers are nearly always the obstructors of society, instead of its helpers; and that in the extremely few cases in which their measures have turned out well, their success has been owing to the fact that, contrary to their usual custom, they have implicitly obeyed the spirit of their time, and have been, as they always should be, the mere servants of the people, to whose wishes they are bound to give a public and legal sanction.[1] [*Loud applause*.]

A vote of thanks to the president having been proposed, seconded, and carried with acclamation, Dickens replied:

I will only say to you, in acknowledgement of your great cordiality, and that of the three gentlemen who moved, seconded, and put the motion just carried, that you never can have a President more truly interested in you, or more determined, at the conclusion of his term, to remain your steady and faithful friend. [*Applause*.]

[1] H. T. Buckle, *History of Civilization in England*, 1902, Longmans, iii. 170.

With this sincere assurance I beg respectfully, but only officially, to bid you farewell. [*Applause.*]

Dickens's restatement of his meaning did not make its implications much more precise. He refused to follow it to a conclusion. It still was not clear who 'the people governing' were supposed to be. The *Saturday Review* sprang to the defence of the administrators of 'the higher departments of the Civil Service', and thought that though his description of the Circumlocution Office had merit as fiction, Dickens ,'like other great authors, . . . has been the victim of his own creation'.[1] The *Standard* equally wished to come to the point:

> Large P or small p, Mr. Dickens still implies that Mr. Gladstone and Mr. Bright are not so wise as the mass of those who place their confidence in Messrs. Gladstone and Bright. This may be perfectly true; but what then are we to think of the people who give their confidence so rashly? Why do the allwise People submit to be governed by the unwise people?[2]

All agreed that Dickens was unsatisfactory as a political philosopher. 'What would Mr. Mill say', asked the *Daily News*, 'who pronounced that splendid eulogium on Mr. Gladstone as the "only Minister who brought forward reforms merely because they were good", to the doctrine that legislators are "the mere servants of the people", whose business it is "implicitly to obey the spirit of their time"?'[3]

Dickens's last word on the subject was to James T. Fields, to whom he wrote on the 14th:

> I hope you may have met with a little touch of Radicalism I gave them at Birmingham in the words of Buckle? With pride I observe that it makes the regular political traders, of all sorts, perfectly mad. Such was my intentions, as a grateful acknowledgment of having been misrepresented.

FAREWELL READING

15 *March* 1870

THE final series of twelve farewell readings was brought to a brilliant close with the *Christmas Carol*, and the *Trial from Pickwick*. It was the largest audience that had ever assembled in St. James's Hall, and hundreds more were turned away at the doors. As Dickens appeared the whole audience rose and cheered for several minutes. Then, says a reporter:

> The hearty applause subsiding, the eyes of all were centred on that one spare figure, faultlessly attired in evening dress, the gas-light streaming down upon him illuminating every feature of his familiar flushed face, lined with literary hard work, the eloquent blue eyes particularly seeming to indicate much recent study.[4]

[1] 'The People', 8 Jan., pp. 36–37.　　[2] 8 Jan., p. 5.
[3] 'In The Recess', 10 Jan., p. 5.
[4] *Penny Illustrated Paper*, 19 Mar., p. 178.

Those who knew how ill Dickens was, had been doubtful whether he would get through the final series of readings alive; and his eldest son had been warned to be in attendance every night, to help the doctor carry his father off in case he should collapse. 'But strangely enough,' he wrote, 'on the very last night of all, . . . I thought I had never heard him read . . . so well and with so little effort.'[1] Others confirm that 'he never read with greater spirit and energy; his voice to the last retained its distinctive clearness'[2]; and 'that he never read better in his life than on that last evening. Evidently enough he was keyed to a crowning effort'.[3]

The applause that followed the conclusion of the *Trial* rang through the hall for several minutes; and when it subsided there was perfect silence, as with unmistakably strong emotion, but in his usual distinct and impressive manner, he addressed his audience for the last time.

L A D I E S and Gentlemen, It would be worse than idle—for it would be hypocritical and unfeeling—if I were to disguise that I close this episode in my life with feelings of very considerable pain. For some fifteen years, in this hall and in many kindred places, I have had the honour of presenting my own cherished ideas before you for your recognition; and, in closely observing your reception of them, have enjoyed an amount of artistic delight and instruction which, perhaps, is given to few men to know. In this task, and in every other which I have ever undertaken, as a faithful servant of the public, always imbued with a sense of duty to them, and always striving to do his best, I have been uniformly cheered by the readiest response, the most generous sympathy, and the most stimulating support. Nevertheless, I have thought it well, at the full flood-tide of your favour, to retire upon those older associations between us, which date from much further back than these, and henceforth to devote myself exclusively to that art which first brought us together. [*Applause.*]

Ladies and gentlemen, in but two short weeks from this time I hope that you may enter, in your own homes, on a new series of readings, at which my assistance will be indispensable;[4] but from these garish lights I vanish now for evermore, with a heartfelt, grateful, respectful, and affectionate farewell.

There was a brief hush as he moved from the platform, followed swiftly by the prolonged thunder of applause.

George Dolby, his Reading manager, sadly recalled the end of their association:

[1] Charles Dickens the Younger, 'Reminiscences of My Father', *Windsor Magazine*, Christmas Supplement, 1934, p. 30.
[2] *Daily Telegraph*, 16 Mar., p. 5.
[3] Charles Kent, *Charles Dickens as a Reader*, 1872, p. 268.
[4] *The Mystery of Edwin Drood.* The first monthly number appeared on 1 Apr.

During the delivery of this short and impressive speech, notwithstanding his visible emotion, he never paused or made an instant's hesitation, and the strength of his feelings was only slightly observable in the words (and the accent accompanying them), 'from these garish lights I vanish now for ever-more'. . . . Leaving the platform amidst acclamations of the most tumultuous kind, he proceeded to his retiring-room with quite a mournful gait, and tears rolling down his cheeks. But he had to go forward once again, to be stunned by a more surprising outburst than before, and dazzled by the waving of handkerchiefs. Respectfully kissing his hand, Mr. Dickens retired for the last time.[1]

A few days later, on 21 March, he sent an account of the reading with a sketch—from a weekly paper—to Charles Fechter's little son, Paul, with the note:

> Mon petit ami Paul, je t'envoie mes adieux au public. C'est fini, je tâcherai d'écrire encore, mais je ne parlerai plus.
>
> Ton vieil ami,
> Charles.[2]

NEWSVENDORS' BENEVOLENT INSTITUTION
5 *April* 1870

BEFORE Dickens had left for the United States, the Newsvendors had written to him sending their best wishes for his journey. On his return they wrote again, asking him to receive a deputation, to which he consented. It was agreed at a committee-meeting, 'to congratulate him on his safe return from, and successful tour in, America; and also to ask him to take the Chair at the Annual Dinner to be held in April or May, 1869'.[3] This they did, informing him 'that they considered he had done more to cement the friendship of the two Countries than ages of diplomacy could effect'.[3] Dickens agreed to preside at the next anniversary dinner, but at the last minute he was taken ill, and his place was taken by Sir Benjamin Phillips. He then agreed to preside the following year.

The dinner was held, as usual, in the Freemasons' Tavern. The cloth having been removed, Dickens rose, and said:

LADIES and Gentlemen, The Newsvendors, who faithfully supply you with the daily history of the gracious lady who rules this land, invite you to drink with loyal acclamations, 'The Health of Her Majesty the Queen'. [*Cheers.*]

After giving the toast of 'Their Royal Highnesses the Prince and Princess of Wales and the rest of the Royal Family', which was also enthusiastically received, the chairman went on:

[1] *Charles Dickens as I Knew Him*, 1885, pp. 449–50.
[2] *Le Gaullois—Supplément Littéraire*, Paris, 12 June 1870.
[3] *Minutes* of the Committee.

We need refer to no remoter precedents than the Chinese expedition, the war in the Crimea, and the Abyssinian enterprise[1] to illustrate the tremendous run that sets in upon the newsman whenever the brave exploits of the Army and Navy are in question. Not that their gallantry is ever to be considered in the light of news, for it is an old, old story that dates from Stonehenge, and will live as long as England lasts. I am to propose to you 'The Army, Navy, and Volunteers'. The characteristic modesty of the Volunteers prevents us hearing their reply. [*Laughter.*] As to the other branches of the service, I may say that this is the only occasion within my experience on which I have known their representatives to be absent when there was duty to be done. [*A laugh.*]

The toast was received with the usual honours, and Dickens then continued:

According to the printed order of our proceedings, with such an appendix as the secretary has placed in my hands, a distinguished friend of mine on my right was to have proposed the next toast, the subject of which I will not anticipate. It was associated with another toast; but I have been informed that the subject of that other toast, a corporate body, would have considered themselves 'snubbed',—to use an expression that has been forwarded to me confidentially [*laughter*]—if they had not been proposed separately. That corporation is the City of London. [*Cheers.*] This is a body represented here by a most distinguished member. For that body we entertain the highest respect, and from it, I for one, have received unbounded hospitality and consideration. I am the more pleased to return this toast, because I have no doubt that this distinguished member of the Corporation unquestionably will now be delighted to tell us what the Corporation is going to do. [*Laughter.*] I have not the slightest doubt that they are going to do something highly creditable to themselves, and something highly serviceable to the whole of the metropolis; and if the secret be not at present closely locked in the blue chamber, I shall be deeply obliged to the gentleman who immediately follows me, if he will let us into it in the same confidence in which I have observed his secret about 'snubbing'. [*Laughter.*] I beg to propose to you to drink, 'The Corporation of London'. [*Cheers.*]

Mr. Alderman Cotton replied, saying that he had always regarded the chairman as one of the warmest friends of the City of London, and that

---

[1] The Chinese expedition followed the seizure of the lorcha *Arrow*, 1857–60. The Abyssinian enterprise was the release of British captives of Theodore III by troops under the command of Sir Robert Napier, early in 1868.

when he remembered that Mr. Dickens went through the Lord Mayor's Show in the lord mayor's carriage, he must feel himself to be, if not quite a lord mayor, at least next to one. After a toast to 'The Sheriffs of London and Middlesex', Dickens rose again, amid great applause, and said:

Ladies and Gentlemen, You have received me with so much cordiality, that I fear you believe that I really did once sit in a Lord Mayor's state coach. [*Laughter.*] Permit me to assure you, in spite of the information received by Mr. Alderman Cotton, that I never had the honour. [*Laughter and cheers.*] Furthermore, I beg to assure you, that I never witnessed a Lord Mayor's Show except from the point of view obtained by the other vagabonds upon the pavement.[1] [*Loud laughter.*] Now, ladies and gentlemen, in spite of this great cordiality of yours, I doubt if you fully know yet what a blessing it is to you that I occupy this chair tonight, because, having filled it on several previous occasions for the society in whose behalf we are assembled, and having said everything I could say about it, and being, moreover, the President of the Institution itself, I am placed tonight in the modest position of a host who has not so much to display himself as to call out his guests—perhaps even to try to induce some among them to occupy his place on another occasion. Therefore, you may be safely sure that, like Falstaff, but with a modification almost as large as himself [*laughter*], I shall try rather to be the cause of speaking in others than to speak myself tonight. Much in this manner they exhibit at the door of a snuff shop the effigy of a Highlander with an empty mull in his hand, who, having apparently taken all the snuff he can carry, and discharged all the sneezes of which he is capable [*laughter*], politely invites all his friends and patrons to step in and try what they can do in the same line. [*Renewed laughter.*]

It is an appropriate instance of the universality of the newsman's calling that no toast we have drunk tonight—and no toast we shall drink tonight—and no toast we might, could, would, or should drink tonight, is separable for a moment from that great inclusion of all possible subjects of human interest which he delivers at our doors every day. Further it may be worthy the consideration of everybody here who has talked cheerfully to his or her neighbour since we sat down at table, what, in the name of Heaven, should we

---

[1] It seems impossible to say how this story arose. Dickens's private opinion of the official ceremonies of City dignitaries was highly uncomplimentary: see *Household Words*, 'Mr. Booley's View of the Last Lord Mayor's Show', 18 Nov. 1850, ii. 217–19, and 'Reflections of A Lord Mayor', 18 Nov. 1854, x. 313–15; also a letter to David Roberts, of 26 Feb. 1854, in which he wrote 'on the subject of the City Corporation as it stands, and the absurdity of its pretensions in an age perfectly different in all conceivable respects'.

have talked about, and how on earth could we have possibly got on, if our newsman had only for this one single day forgotten us! Now, ladies and gentlemen, as our newsman is not by any means in the habit of forgetting us, let us try to form a little habit of not forgetting our newsman. [*Cheers.*] Let us remember that his work is very arduous; that it keeps him employed early and late; that the profits he derives from us, are at the best, very small; that the services he renders to us are very great; that if he be master, his little capital is exposed to all sorts of mischances, from anxieties and hazards; and if he be journeyman, he is himself exposed to all manner of weathers, all manner of tempers, and all manner of difficulties and unreasonable requirements. [*Hear, hear.*]

Let me illustrate this. I was once present at a social discussion, which originated by chance. That subject was, What was the most absorbing and longest-lived passion in the human breast? What was the passion so powerful that it would almost induce the generous to be mean, the careless to be cautious, the guileless to be deeply designing, the dove to emulate the serpent? A daily editor of vast experience and great acuteness, who was one of the company, considerably surprised us by saying, with the greatest confidence, that the passion in question was the passion of getting orders for the play. [*Laughter.*]

There had recently been a great and terrible shipwreck, and very few of the surviving sailors had escaped in an open boat. One of these, a young man, on making land came straight to London, and straight to the newspaper office, with his verbal account of how he had seen the ship go down before his eyes. That young man had witnessed the most fearful contention between the powers of fire and water for the destruction of the ship. He had rowed away among the floating dying, and the sinking dead; he had blistered by day, and he had frozen by night, with no shelter and no food. As he told his dismal tale, he rolled his haggard eyes about him, and when he had finished it, and it had been noted down from his lips, he was cheered and refreshed, and asked if anything could be done for him. Even then, the master passion was so strong within him that he faintly replied—he would like an order for the play! [*Laughter.*] My friend the editor admitted that this was rather a strong case; but he said that during his many years of experience he had constantly witnessed an incredible amount of self-prostration and abasement having no other object, and that almost invariably on the part of people who could well afford to pay. [*Laughter.*]

This made a great impression on my mind, and I lived in this faith for some years, till it happened that, one stormy night I was kindly escorted from a bleak railway station to a little out-of-the-

E e

way town that it represented, by a sprightly and vivacious news-man. To him I propounded, as he went along under my umbrella—he being the most excellent company—the old question, What was the one absorbing passion of the human soul? [*Laughter.*] He replied, without the slightest hesitation, that it unquestionably was the passion for getting your newspaper in advance of all your fellow creatures [*laughter, and Hear, hear*]; and also, if you only hired it, of getting it delivered at your own door at exactly the same moment as another man who hired the same copy four miles off [*a laugh*]; and finally, the invincible determination on the part of both men not to believe the time was up when the boy called. [*Renewed laughter.*]

Ladies and gentlemen, I have not had the opportunity of veri-fying this. I conferred with the managing committee; but I have no doubt my friend was perfectly right. Well, as a sort of beacon in a sufficiently dark life, and as an assurance that among a little body of working men there is a feeling of brotherhood and sym-pathy, which is worth much to all men, or they would herd with wolves; the newsvendors once upon a time established a provident and benevolent institution; and here it is. Under the provident head, certain small annuities are granted to old and hard-working subscribers; under the benevolent head, relief is afforded to tem-porary and proved distress. Under both heads, I am bound to say that the help rendered is very sparing, but if you would like it to be handsomer you have it in your power to make it so. Such as it is, it is most gratefully received, and does a deal of good. Such as it is, it is most discreetly and feelingly administered; and it is encum-bered with no wasteful charges for management or patronage.

You know upon old authority, that you may believe anything except facts and figures [*laughter*], but you really may believe the statistics that during the last year we have granted about £100 in pensions, and some £70 in temporary relief, and have invested in Government Securities some £400. Touching this matter of invest-ments, it was suggested at the last anniversary dinner, on the high and kind authority of Sir Benjamin Phillips, that we might grant more pensions and invest less money. We urge, on the other hand, that we wish our pensions to be certain and unchangeable—which of course they must be if they are always paid out of Government interest and never out of the capital. However, so amiable is our nature, that we profess our desire to grant more pensions *and* to invest more money too. And the more you give us tonight—again so amiable is our nature—the more we promise to do in both departments. That the newsvendor's work is greatly increased, that it is far more wearing and tearing than it used to be, you may infer from one fact. Not to mention that we live in railway times, it is stated in Mitchell's *Newspaper Press Directory* for the present year, that during the last quarter of a century the number of news-papers published in London is more than doubled, while the in-crease in the number of people among whom they have to be disseminated is almost beyond calculation.

I have stated the newsman's simple case, and I leave it in your hands, with the concluding observation that it has had the good fortune, within the last year, of attracting the sympathy and the active support of that eminent man of letters, whom I am proud to call my friend, who now represents the great republic of America at the British Court.[1] Also that it has had the honour of enrolling upon its list of donors and vice-presidents the great name of Longfellow.[2] [*Cheers.*] I beg to propose to you to drink 'Prosperity to the Newsvendors' Benevolent and Provident Institution'. [*Cheers.*]

Charles Dickens, Junior, then proposed 'The Ladies', and Edmund Yates 'The Health of the Chairman', who briefly replied.

ROYAL ACADEMY BANQUET

30 *April* 1870

DICKENS's last public appearance was at the annual dinner of the Royal Academy. But his pleasure in attending it was overshadowed by the loss of his old friend, Daniel Maclise.[3] He had died on 27 April. On

---

[1] John Lothrop Motley (1814–77), author of *The Rise of the Dutch Republic*, 1856, and other historical works; Minister to Austria, 1861–7, and to Great Britain, 1869–70. Motley had first met Dickens at a dinner given by Forster, in 1861, when he wrote, 'I like him exceedingly, . . . and I found him genial, sympathetic, agreeable, unaffected, with plenty of light easy talk and touch and go fun without any effort or humbug of any kind.' (*Correspondence*, 1889, i. 365.)

[2] Henry Wadsworth Longfellow (1807–82). Dickens had met him in America in 1842, and Longfellow visited Dickens in England later in the year. They had a great admiration and liking for each other. They met again on Dickens's second visit to America, and on Longfellow's visit to Europe in 1868 he stayed with Dickens at Gad's Hill Place.

[3] Daniel Maclise (1806–70); he was introduced to Dickens by Forster in 1838, and the three of them soon became close friends. A portrait of Dickens by Maclise was engraved as a frontispiece for *Nickleby*, 1839, and was repeated in the *Life* by Forster. Other portraits of Dickens with his wife and Mary Hogarth, the first four children, Miss Georgina Hogarth as 'A Girl at a Waterfall', and of Mrs. Dickens, are all well known. The friendship between the three com-panions was affectionately maintained for many years, but towards the end of his life, and particularly after 1865, when he was depressed as a result of his exertions in decorating the Royal Gallery of the House of Lords, Maclise

the 29th, Dickens wrote to tell Forster of the shock. 'It has been only after great difficulty', he said, 'and after hardening and steeling myself to the subject, that I have been able to get any command over it or over myself. I shall make a reference to it at the Academy tomorrow'.[1]

Maclise, himself, had refused an offer of the presidency after Landseer, on the death of Sir Charles Eastlake five years before. His last picture, 'Desmond and Ormond', hung in the exhibition. His funeral took place on the morning of the banquet.

The dinner was held in the large central room of the new galleries at Burlington House. The president, Sir Francis Grant,[2] was in the Chair. A brilliant list of speakers included, among others, the Prince of Wales,[3] Gladstone, the Prime Minister, and Disraeli, whose *Lothair* had been published only a few days before.

Gladstone, according to the *Globe*, 'was not happy' and 'was destined to be outshone by the author of *Pickwick*'. In the course of his speech he paid a heavy-handed tribute to 'that half of the human race which is commonly, and I believe justly, called its better half', whom he thought well represented in the exhibition both as 'portrayed by the hands of our artists', and as exhibitors themselves.

Dickens spoke last, in response to the toast of 'Prosperity to the Interests of Literature'. On rising he was received with enthusiastic applause, and said:

MR. PRESIDENT, Your Royal Highnesses, My Lords and Gentlemen, I beg to acknowledge the toast with which you have done me the great honour of associating my name. I beg to acknowledge it on behalf of the brotherhood of Literature, present and absent, not forgetting an illustrious wanderer from the fold, whose tardy return to it we all hail with delight, and who now sits—or lately did sit—within a few chairs of you, on your left hand.[4] I hope I may also claim to acknowledge the toast on behalf of the sisterhood of Literature also, although that 'better half of human nature' to which Mr. Gladstone rendered his graceful tribute is unworthily represented here, in the present state of its rights and wrongs, by the devouring monster, man.[5] [*Cheers and laughter.*]

became a recluse, and they seldom saw each other. Dickens wrote about Maclise's cartoon, 'The Spirit of Chivalry', in *Douglas Jerrold's Shilling Magazine*, Aug. 1845.   [1] F, XII. i.

[2] Sir Francis Grant (1803–78), fashionable portrait painter; A.R.A., 1842; R.A., 1847; P.R.A., 1866.

[3] Later, Edward VII (1841–1910). The prince was so disappointed at not hearing Dickens again at the Royal General Theatrical Fund anniversary on 16 May when Dickens was too lame to attend, that, according to Forster, 'at another dinner a week later, where the King of the Belgians and the Prince were to be present, so much pressure was put upon him that he went, still suffering as he was, to dine with Lord Houghton'. (XII. i.)   [4] Disraeli.

[5] The movement for women's suffrage had been growing stronger, especially since J. S. Mill's election as M.P. for Westminster in 1865. He had presented

All the Arts and many of the Sciences bear witness that women, even in their present oppressed condition, can attain to quite as great distinction and can win quite as lofty names as man. [*Cheers.*] Their emancipation (as I am given to understand) drawing very near, there is no saying how soon they may 'push us from our stools' at these tables, or how soon our better half of human nature, standing in this place of mine, may eloquently depreciate mankind [*a laugh*], addressing another better half of human nature sitting in the president's chair. [*Cheers and laughter.*]

The literary visitors of the Royal Academy tonight desire to congratulate their hosts on a very interesting exhibition, in which risen excellence supremely asserts itself, and from which promise of a brilliant succession in time to come is not wanting. [*Cheers.*] They naturally see with especial interest the writings and persons of great men—historians, philosophers, poets, and novelists— vividly illustrated around them here. And they hope they may modestly claim to have rendered some little assistance towards the production of many of the pictures in this magnificent gallery. [*Cheers.*] For without the patient labours of some among them unhistoric history might have long survived in this place, and but for the researches and wanderings of others among them, the most preposterous countries [*a laugh*], the most impossible peoples [*laughter*] and the absurdest superstitions, manners, and customs, might have usurped the place of truth upon these walls. [*Cheers and laughter.*] Nay, there is no knowing, Sir Francis Grant, what unlike portraits you yourself might have painted if you had been left, with your sitters, to idle pens, unchecked restless rumours, and undenounced lying malevolence. [*Cheers and laughter.*]

I cannot forbear, before I resume my seat, adverting to a sad theme to which his Royal Highness the Prince of Wales made allu- sion, and to which the President referred with the eloquence of genuine feeling. [*Cheers.*] Since first I entered the public lists, a very young man indeed, it has been my constant fortune to number amongst my nearest and dearest friends members of the Royal Academy who have been its grace and pride. [*Cheers.*] They have so dropped from my side one by one that I already begin to feel like that Spanish monk of whom Wilkie tells, who had grown to

a petition in 1867, and published his *Subjection of Women* in 1869. The same year municipal suffrage was extended to women rate-payers. Dickens supported the demand for women's legal and social rights but, caring nothing for a vote himself, refused to take the suffrage question seriously. Mill, who admired *Pickwick* and *Copperfield*, was incensed by what he thought the anti-feminism of *Bleak House*, which he considered 'vulgar impudence', and 'done too in the vulgarest way, just the style in which vulgar men used to ridicule "learned ladies" as neglecting their children and household'.

believe that the only realities around him were the pictures which he loved [*cheers*], and that all the moving life he saw, or ever had seen, was a shadow and a dream.[1] [*Cheers.*]

For many years I was one of the two most intimate friends and companions of the late Mr. Maclise. Of his genius in his chosen art I will venture to say nothing here, but of his prodigious fertility of mind and wonderful wealth of intellect, I may confidently assert that they would have made him, if he had been so minded, at least as great a writer as he was a painter. [*Cheers.*] The gentlest and most modest of men [*hear, hear*], the freshest as to his generous appreciation of young aspirants, and the frankest and largest-hearted as to his peers [*cheers*], incapable of a sordid or ignoble thought [*cheers*], gallantly sustaining the true dignity of his vocation [*cheers*], without one grain of self-ambition, wholesomely natural at the last as at the first, 'in wit a man, simplicity a child'[2] [*cheers*], no Artist, of whatever denomination, I make bold to say, ever went to his rest leaving a more golden memory pure from dross, or having devoted himself with a truer chivalry to the Art-Goddess whom he worshipped. [*Loud and continued cheering.*]

It was fitting that this should be the last of the 'farewell' speeches. Legendary stories soon gathered about it. There is no truth in the tale that 'other toasts and speeches were to have followed', but that, 'when Dickens sat down, the company, moved by a common instinct, rose and departed'.[3] Dickens's speech had been introduced as the last, and the banquet was over. Nor is there any reason to suppose, as Sir Henry Fielding Dickens was told, that his father 'seized the opportunity to pay a tribute to an old and valued friend', because he felt that the President 'had not done full justice to his memory'.[4] He had decided to speak of Maclise the day before, and went out of his way to pay tribute to Sir Francis Grant's 'eloquence of genuine feeling'.

It was the last occasion on which Dickens spoke in public. In less than two months' time his voice was silent for ever.

[1] Sir David Wilkie, Frank Stone, Augustus Egg, and Clarkson Stanfield had all been personal friends, while he had also been well acquainted with C. R. Leslie, David Roberts, and Sir Charles Eastlake.—I have not identified Wilkie's Spanish monk, although Dickens also mentioned him in a letter to Lady Blessington of 24 Jan. 1847.

[2] Pope, epitaph 'On Mr. Gay'.

[3] J. W. T. Ley, annotated edition of Forster's *Life of Charles Dickens*, 1928, p. 854, n. 508.

[4] Sir Henry Fielding Dickens, *Recollections*, 1934, pp. 73–74.

NOTES ON TEXT AND SOURCES

p. 1. *Literary Fund, 3 May 1837*

From the *Morning Post* and the *Morning Advertiser* both of 4 May. The reports in the *Globe* and *Sun* of the same date are the same as the *Morning Post*. The differences between the *Post* and the *Advertiser* are so great that the text is only a compromise between them, and both must have been very imperfect.

p. 2. *Artists' Benevolent Fund, 12 May 1838*

The *Examiner* of 19 May, p. 314, and the *Morning Post* of 14 May report the occasion and the reference to Dickens's speech. Other daily newspapers add nothing further.

p. 2. *Banquet to Macready, 20 July 1839*

No full report. Mentioned in the *Examiner* of 27 July, p. 475, and a reference to what Dickens said from the *Morning Post* of the 22nd.

p. 4. *Southwark Literary and Scientific Institution, 2 December 1840*

From the *Morning Advertiser* of 3 December. Other brief reports in the daily press are of no additional value.

p. 6. *Literary Fund, 12 May 1841*

No report of Dickens's speech: general information from the *Minutes*, and correspondence in the records of the society.

p. 8. *Banquet at Edinburgh, 25 June 1841*

Chiefly from the *Edinburgh Evening Courant* of 26 June. There is also a report in the *Edinburgh Advertiser* of 30 June, probably taken from the *Courant*, and another—much inferior—in the *Scotsman* of the same date.

A reprint of the report of Dickens's main speech, as given by the *Advertiser*, was also edited by William Glyde Wilkins in a *Report of the Dickens Dinner, June 25, 1841*, Cedar Rapids, 1915, in a limited edition of 63 copies. According to the editorial introduction the report in the *Advertiser* 'is very much better as well as more extended than in the other papers'. This is entirely incorrect. Dickens's other two speeches on the same occasion are also reprinted in the *Report*, where they are said to be taken from the *Advertiser*: in fact they were simply given from *Shepherd*. Shepherd's text probably derives from the *Scotsman*.

In letters written immediately after, Dickens mentioned that 'Black-woods . . . intend to publish a corrected account in a pamphlet'. This intention was never carried out. Writing to Forster on the 26th, he said, 'I send you a paper herewith, but the report is dismal in the extreme', and there are similar remarks in letters to Cattermole, Jerdan, and Edward Chapman. This was probably the *Courant;* so that Dickens apparently thought even this account unsatisfactory, although it seems reliable enough. The *Scotsman* of 30 June complained that 'the report of the proceedings in Saturday morning's papers was necessarily very imperfect, and conveyed but a feeble idea of the style and effect of his eloquence'; but this was probably no more than journalistic jealousy, since it offered nothing better in its place.

p. 15. *Presentation to Captain Hewett, 29 January 1842*

From the *Boston Daily Advertiser* of 31 January. Also reported in the *Boston Evening Transcript*, from which it was reprinted by Edward F. Payne, *Dickens Days in Boston*, 1927, pp. 64–67. *Shepherd* has the last three paragraphs only; and all but the last three were reprinted from *Dickens Days in Boston*, by the *Dickensian*, 1942, xxxviii. 102.

p. 17. *Banquet at Boston, 1 February 1842*

From a separately published *Report of The Dinner Given to Charles Dickens, In Boston, February 1, 1842*, by Thomas Gill and William English, reporters of the *Morning Post*, Boston, 1842. Also checked with the report in the *Boston Morning Post*, of 3 February, and the copy of the *Boston Semi-Weekly Advertiser* which Dickens sent to John Forster, and which is now in the Forster Collection. According to the title-page of the pamphlet by Gill and English 'Most of the speeches' were 'revised by their authors'. It is unlikely that Dickens revised his.

According to the *Evening Transcript* of the 3rd, no other newspapers but the *Post* and *Advertiser* were privileged to have reporters present. The account in the *Advertiser* was reprinted, in part, by the *New York Tribune* of the 7th, the *New York American* of the 5th, and no doubt by many others. Given in *Shepherd*.

p. 22. *Banquet at Hartford, 7 February 1842*

From the report in the *New England Weekly Review*, a copy of which was sent to Forster by Dickens and which is now in the Forster Collection. The text of the report in the *New England Review* is the same. Dickens's speech only was also given in the *New York Tribune*, as from the *Hartford Review*: the text is the same, with a few additional mistakes. Given in *Shepherd*.

p. 26. *Banquet at New York, 18 February 1842*

From the *New York American* and the *New York Tribune* of 19 and 21 February, and the *New York Herald* of the 20th. Dickens chose the *Herald* to send to Forster, saying that it was as scurrilous as the English weekly, the *Satirist*, 'but having a great circulation (on account of its commercial intelligence and early news), it can afford to secure the best reporters. . . . My speech is done, upon the whole, with remarkable accuracy. There are a great many typographical errors in it; and by the omission of one or two words, or the substitution of one word for another, it is often materially weakened. Thus I did not say that I "claimed" my right, but that I "asserted" it; and I did not say that I had "some claim", but that I had "a most righteous claim" to speak. But altogether it is very correct.' Yet its report is no better than the *American*. The *Tribune* claimed no more for its account of Dickens's speech than that he 'spoke substantially as follows, . . . ' but asserted that other newspapers copied parts of its early report, and some had relied on it entirely; the editor of the *Saturday* was even said to have professed to have had his account crowded out, when he had never had a reporter in the room at all. The reports of Dickens's speech in the *Herald* and *American*, however, were entirely independent. *Shepherd* is from the *Tribune*.

p. 32. *Private Dinner: Washington, 14 March 1842*

From the account given by Robert Shelton Mackenzie, *Life of Charles Dickens*, Philadelphia, 1870, pp. 139–42, from a diary kept by Benjamin Brown French, lent to Mackenzie by H. M. Keim of Reading. Reprinted by W. G. Wilkins, *Charles Dickens in America*, 1911, pp. 168–71, whence copied by the *Dickensian*, 1941, xxxviii. 39–40. As it was more or less a private affair, and not reported by the press, it falls strictly speaking outside the scope of this collection of the public speeches; but it too clearly belongs with Dickens's other speeches in America to be sacrificed to consistency.

p. 34. *Richmond 'Social Supper', 18 March 1842*

From the *Richmond Enquirer* of 24 March. The speech was preserved partly by chance, and no doubt imperfectly. The *Enquirer* of the 22nd explained that its account, when published, would not be by a professional reporter, but would be 'indebted to a friend who took some notes of the first two speeches for a communication'; and it added the regret at the end of its account on the 24th, 'that so many good things were said by the company at large, which are lost to the Public—that the Toasts were all Improvisatore, and not written or taken down—that some very happy but short Addresses are to be lost in oblivion, for want of a Historian'.

It was reprinted by W. G. Wilkins, *Charles Dickens in America*, 1911, 181–90, and copied from there by the *Dickensian*, 1941, xxxviii. 40.

p. 36. *Printers' Pension Society, 4 April 1843*

From the *Morning Advertiser* of 5 April, except for the toast to 'The Press', which is from 'Popular Portraits xxxvi', *Illustrated London News*, 8 April, pp. 239–40. The speech from the *Illustrated London News* was reprinted in the *Dickensian*, 1918, xiv. 219–20. The report of the *Morning Advertiser* is obviously unsatisfactory.

An alleged extract from Dickens's speech to the society this year was given in *The Printer's Devil, An Account of the History and Objects of the Printer's Pension Corporation*, ed. Walter Hutchinson, and compiled by John Creasey, 1943, pp. 10–12. This was apparently taken from the official *Report* for 1843–4 where it is printed as 'The Address', pp. 14–16. But although it is not unlike Dickens in style, it was clearly not by him: the same 'Address', in exactly the same words, was prefaced to the annual report for many years before 1843.

p. 40. *Hospital for Consumption, 6 May 1843*

From the *Morning Herald* of 8 May.

p. 41. *Deaf and Dumb Charitable Society, 23 May 1843*

From the *Morning Advertiser* and *The Times* of 24 May.

p. 42. *The Sanatorium, 29 June 1843*

From the *Morning Advertiser*, which gives the fullest version; also the *Morning Chronicle*, the *Morning Post*, and the *Morning Herald*—which is based on the same report as the *Advertiser*—all of 30 June.

In her life of her grandfather, *Dr. Southwood Smith, A Retrospect*, 1898, pp. 82–83, Mrs. C. L. Lewes quotes a passage by Dickens as if from a speech on behalf of the Sanatorium, either in this year or 1844. It is, in fact, the third paragraph of the *Old Curiosity Shop*, ch. i. As Mrs. Lewes seems to have thought it came from a speech, she probably quoted from a leaflet issued by the Sanatorium; but this is only conjecture.

p. 44. *Manchester Athenaeum, 5 October 1843*

Chiefly from the *Manchester Guardian* of 7 October; also from the Manchester and Salford *Advertiser and Chronicler*, and the *Manchester Courier*, all of the same date; and *Athenaeum Addresses 1843-8*, Manchester, 1875, which has a report reprinted from the *Manchester City News*.

Replying to Edward Watkin and Peter Berlyn, on 8 October, to thank them for having sent him some local newspapers, Dickens wrote: 'The proceedings of the other night, are remarkably well reported. If you should see, or know, any of the gentlemen who attended for the Press, I wish you would say so from me, in common justice'. Sending two papers to Miss Burdett Coutts on the 17th, 'in a scarlet fever of modesty', he gave the opinion that 'the report in the Guardian, is, upon the whole, the better of the twain'. M.

p. 52. *Liverpool Mechanics' Institution, 26 February 1844*

From the *Liverpool Mercury* of 28 February. There is an illustration of the scene in the hall, in the *Illustrated London News*, 2 March 1844, p. 136, reproduced in the *Dickensian*, 1916, xii, with an article by B. W. Matz, pp. 8–13, 'Christina Weller: A Friend of Dickens'.

p. 58. *Birmingham Polytechnic, 28 February 1844*

The speech was published in a pamphlet entitled *Birmingham Polytechnic Institution.—Report of the Proceedings at the Conversazione, Held in the Town-Hall, Charles Dickens, Esq. in The Chair*. There is no reason to suppose that it was corrected by Dickens. It is in direct speech, but seems to derive from the same reporter who was responsible for the account in indirect speech in the *Birmingham Advertiser* of 29 February. There is the same kind of relation between *Shepherd*'s version, in the first person, and the report in *Aris's Birmingham Gazette*, of 4 March, in the third. There is a further report, from the same source as the *Advertiser*, in a scrapbook of *Newspaper Cuttings collected by Samuel Timmins, 1840–58*, Birmingham Reference Library, 402645.

p. 65. *Governesses' Benevolent Institution, 20 April 1844*

From the *Morning Post* of 22 April. Other reports in the daily press are valueless.

p. 67. *Artists' Benevolent Society, 11 May 1844*

The occasion is reported in *The Times* of 13 May, but none of the daily newspapers gives Dickens's speech. It is the same occasion as one wrongly described as taking place at the 'Royal Academy', J. Lindsay, *Charles Dickens*, 1950, p. 442.

p. 68. *The Sanatorium, 4 June 1844*

From the *Morning Herald* of 5 June. Reprinted from the *Herald* in the *Collected Papers*, ii. 364–7, Nonesuch edition, 1938, with some variations and without the speech to the Ladies.

p. 73. *General Theatrical Fund, 6 April 1846*

Chiefly from *Shepherd*, whose source is not known. He may have used an official report of the proceedings issued as a pamphlet, such as the society certainly published in later years; but I have not been able to trace such a copy. The phrasing is unsatisfactory, and it is even possible that the text that *Shepherd* gives was based on a report in the third person, which he put into direct speech. Reports in the *Morning Post* and *Daily News*, both of 7 April, have also been used. The latter was put together by W. H. Wills, and was reprinted by R. C. Lehmann, *Charles Dickens As Editor*, 1912, pp. 9–11. Other daily newspaper reports, and that in the *Era*, are of no value.

p. 77. *General Theatrical Fund, 29 March 1847*

From an official pamphlet published by the society entitled *Proceedings at the Second Anniversary Festival of the General Theatrical Fund, held at the London Tavern, Bishopgate Street, On Monday, March 29, 1847. W. C. Macready, Esq. in the chair*. A similar report of the annual proceedings was published every year hereafter—with the possible exception of 1848—with the full title in much the same form. The *Morning Post* of 30 March has some extra comments; but the other daily newspapers, and the *Era*, are of no further value. Reprinted in the *Dickensian*, 1918, xiv. 246–8.

p. 80. *Leeds Mechanics' Institution, 1 December 1847*

From the *Leeds Intelligencer* of 4 December; the same report was used by the *Leeds Times* of the same date, and also by the *Daily News* of the 3rd, and the *Morning Advertiser* of the 6th. In *Shepherd*.

p. 85. *Glasgow Athenaeum, 28 December 1847*

From the *Glasgow Chronicle* of 30 December (2nd edition: it has a fuller report than the earlier one), and a separately published *Report of The Speeches Delivered at The Opening Soirée of the Glasgow Athenaeum, Held on Tuesday, 28th December, 1847*, Glasgow, 1848. This report is said to have been reprinted from the *Chronicle*, 'with certain additions from the "North British Mail"'. The editor also added that 'it has been corrected throughout with considerable care, and the Speech of Mr. Dickens, in particular, has undergone careful revision'. No reliance should be placed on this claim. The reports in the *Glasgow Courier, Glasgow Examiner, Glasgow Herald*, and the *Glasgow Saturday Post* are from the same source as the *Chronicle*. In *Shepherd*, probably from the pamphlet report.

In a letter to Miss Burdett Coutts the next day Dickens wrote: 'My presidency went off with great success last night, and was a very grand scene indeed, attended by nearly four thousand people. I would send you a newspaper of this morning with an account of the proceedings, but my speech is so dismally done in the report, that I can't make up my mind to send it.' M.

There is an account of the institution, with a facsimile of the programme of this meeting, and an illustration from the *Illustrated London News* of 8 January, p. 1, in *The Glasgow Athenaeum: A Sketch of Fifty Years' Work (1847–1897)*, by James Lauder, Glasgow, 1897.

p. 92. *General Theatrical Fund, 17 April 1848*

From the *Era* of 22 April. I have not been able to trace any official pamphlet report of the proceedings for this year, and it may be that none was published. What brief reports there are in the daily newspapers are of no value.

The *Era* reporter complained that the 'gentlemen of the press' were placed where it was impossible for them to hear distinctly: 'The reporters for the morning papers generally dismissed the dinner in a brief paragraph, but would have been only too happy to have recorded the brilliant language of the Hon. Baronet who occupied the chair, and the sparkling wit and humour that fell from the talented Boz'.

Reprinted from the *Era*, in the *Dickensian*, 1951, xlvii. 70–71.

p. 94. *General Theatrical Fund, 21 May 1849*

From the official pamphlet report of the *Proceedings*, and the *Era* of 27 May. Reprinted from the official pamphlet in the *Dickensian*, 1939, xxxv. 104–6. The occasion was also reported in the *Morning Chronicle, Morning Post*, and the *Daily News*, all of 22 May.

p. 97. *United Law Clerks, 19 June 1849*

From the *Daily News* of 20 June. This report was republished, with minor alterations, by the *Legal Observer*, xxviii. 141, from which it was reprinted by F. W. Ashley, *My Sixty Years in The Law*, 1936, p. 317, and then, with variations, in the *Dickensian*, xxxiii. 271, and from the

Dickensian, in the *Collected Papers*, ii. 384, of the Nonesuch edition of the complete works, 1938. It is also given, under the heading 'Extract From Legal Observer', in the *United Law Clerks' Society. The Seventeenth Annual Report*, 1849.

p. 98. *Mansion House Banquet, 7 July 1849*

From the *Morning Chronicle* of 9 July. Also given in the *Daily News*, *Morning Advertiser*, and *Morning Herald*, and more briefly in *The Times* and the *Morning Post* of the same date. Reported in the *Illustrated London News* of 14 July, p. 29, with an illustration, in which Dickens is not distinguishable.

p. 100. *Newsvendors, 21 November 1849*

From the *Morning Advertiser* of 22 November, which has the best report, and also the *Morning Chronicle*, *Morning Herald*, *Morning Post*, and the *Globe*, all of the same date. Reports in the *Daily News*, and the *Era* of 25 November, have also been consulted. There is a brief report of no value in *The Times*, reprinted in the official pamphlet published by the association in 1871—*The Newsvendors' Benevolent and Provident Association—Speeches in behalf of the Institution, by the late Mr. Charles Dickens, President*.

p. 104. *Metropolitan Sanitary Association, 6 February 1850*

From the *Morning Herald* and *The Times* of 7 February. There is also a fairly good report in the *Daily News*, and less accurate versions in the *Morning Post* and *Morning Advertiser*, all of the same date. The *Morning Chronicle* is the same as *The Times*. Also from the official account—not a good report—in *The Public Health A Public Question—First Report of the Metropolitan Sanitary Association . . . and containing the Proceedings of the Public Meeting Held at Freemasons' Hall, Feb. 6th, 1850*. The official account was first reprinted in the National edition of the *Speeches*, 1908.

p. 110. *General Theatrical Fund, 25 March 1850*

From the official pamphlet report of the *Proceedings*, and the *Era* of 31 March, which are practically the same. Reprinted in the *Dickensian*, 1939, xxxv. 149–51. What reports there are in the daily press are useless.

p. 113. *Banquet to Macready, 1 March 1851*

From reports in the *Morning Advertiser*, *Morning Herald*, *Morning Post*, and *Daily News*, all of 3 March. In *Shepherd*.

p. 118. *General Theatrical Fund, 14 April 1851*

From the official pamphlet report of the *Proceedings*, the *Era* of 20 April, and the *Daily News*, *Morning Advertiser*, and *Morning Post* of 15 April, each of which is of some value. The main speech only in *Shepherd*.

p. 127. *Metropolitan Sanitary Association, 10 May 1851*

From a manuscript by Dickens, now in the Henry E. Huntington Library, which he made about a week later for his brother-in-law, Henry Austin. He sent it to him from Broadstairs, on 18 May, with a letter saying: 'I have availed myself of a quiet morning here to write the speech—which is, I believe, word for word, *exactly as it was delivered.* I have not put in any hears or cheers; but you heard it, and, if you want them, can shake them out.' M.

It seems probable that Austin was associated with the society, and that the manuscript was written for its official publication; but it does not appear to have been published at the time. It was printed, 'exclusively for Members of the Boston Bibliophile Society', as a *Speech of Charles Dickens. Delivered at Gore House, Kensington, May 10, 1851,* Boston, 1909.

It is in *Shepherd,* in a much inferior version from the *Daily News* of 12 May. It was also reported in the *Observer* of 11 May, and the *Morning Herald, Morning Advertiser,* and *Morning Chronicle* of 12th, from which the 'hears and cheers' are given. There is an illustration of the scene in the 'baronial hall', in the *Illustrated London News* of 17 May, p. 418.

p. 133. *Gardeners' Benevolent Institution, 9 June 1851*

Almost the whole of the first paragraph is from the *Morning Post* of 10 June; otherwise from the *Gardeners' Chronicle and Agricultural Gazette,* 14 June, pp. 372–3. In *Shepherd* from the *Gardeners' Chronicle,* but altered, without comment, from indirect to direct speech.

p. 135. *Newsvendors', 27 January 1852*

From the *Morning Herald* and the *Morning Advertiser* of 28 January. The report in the *Herald* is the better, but it was the account given by the *Advertiser* which was reprinted by the society in its *Speeches in behalf of the Institution, by the late Mr. Charles Dickens, President.*

p. 138. *General Theatrical Fund, 5 April 1852*

From the official pamphlet report of the *Proceedings,* and the *Era* of 11 April. They differ considerably, both being in reported speech; and the text is principally given from the official pamphlet. Reports in the daily press are bad: the best is in the *Morning Post* of 7 April.

p. 142. *Removal of Restriction on the Sale of Books, 4 May 1852*

From the *Morning Post* and *Daily News* of 5 May, and *The Times* of the 6th; also from a pamphlet entitled *A Report of the Proceedings of A Meeting (Consisting Chiefly of Authors) Held May 4th, at the House of Mr. Chapman, 142, Strand, for the purpose of hastening the Removal of Trade Restrictions on the Commerce of Literature,* London, John Chapman, 1853. According to Chapman's preface his account was not so full as he had planned, because the reporter had fallen ill, and there was no one to transcribe his notes: there was some promise of a more complete report to be published later, but it was not fulfilled.

p. 143. *Gardeners' Benevolent Institution, 14 June 1852*

From the *Gardeners' and Farmers' Journal* of 19 June, pp. 389–90, and the *Gardeners' Chronicle and Agricultural Gazette* of the same date, pp. 388–9. In *Shepherd* from the latter only, but altered without comment from indirect to direct speech.

p. 148. *Banquet to the Guild at Manchester, 31 August 1852*

From the *Manchester Courier* and the *Manchester Guardian* of 1 September 1852. The *Morning Herald* of 2 September confessedly took its report from the *Manchester Guardian*; and reports in the *Morning Chronicle* and the *Daily News*, of the same date, probably came from there as well. It was reprinted from the *Guardian* in the *Dickensian*, 1938, xxxiv. 169–70.

p. 151. *Opening of Free Library, Camp Field, 2 September 1852*

From the *Manchester Guardian* of 4 September, the *Manchester Courier* of the same date, and an official account entitled *Manchester Free Library, Report of the Proceedings at the Public Meetings, held in the Library, Camp Field, Manchester . . . (From the 'Manchester Examiner and Times' of September 4th, 1852, Revised*.), Manchester. There were also good reports in *The Times, Daily News*, and *Morning Chronicle*, all of 3 September, and the *Morning Advertiser* of the 4th. Reprinted from the *Manchester Guardian* in the *Dickensian*, 1938, xxxiv. 133–4.

p. 154. *Presentation and Banquet at Birmingham, 6 January 1853*

From the *Birmingham Journal* of 8 January, and *Aris's Birmingham Gazette* of the 10th. The *Morning Advertiser, Morning Chronicle, Morning Post*, and the *Daily News* also give good reports, copied from the *Birmingham Journal*. In *Shepherd*.

p. 162. *Royal General Theatrical Fund, 22 March 1853*

From the official pamphlet report of the *Proceedings*, and the *Era* of 26 March. The pamphlet is wrongly entitled *Proceedings at the Ninth Anniversary Festival of the Royal General Theatrical Fund*. It was the eight anniversary. Reprinted from the pamphlet, as the ninth, in the *Dickensian*, 1946, xlii. 74. There are no reports in the daily press.

p. 163. *Royal Academy Banquet, 30 April 1853*

From *The Times* of 2 May. *The Times* was the only newspaper allowed to have reporters present, but its account was passed on to the others. The *Daily News, Morning Herald*, and *Morning Post*, all of 2 May, all report Dickens's speech in the same words. In *Shepherd*.

p. 164. *Mansion House Banquet, 2 May 1853*

From the *Morning Herald* of 3 May, and the *Morning Advertiser* of the 4th. In *Shepherd* (wrongly dated 1 May) simply from Mrs. Stowe's *Sunny Memories of Foreign Lands*, 1854; the edition published in England by Sampson, Low, Son & Co. was the only authorized one—the others were pirated.

p. 166. *Reading at Birmingham, 30 December 1853*

From *Aris's Birmingham Gazette* of 2 January, and the *Birmingham Journal* of 31 December. The latter has an amusing description parodying Dickens's style. An account in *The Times* of 4 January was recommended by Dickens to his friend W. F. de Cerjat, but it is of slight value. The *Morning Post* of 3 January copied the *Birmingham Gazette*, while the correspondent of the *Daily News* relied mainly on the *Birmingham Journal*. In *Shepherd*.

p. 168. *Reading at Bradford, 28 December 1854*

From the *Bradford Observer* of 4 January 1855.

p. 169. *Commercial Travellers' Schools, 30 December 1854*

The best report is in the *Daily News*, but the *Morning Advertiser* and the *Morning Chronicle*, all of 1 January 1855, have also been used.

p. 176. *Royal Literary Fund: General Meeting, 14 March 1855*

Mainly from the *Morning Herald*, the *Daily News*, and the *Morning Advertiser*, all of 15 March; *The Times* and the *Morning Chronicle* of the same date have also been consulted. The *Athenaeum* of 17 March has quite a good report from the daily papers.

p. 184. *Royal General Theatrical Fund, 2 April 1855*

From the official pamphlet report of the *Proceedings*, and the *Era* of 8 April, which are the same. The daily newspaper reports are bad. Reprinted from the official pamphlet in the *Dickensian*, 1946, xlii. 137–9.

p. 188. *Newsvendors, 21 May 1855*

From a good report in the *Morning Chronicle*, and one almost as good in the *Morning Herald* except that it is in reported speech. It is also given briefly in *The Times*, *Morning Advertiser*, and the *Daily News*, all of 22 May. Not in the society's pamphlet of 1871.

p. 192. *Royal Literary Fund: Special Meeting, 16 June 1855*

From reports in *The Times*, *Morning Advertiser*, *Morning Chronicle*, *Morning Herald*, *Morning Post*, and *Daily News*, all of 18 June.

p. 197. *Administrative Reform Association, 27 June 1855*

Almost entirely from the pamphlet entitled *Speech of Charles Dickens Esq., Delivered at the Meeting of the Administrative Reform Association, at Drury Lane Theatre, on Wednesday, June 27, 1855.—London: M. S. Rickerby, Printer, 73, Cannon Street, City.—1855.* The proofs for this publication were carefully corrected by Dickens, and are now in the Huntington Library. None of the corrections is important enough in itself to deserve a separate note, but some idea of their extent can be gained by comparing the corrected text with another pamphlet version entitled *Speech of Charles Dickens, Esq., Delivered at the Meeting of the Administrative Reform Association, at the Theatre Royal, Drury Lane, Wednesday, June 27, 1855—London: Effingham Wilson, 11, Royal Ex-*

change.— *1855. Price Twopence.* No proper distinction between the two editions has been made before; but Rickerby's was the one for which Dickens corrected the proofs, and it was the one he used when giving copies to his friends; Rickerby was also the usual publisher for the Association. There are good newspaper reports in the *Morning Chronicle* and the *Daily News* of 28 June. In *Shepherd.*

p. 208. *Reading at Sheffield, 22 December 1855*

From the *Sheffield and Rotherham Independent* of 29 December; and also the *Sheffield Telegraph* of 24 December. In *Shepherd* from the *Telegraph.* See W. T. Freemantle, 'Charles Dickens and His Visits to Sheffield', *Dickensian*, 1914, x. 152–7.

p. 209. *Royal Literary Fund, 12 March 1856*

Chiefly from the *Morning Chronicle* and *Morning Advertiser*, and also *The Times* and *Daily News*, all of 13 March. The *Athenaeum* of the 15th, p. 328, has a useful report, taken from the daily press, and a commentary which was by William Hepworth Dixon. In *Shepherd* from the *Morning Chronicle.*

p. 215. *Meeting on Dulwich College, 13 March 1856*

Chiefly from the *Era* of 16 March, p. 10, although the *Morning Chronicle* and the *Morning Post*, both of 14 March, have also been used. They differ very considerably. Reprinted in the *Dickensian*, 1940, xxxvii. 13–17, with several alterations. There is an illustration in the *Illustrated London News*, 22 March, p. 301, reproduced in the *Dickensian.*

p. 220. *Royal General Theatrical Fund, 17 March 1856*

The official pamphlet record of the *Proceedings* and the report in the *Era* of 23 March—which are the same—are the only authority for the second speech. For the first speech the official report is clearly at fault, for although nothing has been left out of the general meaning the phrasing is bad. A number of minor corrections have been made, using the *Morning Advertiser*, *Daily News*, and *Morning Herald*, all of 18 March, and although still unsatisfactory, this is probably the best that can be done. It was also reported in the *Morning Post* and the *Morning Chronicle*, from the same source as the *Era.*

p. 222. *Royal Hospital for Incurables, 5 June 1856*

From the *Morning Post* of 7 June, and also from *The Times* of the 7th, and the *Daily News* of the 6th. There are reports which add nothing further in the *Morning Advertiser* and the *Morning Chronicle*, both of the 6th.

p. 225. *Royal Literary Fund, 11 March 1857*

The text is taken from one in the *Morning Herald*, the *Morning Advertiser*, and the *Daily News*, each of which clearly obtained its account from the same reporter. Nothing useful can be added from shorter

versions in *The Times*, the *Morning Post*, and *Morning Chronicle*, although
The Times says that Dickens made 'a brief speech of much force and
humour'.

p. 228. *Royal General Theatrical Fund, 6 April 1857*

From the official pamphlet report of the *Proceedings*, and the *Era* of
11 April, which are the same. The daily newspaper reports are bad.
Reprinted from the official pamphlet in the *Dickensian*, 1940, xxxvi.
55–57, but giving only Dickens's speech on proposing the health of the
chairman, and omitting his preceding reply on behalf of the trustees.

p. 232. *Royal Hospital for Incurables, 21 May 1857*

From an official report, headed *The Royal Hospital*, made by a reporter
engaged by the institution, and published as a pamphlet of 4 pages the
same month; also from the *Morning Herald* of 22 May. The greater part
of Dickens's speech, from 'One sick man was lying on a sofa . . .' to the
end, was given in the *Memoirs of the Life and Philanthropic Labours of
Andrew Reed, D.D.*, by Andrew Reed and Charles Reed, 1863, 2nd
edition, pp. 443–6—where the dinner at which it was given is wrongly
referred to as the first. The official report has also been reprinted in the
Dickensian, 1948, xliv. 139–40, from a transcript by Professor Edgar
Johnson.

p. 236. *Royal Geographical Society, 25 May 1857*

From *The Times* of 26 May.

p. 237. *Reading at Manchester, 31 July 1857*

From the *Manchester Guardian* of 1 August. Reprinted from the
Guardian in the *Dickensian*, 1941, xxvii, 111.

p. 238. *Final Performance of* The Frozen Deep, *Manchester, 24 August 1857*

From the *Manchester Guardian* of 25 August, and the *Manchester
Weekly Advertiser* of the 29th.

p. 238. *Warehousemen and Clerks' Schools, 5 November 1857*

From the *Daily News* and *Morning Herald* of 6 November. There is a
fairly good report in the *Morning Chronicle* of the 7th. In *Shepherd* from
the *Daily News*.

p. 245. *Reading at Bristol, 19 January 1858*

Principally from the *Bristol Mirror and General Advertiser* of 23 January 1858; also from the *Bristol Times* of the same date. Reprinted from
the *Bristol Times* in the *Dickensian*, 1941, xxxvii. 112.

p. 246. *Hospital for Sick Children, 9 February 1858*

The main speech was printed for the Hospital in a pamphlet entitled
*Speech of Charles Dickens, Esq., As Chairman at the Dinner on behalf of
The Hospital for Sick Children, February 9, 1858*. The *Minutes* of the

Management Committee, for 26 February, show that it authorized 'the printing of Mr. Dickens's speech . . . from the Reporter's copy—proofs to be obtained as speedily as possible'. The pamphlet was kept in print for many years. I have consulted editions only for 1867 and 1874: they show no variation.

The reporter was Thomas Allen Reed (see p. 253). The proofs were sent to Dickens by the honorary secretary. Dickens returned them 'with a few slight corrections' and the remark that the report 'is extremely well done, and with great fidelity. If you should have an opportunity of making my approval of it known to the gentleman who took it down, I would beg you to do so.' [Letter of 21 February 1858, in *Fac-Simile Reporting Notes*, ed. E. J. Nankivell, 1889, i. 11.] Reed printed the original shorthand notes of this speech in *The Phonographic Reporter*, under his editorship, 1858, pp. 38–46. By comparing a transcription of his shorthand with the corrected version passed by Dickens, it can be seen what alterations he made.[1] But, just as with the corrected proofs of the speech on Administrative Reform (27 June 1855), although such a comparison shows the care and frequency with which Dickens made his corrections, none of them is of any particular importance in itself: they consisted chiefly of the addition or omission of single words, which improved the style without materially altering the sense.

The main speech of the present text, therefore, is taken almost without alteration from the pamphlet published for the hospital. The other speeches, and the 'hears and cheers', are from the *Daily News* and *Globe* of 10 February, and the *Morning Post* of the 11th.

p. 253. *Royal Literary Fund, 10 March 1858*

From the *Morning Chronicle*, *Morning Advertiser*, and *Daily News* of 11 March; other reports in *The Times*, *Morning Herald*, *Morning Post*, and the *Observer* are of no additional value. Relying largely, but not entirely, on the *Daily News*, the General Committee published an official version in its pamphlet entitled *A Summary of Facts, . . . Issued by the Committee in Answer to Allegations contained in a Pamphlet entitled 'The Case of the Reformers of the Literary Fund . . .' together with A Report of the Proceedings at the last Annual Meeting, March 12, Under the Presidency of Earl Stanhope*. The pamphlet was prepared by Robert Bell, with the assistance of the secretary Octavian Blewitt: the mistaken date in the title is theirs.

p. 258. *Reading at Edinburgh, 26 March 1858*

From the *Scotsman* of 27 March, and the *Edinburgh Courant* of the same date. *Shepherd* gives only Dickens's speech of thanks after the presentation, almost certainly from the *Scotsman*. His introductory remarks before the reading were reprinted from the *Scotsman* in the *Dickensian*, 1941, xxxvii. 112.

[1] I am greatly indebted to Mr. W. J. Carlton for kindly transcribing Reed's shorthand, and for pointing out to me Dickens's letter to Bathurst, in *Fac-Simile Reporting Notes*, and the letter from Dickens to Reed quoted below, p. 436.

p. 260. *Royal General Theatrical Fund, 29 March 1858*

From the official pamphlet report of the *Proceedings*, and the *Era* of 4 April, which are the same. The *Daily News* of 30 March, and the *Morning Herald* of the 31st, have quite good reports which have also been consulted. Given by *Shepherd*, apparently from the *Morning Herald*.

p. 263. *First Reading for Profit, 29 April 1858*

From the *Daily News*, *Morning Chronicle*, and the *Morning Post*, all of 30 April. In *Shepherd*.

p. 264. *Royal Academy Banquet, 1 May 1858*

From *The Times* of 3 May. According to a protest in the *Morning Advertiser* of the same date, p. 4, no newspaper but *The Times* was ever sent a reporter's ticket, and it was only by the courtesy of its proprietors that the other national papers received a report. The *Morning Advertiser* had declined to accept it. The procedure does not appear to have been changed in Dickens's lifetime, and the protest confirms what one might have supposed from comparing the various reports. The accounts in the *Daily News*, *Daily Telegraph*, *Morning Herald*, and *Morning Chronicle* all obviously derive from the same source. Only the last named made any pretence at revision. There is no report in the *Morning Post*.

p. 265. *Artists' Benevolent Fund, 8 May 1858*

From the *Daily News* of 10 May, and the *Era* (Town edition) of the 9th. They differ considerably in phrasing, although they are both apparently accurate in general meaning. The text given is no more than a compromise made by putting the two together, after reference to other reports. The *Morning Chronicle* and the *Morning Post* both use the same account, in the third person, which is of some value. The *Daily News* reporter made the excuse, in the first paragraph of the main speech, that 'a continued chorus of laughter from the company rendered the taking down of the foregoing passage a task of no ordinary difficulty'. The rest of the daily newspapers have nothing to add. *Shepherd* has the main speech only, from the *Daily News*.

p. 269. *Playground Society, 1 June 1858*

The main speech is given from a pamphlet published by the society, entitled *Speech of Charles Dickens, Esq., at the First Festival Dinner of the Playground and General Recreation Society*. Dickens corrected the proofs, and returned them with a note to the reporter, T. A. Reed, expressing his 'high satisfaction with their great and rare accuracy'. [*Fac-simile Reporting Notes*, ed. E. J. Nankivell, 1889, i. 11.]

The opening and concluding remarks are from the *Daily Telegraph* of 2 June, and the *Daily News*, *Morning Advertiser*, and *Standard* of the 3rd. Reprinted from the society's pamphlet in the *Dickensian*, 1939, xxxv. 227–30.

p. 275. *Foundation of the Dramatic College, 21 July 1858*

From the official report entitled *Royal Dramatic College, For Aged and Infirm Actors and Actresses, and for the Maintenance and Education of the Children of Actors,* and also the *Morning Post* and *Daily Telegraph* of 22 July, and the *Era* of the 25th. In *Shepherd.*

p. 277. *Readings at Edinburgh, 27 and 28 September 1858*

From the *Edinburgh Evening Courant* of 28 and 29 September.

p. 278. *Institutional Association of Lancashire and Cheshire: Manchester, 3 December 1858*

From the *Manchester Guardian* of 4 December and the *Daily News* of the 6th. Dickens's main speech only is given in the *Morning Chronicle* of the 6th; and there is a long editorial about it in the *Daily Telegraph* of the 7th. In *Shepherd.*

p. 285. *Presentation at Coventry, 4 December 1858*

Mainly from the *Coventry Herald* of 10 December. There was a brief account in the *Coventry Standard* of the same date, and a report in the *Daily Telegraph* of the 7th.

p. 288. *Commercial Travellers' Schools, 22 December 1859*

Chiefly from the *Daily News,* the *Morning Advertiser, Morning Chronicle, Morning Herald,* and *Daily Telegraph,* all of 23 December. The *Daily News* is perhaps the best, but all the reports are independent, and something has been taken from each. Their phrasing, however, differs considerably. Thus, although the resulting text gives a good and fairly close idea of what was said, as a *verbatim* report it is only approximately accurate, and no doubt fails to do Dickens justice. The press reports are in the third person; but the second half of the main speech of the evening —which is in direct speech—is largely taken from a broadsheet issued by the society, headed *Opinion of the Commercial Travellers' Schools, kindly expressed by Charles Dickens, Esq., at the London Tavern, 12th Month 22, 1859.* It has been reprinted (under the wrong date of 12 December) from a transcript of the broadsheet by Professor Edgar Johnson, in the *Dickensian,* 1949, xlv. 44–45. Although it is possible that Dickens corrected this part of his speech for publication by the society, there is no proof that he did so. If he did—which is unlikely— he left it very inaccurate.

p. 294. *Royal Society of Musicians, 8 March 1860*

From the *Morning Chronicle* of 9 March. There are passages in the report which are certainly unsound, but in the absence of other versions for comparison—here, as with other speeches—they must stand with the caution that they are more or less corrupt. There is a brief report, in the third person, in the *Daily News* of the 9th, and a general account of the occasion in *The Times* of the same date.

p. 298. *At a Lecture by Layard: Chatham, 17 April 1860*

From the *Chatham News* of 21 April.

p. 298. *Reading at Chatham, 18 December 1860*

From the *Chatham News* of 22 December.

p. 299. *Mansion House Banquet, 1 April 1861*

From good reports in the *Daily News*, *Daily Telegraph*, *Morning Advertiser*, *Morning Herald*, and *Globe*, all of 2 April.

p. 301. *Reading at Chatham, 16 January 1862*

From the *Chatham News* of 18 January. Dickens read again in 1863 and 1865, but his acknowledgements were even briefer. He had also read in 1857 and 1858, but the *Chatham News* was not started until July 1859.

p. 301. *Artists' General Benevolent Fund, 29 March 1862*

From the *Era* (Town edition) of 30 March, which claims to have an 'exclusive' report. There are much inferior accounts in the *Daily News*, *Daily Telegraph*, and *Morning Post*, all of 31 March, and also in *Shepherd*, from which some slight additions have been made.

p. 305. *Newsvendors, 20 May 1862*

From the *Daily News* and the *Morning Advertiser* of 21 May; also reported in the *Morning Post* of the same date. Reprinted, from the *Morning Advertiser*, in the official pamphlet published by the society, *Speeches in behalf of the Institution, by the late Mr. Charles Dickens, President*, 1871.

p. 310. *Royal General Theatrical Fund, 4 April 1863*

From the official pamphlet report of the *Proceedings*, and the 'Gratis Supplement' of the *Era*, of 12 April, which are the same. Also from the *Daily Telegraph* of 6 April. There are quite good reports in the *Morning Post* and the *Morning Herald*, both of the 6th, but they are of no additional value. Reprinted from the official pamphlet, in the *Dickensian*, 1945, xli. 15–20.

p. 319. *Royal Free Hospital, 6 May 1863*

From a pamphlet published by the Hospital entitled *Speech of Charles Dickens as Chairman of the Anniversary Festival Dinner of the Royal Free Hospital*. It was reprinted, from the pamphlet, in *John o' London's Weekly* of 27 December 1930, with an illustration of part of the proofs showing that they were corrected by Dickens; from this it was reprinted in the *Collected Papers*, ii. 460–4, of the Nonesuch edition of the complete works, 1938. There are reports in the *Standard*, *Morning Advertiser*, and *Morning Herald*, all of 7 May. I have been unable to trace the present whereabouts of the proofs.

p. 323. *Printers' Pension Society, 6 April 1864*

From what may have been either a handbill or a proof, entitled *An Address on behalf of the Printers' Pension Society: being a Report of the Speech delivered at the Anniversary Festival on the 6th April, 1864, by the president for the Evening*, CHARLES DICKENS, *Esq.* It is printed on one side only. The copy I have seen is bound in, between pages 6 and 7 of a copy of the Annual Report for 1865 which is in possession of the society.

It was not reported in the daily newspapers. Nevertheless Dickens certainly attended the dinner. *The Times* of 5 April had an advance notice saying that he would preside; and on 29 March Dickens wrote to Forster: 'My dear fellow, Wednesday the 6th, is the day of the Printers' Pension Dinner! And what can the wretched chairman do for his own pleasure, on that dismal occasion!' [FC.]

Part of the speech was reprinted in the *Collected Papers*, ii. 475–6, of the Nonesuch edition of the complete works. It was presumably taken from the handbill or proof printed for the society, but it was somewhat oddly introduced with no other editorial explanation than that: 'The following is from the characteristic speech of Charles Dickens, at the Festival of 1864. From circumstances unnecessary to explain, his speech was never printed, and these extracts are now for the first time published.'

p. 326. *University College Hospital, 12 April 1864*

From a pamphlet published by the Hospital, entitled *North London or University College Hospital. Anniversary Dinner In Aid of the Funds, At Willis's Rooms, Tuesday, April 12, 1864. Charles Dickens, Esq., In the Chair.* Five thousand copies were printed. There is little to be added even from the better newspaper reports in *The Times, Daily News,* and the *Morning Post,* all of 13 April. It was included in the National edition of the *Speeches,* 1908, and the *Collected Papers,* ii. 464–71, of the Nonesuch edition of the complete works, 1938, with considerable variations.

A letter of 15 April, to W. H. Wills, confirms the inadequacy of the press reports: 'But Lord bless you, you have no idea of what I said from those wretched accounts. I hate the thought of anybody's reading them.' But another, to Charles Atkinson, of 21 April, shows that Dickens corrected the proofs of the pamphlet published by the Hospital: 'In reply to your obliging note, I beg to say that I shall be happy to correct the report of what I said at the Dinner, in the Proof, if you will have the kindness to send it to me in due course.'

p. 333. *Shakespeare Schools, 11 May 1864*

From the *Era* of 15 May and the *Daily Telegraph* of the 12th. In *Shepherd.*

p. 337. *Newsvendors, 9 May 1865*

From fairly good reports in the *Morning Herald* and the *Morning Advertiser;* it was also briefly noticed in *The Times, Daily News, Morning Post,* and *Globe,* all of 10 May. In *Shepherd,* apparently from the *Advertiser.*

From an entry in the *Minutes* of the Committee of the Newsvendors Dickens's speech this year seems to have been published separately by the society, since a note from one of the vice-presidents is recorded acknowledging its receipt. But there is no other reference to it, and no mention of expenses incurred in printing. I have never met with, or heard of such a copy; but if it were printed merely as a broadsheet, it might easily have failed to survive. It is given in the pamphlet published by the society in 1871, entitled *Speeches in behalf of the Institution, by the late Mr. Charles Dickens, President*, in a text which varies slightly from the version given by the *Herald*. The variations might possibly represent corrections made by Dickens in 1865, but there is no proof of this, and it seems unlikely. Differences between the pamphlet, the *Advertiser*, and the *Herald* are very slight.

p. 342. *Newspaper Press Fund, 20 May 1865*

From the official annual report, entitled *Newspaper Press Fund . . . Report and Balance Sheet 1865* [*1866*.] Dickens's speech was also printed in the next year's report. There are good accounts in the *Daily News*, the *Morning Advertiser*, and the *Morning Post*, all of 22 May, which differ very little from the official version. Dickens may have corrected the report published by the society, but even if he did not, there is still no doubt that it is practically perfectly correct. In *Shepherd*.

p. 349. *Opening of the Guild Houses at Knebworth, 29 July 1865*

From *The Times* and the *Morning Post*, both of 31 July. There are also reports in the *Daily News* of 31 July and the *Morning Herald* of 1 August, which are the same as the *Morning Post*. In *Shepherd* from *The Times*. The reports differ considerably in phrasing, but there is little to choose between them, and the text is principally based on the report in the *Morning Post*.

p. 352. *Mansion House Banquet, 16 January 1866*

From accounts in the chief national daily newspapers, all of which seem to be from only one reporter.

p. 353. *Dramatic Equestrian and Musical Fund, 14 February 1866*

From the *Era* of 18 February. The *Morning Post* of 15 February has a fairly good report in the third person. Given by *Shepherd* from the *Era*.

p. 358. *Royal General Theatrical Fund, 28 March 1866*

From the *Era* of 1 April, from which the official pamphlet report of the *Proceedings* was taken. There is a full report in the *Morning Post*, and there are good reports of Dickens's speech in the *Morning Advertiser* and the *Daily Telegraph*, all of 29 March, which confirm the accuracy of the *Era*. In *Shepherd*.

p. 359. *Metropolitan Rowing Clubs, 7 May 1866*

From the *Daily Telegraph* of 9 May, from which it is given by *Shepherd*. The occasion was briefly noticed in *Bell's Life* of the 12th.

p. 361. *Railway Benevolent Fund, 5 June 1867*

From a broadsheet published by the society, headed *Railway Benevolent Institution. Ninth Annual Dinner, Charles Dickens Esq., in The Chair*. This is more complete than the account in the *Daily Telegraph* of 6 June, which is the best of the newspaper reports, and which was followed by *Shepherd*. Dickens's speech was reprinted from the broadsheet by W. F. Mills, *The Railway Benevolent Institution*, 1903.

p. 366. *Printers' Readers, 17 September 1867*

From the *Morning Post*, and the *Daily Telegraph*, of 18 September. Also reported, in indirect speech, in the *Morning Herald* of the same date. In *Shepherd*, from the *Herald*.

p. 368. *Farewell Banquet, 2 November 1867*

From the pamphlet prepared by Charles Kent, entitled *The Charles Dickens Dinner—An Authentic Record of the Public Banquet Given to Mr. Charles Dickens, . . . Prior to his Departure for the United States.—With a Report of the Speeches from Special Shorthand Notes*. Dickens is known to have corrected the proofs. He wrote to Kent on 6 November: 'I have gone carefully over my own speech, and have corrected it where it was wrong.' H. There were good reports in all the chief daily newspapers of 4 December.

There is no doubt that Dickens carefully considered what might be the effect of his speech in America; and he probably hoped that the printed pamphlet would have been ready to take with him, if not before. He wrote to Wills on the 22nd: 'Even you, I think, will find it difficult to believe that at this moment Frederick Chapman has not sent out the pamphlet with the Dinner Speeches!!!! Of course, when it does come, it will be waste paper. The American Journals all over the country have taken the account from the English Journals, and I am assured that my speech has given the highest satisfaction to the American people.'

p. 375. *Readings at Washington, 3 and 7 February 1868*

Dickens's remarks on 3 February were referred to by the *Daily National Intelligencer*, the *National Republican*, and the *Evening Express* of the 4th. Those of the 7th were quoted by the *Evening Express* and *National Republican* of the 8th.

p. 376. *Reading at Providence, R.I., 20 February 1868*

From the *Evening Bulletin*, Providence, of 21 February, and the *Providence Journal* of the same date.

p. 377. *Farewell Reading: Boston, 8 April 1868*

From the *Boston Post*, the *Boston Daily Advertiser*, the *Boston Daily Evening Transcript*, and the *New York Daily Tribune*, all of 9 April. *The Times* of 21 April has a report no doubt copied from an American newspaper. *Shepherd* has the farewell speech only. Because of Dolby's mistake (see p. 377 n.) it has usually been thought that the acknowledgement for the flowers, and the farewell remarks, were made on different occasions; but all the Boston papers report them together on the 8th, and none of them mention any remarks in their accounts of the reading of the 3rd. E. F. Payne, *Dickens Days in Boston*, 1927, simply follows Dolby.

p. 378. *Banquet at New York, 18 April 1868*

From the *New York Tribune* of 20 April, and the *New York Herald*—which has not so good a report—of the 19th. The full text of all the speeches was reprinted from the *Tribune*, by W. G. Wilkins, *Charles Dickens in America*, 1911, 258–99. In *Shepherd*.

p. 383. *Farewell Reading: New York, 20 April 1868*

From the *Evening Post*, the *New York Herald*, and the *New York Tribune*, all of 21 April. The account given in the *Tribune* was reprinted in the *Dickensian*, 1916, xii. 236–7. In *Shepherd*.

p. 384. *Banquet at Liverpool, 10 April 1869*

Chiefly from the *Liverpool Daily Courier* of 12 April, and also from the *Liverpool Mercury* of the same date. According to the *Porcupine*, Liverpool, the best report was given by the *Liverpool Daily Post*, but this it has not been possible to consult. There are other reports in *The Times*, *Daily News*, *Morning Post*, and *Morning Herald*, all of 12 April; and there is a descriptive comment in the *Daily Telegraph*, of the same date, p. 3. In *Shepherd*.

p. 394. *Banquet to the Oxford and Harvard Crews, 30 August 1869*

From the *Daily News* of 31 August, which has the best report. In *Shepherd*.

p. 397. *Birmingham and Midland Institute: Inaugural Meeting, 27 September 1869*

From the pamphlet published for the Institute, entitled *Address Delivered at the Birmingham and Midland Institute, On the 27th September, 1869. By Charles Dickens, Esquire, President*. It was apparently based on the report in the *Birmingham Daily Post*, but is known to have been corrected by Dickens, who returned the proofs to John Henry Chamberlain with a letter on 17 November, saying 'I send you the Speech corrected'. He had written to J. R. Robinson, the editor of the *Daily News*, on 21 September, to say that he had no manuscript notes to hand over to his reporter, since 'such notes as I make on such occasions would be illegible to everyone but myself'; but he offered to go over his reporter's notes with him, after the meeting. There is a fairly good report in the *Daily News* of the 29th, but with enough mistakes in it to make it unlikely that any advantage was taken of his offer. Other reports are unimportant. In *Shepherd*. There is an illustration of the scene in the hall, in the *Illustrated Midland News*, of 9 Oct., i. 93.

p. 409. *Birmingham and Midland Institute Prize-giving, 6 January 1870*

From the *Birmingham Daily Post* of 7 January, and, in part, the *Illustrated Midland News* of the 15th, p. 316. Also reported in the *Manchester Guardian* of the 7th, and the *Midland Counties Herald* of the 13th. In *Shepherd*.

p. 412. *Farewell Reading, 15 March 1870*

From the *Daily Telegraph* of 16 March, and the *Penny Illustrated Paper* of the 19th. It was the latter that Dickens sent Paul Fechter; but he may have selected it for the sketch on the cover rather than the accuracy of the report. The sketch was reproduced in the *Dickensian*, 1943, xxxix. 93. The occasion was not well reported, although several newspapers give the bare text of the speech, without variations.

p. 414. *Newsvendors, 5 April 1870*

The text of the main speech is from the pamphlet published by the society in 1871, entitled *Speeches in behalf of the Institution, by the late Mr. Charles Dickens, President.* His other remarks are taken from the *Morning Advertiser* and the *Daily Telegraph*, both of 6 April.

The text published in the society's pamphlet was apparently corrected by Dickens, since he wrote to the secretary on 7 April, 'I shall be happy to correct my remarks for you if you will send me a report of them as you propose.' The *Minutes* of the Committee confirm that this revision was carried out, and that the secretary was instructed to have 1,000 copies printed. I have not seen a copy of this edition, nor come across any other reference to it. The following year, however, the speech was included in the 1871 pamphlet, which was printed in an edition of 2,000 copies, and no doubt the text is the same. There is a version in *Shepherd*.

Fun, of 23 April, has a general article on 'The Newsvenders' Dinner', and an illustration showing Dickens addressing the company. They were reproduced by W. G. Wilkins, *Dickens in Cartoon and Caricature*, Boston, 1924, 165–9.

p. 419. *Royal Academy Banquet, 30 April 1870*

Dickens wrote to W. J. O'Driscoll, biographer of Maclise, on 18 May: 'The remarks I made at the Royal Academy dinner were reported with perfect accuracy in the "Times".' *The Times* no doubt still had a monopoly in reporting the Academy dinner (see note for 1 May 1858), and as it was held on a Saturday, it even had time to have some of the speeches corrected in proof. Dickens wrote his out himself, in full, and sent it to *The Times;* and the manuscript, from which the text is given, is now in the Rylands' Library, Manchester. The 'hears and cheers' are from press reports. The speech is given by *Shepherd*, probably from *The Times*, wrongly dated 2 May.

INDEX

Page numbers printed in **bold** *type refer to main biographical footnotes.*

Absolute, Sir Anthony (*The Rivals*), 139, 382.
Abyssinian expedition (under Sir Robert Napier), 415.
Adams, G. G., 309 n.
Adams, H. G., 301.
Adams, John Quincy, 32–33.
Addison, Joseph, 59, 89.
Adelphi Theatre, meeting at, concerning Dulwich College, 215–20.
Administrative Reform, 187–8; Association for, 190 n.; its meeting (1855), 197–208.
Ainsworth, Wm. Harrison, 1, 51 n., 72, 178 n.
Albert, Prince Consort, xx, 6, 119, 127, 227, 301, 334.
Alexandra, Princess, 311.
Alison, Archibald, 90 n., 91–92.
Alleyn, Edward, 215–19.
Allston, Washington, 22.
Amateur dramatics, 72, 117, 118, 138–40, 148–9, 151, 237–8.
America, 1842 visit, 15–36; 1867–8 visit, 375–84; first impressions, 17; disillusion, 36; controversy over American press, 39; and Mrs. Harriet Beecher Stowe, 164–6; farewell banquet before 1867 visit, 368–74; his speech on America, 370–3, 441; readings at Washington, 375–6, at Providence, 376–7, at Boston, 377–8, at New York, 383–4; banquet in Dickens's honour given by New York press, 378–83; tribute to Americans, 380–1; return home, 384; tribute to Americans represented by Harvard rowing 'four', 394–7.
Anderson, John Henry, 74 n., 221 n.
Ansted, Prof. David T., 210 n.
Answer to the Committee's Summary of 'Facts', 257.
Anti-Corn Law League, 74 n.
Arabian Nights, references to, 19, 33, 35, 39, 60–61, 65, 75, 101, 244, 296, 324, 380, 406.
Argyll, Duke of, xx.
Arkwright, Sir Richard, 48.
Arnott, Dr. Neil, 210 n.
Artists' Benevolent Fund, annual dinner (1838), 2.
Artists' General Benevolent Fund, 211, 225, 268 n.; annual dinner (1862), 301–5.

Arundel and Surrey, Earl of, 40 n.; in chair at dinner of Hospital for Consumption, 40–41.
Ashley, F. W., 428.
Ashley, Lord, *see* Shaftesbury, Earl of.
Athenaeum, The, 176 n., 183, 210 n., 214, 332 n., 390.
Athenaeums, of Manchester, Birmingham, Glasgow, *see* Manchester Athenaeum, &c.
Atkinson, Charles, 439.
Aubrey, John, quoted, 217.
Auldjo, John, 183 n., 193.
Austin, Henry, xvii, 105 n.; letters to, quoted, xxi, 103 n., 109–10, 131 n., 430.
Austin, L. F., 392.

Babbage, Charles, 399 n.
Bacon, Francis (Lord Verulam), 4, 54, 218.
Baines, Edward (Junior), 80 n.
Baines, Edward (Senior), 80 n.
Baker, Mr. (actor), 220–1.
Ballantine, Wm., xix, 98 n., 357.
Bancroft, George, 22.
Banting, Wm., 325 n.
'Bardell and Pickwick', 97–98.
Bateson, Rev. Dr., 385.
Bathe, Mr., 188, 195.
Beard, Thomas, 260.
Bell, Robert, 38 n., 142, 151, 163, 183, 211, 225–6, 257, 337, 435.
Bellew, Rev. J. C. M., 293 n.
Bentley, Richard, 1, 257 n.
Berger, Francesco, 294–5 n.
Berkeley, Right Hon. F. H. F., 162 n.; in chair for Theatrical Fund (1853), 162–3.
Berlyn, Peter, 426.
Bible, quoted, 64, 90, 107, 133, 153, 225.
Birmingham, 52; Athenaeum, 58; Mechanics' Institute, 58; Polytechnic Institution, Conversazione of, 58–65; presentation to Dickens and banquet to literature and art, at, 154–61.
Birmingham and Midland Institute, projected, 160–1; reading for, 166–8; annual meeting, xxi, 397–408; prize-giving, 409–12.
Black, John, 347 n.
Blackmore, R. D., 214 n., 257.

Blackwood, John, 178 n., 183.
Blanchard, Samuel Laman, 3.
Blessington, Lady, 127, 422.
Blewitt, Octavian, 7 n., 213, 226, 435.
Blomfield, Dr. Charles (Bishop of London), 128; in chair at meeting of Metropolitan Sanitary Association, 104–8, 109.
Bloomfield, Robert, 48.
Boffin, N. (the 'golden dustman', *Mutual Friend*), 277.
Boileau, Sir John P., 235 n.
Boileau, Maj.-Gen. Sir John T., 343 n.
Booksellers' Association, 142–3.
Boston, Mass., 23, 41; Dickens's stay there in 1842, 15–22; farewell reading at, 377–8.
'Bottle Conjuror', The, 74 n.
Bowring, Sir John, 45 n.
Boyle, Mary, 209.
'Boz Ball,' 26–27.
Bradbury, Wm., 135, 136 n.
Bradford Educational Temperance Institute, reading for, 168–9.
Bray, Charles, 287.
Brewster, Sir David, 400 n.
Bridgeman, Laura, 41.
Bridgewater treatises, 399 n., 400 n.
Bright, John, xx, 153, 170 n., 406 n., 408.
Bristol Athenaeum, reading for, 245–6.
British Artists' Society, 269.
British Museum, 63, 382.
Brookfield, Rev. W. H., 68.
Brooks, C. W. Shirley, 191 n., 257, 331 n.
Brougham, Henry Peter, Lord Brougham and Vaux, 39 n., 281, 338, 388 n.
Brown, Mrs. Hannah, 148.
Browning, Robert, 42, 393, 394.
Bryant, Wm. Cullen, 31 n.
Buckingham, Leicester, 359.
Buckle, H. T., 411.
Buckstone, John Baldwin, 76 n., 77, 79, 95, 110–11, 113, 123, 138, 162, 220, 222, 228–9, 232, 238, 315–16, 318, 337, 349, 358–9, 374; in chair for Theatrical Fund (1855), 184–8.
Bulwer, Edward, *see* Lytton.
Burdett Coutts, Angela G., *see* Coutts.
Burnett, Henry, 44 n., 50, 52.
Burney, Admiral, 343.
Burns, Robert, 11, 12, 48; quoted, 10, 55.
Butler, Elizabeth Lady, 58.

Cabell, Benjamin Bond, 67 n., 73, 113, 187; in chair for special meeting of Literary Fund, (1855) 193–7, (1856) 209–14.
Cambridge, Duke of, 2, 37, 65.
Campbell, Lord, 142–3.
Canada, visit to (1842), 36, 318.
Carbutt, Francis, 84.
Carlisle, Earl of (previously Lord Morpeth), xxii, 104, 127 n.; in chair at banquet of Metropolitan Sanitary Association, 127–32.
Carlton, W. J., iii, 112 n., 435.
Carlyle, Thomas, xv, 142, 165, 284, 288, 369, 374, 403, 408.
Carpenter, Mary, 67 n.
Carshalton (Surrey), 233, 236.
Case of the Reformers in the Literary Fund, 254, 256.
Castlereagh, Viscount, 128, 131.
Caswell, Charles, 410.
Cattermole, George, 15, 422.
Chadwick, Edwin, 104, 129 n., 132.
Challoner, Mr. (printers' reader), 367.
Chamberlain, John Henry, 397–8, 442.
Chambers, William and Robert (publishers), 258.
Chancery, Court of, 164–5.
Chapman, Edward, 15, 423.
Chapman, Frederick, 441.
Chapman, John, 142 n., 143.
Chapman, Jonathan, 22, 430.
Chapman & Hall, xv–xvi.
Chappell, Capt., 73, 92–93.
Chappell, S. Arthur, 368.
Chappell, Thomas, 368.
Charity Commission, 215–16, 219–20.
Charterhouse Square Infirmary dinner, xxii.
Charteris, Capt., 191.
Chateaubriand, François René de, 195 n.
Chatham, 50; Mechanics' Institute, lecture by Layard, 298; readings given by Dickens for, (1860) 298–9, (1861) 301.
Chaucer, Geoffrey, 6.
China, war in, 415.
Cholera epidemics, 104, 108.
Circumlocution Office, 208.
Clarke, Mary Cowden, 3.
Clay, Henry, 32.
Close, Dr. Francis, 403, 408.
Cobden, Richard, 44–45 n., 50.
Cockburn, Sir Alexander, 374, 388.
Cocker, Edward, 205.
Cockerell, Prof. Charles R., 154 n.
Coleman, John, 114–15, 118.
Collier, John Payne, 218 n., 219 n.
Collins, W. Wilkie, 13 n., 184, 199, 232 n., 238, 256 n., 297, 306 n., 310, 368.

'Commerce of Literature,' meeting for removal of restrictions on, 142–3.

Commercial Travellers' Schools, annual dinner, (1854) 169–76, (1859) 288–93.

Connolly, Dr. John, 235 n.

Consumption and Diseases of the Chest, Hospital for, annual dinner (1843), 40–41.

Cook, Capt., 124.

Cooke, T. P., 315 n., 315–16.

Cotton, Alderman, 415–16.

Coutts, Angela G. Burdett, xxiii, 41 n., 42 n., 65 n., 70 n., 118, 148; letters to quoted, xx, 127, 153, 203 n., 288, 426, 428.

Covent Garden Theatre, 2 n., 3, 79, 221; theatrical fund, 73–75, 77–79, 120–1, 140–1, 221.

Coventry, banquet at, and presentation to Dickens, 285–8.

Crabbe, George, 48.

Creole case, 34 n.

Crimean War, 170–1, 189–90, 197, 319–20, 342; and Committee of inquiry, 187 n., 191 n., 208; and W. H. Russell, 245.

Croly, George, 6.

Cropper, Mrs., 165.

Crossley, James, 51 n., 80, 150, 153.

Crystal Palace, 119, 128, 130, 133–4, 394.

Cubitt, Wm., 299 n., 299–300.

Cullenford, Wm., 112, 122, 275, 315.

Cumming, Rev. Dr. John, 105.

Cunningham, Peter, xxiii, 135, 136 n., 151, 153, 175–6, 178 n., 210, 349.

Curtis, G. W., 373 n., 383.

Cushman, Charlotte, 187.

Cute, Alderman (*Chimes*), 109.

Cuttle, Capt. (*Dombey*), 92–93.

Daily News, xxi, 133, 176 n.; slights Dickens, 99–100; supports Literary Fund 'reformers', 183, 198 n., 199.

Dana, Richard H. (father), 22.

Dana, Richard H. (son), 22, 397 n.

Darwin, Charles, 393, 403 n.

Deaf and Dumb Charitable Society, annual dinner, 41–42.

Deaf and Dumb, Birmingham school for, 160.

De Cerjat, W. F., 168–9, 432.

Delepierre, Mons., 178 n.

'Delta', *see* David Macbeth Moir.

Denman, Lord, 165.

Derby, electoral bribery at, 162 n.

Devonshire, Duke of, 133, 145, 147.

Dexter, Walter, iii, xvi.

Dickens, Catherine Hogarth (Mrs. Charles Dickens), 8, 14, 15, 22, 27, 34, 36, 52, 58, 127, 168; illness (1851), 118; meets Mrs. Stowe, 164–5; separation from Dickens, 263–4 n., 288.

Dickens, Charles (Junior), 360, 413, 419.

DICKENS, CHARLES:
Personal and literary:
Appearance, 3, 8, 18, 44, 143, 166, 245, 263, 366, 369, 375–6, 409, 412–13.

Characters, interest in his own, 9, 21.

Childhood, recollections of, 50–51, 122 n., 240, 323–4, 326–7.

Children, references to his, 25, 33–34, 270–1, 286, 360, 379.

Literature, his choice as a profession, 199, 200–1, 398; as a 'rising author', 1–2; reply to toast of 'literature', 156–8; work on its behalf, 176–7; his aim to be 'true to his calling', 371–2, 389; tributes to Scottish writers, 11–13, and to American literature, 31–32.

Popularity, 2, 3, 8, 15, 18, 26, 50, 57, 80, 85–86, 166, 169–70, 285, 368–70, 393.

Purpose as a writer, 9–10, 19–20, 24–25, 155, 157–8, 209, 262.

Relations between books and speeches; can be misleading, xxiii; 61, 67, 70, 104–5, 109–10, 131, 208, 242, 301, 332.

Reporting days, recollections of, 104, 172, 245, 346–8, 379.

As a speaker, tributes to his ability, xix, xx; method of preparing speeches, xvi, xxi; manner of giving, xix–xx, xxi, 3, 19, 51, 68, 97, 207–8, 214, 253; his manuscripts of, xvi–xvii, xxi, 127, 442–3.

Speeches about and tributes to Dickens, 8–9, 22–23, 33, 35, 43, 64, 91–92, 94, 97, 109, 110, 123, 148, 154, 156, 182, 107, 263, 265, 286–7, 341, 374, 379, 385–6, 389–90.

Opinions and Comments on:
Armed forces and war, 144, 170–1, 239, 247, 288–9, 342–3, 415.

Aristocracy, dislike of, 161, 190, 197, 208, 213, 385–6; acceptance of, 388–9.

Art, 155, 157–8, 163–4, 265–9, 303–5; tributes to Sir David Wilkie, 13–14, John Leech, 136,

Dickens, Charles (*cont.*):
Clarkson Stanfield, 164, Maclise, 419–22.
Capital Punishment, 103, 237 n.
Charity, xxii, 40, 67, 108, 122, 216.
Christianity and religion, 9, 49, 66, 90, 129, 153, 242, 270, 284–5, 293, 326, 329, 398, 399 n., 403–4.
Class division and industrial relations, 49, 56–57, 60, 85, 146, 153–4, 167, 203–4, 286, 366–7, 400.
Copyright, international, 21, 23, 25–26, 28–29, 32.
Crime and delinquency, 47, 60–61, 86, 108 n., 159.
'Dignity of Literature,' belief in, 98–100, 137–8, 156–7, 195, 226; linked with work for Guild, 117, 350–2; *see also* Royal Literary Fund.
Drama, interest in, 3, 115–16, 315–16; expressed at meeting of dramatic profession on Dulwich College, 215–20; at meeting for founding Dramatic College, 257–7; at meeting for Shakespeare Schools, 333–7; at dinner of Dramatic, Equestrian, and Musical Sick Fund association, 353–7; *see also* General Theatrical Fund.
Education, 63–64, 80, 82, 129, 229–30, 249; and Manchester Free Library, 152; and governesses, 65–67; charity schools, 82, 241; in Birmingham, 159–61; and Commercial Travellers' schools, 239–45; private schools, 240–1, 336; public schools, 336; Yorkshire schools, 242; and Playground and General Recreation Society, 269–75; and Dramatic College, 277–9; and medical education, 329–30, 333; and Shakespeare foundation schools, 333–7.
Education, Adult, mechanics' institutes, &c., at Southwark, 4–6; Manchester Athenaeum, 44–52; belief in need for, 44, 60; answer to objections, 47, 55, 57, 62, 81–82, 284; general aims, 49–50; Liverpool Mechanics' Institute, 52–58; Birmingham Polytechnic, 58–65; Leeds' Mechanics' Institute, 80–85; Glasgow Athenaeum, 85–92; Birmingham and Midland Institute, 160–1, 166–7, 397–412; Institutional Association of Lancashire and Cheshire,

278–85; Chatham Mechanics' Institute, 298–9, 301.
Law, the, 97–98, 164–6, 411.
Newspaper press, 39, 102–3, 191–2, 307–9, 339, 344–5, 380–1.
Parliament, 94–95, 106, 189–91, 223, 269, 270, 308; and meeting for Administrative Reform, 197–208; and elections, 162–3; disclaims wish to enter, 228–9; the 'people governing' and 'The People governed', 407–8, 410–12.
Progress, belief in, 62, 81, 157, 340, 361–2, 404–5.
Public Health, 42 n., 103, 104–10, 127–32.
Scorn for 'patronage', 5, 49, 96, 99–100, 137–8, 156–7, 161, 167, 211–13, 254, 338, 373–4, 403.
Self-Help, 48–49, 71, 121, 145, 167, 174, 267–8, 281–3, 401–2, 406.
Strikes, 192, 364.
Working-men and the poor, 63, 107–8, 152–4, 155, 161, 166–7, 279, 319–21, 401.
Works:
All the Year Round, 288, 306; 'The Late Mr. Stanfield', 163 n.; 'The German Chariot' ('Travelling Abroad'), 301 n.; 'Mugby Junction', 361.
American Notes, 17, 27 n., 36 n., 41 n., 129 n.
Bleak House, 110, 131 n., 162 n., 164–6, 421.
Chimes, The, xxiii, 109, 278.
Christmas Carol, A, 61; quoted, 58, 373; readings of, 161, 166–8, 168–9, 208–9, 237–8, 245–6, 253, 258–60, 375, 383, 412.
Cricket on the Hearth, The, 166, 264.
David Copperfield, xxiii, 109, 118, 241, 301, 383.
Dombey and Son, xxiii, 62 n., 242 n., 278.
Hard Times, xxiii, 204, 242 n.
Little Dombey (reading version), 236, 278.
Little Dorrit, xxiii, 187 n., 208, 411.
Martin Chuzzlewit, 27 n., 67, 70, 289; preface to cheap edition, 104.
Master Humphrey's Clock, 8, 21.
Message from the Sea, A (Dickens and Collins), 112 n.
Mugby Junction, 361.
Mystery of Edwin Drood, The, 413.
Nicholas Nickleby, 242 n., 389.
Old Curiosity Shop, 27 n., 29.
Oliver Twist, xxiii, 107–9.
Our Mutual Friend, xxiii.

Pickwick Papers, 97–98, 265.
Reprinted Pieces, 110 n.
Seven Poor Travellers, The, 174 n.
Sketches by Boz, xxii, 379.
Uncommercial Traveller, The, 'Dullborough Town,' 122, 299, 301.
Dickens, Dora Annie, her death, 123–4, 127.
Dickens, Edward Bulwer Lytton (Plorn), 270–1.
Dickens, Frances Elizabeth (Mrs. Henry Burnett), 44 n., 52, 59.
Dickens, Francis Jeffrey (Frank), 306.
Dickens, Frederick, 58.
Dickens, H. C., iii.
Dickens, Sir Henry Fielding, 422.
Dickens, John, his death, 118.
Dickens, Letitia (Mrs. Henry Austin), 67, 105 n.
Dickens, Mary (Mamie), 127, 306, 352, 375, 377.
Dickens, Walter Landor (son in army), 309.
'Dignity of Literature,' 138, 176–7, 178.
Dilke, (Sir) Charles, 210, 374.
Dilke, Charles Wentworth, 2, **176** n., 176–7, 192–4, 209, 214, 225–7, 254–8.
Disraeli, Benjamin, xx, 45 n., 51, 342, 368, 420–1.
D'Israeli, Isaac, 138.
Dixon, G., **398** n.; in chair at meeting of Birmingham and Midland Institute, 398–408, 411.
Dixon, Wm. Hepworth, **210** n., 389–90, 433.
Dodd, Henry, 275–7.
Dolby, George, xxi, 376–7, 377, 378, 384, 393, 413–14, 441.
Dover, Thomas, in chair at Liverpool banquet for Dickens, 385–93.
Doyle, Richard, 99.
Dramatic College, meeting for its foundation, 275–7; later Royal Dramatic College, and connected with starting Shakespeare Foundation Schools, 333–7.
Dramatic, Equestrian, and Musical Sick Fund, 316; annual dinner, 353–7.
Drury Lane Theatre, 79, 113, 115–16; used for Administrative Reform meeting, 197–208; theatrical fund, 73–75, 77–79, 120–1, 140–1.
Dufferin, Lord, 118, **385** n., 386.
Duke, Sir James, 98 n., 244, 352; gives banquet at Mansion House, 98–100.
Dulwich College, meeting of dramatic profession, concerning, 215–20.

Eastlake, Sir Charles Lock, **154** n., 157, 159, 265, 420, 422 n.; in chair for Royal Academy banquet, (1853) 162–3, (1858) 264–5.
Ebrington, Viscount, 128.
Edinburgh, 250; banquet in Dickens's honour, xx, 8–15; readings at, (1858), 277–8; readings for Philosophical Institution, 258–60.
Edinburgh Review, 39.
'Edmunds case', 338.
Elia, 252, 372.
Eliot, George, 142–3, 287.
Ellis, Sir Henry, 99, **183** n.
Elwin, Rev. Whitwell, 7, **196** n., **210** n., 257 n., 258.
Emerson, Ralph Waldo, 52.
English Mercurie (a forgery), 102.
Esquiros, Alphonse, 390.
Estcourt, Thomas H. S. S., **270** n.
Eton College, 335; its provost, 336–7.
Evans, F. M., 135, **136** n.
Evans, Vice-Admiral, 385.
Examiner, 137, 183 n., 191 n.; quoted, 2, 3.
Extra-mural Sepulture, Report on (1850), 131.

Fane, Lady Rose, 236.
Faraday, M., 157.
Fechter, Charles, 368, 414.
Fechter, Paul, 414, 443.
Ferguson, Robert, 48.
Fielding, Henry, 89, 109.
'Field of Forty Footsteps,' 326–7.
Fields, James M., 22.
Fields, James T., **18** n., 373 n., 384, 412.
Fields, Mrs. James T., xxi, 373–4 n., 383.
Fitzalan, Lord, 40 n.
Fitzgerald, Percy, 349.
Fletcher, Angus, 14, 15.
Forbes, Sir John, 183, 193, 196.
Forster, John, 36, 42, 94 n., 96 n., 97, 99, **123** n., 154, 191 n., 419 n.; part in campaign to reform Literary Fund, 2, 176–7, 182–3, 192–4, 209, 214, 225–8, 254–8; as friend of Macready, 3, 92 n., 113; Dickens's 'dear and trusty friend', 288; old friend of Lytton, 349; in chair for Newsvendors (1852), 135–8; health proposed by Dickens, 137–8; speeches mentioned, 40, 79, 118, 123–4, 138, 158, 161; opposed to public readings for profit, 260, 263; *Life of Dickens*, quoted or referred to, xxiii, xxiv, 91 n., 99–100, 420 n.; letters from Dickens quoted, xviii, xxiii, 8, 11 n., 15, 22, 26,

Forster, John (*cont.*):
31 n., 32, 34, 52, 62 n., 85, 92, 93,
100, 148, 151, 168, 187–8, 190 n.,
205 n., 258, 260, 278, 376, 377, 420,
423, 424, 439; letter from Shaftes-
bury, 43 n.; letter to Charles Kent,
368–9.
Forster, Mrs. John, 260.
France, 135, 171, 197, 248, 289.
Franklin, Benjamin, 39, 48.
Franklin, Sir John, 237.
French, Benjamin B., 32, 425.
Frith, W. P., 265.
Froude, J. A., 342, 390.
Frozen Deep, The (Collins), 163 n.,
237–8, 366, 373 n.

Gabriel, Thomas, 374.
Gamp, Mrs. (*Chuzzlewit*), 332.
Gardeners' Benevolent Institution,
annual dinner, (1851) 133–5, (1852)
143–8.
Gay, Thomas, quoted, 391–2; Pope's
epitaph for, quoted, 422.
General Board of Health, 104–5;
Dickens gives toast to, 128–32.
General Theatrical Fund (became
Royal G.T.F., 1853), 275; foun-
dation, 73; annual dinners, (1846)
73–77, (1847) 77–79, (1848) 92–93,
(1849) 94–97, (1850) 110–13, (1851)
118–27, (1852) 138–42, (1853) 162–
3, (1855) 184–8, (1856) 220–2,
(1857) 228–32, (1858) 260–3, (1863)
310–19, (1866) 358–9.
Gibson, Thomas Milner, 50 n.
Gil Blas, 115.
Giles, Rev. John E., 50–51.
Giles, Rev. Wm., 50.
Gladstone, W. E., xix, xx, 361, 368,
408, 412, 420.
Glasgow Athenaeum *Soirée*, 85–92.
Gleig, Rev. G. R., 183 n., 369.
Godfrey, Rev. Dr., 337.
Godwin, George, 265, 269.
Goldsmith, Oliver, 12, 29, 65, 93,
138, 337.
Gooch, Sir Daniel, 361, 366.
Gordon, John Thomson, 11 n.
Goschen, Right Hon. George Joa-
chim, 352 n.
Governesses' Benevolent Institution,
speech for, 65–67.
Gowan, Henry (*Little Dorrit*), xxiii,
177.
Grant, Sir Francis, 374, 420 n., 421–2.
Grant, James, 337, 341 n.
Granville, Lord, xix.
Grattan, T. C., 22.
Gray, Thomas, 'Progress of Poesy'
quoted, 9, 37, 185.

Greeley, Horace, 379 n.; in chair at
banquet given by New York press,
379–83.
Greenwood, Thomas, 228 n.
Grosvenor, Lord Robert, 42, 128 n.,
131, 202 n.
Grote, George, 142, 393.
Guild of Literature and Art, 92 n.,
117 n., 138, 139, 196–7, 387; banquet to at Manchester, 148–51,
153; members entertained at Knebworth, 349–52.
Guizot, François P. G., 99.
Guy, Prof. Wm. A., 41 n.

Haight, Gordon S., 142–3 n.
Hallam, Henry, 99, 178 n., 393.
Halleck, Fitzgreene, 31 n., 32 n.
Halliday, Andrew, 390.
Hamley, Lt.-Col. Edward B., 247–8.
Hammersley, Wm. J., chairman of
Hartford banquet, 22 n., 22–26.
Handel, G. F., 294–5.
Hardinge, Viscount, 163–4.
Harley, John Pritt, 72, 75 n.
Hartford, Conn., banquet at, 22–26.
Harvard and Oxford, banquet to
rowing crews, 394–7.
Haydn, Joseph, 225–6.
Hazlitt, Wm., quoted, 75, 89.
Hedderwick, James, 11.
Helps, Sir Arthur, xx.
Herschel, Sir Wm., 157.
Hewett, Capt., presentation to, 15–17.
Higginson, Thomas Wentworth, 395.
Hill, Matthew Davenport, 42.
Hill, Sheriff, 92–93, 317.
Hogarth, Georgina, 306, 352, 376,
377, 391, 419 n.
Holly-Tree, The (*Household Words*),
372–3 n.
Holmes, Oliver Wendell, 22.
Homer, 39.
Hood, Thomas, 40.
Hook, Dr. Walter F., 165–6.
Horne, R. H., 1.
Hoskyns, C. Wren, in chair at Coven-
try dinner, 285 n., 285–8.
Hospital for Sick Children, dinner
(1858), 246–53, 263.
Hospitals, xxii, 40–41, 42–43, 68–72,
222–5, 232–6, 246–53, 319–23,
326–33.
Hotten, John Camden, iii, xv–xvi.
Houghton, Lord, *see* Monckton
Milnes.
House, Humphry, iii, xxii.
Household Words, xix, 91 n., 158 n.,
214, 287, 306; 'A Few Conven-
tionalities', xx; 'A Child's Dream
of a Star', 62 n.; 'Fire and Snow',

62 n.; 'The Begging-Letter Writer', 110 n.; 'The Raven in the Happy Family', 110 n.; articles on red tape and administrative reform (1855), 190 n.; 'The Royal Literary Fund', 214; 'No Hospital for Incurables', 222–3; 'Highly Proper', 232 n.; articles on Franklin's arctic expedition, 237; 'Drooping Buds', 246; *The Holly-Tree*, 372–3 n.; articles about the Lord Mayor, 416 n.

Houses of Parliament, burnt and rebuilt, 205.

Howard, Miss E., 353.

Howe, Dr. Samuel Gridley, **41** n.

Hughes, Arthur, 309 n.

Hughes, Thomas, **326** n., 397.

Hughes, W. R., 409.

Hunt, Holman, 309 n.

Hunt, James Henry Leigh, 142, 150, 387, 394.

Huntington Library, Henry E., iii, 430, 432.

Hutchinson, Walter, 425.

Incurables, Royal Hospital for, *see* Royal Hospital, &c.

Indian mutiny, 239, 247, 284.

Inglis, Sir Robert Harry, **178** n.

Institutional Association of Lancashire and Cheshire, prize-giving, 278–85.

International Exhibition (1861), 308–9.

Intra-mural Interments, Report on (1850), 131.

Ireland, 277 n.

Irons, Rev. W. J., **270** n.

Irving, Washington, 27 n., 390; chairman of the New York banquet, 26–32.

Jack the Giant Killer, 324.

Jacob's Island, 105, 107–9, 130.

Jaffray, A. W., 332.

Japan, 286, 309.

Jeejebhoy, Sir Jamsetjee, **330** n.

Jeffrey, Lord Francis, 8, 13, 278.

Jerdan, Wm., 1, 15, **104** n., 177, 423.

Jerrold, Douglas, xxii, 40, 76 n., 133, 191 n., **237** n., 315 n.; fund to aid his family, and Dickens's reading for it, 237–8.

Jerrold, Wm. Blanchard, xix.

Johnson, Edgar, 434, 437.

Johnson, Dr. Samuel, 38, 337, 345.

Jones, Dr. F., 338.

Jones, George, **305** n.

Jones, Wm. (headmaster), 240.

Kean, Charles, **94** n.; in chair for General Theatrical Fund, 94–97; in chair at meeting for founding Dramatic College, 275–7.

Kean, Edmund, 94.

Keeley, Robert, 220, 359.

Kemble, Henry, M.P., 4.

Kent, Charles, 349, 352, **368** n., 369, 413, 441.

Kitton, F. G., xix, 208, 253 n., 294 n., 366 n., 409 n.

Knebworth, dinner for Guild of Literature and Art at, 349–52.

Knight, Charles, 135, **136** n., 151, 153, 349.

Knowles, James Sheridan, 150, 387.

Knox, Major J. S., 342–3, **343** n.

Kytch (oboe-player), 294.

Lady of Lyons (Lytton), quoted or misquoted, 117, 281, 400.

Laing, Rev. David, 65 n., 270, 273.

Lamartine, A. de, 45 n.

Lamb, Charles, quoted, 252–3, 372.

Lansdowne, 3rd Marquis of, 42, 178, 182 n.

Landseer, Sir Edwin, 374, 420.

Lauder, James, 428.

Laurie, Sir Peter, **108**–9 n.

Layard, A. H., 157, **191** n., 197–9, 203–4, 206–7, 290, 298, 374.

Leech, John, 99, 135, **136** n.

Leeds, 290; Mechanics' Institution *Soirée*, 80–85, 87.

Lehmann, Frederick, 306, 427.

Lemon, Mark, 99, 127, 133, 135, **136** n., 191 n., 210, 225, 232, 277.

Lever, Charles, 7 n.

Levy, Edward (Lawson), **368** n.

Lewes, Mrs. C. L., 426.

Ley, J. W. T., 422.

Life peerages, 393.

Limbkins, Mr. (*Oliver Twist*), 108.

Lind, Jenny, 112, 212.

Lindley Murray's *Latin Grammar*, 39.

Lindsay, Jack, 427.

Literary Fund, *see* Royal Literary Fund, which it became after 1842.

Literary Fund Club, 2.

Literary Gazette, 104, 183, 197, 214, 227–8.

Little Nell, 8, 10, 20–21, 80.

Liverpool; Mechanics' Institution *Soirée*, 52–58, 59; civic banquet in Dickens's honour, 384–93; his tribute to, 386–7.

Livingstone, Dr. David, 237, **290** n.

Lockhart, John Gibson, **13** n., 99.

London Rowing Club, its banquet to Oxford and Harvard crews, 394–7.

Londonderry, Lord, 43.

Longfellow, H. W., **419** n.; 'Village Blacksmith', quoted, 282.
Lover, Wm., 1.
Lucknow, siege and relief, 239 n., 247 n., 257.
Lushington, Lt.-Gen. Sir James Law, xxii.
Lyttelton, Lord, **158** n., 158–9.
Lytton, Edith, 350 n., 351.
Lytton, Edward G. E. Lytton Bulwer (1st Baron Lytton), 3, **92** n., 151–2, 293, 376, 385, 388; in chair for General Theatrical Fund, (1848) 92–93, 428, (1852) 138–42; in chair for banquet to Macready, 114–18; in chair for Dickens's 'farewell' banquet before visit to America (1867), 369–74; and the 'dignity of literature' controversy, 138; speaks at Manchester dinner to Guild, 148; part in Literary Fund controversy, 178, 182–3, 192, 196–7; entertains Guild at Knebworth, 349–52.
Lytton, Robert, 349 n.

Macaulay, Thomas Babbington, Baron, 99, 157, 165, 385.
McCarthy, Justin, xix, xx.
McClintock, Capt. F. L., 237, **290** n.
Mackay, Charles, 177 n.
Mackenzie, Robert Shelton, xix, 32, 425.
Maclise, Daniel, 42, **419–20** n., 443; Dickens's tribute to, 421–2.
McQuhae, Capt., 96 n.
Macready, Wm. Charles, 2 n., 6, 42, 138, 162, 168, 187, 221, 228 n., 357; banquets in his honour, (1839) 2–3, (1851) 113–18; in chair for General Theatrical Fund (1847), 77–79; story of old actor, 125–6, 266–7; *Diaries* quoted, 3, 6, 77, 79, 113–14; and Lytton, 92 n.; as rival of Charles Kean, 94, 96–97; letters to, quoted, 17, 36, 42, 113, 161, 208, 228, 253.
Macrone, John, 1.
Madden, Sir Frederick, 99.
Manchester; first annual *soirée* of Athenaeum (1843), 44–52, 59; banquet to Guild of Literature and Art at Athenaeum, 148–51; opening of Free Library, 151–4; reading of *Carol* at, 237–8; *Frozen Deep* performed at, 238; prize-giving of Institutional Association of Lancashire and Cheshire, held at, 278–85.
Manchester, Bishop of (1852), 153.
'Manchester School', 152.
Mansion House banquets, (1849) 98–

100, (1853) 164–6, (1861) 299–300, (1866) 352.
Marshall, John, 331.
Marshalsea debtors' prison, 157.
Marylebone vestry, 108–9, 130.
Masterman, John, 174.
Mathews, Cornelius, 32.
Mayhew, Henry, 99.
Mayhew, Horace, **170** n., 175–6.
Mechanics' Institutes, *see* Chatham, Liverpool, Leeds, Sheffield, Sherborne, and Institutional Association of Lancashire and Cheshire.
Mechi, John Joseph, **236** n.
Mendelssohn, Felix, 157.
Message from the Sea, A (Collins and Dickens), 112 n.
Metropolitan Rowing Club, dinner of, 359–61.
Metropolitan Sanitary Association, 104–5; meeting in its support (1850), 104–10; banquet (1851), xxi, xxii, 127–32.
Meynell, Alice, 58.
Mill, John Stuart, 142, 393, 412, 420–21 n.
Millais, John E., 309 n.
Milman, Dean H. H., 142, **163** n., 182, 183 n.
Milnes, Richard Monckton, later Baron Houghton, 99, 153, **194** n., 195–6, 212, 214, 227, 257; at Liverpool banquet, 385–6, 388–91, 420 n.
Milton, John, 5, 39, 157.
Mitton, Thomas, 15, 52 n.
Moir, David Macbeth, 13 n., 80 n., 91.
Moore, George, **170** n., 174–5, 288, 291, 293, 321.
Moore, Thomas, quoted, 210, 386.
More, Sir Thomas, 38–39, 48.
Morgan, Capt. E. E., **112** n., 364–5.
Morgan Library, J. Pierpont, v.
Morley, Henry, 214 n., 246.
Morley, Samuel, **198** n.; in chair at Administrative Reform Association meeting, 198–208.
Morning Chronicle, 219 n., 347 n.
Morpeth, Lord, *see* Earl of Carlisle.
Motley, J. L., 390, **419** n.
Mulgrave, Lord (2nd Marquis of Normanby, 1863), **15** n.
Murchison, Sir Roderick I., **236** n.
Murray, John, 195, 214.
Muta di Portici, La (Auber), 141.

Napier, Sir Robert, 415.
Napoléon, Louis, 135.
Nation, The, 370, 373.
National Gallery, 63.
Nelson, Viscount, 247.

New Adelphi Theatre, used for meeting about Shakespeare Foundation Schools, 333–7.

Newspaper Press Fund, annual dinner (1865), 342–8.

Newsvendors' Benevolent Institution, annual dinners, (1849) 100–4, (1852) 135–8, (1862) 305–10, (1865) 337–42, (1870) 414–19; annual meeting (1855), 188–92.

New York, 6; banquet at (1842), 26–32; banquet in Dickens's honour given by New York press, xxi, 378–83; farewell reading at, 383–4.

New York Herald, 424–5.

New York Tribune, 370, 373.

Nisbet, Ada B., iii.

Normanby, 1st Marquis of, **15** n.

Normanby, 2nd Marquis of (Lord Mulgrave), **15** n.

'North, Christopher', *see* Prof. John Wilson.

Northern Monthly Magazine (Newark, N.J.), 374.

Northcote, Sir Stafford, 198.

Not So Bad As We Seem (Lytton), 117 n., 118, 138.

O'Connell, John, 95 n.

O'Driscoll, W. J., 443.

Olliffe, Lady, 299–300.

Otway, Thomas, 5.

Ouvry, Frederic, 349.

Owen, Rev. J. B., 158.

Owen, Prof. Richard, 96 n., 142.

Owen, Robert, 151.

Oxenford, John, 222.

Oxford and Harvard, banquet to rowing crews, 394–7.

Paget, Lord Henry Alfred, **223** n.

Palgrave, F. T., 309 n.

Palmerston, Henry John Temple, Viscount; takes chair for Artists' Benevolent Society, 67–68; Dickens has no faith in, 190; and the Administrative Reform Association, 198–200, 203–4, 208.

Panizzi, A., 99.

Pasley, Lt.-Gen. Sir Wm. Charles, **210** n.

Paul Clifford (Lytton), 350.

Paxton, Sir Joseph, 119, 130, **133** n., 145, 147, 175, 285; takes chair at Gardeners' Benevolent Institution dinner, 133–5.

Pearson, H. G., 408.

Pepys, Samuel, 201–2, 356–7.

Phelps, Samuel, 228 n.; in chair for Theatrical Fund (1857), 228–32.

Phillips, Benjamin Samuel, **317** n.,

318, 369, 414, 419; gives dinner at Mansion House, 352; in chair for Theatrical Fund, 358–9.

Phipps, Hon. Edmund, **235** n.

Pinner, Commercial Travellers' Schools at, 291–2.

Playfair, Dr. Lyon, 50.

Playground and General Recreation Society, first annual dinner, 269–75.

Pollock, John, 96 n., 150.

Pollock, Lady, 215 n.

Pollock, Sir Jonathan Frederick, **97** n., 183 n.

Pollock, Wm. Frederick, **183** n., 194, 212.

Poole, John, 96 n., 150.

Pope, Alexander, quoted, 47, 77, 422.

Porter, G. R., 42, 99.

Potter, Sir John, **151** n.

Powell, Mr. (puppeteer), 312.

Presented at Court (Coyne), 187.

Priestley, Lady, 259.

Princess's Theatre, meeting at for foundation of Dramatic College, 275–7.

Printers' Pension Society, annual dinner, (1843) 36–40, (1864) 323–5.

Printers' Readers' Association, meeting of, 366–7.

Procter, Bryan Waller, **182** n., 210.

Prout, Father (Rev. Francis Sylvester Mahony), 1.

Providence, R. I., speech about ticket speculation, 376–7.

Punch, 99, 130, 136, 170, 204, 237 n., 331 n.

Puss in Boots, 39, 229.

Queen's College, Birmingham, 159.

Queen's Colleges of Ireland ('Godless colleges'), 329.

Quincy, Josiah, 22.

Quincy, Josiah (Junior), chairman of Boston banquet (1842), **18** n., 18–22.

Rae, Dr., 237.

Ragged schools, 43 n., 47, 129.

Railway Benevolent Institution, annual dinner, 361–6.

Railways, 172–3, 284; and progress, 62.

Raleigh, Sir Walter, 48.

Raymond, Henry J., 383.

Raynham, Lord, 222.

Reade, Charles, 342, 349.

Readings, public; the first (at Birmingham), 166–7; at Bradford and elsewhere, in 1854, 168–9; at Sheffield, 208–9; for the Jerrold fund, at Manchester, 237–8; for Bristol Athenaeum, 245–6; for

Readings, public (*cont.*):
  Edinburgh Philosophical Institution, 258–60; first reading for his own profit, 263–4; in Ireland, 277 n.; two readings at Edinburgh, 277–8; for Chatham Mechanics' Institute, 301; at Washington, 375–6; at Providence, 376–7; at Boston, 377–8; at New York, 383–4; farewell reading at St. James's Hall, 412–13.
Redesdale, Lord, xx.
Reed, Dr. A., **222** n., 223, 236, 434.
Reed, T. A., 253, 435–6.
Reeve, Lovell, 197.
Reformatory school, 159.
Reuter, Baron P. J. von, 339.
Reynolds, Prof. John R., **332** n.
Richmond, Va., 'social supper' at, 34–36.
Ripon, Bishop of (1851), 128–9.
Ritchie, Thomas, chairman of Richmond 'social supper', **34** n., 34–36.
Rivals, The (Sheridan), 94.
Roberts, David, 277, 416 n., 422 n.
Robertson, Patrick, **11** n., 13.
Roby, John, **50** n., 51.
Rob Roy (Scott), 91.
Robinson, J. R., 442.
Robinson Crusoe, 39, 204, 253, 324.
Rochester, King's School, 241.
Roebuck, John, 187 n., 208.
Rogers, Professor Henry, **159** n.
Rogers, Samuel, 99.
Rough Diamond, The (Buckstone), 187.
Royal Academy, 269, 305; banquet, (1853) 163–4, (1858) 264–5, (1870) 419–22.
Royal Dramatic College, *see* Dramatic College.
Royal Free Hospital, annual dinner, 319–23.
Royal General Theatrical Fund, *see* General Theatrical Fund.
Royal Geographical Society dinner (1857), 236–7.
Royal Hospital for Incurables, annual dinner, (1856) 222–5, (1857) 232–6.
Royal Literary Fund, 38 n., 100, 140, 296, 302; anniversary dinners, (1837) 1–2, (1841) 6–7, (1843) 7, 213; general meeting (1855), 176–84; special general meeting (1855), 192–7, 212; general meeting, (1856) 7, 209–14, (1857) 225–8, (1858) 253–8.
Royal Society of Musicians, annual dinner (1860), 294–7.
Ruskin, John, 368.
Russell, Sir Charles, 368.

Russell, George, 368.
Russell, Lord John, 150, 190 n., **244** n., 245, 347, 389, 393.
Russell, Rev. Dr. John, 178, **194** n.
Russell, W. H., 245 n., 319–20, 348.
Ryland, Arthur, 161, 168.

Sadlers' Wells Theatre, 228 n., 230–1.
St. Valentine, 353.
Sala, G. A., xvi, 391.
Sanatorium, The, annual dinners, (1843) 42–43, (1844) 68–72.
Sandford, Rev. John (archdeacon), 156 n.
Sandon, Lord, 42, **65** n.
Sanford, Lucy, 67.
Saturday Review, 214, 393, 412.
Scholefield, Wm., 156 n.
School of Reform (Morton), 200.
Scott, Sir Walter, 11–13, 25–26, 91–92.
Sea-serpent, 96.
Sedgwick, Catherine Maria, **32** n.
Segar, George, 392.
Serle, T. J., 3.
Seymour, Robert, 33 n., **265** n.
Shaftesbury, 7th Earl of (Lord Ashley), 43 n., 104, 132, 151.
Shakespeare, William, 3, 6, 20, 30, 63–64, 74, 157, 202, 216–19; in connexion with Shakespeare Foundation Schools, 333–7; performances for preservation of Shakespeare's house, 387; characters referred to, quoted and misquoted, *passim.*
Shakespeare Foundation Schools, meeting for their establishment, 333–7.
Shaw, Jack, 277 n.
Shee, Sir Martin Archer, 2.
Shee, Sir Wm., **352** n.
Sheffield Mechanics' Institute, reading for, 208–9.
Shepherd, Richard H., iii, xv.
Sherborne Mechanics' Institute, reading for, 168.
Sheridan, R. B., 139, 382.
Sigourney, Mrs. Lydia, 26.
Sikh War, first, 73.
Simmons, W. H., 397.
Skimpole, Harold (*Bleak House*), 177.
Slaney, R. A., 270 n., 273.
Smith, Albert R., 170 n., 175–6, 248.
Smith, Arthur, 170 n.
Smith, C. Roach, 277 n.
Smith, E. T., 222.
Smith, Rev. Sydney, xxi, **144** n., 405.
Smith, Dr. Thomas Southwood, **42** n., 42–43, 129, 426.
Smith, Dr. Wm., **257** n.
Smithson, Charles, 52 n.

Smollett, Tobias, 109.
Somerset, 11th Duke of, 7.
Southern, A., 207–8.
Southey, Robert, 327 n.; his 'The Holly Tree', quoted, 90–91.
Southwark Literary and Scientific Institution, banquet for, 4–7.
Soyer, Mons. A., 127.
Spectator, The (Addison), 59.
Spectator, The (periodical), 393.
Spedding, James, 39 n.
Spring Hill College, Birmingham, 159.
Stanfield, Clarkson, 3, 40, 72, **163** n., 277.
Stanhope, 5th Earl of, in chair for meeting of the Literary Fund, (1857) 225–8, (1858) 253–8.
Stanley, Edward, **54** n.
Stanley, Lord, 194, 212.
Staples, L. C., iii.
Stationers' Company, 40.
Stebbing, Rev. Henry, **332** n., 333.
Stephen, Sir James, 153.
Stephenson, George, 80 n., 84, 105.
Stirling, Mrs. Fanny, 353, **357** n.
Stone, Frank, 151.
Stowe, Mrs. H. B., 164–6.
Stratton, Charles S. (General Tom Thumb), 230 n.
Stuart, Lord Dudley Coutts, **41** n., 41–42.
Summary of Facts (Robert Bell), 257.
Sunday Trading Bill, 202.
Suzannet, Comte de, iii.

Talfourd, Sir Thomas Noon, 3, 41, 73 n., 96 n., 99, 113, 165, 168, 176, 225.
Tatler, The (Steele and Addison), 312.
Taylor, Charles, **222** n.
Taylor, Tom, 99, 337.
Tennyson, Alfred, 56, 157, **194** n., 342, 368–9, 393; 'Lady Clara Vere de Vere', quoted, 56, 133, 146.
Tenterden, Lord, in chair for Theatrical Fund (1856), 220–2.
Thackeray, W. M., xxii, 38 n., 45 n., 99, 114–15, 194 n., 210, 232, 277, 293, 301; his speeches, 118, 153, 212 n., 263, 264–5; and 'dignity of literature' controversy, 138; and Literary Fund, 183; in chair for Theatrical Fund, and his health given by Dickens (1858), 260–3.
Thomas, F. M., xxi.
Thompson, James, 147.
Thompson, T. J., **52** n., 58, 65.
Times, The, xvii, 137, 183, 191, 192, 198, 201, 215, 263 n., 309 n., 342, 345–6, 348, 393, 408; letter from Dickens to, 103 n.

Todgers, Mrs., (*Chuzzlewit*), 289–90.
Tom Jones, 89.
Tooke, Wm., **183** n.
Toole, Mr. (the toastmaster), 185, 188.
Tree, Ellen (Mrs. Charles Kean), 94.
Trevelyan, Sir Charles, 198.
Trollope, Anthony, xix, xx, 337, 342, 374, 389–90.
Truro, Lord, 343, 348.
Tupper, M. F., 342.
Tutor's Assistant, The, 39.

Uncle Tom's Cabin, 164–5.
United Law Clerks' Society, annual dinner (1849), 97–98.
United States, *see* America.
University College Hospital, annual dinner, 326–33.
University reform, 329.
Useful Knowledge, Society for Diffusion of, 42 n.

Vanity Fair, 263.
Verisopht, Lord (*Nickleby*), 389.
Victoria, Queen, 89, 96, 100, 118–19, 143, 170, 207, 239, 247, 270, 373 n.
Victoria Adelaide (Princess Royal), **100** n., 247.
Vincent, Mr. (printers' benefactor), 325.
Virgil, 39.
Volunteer Rifle movement, 289, 331, 326, 415.

Wales, Prince of, 311, 337, 359, 420–1.
Walker, J. Eaton, 161.
Walkinghame, F., 205.
Wallack, James, **126** n.
Walpole, Spencer, 348.
Ward, E. M., 157–8 n.
Ward, F. O., 132.
Warehousemen and Clerks' Schools annual dinner (1857), 238–45.
Warner, Mrs. (actress), 228 n.
Washington, D.C., private dinner for Dickens at, 32–34, 35; first and farewell readings, 375–6.
Washington, George, 33.
Watkin, Edward Wm., **44** n., 50, 426.
Watson, Hon. Mrs. R., xxiv, 166–7, 170 n., 208.
Webster, Benjamin N., **76** n., 222, 277, 308, 349, 374; in chair for Theatrical Fund (1850) 110–13, 125; starts scheme in connexion with Dulwich College, 215, 217, 219–20; scheme for Shakespeare Foundation Schools, 333–7.
Weller, Christina (later Mrs. T. J. Thompson), 57–58, 426.
Wellington, Duke of, 157, 309, 395.
Wellington House Academy, 240.

Westminster Review, 142 n.
Whewell, Dr. Wm., 400 n.
Whiting, Charles, 135, 136 n.
Whittington, Dickens, 229, 299.
Whitworth, Joseph, 388 n., 401.
Widdicombe, Mr. (ringmaster), 122.
Wigan, Alfred S., 308 n., 312.
Wilberforce, Samuel (Bishop of Oxford), xix, **196** n., 212.
Wild, Mr. (newsvendor), 189–90.
Wilkie, Sir David, **13** n., 13–15, 421–2.
Willan, F., 397.
Williams, Rev. David, 177, 210.
Wills, W. H., 133, **158** n., 223, 258–60, 287, 337, 349, 368, 370, 378, 427, 441.

Wills, Mrs. W. H., 258–9, 306.
Wilson, Prof. John, 8 n., 386; chairman of Edinburgh banquet (1841), 8–15.
Wilton, Earl of, 153.
Winter, Mrs. M., xxiv.
'Wizard of the North' (J. H. Anderson), 74, 221 n.
Wood, Sir Wm. Page, **164** n., 164–6.
Woolner, T., 309 n.
Wordsworth, William, 5.
Wrench, Capt., 144.

Yates, Edmund, xix, 263–4 n., **301** n., 317, 337, 341–2, 349, 368, 373, 419.

PRINTED IN GREAT BRITAIN
AT THE UNIVERSITY PRESS, OXFORD
BY VIVIAN RIDLER
PRINTER TO THE UNIVERSITY